TALES FROM THE YAWNING PORTAL

CREDITS

Compilers: Kim Mohan, Mike Mearls
Lead Rules Developer: Jeremy Crawford
Fifth Edition Conversion: Chris Sims, Sean K Reynolds, Jennifer Clarke Wilkes

Managing Editor: Jeremy Crawford
Editors: Kim Mohan, Michele Carter
Editorial Assistance: Chris Dupuis, Ben Petrisor, Matt Sernett

Art Director: Kate Irwin
Additional Art Direction: Shauna Narciso, Richard Whitters

Graphic Designer: Emi Tanji
Cover Illustrator: Tyler Jacobson
Interior Illustrators: Mark Behm, Eric Belisle, Zoltan Boros, Noah Bradley, Sam Carr, Jedd Chevrier, Bud Cook, Olga Drebas, Wayne England, Lake Hurwitz, Izzy, Tyler Jacobson, Titus Lunter, Brynn Metheney, Scott Murphy, Claudio Pozas, Ned Rogers, Chris Seaman, Cory Trego-Erdner, Franz Vohwinkel, Mark Winters, Sam Wood, Ben Wootten
Cartographers: Jason A. Engle, Rob Lazzaretti, Mike Schley, Ben Wootten

Producer: Stan!
Project Manager: Heather Fleming
Product Engineer: Cynda Callaway
Imaging Technicians: Sven Bolen, Carmen Cheung, Kevin Yee
Art Administration: David Gershman
Prepress Specialist: Jefferson Dunlap

Other D&D Team Members: Bart Carroll, John Feil, Trevor Kidd, Adam Lee, Christopher Lindsay, Shelly Mazzanoble, Christopher Perkins, Hilary Ross, Liz Schuh, Nathan Stewart, Greg Tito, Shawn Wood

CREDITS FROM THE ORIGINAL ADVENTURES

Tomb of Horrors (1978)
Design: Gary Gygax

White Plume Mountain (1979)
Design: Lawrence Schick
Editing and Suggestions: Mike Carr, Allen Hammack, Harold Johnson, Tim Jones, Jeff Leason, Dave Sutherland, Jean Wells
Art: Dave Sutherland, Erol Otus, Darlene Pekul, Jeff Dee, David S. LaForce, Jim Roslof, Bill Willingham

The Hidden Shrine of Tamoachan (1980)
Design: Harold Johnson, Jeff R. Leason
Able Assistance: Dave Cook, Lawrence Schick
Editing: Harold Johnson

Editing and Production: Dave Cook, Jeff R. Leason, Lawrence Schick
Illustrations: Erol Otus, Jeff Dee, Gregory K. Fleming, David S. LaForce, David C. Sutherland III

Against the Giants (1981)
Design: Gary Gygax
Editing: Mike Carr, Timothy Jones, Jon Pickens, Lawrence Schick
Art: David C. Sutherland III, David A. Trampier, Jeff Dee, David S. LaForce, Erol Otis, Bill Willingham

The Sunless Citadel (2000)
Design: Bruce R. Cordell
Editing: Miranda Horner

Cartography: Todd Gamble
Illustrations: Dennis Cramer, Todd Lockwood

The Forge of Fury (2000)
Design: Richard Baker
Editing: Miranda Horner
Cartography: Todd Gamble
Illustrations: Dennis Cramer, Todd Lockwood

Dead in Thay (2014)
Design: Scott Fitzgerald Gray
Editing: Ray Vallese
Cartography: Mike Schley
Illustrations: Eric Belisle, Sam Carr, Tyler Jacobson, Miles Johnstone, Mark Winters

Disclaimer: Do we really need a disclaimer to tell you that it's not our fault that your character died because you decided to climb down into a monster- and trap-filled hole in the ground?

ON THE COVER

As proprietor of the Yawning Portal, Durnan has heard amazing tales from adventurers of all sorts from across the multiverse, as seen in this array of characters by Tyler Jacobson.

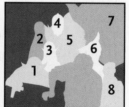

See if you can identify the face and the adventure found in *Tales from the Yawning Portal.*

1. *Gargoyle (Tomb of Horrors); 2. Tarul Var (Dead in Thay); 3. Mialee (Sunless Citadel); 4. Sir Bluto Sans Pite (White Plume Mountain); 5. Tordek (Forge of Fury); 6. Xipe, the oni (Hidden Shrine of Tamoachan); 7. Manticore (White Plume Mountain); 8. Kieren, Chosen of Illmater (Dead in Thay)*

620C2207000001 EN
ISBN: 978-0-7869-6609-7
First Printing: April 2017   (This printing includes corrections.)

9 8 7 6 5 4

CE

Printed in the USA. ©2017 Wizards of the Coast LLC, PO Box 707, Renton, WA 98057-0707, USA. Manufactured by Hasbro SA, Rue Emile-Boéchat 31, 2800 Delémont, CH. Represented by Hasbro Europe, 4 The Square, Stockley Park, Uxbridge, Middlesex, UB11 1ET, UK.

CONTENTS

INTRODUCTION

ELCOME TO *Tales from the Yawning Portal*. Within this book you will find seven of the deadliest dungeons from the history of D&D, updated for the current edition of the game. Some are classics that have hosted an untold number of adventurers, while others are newer creations boldly staking their place in the pantheon of notable D&D adventures.

Just as these dungeons have made an impression on D&D players, so too have tales of their dangers spread across the D&D multiverse. When the night grows long in Waterdeep, City of Splendors, and the fireplace in the taproom of the Yawning Portal dims to a deep crimson, adventurers from across the Sword Coast—and even some visiting from other D&D worlds—spin tales and rumors of lost treasures.

- A wanderer from the distant Shou Empire speaks of strange, leering devil faces carved in dungeon walls that can devour an explorer in an instant, leaving behind not a single trace of the poor soul's passing.
- A bald, stern wizard clad in blue robes and speaking with a strange accent tells of a wizard who claimed three powerful weapons from a city on the shores of a lake of unknown depths, who spirited them away to a slumbering volcano and dared adventurers to enter his lair and recover them.
- A one-eyed dwarf spins tales of a castle that fell into the earth, and whose ruins stand above a subterranean grove dominated by a tree that spawns evil.

These are only a few of the tales that have spread across the Sword Coast from the furthest reaches of Faerûn and beyond. The minor details change with the telling. The dread tomb of Acererak shifts its location from a dismal swamp, to a searing desert, to some other forbidding clime in each telling. The key elements remain the same in each version of the tales, lending a thread of truth to the tale.

The seeds of those stories now rest in your hand. D&D's deadliest dungeons are now part of your arsenal of adventures. Enjoy, and remember to keep a few spare character sheets handy.

USING THIS BOOK

Tales from the Yawning Portal contains seven adventures taken from across D&D's history.

The introduction of each adventure provides ideas on adapting it to a variety of D&D settings. Use that information to place it in your campaign or to give you an idea of how to adapt it.

These adventures provide the perfect side quest away from your current campaign. If you run published D&D campaigns, such as *Storm King's Thunder*, the higher level adventures presented here are an ideal way to extend the campaign.

ABOUT THE ADVENTURES

THE SUNLESS CITADEL

The Sunless Citadel, written by Bruce R. Cordell, was the first published adventure for the third edition of the D&D game. It is designed for a party of four or five 1st-level player characters.

Ever since its publication in 2000, *The Sunless Citadel* has been widely regarded as an excellent way to introduce new players to the game. It's also a great starting experience for someone looking to be a Dungeon Master for the first time.

THE FORGE OF FURY

The Forge of Fury, written by Richard Baker, was published in 2000 shortly after *The Sunless Citadel*. Characters who succeeded in that mission and advanced to 3rd level were now ready to take on the challenges of a ruined dwarven fortress.

Like its predecessor, *The Forge of Fury* is tailored to provide increasingly tougher threats as the characters make their way through the fortress. Those who survive the experience can expect to advance to 5th level—seasoned adventurers ready to strive for greater glory and renown.

THE HIDDEN SHRINE OF TAMOACHAN

The Hidden Shrine of Tamoachan, written by Harold Johnson and Jeff R. Leason, made its debut under the title *Lost Tamoachan* at the Origins game convention in 1979, where it was used in the official D&D competition. The first published version of the adventure was produced in 1980.

The updated version of the adventure presented herein is designed for a group of four or five 5th-level player characters.

WHITE PLUME MOUNTAIN

Lawrence Schick, the author of *White Plume Mountain*, related in the 2013 compilation *Dungeons of Dread* that he wrote the adventure as a way of persuading Gary Gygax to hire him as a game designer. Not only did he get the job, but *White Plume* became an instant favorite when it was first published in 1979.

The version of the adventure in this book is tailored to a group of characters of 8th level.

DEAD IN THAY

Dead in Thay, written by Scott Fitzgerald Gray, was created when the fifth edition D&D game was in the testing stages. In its original form, it was used as the story of the D&D Encounters season in the spring of 2014. Featuring an immense and lethal dungeon known as the Doomvault, the adventure serves as a tribute to *Tomb of Horrors*, *Ruins of Undermountain*, and other "killer dungeons" throughout the history of the game.

The version of *Dead in Thay* presented here is modified for use in home campaigns. It is designed for characters of 9th to 11th level.

Against the Giants

The three linked adventures that make up *Against the Giants* were created and originally released in 1978, during the time when Gary Gygax was still writing the *Player's Handbook* for the original AD&D game. Despite being (in a sense) older than the game itself, these adventures continue to hold a special place in the hearts and memories of D&D players of all ages.

The compilation of *Steading of the Hill Giant Chief*, *Glacial Rift of the Frost Giant Jarl*, and *Hall of the Fire Giant King* was published in 1981 as *Against the Giants*. The version presented here is designed to be undertaken by characters of 11th level.

Tomb of Horrors

Before there was much of anything else in the world of the D&D game, there was the Tomb of Horrors.

The first version of the adventure was crafted for Gary Gygax's personal campaign in the early 1970s and went on to be featured as the official DUNGEONS & DRAGONS event at the original Origins gaming convention in 1975. The first publication of *Tomb of Horrors*, as a part of the Advanced D&D game, came in 1978.

As a proving ground for characters and players alike, fabricated by the devious mind of the game's cocreator, *Tomb of Horrors* has no equal in the annals of D&D's greatest adventures. Only high-level characters stand a chance of coming back alive, but every player who braves the Tomb will have the experience of a lifetime.

Running the Adventures

To run each of these adventures, you need the fifth edition *Player's Handbook*, *Dungeon Master's Guide*, and *Monster Manual*. Before you sit down with your players, read the text of the adventure all the way through and familiarize yourself with the maps as well, perhaps making notes about complex areas or places where the characters are certain to go, so you're well prepared before the action starts.

> Text that appears in a box like this is meant to be read aloud or paraphrased for the players when their characters first arrive at a location or under a specific circumstance, as described in the text.

The *Monster Manual* contains stat blocks for most of the monsters and NPCs found in this book. When a monster's name appears in **bold** type, that's a visual cue pointing you to the creature's stat block in the *Monster Manual*. Descriptions and stat blocks for new monsters appear in appendix B. If a stat block is in that appendix, an adventure's text tells you so.

Spells and nonmagical objects or equipment mentioned in the book are described in the *Player's Handbook*. Magic items are described in the *Dungeon Master's Guide*, unless the adventure's text directs you to an item's description in appendix A.

Creating a Campaign

While these adventures were never meant to be combined into a full campaign—over 30 years separates the newest from the oldest—they have been selected to provide play across a broad range of levels. With a little work, you can run a complete campaign using only this book.

Starting with *The Sunless Citadel*, guide your players through the adventures in the order that they are presented in this book. Each one provides enough XP that, upon completing the adventure, the characters should be high enough level to advance to the next one.

The Yawning Portal, or some other tavern of your own invention or drawn from another D&D setting, provides the perfect framing device for the campaign. The characters hear rumors of each dungeon, with just enough information available to lead them to the next adventure. Perhaps a friendly NPC drawn from the upcoming adventure visits the tavern in search of help, or some element of a character's background pushes the group down the proper road. In any case, these dungeons are designed to be easily portable to any campaign setting.

The Yawning Portal

Amid the bustle of Waterdeep, within the Castle Ward where barristers, nobles, and emissaries battle with word and contract, stands an inn not quite like any other. Before there was a Castle Ward or even what could be recognized as an ancestor of the City of Splendors, there was a dungeon, and in that dungeon begins the tale of the Yawning Portal.

In ages past, the mighty wizard Halaster built his tower at the foot of Mount Waterdeep and delved deep into tunnels first built by dwarves and drow in search of ever greater magical power. Halaster and his apprentices expanded the tunnels they found, worming out new lairs under the surface for reasons of their own. In time, their excavations grew into the vast labyrinth known today as Undermountain, the largest dungeon in all of the Forgotten Realms. Halaster eventually disappeared, as have all his apprentices, but the massive complex he built remains to this day.

For untold years, the secrets of Undermountain remained hidden from the surface world. Everyone who entered its halls failed to return. Its reputation as a death trap grew to the point that criminals in Waterdeep

> ### The Green Dragon Inn
> The Yawning Portal is not the only renowned tavern in D&D lore. In the Free City of Greyhawk stands the Green Dragon Inn, which has been the starting point for some of the most successful expeditions to Castle Greyhawk and beyond. The place is crowded and smoke-filled. Patrons talk in low voices, and anyone attempting to strike up a conversation without making a clear intent to pay can expect a cold reception. Paranoia and suspicion run rampant here, as befits a free city that stands at the nexus between a devil-haunted empire, a vast domain locked in the iron-tight grip of a demigod of evil, and a splintered, bickering host of kingdoms nominally committed to justice and weal. In the battered, weary world of Greyhawk, profit and power take precedence over heroics.

who were sentenced to die were forcibly escorted into the dungeon and left to fend for themselves.

All of that changed with the arrival of two men, a warrior named Durnan and a ne'er-do-well named Mirt. The duo were the first adventurers to return from Undermountain, laden with riches and magic treasures. While Mirt used his wealth to buy a mansion, Durnan had different plans. Durnan retired from adventuring and purchased the land on which sat the deep, broad well that was the only known entrance to the dungeon. Around this well he built a tavern and inn that caters to adventurers and those who seek their services, and he called it the Yawning Portal.

Some of the magic Durnan looted on his successful foray into Undermountain granted him a life span that exceeds even that of an elf. And for decades Durnan left delving into Undermountain to younger folk. Yet one day, something drew him back. Days of waiting for his triumphant return from the dungeon turned to months and then years. For nearly a century, citizens of Waterdeep thought him dead. But one night, a voice called up from the well. Few at first believed it could be Durnan, but folk as long-lived as he vouched it so. The Yawning Portal had passed into the hands of his ancestors, but Durnan returned with enough riches for them to quietly retire. Durnan took his customary place behind the bar, raised a toast to his own safe return, and then began serving customers as if he'd never left.

Adventurers from across Faerûn, and even from elsewhere in the great span of the multiverse, visit the Yawning Portal to exchange knowledge about Undermountain and other dungeons. Most visitors are content to swap stories by the hearth, but sometimes a group driven by greed, ambition, or desperation pays the toll for entry and descends the well. Most don't survive to make the return trip, but enough come back with riches and tales of adventure to tempt other groups into trying their luck.

FEATURES OF THE YAWNING PORTAL

The Yawning Portal's taproom fills the first floor of the building. The 40-foot-diameter well that provides access to Undermountain dominates the space. The "well" is all that remains of Halaster's tower, and now, devoid of the stairways and floors that formed subterranean levels, it drops as an open shaft for 140 feet. Stirges, spiders, and worse have been known to invade the Yawning Portal from below.

Balconies on the tavern's second and third floors overlook the well, with those floors accessed by way of wooden stairs that rise up from the taproom. Guests sitting at the tables on the balconies have an excellent view of the well and the action below.

Entering the Well. Those who wish to enter Undermountain for adventure (or the daring tourists who just want to "ride the rope") must pay a gold piece to be lowered down. The return trip also costs a piece of gold, sent up in a bucket in advance. Once the initial payment is made, a few stairs takes one to the top of the waist-high lip of the well. The rope that hangs in the center of the well is levered over to the lip by a beam in the rafters, and when those who have paid are ready, they mount the rope and take the long ride down.

Oddities on Display. A staggering variety of curios and oddities adorn the taproom. Traditionally, adventurers who recover a strange relic from Undermountain present it to Durnan as a trophy of their success. Other adventurers leave such curios to mark their visits to the tavern, or relinquish them after losing a bet with Durnan, who likes to wager on the fate of adventuring bands that enter the dungeon. Occasionally, something that strikes Durnan's fancy can be used to pay a bar tab.

YAWNING PORTAL TAPROOM CURIOS

d20	Item
1	A key carved from bone
2	A small box with no apparent way to open it
3	A mummified troglodyte's hand
4	Half of an iron symbol of Bane
5	A small burlap pouch filled with various teeth
6	Burnt fragments of a scroll
7	A lute missing its strings
8	A bloodstained map
9	An iron gauntlet that is hot to the touch
10	A gold coin stamped with a worn, hawk-wing helm crest
11	A troll finger, still wriggling
12	A silver coin that makes no noise when dropped
13	An empty jar; when opened, a wolf howl sounds from it and continues until it is closed
14	A clockwork owl; when wound, its head turns and it hoots softly for a minute
15	A blue, glowing crystal shard
16	A statuette of a panther, wooden and painted black
17	A piece of parchment, listing fourteen magical pools and their effects when touched
18	A vial filled with a dark, fizzy liquid that is sealed and cannot be opened
19	A feeler taken from a slain rust monster
20	A wooden pipe marked with Elminster's sigil

A TYPICAL EVENING

On quiet nights, guests in the Yawning Portal gather around a large fireplace in the taproom and swap tales of distant places, strange monsters, and valuable treasures. On busier nights, the place is loud and crowded. The balconies overflow with merchants and nobles, while the tables on the ground floor are filled with adventurers and their associates. Invariably, the combination of a few drinks and the crowd's encouragement induces some folk to pay for a brief trip down into Undermountain. Most folk pay in advance for a ride down and immediately back up, though a few ambitious souls might launch impromptu expeditions into the dungeon. Few such ill-prepared parties ever return.

Groups seeking to enter Undermountain for a specific reason generally come to the tavern during its quiet hours. Even at such times, there are still a few prying eyes in the taproom, lurkers who carry news of the comings and goings from Undermountain to the Zhentarim, dark cults, criminal gangs, and other interested parties.

Starting the Story

Kicking off a dungeon adventure can be as simple as having a mysterious stranger offer the characters a quest while they are at the Yawning Portal (or some other tavern). This approach is a cliché, but it is an effective one. Use the following two tables to generate a couple of details, then tailor the particulars of the quest and the quest giver to suit the adventure you plan to run.

A Mysterious Stranger Offers a Quest

d8	Objective
1	Recover a particular item
2	Find and return with an NPC or monster
3	Slay a terrible monster or NPC
4	Guard a person while they perform a ritual
5	Create an accurate map of part of the dungeon
6	Discover secret lore hidden in the dungeon
7	Destroy an object
8	Sanctify part of the dungeon to a god of good

The Mysterious Stranger's Secret

d8	Secret
1	Intends to betray the party
2	Unwittingly provides false information
3	Has a secret agenda (roll another quest)
4	Is a devil in disguise
5	Has led other parties to their doom
6	Is the charmed thrall of a mind flayer
7	Is possessed by a ghost
8	Is a solar in disguise

Durnan

The proprietor of the Yawning Portal is something of an enigma. Blessed with a seemingly limitless life span by treasures he brought back from his expedition nearly two centuries ago, he is as much a fixture in the taproom as the well.

Durnan is a man of few words. He expects to be paid for his time, and will offer insight and rumors only in return for hard cash. "We know the odds and take our chances," he says, whether he is breaking up a card game that has turned violent or refusing the pleas of adventurers trapped at the bottom of the well who are unable to pay for a ride up. Despite his stony heart, he is an excellent source of information about Undermountain and other dungeons, provided one can pay his price.

Personality Trait: Isolation. It's a cruel world. All people have to fend for themselves. Self-sufficiency is the only path to success.

Ideal: Independence. Someone who can stand alone can stand against anything.

Bond: The Yawning Portal. This place is my only home. My friends and family are long gone. I love this place, but I try not to get attached to the people here. I'll outlive them all. Lucky me.

Flaw: Heartless. If you want sympathy, the Temple of Ilmater is in the Sea Ward. No matter how bad things are, you'll be gone in a blink of an eye.

Other Denizens

The Yawning Portal is host to a variety of regular visitors, most of whom offer services to adventurers. Chapter 4 of the *Dungeon Master's Guide* provides plenty of resources for generating nonplayer characters. The following table provides some possibilities for why an individual is visiting the Yawning Portal.

Denizens of the Yawning Portal

d10	Denizen
1	Devotee of Tymora, encourages adventures to seek out quests, can cast *bless*
2	Bored, retired adventurer, claims to have explored dungeon of note and can describe first few areas (20 percent chance of an accurate description)
3	Heckler, mocks cowards and makes bets that adventurers won't return from an expedition
4	Con artist, selling fake treasure maps (but a 10 percent chance that a map is genuine)
5	Wizard's apprentice, carefully making exact sketches of various curios at her master's command
6	Spouse of a slain adventurer, who pays the toll for anyone wanting to exit Undermountain and plots against Durnan
7	Zhentarim agent, seeks rumors of treasure, tails any folk who return from Undermountain and notes their home base for future robbery
8	Agent of the Xanathar, ordered to "steal the hat worn by the eighth person to enter the taproom this night"
9	Magically preserved corpse in a coffin leaning against the bar; if asked about it, Durnan says, "He's waiting for someone," and nothing more
10	Elminster, incognito; 10 percent chance he is on an errand of cosmic importance; otherwise, he's pressing Durnan for gossip

THE SUNLESS CITADEL

All things roll here: horrors of midnights,
Campaigns of a lost year,
Dungeons disturbed, and groves of lights;
Echoing on these shores, still clear,
Dead ecstasies of questing knights—
Yet how the wind revives us here!

—*Arthur Rimbaud*

HIS ADVENTURE CONCERNS A ONCE-PROUD fortress that fell into the earth in an age long past. Now known as the Sunless Citadel, its echoing, broken halls house malign creatures. Evil has taken root at the citadel's core, which is deep within a subterranean garden of blighted foliage. Here a terrible tree and its dark shepherd plot in darkness.

The tree, called the Gulthias Tree, is shepherded by a twisted druid, Belak the Outcast. He was drawn to the buried citadel twelve years ago, following stories of oddly enchanted fruit to their source. The druid found an old fortress that had been swallowed up by the earth in some sort of magically invoked devastation. With the previous inhabitants long dispersed, vile and opportunistic creatures common to lightless dungeons infested the subterranean ruins. At the core of the old fortress, Belak stumbled upon the Twilight Grove. He discovered at the grove's heart the Gulthias Tree, which sprouted from a wooden stake that was used to slay an ancient vampire.

A perfect, ruby-red apple ripens on the Gulthias Tree at the summer solstice, and the tree produces a single albino apple at the winter solstice. The midsummer fruit grants vigor, health, and life, while the midwinter fruit steals the same. In the years since Belak's arrival, the enchanted fruit has been widely dispersed through the surrounding lands, promoting good and ill. The seeds of either fruit, if allowed to sprout, grow into small plant monsters known as twig blights.

ADVENTURE SYNOPSIS

During their trip through the Sunless Citadel, characters deal with monstrous threats and ancient traps, as well as warring tribes of kobolds and goblins. The adventure is designed for four 1st-level player characters. They should advance through 2nd level to 3rd level before the finale. The adventure has four basic parts:

1. **Oakhurst.** Although it isn't part of the adventure per se, the village of Oakhurst can provide the characters with valuable information about the citadel. They can also use Oakhurst as a place to recuperate and replenish supplies.

2. **Kobold Den.** The characters' foray into the citadel begins with an incursion into the most accessible areas of the fortress, where a tribe of kobolds has taken up residence. The characters can avoid strife with the kobolds by agreeing to retrieve a lost pet for the kobold leader, and they might be able to persuade the kobolds to join their side.

3. **Goblin Lair.** The goblins that live deeper inside the citadel consider themselves the owners of the place. They defend themselves aggressively against intrusion, making it difficult to avoid combat with them.

4. **Hidden Grove.** Eventually, the characters discover the lower level of the citadel and the Twilight Grove that lies within. There, they learn the truth about the enchanted fruit, and they must confront Belak the Outcast and the Gulthias Tree.

RUNNING THE ADVENTURE

To enhance the experience of the players and help you do your best job as Dungeon Master, take the following pieces of advice and information into consideration.

MAPPING

It can be difficult to keep track of all the corridors, turns, areas, and other features of a dungeon setting, and the player characters could soon get turned around without a map. Ask for a volunteer to be the party mapper. It's the mapper's job to listen carefully to your description of each area, noting its size and exits, and to record that information by sketching on a sheet of paper.

> ### PLACING THE ADVENTURE
>
> *The Sunless Citadel* is designed to be easily located in whatever setting the DM prefers. Here are some examples.
>
> ***Dragonlance.*** On Krynn, the citadel was once part of Xak Tsaroth, and it harbored worshipers of Takhisis. When that city was destroyed during the cataclysm, it fell into a rift that opened in the earth. In this setting, consider replacing the kobolds in the adventure with gully dwarves.
>
> ***Eberron.*** Located near the western edge of the Mournland, the citadel was an ancient ruin even during the time of the Last War. Agents of Cyre used it as a way point for conducting espionage against neighboring realms. On the Day of Mourning, the earth opened up and swallowed the place. The Mournland is within sight of the rift.
>
> ***Forgotten Realms.*** On Faerûn, the Sunless Citadel was once a secret stronghold of the Cult of the Dragon, located in the foothills northwest of Thundertree. It plunged into the earth when Mount Hotenow erupted and threw Neverwinter into chaos.
>
> ***Greyhawk.*** The Sunless Citadel is a ruined Baklunish stronghold that was cast into the bowels of the earth when the Suel Imperium unleashed the Invoked Devastation. It is located in northwestern Bissel, in the foothills west of Thornward.

TIME OF YEAR

If you would like the characters to have the opportunity to find a fruit, begin the adventure a few weeks before either the summer or winter solstice. Apart from making a piece of fruit available on the Gulthias Tree, choosing a season provides you with additional details to set the scene, which enhances the adventure.

If you choose summer, the hills are lush with growth, though the heat sometimes grows oppressive. If the characters embark in the winter, temperatures hover just above freezing during the day and plunge below it at night.

ADVENTURE HOOKS

Adventurers can find the Sunless Citadel within a remote and lonely ravine. The characters can be drawn to the dungeon for any of the following reasons. Relate the information below to the players as necessary to get them interested in journeying to the dungeon site.

GOING FOR GLORY

You are eager to make a name for yourself. The legend of the Sunless Citadel is well known locally, and stories indicate it is a place that holds promise for those intent on discovery, glory, and treasure!

RESCUE MISSION

Another party of adventurers, locally based, delved into the Sunless Citadel a month past. They were never seen again. Two human members of that ill-fated party were brother and sister, Talgen Hucrele (a fighter) and Sharwyn Hucrele (a wizard). They were part of an important merchant family based in the nearby village of Oakhurst. Kerowyn Hucrele, the matriarch of the family, offers salvage rights to you and your team if you can find and return with the two lost members of her family—or at least return the gold signet rings worn by the missing brother and sister. She also offers a reward of 125 gp per signet ring, per character. If the characters bring back the Hucreles in good shape (of good mind and body), she offers to double the reward.

SOLVING A MYSTERY

The goblin tribe infesting the nearby ruins, called the Sunless Citadel (though no one knows why) sells a single piece of magical fruit to the highest bidder in Oakhurst once every midsummer. They've been doing this for the last twelve years. Usually, the fruit sells for around 50 gp, which is all the townsfolk can bring themselves to pay a goblin. The fruit, apparently an apple of perfect hue, heals those who suffer from any disease or other ailment. They sometimes plant the seeds at the center of each fruit, hoping to engender an enchanted apple tree. When the seeds germinate in their proper season, they produce a twiggy mass of twisted sapling stems. Not too long after the saplings reach 2 feet in height, they are stolen—every time. The townsfolk assume the goblins send out thieves to ensure their monopoly of enchanted fruit. You are interested in piercing the mystery associated with how wretched goblins could ever possess such a wonder, and how they steal every sprouting sapling grown from the enchanted fruit's seed. Moreover, you wish to find this rumored tree of healing, hoping to heal an ailing friend or relative.

OAKHURST

The community closest to the Sunless Citadel is a village called Oakhurst. Most of its 900 residents (including outlying farms) are human, with a sizable minority of halflings and a scattering of other races.

Significant locations in Oakhurst, and the people to be found within them, include the following:

Village Hall. The center of government in Oakhurst includes the office of Mayor Vurnor Leng, a male human noble.

General Store. The village's main source for supplies and merchandise is the general store, owned and operated by Kerowyn Hucrele, a female human noble.

Shrine. Advice, information, and healing are among the services dispensed at the village's shrine. It is maintained by Dem "Corkie" Nackle, a female gnome priest of Pelor.

Jail. Next to the village hall is a stout building where miscreants serve their sentences. Oakhurst's con-

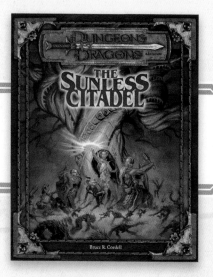

stable is Felosial, a female half-elf veteran. She commands a force of sixteen guards and four scouts who keep the village safe.

Blacksmith. Repairing and forging arms and armor is the job of the village smithy, Rurik Lutgehr, a male dwarf commoner.

Ol' Boar Inn. Garon, a male human commoner, is the owner and barkeep of the Ol' Boar Inn. He serves food and drink, and the place has a few rooms that visitors can rent.

RUMORS HEARD IN OAKHURST

Player characters can discover the following additional information while spending time in the local tavern, or through asking the right questions of the locals.

- No one knows for sure what the Sunless Citadel once was, but legends hint that it served as the retreat of an ancient dragon cult.
- The Old Road skirts the Ashen Plain, a lifeless area. A character who succeeds on a DC 15 Intelligence (History) check knows that the desolation is attributed to the long-ago rampage of a dragon named Ashardalon. A few locals also know this fact.
- Cattle herders don't graze their stock too far afield these days. They're frightened by stories of new monsters that maraud by night. From time to time, cattle and people who have gone out alone at night have been found dead the next day, bearing dozens of needle-like wounds. No one has seen the creatures that cause this mayhem, nor do they leave a discernible trail.
- The missing adventurers include a fighter (Talgen Hucrele), a wizard (Sharwyn Hucrele), a paladin of Pelor (Sir Braford), and a ranger (Karakas). Sir Braford was not a local, and he had a magic sword called *Shatterspike*.
- Sometimes the goblins offer a different apple at midwinter. This apple is corpse-white and poisonous, even to the touch. No samples of either apple are to be had.

- Garon, the barkeep of the Ol' Boar Inn, remembers the last time anyone, aside from Talgen and Sharwyn, asked questions about the Sunless Citadel. About thirteen years ago, a grim human named Belak stopped by, and he had a very large pet frog.

WILDERNESS ENCOUNTERS

If the characters are anywhere between Oakhurst and the Sunless Citadel at night, four **twig blights** attack the party. The blights attack stealthily from out of nearby foliage.

THE CITADEL

See the old Dragon from his throne
Sink with enormous ruin down!

—*Hymn*

Once the characters are ready to leave Oakhurst, the adventure truly begins. The overgrown Old Road winds through rocky downs, near stands of old-growth oak, and past abandoned farms. It is 7 miles from Oakhurst to the Sunless Citadel.

RAVINE

The Old Road passes to the east of a narrow ravine. At the road's closest approach to the cleft, several broken pillars jut from the earth where the ravine widens. Two of the pillars stand straight, but most lean atop sloped earth. Others are broken, and several have apparently fallen into the dark depths. A few similar pillars are visible on the opposite side of the ravine.

A sturdy, knotted rope is tied to one of the leaning pillars on this side of the ravine.

SUNLESS CITADEL OVERVIEW

A dragon cult that valued privacy and defense built the Sunless Citadel on the surface long ago. All record of the cult's name has vanished, though various sources believe that it was associated with the dragon Ashardalon. The cataclysm that killed the cult members sank the fortress at the same time. Because of residual enchantments, much of the structure survived its descent into the earth. With the cultists dead, goblins and other creatures moved in, and they have survived here for hundreds of years.

The goblins, which belong to the Durbuluk tribe ("Dominator" in Goblin), once patrolled the area around the ravine to rob passersby. But now, with the Old Road having fallen out of use, the goblins rarely pay much attention to this entrance anymore. Also, a tribe of kobolds has recently moved in to challenge the goblins' ownership of the fortress. Both groups are skirmishing as they vie for control, and they're not overly concerned about the possibility of intruders. Thus, the cleft offers the characters a good opportunity to gain entry to the dungeon without attracting attention. (The missing party that came here before did much the same; the rope left tied to the pillar near the ravine is theirs.)

Though the kobolds (areas 13–24) and the goblins (areas 31–41) claim the Sunless Citadel as their property, they've never visited all its chambers. They avoid entering the most secluded parts of the grove level. In the past, they feared that the hidden grove was haunted. With the arrival of Belak the Outcast twelve years ago, that belief is vindicated. He orders the goblins to distribute the midsummer fruit each year, and the goblins obey him out of fear.

Monsters on Alert. The kobolds and the goblins respond similarly if attacked. Intruders who fall back to take a long rest before dealing with the leaders of an attacked community allow the creatures time to make preparations. Alerted monsters reinforce cleared rooms with forces previously stationed in other rooms. For example, three kobolds from one area 16 could be stationed in area 15 with orders to set an ambush for returning invaders. Or, four goblins from one area 36 could be redeployed to area 32 to guard against another intrusion. Keep track of such changes, so that the characters don't encounter the same kobolds or goblins twice.

Random Treasure. Each regular kobold and goblin is likely to have 2d10 sp, perhaps in the form of various coins and crude jewelry.

The ravine runs for several miles in either direction, with an average depth and width of 30 feet. At the point where it most closely intersects the Old Road, it widens to 40 feet.

Investigating. The pillars are worn and broken, and graffiti in the Dwarvish alphabet covers most of them. Characters who know Goblin (after translating the letters from Dwarvish) recognize the inscriptions as warnings and threats against potential trespassers.

A successful DC 10 Intelligence (Investigation) or Wisdom (Survival) check reveals that the area in and around the pillars has hosted many small campfires, some of as recent as a month ago. Someone went to some effort to hide the evidence of the camps from casual scrutiny.

Descending. The rope tied to one of the leaning pillars hangs down into the darkness of the ravine. Judging by its good condition, the rope couldn't have been tied there any longer than two or three weeks ago. From the edge of the ravine, older and weathered handholds and footholds can be seen carved into the cliff face. These are goblin-carved.

Adventurers can easily climb down the knotted rope, using the wall to brace themselves. Using the carved indentations is slower but only slightly harder. The descent is 50 feet to the ledge (area 1).

LOCATIONS ON THE FORTRESS LEVEL

The following locations are identified on map 1.1.

1. LEDGE

A sandy ledge overlooks a subterranean gulf of darkness to the west. The ledge is wide but rough. Sand, rocky debris, and the bones of small animals cover it. A rough-hewn stairwell zigs and zags down the side of the ledge, descending into darkness.

The far wall of the chasm is 250 feet to the west, and the bottom of the subterranean vault is 80 feet below where the characters stand.

Creatures. Drawn by the occasional animal that accidentally falls into the ravine, three **giant rats** lurk in the rubble. They try to hide if they become aware of the characters, and they ambush the first character who arrives on the ledge without being quiet about it.

Investigating. A successful DC 10 Wisdom (Survival) check reveals humanoid footprints, as well as rat tracks of unusually large size. The footprints lead down the stairs.

Among the rubble is an old ring of stones that contains (and is covered by) the accumulated ash of hundreds of fires, though no fire has been lit here for a few years. Inside the ash pile are a few rough-hewn spear tips of goblin manufacture and small animal bones.

2. SWITCHBACK STAIRS

The 5-foot-wide stairs that descend from area 1 are roughly carved. They aren't dangerous to traverse, however, except that combat while on the narrow path can be risky. Three small landings lie along the route, the first at 60 feet above the floor in area 3, the second at 40 feet, and the third at 20 feet.

The characters might be able to see area 3 as they descend.

A fortress emerges from the darkness. The subterranean citadel, though impressive, seems long forgotten, if the lightless windows, cracked crenellations, and leaning towers are any indication. All is quiet, though a cold breeze blows up from below, bringing with it the scent of dust and a faint trace of rot.

3. CRUMBLED COURTYARD

The narrow stairs empty into a small courtyard, apparently the top of what was once a crenellated battlement. The buried citadel has sunk so far into the earth that the battlement is now level with the surrounding floor. That floor stretches away to the north and south, composed of a layer of treacherous, crumbled masonry, which reaches to an unknown depth. To the west looms the surviving structure of what must be the Sunless Citadel. A tower stands on the west side of the courtyard.

The stone courtyard, surrounded by crumbled masonry, contains a trap and a wooden door.

Masonry Debris. An expanse of crumbled masonry surrounds the entire citadel. Those attempting to cross it immediately note its unsteadiness. The rubble is difficult terrain. Anyone who moves across the debris must make a DC 10 Dexterity (Acrobatics) check for each 10 feet traversed. On a failed check, the character is unable to move. If the check fails by 5 or more, a slab of masonry below the character shifts, dumping the character into a debris-lined cavity. Climbing back out requires a successful DC 10 Strength (Athletics) check; on a failed check, the victim drops back into the cavity.

Creatures. Each time a creature falls into a cavity, the noise is 10 percent likely to draw 1d4 **giant rats** from the dozens that infest the rubble field. Attracted rats move carefully and stealthily through the rubble to attack.

Hidden Pit. The map shows the location of a concealed trapdoor that covers a 10-foot-square, 10-foot-deep pit. A 2-foot-wide catwalk on the west edge allows access to the door that leads to area 4. It takes a successful DC 15 Wisdom (Perception) check to note the trapdoor's unmortared edge. Then, a successful DC 10 Intelligence (Investigation) check lets a character deduce the location of the catwalk and how the pit operates.

If a creature steps on the trapdoor, the lid flips open, dumping the creature into the pit. With a successful DC 15 Dexterity check, a creature can use thieves' tools to jam the lid shut. A mechanism resets the trap 1 minute after the door opens, pushing it back into the closed position. The mechanism is in the pit wall under the catwalk. A creature can jam it in the open position with a successful DC 15 Dexterity check using thieves' tools. If this check succeeds by 5 or more, the mechanism can be permanently disabled if desired.

Creature. The pit contains two goblin skeletons, one goblin that has been dead for about a day, and one live **giant rat**. The rat, which slipped into the pit to feed on the fresh goblin but was caught when the trap reset, attacks creatures inside the pit or climbs out to attack those nearby.

Treasure. The goblin corpse has a scimitar and a shield, as well as 23 sp and 4 gp in a belt pouch.

4. TOWER SHELL

This circular area is cobbled with cracked granite, upon which sprawl the bodies of four goblins, apparently slain in combat. One corpse stands with its back against the western wall, the spear that killed it still skewering it and holding it upright. Three wooden doors lead from this area. A hollow tower of loose masonry reaches thirty feet into the air, but the intervening floors and stairs are gone, except for a couple of crumbled ledges.

Bodies. Investigation reveals that the four goblins have been dead for quite a while, and rats have gnawed at them. The bodies have been looted. If someone removes the spear pinning the goblin to the wall, the body slumps to reveal Draconic runes on the wall behind it. Those who know the Draconic language can read the runes as "Ashardalon."

Secret Door. A trapped secret door leads to area 5. Finding the door requires a successful DC 20 Wisdom (Perception) check. The door opens by way of a masonry block that also serves as a lever, which can be pushed in on the left side or pulled out from the right.

Needle Trap. If the lever is pulled out, that movement sets off a needle trap. The needle extends 3 inches out of the opening, dealing 1 piercing damage to whoever pulled the lever. Someone who carefully and slowly pulls the lever open can easily see the needle before it strikes. Disabling the needle requires thieves' tools and a successful DC 15 Dexterity check. If the check fails by 5 or more, the trap goes off, stabbing the character unless the character succeeds on a DC 15 Dexterity saving throw.

MAP 1.1: FORTRESS LEVEL

5. SECRET POCKET

This pocket chamber is damp and cold. The skeletons of three long-dead archers slump against rubble-filled arrow slits along the east and south wall.

The skeletons date back to the time before the citadel plunged into the earth. That calamity killed all three archers, at the same time instilling in them the curse of undeath. If anyone enters this chamber, the three **skele-**

tons animate, pinpoints of red fire sparkling in their eye sockets as they rise.

Treasure. Each skeleton has twenty arrows, 2d10 sp, 1d10 gp, and one *+1 arrow* in a special socket on the quiver. Because the skeletons are mindless, they don't use the magical arrows.

6. OLD APPROACH

The masonry walls of this twenty-foot-wide hall are in poor repair. The far end has collapsed, filling the southern section with rubble. The western wall is in much better shape than the other walls, and it holds a stone door with a rearing dragon carved in relief on it. The door has a single keyhole, situated in the rearing dragon's open mouth.

Dragon Door. The door that is carved to look like a dragon has a mechanical lock as well as an *arcane lock* spell cast on it. The Strength (Athletics) check to defeat the arcane lock is DC 30, and the Dexterity check to bypass the magical lock using thieves' tools is DC 25. Casting a *knock* spell on the door suppresses the magical lock for 10 minutes, lowering the DCs by 10 during that time. The mechanical lock remains intact if the magical lock is bypassed, requiring another *knock* spell or the use of the key. The key, which bypasses the magical lock as well as the mechanical one, is in area 21.

Creature. One **giant rat** hides in the rubble. The rat attacks anyone who moves to within 5 feet of the edge of the rubble or anyone left alone in this area.

7. GALLERY OF FORLORN NOTES

As the door opens, a hissing noise and a puff of dust around the door indicate that the chamber beyond has been sealed for ages. Dust, long undisturbed, covers every surface in this large gallery. The air here is stale.

Three alcoves are on the north wall, and one is on the south wall. Each alcove contains a dust-covered stone pedestal with a fist-sized crystalline globe resting on it. The globes in the northern alcoves are cracked and dark, but the globe in the southern alcove glows with a soft blue light. Faint tinkling notes issue from it.

If a character moves within 5 feet of the lit globe, brooding music begins to play throughout the area, and the sound carries into areas 6, 8, and 9 if the doors to those areas are open. Any creature that can hear the music must make a DC 15 Wisdom saving throw. On a successful save, a creature is immune to the music of the globe for 24 hours. On a failed save, a creature becomes charmed and, while charmed in this way, can take only the Dash action and move toward area 3.

The effect on a creature ends once that creature reaches the floor beyond the pit trap in area 3. If an affected creature is prevented from moving to area 3,

the creature can repeat the saving throw at the end of each of its turns, ending the effect on itself on a successful save. The effect ends on its own 1 minute after the creature can no longer hear the music. A creature can escape the music by being on the other side of a closed door that leads to the gallery, or by vacating the area (including adjacent rooms) where the music is audible.

The globe has AC 10 and 10 hit points. If it is attacked or handled, the music becomes louder, audible in areas 4 and 10 if the doors to those areas are open. The DC of the Wisdom saving throw then increases to 20. If the globe is reduced to 0 hit points or taken from the room, it cracks and goes dark and silent. It no longer functions.

8. PRESSURE PLATE

The air is stale in this twenty-foot-long corridor, which leads to another closed stone door.

Arrow Trap. Each time any weight is placed on any part of the center 10-foot-square section of the corridor, a mechanical pressure plate is activated, triggering a trap. An arrow fires from above the western door at the creature who triggered the trap: +5 to hit, 5 (1d10) piercing damage.

With a successful DC 15 Intelligence (Investigation) check, a character can deduce the presence of the pressure plate from variations in the mortar and stone around it, compared to the surrounding floor. Wedging an iron spike or some other similarly sized and sturdy object under the pressure plate prevents it from activating.

9. DRAGON RIDDLE

Dust fills this hall like a layer of gray snow. In the rounded northern end of the chamber stands a ten-foot-tall sculpture of a coiled dragon carved from red-veined white marble.

Dragon Sculpture. If a creature moves within 5 feet of the dragon statue, a *magic mouth* spell causes the dragon to utter a riddle in Common (to viewers, it seems as though the stone jaws are actually moving). The dragon's riddle is as follows:

We come at night without being fetched;
we disappear by day without being stolen.
What are we?
(Answer: stars)

Secret Door. A secret door in the western wall leads to area 10. Finding the door requires a successful DC 20 Wisdom (Perception) check. Under the scrutiny of *detect magic*, the door radiates a faint aura of abjuration magic. The door comes open, pivoting into the room, only if someone speaks the answer to the riddle.

Once the door is opened, it closes on its own 1 minute later, although any obstruction placed in the doorway

walls of the pit are rough, and they offer handholds to climbers. Area 12 begins on its far side.

Creature. A **quasit** named Jot was bound in the southwestern alcove an age ago to guard the contents of the sarcophagus in area 12. It was in suspended animation until a few decades ago, and it now waits on the other side of the arch just out of sight in area 12. Jot is alerted by any light source the characters have, so it can prepare for them. (If the characters have no light source and are stealthy, Jot might not become aware of them.) The quasit darts out of its hiding place and attacks the first creature that climbs out of the pit on the western side.

Development. Jot doesn't fight to the death. If it takes any damage, or if more than one character attacks it, Jot laughs and says, "You broke the binding. My watch over the dragonpriest is over!" It uses its next action to become invisible. It then turns into a bat and flies along the 10-foot-high ceiling across the pit.

If Jot escapes, the characters might see it again. It knows that death on the Material Plane means a return to the Abyss, so it prefers to harass the characters while they are otherwise engaged, laughing and mocking as it does so.

Secret Door. Finding the door on the southern wall requires a successful DC 20 Wisdom (Perception) check. The door opens with a simple push inward.

11. Secret Room

> Dust coats the contents of this tiny chamber, obscuring runes inscribed on the southern wall.

Inscription. If the southern wall is cleared of dust, the runes are revealed to be a message in Draconic. Someone who can read the language understands it as "A dragonpriest entombed alive for transgressions of the Law still retains the honor of his position."

Secret Door. A secret trapdoor in the floor requires a successful DC 20 Wisdom (Perception) check to find. The door opens by pulling it upward. It leads to a 3-foot-by-3-foot crawl space that connects to a similar trapdoor in area 12.

12. Tomb of a Failed Dragonpriest

> Violet marble tiles cover the floor and walls, though all are cracked or broken, revealing rough-hewn stone beneath. Sconces are attached to the walls at each corner. One holds a torch that burns with greenish fire. A marble sarcophagus, easily nine feet long, lies in the room's center. The coffin is carved with dragon imagery, and the head of the sarcophagus resembles a dragon's head. Rusting iron clasps firmly lock down the lid.

Torch. The greenish fire is a *continual flame* spell.
Sarcophagus. Six rusted iron latches hold down the sarcophagus lid. Opening a single latch requires a

---

prevents it from doing so. The door can be opened from the western side with a simple push.

10. Honor Guard

> Dust cloaks the contents of this twenty-foot-wide hall. Six alcoves line the walls, three to the north and three to the south. Each alcove except the southwest one holds a humanoid figure carved of red-veined white marble. The figures resemble tall elves in plate armor. A stone archway at the west end of the hall opens into a wide room from which greenish light glows. A dark pit is situated before the archway.

Southwest Alcove. A successful DC 10 Wisdom (Perception) check reveals that the dust in the room is disturbed by tracks that start in the southwest alcove, though the tracks are filled in enough that the disturbance must have occurred dozens of years ago. A successful DC 10 Wisdom (Survival) check enables a character to determine that the tracks were made by tiny humanoid feet with claw-like nails. They begin in the center of the alcove, move west toward the pit, and then disappear into the pit. A character who enters the pit to follow the tracks must make another successful DC 10 Wisdom (Survival) check to pick up the trail again.

Spiked Pit. The pit is 10 feet deep, and its bottom is filled with spikes that deal 11 (2d10) piercing damage to a creature that falls in, as well as falling damage. The

successful DC 15 Strength check. If the six latches are opened, the lid can be removed with a successful DC 15 Strength check or by the effort of any combination of characters whose combined Strength is 30 or higher.

Inside, a dragonpriest lies imprisoned, kept alive by virtue of a *sequester* spell that is dispelled with a flash of green light when the sarcophagus is opened. If the characters look inside, read:

> In the coffin is a troll! It's dressed in rotted finery, but its jewelry and rings adorned with tiny silver dragons still sparkle. The creature's body is shrunken and elongated, and its flesh is a rubbery, putrid green. Its black hair is long, thick, and ropy. Its beady black eyes flash open, and it snarls.

This dragonpriest delved into magic that the dragon cult deemed profane—he permanently transformed himself from an elf into a troll. For this crime, the cult entombed him alive, though the honor of his station remained. The dragonpriest attacks his rescuers, his mind all but transformed to that of a troll over the ages of his burial. He had a name, but he has forgotten it, although he has not forgotten how to speak Elvish and Draconic.

Creature. In his current state, the dragonpriest is slower and weaker than a normal troll. Use **troll** statistics, but the dragonpriest starts with 30 hit points, regenerates only 5 hit points per round (up to normal for a troll), and can't use Multiattack. If he is defeated in this state, the dragonpriest is worth 450 XP.

Development. The dragonpriest won't pursue fleeing characters. Instead, he continues to repose in his tomb until hunger finally draws him forth to hunt five days later. By that time, he uses the normal troll statistics, retaining his additional languages.

Treasure. The dragonpriest has an ornate ceremonial dagger (worth 125 gp), two silver rings (15 gp each), and a silver amulet (15 gp). Scattered across the bottom of the sarcophagus are 220 sp, 50 gp, and four *spell scrolls*: *command*, *cure wounds* (2nd level), *inflict wounds* (2nd level), and *guiding bolt* (2nd level).

13. Empty Room

Several empty rooms in the fortress have the same characteristics. Nothing of note can be found in any of them.

> This ruined chamber stands empty of all but a litter of rocky debris.

14. Enchanted Water Cache

> The stone relief-carved door sealing this chamber portrays a dragon-like fish swimming.

The door is locked but can be opened with thieves' tools and a successful DC 20 Dexterity check.

RANDOM ENCOUNTERS

In areas 13 and beyond, monsters move through the halls of the Sunless Citadel. For every 12 hours the characters spend in the dungeon, roll a d20 and refer to the following table if the characters are in an accessible hallway or room at that time.

d20	Encounter
1	1d6 **kobolds**
2	1d6 **giant rats**
3	1d4 **goblins**
4	1d2 **hobgoblins**
5	1d4 **skeletons**
6	1d6 **twig blights**
7–20	No encounter

If the door is opened, read:

> This ten-foot-square chamber is hewn from stone. It contains an upright keg fashioned of rusted iron. Rusted pipes lead from the keg into the floor.

If anyone shakes or strikes the keg, the sound of sloshing liquid comes from inside it. The connecting pipes hold the keg in place, preventing it from being detached. The characters can remove a wide metallic bung on the keg's top with a successful DC 15 Strength check, or someone can easily stave in the side of the keg.

Creatures. If the keg is breached, the **ice mephit** and the **steam mephit** confined within it are released. The creatures attack anyone who has disturbed the keg.

Treasure. Within the keg are five tiny sapphires (worth 10 gp each) used to bring about the magic that bound the mephits.

15. Dragon Cell

> Crudely executed symbols and glyphs, scribed in bright green dye, decorate this large and irregularly shaped crumbling chamber. A large pit in the center shows evidence of a recent fire. A metallic cage in the middle of the southern wall contains a gaping hole and stands empty. A small wooden bench draped with green cloth is next to the cage, and several small objects rest on it. A bedroll lies near the wooden bench, and the sound of whimpering comes from inside it.

Until recently, the kobolds confined a white dragon wyrmling in the cage and placed it under heavy guard. Those guards were not strong enough to stand against a sortie by goblins that stole the wyrmling a week ago.

Creature. Meepo, the **kobold** who was his tribe's Keeper of Dragons, is now the sole occupant of the chamber. He is heartsick at the loss of the wyrmling and spends much of his time nowadays in nightmare-ridden sleep in his bedroll. With the loss of his charge, Meepo's status is in the gutter. He doesn't react to anything short of loud noise or direct prodding.

If he is disturbed, Meepo is frightened but willing to talk. He is weepy. His numerous obvious scars are souvenirs of his job as Keeper of Dragons. If he is asked about the cage or queried in any way that mentions a dragon, he says, "The clan's dragon ... we lost it. The wretched goblins stole Calcryx, our dragon!"

To all other questions, Meepo responds by saying, "Meepo don't know, but Yusdrayl does. Meepo take you to meet Yusdrayl, our leader, if you make nice. You get safe passage, if you promise to make nice. Maybe if you promise to rescue dragon, Yusdrayl make nice to you, answer questions."

Meepo perks up as he senses the possibility of getting the dragon back. True to his word, he guides the characters to area 21. Along the way, he shouts out "Ticklecorn!" (in Draconic) from time to time, explaining that it's a password that tells other kobolds the characters are friendly. If the characters leave Meepo behind, or if they are antagonistic toward him, the characters don't learn the password, and all other kobolds are hostile toward the party.

Development. If combat occurs in this chamber, the kobolds in the nearby area 16 are alerted, and they rush out to meet enemies.

Investigating. The symbols on the walls are crudely formed in Draconic and read, "Here There Be Dragons." The metallic cage is all but destroyed and can't be used to restrain captives. A search of the cage reveals white scales that someone who has proficiency in Nature or Survival can determine to be from no natural animal. A successful DC 15 check using either skill identifies the scales as those of a white dragon wyrmling. The firepit, if its ashes are sifted, is found to hold charred bits of kobold bones and armor.

Treasure. The bench serves as a sort of tiny altar. Resting on it are containers of green dye, a paintbrush made of goblin-hair bristles, and four tiny jade figurines of dragons (worth 15 gp each). A thorough search of the firepit and a successful DC 15 Wisdom (Perception) check reveals another jade figurine.

16. KOBOLD GUARDROOM

Three rooms in the fortress serve as kobold guard stations. All have the same characteristics.

Door Trap. The door leading to the room is trapped with a tripwire that the kobolds connect after shutting the door. Hitting this tripwire, 2 inches off the ground stretched between opposite door frames and running up the frame, causes the trap to trigger. A character who succeeds on a DC 10 Wisdom (Perception) check spots the wire. If a character then succeeds on a DC 10 Dexterity check using thieves' tools, the tripwire is cut without triggering the trap. A character can attempt this check using any edged weapon or edged tool in place of thieves' tools, but does so with disadvantage.

On a failed Dexterity check, the trap triggers, tipping over a clay pot of offal, garbage, and dragon droppings that falls on any creature in the doorway and splatters in a 5-foot radius. A creature hit by the stuff must succeed on a DC 10 Constitution saving throw or be poisoned for 1 minute. An affected creature can repeat the saving throw at the end of each of its turns, ending the effect on itself on a successful save.

The kobolds release the tension on the tripwire when they exit, meaning that any guardroom that has been vacated can be entered safely.

> A small pit of embers, built of broken masonry and portions of shattered stone sculptures, smolders in the center of this chamber. Arrayed around the pit are several small rugs woven of matted hair and dead fungi.

Creatures. The room serves as a barracks and guard post for the kobold tribe's warriors. Three **kobolds** stand guard inside, unless they have already come forth to reinforce other kobolds.

If the characters try to talk and the interaction is successful, the kobolds direct the characters to head toward "Yusdrayl on her dragon throne," giving them simple directions to area 21 and warning them to avoid rousing the ire of Yusdrayl's elite guards.

17. DRAGON CHOW

A character who approaches the door can smell the stench of what lies beyond. If the door is opened, read:

> Rats fill the room, trapped among their own waste. A small half-barrier prevents the rats from easily escaping when the door is open.

Creatures. The rats are used as food for the dragon wyrmling that was once stabled in area 15. Since the abduction of the dragon, the kobolds have neglected the rats, and in the meantime the rodents have chewed away the fastenings of the barrier. One round after someone opens the door, the rats knock the barrier over and rush out, attacking as a **swarm of rats** for 1 round, after which they disperse into the dungeon.

18. Prison

Each door that lead to the prison chamber is locked, requiring a DC 15 Dexterity check using thieves' tools to unlock, and also barred on the outside with an iron rod. If a character attempts to open either door while any kobolds are present, the kobolds warn against doing so. Opening a door in spite of this warning turns the kobolds hostile.

> Four small humanoids are shackled by thick, rusted chains attached to a large iron spike set in the floor. Several broken weapons and sundered shields lie in one corner.

Creatures. Four **goblins** are chained here, taken prisoner during the course of several skirmishes. Every so often, the kobolds remove a goblin from the room and ransom it back to the goblins (for a price of 2d10 sp). Those who can't be ransomed are bound for the kobold cook pot. The goblins whine and cower pathetically if any characters enter the room. A character who succeeds on a DC 15 Dexterity check using thieves' tools can open the lock on the chains, or the chains can be broken (Strength DC 20) or sundered (AC 15, 60 hit points).

The goblins promise anything and everything in exchange for their release, including safe passage for the characters to their chief. The creatures have no power to guarantee their promises, however. In addition, if the goblins are released, any understanding the characters have with the kobolds is voided. Freed goblins flee at the first hint of trouble, and they double-cross their rescuers if threatened by other goblins.

19. Hall of Dragons

> A double row of relief-carved marble columns march the length of this long, large hall. The worn carvings depict entwining dragons.

Creatures. An elite squad of three **kobolds** (each with 7 hit points) patrols the hall, considering the duty an honor. The guards pay particular attention to the door that leads to area 24, which is along the route traditionally used by goblin raiders. These kobolds react to the character's presence in the same way as the ordinary ones described in area 16. If the characters head for area 21 without causing hostilities, these guards follow the characters into Yusdrayl's presence.

Development. If combat erupts here, the result is likely to be deadly for the party. Any kobolds remaining in the areas nearby enter the room as reinforcements. Yusdrayl and her two guards arrive from area 21 at the start of the second round of combat. At the start of the fifth round, the kobolds in the area 16 to the southwest of this room come on the scene. At the start of the eighth round, the kobolds from area 23 enter the fray. (Kobolds that leave their original area and are slain here should be noted for possible future reference.)

20. Kobold Colony

The strong wooden door that leads to the kobolds' living quarters is barred from the inside. Characters who give the proper password ("Ticklecorn!" spoken in Draconic; see area 15) or who make a successful DC 15 Charisma (Deception) check can convince the kobolds within to unbar the door. Otherwise, the kobolds open the door only when guards return to the room for a shift change.

> Several small but smoky fires light this wide and high chamber. Spits, tanning racks, and other implements of a primitive culture are visible through the haze. Several small figures busily work and play within the chamber.

Twenty-four kobolds occupy the room, but only three **kobolds** are capable warriors that challenge unescorted intruders. Seven other kobolds are **commoners**, but with 3 hit points each, and a −1 reduction to hit and damage compared to the *Monster Manual* statistics. The other tribe members here are too young, too old, or too cowardly to defend themselves; they flee if combat breaks out and are worth no XP. Even the kobolds capable of fighting run away if they are outmatched.

The kobolds here answer all questions with a quick "Yusdrayl knows."

An attack on these kobolds brings reinforcements, as described in area 19, though each group arrives 1 round later because of the extra distance it must traverse.

21. Dragon Throne

> A short throne stands near the west wall, constructed of fallen bits of masonry stacked against an old altar. On the top of the altar sit a variety of small items. The portion of the altar that serves as the throne's back features a carving of a rearing dragon. A metallic key is held firmly in the dragon's open jaws.

Creatures. Normally sitting on the throne is the kobolds' leader, **Yusdrayl** (see appendix B). Two elite **kobolds** (7 hit points each) guard her. Those who come to Yusdrayl's chamber can talk to her; she is hostile only if she knows that the characters have slain other kobolds. Characters who antagonize her while talking earn the leader's ire and a savage attack.

Yusdrayl can speak to the following questions:

Why are kobolds in this place? "Kobolds are heir to dragons. As the mightiest among my people, I have led a brave few to this ancient holy site, where dragons were worshiped long ago." Yusdrayl knows nothing else about the history of the fortress, except the name of the dragon that was once revered here, which is Ashardalon.

What about the goblins/fruit/Belak? "The Outcast, he lives below. He grows the fruit, which he gives to the goblins. The dragon-thieving goblins are his servants!"

What about the twig monsters? "The twig blights are pets of the Outcast. They are more numerous below, in the Twilight Grove."

What about the lost human adventurers? "They went to fight the goblins and never returned."

What about the stolen wyrmling dragon? "The goblins stole our dragon! If you return Calcryx to us, I shall grant you a reward. Meepo can accompany you if you desire."

If the characters decide to go looking for the dragon, the kobolds direct them toward the passage that connects area 15 and area 25, which is the "back way" into goblin territory. Yusdrayl and her followers know nothing useful about the goblin lair. If the characters take Meepo with them, he can serve as their guide to that location. If Meepo goes along and is slain, the kobolds count it as a small loss as long as the dragon is rescued.

Possible rewards include the key in the carved dragon's mouth, or any two of the items on the altar. Yusdrayl is also willing to sell the key for 50 gp.

Development. If hostilities break out, reinforcements arrive in the manner described in area 19.

If the characters return Calcryx, Yusdrayl can be convinced to aid them in an assault on the remaining goblins. You determine the nature of the aid.

Treasure. The key clenched in the mouth of the carved dragon opens the door to area 7. Yusdrayl has keys to area 18 and the chains there, a key to the doors in area 24, and a key that once fit the cage in area 15. She also has 35 gp.

The items assembled on the altar include a *Quaal's feather token* (tree), three *spell scrolls* (*mage armor*, *spider climb*, and *knock*), and a small flask that contains three doses of *elixir of health*.

22. Larder

> The odor of rotting meat permeates this chamber. Most of the rusty iron hooks in the ceiling are empty, but a few hold the skinned carcasses of large vermin, huge fungoid stalks, and several massive insect carapaces. On a small, battered bench along the south wall are pieces of nearly useless cutlery and rusting skinning knives.

The kobolds bring food for their tribe up from the Underdark and store it in a nearby chamber. The rotting flesh is that of rats, bats, overlarge cave crickets, beetles, goblin parts, and spiders. The room also has a selection of fungi and mushrooms.

23. Underdark Access

> The floor is partially collapsed on the east side of this room, revealing a tunnel. The passage is unworked, and it fluctuates widely in width, height, and direction as natural tunnels do. Within the room, hunting gear is racked on the wall, and several pallets lie nearby.

The kobolds used the natural passage to first enter the Sunless Citadel, and they continue to travel through it for hunting and gathering forays into the Underdark.

The tunnel leads beyond the scope of this adventure, but it could be a route to a site you have designed.

Creatures. If they have not come forth as reinforcements, three **kobolds** camp here, serving as hunters and guardians of the tunnel. They react as described in area 16.

24. Trapped Access

The doors on both ends of the corridor are locked and can be opened by a character who succeeds on a DC 20 Dexterity check using thieves' tools.

> At the other end of a twenty-foot-long corridor is another closed door.

Hidden Pit. The map shows the location of a concealed trapdoor. A 2-foot-wide catwalk along the pit's center allows safe passage over the pit. With a successful DC 15 Wisdom (Perception) check, a character notices the door's unmortared rim. After that, a character who makes a successful DC 10 Intelligence (Investigation) check deduces the location of the catwalk, as well as how the pit operates.

If a creature steps on the pit cover, the lid flips open, dumping the creature 10 feet into the pit. With a successful DC 15 Dexterity check, a creature can use thieves' tools and an object, such as an iron spike, to wedge the lid shut.

Kobolds regularly check the trap and manually reset it when necessary.

25. EMPTY CHAMBER

Two empty chambers in the eastern end of the fortress have the same characteristics.

> This empty chamber is home only to rat droppings, crumbled flagstone, and stains.

Investigating. A character who succeeds on a DC 15 Wisdom (Perception) check notices tracks in the dust. Some tracks were made by rats and some by humanoids. A character who then succeeds on a DC 15 Wisdom (Survival) check ascertains that the rat tracks are very recent, maybe a day old, and that the humanoid tracks are almost a month old and were made by three or four human-sized humanoids moving across the area to the north.

Trap. The door that connects the northernmost empty chamber with area 31 contains a trap. See area 31 for more details.

26. DRY FOUNTAIN

> Dust and odd bits of stony debris and rubble lie scattered on the floor. An ornate fountain is built into the eastern wall. Though cracked and stained, the fountain's overarching carving of a diving dragon retains its beauty. A relief-carved stone door stands on the western wall.

Investigating. The debris and dust covering the floor display the same tracks described in area 25.

Fountain. A thin layer of scum coats the fountain's basin, but it is otherwise dry. Under the scrutiny of a *detect magic* spell, the fountain emits an aura of conjuration. A character who makes a successful DC 15 Wisdom (Perception) check notices a mostly worn-away inscription in Draconic on the basin's front. It reads, "Let there be fire."

If a character speaks the phrase aloud, the magic of the fountain functions one last time. Reddish liquid begins to well from the diving dragon's mouth, slowly accumulating in the basin. If the liquid is collected, it can be used as a *potion of fire breath*. After it is used in this way, the fountain loses its magic.

Western Door. Carvings on the western door show skeletal dragons. A Draconic inscription on the door reads, "Rebuke the dead, open the way." Within 5 feet of the door, the air is noticeably cooler, and the door itself is cold to the touch.

The locked door opens only when someone targets it with a *knock* spell or an effect that turns undead. If someone does so, the door glows ghostly blue and swings open silently.

Scythe Trap. If someone tries to open the door without first deactivating the lock, a scythe blade springs forth, targeting the area immediately in front of the door: +5 to hit, 4 (1d8) slashing damage.

The blade is concealed in a slot in the ceiling, 10 feet up. A character who succeeds on a DC 20 Wisdom (Perception) check can find the slot before the trap is sprung.

The opening, once discovered, can be blocked with an iron spike or a similar object. A character who does so must make a DC 15 Dexterity check or Strength check. On a failed check, the blockage falls out when the trap is sprung. Alternatively, a character can use thieves' tools and a successful DC 20 Dexterity check to pull the trap mechanism out of the slot and dismantle it. Either task takes about a minute.

27. SANCTUARY

> Five dusty sarcophagi, three to the north and two to the south, stand on end in this silent chamber. Each of the carved stone coffins resembles a noble, elf-like humanoid in ceremonial robes. An altar, with images of dragons carved into its black obsidian, is set in the center of the west wall. A single candle burns brightly on the altar. Next to the candle are a small whistle and a crystal flask.

Creatures. Five **skeletons** emerge en masse from the sarcophagi to attack those who disturb the altar or open any sarcophagus. These creatures pursue characters who flee.

Treasure. The candle has a *continual flame* spell cast on it. In the flask is a *potion of resistance* (fire). The whistle, made of crystal, has the name *Night Caller* inscribed on it in Dwarvish. See appendix A for a description of this item. A secret compartment in the shrine, requiring a successful DC 20 Wisdom (Perception) check to find, holds a coffer containing six peridot jewels carved in a likeness of a dragon (worth 10 gp each).

28. INFESTED CELLS

> This section of hallway contains six doors, all slightly ajar. The area smells musky.

The doors lead to small cells. Each door is open just wide enough to enable Small and smaller creatures to slip through without having to open it farther.

Creatures. The two southernmost cells and the one to the northeast contain abandoned giant rat nests. One **giant rat** lives in each of the other cells. Any noise or light in the area attracts all three creatures.

Investigating. A character who succeeds on a DC 15 Wisdom (Perception) check notices tracks in the dust here. Some tracks were made by rats and some by humanoids. A character who then succeeds on a DC 15 Wisdom (Survival) check ascertains that the rat tracks are recent, perhaps a few minutes old, and the humanoid tracks are almost a month old and were made by four human-sized individuals moving across the area to the north. Only three of those individuals returned south.

Treasure. The occupied rat nests contain shiny bits collected by their current owners. Poking through each nest turns up 2d6 − 2 sp, 1d6 − 1 gp, and 1d4 − 1 gems (worth 5 gp each).

29. DISABLED TRAPS

> The cobblestone floor contains two trapdoors blocked open by iron spikes. The north wall holds a dry fountain carved with an overarching diving dragon. A faint rotten stench pervades the room.

Investigating. The two marked areas on the map are traps that were jammed open by the lost adventuring party. Examining each one reveals a 20-foot-deep pit containing only rat bones, rusted metal bits, and filth.

Chances to find or follow the trail noted in area 28 are similar here. The trail of the missing adventuring party skirts around the traps and leads to the western wooden door.

Development. Those who spend more than 3 rounds in the chamber conversing in normal tones, or otherwise making noise, draw the attention of the inhabitants of area 30, who hide to ready an ambush.

Trapped Fountain. The dry fountain on the northern wall looks remarkably like the one described in area 26. Under the scrutiny of a *detect magic* spell, the fountain emits a faint aura of evocation. A successful DC 20 Wisdom (Perception) check reveals suspicious metallic tubes in the carved dragon's mouth, as well as a small, rusted iron canister. A character who makes a successful DC 15 Wisdom (Perception) check notices a mostly worn-away inscription in Draconic on the front of the basin. It reads, "Let there be death."

Anyone who speaks this phrase aloud in Draconic triggers the trap. A poison mist sprays forth from the dragon's mouth, filling a 20-foot cube and expending the canister's last charge. Those in the area must make a DC 10 Constitution saving throw. On a failed save, a creature takes 5 (1d10) poison damage and becomes poisoned for 10 minutes. On a successful save, the creature takes only half the poison damage and is poisoned for 1 minute.

Western Door. A character who approaches the western door can smell the stench of rotten meat coming from the other side.

30. MAMA RAT

> An oppressive smell suffuses the air, rising from chewed carcasses of cave rats, smaller vermin, and a few humanoid-looking creatures. The bodies lie upon a floor of filth, old bones, hair, and fur that combine to make a particularly large and vile nest.

Investigating. The humanoid corpses in the chamber include two goblins, a kobold, and one human male—a member of the lost adventuring party (Karakas the ranger).

Creatures. Three **giant rats** occupy the area, along with a monstrously swollen female **diseased giant rat** (Medium [6 feet long], 16 hit points, +5 to hit, challenge rating 1/4 [50 XP]) that the goblins call Guthash (Bloated One). The giant rats that hunt in the Sunless Citadel all descend from her. These creatures attack and attempt to eat all trespassers.

Treasure. Poking through the refuse over a period of 10 minutes uncovers 312 sp, 68 gp, and 3 gems (worth 25 gp each). On and around the ranger's corpse are several items: studded leather armor, five daggers, a longbow, a backpack (containing a water skin, one day's rations, a bedroll, a tinderbox, and three torches), a quiver with six arrows, a *potion of healing*, and a pouch that holds 17 gp. A gold ring (worth 10 gp) on Karakas's finger is engraved (in Common) with his name.

31. CALTROP HALL

The door that leads north into this hallway is closed and fitted with a bell that clangs if someone opens the door without doing so very slowly.

With a successful DC 15 Wisdom (Perception) check, someone who carefully opens the door might spot the bell attached to the door about 3 feet off the ground. A character who examines the space around the door before opening it and succeeds on a DC 15 Wisdom (Perception) check notices the damage done to the door when the goblins fastened the bell to it.

If the bell rings, the noise alerts the goblins in area 32. They duck behind the low wall and wait to ambush intruders that enter the corridor.

> The ten-foot-wide hall is liberally strewn with sharp caltrops. On the northern wall, passage to the room beyond is partially blocked by a roughly mortared, three-foot-high wall, complete with crenellations.

Caltrops. The floor in the hallway is strewn with caltrops; see "Adventuring Gear" in chapter 5 of the *Player's Handbook*.

Creatures. Two **goblins** in area 32 pop up over the wall if they are alerted to the characters' presence. The creatures use ranged attacks as the characters move through the hall.

Treasure. About two hundred caltrops are strewn on the floor.

32. GOBLIN GATE

> The filth on the floor, stains on the walls, shabby hides, and firepit attest to the years of use this room has seen at the hands of creatures unconcerned with hygiene. On the eastern side of the southern wall is a crudely mortared half-wall, complete with crenellations.

Creatures. Two **goblins** are stationed behind the rough, 3-foot-high wall. They are hostile to intruders, but unwilling to die facing a superior force. If captured, these goblins know the same information that Erky Timbers in area 34 does.

Development. If one of the goblins gets away, it warns the goblins in area 33. The alerted goblins prepare an ambush for intruders in that area.

Investigating. A search of the room turns up putrid jerky, vinegary wine in poorly preserved water skins, and other worthless bits of clutter.

33. PRACTICE RANGE

The sound of goblins engaged in target practice might be heard from outside any of the doors to the practice range.

> Dozens of blunted and broken arrows lie on the cracked cobblestone floor, and a few protrude from three crudely sewn, human-sized targets hung along the center of the south wall. The northern third of the room is separated from the south by a crudely mortared and crenellated half-wall. A permanent camp of sorts lies north of the wall, complete with a fire ring and several small iron cook pots.

Creatures. The three **goblins** assigned to watch the room spend some of their time shooting at the hair-and-fur-filled burlap dummies that look vaguely like humans and elves. The rest of the time they drink too much goblin wine.

When fighting, the goblins try to use the 3-foot-high wall for cover while shooting their foes.

Treasure. One goblin has a silver flask of dwarven make (worth 50 gp) filled with vile goblin wine. Another goblin has a key to open the locked door to area 34.

Development. If things go badly for the goblins, one of them attempts to warn the goblin warriors in area 39.

34. GOBLIN STOCKADE

The wooden door is closed and locked. It can be opened by a character who succeeds on a DC 15 Dexterity check using thieves' tools.

> Squalor reigns in this low-ceilinged room. A large iron spike is driven into the floor near the door, and a small iron cage is set farther back. Several sets of corroded manacles are connected to the walls, and some still bind a few crumbling skeletons.

Creatures. Three **kobolds** are bound with crude rope to the iron spike. A battered gnome lies in the cage, which is almost too small for him. It's easy to untie the kobolds. Freeing the caged gnome requires either a successful DC 15 Strength check to bend the bars or a successful DC 15 Dexterity check using thieves' tools to open the cage lock.

The kobolds are aware that the goblins might try to ransom them back to the other kobolds. Uncertain of their chances with the characters, the kobolds are unhelpful and reluctant to be set free. If they are released and shown a clear line of retreat, the kobolds flee. They know very little, but they react positively to Meepo's presence or if they are told that the characters intend to free Calcryx.

The gnome is named Erky Timbers, an **acolyte** with 17 (5d6) hit points who knows Common, Draconic, Gnomish, and Goblin. He has the cleric's Channel Divinity: Turn Undead feature, which he can use once after each short or long rest.

If he is released, he helpfully answers questions. He knows the following information:

Why are you here? "Months past, I was on my way to seek my fortune and took the Old Road. My bad luck that the goblin bandits caught me; I've been here ever since. My deity's blessings have kept me healthy; otherwise I'm sure I'd be dead from starvation and abuse."

What about the goblins/Belak? "I've heard the goblins talk about the Twilight Grove down below. A wicked old human called Belak—a spellcaster, I suspect—tends an enchanted garden and harvests fruit from something the goblins call the Gulthias Tree, but they speak of it only in the most terrified of whispers. The enchanted fruit grows on the Gulthias Tree."

What's the deal with the fruit? "The midsummer fruit restores spirit and vigor to those who eat it; the pale midwinter fruit steals the same. Belak allows the goblins to sell the fruit on the surface, but I don't know why."

What about the twig blights? "Twig blights live in the level below, with the Gulthias Tree."

What about the lost human adventurers? "The goblins caught three of them over a month ago, and they were captives with me in here for a while. They said their names were Talgen, Sharwyn, and Sir Braford. The goblins kept them in here only about a week before they removed them. Belak wanted them, and that's the last I've heard about that."

Development. If the characters fail to suggest it, Erky Timbers asks to join the party as a temporary member. The gnome serves as a loyal friend. Currently, though, he has no gear. Those who free Erky gain XP as if they defeated him in combat.

Manacles. The rusted iron restraints can bind a Small or Medium creature. If the characters are taken prisoner (see area 36) and bound here, escaping from the manacles requires a successful DC 20 Dexterity check. A set of manacles can be broken with a successful DC 20 Strength check, or a character proficient with thieves' tools can pick the lock on a set of manacles with a successful DC 15 Dexterity check. Manacles have AC 15 and 15 hit points.

35. TRAPPED CORRIDOR

Hidden Pit. The map shows the location of a concealed trapdoor. A 2-foot-wide catwalk along the pit's center allows safe passage over the pit. With a successful DC 15 Wisdom (Perception) check, a character notices the door's unmortared rim. After that, a character who makes a successful DC 10 Intelligence (Investigation) check deduces the location of the catwalk, as well as how the pit operates.

If a creature steps on the pit cover, the lid flips open, dumping the creature 10 feet into the pit. With a successful DC 15 Dexterity check, a creature can use thieves' tools and an object, such as an iron spike, to wedge the lid shut.

Development. If characters fall into the pit or otherwise make excessive noise, the goblins in the area 36 to the north are alerted. Alerted goblins respond in 2 rounds. These goblins also check the trap and manually reset it.

Treasure. A successful DC 15 Wisdom (Perception) check made while searching around the pit uncovers a long-lost gold ring with an inset sapphire (worth 25 gp).

36. GOBLIN BANDITS

Three rooms in the northern part of the fortress serve as living quarters for goblin bandits. All have the same characteristics.

> The stench, garbage, and carrion here are evidence of years of use by unsanitary tenants. Tattered hides stretched on frames form six unstable hammocks around a much-used firepit. Battered cooking equipment is mixed indiscriminately with broken or worn arms and armor.

Creatures. Three **goblins**, who proudly call themselves bandits, are in the room when the characters enter. In better times, two or more bandit groups would

hunt the Old Road together, preying on travelers. Now, the bandits content themselves with an occasional hunt in the wilds of the Underdark (see area 43), as well as preying on the kobolds.

Development. The goblins might try to knock the characters unconscious and imprison them in area 34, locking victims into manacles. They take captured equipment to the goblin chief in area 41. The bandits are likely to try to ransom the prisoners to someone in Oakhurst. Kerowyn Hucrele is prepared to pay such a ransom, taking it out of the characters' prospective reward.

If things go badly for the goblins, one of them attempts to warn the goblin warriors in area 39.

Investigating. A search of the room turns up putrid jerky, vinegary wine in poorly preserved water skins, and worthless bits of clutter.

37. TROPHY ROOM

Both of the wooden doors that offer access to the trophy room are closed and locked. Either door can be opened by a character who succeeds on a DC 15 Dexterity check using thieves' tools.

> Mounted and stuffed animal heads adorn the walls. The mounting job is sloppy, and the assortment of heads includes cattle, rats, and other not particularly impressive specimens. A few grisly trophies share the wall with the animals, including a couple of kobold heads. Smashed and broken cabinets and small tables litter the periphery of the room, mute victims of some sort of rampage. A rusted iron spike stands in the center of the room, trailing a broken chain. Thin patches of frost coat sections of the walls, floor, and debris.

Creature. Calcryx, the **white dragon wyrmling**, is initially out of view, resting behind a broken table. The goblins used the iron chain to bind her, but she broke free and rampaged through the room, destroying the floor displays. Balsag, the bugbear responsible for capturing the dragon, hasn't returned to bring her under control, and the other goblins fear to enter.

The wyrmling finds her current situation superior to her station as the kobolds' pet. She is hostile to those who enter this chamber. If battle breaks out and Meepo accompanies the party, the dragon targets him first.

Treasure. The wyrmling has scoured the room and gathered all items of worth into a nest she made behind the table. The valuables include a dragon-shaped, jade figurine (worth 20 gp), a crystal goblet (5 gp), and twenty-four pieces of fine silverware (1 gp each).

Of particular note is a sealed scroll case carved of bone, carrying an inscription. Runes in the Dwarvish alphabet spell out the word "Khundrukar." An old parchment is within the case. Age and water damage have destroyed most of it, but a short message in Dwarvish remains: "... the remaining few. By order of Durgeddin the Black, we have created a secret dwarven redoubt. None shall find us; however, ..." Though the information

makes little sense, even to most dwarves, the case and the parchment can fetch up to 100 gp if sold in a dwarven community.

38. Goblin Pantry

The north and south walls of this chamber are stacked halfway to the ceiling with ill-made barrels, boxes, and crates. A clear path allows easy access between the west and east doors.

The goblins store water, wine, and food, none of which is of good quality, in a pantry accessible through two doors. The stockpile includes five pints of oil, along with a few small barrels labeled "Elf Pudding" in Goblin.

39. Dragon Haze

Several torches mounted in crude sconces burn fitfully around this chamber, filling the air with a haze. A double row of marble columns carved with entwining dragons runs the length of the hall.

As long as the torches burn, the hall is lighted, but the haze makes the area lightly obscured. The haze never builds to suffocating levels, thanks to natural ventilation.

Any loud noise in the chamber attracts the attention of goblins in the area 36 to the south, as well as in area 40. The goblins in area 40 prepare for danger but don't leave their stations, while those in area 36 come to investigate within 2 rounds.

40. Goblinville

Anyone who stands within 10 feet of a door leading to the goblins' main living area can hear the voices of the goblins inside, unless they have been alerted to danger.

What might once have been a cathedral is now a goblin lair, thick with the filth of years of goblin life. Scores of wall- and floor-mounted sconces filled with violet-glowing fungi provide illumination. Dozens of goblins go about their daily business, which involves a lot of rudeness and violence. Along the southern wall is a heaping pile of assorted items, including wagon wheels, broken armor and rusted arms, chests, small statues, antique furniture, and artwork.

Creatures. Thirty-four goblins are at home when the characters arrive, but only four of the **goblins** are warriors. Ten of the other goblins are **commoners**, but with 3 hit points each and a −1 reduction to hit and damage compared to the *Monster Manual* statistics. The other twenty creatures are noncombatants, too feeble or too fearful to defend themselves; they try to flee through the northernmost or the eastern exit. This stampede should dominate the first moments of battle, and even the goblins capable of fighting refuse to stick around just to lose their lives. Noncombatants are worth no XP.

These goblinoids know the same information, in cruder form, that Erky in area 34 knows.

Development. An attack on the goblins brings reinforcements from area 36 and warns the goblin chief in area 41 that something is amiss. Grenl, the goblin shaman in area 41, might emerge to protect the tribe.

Investigating. The goblins collect the phosphorescent fungi from the grove below. They need its light for close work, such as reading, and the fungus is edible. Crude equipment for cooking, skinning game, tanning hides, and other basic gear fills the area. Food is usually collected from the Underdark through area 43.

Treasure. Among the tribal equipment, near the shaman's bedding, is a healer's kit and a poisoner's kit.

The pile along the southern wall contains the tribe's loot, mixed in with lots of other stuff taken from the goblins' victims. The characters can find almost any piece of mundane gear that has a value of 5 gp or lower. Two items of considerable value can be unearthed by separate successful DC 15 Wisdom (Perception) checks: a fine agate statue of the elven deity Corellon Larethian (worth 30 gp) and a Medium chain shirt.

41. HALL OF THE GOBLIN CHIEF

If the goblinoid guards in the chief's hall have been alerted, or if they hear conflict in area 40, they cover the door for 10 minutes, then investigate the source of the disruptions at their leader's behest.

> A circular shaft pierces the floor of this forty-foot-diameter domed chamber. Dim violet light shines out of the shaft, revealing sickly white and gray vines that coat the walls of the shaft. The light is supplemented by four lit wall torches set equidistant around the periphery of the chamber. A crudely fashioned stone throne sits against the curve of the northwestern wall. A large iron chest serves as the throne's footstool. A sapling grows in a wide stone pot next to the throne.

Creatures. The chief of the Durbuluk tribe is Durnn, a **hobgoblin**. He wears splint armor (AC 19) and has 18 hit points, a +4 bonus to hit, a +1 bonus to damage, and Strength 15 (+2). These changes raise his challenge rating to 1 (200 XP). When not in combat, Durnn sits on the throne, and three other **hobgoblins** stand nearby or lounge on stone benches.

The shaman Grenl advises the chief. She is a **goblin** with 10 (3d6) hit points, a Wisdom of 13 (+1), and the following trait:

Spellcasting. Grenl is a 1st-level spellcaster. Her spellcasting ability is Wisdom (spell save DC 11, +3 to hit with spell attacks). She has the following cleric spells prepared:

Cantrips (at will): *poison spray, thaumaturgy*
1st level (2 slots): *bane, inflict wounds*

A **twig blight**, a gift from Belak the Outcast and a pet of Durnn's, is in the stone pot, and goblins from area 40 occasionally enter the chamber to see to the needs of the tribe's elite that languish here.

Development. Durnn has a *potion of healing* and two vials of antitoxin. Grenl has a *spell scroll* of *faerie fire* and another of *expeditious retreat*.

The goblins in area 40 don't join the battle if they hear sounds of violence coming from the north. If the fight turns against the chief, however, he might open the door to area 40 and call for aid, or withdraw to area 40 to continue the fight.

Durnn can't surrender for fear of losing face. He won't give up if the opposition includes kobolds. Otherwise, he might call for parley if doing so allows him to avoid death. But he must still look strong while negotiating, so he's unwilling to capitulate in an arrangement that makes him look weak.

Because Durnn and his hobgoblins usurped control of the Durbuluk tribe, Grenl hates them. She also wants to protect her tribe, so she is willing to negotiate a truce if Durnn falls. Grenl also hates and envies Belak, and she wants him gone from the citadel so she can control the Gulthias Tree.

If captured and interrogated, the goblinoids here know what Erky in area 34 knows, with the following addition: Belak wanted all the living human prisoners sent down to him, but in a fit of anger, Durnn slew Talgen. Thus, Durnn sent only Sharwyn and Sir Braford down to the Twilight Grove.

Shaft. The shaft has a 2-foot wall around it, much like the upper end of a well. Because of the wall, a creature pushed toward the shaft can avoid going over the edge by falling prone and succeeding on a DC 10 Dexterity saving throw. Thick, pale vines line the shaft. The vines are as good as knotted rope for the purpose of climbing.

A creature that falls into the shaft can make a DC 15 Dexterity saving throw to catch the vines. On a failed save, the creature falls 80 feet to the floor of area 42.

Trapped Chest. Durnn's iron chest rests in front of the throne. It is locked (Dexterity DC 15 using thieves' tools) and trapped with a poisoned needle. A character who succeeds on a DC 15 Intelligence (Investigation) check deduces the trap's presence from alterations made to the lock. A character can then remove the needle from the lock by succeeding on a DC 15 Dexterity check using thieves' tools. On a failed Dexterity check, the trap is triggered.

When the trap is triggered, the needle extends 3 inches straight out from the lock. A creature within striking distance takes 1 piercing damage and must succeed on a DC 10 Constitution saving throw or take 3 (1d6) poison damage.

Treasure. In addition to the valuables mentioned in the "Development" section, Durnn wears Talgen's gold signet ring (worth 20 gp) and splint armor, which is identifiable by the Hucrele family crest worked into the chest pieces. The chief also has the key to his iron chest. Grenl has keys to areas 34 and 37. One of the other hobgoblins wears silver earrings set with moonstones (20 gp each), and another wears a matching necklace (50 gp).

Inside Durnn's iron chest are 231 gp and two onyx gems (30 gp each).

GROVE LEVEL

1 square = 5 feet

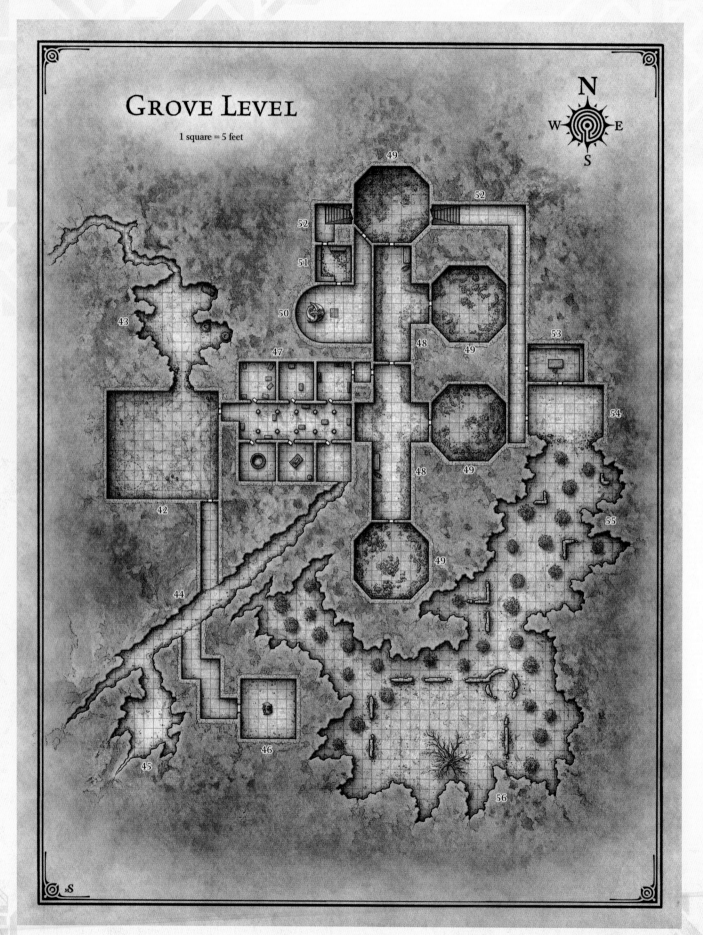

Locations on the Grove Level

The grove level and the fortress level connect through the shaft that leads from area 41 to 42. The following locations are identified on map 1.2.

42. Central Garden

> Luminescent fungus, shedding violet light, clings to the walls and ceiling of this wide cavern. The air is damp, chilly, and redolent with the odors of loam and decay. A layer of earth, mixed with rotting vegetation and the remains of cave animals, covers the floor. Several varieties of mushrooms and fungi grow on the detritus, as well as a few saplings.

Creatures. Two robed **skeletons** (AC 12) serve Belak by tending a fungus garden, using shovels and a rusted wheelbarrow to turn the soil and spread compost. In addition, two mature **twig blights** are rooted in the garden. The twig blights ambush intruders that aren't goblinoids, and the skeletons attack (with shovels, 1d6 bludgeoning damage) anything that the twig blights target.

Development. The creatures in area 43 investigate any disturbance in the garden after 3 rounds.

43. The Great Hunter's Abode

> The floor of this rough cavern is stained and smells of blood and animal musk. Light from glowing fungus reveals the eastern niche, which holds a pallet of matted furs, a wide wooden board on which a variety of weapons are affixed, and a great cloak of patchy black fur hung on a slender pole. To the edge of the niche are two large nests made of hair, dry fungus, and refuse.

Creature. Balsag the **bugbear** and his two **giant rat** "hounds," named Grip and Fang, reside in a natural stone chamber when they're not hunting (25 percent chance of being absent when characters arrive). The bugbear wears a crown of antlers on his head to enhance his frightening appearance. Balsag considers all non-Durbuluk creatures to be potential prey, so he attacks any he meets, roaring in Goblin, "Get ready to meet the cook pot!"

Underdark Access. In the dark of the northern cavern section, a crude tunnel leads away, angling west and downward. The tunnel is like the one in area 23.

Treasure. Two spears, six javelins, one longsword, one greatsword are affixed to the weapon rack. A box hidden under one of the furs in Balsag's bedding, requiring a successful DC 15 Wisdom (Perception) check to notice, contains 241 sp and 54 gp.

44. Rift

> A rift opens here, its debris-strewn floor two feet below that of the corridor. No phosphorescent fungus grows in the rift. The corridor continues past the rift, though the opening of the rift has caused it to shift 10 feet to the west. A number of two-foot-diameter holes riddle the floor of the rift. The smell of burnt earth hangs in the air.

The small holes in the floor extend as far down as anyone is capable of probing.

45. Rift Node

> The rift widens, creating a cavern-like chamber. Small, two-foot-diameter holes riddle the node. A dim fiery glow shines out of one such hole.

Creature. In the glowing hall rests a **fire snake**. Belak used magic to call the creature forth and hopes to train it to be a loyal servant before it matures.

Treasure. Belak has already appealed to the snake's greed with a small gift. In its nest, the adventurers find two sapphires (worth 50 gp each).

46. Old Shrine

The stone door at the end of the corridor is closed and stuck, requiring someone to make a successful DC 15 Strength check to pull it open.

> Faded mosaic tiles still decorate parts of the wall, but most have fallen to the dust-covered floor and shattered. Situated at the center of the chamber stands a slim pedestal of rusted iron shaped like an upright dragon. In the dragon's mouth rests an empty tray.

The room once held items of importance to the old dragon cult. The remaining features are dust-covered and worthless.

47. Belak's Laboratory

> Two rows of dragon-carved marble columns march the length of the hall, most completely covered in luminescent fungus. The cobbled floor is cracked and stained, and on it sit many small wooden tables. The contents on the tables include mortars and pestles, small tools, bowls filled with crushed leaves, chopped fungus stalks, and other plant specimens. The many doors leading off this hall are all partly open.

Belak prepares various experimental concoctions in his laboratory and the small chambers that lead off it (see the sections below), with the fumbling aid of goblins that

serve him. Any noise or disturbance in the main area draws all the monsters, although those in the northwest chamber respond most slowly.

Investigating. The containers on the small tables in the main area hold mashed leaves, fungus, bark, and powdered roots. A character who makes a successful DC 10 Intelligence (Nature) check identifies many common varieties of tree, shrub, and fungus, although all have a pronounced pallor, as if sun-starved.

Treasure. One pile of herbs and supplies in the main chamber contains the ingredients of a healer's kit. An assortment of tools and herbs can be salvaged to make up a herbalism kit and a set of alchemist's supplies.

Northwest Chamber. Snores are audible from the room to the northwest, which is a rough barracks. Sixteen small pallets of matted fur cover the floor. Two pallets currently hold a sleeping **goblin** and two goblin **commoners** (like those in area 40).

Southwest Chamber. The goblins use a crude mashing, straining, and casking facility to create goblin wine, which they and Belak are quite fond of. Two goblin **commoners** currently stand barefoot in the mashing-tun, squashing roots and fungi into pulp. A dirty straining bin stands nearby, as well as ten 2-gallon casks of the end product.

North Central Chamber. Two goblin **commoners** currently repair dirty goblin armor with cord, iron needles, leather patches, and other crude implements of tailoring.

South Central Chamber. One **goblin** and two goblin **commoners** monitor the health of a diseased giant rat, which is strapped spread-eagled onto a wooden bench. The rat suffers from horrible tumors that look woody and fruit-like. Its tumors stem from an elixir Belak created to infuse twig blight traits into giant rats.

On a stand in the corner is a fancy crystal vial (worth 5 gp) that contains the elixir. Drinking the elixir exposes the drinker to the same disease that the diseased rat might impart with its bite, except the initial saving throw DC is 15.

Northeast Chamber. Extra weapon stores include five battered scimitars, six shortbows, and forty arrows.

Southeast Chamber. The room stands empty, and the caved-in back wall leads to a natural rift in the earth (see area 44).

48. Garden Galleries

The two galleries that lead to the arboretums have the same characteristics. The doors to all connecting areas are closed.

> Nodules of luminescent fungus hang from the ceiling and walls and grow in clumps on the flagstone floor. The light illuminates portions of grand bas-relief carvings on the stone walls that aren't covered with the fungus. The carvings depict dragons in various stages of raining fire down upon terrified people. Soil and compost cover half the chamber's floor, which allows a variety of feeble plants to grow. A bench containing simple gardening implements stands along the west wall.

Belak is using the galleries to grow aboveground vegetation using the light of luminescent fungus.

Creature. A **bugbear** gardener roams both galleries, tending the grasses for Belak. She is armed with a sickle-bladed glaive; she has a reach of 10 feet and deals 2d10 + 2 slashing damage with it.

Treasure. The bugbear carries a *potion of healing*.

Development. The neighboring arboretums (area 49) contain additional monsters. The closed doors and stone walls prevent sound from entering these four areas. The creatures within join the battle here at your discretion.

49. ARBORETUMS

> Luminescent mist blurs the edges of this octagonal chamber. Nodules of glowing fungus dot the stone walls and ceiling, as well as the caps of toadstools and mushrooms, small polyps, puffballs, and lichen. The humid air reeks with rot.

The arboretums hold small samples of traditional Underdark ecosystems, which aren't difficult for Belak to nurture. The stone doors leading to them are unlocked.

Southern Arboretum. A **goblin** and three goblin **commoners** gather fungus for use in area 47.

Southeast Arboretum. Several growths in the chamber are scorched and dead. Fungus shrouds holes similar to those found in area 45, and a **fire snake** lurks inside one of these openings. It emerges if anyone pokes into or closely examines the holes. If the snake comes out, a character who reaches into the snake's burrow can recover two sapphires (worth 50 gp each).

Northeast Arboretum. Three **skeletons**—AC 12, 3 (1d6) bludgeoning damage with shovels or rakes—are at work, clearing scorched plants. One **twig blight**, which is hostile to the adventurers, is with them. The skeletons attack anything the twig blight attacks.

Fungus shrouds holes similar to those in area 45.

Northern Arboretum. The northern room contains only its plants.

50. ASHARDALON'S SHRINE

> Dragon-carved granite blocks line this chamber's walls and ceiling, though many are crumbled and broken, leaving stony debris on the floor. A huge marble statue of a rearing red dragon stands in the curve of the western wall. The eye sockets of the dragon are empty, but a red glow lingers there, providing reddish light throughout the chamber. The radiance casts an inky shadow behind the statue's wide wings. A five-foot-diameter, circular tile of dark stone is set in the floor in front of the dragon statue. Runes are carved around the circular tile's inner edge.

Investigating. Viewed in white light, the circular tile is red. A *detect magic* spell can reveal that the tile and statue give off an aura of transmutation. The runes on

the tile's inner edge read, in Draconic, "Let the sorcerous power illuminate my spirit." If anyone speaks this sentence aloud while standing on the tile, a puff of spectral flame harmlessly envelops the speaker, granting the target advantage on Charisma checks for 24 hours. Once the tile is activated, it is dormant for 24 hours.

Creature. A **shadow** hides in the gloom behind the dragon statue. It attacks only those who spot it or who attempt to investigate the circular tile or claim the treasure. The creature doesn't pursue those who flee.

Treasure. A loose stone is in the wall behind the statue, requiring a successful DC 15 Wisdom (Perception) check to find. Inside are 34 gp and two flasks of alchemist's fire.

51. DRAGON LIBRARY

> Leaning and fallen stone bookshelves fill this chamber, though a clear path connects wooden doors on opposite walls. Torn and burnt pages, bindings, and scrolls form disordered piles in the corners.

Treasure. Rooting around in the wreckage, separate successful DC 15 Wisdom (Perception) checks uncover a *spell scroll* of *scorching ray*, a *spell scroll* of *Melf's acid arrow*, and a tome of dragon lore bound in dragon scale and written in Draconic (worth 150 gp).

52. UNDERPASS

> Damp and crumbled steps descend sharply.

The steps descend 15 feet. An 8-foot-high stone corridor passes about 7 feet below the northern arboretum (area 49), connecting the stairways on either side.

53. BELAK'S STUDY

The wooden door leading to Belak's study is closed and locked. The lock can be undone by someone who uses thieves' tools and succeeds on a DC 20 Dexterity check.

> A layer of soil covers the floor. Rough wooden shelves, filled with a scattering of tomes and scrolls, line the north and east walls, and a rough-hewn desk stands in the center of the chamber. Fungus on the ceiling provides light, apparently in sufficient quantity to nourish several small bushes and pale saplings that grow in the soil.

Investigating. In his study, Belak stores seasonal records of growth, precipitation, harvests, and similar notes for the surrounding lands for the last dozen years. One interesting tome titled (in Draconic) *Treasures of the Fire Lords* has a *glyph of warding* spell with an explosive runes effect on it. The glyph is on the second page, and it's triggered when someone opens to that page. Otherwise, the book is blank.

If the glyph is triggered, it erupts with magical energy in a 20-foot-radius sphere centered on the book. The sphere spreads around corners. Each creature in the area must make a DC 12 Dexterity saving throw. A creature takes 22 (5d8) cold damage on a failed saving throw, or half as much damage on a successful one. The cold doesn't damage the other works here.

Development. If any obvious disturbance occurs here, the goblins in area 54 set an ambush for intruders. They wait at least 10 minutes before coming to investigate.

Treasure. Separate successful DC 15 Wisdom (Perception) checks uncover a *spell scroll* of *entangle*, a *spell scroll* of *protection from poison*, and a tome on druidic theories on the cycle of life and death (worth 150 gp). Cubbyholes in the desk hold 365 gp and four agate gems (20 gp each).

54. Grove Gate

> Twigs and roots are piled on the floor of this sagging chamber. The collapsed southern wall opens into a vast cavern. Luminescent fungus on the rough walls and the high roof loom over a twilight grove of sickly briars, bushes, saplings, and other woody plants. Ruined walls and hollow towers protrude from the briars.

Creatures. Four **goblins** sort the specimens for Belak. They are hostile to intruders. If things go badly for them, they cry out in Goblin, saying, "Aid us, Protector of the Twilight Grove!"

Development. Sometimes the twig blights in area 55 attack the goblins out of sheer malice. Thus, a call from the goblins doesn't bring all the forces of the cavern down on the characters. But if the goblins do call, four **twig blights** arrive from area 55 and attack.

Investigating. Any character who gazes into area 55 and succeeds on a DC 10 Wisdom (Perception) check spots the blackened top of the Gulthias Tree in the distance. If the check succeeds by 3 or more, the character also spots the twig blights creeping around in area 55.

55. Twilight Grove

> Pale, spindly briars press close, casting twisted shadows on the earth floor in the violet light.

Briars. The most successful aboveground plants that Belak has transplanted in the Twilight Grove are the briars, though they appear sickly and pale, with blighted leaves. Other common plants and bushes are also represented, though they are equally afflicted.

The briars don't hinder Small and smaller creatures. Larger creatures must either spend 2 feet of movement for every 1 foot moved or make a DC 10 Constitution saving throw for every 10 feet moved. On a failed save, the creature takes 1 piercing damage from the briars.

A 5-foot-by-5-foot area of briars can be cleared if it takes 20 damage of any type other than psychic.

Creatures. Ten **twig blights**, less any that were dispatched in area 54, are spread about the grove. After moving 50 feet into the cavern, the characters come upon 1d4 of the hostile creatures. Any significant noise, such as from combat or clearing the briars, also attracts 1d4 − 1 twig blights (minimum 0) each round.

Development. If the characters get to area 56 before all the twig blights have engaged, the rest of the monsters hold off their attacks. Any conflict that involves yelling in a language other than Goblin, the use of flashy magical effects, or similar noticeable elements alerts Belak in area 56 to the approach of invaders.

56. The Gulthias Tree

> A walled clearing is here among the briars. The walls are about twenty feet high, which is less than half the height of the cavern's ceiling. Several varieties of plants grow around the perimeter of the clearing, including a few suspicious-looking saplings, but their importance pales before that which stands at the courtyard's center. Beneath the fungal light grows an evil tree. Its blackened, twisted limbs reach upward, like a skeletal hand clawing its way out of the earth. Before it stand a few twig blights; a heavily armored, young human male with a shield and sword; a blonde, young human woman in a robe fit for a noble; and a middle-aged, bearded human male wearing a hooded brown robe and armed with a staff and sickle. The younger humans have black eyes and gray skin with the texture of bark.

Creatures. Belak the Outcast spends much of his time studying the Gulthias Tree, but he is well aware when the characters are approaching. He is a human **druid**, and he has the following spells prepared:

Cantrips (at will): *druidcraft*, *poison spray*, *shillelagh*
1st level (4 slots): *cure wounds*, *entangle*, *faerie fire*, *thunderwave*
2nd level (3 slots): *barkskin*, *flaming sphere*

Standing with Belak are **Sir Braford** and **Sharwyn Hucrele** (both described in appendix B). Belak's **giant frog**, Kulket, lurks stealthily in the branches of the Gulthias Tree. A character who has a passive Perception score of 15 or higher or succeeds on a DC 15 Wisdom (Perception) check spots the frog. If combat breaks out, the frog jumps down and joins the fight in the second round. Three **twig blights** are here, too.

Interaction. When the characters arrive, Belak says loudly, "Hold a moment, you know not what you do!" If the characters engage him in conversation, he can share the following information:

What are you doing? "I am Belak, called the Outcast. My circle expelled me, the fools. Why? Because I dared to expand nature's reach in ways they couldn't grasp. I have found what I sought in the Gulthias Tree."
What is the Gulthias Tree? "It's beautiful, no? It lives, though it looks dead. In an age long past, someone

THE GULTHIAS TREE

A Gargantuan plant, the Gulthias Tree has AC 10 and 35 hit points. It is immune to necrotic, poison, psychic damage, and it has resistance to piercing damage. The tree has vulnerability to fire damage.

Fruit. Two magical fruits (evocation school) ripen on the tree each year. Each fruit resembles an apple, but it slowly extrudes from the tree like a cyst.

Up to a week before the summer solstice, a ruby red fruit grows. Someone other than a construct who eats a quarter or more of it regains 70 hit points. In addition, any blindness, deafness, and diseases affecting the eater end.

Up to a week before the winter solstice, a sickly white fruit grows. Someone who eats a quarter or more of it takes 70 necrotic damage. Each fruit has 1d4 seeds that, if planted, grow leafless woody shrubs that animate as twig blights after one year.

Tree Thralls. If a humanoid is bound to the bole of the Gulthias Tree, over the next 24 hours the victim is sucked completely into the tree. Once the victim is completely absorbed into the tree, it becomes the tree's thrall, and is expelled over the course of 1 hour. The Gulthias Tree can have only four thralls at any one time. A victim's skin is rough, gray, and bark-like. A thrall is totally corrupted, becoming neutral evil. Such a creature exists only to serve the Gulthias Tree and those who tend it (such as Belak). It possesses all of its former abilities and gains the following traits:

Barkskin. The thrall's AC can't be lower than 16.

Tree Thrall. If the Gulthias Tree dies, the thrall dies 24 hours later.

staked a vampire on this very spot. The stake took root. And so grew the Gulthias Tree, reverberating with primal power for those who can tap it."

What's with the stick-monsters? "The twig blights grow from seeds of the tree's fruit."

What's going on with the fruit? "I give fruit to the goblins with orders to disperse their seeds on the surface. Deceitful beings that they are, the goblins barter the fruit, but the seeds are dispersed all the same. My plan for colonizing the surface with the children of Gulthias continues."

What did you do to the other adventurers? "They were the first supplicants. The Gulthias Tree has accepted them, and they are mine to control, just like the twig blights. You can't save them."

Why are you talking to us? "Though your remains would enrich the compost, you'll serve my needs better as supplicants. You shall retain your lives, after a fashion. Surrender and submit peacefully, or perish!"

While this interaction proceeds, Sir Braford, the three twig blights, and Belak's frog position themselves between the characters and Belak (Sharwyn stands next to Belak).

Combat. If a fight breaks out (which will happen unless the characters actually submit to Belak), the twig blights, the frog, and Sir Braford attack the characters physically. Sir Braford uses *Shatterspike* (see appendix A) to destroy his foe's weapon, if possible.

Belak casts *barkskin* on himself, possibly before melee occurs. He also makes early use of his *wand of*

entangle (see appendix A), attempting to hold the transgressors in place. If Braford looks like he needs healing, Belak casts healing spells on him, as well. Sharwyn uses her repertoire of spells to best advantage, resorting to her dagger only in desperation.

Development. During a battle, if any twig blights remain in area 55, 1d4 − 1 of them (minimum 0) enter this area each round.

Targeting the Tree. A successful DC 15 Wisdom (Insight) check or Intelligence (Arcana or Nature) check allows a character to deduce that destroying the tree might have an effect on Sir Braford, Sharwyn, and the twig blights. If anyone attacks the Gulthias Tree, Belak and the twig blights try to kill the aggressor. If the Gulthias Tree dies, Belak loses his influence over the twig blights, Sharwyn, and Sir Braford. These monsters turn on Belak before targeting the characters again.

Walls. The courtyard's walls stand 20 feet tall, and the cavern's stalactite-dotted ceiling is 50 feet up.

Treasure. Belak has a key (to area 53), three *potions of healing*, two doses of antitoxin, and his *wand of entangle*. Sharwyn wears her gold Hucrele signet ring (worth 20 gp).

AFTERMATH

If the characters kill the Gulthias Tree, Sharwyn and Braford die 24 hours later (unless you decide they can be saved somehow). If Belak survives, his former servants turn on him, and he attempts to escape. If he succeeds in getting away, he might appear later to trouble the characters.

If the characters reveal the truth about the fruit's seeds to the villagers of Oakhurst, those folk cut down and burn all growing saplings.

> As the villagers set the evil saplings alight, the mayor turns to you with a frank expression. "You realize that our actions have set loose several of these abominations upon the world. Who knows what these twisted plants are doing now?"

The mayor is right. Twig blights that are already loose in the world can still reproduce through root sprouts, as aspen trees do. Although it is likely a hopeless task, the characters can search out these twig blights and destroy them. It's up to you and your players to determine what happens next. At any rate, if the characters warn Oakhurst's residents about the seeds, they have taken their first steps toward gaining a measure of fame and establishing a rapport with local residents.

In addition, if the characters return the Hucrele signet rings to the family matriarch, they receive the promised monetary award. If they bring back the remains of Sharwyn and Sir Braford, the matriarch begins funeral arrangements and invites the characters to attend. If they accept, they can begin to establish a long-term relationship with the Hucrele family, which can prove useful in later adventures. ⚑

THE FORGE OF FURY

TWO CENTURIES AGO, THE GREAT DWARF smith Durgeddin the Black and his clan were driven from their home by a horde of fierce orcs and trolls. They plundered the dwarves' ancestral halls and slew all they could catch. Fleeing his enemies, Durgeddin led the destitute remnants of his clan in search of a new home. After years of wandering, the dwarves discovered a great cavern system beneath the Stone Tooth: a rugged, forested hill crowned by a bare rocky crag. There Durgeddin and his followers founded the stronghold of Khundrukar.

About a century ago, a member of Durgeddin's clan was captured by a powerful orc tribe during a raid, and the orcs learned of their enemy's hidden stronghold. The orc chieftains raised a great army and marched on Khundrukar. In a hard-fought siege lasting months, the orcs tunneled around the dwarven defenses. When they finally stormed the place, they put all within to the sword, then carried off wagonloads of booty.

In the years since the great battle, various creatures have occupied the stronghold and used the place as a base for their raids. At other times, the caverns have lain empty except for the mindless and bloodthirsty monsters that haunt such places. Today legends of Durgeddin's Vengeance (or the Smith's War) and the extraordinary blades the dwarves forged in anger still surface from time to time in the lands near the Stone Tooth.

ADVENTURE SYNOPSIS

The Forge of Fury is set in the ruined stronghold of Khundrukar. It is designed for four 3rd-level player characters. They can advance to 5th level with good play.

The characters come to the Stone Tooth in search of a reputed cache of Durgeddin's superior blades and find the stronghold inhabited by dangerous monsters. The complex consists of the following five sections:

The Mountain Door. The Mountain Door comprises the uppermost level of the cavern complex. It is currently inhabited by a tribe of fierce orcs, led by a brutal ogre known as Great Ulfe.

The Glitterhame. The largest level of Khundrukar, the Glitterhame is an expanse of beautiful natural caverns now infested by troglodytes and other cave-dwelling monsters.

The Sinkhole. Streams in the Glitterhame descend to an underground river, which runs through a corner of the caverns forgotten by the denizens above.

The Foundry. Beyond the Glitterhame lies a complex of chambers and passageways carved by Durgeddin's folk. A small band of duergar (gray dwarves) currently hold Durgeddin's hall, working to uncover the secrets of the smith's ancient forge. A great crevasse drops to the Black Lake.

The Black Lake. The most dangerous denizen of the caverns under the Stone Tooth lairs in the cold, still waters of the Black Lake. Nightscale, a young black dragon, discovered a passage into the lake through an underwater siphon connecting to a mere on the far side of the hill. The dragon has claimed the ancient wealth of Khundrukar as her hoard.

CHARACTER HOOKS

You can place the Stone Tooth and its caverns anywhere you like in your campaign world. *The Forge of Fury* works well if you pick a remote range of rugged hills or highlands several days from the nearest community.

The town of Blasingdell is briefly described in this adventure, if you need a location where the characters can make their final preparations.

Your next task is to decide how the party learned about Khundrukar. Pick one of the following options that suits your campaign, or make up an explanation.

FOLLOW THE MAP

The party has acquired a map showing the location of a secret dwarven stronghold named Khundrukar. Perhaps the characters discovered the map and other lore about the place during a previous adventure, or it turned up in a forgotten corner of a library. Tales attributed to a previous, failed expedition make reference to a hoard of wondrous arms and armor.

PLACING THE ADVENTURE

Any setting that includes a mountainous region has a ready-to-use location for the dwarven stronghold in *The Forge of Fury*.

Dragonlance. On Krynn, Khundrukar can be placed anywhere in the Kharolis Mountains. An independent stronghold that has no direct tunnels connecting it to Thorbardin, it was overrun by attackers during the Age of Might. During the Age of Despair, it was seized by Highlord Verminaard's forces. Consider replacing the orcs in the adventure with hobgoblins and the duergar with Theiwar dwarves.

Eberron. Once an outpost in the western Mror Holds, Khundrukar was besieged and cleared of its inhabitants when the Kingdom of Galifar invaded that land. The aggressors left the place unoccupied after their victory. Since then, it has fallen into the hands of various groups of monsters.

Forgotten Realms. Located northwest of Mirabar in the Spine of the World, Khundrukar was a shield dwarf stronghold that became overrun by renegade orcs from the Many-Arrows tribe, unhappy with what they saw as their kingdom's betrayal of the old ways.

Greyhawk. Khundrukar stands in the Pomarj, in the western Drachensgrab Hills. The fortress fell shortly after the Hateful Wars, when a wave of orcs and other evil humanoid invaders swept over the region.

TRACK THE BROKEN BLADE

Baron Althon, a local noble, hires the party to search for the legendary cache of weapons forged by Durgeddin the smith. He shows the characters a broken blade bearing the smith's mark, and tells them that it was discovered near a rocky hill called the Stone Tooth. Baron Althon provides directions and promises to reward the characters richly for each of Durgeddin's blades they recover. He will pay the characters 20 gp each just for bringing back information about the dwarven complex, and an additional 100 gp if they provide detailed maps.

VANQUISH THE ORC RAIDERS

In the mining town of Blasingdell, the characters learn that orc raiders have been pillaging isolated farmsteads and camps in the hills north of the town. The local militia captured an orc warrior left for dead by its comrades

THE MINING TOWN OF BLASINGDELL

Blasingdell lies about 30 miles south of the Stone Tooth, a journey of three days on foot or two days on horseback due to the surrounding rugged terrain and dense forests. Although it isn't close enough for the characters to use as an overnight rest stop while they explore Khundrukar, Blasingdell is still useful as a place to purchase equipment, stock up on supplies, and train between excursions into the caverns.

The town's population of around 2,000 is quite diverse; although humans are the largest group, almost any player character race can be found here.

The town's mayor is **Sir Miles Berrick** (male human **noble**).

Sergeant Grendar Kuln (male half-orc **veteran**) is in charge of the town watch; **Constable Dara Whitewood** (female human **veteran**) is the senior officer. The town watch consists of two full-time guards in addition to its officers. A militia force of around 100 commoners can be mustered in emergencies.

Kheldegan Tolm (male dwarf **commoner**) owns Tolm's Superior Outfitting and Dry Goods.

Sarel Bankdown (female half-elf **commoner**) is the proprietor of the Griffon's Nest inn and tavern.

Sister Alonsa (female human **priest**) heads up the town's small temple (its primary deity is left to you). Sister Alonsa is assisted in her duties by two acolytes.

and brought it back for questioning. Under the influence of a *charm person* spell, the orc divulged the location of the monsters' lair, a lonely hill called the Stone Tooth. The mayor offers a bounty of 25 gp per orc, dead or alive, and the gratitude of the townsfolk to any who can permanently end the threat.

APPROACHING KHUNDRUKAR

At the start of play, the characters are trekking through the wilderness and have just reached the outskirts of Blasingdell (or some other community), When you're ready to begin, read:

> Durgeddin was a master smith who forged blades of surpassing quality and power. Centuries ago, his home was sacked by orcs. Durgeddin led the remnants of his clan to the mountains north of the town of Blasingdell and established a small, secret stronghold somewhere in the trackless wilderness.
>
> From his hidden redoubt, he waged a decades-long vendetta against all orc-kind, until his enemies discovered his fortress and attacked it after a long siege. Durgeddin and his followers perished, and much wealth was carried away by the conquering hordes. But it's said that the deepest and best-hidden vaults and armories escaped the looting, and that some of Durgeddin's extraordinary blades still wait in the darkness for a hand bold enough to claim one.
>
> You've come to Blasingdell, a small mining town on the northern frontier, to see if there's anything to these stories. Your map shows that the old dwarf-hold lies about three days' march to the north of the town. Dark, deeply forested hills rise beyond the town's outskirts

The characters can spend time interacting with the townsfolk, gathering equipment and provisions, and otherwise preparing before they set out.

ABOUT THE ORIGINAL

The Forge of Fury, by Richard Baker, was originally published in 2000 as an adventure for the third edition of the D&D game.

The adventure was published shortly after *The Sunless Citadel* and was designed as a follow-up to it. Characters who succeeded in that mission and advanced to 3rd level were now ready to take on the challenges of a ruined dwarven fortress.

THE STONE TOOTH

When the characters set forth on their journey, read:

> As you travel north from the mining town of Blasingdell,
> you pass through brooding pine forests and deep vales.
> From where you stand now, you catch sight of a tall,
> steep hill that rises to a prominent bare knob of rock—
> the Stone Tooth. A thin spire of smoke rises from some
> unseen point high on the hill's slopes, and you can make
> out a steep, narrow road or track that runs back and forth
> across the face of the mountainside.

Refer to map 2.1. The characters have several options: follow the path, scout the area, or wait and watch.

FOLLOW THE PATH

At the foot of the Stone Tooth, a carefully constructed path winds up the hillside to some unseen height above. Durgeddin's clan concealed its presence as much as possible, but years of wind and rain have eroded away its cover, leaving the path exposed and visible from the valley floor below.

The path climbs to the Mountain Door, at the location marked A on the map. This is the route used by the orcs in Great Ulfe's tribe to come and go from their lair.

If someone checks the path for tracks, a successful DC 10 Wisdom (Survival) check reveals that four booted humanoids came down it within the last day and headed into the forest. The trail joins older tracks in the woods and becomes indistinguishable after about half a mile. These tracks belong to orc foraging parties; see "Wait and Watch," page 36, for more information.

SCOUT THE AREA

Ambitious characters might choose to ignore the path and scale the Stone Tooth's slopes. The going is very hard, with steep slopes and heavy undergrowth, reducing the characters' travel pace to roughly 100 feet per minute. Thoroughly exploring the hillside could easily take hours.

Heavy woods block the view upslope, making it difficult to ascertain the origin of the smoke (a natural chimney). Have the party's guide make a DC 10 Wisdom (Survival) check when the group first enters the hillside. On a successful check, the characters travel in the general direction of the chimney. Otherwise, they lose their way (see "Becoming Lost" in chapter 5 of the *Dungeon Master's Guide*).

(A) The Mountain Door. This is the front entrance to the Glitterhame. The old dwarf-path leads up to a bare shoulder of rock and then turns into a deep cleft in the hillside. If the characters enter this way, the expedition begins in area 1 of map 2.2, the Mountain Door.

(B) Chimney. When the characters reach the area marked B on the map, they can discover the source of the smoke. A natural rock chimney leads down into the caverns below, and a thin stream of smoke rises through it. The smoke spreads out and isn't easy to pinpoint in the rugged terrain.

THE STONE TOOTH

MAP 2.1: THE STONE TOOTH

A character who searches for the source of the smoke finds the rock chimney with a successful DC 10 Wisdom (Perception) check. If the characters pass nearby without searching, anyone who has a passive Perception score of 15 or higher notices the fissure.

If the characters descend the chimney, the expedition begins in area 7 of map 2.2, the Mountain Door.

(C) Orc Tunnel. On the other side of the Stone Tooth, a few hundred yards from the Mountain Door, the orc army burrowed into the hillside to circumvent the dwarven defenses. The tunnel is still passable, but its entrance is choked with brush and debris. If the characters enter this area, someone who has a passive Perception score of 15 or higher discovers the orc tunnel. The characters locate the tunnel automatically if anyone searches the area; it leads to area 21 of map 2.3, the Glitterhame.

The tunnel entrance is about 6 feet high and 4 feet wide. Anyone who succeeds on a DC 10 Wisdom (Sur-

---

WILDERNESS ENCOUNTERS AND CAMPING

If you want to make the trek from Blasingdell to the Stone Tooth more interesting, you can create random encounters with orc raiding parties (see "Wait and Watch," page 36) or with creatures native to forest or hills. See appendix B of the *Dungeon Master's Guide* for lists of monsters by environment.

The characters might be forced to retreat outside the stronghold to recuperate after difficult battles. The party can readily find defensible campsites in the forest near the Stone Tooth.

vival) check can spot old tracks passing in and out of the tunnel—reptilian footprints (from the troglodytes inhabiting the Glitterhame) and the paw prints of a very large bear.

(D) Hilltop. An hour or two of hard hiking brings the party to the summit. The Stone Tooth is about 1,450 feet in height, towering over the neighboring hills by 500 feet or more. The last 100 feet or so are a sheer point of rock, requiring DC 15 Strength (Athletics) checks to climb successfully. The view is spectacular, but the hilltop is otherwise unremarkable. (No entrance to the fortress is to be found here.)

(E) The Dark Mere. The eastern slopes of the Stone Tooth descend into a damp valley where water is trapped by the terrain. A dark tarn pools under the hill's slopes, surrounded by numerous smaller lakes. A hidden drainage channel deep underwater connects to the subterranean Black Lake, providing access to Nightscale's underground lair.

The opening is about 40 feet down, and it lies about 100 feet from the western lakeshore. Player characters exploring around the lake can't find this outlet unless they conduct extensive dives to plumb the mere's depths, requiring DC 10 Strength (Athletics) checks to swim underwater. If any characters are capable of staying this deep without suffocating and conduct a thorough search of the lake, they discover the passage with a successful DC 12 Wisdom (Perception) check. If the characters enter through this watery passage, they emerge in area 54 of map 2.6, the Black Lake.

WAIT AND WATCH

The characters might choose to observe the path for some time before braving the Stone Tooth. When they arrive, two foraging parties from Great Ulfe's tribe are searching the nearby hills for loot. The first party of four **orcs** returns two days after the characters arrive, and the second group three days after that. These orcs sleep by day and travel by night, so they arrive in the party's vicinity just before dawn.

If the party sets up camp at least 90 feet from the path and doesn't take any action that might draw attention, the returning orcs pass by without spotting the campsite. Otherwise, the orcs notice the camp when they

---

KHUNDRUKAR: GENERAL FEATURES

The following aspects of Khundrukar are true unless otherwise noted in a particular area description.

Doors. Most doors are made of wood or stone. Characters can attempt various tasks before trying to open a door, including listening for sounds from the other side and checking for traps. If characters elect to listen at a door, check the description of the room beyond to determine if any creatures inhabit that area. If no instructions are otherwise provided, a character who listens at a door and succeeds on a DC 10 Wisdom (Perception) check can hear sounds of activity through the door; increase the DC to 15 for quieter sounds.

Light. Within the confines of Khundrukar, all areas are dark unless a room's description says otherwise.

Ventilation. All keyed areas contain an adequate air supply. The air is renewed through vents that lead to the surface. These vents are individually too small for any but Tiny creatures to navigate.

---

come within 90 feet (or within twice as far if a campfire is burning or the party isn't attempting to be quiet).

A lookout whose post overlooks the trail and who has a passive Perception score of 10 or higher detects the orcs as they approach. The orcs aren't likely to notice a hidden lookout; compare their passive Perception scores to the character's Dexterity (Stealth) check.

> Four hunched humanoids in dirty hide armor approach along the trail, snarling and muttering to each other in a guttural tongue. Yellow tusks jut from their bestial faces.

If the orcs come across the camp and aren't spotted, they attempt to take out anyone on watch or creep into the camp to attack sleeping characters.

If an orc party moves past the characters unchallenged or fights its way through, the survivors reinforce the defenses in the complex (see area 5 and area 14).

Captured orcs can describe in some detail the general arrangement of the Mountain Door. They don't know anything about the rest of the complex, or that it's possible to enter through the chimney. The orcs defending the Mountain Door refuse to negotiate for their return.

The characters might disguise themselves as orcs using captured gear. Doing so can let them try to bluff their way past sentries in the dungeon, using Charisma (Deception) checks contested by the orcs' Wisdom (Insight) checks.

Treasure. Each orc carries a sack of mundane supplies looted from the countryside, as well as coinage totaling 4d6 sp and 1d4 gp.

Development. No more dungeon denizens emerge from the dungeon during this time, and no more orcs leave for a week after the second patrol returns.

THE FORGE OF FURY

Once the party enters Khundrukar, start at the appropriate area on map 2.2, the Mountain Door, or map 2.3, the Glitterhame.

THE MOUNTAIN DOOR

The uppermost level of Khundrukar, called the Mountain Door, is a natural cavern that was expanded and improved upon by Durgeddin's folk, who created a series of halls and guard chambers that protect the entrance to their realm. The place is still well fortified, even to this day.

This former dwarven strongpoint is now occupied by a band of orc raiders, led by a fierce ogre who calls himself Great Ulfe. These raiders emerge from the Mountain Door to hunt and pillage in the surrounding area. To keep their lair secure, the orcs have blocked access to the lower levels of Khundrukar, and they rarely encounter the other denizens of the cave system.

The following locations are identified on map 2.2.

1. END OF THE TRAIL

The old dwarven path ascends to a cleft in the hillside and ends at the front door of Khundrukar.

MAP 2.2: THE MOUNTAIN DOOR

The path climbs up one last steep switchback toward a bare shoulder of rock. The hillside rises steeply on your right and drops away precipitously on your left. Debris and rubbish lie scattered over the last hundred yards or so—discarded water skins, bits of charred bone, and splintered casks or kegs. Up ahead, the path opens onto a wide ledge and then doubles back sharply into the mountainside.

Two bestial humanoids in hide armor stand watch on the ledge. They appear inattentive and bored.

Creatures. Two **orcs** stand guard along the northern edge of the ledge, though they aren't paying as much attention to their duties as they should. The characters (or their advance scout) can spot them from as far as 60 feet away. The sentries, Wark and Thark, are grumbling in the Orc language about someone named Ulfe. Apply a −2 penalty to the orcs' passive Perception scores.

Arrow Slits. When the characters move around the corner into the eastern part of the ledge, they might discover a row of hidden arrow slits in the rocky wall to the east about 15 feet above the floor. By examining the wall and making a successful DC 15 Wisdom (Perception) check, a character notices the slits.

Developments. If they are attacked or confronted by more than one character, Wark and Thark call out a warning that's heard by the orc in area 4 and then attempt to flee to area 3. See the "Mountain Door Defenses" sidebar.

If the archers are alerted to the party's presence, they open fire on intruders on the ledge and in area 2. See area 4 for more information.

2. THE DWARF-DOOR
Moving eastward from the ledge, the trail turns south and rises steeply through a cleft in the rock toward a grand entrance.

Shallow steps lead up through a steep fissure to the south and turn east into the mountainside. Here, a broad entranceway has been carved out of the stone. Marble steps cracked with age and veined with green moss lead up to a strong double door of carved stone, eight feet wide and almost ten feet tall. Arrow slits high on the north and south walls command this area.

If the characters quietly dealt with the orcs in area 1 using stealth or disguise, the door is open. Otherwise, the orcs have been alerted to intruders, and the door is shut and barred from the inside. Forcing open the barred door is very difficult, requiring a successful DC 20 Strength check.

MOUNTAIN DOOR DEFENSES
The orcs are well prepared for a frontal assault on the Mountain Door. They follow the sequence of activity described below to the best of their ability unless prevented or interrupted by the player characters.

Round 1. After sounding the alarm, the sentries in area 1 (Wark and Thark) flee south to area 2.

Round 2. The orcs in area 4 fire at any exposed characters in area 1 if they have been alerted by the sentries. Wark and Thark flee through the door into area 3.

Round 3. Wark and Thark cross the rope bridge in area 3. The orcs in area 4 continue to fire at characters in areas 1 and 2. One orc from area 4 moves through the secret door leading to area 3, intending to close and bar the double doors leading to area 2.

Round 4. Wark and Thark slip through to area 5 to spread the alarm, alerting the orcs in areas 11 and 14.

Round 5. The orc that shut the double doors in area 3 moves to area 4 or 4a while the other archers continue to fire at exposed characters. The orcs in the eastern half of area 3 cut the rope bridge and prepare to defend the doors that lead to area 5.

Round 8. The orcs in area 14 arrive in area 5.

Round 12. Great Ulfe and the orcs from area 11 move to area 5 to ready a counterattack.

Creatures. If the orcs have been alerted, the orcs in areas 4 and 4a fire arrows until the characters either retreat or succeed in bypassing the door.

Development. If the characters are repelled, they must deal with additional reinforcements if they try this approach again. Two orcs from area 11 stand watch at the doors on the west side of area 3, while the orc Eye of Gruumsh from area 9 backs up the orcs in area 4 or 4a.

3. THE RIFT HALL

> The great door opens into a large hall. A narrow ledge overlooks a deep, dark crevasse that cuts the room in two. A dangerous-looking rope bridge, frayed and thin, spans the gap. Water gurgles and rushes somewhere far below. Two copper braziers burn brightly on either side of the door, illuminating the western half of the room. Another ledge is barely visible on the other side of the chasm.

The hall beyond the doors, and the great crevasse that runs through it, once served as the last line of defense for Khundrukar's dwarves.

Creatures. Two **orcs** guard the eastern side of the room. They do everything in their power to prevent the characters from getting across the bridge. If any of the party members have darkvision or a means of illuminating the far side, read:

> Two brutish humanoids stand watch on the other side of the crevasse. They snarl a challenge, revealing yellowed tusks, and prepare to hurl javelins at you!

Rope Bridge. The bridge is safe structurally, despite its appearance. Crossing under fire is difficult enough to require DC 10 Dexterity (Acrobatics) checks. On a successful check, a character can move at half speed. On a failed check, a character makes no progress. If the check fails by 5 or more, the character must make a DC 10 Strength or Dexterity saving throw. On a failed save, the character plummets almost 200 feet to the underground river below and is swept away. The characters can prevent falls by roping themselves to a stable attachment point before crossing.

Secret Doors. Two secret doors on the north and south walls lead to areas 4 and 4a. The doors are well made, each requiring a successful DC 15 Wisdom (Perception) check to discover. A door can be opened by simultaneously pushing in two concealed stone plates in the wall about 1 foot above it. The plates can be found with a successful DC 15 Wisdom (Perception) check.

Developments. The orcs use the rock outcroppings on their side for shelter from attacks, gaining half cover. They throw their javelins at characters trying to cross the bridge, or at those who hang back to cast spells or make ranged attacks. A character on the bridge who is hit by an attack must make a saving throw to avoid a fall, just as if the character's Dexterity (Acrobatics) check to move along the bridge had failed by 5 or more.

If an intruder gets at least two-thirds of the way across the bridge, one orc breaks cover to move through the double doors into area 5 and get help. The other tries to hinder the characters by chopping at the bridge's support ropes with its greataxe. Each rope has 8 hit points and AC 11. If one support rope is cut, the DC of the Dexterity (Acrobatics) check to cross the bridge increases to 12, and characters on the bridge must immediately make a saving throw to avoid falling as described above. If both ropes are cut, the east end of the bridge drops into the crevasse and slams into the cliff wall on the west side. Any characters on the bridge take 7 (2d6) bludgeoning damage from the impact with the wall and must make successful DC 12 Strength or Dexterity saving throws to avoid losing their grip and falling if they aren't otherwise secured.

Development. If the orcs destroy the bridge but repel the invaders in doing so, Great Ulfe's followers rebuild it within three days. Any orcs killed here are replaced by orcs from area 11.

4 AND 4A. ARCHERS' STATIONS

The dwarves carved out chambers on either side of the entryway so they could rain arrows down on attackers that approached the front door of their stronghold. The arrow slits are 15 feet or more above the floor of areas 1 and 2 and are impassible for creatures larger than Tiny. They grant three-quarters cover to the orcs stationed behind them.

The secret doors in area 3 provide access to these locations.

> The door slides aside to reveal a narrow passage that descends a flight of stairs into a small chamber. Light from outside slants into the room through a series of narrow embrasures.
>
> The area is littered with well-gnawed bones, cobwebs, and rat droppings. Poorly cured hide blankets are carelessly scattered over the floor.

Secret Door. In the north end of area 4, a secret door connects to area 14. A character can find the door by succeeding on a DC 18 Wisdom (Perception) check. The orcs are unaware of this passage and don't use it.

Creatures. Four **orcs**, three in area 4 and one in area 4a, overlook the stairs leading up to area 2. These orcs aren't particularly vigilant, but they do start shooting if the sentries in area 1 call for help. The orcs are armed with longbows instead of javelins: +3 to hit (range 150/600 ft.); 5 (1d8 + 1) piercing damage on a hit.

When the characters turn the corner into area 2, the archer in area 4a joins the attack while one of the archers from area 4 circles around through the secret door in an attempt to shut the double doors to area 3 (see "Mountain Door Defenses," page 37).

If the heroes attack by coming through the secret doors that lead to these areas, the archers fire at characters descending the stairs, then switch to greataxes and move up to block the stairways.

Development. If the characters dispose of the sentries in area 1 quietly, the orcs in area 4 might not notice them. Characters can attempt to sneak past the row of arrow slits by comparing their Dexterity (Stealth) checks to the orcs' passive Perception scores. If the characters successfully sneak past the sentries, they reach area 2 without alerting the archers.

If the characters defeat these orcs but withdraw from the dungeon before overcoming the rest of them, the archers are replaced by orcs from area 14 and reinforced by the orc eye of Gruumsh from area 9.

5. ORC CAVE

> The walls and floor of this natural cave have been carefully smoothed. You can discern at least four routes leading off into darkness. Red coals glow from within the southeastern passageway, and a crude wooden cage door closes off the southern exit. The floor is covered with sleeping furs, crates, sacks, and rubbish.

The second orc raiding party normally lairs in the open area east of the doors. These orcs are currently out of the dungeon unless the party spent several days observing the hillside (see "Wait and Watch," page 36) before entering.

Cage Door. The cage door to the south leads to area 6, where two prisoners languish under the orcs' indifferent care. The prisoners leap to their feet and rush to the cage door to cry for help when the characters enter area 5.

Treasure. The crates and sacks in this room contain mundane supplies looted from the countryside—flour, grain, nails, and so on. The total value is about 20 gp for about 500 pounds of material. Additionally, if characters are held captive in area 6, their equipment is stored here.

Development. When the second orc raiding party returns (five days after the characters arrive at the Stone Tooth), they take up residence here. Add four orcs to this room after their return.

6. PRISONER CAVE

The orcs occasionally capture miners, settlers, and merchants traveling through the forests north of Blasingdell. They keep their captives in a small pen until they put them to death or ransom them.

> A row of rough-hewn sapling trunks forms a crude but serviceable barrier across the mouth of this small cave. A door locked with an iron padlock secures the room. Inside, you see two filthy prisoners dressed in tattered rags, crowding close to the door. "Thank Yondalla!" one cries out. "We're rescued!"

Creatures. The prisoners are a pair of human **commoners** named Geradil and Courana. They hail from a small settlement a few miles from Blasingdell, and the orcs have held them captive for almost a month now. Neither one's family could raise the ransom demanded by their captors, so both await a terrible death at the orcs' hands.

Opening the cage door requires a successful DC 12 Dexterity check using thieves' tools, the key from Old Yarrack's pocket (see area 14), or a sharp axe and a little time. (The padlock has AC 19 and 5 hit points.) Geradil and Courana are extremely grateful for their rescue, but they will not join the characters in their quest—neither is skilled at fighting, and they just want to go home.

Treasure. The characters can free the prisoners and escort them back to their homes (about a day's travel away). The grateful families reward them with two *potions of healing*. Taking the time to see Geradil and Courana to safety, however, gives the orcs a chance to prepare for the next assault.

Development. Any characters captured by the orcs eventually wind up in the cage, unless they demonstrate that they're too much trouble to be left alive. Their gear is stored among the other supplies in area 5. New characters joining the party might also be introduced as prisoners here.

7. FIRE IN THE HOLE

The irregular chamber southeast of the main cave holds the main cooking fire of the tribe. A crevice in its ceiling winds up through the rock to the natural chimney on the hilltop above (see "The Stone Tooth," page 35).

> A large, smoky fire crackles in the center of this room. Battered pots and kettles are stacked all over; clearly, this space serves as a crude kitchen. You feel a distinct draft drawing the smoke up through a rough hole in the ceiling.

The characters might attempt to descend into the area through the chimney. The shaft is about 80 feet long; its walls are irregular and rough but slippery, requiring successful DC 15 Strength (Athletics) checks to climb. Anchoring a rope at the top of the shaft reduces the check DC to 5. A careful climber can easily avoid the fire on the way down.

If a character's check fails by 5 or more, the character must succeed on a DC 10 Strength saving throw or fall the rest of the way down the chimney. In addition to falling damage, the character takes an extra 3 (1d6) fire damage from the hot coals and makes enough noise to alert any orcs in area 5.

8. ORC COMMONS

> Haphazard stacks of crates, barrels, sacks, and bundles crowd this long cavern. To the north, two finished stone passageways open to the east and west; a narrower opening leads south. In the southeast corner is an old well full of murky water.

The cavern is full of plunder from the orcs' raids through the surrounding area: foodstuffs, ale, blankets, tools, timber, pitch, nails, wool, and similar goods.

Iron Gate. The passage leading east is blocked about 10 feet in by tightly packed crates and sacks of flour. Removing this material allows travel for another 20 feet to the east, where the tunnel ends at an iron gate stuffed with blankets and straw pallets. The orcs created these barricades to prevent the stirges in area 10 from getting out.

The iron gate's lock is rusted shut; it can be picked with a successful DC 12 Dexterity check by a character using thieves' tools or forced open with a successful DC 15 Strength check.

Secret Doors. The passage to the south branches in a Y shape. The southwest branch connects to area 5, and the southeast one leads to a secret door cleverly constructed to blend into the natural rock of the cave. A character who makes a successful DC 15 Wisdom (Perception) check discovers the door.

On the other side, a worked passage continues up to what appears to be a blank wall, marked with hexes and curses in Orc. The markings conceal another secret door, which requires a successful DC 12 Wisdom (Perception) check to find.

Treasure. The mundane supplies have a total value of about 20 gp for about 500 pounds of material.

With a successful DC 10 Wisdom (Perception) check, a character finds a loose stone. Behind it is hidden a small locked strongbox containing 180 gp and a flask of holy water. This is the personal treasure of Old Yarrack (see area 11).

9. SHAMAN'S LAIR

> The secret door pivots open to reveal a chamber of finished stonework. The room is cluttered with crude furnishings, and the air is hazy with the smoke of a small cooking fire. Dozens of yellowed skulls are suspended from the ceiling by fraying ropes strung through holes punched in the bone. An orc in a ragged black robe looks up from her work, her face twisted in an expression of rage.

Creatures. Burdug the shaman, an **orc Eye of Gruumsh**, has commandeered a chamber as her private domain. She lives here with her two followers, female **orcs**, separate from the rest of the tribe.

The door to area 10 is locked, but the key is inserted in the keyhole on this side. Burdug keeps the door closed because she wants to confine the stirges on the other side. (She calls the stirges her "little stingies" and occasionally captures one to use in her potions and brews.)

Burdug orders her two followers to engage intruders while she attempts to neutralize a dangerous-looking combatant with a *command* spell. Then she casts *bless* on herself and the others, and finally casts *spiritual weapon* before joining battle.

If the fight goes poorly, Burdug throws alchemist's fire (she has three flasks) and opens the door to area 10, releasing the stirges. She takes advantage of the confusion, using more alchemist's fire if necessary, to escape and seek help.

Treasure. A character who makes a successful DC 10 Wisdom (Perception) check finds two leather sacks among the clutter, each containing 160 sp. If Burdug is defeated, the characters can recover any of her three flasks of alchemist's fire that weren't used.

Secret Exit. A successful DC 12 Wisdom (Perception) check is required to find the secret door on the west wall. It connects to the passage leading toward area 8; the secret door farther along the passage to the west isn't concealed from this side.

10. The Grand Stair

> The ceiling soars thirty feet high in the center of this impressive chamber, and the walls are carved with images of dwarves at their forges. Two large stone doors exit to the north and south. Several old skeletons lie scattered near the northern door. A gate of wrought iron stands in the western wall.
>
> In the center of the floor, a natural rift descends sharply. Dozens of stone steps lead down into darkness. You can hear the distant sound of running water and a curious buzzing coming from far below.

The easternmost chamber in the Mountain Door complex formerly served as the main entrance to the Glitterhame, which occupies the great natural caverns deeper in the hillside.

Creatures. If the characters aren't trying to be quiet, four hungry **stirges** attack.

> The buzzing grows louder, and then four things resembling insectoid bats emerge from the stairwell and fly toward you!

Large quantities of smoke discourage the stirges, and they don't move closer than 5 feet from a source of fire (including characters set alight by the trap described below). Sated stirges flap off to digest their meal down in area 15a of the Glitterhame.

The iron gate blocks entry from area 8 (see it for more information). The stairs in the rift lead down to the northwest end of area 15 in the Glitterhame.

The door to the south connects to area 9 and is locked from the other side. The lock can be picked from this side by someone who makes a successful DC 10 Dexterity check using thieves' tools, but doing so pushes the key out on the other side and warns Burdug the shaman that someone's coming.

Fire Trap. The door to the north is carved in the image of a glowering dwarf's face. Hinges are visible. On either side of the door, eight small spouts are carefully worked into the stonework about 10 feet above the floor.

The skeletons near the door are those of orcs killed by the trap long ago; their remains show signs of severe scorching. Rusted axe heads lie near the bodies, with no sign of the weapons' hafts.

If the door is pulled open before the trap is disabled, a counterweight drops and pumps a flammable substance resembling alchemist's fire from the spouts. Each creature within 15 feet of the door takes 10 (4d4) fire damage, or half damage with a successful DC 10 Dexterity saving throw. At the start of each of its turns thereafter, an affected creature takes 5 (2d4) fire damage. A creature can fight the flames around itself by making a successful DC 10 Dexterity check as an action; a successful check reduces the fire damage it takes at the start of each of its turns to 2 (1d4). Making another successful Dexterity check as an action quenches the flames around the creature entirely.

After the door is opened, the counterweight pulls it shut again in 2 rounds, resetting the trap. The characters can prevent this from happening by jamming the door open. If the trap resets, it can be activated only once more before its fiery substance is depleted.

The spouts on the wall can be detected by someone who succeeds on a DC 15 Wisdom (Perception) check. With a successful DC 10 Intelligence (Investigation) check afterward, a character deduces that they form part of a trap mechanism. A character who makes a successful DC 12 Dexterity check using thieves' tools, or someone who tightly plugs the holes with durable material, renders the trap inactive. Someone who succeeds on a DC 10 Intelligence (Investigation) check while examining the door identifies the counterweight mechanism that activates the trap; it can be deactivated afterward by someone who makes a successful DC 10 Dexterity check using thieves' tools.

Development. Inspecting the small room behind the door reveals the full extent of the trap's counterweight mechanism, as well as a system of pipes that connect the spouts to two 20-gallon copper drums (containing the substance for the fire trap).

A character who is proficient in the use of alchemist's supplies might be able to craft alchemist's fire from the dregs of the tanks. Doing so requires a successful DC 15 Intelligence check after the character finishes a long rest. On a successful check, the character salvages 1d4 flasks of alchemist's fire. On a failed check, the reagents are mixed improperly, spoiling the batch; no further attempt to use these reagents can be made. If the check fails by 5 or more, the character is affected as though hit by alchemist's fire.

11. Orc Quarters

> Barrels, crates, and sacks line the walls of this chamber. Among the loot, four oversized straw pallets and other simple furnishings show that it now serves as a bunk room. Four bestial humanoids with feral eyes are cleaning their weapons and mending their gear; they spring to their feet and roar in challenge.

Creatures. Four **orcs** live in an old guardroom. These orcs fight dirty. They team up into pairs, each focusing on one character. One orc in the pair attempts to shove the character, then the other attacks, hoping for a prone target.

Treasure. The supplies stockpiled here are the same as those in areas 5 and 8: trade goods and staples raided from travelers and nearby settlements.

The orcs have 210 gp stashed in an old iron cauldron under vermin-infested bedding. A small pouch in another orc's bedding contains a topaz worth 200 gp and two onyx stones worth 50 gp each. This loot isn't well hidden; anyone searching the room can uncover it.

Development. If the characters leave the complex before they have defeated Great Ulfe, two of these orcs move to reinforce area 2 (reducing the number in this room to two) before the characters return.

12. Great Ulfe

> A short flight of stairs leads up to a large, iron-bound door. A bloodstained human skull is fixed to the center of the door by an iron spike.

The door isn't locked, but it is heavy and hard to move; a successful DC 17 Strength check is needed to force it open.

> Beyond the door lies a small chamber covered in poorly cured animal hides and illuminated by smoking torches in bronze sconces. The smell is indescribable. A monstrous creature about ten feet in height steps forward, a massive axe in one hand. Two huge wolves strain at

chains held closely in its other hand. "You think to challenge the Great Ulfe?" the creature booms. "Vak! Thrag! At them!"

It drops the chains and, as the wolves spring forward, it charges at you with a roar of rage.

Creatures. Great Ulfe is a fierce **ogre** who leads the orcs of the Mountain Door. The chamber he claims as his own once belonged to the dwarf watch-captain.

If the characters fail to open the door on the first attempt, Great Ulfe is alerted to their presence. He releases his two **dire wolves**, Vak and Thrag, and takes the Ready action to attack the first enemy who enters the room. He is armed with a greataxe instead of a greatclub: +6 to hit; 17 (2d12 + 4) slashing damage on a hit.

Great Ulfe neither asks nor gives quarter, but if the ogre falls, the wolves attempt to flee.

Development. If the characters defeat Great Ulfe but leave any orcs alive, one of the surviving orcs claims leadership of the tribe. If at least half the orcs in the tribe are slain in addition to Ulfe, any survivors abandon the dungeon after the party leaves. They become roving bands of raiders that the adventurers might have to deal with later.

Treasure. Great Ulfe keeps his hoard in two large wooden chests against the south wall: 440 gp, 1,600 sp, a *potion of climbing*, and a *+1 rapier*. (The ogre would never stoop to wielding the delicate blade like some prancing bard.)

13. Dwarven Statue

> At the end of the passage stands a statue of a fierce-looking dwarf in heavy mail armor. The stone warrior holds a sword in one hand and a smith's hammer in the other. The statue is about seven feet tall and stands on a large stone pedestal.

The statue is part of another trap designed to thwart invaders of the citadel. All the denizens of the Mountain Door know about the trap and avoid triggering it.

If any character approaches within 5 feet of the statue without disarming the trap, read:

> Suddenly, you feel a small click from the floor beneath your feet. The statue's bearded face slides open, like an oversized nutcracker, and greenish gas billows forth.

Poison Gas Trap. A pressure plate is set into the floor about 5 feet in front of the statue. When at least 20 pounds of weight is placed on the pressure plate, it depresses into the floor, opening the statue's face to reveal a nozzle from which poison gas sprays out in a 15-foot cone. Each affected creature must succeed on a DC 12 Constitution saving throw or become poisoned until the creature finishes a short rest.

Someone who examines the proper location and succeeds on a DC 15 Wisdom (Perception) check notices the pressure plate. A successful DC 12 Dexterity check by a character using thieves' tools disarms the trap; the pressure plate can also be deactivated by physically jamming it so that it can't move.

If the trap isn't deactivated, it resets automatically after 1 minute.

14. Bunk Room

A large chamber, once the principal bunk room for dwarf guards posted in this part of the dungeon, has been appropriated by Great Ulfe's orcs. Up to eleven of the creatures live here, but at the moment a group of them are out raiding the countryside nearby, and three others are on duty in area 4.

> This chamber is filled with rough-hewn bunks, tables, and chairs, and the floor is strewn with filthy pelts. At first glance it appears that a dozen or so humanoids might use this area as a sleeping quarters.

Creatures. Only Old Yarrack the **orog** and four **orcs** are at home when the characters enter the chamber. They enter combat as soon as they're aware of intruders.

If the battle goes poorly for the orcs, Old Yarrack orders an orc to break off and summon help from area 9. If things get desperate, he sends for help from the orcs in area 11. If the orcs here fall, Yarrack attempts to join Great Ulfe's forces in area 12. The orog carries a *potion of healing* and drinks it if his current hit points drop to one-fourth his hit point maximum or lower.

Secret Door. The orcs don't know about the secret door in the western wall, but a character who searches the spot can discover it with a successful DC 15 Wisdom (Perception) check.

Development. Two days after the characters arrive, the first raiding party returns and reinforces this room with four more orcs. Thus, the party might encounter as many as nine creatures in this room.

Any orcs slain in area 4 are replaced by orcs from this room, if any survive.

Treasure. A successful DC 10 Wisdom check reveals a loose stone on the south wall, concealing a sack that holds 250 sp and 40 gp. Aside from his *potion of healing*, Old Yarrack keeps his personal treasure in area 8.

Old Yarrack carries the key to the cage door in area 6.

The Glitterhame

Below the Mountain Door lies the Glitterhame, a large series of natural caverns in the heart of the Stone Tooth. The caverns are beautiful: the walls sparkle and glisten with flecks of semiprecious stone, and millennia of sculpting and erosion by water have created sheets of fluted flowstone, delicate stalactites, and majestic stalagmites. Water streams down through the caverns toward an underground river far below.

The Glitterhame is now home to a band of troglodytes, dangerous reptilian savages that haunt underground places. The troglodytes and Great Ulfe's tribe maintain

an uneasy peace, although skirmishes occur. The troglodytes usually use the old orc tunnel (see area 21) to hunt on the surface and leave the orcs alone. In return, Great Ulfe's followers rarely invade the troglodytes' domain.

The following locations are identified on map 2.3.

15. The Cold Stream

If the characters take the steps down from area 10, they emerge into a narrow tunnel with a subterranean stream flowing across it.

> The stairway twists and turns a long way downward. The floor has been cut into hundreds of shallow steps, but the walls and ceiling are still natural rock. About sixty feet down, a rushing stream spills from a narrow crack to the south and crosses the stairway, disappearing into a narrow, winding tunnel to the north. The rill is only two or three feet wide.

If the characters explore the route taken by the stream, they have to go single file as they wade through the water. The bed of the fast-moving stream slants sharply; each character must make a successful DC 8 Strength (Athletics) or Dexterity (Acrobatics) check to descend safely. If the check fails by 5 or more, the character falls, tumbling 20 feet downhill and taking 3 (1d6) bludgeoning damage.

> ### Vision in the Glitterhame
> Range of vision is important in the characters' exploration of this level. Most light sources don't illuminate beyond 60 feet, and many of the chambers and passages in the Glitterhame are much larger than that. The darkness hides many perils.

1 square = 5 feet

MAP 2.3: THE GLITTERHAME

15A. STIRGE COLONY

Creatures. Stirges have made their nest in a small cave overlooking the stream, about halfway down the passage. Fissures at the back of the cave run 150 feet to the surface, but nothing larger than a stirge can fit through. Six **stirges** are sleeping in the nest, but any noise or light from a party descending the streambed wakes them. Each round after the characters enter the cave, 1d4 stirges wake and attack, until all are active.

Treasure. On the floor at the back of the stirge cave lies the desiccated corpse of a dwarf explorer who died here many years ago—part of the failed expedition. A leather pouch on its belt contains 35 gp.

16. HIGH CAVERN

The first chamber of the Glitterhame proper is bisected by the stream and has a number of routes leading away from it.

> The descending fissure opens up abruptly into a very high cavern, its ceiling easily forty feet or more overhead. The stairway continues to wind down along a ledge that follows the north wall of the chamber. A fast-moving stream about five feet wide runs across the floor of the chamber from the north and disappears under a low stone overhang to the south, and larger passageways exit to the southeast and the northeast.

Creatures. Four **stirges** are clinging to the chamber walls high overhead. They can see any light source that is brought into this chamber, but they are very hard to spot in turn, owing to the height of the ceiling. The stirges have advantage on Dexterity (Stealth) checks made to hide unless a character specifically looks for danger overhead, so they might surprise the party.

The stream exits the south wall of the cavern through a passage only 3 feet high, half filled by water, which serves as an entrance to the troglodytes' lair (area 17). Anyone who searches the stream's banks finds the footprints of Medium reptilian creatures and tracks left by tails with a successful DC 10 Wisdom (Survival) check.

To reach area 17 from this cave, a Medium or larger character must crouch down and then wade or crawl through the stream. Torches and lanterns are difficult to keep lit, since the lowest point of the ceiling in this passage is only about 6 inches above the water's surface.

17. TROGLODYTE CAVERN

The troglodytes that infest the Glitterhame have claimed one of the largest caverns as a common room and food storage area. They defend it against all intruders. Characters coming from area 16 might not be able to see everything at first.

> Floundering through the cold, swift stream, you emerge in a huge cavern. The ceiling must be thirty feet overhead, and the far end of the cave is lost in darkness. A foul stench assaults your nostrils immediately. The remnants of butchered game animals hang from crude wooden stakes along the cavern walls, and you spot a pair of orc corpses treated in the same fashion.

The grisly trophies that decorate the room represent about two or three weeks' worth of meals for the troglodyte tribe. The troglodytes like to let their meat age a bit before eating it, so most of the carcasses here are appallingly decayed.

Creatures. Two **troglodytes** are hiding in the northern end of this area, one on each side of the stream. Their Chameleon Skin trait gives them advantage on Dexterity (Stealth) checks made to hide. They attack as soon as two characters have entered the area, likely achieving surprise.

Mud-and-Wattle Door. The troglodytes have blocked the southwest passage leading to the main warren (area 18) with a crude plug made of mud and wattle. A successful DC 10 Strength check is required to pull it open. If alerted by the sounds of battle, the troglodytes on the far side secure the door, increasing the DC of the check to 15.

Pool. The stream flows through the center of the cavern, growing somewhat wider and deeper until it reaches the southeast corner. The pool in that location is about 20 feet across and about 10 feet deep in the middle.

Along the eastern edge of the pool, a short passage leading to area 23 has been blocked up with loose rubble and mud, creating a rough stone wall 10 feet across. Characters can break through this barrier with some effort; it has AC 16 and 50 hit points per 5-foot segment.

18. TROGLODYTE WARREN

Most of the troglodytes dwell in a group of dismal caverns, occupying three caves that branch off the warren's central area to the northwest, southwest, and southeast.

> The passage opens into a long, low cavern that has three narrow, twisting passages leading off into darkness. Numerous rock columns rise to meet the stone overhead. The air is thick with troglodyte stench, and the floor is littered with refuse from the monsters' meals and gnawed bones of dubious origin.
>
> Something scrapes and hisses in the dark, and you hear the soft padding of scaly feet on rock.

Characters who are being stealthy might catch the troglodytes unawares. If the characters are carrying any light sources or making a lot of noise when they enter, the troglodytes in the west and southeast chambers are alerted. As soon as any fighting begins, one troglodyte attempts to escape to the north, toward area 19, and summon Kaarghaz, the chieftain.

Northwest Chamber. Two **troglodytes** are sleeping in the small cave to the northwest when the characters enter area 18.

Southwest Chamber. The females tend the colony's eggs and raise hatchlings in the southwest cave. Six **troglodytes** defend the hatchery and fight to the death to defend their young.

The chamber also contains two dozen noncombatant hatchlings, which scurry away from intruders. Characters receive no XP for slaughtering them.

Southeast Chamber. Three **troglodytes** recently returned from the hunt are relaxing in the southeast cave. Unless they are alerted to the characters' presence, they are concentrating on devouring what's left of a small deer.

Tactics. If the characters attack the troglodytes in the northwest or southeast chamber, those in the other chamber hear the sounds of battle and rush to assist. The troglodytes in the southwest chamber remain there to protect the hatchlings; if the characters attack the hatchery first, all the troglodytes from the other chambers come to join the fight.

19. CHIEFTAIN'S CAVE

The door leading north from area 18 is a mud-and-wattle barrier wedged in place; a successful DC 10 Strength check is required to pull it aside.

> Glowing coals in a crude hearth illuminate this large cave. The ceiling here rises about fifteen feet above the floor, and rubbish and skins cover the floor. A lizard the size of a small horse rises and slowly slithers toward you.

Creatures. The chief of the troglodytes, Kaarghaz, occupies the chamber along with his pet **giant lizard**. Kaarghaz is a **troglodyte** with the following changes, which increase his challenge rating to 2 (450 XP):

- His AC is 13 (natural armor).
- He has 39 (6d8 + 12) hit points.
- His Charisma is 15 (+2).
- He can speak Draconic and Troglodyte.
- He has an additional trait:

Spellcasting. Kaarghaz is a 4th-level spellcaster. His spellcasting ability is Charisma (spell save DC 12, +4 to hit with spell attacks). He knows the following sorcerer spells:

Cantrips (at will): *fire bolt, mage hand, poison spray, prestidigitation, ray of frost*
1st level (6 slots): *burning hands, shield, sleep*
2nd level (3 slots): *invisibility, scorching ray*

If the characters make a lot of noise or tip off their presence in some other way, Kaarghaz begins this encounter invisible (see below). Otherwise, read:

> Behind the lizard, a hulking, scaly-skinned creature easily a foot taller than any of the others you've seen glares at you and snarls.

If Kaarghaz is alerted to the party's approach, he casts *invisibility* on himself before they enter. If he loses at least half his hit points, he tries to escape (using *invisibility* if possible). If his escape succeeds, he soon afterward rounds up a war party of surviving troglodytes from other areas to track down and ambush the party.

Negotiation. Kaarghaz starts out hostile and won't become friendly to the characters. Nevertheless, a character who speaks Draconic might be able to stave off combat by parleying with the chieftain. For example, the characters might have captured some of the hatchlings in the southwest chamber, intending to ransom them back to the troglodytes in exchange for treasure. Even if Kaarghaz can be convinced to give up some of his wealth, he doesn't let the matter rest—he forms a war party (as described above) and goes after the characters.

Treasure. The chief's chamber is strewn with trophies, including the skulls, bones, hides, and weapons of defeated foes. Amid the mess, a small square of black silk hides a ruby worth 300 gp. It can be found with a successful DC 10 Wisdom (Perception) check. A battered wooden chest with leather hasps holds 1,500 sp.

20. SCALY LAIR

> The swift stream passes over a steep slab of bedrock in front of a short passage. The cave beyond is long and low, with an uneven ceiling about ten feet high. In the southern end of the room, an enormous white-scaled lizard lunges and snaps, but you can see that a sturdy chain around its neck tethers it in place. The agitated creature twists in frustration, its tail lashing.
>
> Behind the lizard lie a couple of iron chests.

Creature. The cavern holds the troglodytes' secret weapon—a freshly captured **giant subterranean lizard** (see appendix B). Although the lizard is chained, it can attack anyone who comes within its reach. It strikes with its tail first, hoping to knock a target prone, then snaps at it with its powerful jaws to gulp it down.

Treasure. The two chests contain a total of 2,200 sp. One holds a *potion of climbing*, and the other a *potion of water breathing*.

21. ORC TUNNEL

> Several passages branch away from this large, high-ceilinged cavern. To the north, a carved, square-mouthed tunnel shows that someone has been at work in these caves. A gate of rough-hewn timber blocks a small passage to the northeast. Three other passageways wind off toward the south. A heavy animal smell lingers in the air.

A hundred years ago, the orcs besieging Khundrukar tunneled into the dwarven stronghold. The cavern they emerged in now serves as a guard post and a mustering point for troglodyte raiders.

The tunnel in the northern end of the area runs about 500 feet and opens on the hillside (see the "Orc Tunnel" subsection of "Scout the Area," page 35). The troglodytes use the opening to raid and hunt on the surface.

Creatures. In the northern part of the cavern, near the passages that run east and west, two **troglodytes** are hiding. From their Chameleon Skin trait, they have advantage on Dexterity (Stealth) checks to hide. The troglodyte on the west side waits for an opportune moment to attack intruders with surprise. The other moves east to the gate and opens it to release a **brown bear**, which attacks any non-troglodyte in the next round (roll initiative for the bear when it is released).

Bear Pen. A sturdy timber gate, latched on the outside, seals a smaller cave to the east. The bear attacks any non-troglodyte that opens the cage door, then tries to escape through the tunnel.

The animal isn't trained but has come to expect food from the troglodytes. It is hostile toward strangers, but someone proficient in Animal Handling might be able to calm it down with a DC 15 Wisdom check. If the check succeeds and no troglodytes remain nearby, the characters can release it safely and let it depart.

22. FUNGUS CAVERN

> A trickle of water seeping down from the hillside above reaches this irregular cavern, nourishing a profusion of fungus—weird puffballs, tall caps, and patches of fuzzy mold in a variety of colors. A golden-brown carpet of mold covers an old skeleton in rusted mail in the southern part of the room, and a narrow passageway leads to another small room beyond this one. A surprisingly bright sword gleams in the skeleton's bony grasp.

Hazard. The skeleton that the characters first see is that of a dwarf. From its location, it's possible for someone to see a second skeleton (human) in the south end of the chamber. Both skeletons are covered with a particularly virulent form of mold. A character can identify the threat with a successful DC 10 Intelligence (Nature) or Wisdom (Survival) check.

If either skeleton is touched, the mold ejects a cloud of spores that fill a 10-foot cube originating from the skeleton. Any creature in the area must succeed on a DC 15 Constitution saving throw or take 10 (3d6) poison damage and become poisoned for 1 minute. At the end of this time, unless the poisoned condition is removed, the creature must repeat the saving throw, taking 17 (5d6) poison damage on a failed save, or half as much damage on a successful one. Exposing a patch of the mold to sunlight or dealing any fire damage to it destroys it.

Treasure. The dwarf skeleton clutches a *+1 longsword* that bears Durgeddin's smith-mark. The human skeleton wears a steel helmet chased with silver, worth 110 gp.

23. Dwarven Sepulchers

> You gaze into an extremely large cave faintly lit by natural phosphorescence. Its ceiling rises fifty feet high in places. Crystals glimmer softly in the eerie light. Weird, beautiful flows and structures of delicate stone grace the chamber. The western portion of the great cave is separated from the rest by a steep bluff; the ceiling here is half the height of the rest of the chamber.
>
> A couple dozen large stone sepulchers line the cavern walls, each carved with intricate reliefs and designs and marked with Dwarvish runes.

The upper portion of the great cavern was intended to be the final resting place of Durgeddin's clan.

Durgeddin and his followers feared that their war against the orcs would ultimately claim them all, so they built their own tombs during the first phase of carving out the stronghold. Ironically, only a handful of the dwarves were ever interred here; the rest lie where they fell when the orcs stormed Khundrukar.

The troglodytes have a superstitious fear of the tombs and refuse to set foot in this part of the Glitterhame. They don't pursue characters who enter this area.

If the characters investigate the tombs at greater length, read:

> Twenty-three sepulchers stand here. The lids are carved in the likenesses of grim dwarves in armor. Dwarvish runes on the front of each tomb appear to represent the names of the occupants or the intended occupants. Three of the stone coffins have additional runes carved into them.

If someone in the party can read Dwarvish, the following details become apparent:

> The additional runes record the occupant's date of death and the great deeds the dwarf performed in life. Also carved into these three coffins is a warning that doom awaits any who dare to defile the honorable dead.
>
> The names on these three sepulchers are those of Borgol the Old, Gharin Orc-Doom, and Numik the Unlucky.

Treasure. Each tomb is a marble vault 6 feet long, 4 feet high, and 3 feet wide, with a heavy stone lid. Despite the warnings carved on the tombs, there is no danger here. Even if the characters disturb Borgol, Gharin, or Numik, all they find are old bones and no undead.

The three dwarves were buried with little funerary wealth; Durgeddin's folk believed in honoring their dead with stone, not riches. Borgol's remains include a ring of gold in the shape of a dragon holding its tail in its mouth, worth 120 gp. Gharin was buried with a finely crafted warhammer inset with a garnet, worth 110 gp.

24. The Glitterhame

> This great cavern glimmers with a faint phosphorescence. The ceiling is almost fifty feet overhead, and bright flecks and gleaming stone formations are visible in the distance. Patches of strange fungi dot the floor, including capped stalks standing as tall as a human and glowing puffballs almost a yard wide.
>
> High ledges rise fifteen to twenty feet above the floor on the north, south, and west walls. Narrow passageways lead off to the north and the south, and a flight of carved stone stairs descends from the western ledge to a path that meanders through the center of the chamber toward a small iron door in the eastern wall. Audible throughout the entire chamber is the sigh of a soft, cool breeze that rises toward the surface far above.

The fungal growths are harmless. In fact, the stalks and the puffballs are edible, if not especially tasty. The danger lies in the grick nest that overlooks the path.

Creatures. Two **gricks** lurk in the 20-foot-high rockfall that spills down from area 26, at the place where the path leading east comes closest to the slope. They are wedged into spaces between boulders, 6 to 8 feet above the cavern floor. Their Stone Camouflage trait gives them advantage on Dexterity (Stealth) checks made to hide, so they might surprise the party.

The gricks attack anyone who travels on the path next to the rockfall or climbs anywhere along the slope that leads to area 26. Any character trying to scale the rockfall while under attack must succeed on a DC 8 Strength (Athletics) check to make progress. If the characters reach area 26 by some other means, the gricks move to attack them there.

25. LONG CAVERN

> The thunderous roar of falling water fills this long, low chamber, and spray makes everything slick and wet. A fast stream rushes through the center of the cavern, emerging from beneath a crude dam of rock and mud in the western wall. The stream disappears into a dark shaft at the cavern's eastern end. A rough, winding path follows the stream toward the east.

The chamber runs from the troglodyte warrens to a natural shaft on the east end that leads down into the Sinkhole (see area 28). The stream spills over the edge of the shaft in a subterranean waterfall, and near the waterfall a narrow, winding stairwell leads down.

Slippery Slope. The smooth cavern floor slopes down toward the stream, and much of the area immediately north of the stream is covered with a thin layer of slime. The slime makes the floor very slippery. Its presence can be discerned with a successful DC 15 Wisdom (Perception) or Wisdom (Survival) check.

Any creature that enters the slippery slope or starts its move there must make a DC 12 Dexterity (Acrobatics) check. A creature that fails the check falls prone and slides southward toward the stream at half its walking speed. The stream is flowing fast enough that anyone who falls in must succeed on a DC 10 Strength saving throw to avoid being swept over the waterfall.

A creature that goes over the waterfall lands in a pool 60 feet below (see area 28), taking 10 (3d6) bludgeoning damage and suffering one level of exhaustion.

26. GRICK LAIR

> A rocky ledge sits at the top of a steep, irregular rockfall about twenty feet high. The mouth of a side cavern leads into darkness beyond.

Creatures. The two **gricks** hidden in the rockfall (see area 24) make their lair at the end of a passage that winds north from the ledge. They are encountered here if they retreated to attack characters who got past them.

Treasure. The gricks discarded the inedible portions of their victims in the back of the cave. Rooting through the grisly remains uncovers a suit of scale mail and scattered coins totaling 200 cp, 180 sp, and 60 gp.

27. IRON DOOR

The entrance to Durgeddin's halls and forges lies behind a sturdy locked door.

> Cut into the cavern wall is a small but strong-looking door of iron plates, about five feet tall and four feet wide. Heavy rivets stud its surface, and a tarnished silver rune—Durgeddin's smith-mark—gleams on the door's rusted face.

The door consists of two pieces of sheet iron bolted to a strong frame. A pintle is fitted through the door's middle, so it has no hinges. It can be opened with the key on the dwarf skeleton in the prison (see area 34). A character can pick the lock with thieves' tools and a successful DC 18 Dexterity check. Breaking the door down is very difficult, requiring a successful DC 25 Strength check.

On the other side of the door is a steep staircase that leads up to area 35 in the Foundry.

THE SINKHOLE

The stream that flows through the Glitterhame descends through the chasm in area 25 to an even lower level of caverns—the Sinkhole. Here it joins a subterranean river that traverses dark caverns and forgotten storerooms before connecting with the Black Lake.

None of the monsters that inhabit the complex regularly visit this place. The black dragon Nightscale sometimes swims through its submerged areas, using the river as a back door to its lair.

A narrow staircase winds down along the chasm walls until reaching bottom, where it offers access to area 28.

The following locations are identified on map 2.4.

28. WATERFALL CAVERN

> A loud waterfall spills down the northwest wall of this cavern into a deep pool. The rocky walls glisten with spray, and a weird array of colorful minerals and strange lichens lend an unearthly beauty to this spot. A fast-moving stream runs south from the pool at the base of the falls, and a nearby natural passage heads in the same direction. A set of narrow stairs cut into the rock wind up to the north, and two old wooden doors stand in a wall of dressed stone to the east.

The stream flowing from area 25 in the Glitterhame pours down into the chamber.

The pool is populated by harmless blind fish and white crustaceans but contains nothing dangerous. The outflowing stream drains into the river in area 29. Any characters who fell into the pool are carried by the current toward the outflow at about 20 feet per round. A character who ends up in the river might be swept away; see "Fast-Flowing Water," page 51.

29. RIVER CAVERN

> This long, narrow cavern is half-filled with an underground river, flowing along at a rapid pace. A narrow ledge on the north side overlooks the river. A bridge of stone spans the river, leading to a larger ledge on the south side that follows the course of the river to the east.

The underground river flows swiftly from east to west. The bridge is sturdy and sound; there's no danger in crossing it.

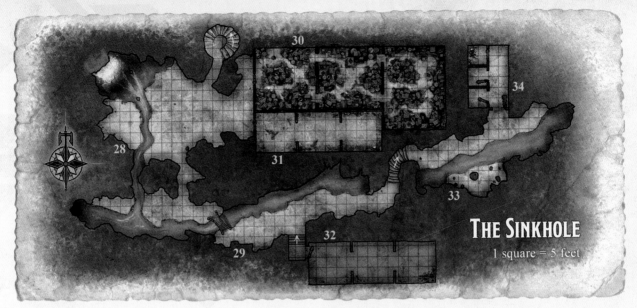

Watery Peril. At the west end of the cavern, the ceiling lowers to meet the surface of the river. Any creature swept past this point by the current is trapped in a long, airless underground channel and is likely to drown (see "Suffocating" in chapter 8 of the *Player's Handbook)*. In addition, the creature must make a successful DC 12 Strength saving throw each round or take 1d6 bludgeoning damage as it is battered by rocks. Even creatures that can breathe water aren't likely to survive for long.

The stream runs underground for about 5 miles before emerging on a hillside to the west of the Stone Tooth.

30. Old Storeroom

The northern door in area 28 has swollen shut from dampness. A successful DC 10 Strength check is required to force it open. Durgeddin's folk formerly used the large chamber beyond as a storeroom.

> The door gives way grudgingly, revealing a low chamber of dressed stone. This chamber is filled with what appears to be rotten food—barrels of salted meat gone bad, sacks of flour or grain covered in russet-colored mold, tuns of cider turned to vinegar.
>
> Two open archways in the east wall lead to a similar room, and two more openings are dimly visible beyond. The floor just past the first archway gleams wetly.

Creature. None of the supplies are salvageable. While searching, the characters might blunder into a **gray ooze** that occupies the middle chamber of the three.

While motionless, the ooze is indistinguishable from a patch of wet stone. It is alerted when characters force open the door, and it strikes at the first character who enters the middle chamber, attacking with surprise.

> What appeared to be a wet patch on the floor suddenly twists like a snake and lunges toward you!

31. Empty Storeroom

The southern door in area 28 is swollen shut and requires a successful DC 10 Strength check to open. The chamber on the other side of the door resembles area 30, but it is empty. The orcs broke in and carried off most of its contents during the fall of Khundrukar.

32. Flooded Storeroom

A year or so ago, a season of heavy rains on the surface raised the level of the subterranean river to create a minor flood. Water still stands at the bottom of the stairs.

> A short flight of stone steps leads down to a wooden door that stands half-open. Dark, stagnant water pools in the small landing at the base of the steps and in the doorway, presumably filling the room beyond as well. The area smells of rot.

Diseased Pool. The water is about 5 feet deep and is tainted by disease. Anyone who drinks the water or wades into it is exposed and must succeed on a DC 10 Constitution saving throw to avoid infection. Symptoms manifest one day after exposure and include high fever, muscle spasms, and eventual paralysis.

An infected creature suffers one level of exhaustion when it finishes the first long rest it takes after being exposed. Whenever it finishes a long rest thereafter, it must make a DC 10 Constitution saving throw. On a failed save, the creature suffers another level of exhaustion. On a successful save, its exhaustion level is reduced by one. If its exhaustion level reaches 5, the infected creature becomes paralyzed until the disease is cured or the effect is removed with a *lesser restoration* spell or similar magic. If a successful saving throw reduces the infected creature's exhaustion level to 0, the creature recovers from the disease.

Treasure. Submerged in the corner of the eastern vault is the skeleton of an orc killed a century ago. The skeleton rests atop a rotted leather pouch that contains a *potion of water breathing* and a *potion of invisibility.*

33. Roper's Cavern

> The rock stairs climb steeply, turn north, and then descend toward the east into a cavern very much like the one you just left, but smaller. A ledge along the river continues east to a door on the north wall, and the rushing river separates you from a ledge on the southern side.
>
> A large, strange-looking stalagmite stands in the middle of the southern ledge. A cave fish flops helplessly on the bank nearby.

Creature. The southern ledge is the home of a ravenous **roper** that has been feeding on fish from the stream. Unsatisfied with this diet, the roper is eager for larger prey.

Even characters who look closely at the roper can't tell that it's anything other than a stalagmite unless it moves. The roper is difficult to sneak up on. If a character manages to approach without alerting it, continue:

> A strand extends from the stalagmite, with the thrashing cave fish in its grasp. It pulls the fish toward the rock formation—and then, suddenly, a fang-filled maw gapes open in the stalagmite and devours the fish in one bite.

The roper attacks when any character gets at least 20 feet into the cave, gaining surprise if its presence hasn't been revealed. It can target up to four characters with its tendrils, possibly pulling those it has grappled into the rushing river. Characters in the water have advantage on checks to escape the grapple due to the force of the current. The river poses a severe hazard in itself, though; see "Fast-Flowing Water," page 51.

Development. The roper is satisfied, ending the attack, after it devours one Small or larger creature. It can't speak or understand languages, but it has a bestial intelligence and might be persuaded to accept a substitute meal. As long as the food is alive, the roper isn't picky.

Treasure. Cutting open the roper's stony gizzard reveals a *ring of spell storing* and six gemstones: a ruby worth 1,000 gp, two emeralds worth 400 gp each, and three serpentines worth 60 gp apiece.

34. Prison

If the characters get past the roper in area 33, they can explore an area that was used as a prison in Durgeddin's day.

> A sturdy door of iron plate stands open in the north wall of the cavern. Inside you see a short passageway with three small iron doors set into the west wall. The first two are open, but the door at the end of the hall is closed.

The door to the northern cell is locked. With a search of the grimy floor and a successful DC 10 Wisdom (Pereption) check, a character discovers an old jailer's key that fits the lock. Otherwise, the lock can be picked by someone who succeeds on a DC 15 Dexterity check using thieves' tools.

The first two cells are empty. The locked cell holds the skeletal remains of a dwarf in rusted plate armor. This individual was one of Durgeddin's chief lieutenants; the orcs captured her during the final battle and threw her in this cell for interrogation later. Afterward, the unfortunate warrior was forgotten and left to starve.

Treasure. The suit of plate is too corroded to be of any use, but a search of the corpse produces a small silk purse containing 8 pp and a key that opens the iron door in area 27.

THE FOUNDRY

Durgeddin's followers lived and worked in a series of carved halls and chambers beyond the Glitterhame. Most of this part of the complex was thoroughly ransacked when the dwarven citadel fell.

Unlike the Mountain Door or the Glitterhame, which offer exits to the surface world, the Foundry isn't readily accessible. The area isn't abandoned, though. Undead horrors wait in its darkest recesses, and dwarf-crafted traps still work perfectly well despite their age. In addition, a small number of duergar have come here to breathe life into Durgeddin's old forges and decipher the secrets of the master smith's work.

If the characters come to this part of the complex from the Black Lake (see the "Dark Mere" subsection of "Scout the Area," page 35), they begin in area 38.

The following locations are identified on map 2.5.

35. CHAMBER OF STATUES

In the corridor behind the iron door in area 27, a flight of steep stone stairs climbs 30 feet northward.

> The stairs end at the entrance to an octagonal chamber. The floor is inlaid with cracked, dusty blue tiles, and the walls are dressed with polished marble. Large doors of iron-bound oak exit to the northwest and northeast.
>
> Three cast bronze statues, almost ten feet tall, stand by the west, north, and east walls. Each depicts an armed dwarf. The eastern and western ones carry axes and shields. The center statue is armed with two axes. The ceiling rises in a dome almost thirty feet above the floor.
>
> From somewhere in the distance, you can hear the faint ringing of hammer on anvil.

The sound of the hammering comes from beyond the east wall, as can be determined with a successful DC 13 Wisdom (Perception) check. Anyone who examines the floor notices that the dust is somewhat disturbed. A successful DC 13 Wisdom (Survival) check reveals an infrequently used trail that leads from the entrance stairs to the stone wall behind the east statue.

Statue Trap. The obvious exits to the northeast and northwest are false doors that open onto blank stone. Pulling on either door releases a catch that causes the

axe-wielding hands of the two closest statues to drop. Any creature within 5 feet of a door when it is opened is subjected to two melee attacks: +5 to hit; 9 (2d8) slashing damage on a hit.

With a successful DC 15 Wisdom (Perception) check, a character can discern small scorings on the floor in front of a door, left by earlier axe strokes. A successful DC 15 Intelligence (Investigation) check enables a character to deduce that the doors aren't what they seem, through small clues showing that they are unused. The same check focused on a statue can reveal a small line on the arm that holds an axe, indicating the arm's ability to move.

> ### FAST-FLOWING WATER
> The underground river that cuts through this level of the dungeon presents a serious hazard. Those who fall in risk being swept away by the current.
>
> A creature that falls in the river and is within 5 feet of the water's edge must succeed on a DC 10 Strength saving throw to catch itself on the rocky bank. On a failed save, or if the creature is too far away from the bank, it is drawn into the main current.
>
> A creature in the main current that takes no other action is swept 60 feet downstream (to the south or to the west, depending on location) each round. If it spends its action to make a DC 10 Strength (Athletics) check and the check is a success, it can reduce the distance traveled by the amount of its walking speed and move toward a bank.
>
> On a failed check, the creature must succeed on a DC 10 Constitution saving throw or suffer one level of exhaustion. Creatures that have a swim speed can take the Dash action and use their full swim speed without making a Strength check. A creature within 5 feet of a bank can pull itself out of the current as part of its move.

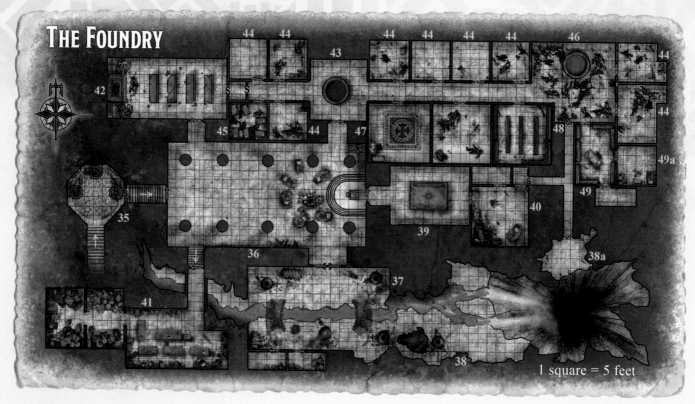

THE FOUNDRY

Map 2.5: The Foundry

A character who makes a successful DC 10 Dexterity check using thieves' tools can jam a statue's arm so that the axe can't swing. Destroying a statue (AC 18, 60 hit points, immunity to necrotic, poison, and psychic damage) also disables its attack.

Once a statue has attacked, the trap must be reset manually. If any duergar survive and remain here, they reset the trap within a day after it has been triggered.

Secret Stairwell. The secret door behind the east statue is well hidden, requiring a successful DC 18 Wisdom (Perception) check to spot. If the characters detected the faint trail that leads there, a successful DC 10 Wisdom (Perception) check locates the door. Beyond is a flight of stone stairs that leads upward.

The stairs have been warded with a magical alarm. When a creature ascends past the halfway point of the staircase, a *magic mouth* spell calls out in Dwarvish, "Alert! Alert! Intruders approach!" This sound warns the duergar guards in area 36.

36. THE GREAT HALL

At the top of the stairs from area 35 is a stone door carved with a glowering dwarf's face. It opens easily.

> This enormous hall is lined with ten great pillars, carved into the forms of giants and dragons, that support the vaulted ceiling high above. Guttering orange torches set in sconces along the walls illuminate the room, and a mighty throne sits on a dais at the opposite end. The walls were once covered with tile mosaics, but they have been smashed and defiled by graffiti. Tiny fragments of tile litter the floor. You can see five other exits.

> A small fire smolders on the floor before the dais, where six sleeping pallets lie empty, surrounded by packs and supplies. The sound of hammers ringing on iron comes from beyond the doors to the south.
>
> Suddenly a harsh voice calls from the shadows of the pillars, "Go back the way you came! This is the only warning you'll get!"

The cavern was formerly Durgeddin's throne room, banquet hall, and center of authority. Its ceiling is 30 feet high, and the sconces are 10 feet above the floor. The throne is unremarkable: a short bench of stone that might have been decorated at some point in the past. The graffiti consists of crude epithets in the Orc language insulting dwarves and their ancestry.

Creatures. Two **duergar** guards and Ghared, a **duergar spy** (see appendix B), stand watch here. Unless the party climbed the stairs from area 35 without triggering the *magic mouth*, the duergar are invisible.

Negotiation. The duergar start hostile but wait to see if the characters attack. Ghared shouts the initial warning and speaks for the group; she's suspicious, greedy, and arrogant, but not stupid. She is willing to give information to the party if a character succeeds on a DC 20 Charisma (Persuasion) check. The characters can change her attitude to indifferent, reducing the check DC to 10, with a suitable bribe (at least 100 gp).

Ghared can share any of the following information if the party succeeds in getting her to converse:

- The doors to the north lead to halls infested with undead and cursed magic.

- The door to the southwest leads into the old kitchens, guarded by more cursed magic.
- A dragon lives in a large lake cavern deep below.
- The subterranean river flows from the lake through other parts of the complex below the Glitterhame. It's fed from a lake on the surface.

If negotiations are successful, the duergar are willing to let the party enter the rooms to the north. With a sufficiently high Charisma (Persuasion) check and an indifferent attitude from Ghared, the characters can get the duergar to escort them to the entrance to the dragon's territory (the chasm in area 38). The duergar will not allow the party into the bladeworks (area 37) without an escort, and they prohibit entry into area 39.

If the characters don't negotiate, or if talks go badly, combat ensues.

Tactics. If combat occurs, the duergar guards first attack with their javelins. They use their Enlarge ability in the next round, taking cover behind two of the pillars before wading into melee.

Meanwhile, Ghared remains invisible and maneuvers to make a sneak attack, then enlarges herself after she becomes visible. She has a *potion of healing*, which she uses if her current hit points drop to half her hit point maximum or lower.

If two duergar fall in battle, the survivor tries to retreat to area 37 or 39.

37. The Bladeworks

In what was Durgeddin's smithy and workplace, the duergar are currently engaged in a secret project, hoping to capture a spark of the master smith's vengeful magic.

> Double stone doors lead into a barrel-vaulted area containing several furnaces. The eastern end of the chamber continues into a large, dark cave, from which a cold wind moans. A stream of water rushes from west to east through the center of the room, crossed by two stone bridges. On the other side of the stream, three bald, gray dwarves work at a roaring forge, beating a white-hot blade into shape on an old anvil.

Creatures. Two **duergar** smiths are forging a blade at the forge in the center of the south wall. The work is overseen by Snurrevin, a **duergar** with the following changes, which increase his challenge rating to 2 (450 XP):

- He has 45 (7d8 + 14) hit points.
- His Intelligence is 14 (+2).
- He has an additional trait:

Spellcasting. Snurrevin is a 3rd-level spellcaster. His spellcasting ability is Intelligence (spell save DC 12, +4 to hit with spell attacks). He has the following wizard spells prepared:

Cantrips (at will): *fire bolt, mage hand, minor illusion, shocking grasp*
1st level (4 slots): *color spray, shield, silent image*
2nd level (2 slots): *hold person, shatter*

Snurrevin has a familiar, a **rat** named Browngnaw, that hides in the shadows near the unlit forge to the east. The duergar are preoccupied with their task and don't notice the party's entrance unless the characters make themselves known. They object violently to intruders who aren't escorted by duergar.

If a threat becomes apparent, the two smiths grab their weapons, use Enlarge, and move to guard the two bridges. If the fight goes against them, they turn invisible and try to slip out to area 36, then join the other duergar in area 39.

In combat, Snurrevin might cast *shocking grasp* through his hidden familiar, and he might use *silent image* to confound enemies with realistic-seeming threats.

Treasure. In the cold forge in the northwest corner of the room, Snurrevin has stashed 320 gp, 1,100 sp, a gold necklace set with ruby stones worth 900 gp, and a *potion of hill giant strength*.

38. The Chasm

> The stream running through the old dwarven bladeworks meanders through a natural cavern before tumbling into a great chasm. You can see nothing but darkness below, although the splashing of waters deep below is barely audible over the roar of the waterfall.
>
> To the north of the chasm, a small ledge is partially hidden by a spur of rock.

The chasm is 120 feet deep. Anyone who falls in takes 42 (12d6) bludgeoning damage and ends up in area 50 of the Black Lake level. Climbing down the slippery stone next to the waterfall requires several successful DC 15 Strength (Athletics) checks, or DC 5 checks for a character who uses a rope.

38a. Chain Ladder

The rock spur on the northern ledge partially conceals an old chain ladder that leads down to area 51 of the Black Lake. The ladder isn't immediately obvious from the southern ledge, but a character who makes a successful DC 10 Wisdom (Perception) check can spot it.

39. Council Chamber

The duergar have set up a guard post in what was once the council room of Khundrukar.

> The door behind the throne leads into a small audience chamber. A large table made of a single stone slab dominates the room's center, and old tapestries cling to the walls. A stone door in the far wall is carved with the dwarf's visage that you've seen elsewhere.
>
> One gray-skinned dwarf in scale mail and shield stands watch by the far door. He shouts and raises a javelin.

Creatures. Unless the party is under Ghared's protection (see area 36), the lone **duergar** on duty fights to the death to protect his leader, who is in area 40.

If the characters engage the duergar guard, the sounds of battle alert the leader, Nimira. She is a **duergar** with the following changes, which increase her challenge rating to 3 (700 XP):

- Her AC is 17 (splint armor).
- She has 52 (8d8 + 16) hit points.
- She has additional traits:

Multiattack. Nimira makes two greatsword attacks.

Greatsword. *Melee Weapon Attack:* +4 to hit, reach 5 ft., one target. *Hit:* 9 (2d6 + 2) slashing damage, or 16 (4d6 + 2) slashing damage while enlarged.

Nimira uses Enlarge and comes out to join the fight in the next round. If her guard falls or she faces at least three enemies, and negotiation isn't an option, she turns invisible and tries to escape into area 36 or through the secret door that leads east out of area 40.

Negotiation. Nimira is an excellent fighter, but she is pragmatic and willing to negotiate in the right circumstances. She knows the same information as the duergar in area 36 and might be convinced to guide the party to the chasm that leads to the dragon's lair (area 38).

40. DURGEDDIN'S QUARTERS

Durgeddin led a spartan lifestyle, eschewing rich decorations and treasures in his personal quarters. Nimira has appropriated the room for her own use.

> This room appears to be a bedchamber. In one corner to the south stands a large wooden sleeping platform, badly gouged by axe blows and partially burned. A table, a bench, and a writing desk have been similarly treated. In the middle of the southern wall, a space has been cleared for a simple sleeping pallet and a pair of large satchels. Two doors exit the room to the north.

If the party enters the room through the secret door in the closet (see below), or if the characters avoided or quietly dealt with the guard in area 39, Nimira is here, resting on the pallet. Otherwise, the room is empty. The satchels contain mundane supplies: extra clothes, food, lamp oil, and similar stuff.

The door in the northwest corner leads to a bathing area, fitted with two small clay tanks to hold wash water. The northeast door opens into a closet containing the mildewed remnants of several cloaks.

Secret Door. The east wall of the closet conceals a secret door. The door isn't well hidden, requiring a successful DC 10 Wisdom (Perception) check to find. Nimira knows about the secret passage and escapes through it if pressed.

41. KITCHENS

> The stairs leading south from the pillared hall end at a wooden door. Beyond is a corridor that opens up into a large room lined with hearths. This room must once have served as the kitchen: pots, pans, cauldrons, and kettles lie scattered on the floor and strewn across several tables. An archway to the west leads into a pantry filled with rotted foodstuffs. Suddenly, you hear a scraping sound, and a big wooden table shudders and begins to move, heading right for you!

Creature. An **animated table** (see appendix B) activates when someone enters the main part of the room. It fights until destroyed but won't attack a dwarf. See the "Arundil's Animated Objects" sidebar.

The room is full of old, rusty iron pots, pans, cutlery, and cooking utensils, none of which are worth much.

42. DESECRATED SHRINE

Durgeddin made his last stand in Khundrukar's shrine, laying enemies low until the orcs finally overwhelmed him. Orc shamans pronounced dire curses over his remains to ensure that their terrible foe would never return. Then they entombed a fierce orc warrior to defend it forever in undeath.

The door leading from area 36 bears an inscription in Orc: "Beyond this door the Maker of Death is chained. May he gnaw on his own hate until the sun dies and all things end."

> This room was once a shrine to the gods of the dwarves. The walls are carved with their dour images, and a low stone altar stands at the western end of the room. Stone benches have been smashed and thrown askew, and the icons of the gods have been defaced.
>
> Atop the altar, arms folded over his chest, lies the ancient corpse of a dwarf warrior in plate armor. Bones lie heaped around the altar's base, and at its foot crouches the desiccated body of an orc in studded leather.

Creatures. The orc champion is now a **wight**, an undead monster that thirsts for life essence. Two of the piles of bones are ogre skeletons (use the **ogre** stat block; give it the undead creature type, vulnerability to bludgeoning damage, immunity to poison damage, and immunity to the exhaustion and poisoned conditions; and remove its ability to speak). The ogres were slain during the final battle and later animated to join the orc warrior in his watch.

The wight and skeletons lie immobile until someone enters. They can't pursue characters outside room.

> Some of the bones at the foot of the altar stir and form into a pair of towering skeletons clutching greatclubs. The dead orc warrior looks up at you and grins evilly, green fire burning in its hate-filled eyes as it stands.

Treasure. The orcs looted the shrine after the fall of Khundrukar, but two members of the previous expedition fell to the undead defenders with valuables in their possession. Under a scattering of bones near the altar can be found a sack that holds 280 gp and a bone case that contains a *spell scroll* of *web* and a *spell scroll* of *spider climb*.

43. ENTRANCE TO THE DWARF-HALLS

The dwarves of Khundrukar once resided in private rooms to the north of the great hall. When the orcs came through, they cut down all the dwarves they found and stripped the treasure out of the place.

> The door opens into a large chamber with a dark pool in the center. Bits of smashed furniture and other debris are scattered about the floor. Hallways lead off to the east and the west.
>
> A weird moaning fills the area, slowly becoming recognizable as Dwarvish curses. The sound rises to angry shouting and grows closer. Then the translucent form of an armored dwarf appears through a wall and attacks!

Creature. Area 43, area 46, and all the rooms marked 44 are now the demesne of the dwarf mage Arundil, who lingers as an insane **ghost**.

The ghost relentlessly attacks anyone who enters its territory (most likely in either area 43 or area 46) but can't pursue characters who retreat beyond its domain. If the ghost is turned, it flees to one of the empty rooms labeled as area 44.

Development. Arundil's ghost is tormented by grief and shame over abandoning his kin to die (see area 47). The spirit might be laid to rest if the characters can convince it that they have cleansed Khundrukar.

44. LOOTED ROOMS

Severak chambers in the Foundry were once living quarters, drawing rooms, barracks, armories, storerooms, and so on. Now they contain only smashed furniture and debris from the final battle, graffiti in the Orc language, and skeletal remains of dwarves and orcs.

Treasure. Here and there a remnant of something valuable can be salvaged from the trash. Roll a d10 the first time a character searches a given room; on a result of 10, the character uncovers a semiprecious stone (see the 10 gp Gemstones table in chapter 7 of the *Dungeon Master's Guide*).

45. SKELETON ROOM

One of the smaller chambers once served as a small barracks. Half a dozen dwarves perished here and were later animated by Arundil (see area 47). He ordered them to defend their post against all intruders.

This chamber might once have been a barracks. The remains of six wooden bunks lean against the walls, burned and hacked by pillagers, and half a dozen skeletal dwarves lie here and there on the floor. With clicking and scraping sounds, the skeletons rise and advance on you.

Creatures. The six **skeletons** attack any non-undead creature that enters. They don't pursue anyone beyond this chamber.

Treasure. The rogue from the failed expedition lies in this room, her desiccated corpse half-buried under wrecked furniture. A pouch on her belt contains 670 sp.

46. COMMON AREA
The open courtyard in the east end of the residential area was the site of a pitched battle between dwarves and orcs.

The hallway leads to a large open chamber. Three doors open into it, and a dark pool fills a low stone basin in its center. The chamber is littered with the remains of old warriors. Seven dwarf corpses lie where they fell a hundred years ago, surrounded by the remains of at least a dozen orc warriors. The dead have been stripped of their arms and armor; only a handful of broken weapons and shattered shields remain.

Creature. If the characters approach this area from the secret door to the south before entering area 43, Arundil the **ghost** confronts them here; refer to the encounter in area 43. Otherwise, there is nothing dangerous or valuable in the area.

47. ARUNDIL'S CHAMBERS
Arundil, the leading mage of Khundrukar and Durgeddin's trusted advisor, lived in a spacious room close to the great hall. During the final assault of the orcs, Arundil used his magic to escape the slaughter. He returned to find all his kinfolk dead. Driven insane with grief, he tried to repair some of the complex's defenses, animating dead warriors and various objects to kill any intruders that returned. In his madness, he even summoned a fiend (see area 49), and he perished at its hands not long after.

This chamber must once have been the personal quarters of an important dwarf. It is decorated with tapestries and furnished comfortably, although age has taken its toll on the contents. Apparently, the room has not been looted. A beautiful rug covers the center of the floor, and a simple bed and writing desk stand in the southwest corner.

Creature. The rug, 20 feet square, is actually a Gargantuan **rug of smothering** that activates when any non-dwarf sets foot on it. It fights until destroyed but doesn't attack a dwarf under any circumstances. See "Arundil's Animated Objects," page 54.

Treasure. Beneath the bed is a small wooden chest containing 1,200 sp, 3,000 cp, and a square of silk in which are wrapped a star sapphire worth 500 gp and a pair of matched blue topazes worth 90 gp each.

48. LOOTED ARMORY
Khundrukar's armory was looted long ago. Its door is made of iron plates, but the lock was broken during the pillaging—it can be forced open with a successful DC 15 Strength check.

Rows of empty weapon racks and a dozen or more armor stands indicate that this room was once an armory. Some debris litters the floor, but nothing of value is readily apparent.

Creature. One of the armor stands is actually an animated object (use the **animated armor** stat block), which activates when a non-dwarf enters the room. It fights until destroyed. See "Arundil's Animated Objects," page 54.

49. IDALLA'S DEN
The mad dwarf Arundil used every magical tool at his disposal to protect the complex. He not only animated objects and the bones of the dead but called upon more dangerous magic in his futile attempt to make the place safe. In the former chambers of a dwarf scholar, tucked away in the eastern end of Khundrukar, he found a scroll that he tried to use to bind a fiend to his service.

This room was once a library or a study. Bookshelves stand against the walls. Piles of books rest on a reading table in the middle of the room. The air reeks of moldy paper. Doors exit to the north, east, and south.

A beautiful, slender woman with long black hair sits in a chair at the table, looking extremely sad. Her clothing, though well worn, does little to detract from her appearance.

Creature. Arundil summoned a **succubus** and commanded it to guard the area that is now the domain of Arundil's ghost (see area 43). But the fiend easily overpowered Arundil's will, then toyed with him cruelly until it finally drained his life force.

The succubus, which calls itself Idalla, claimed the scholar's library for its own and spends much time here reading through the collected lore. It learned of Khundrukar's history from the scholar's records and realized that the legends of wondrous treasure would lure greedy souls. It consumed the wizard from the previous expedition, who took refuge in this library after his companions were killed. Since that time, it has spread rumors to draw more adventurers to its lair.

Idalla takes the form of a human woman. When the characters enter, the fiend jumps up and begs to be released from imprisonment. Idalla tells the characters that she is a captive of a wizard who resides below this level. The succubus plays the role to the hilt, trembling and crying as it spins a tale of woe. It tries to split up the group, persuading one character to remain (using its Charm attack if necessary) while the others deal with the wizard. If they leave anyone alone with Idalla, the fiend attempts to kiss and drain the hapless dupe. The succubus is an adept liar and mixes in just enough of the truth to be convincing; see the "Idalla's Story" sidebar.

If the characters attack, Idalla attempts to charm the most dangerous-looking character and turn him or her against the party while the fiend fades into the Ethereal.

49a (Bedchamber). The adjoining room was the sleeping quarters of the dwarf scholar. It is moldy and very stuffy. Anyone who looks around the room finds a secret compartment in one of the walls with a successful DC 15 Wisdom (Perception) check.

Treasure. The dwarf scholar amassed a small amount of treasure, which he kept in the secret compartment: 110 gp and a cat's-eye gem worth 70 gp. In the library, in addition to an extensive collection of dwarven lore, the characters can find four *spell scrolls* (of *alarm*, *disguise self*, *enlarge/reduce*, and *shield*). The shelves might also include more scrolls, useful information tying in to future adventures, items of value to a collector, or other interesting lore, as you see fit.

THE BLACK LAKE

The darkest and most remote corner of the Glitterhame's cavern system, the Black Lake is a large, winding cavern filled with water that drains from the Dark Mere through a submerged siphon. From the lake, the subterranean river flows west through the Sinkhole, across the bottom of the chasm in area 3 of the Mountain Door, and onward for about 5 miles until it emerges at the surface.

The dwarves of Khundrukar never settled these caverns, although Durgeddin had his followers begin work on an escape route through the depths.

The Black Lake is now the domain of Nightscale, a young black dragon. Here she has built her hoard, having slowly collected most of the remaining loot from Khundrukar. From the lake, Nightscale can swim to the Sinkhole, climb up to the Glitterhame, or fly up to the Foundry through the chasm there. The troglodytes fear and worship the dragon. The duergar have negotiated an uneasy truce with Nightscale, paying her a modest tribute to leave them alone.

The following locations are identified on map 2.6.

50. THE CASCADE

The stream in area 38 flows over the edge of the chasm and pours down into a turbulent pool.

> A thundering spray of water fills this chamber, pooling and flowing out to join a larger river to the north. The air is damp, and the roar of the waterfall is deafening. A broad ledge heads north toward the river and then turns out of sight to the east. The muddy bank of the pool looks disturbed by tracks of some kind.

A character who makes a successful DC 10 Wisdom (Survival) check identifies the tracks as those of a Large reptilian creature with four feet and a long tail. The tracks lead away from the hard stone of the ledge to the north (where they can't be seen) and into the water.

51. DWARVEN BRIDGES

Durgeddin's followers built two stone bridges when they started work on the escape route through this level. The chain ladder that drops from the north ledge of area 38 ends just above the ground in the area south of the western bridge.

If the characters reached this area by using the chain ladder or otherwise descending through the chasm, read or paraphrase the following text. Adjust the information as needed if they arrive here by a different route.

> A fast-moving underground river roars from east to west under a stone bridge. The bottom of the chain ladder is near the south bank of the river. On the north side of the bridge, a ledge continues to the east.

If the characters go north and cross the bridge, read:

> After a short distance, the ledge leading east bends to the south, and a second bridge surmounts the river.

The western bridge is safe, but the bridge to the east is not. It has settled considerably, some of its stone blocks leaning precariously. Also, the stone has a curiously pitted appearance (which was caused by Nightscale's acid breath). A character who succeeds on a DC 10 Intelligence (Investigation) check can determine that the stone was affected by acid, although the source of the acid isn't apparent.

Hazard. The weakened bridge can't take much weight before it collapses. If more than one Small or larger creature is on the bridge at one time, or if a character in heavy armor steps onto it, the arch fails. Any creature on the span must succeed on a DC 10 Dexterity saving

THE BLACK LAKE

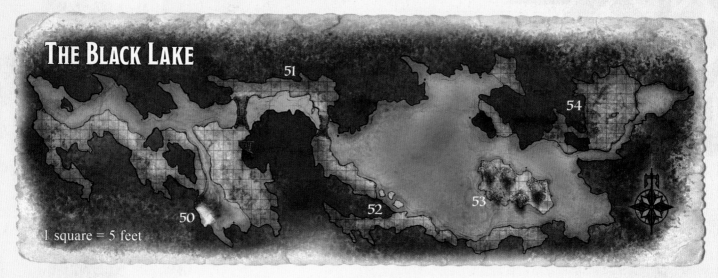

MAP 2.6: THE BLACK LAKE

throw to catch itself on the ledge. On a failed save, a creature falls, takes 7 (2d6) bludgeoning damage from falling timbers and stones, and is caught in the river's current (see "Fast-Flowing Water," page 51).

52. NIGHTSCALE'S LAIR

When the characters first approach the southeastern shore of the lake, Nightscale is dozing on her hoard on the island (area 53). The dragon is immediately alerted to their presence if the characters make noise, carry light sources, or trigger the collapse of the bridge. Otherwise, the characters don't draw the dragon's attention unless they move all the way to the ledge directly south of area 53.

> The dilapidated bridge leads to another ledge that winds southeast alongside a very large lake, apparently the source of the underground river. The cavern is quite large; the lake's far shore is lost in shadow, and the echoes of water seem to indicate a very sizable cave.

Creature. When Nightscale becomes aware of intruders, the **young black dragon** slips into the water, quietly swimming to a point near the three stepping stones shown on the map. Any character watching the lake can make a Wisdom (Perception) check contested by the dragon's Dexterity (Stealth) check. On a successful check, the character catches a glimpse of a serpentine form moving in the darkness.

The dragon takes full advantage of her aquatic environment and never offers an easy target to enemies. She begins combat at a range of 20 to 30 feet, raising only her head and part of her neck above the water (granting her three-quarters cover) and breathing acid. Then she submerges and waits for her breath weapon to recharge. Nightscale doesn't resort to melee combat unless she is confronted underwater. If the dragon is reduced to 40

hit points or fewer, she tries to escape through the passage in area 54.

Negotiation. Nightscale isn't inclined to parley with the characters unless they surrender, give her all of their treasure, and throw their arms and armor in the lake. If the characters seriously injure her, Nightscale might bargain to buy time so she can later move her hoard. Only when she is near death does she abandon her treasure.

53. NIGHTSCALE'S HOARD

When the characters come into view of the island for the first time, read:

> A short distance offshore sits a small isle thirty or forty feet across. Stalagmites thrust up at the ceiling above, and the dark waters lap quietly at its shores. Several spots on its surface glimmer even in the gloom, suggesting the promise of treasure to be had.

Nightscale keeps her treasure on the small island in the lake, and she spends most of her time resting here. If the characters have avoided attracting her attention so far and want to approach the island, they can do so quietly if every character's Dexterity (Stealth) check meets or exceeds the dragon's passive Perception score.

Treasure. Nightscale has accumulated considerable wealth from her plunder of Khundrukar. Her hoard contains 6,200 sp, 1,430 gp, two garnets worth 20 gp each, a black pearl worth 50 gp, a *wand of magic missiles*, a *+2 greataxe* bearing Durgeddin's smith-mark, a *+1 shield*, a *potion of healing*, and a *potion of flying*.

54. THE DRAGON'S PASSAGE

Beneath the surface of a small pool is an underwater passage that links the Black Lake to the Dark Mere on the east side of the Stone Tooth. The submerged passage is about 700 feet long.

Aftermath

The characters have overcome Khundrukar's dangerous inhabitants and looted the dragon's lair. What next?

Resolving the Character Hooks

If the characters return to Blasingdell, their fame as adventurers spreads. Townsfolk hail them on the street, and some might approach them with problems that can lead to further adventures. The characters can continue to use the town as a base of operations. Other developments depend on what got them here and how they leave.

Follow the Map

While the characters are exploring the stronghold, they might find another map, perhaps on the body of an adventurer from the previous expedition, or in the library in area 49. It could lead to a different dungeon, a city in some land far away, or an as-yet-unknown location rumored to hide a fabulous treasure.

Track the Broken Blade

If the characters were sent to retrieve weapons for Baron Althon, they can bring him the *+1 longsword* from area 22, the *+2 greataxe* in area 53, the handaxe from area 14, and the warhammer from area 23. All bear Durgeddin's smith-mark; Baron Althon pays 500 gp above the market price for each mundane weapon, 1,000 gp for the *+1 longsword*, and 6,000 gp for the *+2 greataxe*, if the characters are willing to sell.

Vanquish the Orc Raiders

The characters can return to Blasingdell at any time to collect the bounty for orcs they kill or capture. If the characters eliminate all the orcs in the stronghold, the mayor honors them with a celebration attended by the eminent citizens of the town. The characters have established valuable contacts who can aid them in their later endeavors.

Further Adventures

You can build an entire campaign around the duergar that occupy the Foundry. Perhaps they came here from a hidden city in even deeper caverns beneath the Sinkhole and the Black Lake. Your answers to the following questions form the basis for further adventures:

- How did the duergar get into the complex?
- What is the mysterious project they are working on?
- Did Durgeddin know of the duergar's existence?
- Do the duergar have some of Durgeddin's items? If so, are they guarding them or using them?

You can also use this adventure to sow the seeds of the characters' next activity. Perhaps the party encounters a legend of a magical treasure from Khundrukar's fall, buried in the tomb of an evil knight. Maybe Great Ulfe's ogre clan is terrorizing a nearby area, or an orc war chief wields a legendary weapon that was crafted by Durgeddin.

Whatever form they take, the repercussions of the characters' descent into Khundrukar have the potential to affect their lives for years to come.

THE HIDDEN SHRINE OF TAMOACHAN

THE ANCIENT RUINED CITY OF TAMOACHAN is familiar to a select few scholars and fortune seekers, who know of it but not always exactly where it is. Even more secluded, lying somewhere within or beneath the ruins, is a hidden shrine said to be dedicated to Zotzilaha, the vampire god of the underworld. Adventurers who catch wind of the place are likely to find its lure irresistible.

If the characters find their way to the environs of the ruined city, their next order of business might be to set up a camp nearby. After a few hours of searching, they can find an easily defended glade with an artesian spring.

Most of the city is toppled and almost completely covered in undergrowth. Intruders who enter the ruins will discover that the ancient streets now serve as overgrown "valleys" between the debris of the crumbled buildings. The largest of these valleys all lead to the central clearing where a great pyramid stands.

In the south side of that clearing is a newly collapsed area, revealing a jagged hole with a debris-covered slide, leading down into darkness.

RUNNING THE ADVENTURE

The adventure, which is designed for a group of four or five 5th-level player characters, gets under way the morning after the characters arrive in the vicinity of the ruins and make camp. When all of them have risen and finished preparing for the day's travel, read:

> As you head toward the pyramid temple, you tread across cracked and overgrown flagstones, stepping over fallen and shattered pillars, pushing aside vines and briars.
>
> When you are nearly at the temple, the sound of creatures crashing through the underbrush comes from behind you. You turn around to see people moving through the woods toward the clearing around the pyramid.
>
> Then, suddenly, the earth shudders and gapes open beneath your feet and you are falling amid the roar of collapsing masonry. Dust fills the air and the sunlight disappears as the darkness swallows you.

The party has fallen into area 1 of the dungeon, which is where play begins.

THE RUINS OF THE SHRINE

Map 3.1 shows the layout of the shrine, and later sections of this adventure describe what can be found there.

THE RUINS: GENERAL FEATURES

The walls inside the ruins are constructed of blocks of unmortared stone covered by stucco. The ceilings are of the same material, supported by corbel arches.

Ceilings. Most of the hallways have 20-foot ceilings. Some rooms have ceilings of 20 to 40 feet in height.

Doors. Doors are made of beaten bronze or slabs of stone. While heavy, they can be opened without a check.

Unsafe Stonework. In some places, the corbel arches that hold up the ceiling aren't structurally sound. As a result, some spells might have disastrous effects. A spell like *fireball* (an explosion) or *thunderwave* (an area of thunder damage) has a 25 percent chance to cause a ceiling collapse within the spell's area, dealing 16 (3d10) bludgeoning damage to creatures in the area. This collapse might block or bury objects or exits.

Poisonous Gas. The lower levels of the ruins, including the rooms and passages of encounter areas 1 through 38, are filled with poisonous gas. The gas is an amber color, and its area is lightly obscured. Anyone can tell that the gas is irritating, but it takes a successful DC 15 Intelligence (Nature) check to discern the gas's toxicity. Flames in the gas sputter and glow redly, and any attempt to use natural means to ignite a fire has only a 50 percent chance of success. Fire used as a light source has an effective radius only half normal.

A creature takes 3 (1d6) poison damage every hour it spends in the gas. The gas is light, so it accumulates closer to the ceiling. Inhabitants of the dungeon have immunity to the poisonous effect of the gas.

PLACING THE ADVENTURE

In the original adventure, set in the world of Greyhawk, the Hidden Shrine is part of the ancient ruined city of Tamoachan, once the northernmost capital of the Olman empire. The civilization of the Olman people covered much of the southern continent centuries before current history began. Tamoachan is located in the savage lands south of the Olman Islands and southeast of the Holds of the Sea Princes. The climate is subtropical and very damp; it rains nearly every afternoon.

In other worlds, similar possibilities can be found.

Dragonlance. The hidden shrine might not be part of an ancient city on Krynn, but instead an isolated temple for a weird dead cult devoted to the god Chemosh. The site could date back to the Age of Dreams, and might be on an isle or in an isolated region near the Blood Sea of Istar.

Eberron. On Eberron, the site might be the ancient seat of an elven cult, possibly connected to the line of Vol. Alternatively, Tamoachan could be a truly primeval location in Q'barra, and the Olman "gods" actually fiends from the Age of Demons.

Forgotten Realms. Because the people of Maztica closely resemble the Olman, that region is a likely place for the ruined city and the shrine. Tamoachan might instead be a lost city in the jungles of Chult.

Side View of Temple

Temple

Third Tier

Second Tier

First Tier

Lower Chambers

Temple

Second Tier

Third Tier

First Tier

CHAPTER 3 | THE HIDDEN SHRINE OF TAMOACHAN

The Hidden Shrine
of Tamoachan

1 Square = 5 feet

Door	Stairs
Double Door	Statue
Secret Door	Stuffed Animal
False Door	Bas-Relief, Wall Sculpture
Trap Door in Ceiling	Divan
Trap	Curtain
Trigger Mechanism	Water
Open Pit	Underwater Ledge
Covered Pit	Smokehole or Chute
Fountain	Iron Bars
Well	Rubble
Pillar	Vertical Shaft

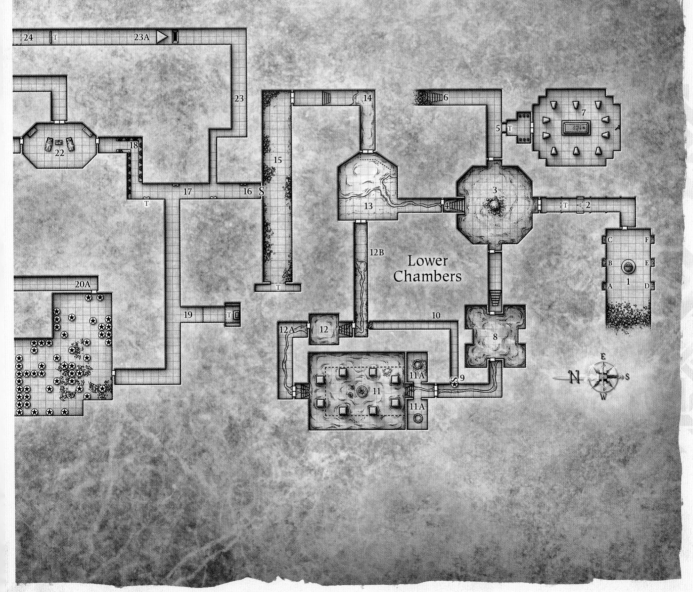

Lower
Chambers

Map 3.1: The Hidden Shrine of Tamoachan

The gas rises up and out of the ruins if the doors to area 39 are opened. It takes one month for the lower levels to clear completely. If the doors are closed again, the lower chambers refill with gas in two weeks.

Dried Potions. In some locations, characters discover the remains of a potion in the form of sediment in the bottom of a container. It is possible to mix this powder with water or wine and restore the potion. Wine creates a potion with full effect, but water shortens the potion's duration (if it has one) by half. If the powder is consumed by itself, there is a 1 in 8 chance that it acts as a *potion of poison*; otherwise, the powder has no effect.

Pressure Plates. Several areas have traps that are triggered by the operation of a pressure plate, which depresses when a certain amount of weight is put on it.

A character who succeeds on a DC 20 Wisdom (Perception) check can find a pressure plate. The plate can be blocked, preventing the trap from triggering, by wedging it in the upper position with pitons or similarly strong shims. Doing so takes one character at least 5 minutes, and the character must make a DC 15 Dexterity check using thieves' tools. If the check fails by 4 or less, the character knows the shims aren't properly placed. If the check fails by 5 or more, the character doesn't realize the shims will fail to hold up the plate.

RANDOM ENCOUNTERS

Each hour the party is in the ruins, roll a d12. On a roll of 1, an encounter occurs. Then roll a d10 and see the following table to determine which monsters show up.

d10	Encounter
1	1d3 **swarms of rats** (diseased, as giant rats)
2	1d3 **swarms of bats**
3	2d4 **giant fire beetles**
4	1d6 **zombies**
5	1 **will-o'-wisp**
6	2d4 **baboons**
7	1 **swarm of poisonous snakes**
8	1d4 **giant frogs**
9	1d2 **panthers**
10	1d3 **giant wolf spiders**

These wanderers are extra and aren't from any of the areas in the ruins. If an indicated monster doesn't fit the situation, check again or choose a different result.

LOCATIONS IN THE LOWER CHAMBERS

The following locations are identified on map 3.1.

1. THE VAULT OF CHICOMOZTOC
(Chee-koh-MOZ-tok, the place of seven caves)

The poisonous gas is present here, affecting fire and breathing.

Relate the following information to the characters gradually as they examine their surroundings.

> You are in a long, narrow chamber, running east-west. In the center of this apartment is a domed shape on the floor. In the east wall is a blank-faced stone door. The west end of the room is blocked by fallen stone and rubble, apparently the result of a collapse. The two side walls appear to have several niches cut into them.
>
> The shape in the center of the chamber appears to be a small alcove, protected by a half-dome with the open end facing toward the door in the east wall. This alcove is set in a recessed, shallow, tiled well, one foot deep and ten feet wide. The alcove itself is four feet high. The recess contains some sort of display.
>
> The display appears to be a diorama depicting a hunting party of Olman warriors, in feathers and deer-hide garments, in a mountainside scene. Some have pulled down a stag with the aid of a dog, another group is cleaning a small mule deer, and others have cornered a panther with their spears. A scout watches the panther from an outcropping above. He holds a metal staff with a loop in its end. It looks like a shepherd's crook.
>
> The three niches on both the northern and southern walls are five feet wide and about three feet off the floor.

ABOUT THE ORIGINAL

The Hidden Shrine of Tamoachan, by Harold Johnson and Jeff R. Leason, was originally published in 1980 as an adventure for the first edition of the D&D game.

The design of the temple draws heavily on Mayan and Aztec/Toltec mythology and society. In the original publication, Dungeon Masters were encouraged to research these real-world background elements to add depth and realism to the characters' experience.

Each niche contains a diorama depicting some aspect of tribal life. The six-inch-tall figures in all of the displays appear to be made of stucco, realistically and brightly painted. The scenes portrayed represent fishing, farming, religion, warfare, the creation story, and crafting.

A cave-in completely blocks the west end of the chamber. At short intervals, small amounts of rubble and dirt come spilling into the room. Several large stones appear to have wedged themselves tightly, closing the collapse.

The figures of people and animals in all of the dioramas are loose and can be picked up and manipulated. If any of the people, and some of the animals, are removed from a display and placed on the floor of this vault, the item grows to full-size dimensions immediately, and spirits of the ancestors animate the creature and it attacks. These beings are constructs, but otherwise function according to the statistics for a certain kind of creature, as noted below.

Center Display. The diorama in the alcove holds twelve **tribal warriors**, one **scout**, a **mastiff**, and a **panther**. The deer don't animate.

Niche A. In a river scene, a dozen **commoners** gather rushes, fish with nets, and carve a dugout.

Niche B. Twelve **commoners** are engaged in farming, planting maize and harvesting wheat. Five **tribal warriors** stand guard, and a **cult fanatic** (priest) in a bird costume is blessing the fields.

Niche C. The display portrays a temple upon a tiered pyramid. Seven **commoners** are bringing small offerings of gold and jade. Before the temple stands a **cult fanatic** handling a **constrictor snake**. Around him stand three costumed **tribal warriors**. One, dressed as a winged serpent, holds a spear; another is dressed as a bear with razor claws; the third represents a coyote holding a torch. There are also several stone statues of the gods. The bits of gold and jade are worth 5 gp each, and there are fifteen such items.

Niche D. A scene of tribal warfare involves twenty **tribal warriors** in combat. The ten warriors of one side are painted black, while the ten others are done in red. Warriors that are animated will fight animated enemy warriors first, but once they vanquish their foes they turn on the characters.

Niche E. In the display that depicts the creation of the world, all the statuettes are stylized and obviously nonhuman. These figures can be removed, but they don't animate. A god, adorned in green quetzal feathers, is mixing ashes with blood to form sculptures of a man and woman, while four towering figures painted red, black, blue, and white are standing about a fire committing suicide with their daggers. Two smaller figures are ringed by the four—the modest "Pimply One" is being consumed by the fire, while the braggart "Lord of Snails" cowers in fear.

Niche F. In a scene that shows various forms of crafting, twelve **commoners** are busy weaving rugs and baskets, carving totems, making pots, grinding stones for weapons, and making clothes.

Treasure. The staff held by the scout figure in the central diorama is actually a key and may be separated from the figure without affecting it. The key (worth 2 gp) is used to open the door to this room.

Cave-In. Attempting to dig upward through the rubble in the west end of the room results only in more detritus falling into the area.

Any further collapse deals 2 (1d4) bludgeoning damage to each digger. Each digger must also succeed on a DC 13 Dexterity saving throw or be buried by the rubble and take another 7 (3d4) bludgeoning damage. If the saving throw fails by 5 or more, the rubble engulfs the digger completely, and the trapped character can't breathe until dug out. Struggling out on one's own requires a successful DC 15 Strength (Athletics) check, and doing so takes 1 minute.

Door. When the characters investigate the door that offers an exit from the chamber, read:

The door is carved with a sun symbol and appears to open into the room; there are hinges on this side and scratches on the floor. There is no visible lock or handle on it, although a slight gap stretches across the top of the door. Eight holes seem to have been bored into the door; they are about an inch in diameter, but nothing can be seen in them. The door seems to be fairly thick. The lintel is arched, with a keystone at the top.

This door can be opened in a number of ways.

The key found in the diorama about hunting can be used to spring the door open when it is turned in the keyhole hidden under the keystone over the door. The keyhole can be found with a successful DC 20 Wisdom (Perception) check.

Pitons or similar tools can be driven into the door to provide handles. Driving pitons into the door takes 1 minute and requires a successful DC 10 Strength check. With such a grip, the door can be opened with some force, but with no check needed. (Objects inserted into the holes that are already bored won't stay in the door.)

The two hinge pins can be broken (each has AC 12 and 20 hit points) and removed, but the door falls inward. Someone who holds the door and succeeds on a DC 15 Strength (Athletics) check can keep the door up and lower it to the floor. Otherwise, the door falls, and those within 5 feet of it must succeed on a DC 15 Dexterity saving throw to avoid the falling door. On a failed save, a creature takes 7 (2d6) bludgeoning damage.

2. The Hall of Thrashing Canes

> The stone walls of this corridor are carved to resemble a stack of bamboo-like logs. The passage slopes down from a single door on its western leg, the lintel of which has been crafted to represent a stylized cavern entrance. It leads to double doors of beaten bronze, worked to resemble a forest of seaweed.

Pressure Plate. There is a pressure plate halfway down the hallway that triggers a trap when weight equivalent to that of three or four humanoids is on it. See "The Ruins: General Features" at the beginning of the adventure for details about pressure plates.

If the trap triggers, several of the logs swing out from either wall and buffet the party. Those in the plate's area when the trap triggers take 7 (2d6) bludgeoning damage and are pushed 5 feet down the slope toward the double doors. Once they swing out, the stone logs don't swing back and thus effectively block the passage, since they bar the way from ceiling to floor with only a 6-inch gap remaining between the logs.

3. Roost of the Conch

> This room is constructed of large stone blocks, buttressed in the corners. The walls are wet and slimy, and mud covers most of the floor in a thin coating. To the east and west may be seen stone doors recessed in the wall, and to the north a set of stairs leads down.
>
> In the center of the chamber sits a large polished boulder amid a pile of smaller rounded rocks. The boulder is five feet tall and colored brown with dark streaks and spots. Leaning against it is what appears to be a bamboo staff.
>
> In the mud around the base of the boulder is a moving shape, looking like a crayfish. It is facing you and seems to be aware of your presence.

Slippery Mud. The floor of the chamber is very slippery, counting as difficult terrain. Any sudden actions, including those necessary for combat, may result in the character taking a spill. A character who uses the Dash action or tries to fight within the room must succeed on a DC 10 Dexterity saving throw or fall prone. The saving throw should be made before attacks are made. Creatures encountered here are unaffected by the mud.

Guardian. The creature at the base of the boulder is a **giant crayfish** (see appendix B). If it is approached, it will advance waving its claws in an aggressive manner and speak. If any member of the party can understand Olman, an ancient language, the crayfish will be heard to say, "Who is this? Who dares to enter the chamber of the guardian? You had better go, or I will have to discharge my sacred duty! Be off with you before I lose my temper!"

If the party retreats, the crayfish will not follow, but will take to marching back and forth in front of the boulder and will continue to threaten the party if they approach again. If the crayfish is attacked, it will immediately call forth its companion.

Creature. The boulder is in reality a huge shell inhabited by **Kalka-Kylla** (see appendix B), a giant hermit crab. The bamboo staff is one of its legs; a successful DC 15 Intelligence (Nature) check enables a character to discern this fact and get a hint as to Kalka-Kylla's nature before the crab moves.

When the characters enter the room, Kalka-Kylla is asleep and will not awaken unless the crayfish is attacked. Once it is awake, it may attack or bargain. It speaks Olman.

The crab can be reasoned with, if the party doesn't attack it and can come to terms with it. The crab denies any knowledge of this place, stating that it was brought into these warrens when very young. If asked for directions, it first sends the party to the rubble-filled staircase to the east, and then, if asked a second time, it sends the party to the west.

4. Mud-Filled Doorway

Southern Approach. If the characters come upon the doorway from the south, read:

> The landing at the foot of a short flight of steps is filled with mud and silt that partially blocks the door leading north. The door is meant to open inward, for there are hinges on this side and a large grip to pull on.

Any attempts to open the door will meet with failure until the blockage is removed. Probing the silt will reveal its depth to be about 18 to 24 inches and its consistency as tenacious as quicksand. The silt can be scooped out of the stairwell, but it is semi-liquid and will quickly flow back. If water is forced, in quantity, through the silt, it will wash the silt under the door jamb and down the hall beyond, alleviating the blockage.

Northern Approach. If the characters come upon the doorway from the north, read:

> The thin, muddy stream that trickles through the hallway here flows out from underneath the door that lies ahead.

The door can be forced open only a few inches, enough to see it is blocked on the other side by a mass of silt.

5. Tomb Stone and Wet Lime

> The walls of this corridor are wet and slimy. The stucco covering has become saturated with water and is decomposing and sloughing off in spots on the southern wall, exposing the seams of one of the large stone blocks from which this structure was built.

The tightly fitted stone seals off a tomb. The block is made of limestone, and the entire face of the plug is covered with wet, caustic lime.

Wet Lime. Any flesh that comes in contact with the lime will take 1 acid damage per round. The lime must be removed from the skin to stop the damage, and it can either be wiped off or washed away.

If cloth or soft leather is used to protect flesh from contact with the wet lime, the lime will soak through in 2 rounds. Nonmagical leather armor won't absorb the lime, but each hour of contact with it reduces the armor's AC by 1, making the armor useless if its AC becomes 10. The lime can't be removed from the stone, since it isn't a coating.

Moving the Block. After the stucco is scraped away from the seams, the block can be pushed inward by the combined effort of up to four characters with a total Strength of 48 or higher. The stone is about 6 feet tall, 3 feet wide, and 3 feet thick. It takes 1 minute to push the plug 10 feet, after which it can be circumvented.

6. Rubble-Filled Staircase

> This staircase goes up for only a few steps, and then it seems that the rest is filled in with clay and stone rubble.

One or more characters can try to dig this staircase out. Any digging, however, will result in further movement of the rubble, dealing 2 (1d4) bludgeoning damage to each digger. Each digger must also succeed on a DC 13 Dexterity saving throw or be buried by the rubble, taking another 7 (3d4) bludgeoning damage. If the saving throw fails by 5 or more, the rubble engulfs the digger completely, and the trapped character can't breathe until dug out. Struggling out on one's own requires 1 minute of effort and a successful DC 15 Strength (Athletics) check. The staircase is completely blocked and leads nowhere.

7. The Sepulcher of Tloques-Popolocas
(Tloh-kays Poh-poh-LOH-kahs, master of the outsiders)

Once the stone entrance block (area 5) is pushed out of the way, the characters have enough space to get past it.

> Beyond the plug is a small foyer holding three sealed urns on the east and west sides. To the south are double doors of bronze with glyphs worked into their faces.

The ancient glyphs are scribed in Olman. If anyone in the party can read this language, or if the message can be understood by other means, the glyphs will translate as "Here lies Tloques-Popolocas, master of the others, who is like the wind and the night!"

Trapped Doors. The doors are locked (DC 15 Dexterity check to pick with thieves' tools) and trapped. Opening the lock disables the trap. Forcing the doors open can be done with a successful DC 20 Strength (Athletics) check, but the act causes a glass sphere on the other side of the doors to break. This sphere is attached to the doors just above the lock, and opening the lock pushes the sphere aside, putting it out of harm's way.

Someone who examines the door closely with a light source notices the glint of glass in the seam between the doors with a successful DC 20 Wisdom (Perception) check. Even with the lock still in place, the lever on which the sphere rests can be moved by someone who succeeds on a DC 20 Dexterity check using thieves' tools. The painstaking process in the narrow space takes 5 minutes, and if the check fails by 5 or more, the sphere breaks at the end of the attempt.

Sleep Gas. If the glass sphere breaks, it releases green, swirling sleep gas throughout the area. Each time a creature ends its turn in this chamber, the creature must succeed on a DC 10 Constitution saving throw or become poisoned for 5,000 years. While poisoned in this way, a creature is also unconscious, and it is unaffected by the passage of time or by other poisons. If magic is used to cure the poisoned condition, the recipient is immune to the poison for 1 hour. A casting of *dispel magic* using a spell slot of 7th level or higher can also end the effect. The vapors linger for a month unless they are cleared away by a strong wind.

Treasure. The seal on the urns is made of beeswax and may be broken so that the lids can be removed. Each of the six urns contains the equivalent of twenty flasks of oil. A filled urn weighs 25 pounds.

> Behind the doors is a chamber cut out of the rock with a veil of calcite and stalactites covering the walls. Buttresses rise from the corners, brown shot through with black, and triangular stone pillars support the high ceiling. Occupying the center of the chamber is a colossal monument resembling a giant's table, covered on all sides with intricate carvings and glyphs. Engraved on the floor in front of the entrance is a seal that displays more glyphs. Opposite the entrance, a battleaxe is embedded in the wall, six feet above the floor.

The glyphs in the floor seal are written in Olman and translate as "Ah, defilers! Now you shall join me in my eternal resting!"

The monument is constructed from several parts. A great stone slab, 20 feet long by 10 feet wide, rests upon a 4-foot-thick monolith of rock of similar dimensions, and this, in turn, is supported by six huge blocks of dolomite. Every component has been covered with intricate carvings and glyphs. The top of the slab depicts a struggle between a dark-skinned man and a mighty, knotted serpent.

Engraved alongside this illustration are glyphs identical to those found on the door. Under these sigils are etched a series of four face-glyphs in a line. At the foot of the slab is a row of eleven of these symbols, all different in form.

The carved block is the resting place of Tloques-Popolocas, a servant of the shadow-loving Zotzilaha. The glyphs on the top of the slab give his name, and the date he died, 54–3–9, is written in the face-glyphs. One glyph is a *glyph of warding* (save DC 17), which casts *bestow curse* on everyone in the tomb if the crypt is opened by those who don't serve the god Zotzilaha. The curse lasts until it is dispelled, and 4d10 days after this tomb has been broken into, every cursed violator receives a visit from either Tloques or some other agent of Zotzilaha seeking retribution.

The eleven face-glyphs at the foot of the block correspond to the numbers 0 through 10. The tomb is opened by pressing the glyphs that correspond to the numbers of the date carved on the top, in order. When the 9 glyph is depressed, a grating sound issues forth and the top slab slides back a bit. The tomb lid can then be opened the rest of the way by the combined effort of one or two characters with a total Strength of 20 or higher.

> The block beneath the slab is hollow, and inside is a crumbling skeleton decked out in decayed finery. It appears to have been a man of taller than average stature,

> obviously of great importance. Gems and other small adornments of obvious value lie on and around the body. Covering the skull is a mask of jade with cowrie-shell eyes and obsidian pupils. About the corpse's neck is a jade pendant carved with the face of a humanlike bat.

Creature. The corpse is the body of Tloques-Popolocas, a **vampire spawn** with special qualities (see below).

If the characters examine the contents of the tomb, see "Treasure" for details. Any of the items can be lifted off or out if the characters so desire. If the mask and the pendant are both removed, Tloques starts to awaken. Dust is stirred up into clouds and begins to gather on the bones as they knit back together. His wasted form then sits up and gazes about. This part of the regeneration process requires 2 rounds, during which time the corpse has AC 12 and 27 hit points. (If they have not been removed, the corpse benefits from the *bracers of defense* and the *ring of protection* he is wearing; see "Treasure.") If either the mask or the pendant is forced back upon him before the 2 rounds elapse, he returns to death. If not, he then sits for 2 more rounds, while his flesh knits and swells out with the apparent vigor of the living. He gains 27 hit points in the first round and 28 hit points in the second round, and he has his normal AC of 17 but remains prone. He can use Multiattack to make two claw attacks in either of these rounds, but being prone, he does so with disadvantage. Within this period, if both the mask and the pendant are forced back on him, he can resist returning to death with a successful DC 10 Wisdom saving throw. When he is whole again, he attacks.

Tloques, having gained his power from his allegiance to Zotzilaha, isn't a typical vampire and doesn't bite. He has the Shapechanger trait of a true vampire, except he can't change into mist. Tloques also has the Children of the Night action option of a true vampire, but he calls only bats. He can innately cast the *hold person* spell at will, requiring no components, but his target must be able to see him. When he has a chance to do so, Tloques pulls his axe from the wall and then uses it for each of his two attacks per round.

He is a blood-drinker and attempts to subdue opponents, if not vastly outnumbered, so as to assure himself a constant supply of blood. To drink blood, Tloques must first drain it into a receptacle and then drink it, which can reduce the target's hit point maximum as a normal vampire spawn bite does.

Tloques will not pursue fleeing grave robbers from his tomb immediately, but instead will seek to regain his bearings in the world of the living for several days. He can track down cursed thieves later, or invoke the power of Zotzilaha to locate any treasure stolen from this place. In the intervening time, he might regain some of his former power.

Battleaxe. The battleaxe has a blade of bronze, and the haft is wound with snakeskin wrappings. The weapon detects as magical. It casts an ominous shadow in the shape of what appears to be a withered arm.

Those who approach within reach of it feel a cold chill run up and down their spine, and anyone who tries to pull the axe from the wall finds it impossible to do so.

The weapon is a *berserker axe* that has a +2 bonus to attack and damage rolls instead of the normal +1. The axe can't be picked up by another as long as its current owner, Tloques, remains alive. Concealed beneath the wrappings around the handle is a parchment containing the spells *passwall*, *burning hands*, and *gust of wind*. When the attuned wielder uses an action to say the correct words of power, which are engraved in Olman on the axe blade, one of these spells can be cast.

The axe has 12 charges and regains 1d6 + 4 expended charges daily at dawn. Casting a spell from it takes a number of charges equal to the level at which the spell is cast (5th for *passwall*, 2nd for *gust of wind*, and 1st or higher for *burning hands*; spell save DC 15). If the parchment is removed from the axe, the axe loses the capability of casting these spells forever.

Treasure. The mask has a value of 200 gp, and the pendant is worth 50 gp. Describe the other contents of the tomb if the characters examine portions of the corpse more closely:

- Beneath the mask are fragments of bone, as though the skull has been crushed. Within the fragments of the jaw is a spherical white onyx (15 gp).
- Strands of hair still remain on the skull, gathered into black obsidian and red pipestone tubes (worth 50 gp as a bunch).
- Above the mask, on the corpse's forehead, is a diadem of dark opals and jade discs (worth 200 gp).
- To either side of the mask are jade earplugs carved in several pieces to resemble budding flowers (the pair worth 30 gp).
- Draped over the rib cage is a breastplate made of loops of tubular jade interspersed with bone dividers (protects like studded leather, worth 200 gp).
- Scattered around the neck and through the rib cage of the corpse are one hundred fifty-six jade beads (each worth 1 gp) shaped like spheres, cylinders, tri-lobed beads, floral buds, open flowers, pumpkins, melons, and a snake's head.
- About the wrists are wide jade bead bracelets (*bracers of defense*).
- On the middle finger of each hand are carved jade rings, one in the form of a man holding the moon (a *ring of protection*) and the other a panther ready to strike (a *ring of animal influence*).
- Pressed into the fingers of each hand is a large bead, a jade cube (150 gp) in the right hand and a spherical agate (50 gp) in the left hand.
- At the feet of the skeleton lie two small containers, apparently of glazed clay, one fitted with flower-shaped plugs in both ends (it contains the dried remains of a *potion of invisibility*), the other holding a 1-inch-diameter piece of mother-of-pearl (5 gp).
- Lying among the hip bones is a 6-inch-long statue of a faceless man with large pointed ears. Plugged at the bottom, it is a bottle that contains an *elixir of health*.

8. Courses of the Gods

This room is wet, and the walls are covered with a slimy, white buildup. There is about an inch and a half of water and mud blanketing the floor. Many overturned pedestals and pieces of broken statuary lie on the floor, partially buried in the mud. Opposite the entrance to this room is another door.

Only one pedestal remains standing, in the northwest corner. On it sits a small, metallic, three-sided pyramid. Overhead in the shadow-draped ceiling are inlaid colored tiles depicting a starry sky and forming strange patterns in the areas above the pedestals.

A dark, wet mass clings to the wall above the western door. Upon closer inspection, it appears to be green in color. The mass is a large colony of algae, though it resembles green slime; a successful DC 15 intelligence (Nature) check enables a character to tell the difference. Fire will have little effect on it, because the algae is oozing wet and fire doesn't burn with much vigor in the presence of the poisonous gas that fills this level. Attempts to dislodge the slime will result in slippery sections of it dropping on the characters.

Caustic Lime. The walls of this room are heavily coated with caustic lime. Any flesh that comes in contact with this lime will take 1 acid damage per round. The lime must be removed from the skin to stop the damage, and can be either wiped off or washed away.

Treasure. The small pyramid is made of silver (worth 5 gp). It represents the god of the moon and lightning, Apocatequil (A-poe-ka-TAY-kel). The fallen statuary was made of stucco and depicted other Olman gods. These include a coyote, a crab-headed figure, an alligator-headed god, a feathered warrior, and a jaguar.

9. Stone Statue

The walls and ceiling of this hallway are coated with slime, and the floor of the passage is covered with a layer of mud. Through this muck a steady stream of water trickles northward. The stucco on the walls is flaking off, and there are glowing silver tracks in the slime crisscrossing the walls and ceiling.

Along the east wall of the passage stands a twelve-foot-tall stone statue of a man outfitted in fine clothing and holding a stone tray in his raised arms. Its eyes appear to be black gemstones; the right one droops out of its socket, balancing on the statue's cheek. From behind the left shoulder protrudes the hilt of a weapon, most likely a sword. The stone tray, as well as the forehead and the nose of the statue, are chipped and scratched.

The easiest way to reach the sword or the gems is to climb up on the statue and stand on the tray. A character who succeeds on a DC 15 Intelligence (Investigation) check realizes the statue is top-heavy; proficiency with mason's tools and a dwarf's Stonecunning trait apply to this check. If a weight of more than 100 pounds is applied to the tray, or someone pushes on the statue anywhere above the tray and succeeds on a DC 10 Strength check, the statue overbalances and topples into the hall. Anyone on the statue, or under it, must succeed on a DC 15 Dexterity saving throw or take 7 (2d6) bludgeoning damage from the falling statue. Behind the toppled statue is a narrow passage 4 feet above the floor (see area 10).

Treasure. The eyes of the statue are pieces of polished obsidian worth 10 gp each. The sword is a *+1 long-sword* in fine condition, made of laminated wood, inset with jagged teeth of obsidian. It deals an extra 2d6 damage to any creature of the plant type. The sword comes free easily, if any character pulls it up and out.

10. Secret Passage

> Water beads collect upon the walls of this narrow passage, and the flooring is cold and damp. A low ceiling, only five feet tall, further cramps this dank place.

The northern entrance to this passage is a block of stone mounted on a central pivot, which has been wedged partially open by accumulated debris.

The location of the southern entrance appears to be a blank wall when initially viewed from within the passage. The portal can be opened from inside the passage by releasing a concealed catch at the intersection of the wall and the ceiling. Finding the catch requires a successful DC 15 Wisdom (Perception) check.

11. The Court of Cemanahuac
(*Say-man-AH-wok, place surrounded by water*)

Describe the features of this room as the characters become able to see them or examine them. The text assumes the characters are approaching from the south.

> The doors to this room are made of bronze and are tinted blue from oxidation. Just inside the doorway are two small alcoves. Each space contains an old fountain, cracked and crusted with lime. Around the fountain in the eastern alcove, a heap of rubbish litters the floor. The fountain in the western alcove still holds some green scummy water, in which something moves.
>
> A short hall ending in descending steps leads to the central chamber, which is flooded. A dark, foul pool covers the entire floor. A central hall, flanked by narrow aisles, is defined by two rows of massive square columns. The walls are coated with slime, and there are glowing silver lines etched across them. From what you can see

of the chamber's walls, the stone appears to be crudely worked.

Two corroded bronze braziers stand in the pool. Toward the middle of the room, two broken urns, each apparently once about four feet tall, poke up out of the water. In the darkness on the eastern wall appears to be an enormous growth of an overall greenish hue that gives off the same silvery gleam as the slime trails.

The water in the central area of the floor is 2 feet deep, and the floor is very slippery—moving across this difficult terrain costs 3 feet of speed for every 1 foot traveled). Any sudden actions, including those necessary for combat, might result in the character taking a spill. A character who takes the Dash action or tries to fight while in the room must first succeed on a DC 10 Dexterity saving throw or fall prone.

Moat. The 10-foot-wide section of floor that runs along the east, west, and north sides of the room is 10 feet lower than in the rest of the room, creating a 12-foot-deep moat. Characters who don't probe ahead will be unable to detect the drop-off until it is too late.

Lime. The walls are heavily coated with lime, which also pollutes the water. If a character stands in this water for more than 30 minutes, the soaked portions of the character's clothing begin to rot away.

Creature. The phosphorescent glow on the eastern wall is actually a giant slug named **Tecuziztecatl** (see appendix B), the Lord of Snails. Tecuziztecatl (Tay-COO-zeez-tay-COT-el) is highly intelligent and quite the boaster. In ancient lore it was considered to be related to the moon, a fact of which it is quite proud. During combat the slug will detail, in Olman, what it has in store for the characters and how hopeless their situation is.

If it begins to lose the combat, the slug will either "surrender" and after bargaining agree to help the party, or else it will flee and conceal itself in the moat. If the characters allow themselves to be helped, the slug will precede them to the north side of the moat and stretch its body across the gap, making it appear to be solid ground. Those who step on the slug without taking precautions will plunge into the moat.

The slug will lead the party toward the Tomb of Hurakan (area 12) and instruct them to open the door. Once the door is open, Tecuziztecatl will flee from the party and hide in the bottom of the moat.

Eastern Alcove. The eastern fountain has a small amount of concentrated lime solution near the bottom (dealing damage as the lime in area 5). It looks like cloudy water. A small amulet lies beneath the caked lime. The amulet (worth 65 gp) is made of brass and chrysoprase, engraved with the words "Lord of Snails." It is possible to use the amulet as a bargaining tool with the giant slug, which will accept it in return for allowing the characters passage to the Tomb of Hurakan.

In the southeast corner of the eastern alcove, a **swarm of rats** nests in the rubbish. The swarm is made up of diseased giant rats.

Western Alcove. The western fountain is filled with algae, and some bullfrogs are raising a brood of tadpoles in the water.

12. THE TOMB OF HURAKAN
(Ewe-RA-kan, god of the flood)

If the characters approach from the north (through the corridor marked 12A), read:

> This passageway is slime-covered, and a stream of water trickles away from the door. There is condensation on the walls, door, and ceiling, some of which drips down on you. A quiet sound of dripping and splashing echoes in the corridor. This door is tightly sealed and appears to be warped outward or wedged shut. The door's hinges are mounted on this side.

The door requires a successful DC 20 Strength (Athletics) check to pull it open. The difficulty is due to the fact that the room behind the door is entirely filled with water, which has bowed the door and jammed it shut. Those who listen at the door will hear a slight splashing and gurgling, if they hear anything at all.

Opening the door will release a wave of water. Those hit by the water take 2 (1d4) bludgeoning damage and must succeed on a DC 15 Strength saving throw or be knocked down and washed along the passage to the north, then westward. A creature that succeeds on a DC 15 Strength (Athletics) check while moving around a corner can grab onto the stonework there and halt its movement. When the flood washes to area 11, the water bursts open the doors there (if they weren't open already), and anyone in the water is dumped into the moat.

A character who is washed down the hall must succeed on DC 15 Dexterity saving throw to keep a hold on anything in hand. Heavy objects sink to the floor in the hall, but lighter ones are washed into the moat.

12B. TOMB, SOUTH ENTRANCE

If the characters traverse the corridor from east to west, describe the area as they advance.

> This hall is strewn with mud and flotsam. Water accumulates in the center of the corridor and flows westward to where a stone block in the southern wall has shifted out of place. The corridor turns north, and the flow of water follows it, then goes under a door made of bronze-bound wood. The door has a handle and a keyhole.

Opening the door will reveal stairs going down into a small room. A pool of water fills the entire chamber. Another door is across the way, but only the top 3 inches of it can be seen above the water.

13. CHILD OF ZOTZILAHA

> A faint, melodious sound comes from ahead. It is difficult to tell whether it is someone singing or the echoing of dripping water in a great cavern.

If the characters burst into the room, they immediately hear a surprised squeal and a splash.

> The room is lit by a soft light that reveals a section of rocky beach. Beyond the beach is a pool of glowing water, filling half the room and framed by a crystal cavern. Green fronds can be seen in the pool. Light seems to flow from everywhere, the pool and walls glistening like soft moonlight. On the far side of the pool is a set of doors carved with a sun symbol.

If the characters approached quietly, they might glimpse the singer.

> Sitting on the beach in front of the crystalline pool is a woman, young and slim, with long golden hair and pale white skin. She radiates a soft silvery light even through her shawl, white as the froth of waves. She is singing a strange melody in an unrecognizable language. After finishing her song, she enters the water in a long, arching dive.

Water covers more than half of the cavern. The floor drops off sharply, creating a pool that is 12 feet deep. A ledge runs from the southern wall to a set of doors that lead east. Above the ledge, the water is only 2 feet deep, but the area counts as difficult terrain.

The doors that lead east have keyholes in them but are unlocked.

Creatures. The young woman is actually a **nereid** (see appendix B) named Dasa Zotz. Whether startled or not, eventually the nereid surfaces and a silvery laugh is heard. This creature is an agent of Zotzilaha. Unlike most other nereids, she is chaotic evil in alignment, and she speaks Olman instead of Common. She possesses an insidious and clever mind, concealed beneath her alien beauty and seeming naiveté. She retreats from close combat and conceals herself in the water.

The nereid has a pet named Chac, a **giant lightning eel** (see appendix B). If she calls to Chac for aid, she does so on her turn when she uses Water Lash. The waters begin to heave and boil, and the watery form of a human with an elephantine head, wearing an elaborate headdress and holding a trident, rises up. The eel comes near the surface and strikes when the watery "god" levels its trident at a character.

Treasure. If seriously threatened, the nereid might reveal the location of her treasure. At the deepest part of the pool is a grotto hidden behind a bed of kelp. In this cave are six golden statuettes (worth 50 gp each) and a golden mask (worth 250 gp). Also lying in the cache are two crystal scroll cases (worth 25 gp apiece), though water has destroyed the scrolls in them; a silver idol (worth 15 gp), which is actually a bottle holding a *potion of clairvoyance*; and a pair of *gloves of missile snaring*.

14. FLOODED HALL

Half of the L-shaped corridor is flooded. The water is 3 feet deep and cold, and the bottom is very slippery; moving across this difficult terrain costs 3 feet of speed for every 1 foot traveled. Any sudden actions, including those necessary for combat, might result in the character taking a spill. A character who takes the Dash action or tries to fight within the room must first succeed on a DC 10 Dexterity saving throw or fall prone.

The water becomes shallower to the east. After the corridor turns north, a set of stairs rises up out of the dampness, and the path ends at a set of bronze doors. The doors have keyholes but are unlocked.

15. THE GREAT HALL

> This hallway is twenty feet wide and has piles of rubble and debris scattered along its length. The walls are covered with frescoes. The south wall displays scenes of a battle between natives and invaders.
>
> The north wall depicts people questing for a new land; their experiences during the journey include crossing treacherous mountains, sailing over storm-tossed seas, and receiving the guidance of the gods in their battles to keep their homeland free from invasions. In the center of the wall is a painting of a pyramid with a temple atop it and the sun shining over the land.
>
> Double bronze doors stand in the eastern end of the south wall. Down the hall to the west is an archway carved in the form of twining serpents. Beyond it, the corridor continues on into shadow.

The hallway extends only 5 feet beyond the arch. The western wall is a cleverly painted mural designed to give the illusion of depth and reality, and the obscuring effect of the poison gas contributes to this impression. If characters attempt to go in this direction, they walk straight into the wall unless someone succeeds on a DC 15 Wisdom (Perception) check. The space beyond the arch immediately in front of the mural is where creatures arrive after being teleported from the south end of area 32.

To either side of the arch is a 5-foot-deep niche. A character who steps into either niche triggers a pressure plate (see "The Ruins: General Features" at the beginning of the adventure) that releases a set of horizontal bars—closing off the archway and trapping the interloper.

The character can instead take 10 minutes to remove the plate from the floor, requiring the same sort of check as for an attempt to block the plate from moving. A failed check in this case means another 10 minutes of work is required, followed by another check.

Sun Painting. The painting of the pyramid and the sun conceals a secret door. A character who makes a successful DC 15 Wisdom (Perception) check discovers that the portion of the work that depicts the sun is separate from the rest and can be depressed. Pushing it inward reveals and opens a secret door in the wall. The floor of the passage that leads north is 8 feet above the floor of the great hall. Accessing this secret exit causes any bars over the niches to retract into the walls and the pressure plates to reset.

16. SECRET DOOR

This description assumes an approach from the north. The south side of the secret door is described in area 15.

> The wall at the end of this corridor has a bas relief sculpture of a warrior armed with a spear and shield. The shield, which rests on the floor, resembles a sundial, complete with a marker standing out from the wall. Etched on the shield's surface are runes in Olman script.

The message on the shield reads, "Turn back!"

Instead of being part of a solid carving, the shield has a seam that a character can discover with a successful DC 15 Wisdom (Perception) check. Chips around the seam suggest that the shield can be pivoted. Experimentation thereafter reveals that the sundial marker is movable. When it's in its current position, leaning to the right, the secret door is closed. If the marker is pushed to the left, the shield pivots, and the exit opens.

The floor of the area beyond the door is 8 feet lower than the floor in the corridor.

17. HALL OF THE GREAT SPIRITS

> This corridor is high-ceilinged and decorated with sculptures mounted on the walls. Two corridors branch off from the main hall, a narrow one to the east and another to the west. The statuary that adorns the walls consists of four sculpted heads of animals. Each one is six feet above the floor and two to three feet in diameter. Opposite the passage that leads east is the stylized head of a coyote, and across from the hallway going west is the head of a grinning bear. Near the south end of the corridor, the head of a bison is mounted on the east wall.
>
> At the north end of the area, on the west wall, is what appears to be the head of an eagle, with its beak open. Something shines from within the eagle's mouth.

Wedged in the eagle's throat is an intricately crafted golden bracelet. To remove the item, a character must either reach into the mouth or attempt to push the bracelet out with another object.

Snapping Trap. Disturbing the bracelet in any way will cause the beak to snap shut instantly. Whatever was inserted into the mouth will be pinned, and the hinge of the mechanism will jam.

The hinge can be loosened with oil, after which the beak opens easily, or the beak (AC 16, 25 hit points) can be broken off by dealing bludgeoning damage to it that reduces it to 0 hit points. If a character's arm is caught in the beak when the beak is struck, that character takes one-quarter of the damage dealt to the beak and the beak takes the remainder.

Treasure. The golden circlet is a *bracelet of rock magic* (see appendix A) that was originally a ring, an earring, or some other piece of stone giant jewelry.

18. HALLWAY OF THE ANCESTORS

> Along both sides of the corridor, deep in shadows, human figures appear to be floating above the floor. As you approach, you see that the figures seemingly suspended in the air are actually withered corpses standing upright on a ledge two feet above the floor.

Creatures. Once the lead character in the party reaches the midway point of the east–west passage, fifteen **zombies** animate and attack. These corpses don't register as undead to a casting of *detect evil and good* until after they animate.

Disease. After combat with the zombies is finished, each character who took damage from the monsters must succeed on a DC 11 Constitution saving throw or contract sewer plague (see "Sample Diseases" in chapter 8 of the *Dungeon Master's Guide*). Unlike the normal disease, symptoms of this disease manifest in an infected creature after 1 hour rather than 1d4 days.

19. Silver Coffer

At the end of the corridor is a small alcove holding a three-foot-tall stone pedestal on which rests a small silver coffer. Fifteen feet in front of the alcove, there is a single small step up in the stone floor. Inside the alcove, the floor is elevated an additional two feet.

Hinged Floor. A character who examines the base of the 2-foot step along the edge of the raised floor and succeeds on a DC 15 Wisdom (Perception) check notices a metallic glint coming from a hinge that runs across the full width of the floor. The hinge can be dismantled by someone who uses thieves' tools, takes 5 minutes to do so, and succeeds on a DC 15 Dexterity check. On a successful check, the trap (see below) is prevented from triggering. On a failed check, the character hasn't managed to dismantle the hinge but can try again.

Shifting Slab Trap. If the hinge in the floor isn't dismantled, a trap is triggered if more weight is placed on the floor of the alcove than on the space immediately in front of the step up. The floor inside the alcove sinks 10 feet. At the same time, the 15-foot slab of floor north of the alcove (as shown on the map) rises up, pivoting along its south edge. The northern side of the slab now seals off the passage to the north, while the southern side slopes down toward the alcove. Those who were on the slab when it pivoted fall prone and roll to the bottom of the slope on the alcove floor, 13 feet below where the coffer sits on its pedestal. Each creature that falls in this way takes 3 (1d6) bludgeoning damage.

When the slab finishes moving, it locks into place, so the floor remains steeply sloped and the passage north remains blocked. The locking mechanism is hidden by the northern (elevated) edge of the floor, and it's in a very narrow space. The stone around it can be chipped away over several hours of tedious labor until the edge of the slab no longer holds in place. A *knock* spell can also defeat the locking mechanism.

Treasure. The silver coffer is unlocked, but it is latched, so the lid will not come open unless the characters touch the box.

Inside the coffer is a strange copper figurine, narrow, with fins, looking somewhat fish-like. Written on the side of this figurine are strange runes. On the slimmer end is a small arched square panel.

The runes are in a script similar to Elvish and spell out the name *Ilnedraw*. Deft fingers will be able to open the small panel, revealing a hollow inside which is a wall of lighted, colored beads.

Touching any of the beads will cause the panel to close. A few seconds thereafter, the figurine will rise into the air and start to fly about the alcove, hovering at times and avoiding being touched by characters or missiles. Once an exit is available, the figure will fly from the party and move randomly through the ruins, stopping at doors and pausing for a minute. This floating statuette serves no purpose and is more or less a false lead.

The silver coffer weighs 15 pounds and is worth 150 gp due to its fine workmanship. The copper figure is worth 50 gp and weighs 5 pounds.

20. Spirit Guard of Ayocuan
(A-YO-kwan)

A massive bronze door opens into this grand chamber. The place is filled with rubble and life-sized statuary, much of it broken. Standing in ranks is an army of clay statues, in what must have once been an impressive array. Now, half of them are fallen and crumbled. Near the door are spear-wielders, perhaps twenty of them, outfitted only in scraps of leather now. At their feet lay obsidian spearheads and bits of rotted wooden shafts. Behind these figures are archers, in a scattered formation. Few of them remain standing. Their arrows are gone, but they hold laminated bows, dried and worm-eaten.

Farther into the room are figures of warriors with war clubs and handaxes, wearing scraps of lacquered leather, sandals, and caps. Beyond all of this in the north end of the chamber are a group of statues that must have been an honor guard. These warriors wear feathered robes and headdresses and are armed with pitted bronze spears. Each of these figures wears a breastplate of shells. They are standing near a domed structure. The stuccoed dome has no apparent openings.

On the east wall of the room are two carved stone columns flanking the remains of a covered sedan or litter, with statues of attendants standing nearby.

Treasure. The stuccoed dome is a cairn. It is a weak construction and can be broken into in 1 minute, using any bludgeoning instruments. If the characters work in concert, the time can be divided among multiple workers. Inside are six sets of worthless bones and six jade bead pectorals, worth 50 gp each. In a dusty corner is a pendant made of silver and turquoise, which is an *amulet of protection from turning* (see appendix A). In the center of the floor of this cairn is a bronze and chrysoprase lamp set into the stucco, worth 15 gp.

Creature. Lifting the lamp will open a hidden door in the floor, releasing a **wight** called Ayocuan from the compartment in which he has been trapped. Ayocuan wears another *amulet of protection from turning*.

Covered Sedan. Inside the curtained portion of the litter are the skeletal remains of a human, his arms are shackled to an arm of the sedan. In his rib cage can be found three arrowheads. Mixed throughout the broken clay in the immediate area are nearly five thousand beads of coral and shell worth 1 cp each.

20A. Behind the columns along the east wall is a bronze door barred shut with a pitted copper bar so that it can't be opened from the outside. From inside this room, one has merely to remove the bar.

21. STONE BLOCK

A large block of stone obstructs the corridor ahead. It doesn't seem to have been a part of the original construction, for its composition is more sandy than the stones that make up the walls of these ruins. Furthermore, a gap of several inches is visible along the sides of the block and between the stone and the ceiling.

This block was placed by the ancient architects to prevent access into the lower chambers and deter grave-robbers.

To reach its current position, the stone was slid southward down the gently sloping passage to the north. That passage has several rollers built into the floor to aid in moving the stone across it. The block can be pushed back up the rollers by the combined effort of up to four characters with a total Strength of 45 or higher, or moved out onto the bare stone floor by the combined effort of up to four characters with a total Strength of 50 or higher. In either case, the stone can be moved a number of feet per round equal to half the walking speed of the slowest individual among the workers.

If the block is pushed up the rollers, it will roll back next round to block the corridor if not braked with a large object.

22. CHAMBER OF THE NACEHUAL
(Nah-SAY-wal, the achieved ones)

All the doors bordering this lozenge-shaped room are made of heavy bronze. Colorful glyphs are scribed on the western wall. There are two sideboards against the walls to the east.

In the middle of the chamber are two stone divans, each with a human figure stretched out on it. Between the divans is a low stone table holding a flask and two goblets, all made of crystal. In the bottom of the crystal flask is a quantity of silvery dust.

The figures on the divans are a male and female, each about middle-aged and perfectly preserved. They are very still, dust-covered, and apparently dead. Their bodies are covered with dry snakeskin. The female wears a silver bracelet and holds what looks to be an ivory wand. The male has an amulet of electrum resting on his chest, inset with a red stone of considerable size.

The glyphs, in Olman, read, "Beware ... many-eyed god will bring down a fiery death."

Poison Dust. Mixing the silvery powder in the flask with any liquid will create a special potion. A creature

that drinks it must succeed on a DC 20 Constitution saving throw or become poisoned for 5,000 years. While poisoned in this way, a creature is also unconscious but semi-aware of its surroundings, and it is unaffected by the passage of time or other poisons. If magic is used to cure the poisoned condition, the recipient becomes immune to the poison's effect for 1 hour. A casting of *dispel magic* using a spell slot of 7th level or higher can also end the effect.

Creatures. The two bodies are **martial arts adepts** (see appendix B) in suspended animation. The male is named Cipactonal (See-PAK-ton-al), and the female is Oxomoco (Oks-OH-mo-koh). They used the potion that the flask once contained to feign their death. If either is disturbed, they both instantly awaken and stand. Oxomoco says, first in Olman and then in an ancient dialect of Common, "You have broken our glorious sleep; for this you must atone."

The two then assume fighting stances, and if either is threatened or harmed, they attack. If the party negotiates, the two demand payment of 500 gp or one uncommon or rare magic item. If they aren't paid, the monks attack.

If the monks are questioned about the ruins, they know nothing to tell, except that they can translate the message on the western wall. They will not leave their chambers.

Treasure. The ivory "wand" that Oxomoco holds is actually a folded fan worth 50 gp, and her platinum bracelet is worth 250 gp. Cipactonal's amulet, made of electrum and garnet, is worth 100 gp.

23. Light Ahead

> As you peer down the corridor, a faint flickering light becomes visible. The light begins to move through the hallway away from you, sputtering and wavering just at the edge of your perception.

The bobbing light is a **will-o'-wisp**. It will attempt to lure the party into a trap, then use Consume Life on a victim. The creature will lead parties coming from the west toward and then into the north–south corridor. Characters approaching from the north, who might already be familiar with the will-o'-wisp (see area 24), will be led on a zigzag route through the passages toward area 19.

23A. Triangular Stone

If the characters approach from the south, read:

> You come upon a ten-foot-wide pit that stretches across the corridor. Beyond it is a wedge-shaped stone block or pillar that blocks the passage. The light ahead of you that you had been following is nowhere to be seen, as though it somehow passed through the pillar.

The pit is 10 feet deep and contains several humanoid skeletons.

The triangular pillar's apex points toward the pit. Scratches on the floor and ceiling, scribing short arcs on either side of it, are easy to see. Someone who examines the pillar notices that it can be pivoted to either the left or the right, which will open a passage 2 feet wide that offers access to the north. If the characters move through this opening, they once again see the light of the will-o'-wisp in the distance.

If the characters approach from the north, read:

> The hallway abruptly ends at a blank stone wall.

If the wall is hammered on, it will sound solid. A character who examines the floor or the ceiling finds scratches that scribe an arc from one corner to the other. Pushing on one side of the apparent dead end causes the triangular pillar to pivot as noted above. If the characters move through the opening, they discover the pit. If they proceed to the south, continue with area 23.

24. Sandbox

The two thick lines on the map mark the boundaries of a trap. A character who examines the ceiling 20 feet overhead as the party passes under one of the marked areas and makes a successful DC 15 Wisdom (Perception) check notices a narrow band of copper extending from wall to wall. A gap between the copper and the surrounding stone suggests that the metal might be part of a door or a portcullis. This object can be prevented from coming down by wedging it in place as if it were a pressure plate.

Pressure Plate. The 10-foot-square section of floor marked on the map is the location of a pressure plate (see "The Ruins: General Features" at the beginning of the adventure). If an amount of weight equivalent to that of three or four humanoids is placed on it, the trap described below is triggered.

Falling Door Trap. If the characters set off the trap by activating the pressure plate in the floor, they hear a click and then a crash as both portcullises, made of timber bound in copper, come crashing down, sealing off the indicated area. These barriers are a foot thick; each has an AC of 15 and 100 hit points. Lifting a door requires a successful DC 25 Strength (Athletics) check, and any such check is made with disadvantage, since getting a good grip is difficult. If a door can first be pried up slightly with a crowbar or similar lever, requiring a successful DC 20 Strength (Athletics) check, someone not using the lever can get a grip on the bottom of the door, eliminating the disadvantage.

After 5 rounds, characters confined by the trap hear the sound of stone slowly grating on stone. Small panels near the ceiling move to expose four holes the size of a human fist on each wall. Dust trickles from the holes. After another 5 rounds passes, golden sand starts to pour rapidly through the holes. The floor is swiftly covered by the sand, which builds up at a rate of 2 feet per minute. Therefore, it takes 10 minutes for the sand to completely fill the hallway.

The area becomes difficult terrain after 1 minute. After 3 minutes of accumulation, a creature that moves through the sand must make a DC 10 Strength or Dexterity saving throw, becoming restrained on a failed save. (A creature that crawls need not make the saving throw, and creatures that have more than two legs have advantage on the saving throw.)

A creature can end the restrained condition on itself by using an action and succeeding on a DC 10 Strength or Dexterity check. Another creature can use an action to make the check and pull a restrained creature free. After 5 minutes of accumulation, the DC of the saving throw increases to 15. Once the sand is flowing, it must be scooped away from a closed door for someone to try to lift that door, and the sand flows through open doorways.

The dust that fills the air as the sand falls causes choking. Unless it need not breathe, a creature in the dust must make a DC 13 Constitution saving throw at the start of its turn. On a failed save, the creature spends its turn coughing, able only to move at half speed or to make a check (with disadvantage) to free itself from the restrained condition.

Creature. As soon as the sand begins flowing, the **will-o'wisp** that frequents this part of the ruins (see area 23), if it remains alive, moves through one of the doors into the trapped area. It harries those who are having the most success at escaping the trap.

25. THE NEST OF THE WARRIORS

> A bitter stench assails the senses as you lay eyes on the room ahead. Inside, amid a pile of rubbish, offal, and bracken, ghostly lights move across the floor.
>
> Closer observation reveals that the light is emitted by giant beetles. There seem to be around a dozen of these creatures in the room, each about three feet in length. They don't appear to take notice of you. From within the largest pile of trash, where most of the beetles are clustered, come glints of something shiny.

Creatures. The garbage-infested room is home to thirteen **giant fire beetles**. They lack the two light-emitting glands behind the eyes that are normal for such creatures. They do give off a soft glow that emanates from their abdomens but doesn't provide significant illumination. The beetles are nonaggressive unless their nest is threatened. Any sudden noise will bring a beetle or two to investigate. They examine any strange object with their feelers, and if it is edible, they bite it. Other beetles move toward the sound of their comrades fighting.

Treasure. The shiny objects in the beetles' nest are odd pieces of metal, polished rocks, broken crystal, three large turquoises (worth 20 gp each), and a *+1 dagger* that looks like junk. When it is used, its grip frays, its blade chips, and it flakes rust. If a character wielding this weapon gets a natural 1 on an attack roll, the dagger breaks and becomes nonmagical.

LOCATIONS ON THE FIRST TIER

Ascending either of the routes out of the lower chambers brings the characters to the first tier of the temple proper. The following locations are identified on map 3.1.

26. RAMP

If the characters approach from the north, read:

> A ramp slopes gently down from north to south. Set in the floor at two-foot intervals are smooth stone cylinders that apparently function as rollers.

If the characters approach from the south, read:

> A ramp leads gently up from south to north. Set in the floor at two-foot intervals are smooth stone cylinders that apparently function as rollers.

27. STAIRS

This corridor ascends from south to north in a series of short, gently sloped staircases.

Pressure Plate. The 10-foot square indicated on the map is the location of a pressure plate (see "The Ruins:

General Features" at the beginning of the adventure). If more than 30 pounds is placed on the plate, the trap described below triggers.

If the characters detect the presence of this plate, they can remove it from the floor with 10 minutes of work and a successful check as for an attempt to block the plate from moving. A failed check means another 10 minutes of work is required, followed by another check.

Rolling Stone Trap. A millstone, concealed in the wall behind a layer of stucco, lies at the top of the steps. No nonmagical means can detect the hidden stone. If the trap is triggered, the mechanism pushes the millstone through the wall and sends it rolling down the stairs. When this occurs, anyone who has a passive Perception score of 14 or lower is surprised. Everyone rolls initiative, including the stone, which has a +10 bonus to the roll. On its turn, the stone moves 60 feet. Anyone in its path must succeed on a DC 15 Dexterity saving throw or take 27 (5d10) bludgeoning damage and have a 50 percent chance to drop anything carried in hand. A character whose saving throw fails by 5 or more takes maximum damage, is knocked prone, and drops anything held in hand. Dropped objects take damage from hitting the stone and end up somewhere on the stairs.

The stone ultimately crashes into the doors to area 25, breaking them open and destroying them. If beetles remain in the room, some or all of them come into the stairway agitated and looking for a fight.

28. THE ARC OF NANAHUATCIN
(Na-na-WA-tzen, the Pimply One)

> This is a spacious, vaulted hall, weathered and cracked from the ravages of time. The walls are charred and scored. Scattered around the floor are several stone statues of baboon-like creatures, chipped and tipped over. The remains of a few once-living baboons, partially eaten, lie nearby, with fungus covering their corpses.

As the area is further penetrated, it is discerned that this was once a processional hall. Little remains to identify its past purpose except for a carving etched in the center of the worn floor that depicts a silver sun with a single eye. The beast that lairs here will not attack until the party sights it.

> Ahead, something spherical floats in the air at about chest height. The sphere has a central eye and about a dozen tentacles growing out of its top. Each appendage has a white sphere with a black pupil at its tip.

Creature. The spherical creature is a **gas spore** that represents Nanahuatcin, the "sun."

Treasure. Near the center of the south wall is a sack made of fish skin. It contains seven silver pellets, each about the size of a sling bullet and worth 1 gp.

29. The Tomb of Pelota

As you approach a bend in the passage, you see a series of faint line drawings on the walls depicting people playing a game that uses a ball and has goals on either end of the playing field.

At the place where the corridor bends is a capstone that seemingly covers a hole in the floor. Etched into the top of the slab are several glyphs obscured by a layer of dust. This writing, in Olman, reads, "Dare not open this pit unless you be willing to meet the challenge of pelota."

Five feet above the capstone in the southern wall is a hemispherical depression 1 foot in diameter.

Lifting the capstone requires the application of leverage and the combined effort of up to two characters with a total Strength of 25 or higher. Beneath the stone lid is a pit filled with the skeletal remains of the losers of a previous game of pelota in this area. Atop the bones rest several figurines and a plaque, all made of jade, and a glistening black ball 1 foot in diameter.

Cursed Treasure. If any treasure is removed from the pit, a curse will fall upon its bearer 1 hour later. The victim must succeed on a DC 15 saving throw, or it has disadvantage on Strength and Dexterity ability checks and saving throws until the curse is dispelled.

The jade plaque depicts two men, wearing padding on their arms and hips, with a large ball traveling between them. The figurines are carved in the image of a sun-god in a feathered robe. There are seven jade items in all, weighing 1 pound and worth 30 gp each.

Buried beneath the skeletons is a chalice of beaten gold, inset with six amethysts, that weighs 1 pound and is worth 150 gp.

Pelota Ball. The ball, made of rubber wound around a balsa core, is used in the game of pelota. It is the same size as the depression in the wall, which is one of the goals on this playing field. The ball is cool to the touch. If it is picked up, it suddenly jerks free of the holder's grasp and rebounds off the south wall, then speeds 30 feet to the north and hovers. It animates for the purpose of challenging the violators of the tomb to a game.

The ball can fly up to 30 feet on its turn, and it can hover. It makes melee weapon attacks with a +5 bonus, dealing 1 (1d4 − 1) bludgeoning damage on a hit. The ball has AC 13 and 50 hit points. It is immune to all damage except for magical effects that deal acid, fire, force, piercing, or slashing damage. The ball is immune to most conditions, but it can be grappled or restrained by effects that work on objects. It makes ability checks to escape such entanglements with a +5 bonus.

Start of the Game. Roll initiative. The ball uses its initial actions to bounce off the walls and strike at characters, trying to get them to strike back. When a character's attack hits the ball, it bounces off the south wall, and the depression in the wall briefly glows orange. After the second such occurrence, the ball will break off its attacks. A sound like that of a trumpet indicates that the game is about to start. The goal above the pit and another goal at the northern end of the hall 140 feet away are limned in orange light that remains until the game ends. When the characters hit the ball, it flies to the south and the southern goal flashes briefly. When the ball moves, it flies to the north, and the northern goal flashes.

How to Win. The characters win the game by propelling the ball into the goal above the pit while preventing the ball from reaching the northern end of the hall. If all the characters fail to hit the ball for 1 round, the faint sound of a drum dirge will be heard.

A character who attacks the ball successfully sends it flying south up to 15 feet. To knock the ball into the southern goal, the ball must be within 15 feet of the goal, and a player must declare that the character is trying to score. If the character's attack roll exceeds the ball's AC by 4 or more, the ball goes into the goal.

If the ball moves to within 5 feet of the northern wall, it can bounce itself into its own goal. To do so, the ball must make a successful attack roll against AC 15.

Once the ball is knocked into a goal, it sticks there for 1 round, impossible to remove without destroying it. If the ball enters the goal to the north, a number of *magic missiles* erupt from the goal equal to the number of conscious characters in the corridor. Each missile strikes a different character for 3 (1d4 + 1) force damage.

When the ball moves out of a goal, it flies to the center of the corridor and hovers, awaiting the start of another point. The game continues until the characters die or score a goal that puts them 2 points ahead of the ball.

Spoils of Victory. If the characters win, the ball becomes inert. The sound of triumphant drums erupts briefly, then the area goes silent. The southern goal goes dark, but the northern goal continues to glow orange.

Investigation reveals that a small panel has opened in the back of the depression. Within the space beyond is a pouch made of fish skin that holds ten pink pearls (worth 20 gp each), a topaz and shell necklace (worth 50 gp), and a whistle made of an eagle's bone with feather decoration, which is an *eagle whistle* (see appendix A).

30. The Guardian Beast

> This oddly shaped room is decorated in a cat motif. The center of the southeastern wall is carved to resemble the face of a snarling tiger with hollow eyes. Near the center of the room is a stuffed tiger, posed as if on the prowl. The tiger's left ear has been torn off, leaving a jagged scar on the head. Also near the middle of the room stands a stone statue of a tiger-headed man holding a spear.
>
> In several other spots on the floor are stuffed domestic cats in various poses: sitting, stalking, pouncing, and one is begging, pawing the air. One of these cats in the center of the room has been knocked over and chewed on; its stuffing is falling out.
>
> Hung on the walls are several skins of lions and leopards, tiger heads, and a cat-of-nine-tails. Along the northwest edge of the chamber a large calendar stone is mounted on the wall above a stone table or altar.
>
> The statue of the cat-man depicts a tall human male with two extra sets of nipples. He seems to be wearing a tiger-faced mask and is clad only in a loincloth. A jagged scar runs across the left side of his chest, above the heart, and his chest is sunken and bony. The spear is stone-hafted, but bears a silvery head.

All the items hanging on the walls are actually realistically painted stucco sculptures. If the characters investigate the calendar stone, see area 31.

Creature. The statue is a petrified werejaguar (use the **weretiger** statistics). If the altar is molested or any of the room's contents are abused, the werejaguar becomes aware and seizes the first opportunity to attack with surprise. It can turn to flesh as a bonus action and then transform into cat shape, dropping its spear. (The magic on the creature renders it strongly related to earth and stone with regard to the curse on the *bracelet of rock magic*, described in appendix A.) Its first choice of targets is always the weakest member of the party. If the werejaguar is reduced to 0 hit points, it reverts to human form and becomes petrified again.

The werejaguar's heart has been removed by magical surgery and is hidden in the head of the stuffed tiger (hinted at by the scars on man and tiger). Therefore, the cat-man might take damage or even die, but unless its heart is destroyed, it is reborn again whole in one day's time. If the lycanthrope's heart (AC 10, 2 hit points) is destroyed, the creature dies and turns to dust.

Treasure. In the belly of the stuffed tiger are 500 gp.

Eye of the Tiger. A secret door is concealed in the mouth of the wall carving. The catch to open it is hidden in the hollow of the right eye. The door and the catch each require a successful DC 20 Wisdom (Perception) check to find.

31. Calendar Stone

> The calendar, a great wheel of stone, is carved from limestone. In the center of the calendar is a symbol of the sun surrounded with various sigils depicting seasons of the year. The stone is ten feet across and is mounted five feet above the floor over a stone altar. On the altar rests a ceremonial dagger of flint and a jade statue of a cat. At the foot of the altar is a stuffed cat, posed as if begging or attempting to catch something in the air.

Secret Passage. The calendar stone covers a door and a secret passage to a hidden tomb. A character who examines the calendar and succeeds on a DC 15 Wisdom (Perception) check can see that it is held onto the wall by a smaller rod of stone behind it. The gap between the calendar and the wall is a few inches wide, so characters looking at the calendar in a specific way might notice the unusual mounting without making a check. In order to open the door, the sun symbol must be pushed into the wall. The calendar stone and the wall behind it then swing to one side on a set of hinges.

Treasure. The sacrificial knife on the table is a *+1 dagger*. The jade statue is worth 200 gp and weighs 9 pounds. In the tail of the stuffed cat is a *scroll of protection* (feline beasts and feline lycanthropes).

32. The Portal to Death

> Behind the concealed entrance is a narrow tunnel that slants down and away. The passage is barely four feet in diameter, and the walls are carved with a profusion of ancient and weird glyphs. The floor of the tunnel is slick with a molten, glassy glaze.

These nonmagical glyphs are of two types. Some are Olman curses cautioning and cursing trespassers; others are arcane symbols of abjuration, which is apparent to anyone who has proficiency in the Arcana skill.

> The tunnel opens out two feet above the floor of a corridor running north and south. Three exits are visible, one at either end of the hallway and a set of double doors on the midpoint of the western wall.
>
> The door to the north is barred, though it seems to have no latch. The image of a bear holding a disk of obsidian is set in its face. The lintel of the door is carved in the form of entwined serpents.
>
> The southern door is plated in bronze. Etched on it is a symbol of two circles joined. The path leading up to it has a depression in the stone floor, as though it has been worn smooth by the passage of countless feet.
>
> The floor in front of the central doorway is sunken and glazed. Affixed across the double doors is a golden seal one foot in diameter with ancient glyphs scribed into it. To open this door, it appears that the golden seal must be broken. Ancient glyphs are scribed on the seal. To either side on the lintel of the door are barely discernible scratches, and brown stains stipple the wall and floor.

Northern Door. Even after the bar is removed, the false door will not open. It appears to open outward, but when a character pushes against it, three arms spring out from the lintel and surround the character. Spotting these arms among the entwined serpents in the lintel requires a successful DC 20 Wisdom (Perception) check. The arms are treated as a pressure plate (see "The Ruins: General Features" at the beginning of the adventure) if a character attempts to jam them in place to keep them from moving.

A character caught in the trap can wriggle free only with a successful DC 20 Dexterity (Acrobatics) check. Otherwise, unconfined characters can attempt to free a victim. The combined effort of two characters with a total Strength of 30 or higher is needed to pry back each arm, taking 1 round to move each one.

After a victim has been trapped for 5 rounds, the cover to a 5-foot-square pit starts to drop open. The pit is lined with spikes. The cover fully opens in 2 rounds, at which point the arms swiftly spring back into the lintel, releasing any victims to plummet into the 15-foot-deep pit. A fall into the pit deals 11 (2d10) bludgeoning damage. The spikes are hard rubber wrapped around balsa wood, placed for artistic effect.

Southern Door. The image on the southern door is the infinity symbol, representing the dual-god, the supreme god of creation. The door isn't latched, but it is stuck shut. A *detect magic* spell cast on it reveals that an aura of conjuration magic emanates from beyond the door. It takes a successful DC 20 Strength (Athletics) check to bash the door open. If a creature does so, the door gives way suddenly, dumping the gate-crasher into a narrow space ahead. Any creature that enters this space is teleported to the west end of area 15, just outside the painted mural on the wall.

Double Doors. The message on the seal, written in Olman, reads, "Beware! Beyond this door is death!" Once the seal is broken by opening the doors, it may not be used to reseal the doors. The gold in the seal is worth 250 gp.

The door is trapped, but the only evidence of this fact is concealed within the door frame and under the stucco on the ceiling, completely hidden. When the doors are pushed open, five heavy crossbows, set in the ceiling of the room beyond, fire. Two are aimed toward each door, and the last is aimed down the center of the two doors. The crossbows have a +6 bonus to hit, and each deals 5 (1d10) piercing damage.

33. The Tomb of Tlacaelel
(Tlah-kah-AYL-ayl)

> Beyond the door is a pillared porch overlooking a chamber that contains a model of a city. Arrayed on the porch are numerous clay statues of guards holding bronze-headed spears. The face of each statue is different, as if they were modeled from different subjects. Next to each statue is a small, glazed clay pot. The walls are decorated with brightly colored frescoes depicting a royal court in ceremonial garb and a king arrayed with his armies.
>
> There is a chill in the chamber beyond, like that of a brisk winter morning. In the center of the room is an enormous, tarnished copper raft, crafted to resemble a dragon, bearing a copper coffin. The raft is afloat on a sea of silvery-white, flowing metal, fed by several rivers that trail along the floor of the room. The flowing liquid appears to be cool.
>
> Between the waterways, stepped pyramid-temples rise skyward in mute paean to the gods of ancient Olman. Three of the pyramids appear to have tops that can be removed. In the rest of the area, a royal complex sprawls across verdant fields, and courtyards and ringed marketplaces dot the miniature countryside. There is a blight on this spectacle, however, for several of the models have been smashed and melted.

Fire Trap. On the floor just inside the doorway is a *glyph of warding* (save DC 17). The first character to step through the door and onto the glyph causes a *wall of fire* spell to spring up in the doorway, with the damaging side facing away from the character who entered. The wall remains in place for 1 minute.

Creature. Within the copper coffin is a **doppelganger**. The creature emerges from the coffin through a hole in the side facing away from the entrance as soon as the glyph is triggered. It assumes the form of any character trapped alone in the room and tries to attack with surprise. If it succeeds in slaying the character before the *wall of fire* expires, then it hides the body in the coffin.

The doppelganger is unfamiliar with the rest of the ruins but tries to act like the character it has killed until it is discovered. If the doppelganger is forced to fight the party, it assumes the shape of a creature of molten metal that shrouded in flames. The fire is an illusion and doesn't burn.

Liquid Fire. The first time a creature or an object enters or touches the silvery liquid metal of the sea or the rivers on a turn, or a creature starts its turn in such a place, the creature or object takes 3 (1d6) fire damage. If any of this fluid is carried out of this room, it evaporates in 1 minute. The ships and the coffin floating on the liquid deal similar fire damage if they are touched.

Treasure Chests. Three of the pyramid-temples, which are fastened to the floor, conceal treasure. The top of each temple is hinged like the lid of a chest, and the catch is released by pressing down on the altar at the top. Each of these chests holds several coin necklaces, each made of three hundred sixty silver coins pierced and threaded on a piece of gut, and other assorted valuables.

Chest 1. The lid is jammed on the first chest that the characters examine, requiring a successful DC 15 Strength (Athletics) check to pry open. The chest holds ten coin necklaces, six pairs of jade earplugs (worth 15 gp a set), an alabaster statuette (worth 50 gp), and an agate ring (worth 5 gp).

Chest 2. The second chest is trapped. When hands are thrust into the treasure, a mechanical vise in the wall of the chest grabs the limbs within. A character must succeed on a DC 15 Dexterity saving throw or become grappled by the device (escape DC 15). A creature is restrained while grappled in this way. Roll initiative. Six mechanical needles spring out from the sides of the chest on initiative count 0. The needles can be attacked (AC 12, 5 hit points). Each needle deals 1 piercing damage.

A creature struck by one or more of the needles must make a DC 15 Constitution saving throw. The creature takes 21 (6d6) poison damage on a failed save, or half as much damage on a successful one. In either event, the creature is poisoned. The poisoned creature must repeat the saving throw every 24 hours, taking 3 (1d6) poison damage on a failure. The poison ends when the creature makes five successful saves against it. Until the poison ends, any hit points lost to it can't be regained. The poisoned creature is feverish and occasionally trembles, gibbers, or retches.

The chest holds nine coin necklaces, eight bracelets of beads (5 gp apiece), four small figurines of jade and coral (25 gp each), and three rings carved of jade and alabaster (10 gp each).

Chest 3. Operating the catch of the third chest requires more force than with the other two. If the catch is pressed, the chest lid sprays perfumed oil on anyone within 5 feet of it. The nozzles that produce this spray can be discovered by someone who succeeds on a DC 15 Wisdom (Perception) check. The only way to disarm the "trap" is to disassemble the chest lid and remove it without pressing the catch. Doing so takes 10 minutes of work with thieves' tools.

When the catch is pressed, a lever wedged in the lid pops up, triggering the launch of darts. The tubes that hold these darts are sealed with a thin layer of stucco, so they're all but impossible to discover without damaging the chest. Someone who cautiously opens the chest can feel the pressure from the lever and see it by peeking into the chest. If someone can reach the lever through the half-open lid and hold it in place, the trap doesn't function. Holding the lever in place as the lid is opened requires a successful DC 12 Strength check. This check must be repeated in every round that the lever is held down. If the trap triggers, four darts fire from each of the chest's front and back sides. Each dart flies up to 60 feet, has a +6 bonus to hit, and deals 5 (2d4) piercing damage on a hit.

The third chest holds eleven coin necklaces, fifteen bracelets of obsidian, bronze, and shell (10 gp each), and two piles of gems (tourmalines, spinels, and topazes; sixty gems worth 5 gp each) lying upon two silver platters 15 gp apiece).

Other Treasure. The clay pots on the porch are sealed with wax, and they hold scented oils and perfumes—there are twenty such containers, each weighing 10 pounds and with contents worth 15 gp.

Several places that represent royal granaries in the modeled city are actually stone bins that hold aromatic woods and spices (cinnamon, nutmeg, vanilla, quince, cinchona, sandalwood, and pepper). This haul is worth a total of 250 gp and weighs 10 pounds.

Inside the coffin are the bones of Tlacaelel, for the doppelganger has eaten the flesh. Scattered around the interior are the ornaments once worn by the corpse. These items include a stone box, two jade bracelets (worth 20 gp apiece), and an alabaster statuette of Coatlicue (Koh-WA-tlee-cue), the snake woman, mother of the gods (worth 25 gp). The stone box (worth 75 gp) holds five small figurines carved of coral (25 gp each), a large jade thumb ring (10 gp), and eight ceramic miniature flasks of perfumes and essences (10 gp apiece).

Cradled in the crook of the elbow of the corpse's right arm is a baton of granite. The baton is a scroll case with a cleverly fashioned plug. Within the case is a piece of faded parchment—a *spell scroll* of *stone shape*, written in astrological symbols of the Olman.

Upon the skull is a ferret-faced, feathered mask that functions as a *hat of disguise*.

33A. Sacrifice to the Sun

When the characters can see the northern end of the chamber, read:

> In an alcove framed by pillars stands a stone bench on which a shriveled corpse huddles. Scattered around its feet are various trinkets.

This figure is the preserved body of an adolescent male, whose heart has been cut out. He was a *guesa*, a boy chosen at birth to be sacrificed to the sun upon his coming of age.

Treasure. The items at the corpse's feet include an agate carved in the shape of a heart (worth 15 gp) that is actually a *stone of ill luck* (see appendix A), a miniature gold llama (worth 50 gp), a ring of polished pink granite (worth 10 gp), and a silver plaque bearing the face of the sun (15 gp).

34. Guardians Bar the Way

> The passage leads toward a set of double bronze doors bearing the engraved face of the jaguar god. Both walls of the corridor are carved to represent two lines of warriors in profile, holding hatchet-headed polearms and facing the western doors. These figures are painted with vivid, lifelike colors: red, black, white, green, and yellow.

Pressure Plate. Near the midpoint of this corridor is a 10-foot-square pressure plate (see "The Ruins: General Features" at the beginning of the adventure) that triggers if more than 30 pounds is placed on it.

Shocking Blades. If the pressure plate is depressed, two of the carved warriors pivot out from the walls in front of the party, crossing their metal halberds before them to bar the way to the northern doors. The blades spark and hum when they are brought together. A creature that touches either of the blades takes 5 (2d4) lightning damage and must succeed on a DC 15 Constitution saving throw or become paralyzed while it is in contact. A paralyzed creature takes the damage again at the start of each of its turns.

There is barely enough room for a Medium humanoid to crawl under the crossed polearms and between the statues. Doing so without touching the blades requires a successful DC 10 Dexterity check.

35. Xipe's Audience Chamber
(Zee-PAY)

> When the door comes open, a rush of warm, fetid air greets you. The room is lit with a sanguine glow. On the wall opposite the door are tacked several human skins. A cat-o'-nine-tails hangs beside them.
>
> To the west the room widens to accommodate a statue that towers almost to the ceiling. The statue is an ogre-like figure, outfitted in flayed skins and adorned with skulls, with a gaping mouth wide enough to swallow a horse whole. It is seated atop a huge basin of red-hot coals, more than ten feet in diameter.
>
> Around the statue is a pile of splintered bones, skulls with cracked pates, and broken weapons. In front of the display crouches a panther, deathly still, facing away from the statue.
>
> To the east the walls are highly polished. They loosely enclose an intricately carved well that seems to be illuminated from within. Beyond the well, mounted on the wall, is a blackened mirror with a richly ornamented frame. Directly above the well, in the twenty-five-foot-high ceiling, a five-foot-wide opening can be discerned in the red light of the room.

The statue represents Xipe, "Our Lord of the Flayed Skins." The chamber serves as the foyer to his lair, which lies beyond the opening in the ceiling.

Statue Guardian. If the characters approach the statue, the **panther** will stand and pad menacingly in their direction ... and then continue on past them. The panther has a mental block that prevents it from being able to see humans, which initially applies to other humanoids as well. It likewise ignores familiars, but it attacks any beast companion or other non-humanoid present with the party.

If the panther is not attacked and is unable to find a target, it takes to pacing in front of the door. If the party attacks the cat, its mental block regarding other humanoids fails, and the panther attacks any such creature it can see. If it can see no target, the bewildered panther resumes its pacing.

Treasure. Almost all the weapons around the statue are useless, though the head of a *+1 mace* attached to a broken haft can be found.

Well of Light. The illumination inside the well comes from liquid light, a fluid that clings like oil if touched to a given surface and in the presence of other light eventually spreads to cover the entire surface.

If a creature falls into the well and is pulled out, the liquid light clings to a small portion of its body, then spreads to cover an additional 5 percent of the body every round. Eventually the liquid covers its eyes, nose and mouth. If this happens, the character can't breathe until the liquid is removed by immersion in water. In the absence of a light source, the liquid light doesn't spread, and a *darkness* spell renders it inert for 1 hour.

If anything is tossed into the well, brilliant light flashes upward and a bellowing voice fills the chamber. The voice belongs to Xipe, and he asks (in Giant) who has come and for what purpose. Nothing else happens, for Xipe can't be bothered to leave his lair to investigate.

Ceiling Tunnel. The hole in the ceiling leads to Xipe's lair. If the characters try to climb the walls, they discover the walls are too slick to be ascended in this way.

A surefire way of getting in is to tie a grappling hook to an arrow and shoot the arrow up through the hole. This method never fails to anchor the hook on something, for Xipe grabs the rope once it is fired through his front door. If a creature then decides to climb the rope up into the lair, Xipe starts to reel in the climber when it has ascended halfway.

A creature being hauled up into the tunnel can release the rope and drop into the well, taking no immediate damage (other than being covered in the liquid light), or it can swing its body outward and drop onto the floor, taking falling damage. Otherwise, Xipe pulls the climber into his lair in 1 round.

Creature. Beyond the hole in the ceiling is a chamber that measures 30 feet in each direction. It is the lair of Xipe, an **oni**. Xipe can't cast *cone of cold*, but he can cast *sleet storm* and *fear* once per day each. When he casts *fear*, he unleashes a great bellow that shakes the room.

Treasure. Xipe's treasure includes a wooden cylinder that holds a *spell scroll* of *detect magic*. Also in his lair are piles of rich cat furs, eight of the furs worth 5 gp each. Two leather bags beneath the furs hold 1,000 sp each.

Lastly, an intricately carved ivory cube about 1 foot tall stands on an ornamental table. The cube (worth 100 gp) is a trick box. To open it, two plugs on either side of the cube must be pushed in, and then its center slides out of a frame formed by the other four sides. This inner box opens like a chest. Within it is a silver and aquamarine necklace (worth 125 gp) and a parchment packet that holds three pinches of *dust of disappearance*.

36. Apartment of the Dust of Ages

> The floor of this room is covered with a layer of fine gray dust and ash, three inches deep. Across the room, opposite where you entered, is another set of double doors. There are two empty alcoves to the north and south. On small ledges in each corner of the room are pieces of what appear to be broken pottery.
>
> As you move into the room, your steps send motes of dust and ash swirling into the air, and these clouds form into shapes.
>
> First, from the ash, a dusty phantom assumes the shape of a woman. Her face is forlorn and tear-streaked. She throws up her hands in despair, rushes into one of the alcoves, and disappears.
>
> Immediately afterward, two more dusty phantoms emerge—mighty warriors armed with jagged-edged swords and bearing fierce countenances. They move to block the doorway opposite where you entered.

If the characters approach the phantom guards, they raise their swords threateningly. But they can cause no harm, for they are just images of the long-dead past. For as long as the characters remain in the room, other phantoms—in the shapes of priests, sages, and mourning young women—briefly form out of the dust and then dissipate. Moving through any of these phantom forms causes them to collapse.

37. Bed of Xilonen
(Zeel-OAN-an)

> In the center of this room is a withered tree that looks like a leafless willow, rooted in a terraced depression. The bottom of this hollow is filled with oily water, a few inches deep. Across the room, beyond the dead tree, is another door. Around the sides of the room, a five-foot-wide ledge encircles the tree. The walls of the room are beaded with condensation.

The water in the bottom of the depression makes the floor in that area difficult terrain.

Creature. The "tree" is Xilonen, a semisentient (Int 2), gigantic variety of polyp, similar to a sea anemone, once revered as the hairy mother goddess of corn. The polyp, which functions similarly to a **roper**, is very hungry. Its mouth is concealed among a nest of flailing tentacles and protected by sharp spines.

Treasure. Within the polyp's gut are twelve pieces of blue jasper (worth 10 gp each) and a silvery rod, actually a copper-nickel alloy, which is a *wand of lightning bolts*.

38. Barred Pit

The walls of the passage glow magenta, bathing the corridor with a ghastly hue. After fifteen feet, the floor drops away to a pit that fills the hallway ahead. The pit is twenty-five feet deep. Eight large, spidery bushes with thorny stems, white leaves, and enormous yellow blossoms grow across its bottom.

Five feet beyond the nearest edge of the pit is a bronze bar, set level with the floor and embedded in the pit walls to either side. Farther out over the pit can be seen other similar bronze rungs, set at five-foot intervals. On the floor by the edge of the pit is a scattering of broken, rotting wooden planks.

Bridge of Bars. A character can attempt to cross this pit by leaping from one bar to the next. There are a total of eight bars and 45 feet of pit. Moving across the bars is akin to moving across difficult terrain; moving 5 feet onto a bar, or between two bars, costs 10 feet of movement. If a creature attempts to move more than half of its base walking speed on any of its turns, it must make a DC 10 Dexterity (Acrobatics) check. On a successful check, the creature can keep moving. On a failed check, the creature stops moving to regain its balance and can move no farther on that turn. If the check fails by 5 or more, the creature falls into the pit.

The third and sixth bars along the way are corroded. When a character moves onto one of these bars, roll a d20. On a roll of 5 or lower, or 2 or lower for a Small character, the bar breaks. If the bar doesn't break and the roll is 10 or lower, some obvious sign of the bar's weakness becomes evident, such as chipping or bending.

Hazard. The bushes growing in the pit are carnivorous **thorn slingers** (see appendix B). Each plant lies beneath one of the bronze bars and casts its projectiles directly upward against anyone attempting to traverse the bars. A creature balancing on a bar when it is hit by thorns must make a Dexterity saving throw with a DC of 6 + the damage taken. If the saving throw fails by 4 or less, the creature falls prone, catching itself on the bar. (To stand up on the bar afterward, a character must make a Dexterity check as if attempting to move on the bars.) If the saving throw fails by 5 or more, the character falls in the pit.

Someone who falls into the pit always comes down on a bush, cushioning the impact. The fall deals only 3 (1d6) bludgeoning damage, but the character lands on a plant's adhesive blossoms.

39. Chamber of the Second Sun

This enormous chamber is thirty feet tall with mighty buttressing and a vaulted ceiling. Parts of the ceiling and walls have collapsed, and raw earth has spilled down from a gaping hole in the east wall. Crushed beneath a fallen block in the center of the room are humanoid remains. Elsewhere around the floor are the chewed and decayed corpses of baboons. Through a hole in the eastern ceiling, daylight and fresh air filter in. Above, through this gap, can be seen four baboons. They jump around the hole and and scream in agitation, and as they do, dirt begins to slide down the banks and rocks in the walls shift slightly.

There is no poison gas in the room, or in any of the upper areas (40 and higher), because the gas escapes out the hole in the ceiling. The floor is strewn with rubble, so it is difficult terrain. Larger rubble piles are 1 to 4 feet high. Any loud noise (such as an explosion, shouting, or fighting) causes a minor cave-in: at the start of each creature's next turn after the noise, that creature is subjected to an attack from falling rocks and earth (+5 to hit, dealing 3 (1d6) bludgeoning damage on a hit).

Creatures. Hidden in a pile of rubble in the center of the room is an amphisbaena—a giant, two-headed snake. It fights as a **giant constrictor snake** that can make two melee attacks on each of its turns, only one of which can be a Constrict attack. This ability increases its challenge rating to 3 (700 XP).

If the snake is slain, the four **baboons** leap through the hole in the ceiling and down upon the party. (They remained outside the room because of their fear of the snake.)

Treasure. The bones crushed beneath the fallen block belonged to two humans. This block can be moved by the combined effort of up to three characters with a total Strength of 30 or higher. A pouch tied on the waist of one corpse holds 40 ep. One of the humans wore a brooch of bronze and green quartz in the shape of a lizard (worth 25 gp). A silver and beryl-emerald ring (50 gp) is worn on a bony finger. A silvery dagger, actually made of a copper-nickel alloy and worth 10 gp, is stuck in the left boot of one figure. A scroll case holds a map of the territory in which these ruins are located. Finally, a crystal sphere, cracked in the catastrophe, has rolled into the shadow of some nearby rubble. It is made of polished quartz, 3 inches in diameter, and is worth 45 gp.

Crumbling Exit. If characters attempt to climb up the dirt embankments to the hole in the ceiling, they discover that the surface supports only 50 pounds. More weight than that on any space along the slope causes further collapse—each climber must succeed on a DC

13 Dexterity saving throw or be buffeted by dirt and rubble, taking 7 (3d4) bludgeoning damage. If the save fails by 5 or more, the rubble engulfs the digger completely, and the trapped character can't breathe until dug out. Getting out on one's own requires a successful DC 15 Strength (Athletics) check, and doing so takes 1 minute.

Serpent Doors. The southeast exit from this chamber is a set of double bronze doors in the north wall at the end of a short corridor. Above them hangs a plaque inlaid with jade (worth 25 gp). The plaque depicts a two-headed serpent, with its second head where its tail should be.

LOCATIONS ON THE SECOND TIER

The staircase at area 40 provides access to the second tier of the temple. The following locations are identified on map 3.1.

40. DRAGON BREATH

When the party reaches the bottom of the stairs, read:

> A staircase leads upward into the gloom. It seems as though you have found the entrance to another layer within the complex.

The second 10-foot square along these stairs is warded by magic like that of a *glyph of warding* spell (save DC 17). If the glyph is triggered, nothing happens until a creature moves onto the uppermost 5 feet of the stairs. When that occurs, a stone statue of a dragon, hidden in the secret room at the top of the stairs (see the "Second Tier" portion of the map), pops out and rolls forward to the head of the steps. The statue has the statistics, defenses, and traits of a **stone golem**, but it has no action options. As soon as it stops after emerging, it opens its mouth and breathes a gust of steam 30 feet long and 10 feet wide. Those in the area must make a DC 15 Constitution saving throw, taking 7 (2d4 + 2) fire damage on a failed save, or half as much damage on a successful one.

Thereafter, the statue breathes the next three times someone moves into or through the warded area. After four breaths, the statue retreats to its room and the door closes. (The statue's resting place is connected to a hot water geyser in the bedrock, through which it replenishes itself.)

Slippery Steps. After the statue breathes for the first time, the condensing steam makes the stairs slippery difficult terrain. A character who moves on the stairs must while they are slippery must succeed on a DC 10 Dexterity (Acrobatics) check or fall prone.

Secret Door. If the characters get to the top of the stairs without triggering the glyph, someone can discover the secret door here with a successful DC 20 Wisdom (Perception) check. The door can't be opened from the outside, however.

41. FREE GOLD

> At the western end of this corridor is a pile of golden coins heaped on the floor. On top of the gold rests a skull missing its lower jaw. In the right eye socket, a black spider has made a home. Several bones are piled with the coins, and the hilt of a broken sword thrusts up from the mass.

This apparent pile of gold is covered with a pale yellow dust. The entire pile of coins is actually yellow mold (see "Dungeon Hazards" in chapter 5 of the *Dungeon Master's Guide*) covered by a permanent *major image* spell (save DC 15). The bones, spider, and sword hilt are real.

Eastern Door. Close examination reveals that the stone in the center of the corridor is smoother than the surrounding wall. Because of this clue, it takes only a successful DC 15 Wisdom (Perception) check to find the secret door. The door can be opened by stepping forcibly upon an obvious cobblestone that is slightly raised from the floor. The door has two facing panels that pivot inward when it is opened.

Western Door. In front of the secret door is a dark stain on the floor, which makes the door as easy to find as the eastern one. This door swings on a horizontal pivot in the middle of the slab. Pushing in at either the top or the bottom of this secret panel causes the opposite end to swing outward, providing enough space to crawl through into the secret passage beyond.

42. THE CHAPEL OF KUKULKAN
(Koo-KOOL-kahn, the feathered serpent)

> Beyond the secret door, the passage bends around to the left. At the end of a narrow corridor hangs an ornate mirror, and a door is set in the eastern wall next to it.

Magic Mirror. The first creature to come within 10 feet of the mirror at the end of the corridor must make a DC 15 Wisdom saving throw. On a failed check, the creature believes that it is in deadly combat with a feathered warrior that has emerged from the mirror. This effect is like that of a *phantasmal force* spell, with the character battling a warrior that has a +6 bonus to hit and deals 3 (1d6) psychic damage, as described in the spell. The effect ends if the affected creature deals the imaginary warrior a total amount of damage equal to the creature's own hit point maximum.

While under the effect of this magic, the creature is actually paralyzed, appearing to others as if it were just standing there staring into the mirror. If someone disturbs the affected creature, that creature can repeat the saving throw, ending the effect on a successful save.

The Door. When anyone get close to the door, read:

> The door seems to be very heavy, and it has many glyphs carved upon it. In the center of the door is carved an eagle killing a serpent. Two stone warriors dressed in loincloths and wearing panther masks are sculpted into the door posts.

The glyphs on the door tell a story in ancient Olman of a journey to find truth and light, which ended in failure and imprisonment in the land of the dead.

The door opens outward. When the characters pass through the doorway, read:

> Beyond the door is a wide foyer that leads into a circular room. On the south wall of this hall is a jade death mask affixed at chest height.
>
> Taking up the middle of the chamber is a cross-shaped dais with sets of stairs leading up to it along each of the four ends. In the center of the dais rises a cylindrical structure that appears to be made of transparent walls of crystal enclosing an oddly carved, stone pillar.
>
> The stairs that face the room's entrance are carved with the heads of many gods. The steps on the north side are bloodstained, and atop the landing stands a statue of a warrior. The stairs to the east, across the room, are partly obscured by shadow. The southern staircase is luminescent, appearing to change colors in the light.

> Tucked into each nook where the arms of the cross come together is a low shelf on which are placed small offerings: silver bracelets, earrings, neck collars, anklets, piles of coral beads, and silver and jade statuettes.

Trapped Mask. The mask (worth 25 gp) is the trigger to a trap. If the mask is taken off the wall, the lever it hangs on pivots up and three sets of iron bars drop, caging whoever is in the square in front of the mask. The bars are old, and they can be bent or lifted away from the floor with a successful DC 20 Strength (Athletics) check.

Trapped Treasure. If any of the items on the shelves (worth a total of 450 gp) are touched, the exit door seals with an effect like that of an *arcane lock* spell, requiring the use of magic or a successful DC 25 Strength (Athletics) check to force the door open.

Creature. Coiled about the pillar, trapped within the magic walls of the crystal cylinder surrounding it, is a **couatl**. Because of its especially potent Shielded Mind trait, it is effectively invisible.

If the characters disturb any of the items on the shelves, the couatl speaks to the party in Common, its voice seeming to come from everywhere in the chamber.

> "Interlopers, you have trespassed on my sacred chapel. For this affront, retribution has already begun, for you are now breathing a toxic gas which will kill you shortly. It is possible your actions were not from malice or greed, but just idle curiosity. Therefore, you will find the cure upon the stone in the middle of the dais, if you can solve the puzzle to reach it by the proper route. Choose your path wisely, and act quickly."

There is actually no poison gas in the room, but as the characters spend time in here trying to get to the cure, describe how they seem to be getting weaker and weaker. They should feel as if time is running out.

Aura. A *detect magic* spell reveals an aura of evocation magic emanating from inside the crystal cylinder.

The Right Path. To reach the "cure," the characters must first face the challenge of ascending the northern steps, where the warrior stands. The warrior, a **helmed horror**, animates and attacks when it is approached. Once the construct is defeated, the characters can proceed to the center of the dais.

A character who attempts to reach the dais another way has no luck:

- Someone who tries climbing up the shelves takes 2 (1d4) force damage and is pushed back 10 feet.
- The heads carved into the western stairs babble when a character steps on them. That character feels too weak to continue, and sits down until helped away from the stairs.
- The eastern stairs are shrouded in dim light, which can't be made brighter by any means. Any character

who mounts the stairs falls down and rolls back onto the floor, taking 3 (1d6) bludgeoning damage.

- The southern stairs change color constantly. Anyone who tries to ascend them makes no progress (though they can be descended normally).

Once the characters reach the crystal cylinder, the couatl again speaks to them, still hidden from sight:

> "So you have passed the first test. Perhaps you are not the fools you first seemed. But it will take the best tool of your most clever person to breach these crystal walls. Your time is running out."

The surface of the crystal cylinder is cold to the touch and impervious to all blows. The enclosure has no visible gaps.

A gap appears in the wall if someone who has proficiency with thieves' tools touches the tools to the surface with the intention of finding a portal or a lock. The players might come up with other valid solutions, such as a wizard (clever person) touching the crystal with a wand (tool). It's up to you which alternative attempts work.

Cure in Sight. By the time the characters reach the pillar inside the cylinder, they feel very weak. On the top of the pillar in front of them is a potion bottle, but an invisible barrier prevents anyone from touching it. A glyph is etched into the side of the pillar just below the bottle. One more time the couatl speaks, its voice now seeming to come from the stone:

> "So you have reached my altar, but your time is nearly exhausted and the cure is just beyond your reach. Trust your souls to the gods, foolish mortals."

The top of the pillar is shielded by a wall of force that must be breached to reach the potion bottle. The wall can be destroyed by a *disintegrate* spell or by damaging the glyph inscribed below it. If someone pours holy water on the glyph, touches it with a holy symbol, or casts a divine spell on it, the *wall of force* disappears.

Aftermath. When the characters claim the potion bottle, the couatl becomes visible and flies out into the chamber. If the characters immediately attack it, the couatl calls them ingrates and fools, and then attacks back.

If the characters don't attack, the couatl smiles and thanks them for freeing it from its long imprisonment.

Treasure. Inside the bottle is a *potion of healing*. The mask, if it is claimed, weighs 30 pounds and is worth 25 gp. Miscellaneous items on the shelves have a total value of 450 gp.

Special Treasure. If the couatl and the characters are on good terms at the end of the encounter, the couatl provides them with special treasures: a *balance of harmony* (see appendix A) and the gems needed to operate it, a *mirror of the past* (see appendix A), and a *periapt of wound closure*.

In addition, if the characters ask, the couatl might be willing to use its spells to help the party. It has been imprisoned a long time and doesn't know anything about the ruins. It returns to the celestial planes after giving the characters their rewards.

43. The Smoking Mirrors

> An amber haze drifts in this room, which is unoccupied. Strangely shaped and colored mirrors hang on the walls, and a large, oblong stone basin stands in the middle of the floor. The basin is about ten feet long, five feet wide, and three feet tall. It is filled with a steaming golden liquid.
>
> The red mirror on the eastern wall seems to be composed of fiery glass and framed in bronze. Light beams are broken by the mirror into myriad flames, and ghostly shapes seem to flicker in its depths.
>
> On the northern wall are two mirrors: a striking black one of obsidian framed in lacquered wood, and a stark white mirror with a wrought iron frame. The black mirror has a distinctive earthy odor and the blackness of subterranean caverns, but it seems of crude construction and reflects objects only when they are close to it. The white mirror has a pungent odor of nutmeg and spice, and its depths are gelid and smoky.
>
> The mirror that hangs on the western wall is in a stone frame and is blue in color. Reflections in this mirror ripple as if the viewer were looking into a pool of water.

Red Mirror. A creature that looks into the red mirror sees a ghostly white form next to its own reflection. This mirror falsely predicts the viewer's death. The ghostly image takes on the appearance of a monster or a trap from this adventure. The image then assaults and kills the viewer's reflection. The mirror functions only once per character; after a character has this vision, the mirror becomes a normal mirror for that individual.

A creature that touches the red mirror for the first time on a turn takes 2 (1d4) fire damage.

Black Mirror. A creature that looks into the black mirror sees its reflection blur and then reappear in ancient garb as if depicting a previous incarnation. The image says, in Olman, "Command me to answer, and I shall."

The image of a long-dead Olman is superimposed on the character's reflection. A *command* spell can cause the spirit to answer three yes-or-no questions (the one-word command is "Answer"). The spirit answers only questions spoken in Olman, and nods or shakes its head in response.

Any creature that touches the black mirror must succeed on a DC 13 Charisma saving throw, or all valuable metals and gems in its possession turn into lead and glass.

White Mirror. Reflections in the white mirror are blurred by what looks like a fine mist. Any creature that steps before this mirror and looks into it must make a successful DC 13 Wisdom saving throw or be stunned until the end of the creature's next turn. If the saving throw fails, the mirror, which is really an **ochre jelly** of unusual color, comes out of the frame and falls upon the character. Behind this false mirror is a door, which can be opened once the jelly is removed.

Blue Mirror. The mirror on the western wall is actually a window of magical glass that offers a view of a pool of water. Any character who touches the glass must succeed on a DC 13 Charisma saving throw or be drawn through the glass, becoming submerged in the water. Weapons can be used to break the glass (AC 15, 20 hit points). If the glass is destroyed, the water in the pool and those trapped in it spill out into the room.

Golden Liquid. Any nonmagical object immersed in the basin reacts with the fluid inside, which turns the object into gold for 1 hour. If any of the golden liquid is removed from the basin, it becomes colored water.

44. SUN OF MOTION

In the center of this diamond-shaped room is a dais on which a weirdly formed altar rests. The altar is made to resemble a many-armed and beaked octopus-like creature with a large purple-red stone its forehead. The altar and floor are covered with dust. The walls of the room are decorated with paintings of the sun and moon in motion. Other images show people standing about a temple making sacrifices of flesh and blood, while the figure of a priest holds the heart of his latest victim above his head.

Trapped Altar. The altar radiates an aura of transmutation magic if *detect magic* is cast on it. Any creature that touches the octopus figure sticks to the stone, becoming grappled (escape DC 15). Once a creature is stuck, the octopus-altar starts to spin, dragging the victim about the room. Within 1 round, the speed is too great for the victim to maintain footing, and the creature is dragged and bashed about, taking 3 (1d6) bludgeoning damage at the end of each of its turns. A creature that comes free while the altar is spinning tumbles away from it and takes another 2 (1d4) bludgeoning damage.

The gem in the center of the altar has AC 17 and 15 hit points. If it is destroyed, the altar stops spinning and the character is released. The gem is a cursed stone, but it appears to be a jewel of value, and it can be pried from the altar. If the gem comes in contact with a creature's flesh, that creature must succeed on a DC 16 Wisdom saving throw or be affected as if by an *Otto's irresistible dance* spell, going into a spinning dance that lasts until the stone is released. To let go of the stone willingly, the creature must be the target of magic that removes a curse or breaks an enchantment.

If the creature dances for a number of minutes equal to its Constitution score, it must succeed on a DC 10 Constitution saving throw or suffer one level of exhaustion. The creature repeats the saving throw whenever the same number of minutes elapses again, suffering one more level of exhaustion on a failed save.

45. MICTLAN
(Meek-TLAN, Land of the Dead)

This room is decorated with a bizarre diorama depicting the land of the dead. Small, brightly painted clay statues have been placed about the room to represent the inhabitants of this realm and the unfortunate people they have taken into their care.

In the center of the room, the floor rises to form a small hill. A group of small figures seem to be struggling to roll a boulder up the hill, while a devil drives them on. Above the hill in the ceiling is a glowing spot that illuminates the entire chamber with an eerie silver light.

A cobblestone path leads from the western door to the foot of the hill. A similar path runs eastward and then veers south. Sections of the diorama around the perimeter of the room depict different environments in the land of the dead.

In the western end of the room is a region of burning sands. There devils torture those who have been unfortunate enough to fall into their hands.

Along the southern side is a grassy plain where people frolic and hunt antelope and deer.

North of the grassy plain and south of the hill, the floor opens into a model of a canyon. A river of lava flows down it while flames lick the walls.

East of the hill, in a side area of the room, is a counterpart to this fiery canyon—an icy waste.

To the north of the hill is a putrid, bubbling marsh where figures strive to keep their heads above the surface.

From out of the marsh a black, torpid river wends its way past the northern edge of the hill and flows west to pour over the lip of a steam-filled chasm in the northwest corner of the room. Within this dark chasm, worms pursue the fleeing forms of naked people.

In the south corner of the room on the eastern wall is a barred door.

The light in the ceiling comes from the walls of a chute that glows in the dark. The chimney can be reached by someone who climbs on the shoulders of another character, but to enter it, the character must brace back and legs against opposite walls because there are no protuberances to hold onto. The steeply inclined passage beyond is full of cobwebs and leads eventually to area 48.

Each section of the diorama in this room has a magical aspect that affects any creatures that walk into the region. If the effect isn't instantaneous and isn't related to a spell, it can be dispelled with *dispel magic* cast as a 5th-level spell (or at a level stated in the effect). A creature on which a region's effect is dispelled is immune to the effect for 1 minute.

The two paths are free of magical effects. If characters veer off the paths, either unwittingly or with the intent of exploring, apply the effects described below according to the areas they enter. Unless otherwise noted, creatures can leave an area whenever they desire, by either moving onto one of the paths or into an adjacent area.

Hill. A magical force pushes those who climb to the top of the hill in a random direction. A creature that ends its turn on top of the hill must succeed on a DC 15 Strength saving throw or be pushed 5 feet off the top of the hill and knocked prone. If a creature slips, roll a d4 to see which direction it rolls off the hill.

Burning Sands. Any creature that ends its turn in this region must succeed on a DC 15 Constitution saving throw or start to bleed profusely from the nose. This hemorrhaging causes a loss of 1 hit point at the end of each of the creature's turns thereafter. If the creature leaves the area, the bleeding stops at the end of its next turn.

Grassy Plain. Any creature that enters this region must succeed on a DC 15 Charisma saving throw or refuse to leave it. A creature affected by the magic is allowed another Wisdom saving throw every 24 hours while the magic persists. A creature can repeat the saving throw every time it takes damage. If companions outside the area try to talk the creature into leaving, you can decide to allow the victim another saving throw. In any case, each time the saving throw is repeated, the DC increases by 1.

Flames. Creatures that enter this section are affected as if by a *heat metal* spell cast at 3rd level (save DC 15).

Ice. Creatures that enter this area are affected as if by a 3rd-level *heat metal* spell (save DC 15), but the damage is cold instead of fire, and the creature has no chance of dropping a chilled object.

Marshes. Any creature that enters this area feels a shortness of breath after 3 rounds and begins to suffocate after 3 more rounds.

River. Those who enter the river for the first time on a turn must succeed on a DC 15 Intelligence saving throw or forget how they came to be here and why they are here. A spellcaster also forgets how to cast one level of spells for each point by which the saving throw failed, starting with the highest level the character knows. Forgotten spells can be prepared again. *Dispel magic* doesn't remove this effect, but *remove curse* or *greater restoration* can.

Pit of the Worms. Any character who enters this region must succeed on a DC 15 Wisdom saving throw or be affected as if by a *fear* spell.

46. TLAZOTEOTL
(Tlaz-ohl-TAH-oh-tel, mother goddess of the earth)

Beyond the door is a modest-sized room with a lumpy pile of earthy material in the middle of the floor. Across from the door in the southeast corner, a glazed flask rests on a small shelf. In the northwest and northeast corners are two more shelves on which rest a small urn and a thin stone cylinder.

Creature. When any character starts into this room the pile of earth, which is a **gibbering mouther**, opens one eye, and then another and another, until many eyes of different shapes and sizes stare at the party. All about the eyes are fanged, drooling mouths that begin a cacophony of babbling. The creature attacks until destroyed but doesn't leave the room.

Treasure. The flask contains a dried *potion of hill giant strength*. The stone cylinder is a *+1 rod of the pact keeper*.

The urn holds the dried heart of a mighty yuan-ti that radiates transmutation magic if *detect magic* is used on it. Any character who eats the entire thing gains the permanent ability to understand the speech of snakes and yuan-ti.

47. SPIDER IN HIDING
Creature. In a web-covered opening in the wall of the steeply inclined chute, 30 feet above the where the lower end meets the ceiling of area 45, lurks a **giant spider**. The spider's lair is 10 feet long, 4 feet wide, and 4 feet tall. A character must succeed on a DC 17 Wisdom (Perception) check to notice the tunnel or its occupant before the spider attacks. If the spider paralyzes its prey, it retreats into its lair with the prey to feed.

In the Chute. The cramped quarters of the tunnel impose disadvantage on weapon attack rolls.

Also, a creature in the chute struck by the spider must succeed on a DC 11 Dexterity or Strength saving throw (player's choice). On a failed save, the creature slips down the chute 5 feet for every point by which the saving throw failed. If a creature falls 30 feet, it plummets out of the chute, taking falling damage accordingly and rolling in a random direction (roll a d4) after landing prone in area 45. The spider pursues prey into the chute, but is unlikely to emerge to fight in an open area.

Upper End. The top of this passage is covered with a pewter basin, which requires a successful DC 10 Strength (Athletics) check to move.

LOCATIONS ON THE THIRD TIER

The tunnel that leads up from area 45 opens onto the third tier of the temple. The following locations are identified on map 3.1.

48. HOUND OF THE BAT

The description below assumes that the characters entered the room by traveling through the chute and pushing aside the pewter cover. The tunnel comes out at the bottom of a stone ring that, from inside the room, resembles a well. (If they entered from the west, the pewter cover is still in place.)

> This room is small and plainly decorated. On the north and south sides are fountains made of bronze-inlaid marble. The southern one is cracked, and only dry limy deposits remain in it. The northern one contains about two feet of dark water, fed by a trickle that falls from the top of the fountain. In the water, the white, gauzy form of a crayfish lies on a bed of lime encrustations.
>
> To the west, stairs lead up out of the room, and to either side of the stairs along the west wall are narrow, dust covered ledges.

Creature. The fouled water in the fountain contains a neutral evil **water weird**. It rises up and attacks characters who disturb the water.

Treasure. The "crayfish" is nothing more than the shed shell of a long-expired resident of the fountain. Beneath it is a platinum key and chain (worth 20 gp). The key unlocks the portcullis that blocks the exit in area 53.

49. SACRED CHITZA-ATLAN
(SHEET-zah AY-tlan)

> In the middle of this chamber is what appears to be the withered, preserved form of a centaur mounted on a slab of marble. Tinted green and decked out in lacquered leather, feathers, and copper wire jewelry, he faces the western entrance to this chamber. The centaur holds a bronze-hafted pike tipped with a broad, blue-gray, flame-shaped spearhead.
>
> Scattered around the room are jewelry and knick-knacks, made of beaten copper, cut and polished obsidian, shells, quartz, and coral. Much of this treasure is at the feet of the centaur, symbolically being trod underfoot. Two tall urns shaped like wicker baskets stand along the north wall, each one filled with river stones.

Creature. The centaur figure is the mummified remains of a sacred offspring of Chitza-Atlan, the guardian of the gateway to the underworld. This guardian has two functions: to prevent any but the dead from entering these ruins, and to keep those creatures in the ruins confined there. Thus, if any character tries to exit this room by any door other than the one entered from, the **centaur mummy** (see appendix B) animates and attacks the characters. The mummy will also defend itself if attacked. A word or a pass from Zotzilaha will gain free passage.

Treasure. If all the junk jewelry is taken (eight hundred pieces), the total value of the haul is 80 gp. The real treasure is concealed in the bottoms of the two urns. Buried beneath the stones are two crushed silver masks (worth 25 gp each), an electrum serpent bracelet (worth 50 gp), a broken marble statue of a monkey (50 gp), and four silver hairpins set with jade worth (5 gp each).

50. JADE WALL

> Here a wall of green, polished stone blocks the way.

This wall, which is 7 feet wide and 7 feet tall, is a trap for those attempting to break into the ruins. If any tampering is done to the wall, it falls west out into the anteroom. If the wall falls on a creature, the creature must make a DC 10 Dexterity saving throw. On a failed save, the creature takes 9 (2d8) bludgeoning damage and is knocked prone under the wall, restrained. A successful DC 15 Strength (Athletics) check is needed to lift the stone wall off any trapped beneath it.

51. WIND TUNNEL

> This five-foot-diameter passage is dry and dusty, and it shows no sign of having been used for ages. Near the top of the corridor walls, about three feet from the ceiling, stone lintels run the length of the passage. The corridor abruptly widens to a cube fifteen feet on a side with a corrugated floor. In the ceiling of this area, a bronze, circular trapdoor is set. The cover is latched shut.
>
> In the four corners of this foyer are sets of metal rungs forming a ladder that leads up and across the arched ceiling to the trapdoor. The rungs are broken in several places, leaving rusty spikes. On the other side of this area, the corridor continues.

Hazardous Hatch. Opening the hatch releases a whirlwind. The character who climbed up to open the hatch is hurled to the floor and takes 3 (1d6) bludgeoning damage as the wind emerges and fills the 15-foot chamber. Thereafter, it costs 3 feet of speed to move 1 foot in the room. The hatch can't be shut, and the wind doesn't die down.

Each creature that starts its turn in this area must make a DC 13 Strength saving throw. (A character grasping the rungs of one of the ladders has advantage on the saving throw.) On a failed save, the wind throws the creature 10 feet in a random direction, the creature takes 3 (1d6) bludgeoning damage, and it is knocked prone. If the saving throw fails by 5 or more, the creature strikes one of the rusty spikes, taking an additional 3 (1d6) slashing damage.

If a target thrown by the wind strikes an object, such as a wall, the target takes another 3 (1d6) bludgeoning damage. If a target is thrown into another creature, that creature must succeed on a DC 13 Dexterity saving throw or take 3 (1d6) bludgeoning damage and be knocked prone. On a successful save, the creature takes half the bludgeoning damage and isn't knocked prone.

A creature that moves only by crawling on the floor, using the corrugated surface to maintain one's grip, is safe from the wind.

52. The Hidden Room of Nahual
(NAH-wahl, alter ego)

A character can discover one of the secret doors to this room by succeeding on a DC 20 Wisdom (Perception) check. Each door can be opened by reaching up above it, grabbing the lintel or the molding on the wall about 8 feet above the floor, and pulling down. The secret door then swings inward, but it closes 30 seconds later. These doors are counterweighted and can't be spiked open. From the inside, either of the doors can be opened by pressing down on a stone projection to the right of it.

When the characters exit one of the antechambers and pass into the room beyond, read:

> The walls of this chamber are painted flat black, while the floor is inlaid with a colorful mosaic of strange gods cavorting and leaping around a sun. An alcove in the center of the eastern wall is masked by a curtain of shells and beads.

If the characters push aside the curtain, read:

> Behind the curtain is the chalky form of a statue seated on a stone throne with its surface carved to depict feathers. The statue is wearing a feathered headdress and a feathered robe. Lying across its lap in its open palms is a scepter of gold and silver with an eagle's head crafted on one end and the talons of a bird holding a blazing sun on the other. The most remarkable thing about the statue is its face.

The statue duplicates the face of the first person who enters this room. The scepter is worth 200 gp. It is stuck to the palms of the statue, and only the character with the same face as the statue can lift the scepter.

Once that character picks up the scepter, it provides its holder with visions of great battles of the past. The holder is transfixed by the visions; others see the character lose focus and begin to sweat. After 30 seconds, if

still holding the scepter, the holder becomes petrified. At the same time, the statue becomes flesh and blood.

Creature. The figure on the throne is a nahual, or alter-ego. It is essentially a **doppelganger** of chaotic evil alignment that is also a fiend (demon). It possesses the memories of the petrified character and tries to convince the party that it has just merged with the spirit of one of the character's earlier incarnations. Given a chance, the nahual leads the party to their deaths with false information gained from "memories" of its former life.

The nahual must be slain and the scepter touched to the nahual's corpse to restore the petrified character. A *greater restoration* spell also works, before or after the nahual has been slain.

53. The Valve

> Before you is a foyer, ten feet wide and twenty feet long. A narrow hall connects with this area on the south side, and on the north end a five-foot-wide staircase leads up.
>
> A wheel is set horizontally half into the wall in the southwest corner. This wheel appears to be a crank. Above the wheel, a bronze lever is set in the wall, angled downward.

Open and Shut. The stairs lead up to a blank wall that is the location of a secret door. This door can be opened by turning the wheel in the foyer. The wheel turns only after the lever is pushed up, and then only in one direction. Rotating the wheel opens the secret door, but it also opens the floor in front of the wheel to reveal a 10-foot-square pit, at the bottom of which can be seen a pale shimmer of bones. There is a 1-foot-wide ledge along the west edge of the pit for someone to stand on while working the wheel, and a 6-inch-wide footbridge of polished marble spans the center of the pit from west to east.

Crossing this beam, which is difficult terrain, requires a DC 10 Dexterity (Acrobatics) check. On a failed check, the character can't move farther during that turn. If the check fails by 5 or more, the character falls off the beam 30 feet to the bottom of the pit.

If the crank is released once the secret door is open, it unwinds quickly, pulling the door shut. To prevent this, the lever can be pulled down to lock the wheel in place—but doing so causes a portcullis to fall across the entrance to the stairs. The portcullis can be lifted by a character who succeeds on a DC 20 Strength (Athletics) check.

Easy Way Out. If the characters search the walls beside the portcullis, a keyhole can be discovered. The key from room 48 fits the lock, enabling the portcullis to be opened like a gate.

Hard Way Out. In the ceiling directly above the pit, a thin slab that looks like ordinary stonework conceals a sloping tunnel that leads upward. The slab can't be detected or manipulated from this side.

TEMPLE GROUNDS

The inset on map 3.1 depicts what is left of the shrine at ground level.

54. TEMPLE RUIN

This was apparently a large temple of some sort. Once a major building, all that remains are the back wall and enough of the roof to shelter the altar. All else seems closed off by fallen debris. Several pillars have fallen and they litter the floor. Sunlight filters through holes in the roof, thirty-five feet overhead, which is a maze of chips and cracks. The back wall is covered by a bas-relief of a giant bat-thing, nine feet tall, with a wingspan of twenty feet. In front of this wall is an altar stone, carved to represent a mass of squirming rats, weasels, and worms. On the front of the altar is the head of a screaming bat. Jutting above the altar on either side are a pair of sharp-edged, metal bat-wings, eight feet long. The floor in front of the altar is worn smooth.

Field of Rubble. The temple area is filled with debris that offers no obvious passage to the interior. In the center of the south edge is an area where rubble is heaped over an opening that seems to lead down deeper into the debris. It is shaky and can be collapsed easily—any force applied to the heap by a creature with Strength 15 or higher will bring the rocks down. This rubble can also be caused to collapse by hurting a weighty object at it or using a spell such as *thunderwave* to create the needed force. Those within 10 feet of the collapse must succeed on a DC 10 Dexterity saving throw or take 5 (2d4) bludgeoning damage from falling debris.

Climbing elsewhere on the debris causes a minor collapse, dealing 2 (1d4) bludgeoning damage to each climber. Each climber must also succeed on a DC 13 Dexterity saving throw or be buried by the debris, taking 7 (3d4) more bludgeoning damage. If the saving throw fails by 5 or more, the debris engulfs the digger completely, and the trapped character can't breathe until dug out. Struggling out on one's own requires a successful DC 15 Strength (Athletics) check, and doing so takes 1 minute. Any of these sorts of collapses open no access to the inside.

Fragile Roof. Each time a creature ends its turn on the portion of the roof that remains standing, there is a 20 percent chance that the roof beneath its feet gives way. The creature falls 35 feet, to the rubble below, taking 14 (4d6) bludgeoning damage.

Trapdoor Entrance. If the characters begin their investigations of the hidden shrine by arriving at the temple, they need to find a way in. One route is by way of a trapdoor in the floor about 10 feet in front of the altar. A character can discover the seam of the door with a successful DC 15 Wisdom (Perception) check. Any creature that walks across the top of the door has a 1-in-12 chance of triggering it, for the mechanism is old, and long disuse has made it unreliable. Any skilled character's reasonable attempt to keep the door from opening works. Forcing the door to stay open requires a successful DC 10 Strength (Athletics) check. The trapdoor opens onto a slide that emerges above the pit in area 53. Anyone who slides down the tunnel to the hidden hatch at the other end is dumped into that room.

Secret Entrance. The second way to enter the tombs below is through a secret door hidden behind the left wing of the giant bat-thing carved upon the wall. A character can locate the door with a successful DC 20 Wisdom (Perception) check.

The door can be opened if a character places a limb into the mouth of the carving. If this occurs, the mouth clamps shut; the teeth puncture the limb, dealing 11 (2d10) piercing damage; and a giant batwing folds out from the wall to reveal the passage. A creature trapped in the bat's mouth is grappled (escape DC 12) but doesn't take further damage.

The mechanical nature of the latch becomes apparent to any creature that examines the mouth of the bat sculpture and succeeds on a DC 10 Intelligence (Investigation) check. If the check succeeds by 10 or more, the creature deduces that the function of the mouth can be activated by placing any object (not necessarily an extremity) into it. This information can also be obtained by a creature that examines the mouth further and then succeeds on a DC 15 Intelligence (Investigation) check.

Once the wing has moved to reveal the secret door, it veils the lower half of the carving's face and the bat's black eyes start to glow. Any character who looks at them must succeed on a DC 15 Charisma saving throw or be paralyzed. A creature can repeat the saving throw at the end of each minute or whenever it takes damage, ending the effect on itself on a successful save. The effect ends after 1 hour, or earlier if any magical light is shone on the altar.

Development. After the secret door to the shrine is opened, a **giant hyena** moves into this area. It makes a lair behind a fallen pillar to the east, waiting to ambush any who emerge back through the door.

Hinged Altar Trap. Close inspection of the altar reveals handholds along the front side and hinges at the back, indicating that the altar can be lifted from the front and tipped on its side. This can be accomplished by the combined effort of up to three characters with a total Strength of 30 or higher. If the altar is lifted quickly by characters in a standing position, the metal wings whip through an arc from the sides of the altar to the front center about 4 feet off the floor. Each wing's leading edge is razor-sharp. Anyone in the path of a wing must succeed on a DC 15 Dexterity saving throw or take 13 (3d8) slashing damage. If a wing misses its first target, it sweeps past that creature with the possibility of striking another creature along the same path.

If the altar is tilted by characters while they are in a kneeling position, the wings whistle harmlessly overhead. The other way to avoid the trap is by being careful in the lifting.

The mechanism for the trap is inside the altar. Characters who lift the altar slowly and look underneath it can easily spot the levers and joints that connect with the bladed wings. The characters can prop the altar up, enabling someone to crawl under and disable the trap. Doing that requires 10 minutes of work and a successful DC 15 Dexterity check using thieves' tools.

Treasure. Beneath the altar is an 8-foot-deep pit in which are many items of value and two bodies cut in half. The treasure is very bulky. Resting on and buried in a pile of 20,000 silver pieces are the following items: fifty silver chased goblets (worth 5 gp each), twenty gold-plated statuettes (10 gp apiece), forty embossed silver chalices and servings (5 gp each), eighty pieces of jewelry (5 gp apiece), fifty mother-of-pearl pieces (1 gp each), a jade placard bearing the image of Zotzilaha (100 gp), and a marble statue of a reclining figure (50 gp).

It is very likely that if large portions of this treasure are taken, Zotzilaha finds out about it and sends a vampire or a giant bat to seek retribution.

beyond to the lair of
dragotha
the undead dragon,
where fabulous riches
and hideous death await
THE HUT OF THINGIZZARD! BEWARE HER POTIONS!!
The Great Swamp
THE CURSED RUINS OF CASTLE MUKOS. WHO KNOWS WHAT LIES WITHIN ?
THE TWISTED THICKETS SKITTERING SLITHERS
White Plume Mountain
TO TOWN
HERE BE THE DEAD GNOLL'S EYE SOCKET

WHITE PLUME MOUNTAIN

HITE PLUME MOUNTAIN HAS ALWAYS been a subject of superstitious awe to the neighboring villagers. People still travel many miles to gaze upon this natural wonder, though few will approach it closely, as it is reputed to be the haunt of various demons and devils. The occasional disappearance of those who stray too close to the Plume reinforces this belief.

Thirteen hundred years ago, the wizard Keraptis was searching for a suitable haven where he could indulge his eccentricities without fear of interference. He visited White Plume Mountain, going closer than most dared to, and discovered the system of old lava-tubes that riddle the cone and the underlying strata. With a little alteration, he thought, these would be perfect for his purposes. The area already had a bad reputation, and he could think of a few ways to make it worse. So he disappeared below White Plume Mountain and vanished from the knowledge of the surface world.

Today, the once-feared name of Keraptis is not widely known even among learned scholars. Or it *was* not widely known, that is, until several weeks ago, when three highly valued magic weapons named *Wave*, *Whelm*, and *Blackrazor* disappeared from the vaults of their owners. Rewards were posted, servants hanged, even the sanctuary of the thieves' guild was violated in the frantic search for the priceless arms, but not even a single clue was turned up until the weapons' former owners each received a copy of the following note:

Search ye far or search ye near
You'll find no trace of the three
Unless you follow instructions clear
For the weapons abide with me.

North past forest, farm and furrow
You must go to the feathered mound
Then down away from the sun you'll burrow
Forget life, forget light, forget sound.

To rescue Wave, you must do battle
With the Beast in the Boiling Bubble
Crost cavern vast, where chain-links rattle
Lies Whelm, past water-spouts double.

Blackrazor yet remains to be won
Underneath inverted ziggurat.
That garnered, think not that you're done
For now you'll find you are caught

I care not, former owners brave
What heroes you seek to hire.
Though mighty, I'll make each one my slave
Or send him to the fire.

All the notes were signed with the symbol of Keraptis.

White Plume Mountain has tentatively been identified as the "feathered mound" of the poem. The former owners of *Wave*, *Whelm*, and *Blackrazor* are outfitting a group of intrepid heroes to take up the challenge. If the adventurers can rescue the weapons from this false Keraptis (for who can believe it is really the magician of legend, after thirteen hundred years?), the wealthy collectors have promised to grant them whatever they desire, if it is within their power to do so.

RUNNING THE ADVENTURE

This version of *White Plume Mountain* is designed for a group of 8th-level player characters. Your players will need both brains and brawn to successfully complete their mission, as there are situations here which cannot be resolved by frontal assault. If your players are unused to hack-proof dilemmas, they may find this adventure frustrating or even boring. But if your players are used to using their wits, they should find this an intriguing balance of problems and action. Unless you are used to mastering lengthy adventures, it will probably take more than one session for a party to investigate all three branches of the dungeon. If this is the case, it would be best if the party were required to leave the dungeon and reenter upon resumption of the game. If they stay in the nearest village (several miles away) they will be relatively safe, but if they camp near White Plume Mountain it would be a good idea to roll for random encounters.

ADVENTURE START

The party has arrived at White Plume Mountain, which stands alone in a vast area of dismal moors and tangled thickets. They will probably arrange to leave their horses and possessions either at the nearest village (about 5 miles from the mountain) or hidden in the Dead Gnoll's Eye Socket, a small natural cave in the side of a hill about 2 miles from the Plume. There is really no

---

PLACING THE ADVENTURE

White Plume Mountain is located in the Greyhawk campaign setting, in the northeastern part of the Shield Lands, near the Bandit Kingdoms and the Great Rift.

Here are suggestions for where you can place the mountain in another world. Wherever you place it, the party may be required to journey to the vicinity through the wilderness. How they get there is up to you.

Forgotten Realms. The mountain can be placed near Mount Hotenow in the region of Neverwinter.

Dragonlance. Found near Neraka in the Khalkist Mountains, the mountain might be a place of interest not only to adventurers, but also to the armies of Takhisis.

Eberron. On the continent of Xen'Drik, the mountain could stand in the range known as the Fangs of Argarak.

other shelter available. The villagers know about the cave and may have mentioned it. If the party leaves no guard, they will just have to trust the villagers not to steal their belongings. (Dishonest villagers will have to weigh their fear of White Plume Mountain against their certain belief that the party will never be seen again.) The cave is easily barricaded to keep out unintelligent wandering monsters.

White Plume Mountain is an almost perfectly conical volcanic hill formed from an ancient slow lava leakage. It is about 1,000 yards in diameter at the base, and rises about 800 feet above the surrounding land. The white plume that gives the mountain its name and fame is a continuous geyser that spouts from the very summit of the mountain another 300 feet into the air, trailing off to the east under the prevailing winds like a great white feather. The spray collects in depressions downslope and merges into a sizable stream. Steam vents are visible in various spots on the slopes of the mountain, but none of them are large enough to allow entry.

Map 4.1 depicts a cross-section of the mountain, showing the lava pool and the shaft of the geyser. The numbers refer to key areas inside the mountain, showing their orientation with respect to one another.

The only possible entrance into the cone is a cave on the south slope known as the Wizard's Mouth. This cave actually seems to breathe, exhaling a large cloud of steam and then slowly inhaling, like a person breathing on a cold day. Each cycle takes about 30 seconds. Approaching the cave, the party will hear a whistling noise coinciding with the wind cycle. If it were not for the continuous roaring of the Plume, this whistling could be heard for a great distance.

The cave is about 8 feet in diameter and 40 feet long. At the end of the cave, near the roof, is a long, horizontal crevice about a foot wide. The air is sucked into this crack at great speed, creating the loud whistling noise and snuffing out torches. Shortly the rush of air slows down, stops for a couple of seconds, and then comes back out in a great blast of steam. This steam is not hot enough to scald anyone who keeps low and avoids the crevice, but it does make the cave very uncomfortable, like a hot sauna bath interrupted by blasts of cold air.

The ceiling and walls of the cave are slick with the condensed steam that runs down them. The floor is covered with several inches of fine muck. Only careful probing of the muck near the back of the cave will reveal a small trapdoor with a rusted iron ring set in it. Once the muck has been cleared away, a successful DC 20 Strength check is required to pull up the encrusted door. Magic such as *knock* or *passwall* can also help open or bypass the door.

Directly beneath the door is a 20-foot-square vertical shaft and the beginning of a spiral staircase that leads down.

DUNGEON: GENERAL FEATURES

All corridors in the dungeon are 10 feet in height, and have been carved out of and, in some places, seemingly melted through solid rock. Unless otherwise noted, doors are 8 feet by 8 feet, made of oak and bound in iron. Though the doors are swollen by the dampness, and thus difficult to open (requiring a successful DC 15 Strength check), the wood is not by any means rotten.

The water on the floor is about 1 foot deep, and the floor itself is covered with slippery mud. Except where flights of steps lead up out of it, this scummy water covers the floors of all rooms and corridors. The water and mud reduce average movement by one-third (speed 30 becomes 20, speed 20 becomes 15), and will necessitate continuous probing of the floor by the party as they advance. It will be very difficult to keep silent, run (without falling), or depend on invisibility (waves and foot-shaped holes in the water give one away).

RANDOM ENCOUNTERS

Check once every 10 minutes for random encounters by rolling a d12; an encounter occurs on a roll of 1. If an encounter is indicated, roll a d6 and refer to the table below.

These are monsters that Keraptis has released into the dungeon specifically for the purpose of giving the intruders a hard time. All will attack immediately. The ogres and the bugbears are magically controlled and cannot be persuaded to betray Keraptis.

ABOUT THE ORIGINAL

White Plume Mountain, by Lawrence Schick, was originally published in 1979 as an adventure for the first edition of the D&D game.

Schick related in the 2013 compilation *Dungeons of Dread* that he wrote the adventure as a way of persuading Gary Gygax to hire him as a game designer.

d6	Encounter
1	1 black pudding
2	1d4 + 1 bugbears
3	2 gargoyles
4	1 invisible stalker
5	1d3 ogres
6	1d2 wights

LOCATIONS IN THE DUNGEON

The following locations are identified on map 4.2.

1. SPIRAL STAIRCASE

> The staircase is badly rusted but appears to be sturdy. The air inside the passageway is warm, humid, and rather foul. You reach the bottom of the stairs with a splash— the floor is submerged beneath a foot of water!

The spiral staircase descends about 100 feet before ending in area 1. Sensitive characters will feel it thrumming to a continuous low vibration (this vibration from the Plume geyser will be noticeable everywhere in the dungeon). In the humidity, lamps and torches will burn fitfully and give off a lot of smoke.

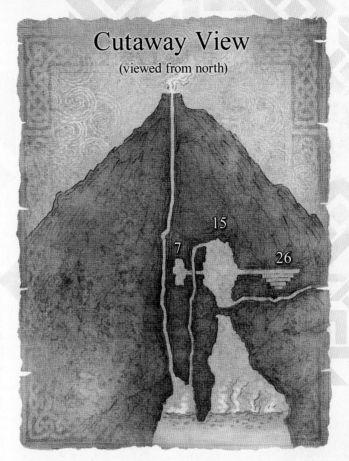

Cutaway View
(viewed from north)

MAP 4.1: CUTAWAY VIEW

THE LEGEND OF KERAPTIS

In the original publication of *White Plume Mountain*, "The Legend of Keraptis" was presented on the inside back cover. Although these details of the wizard's former life don't play a direct part in the adventure, a DM who shares this information with the players can deepen the characters' understanding of the situation and strengthen their motivation for delving beneath the mountain.

* * *

Well over a millennium ago, the wizard Keraptis rose to power in the valleys of the northern mountains, bringing the local warlords under his thumb with gruesome threats—threats that were fulfilled just often enough to keep the leaders in line. Under Keraptis's overlordship, the influx of rapacious monsters and raids from the wild mountains decreased markedly, dwindled, and then almost stopped. Seeing this, the populace did not put up much resistance to paying the wizard's heavy taxes and tithes, especially when stories were circulated of what happened to those who balked. Any nobles who protested disappeared in the night and were replaced by the next in the line of succession, who was usually inclined to be more tractable than the previous lord.

Gradually, as dissension was stilled, the taxes and levies became even more burdensome, until eventually the wizard was taking a great piece of everything that was grown, made, or sold in the valleys, including the newborn young of livestock. Around this time, numerous reports arose in the land concerning sudden madness, demonic possessions, and sightings of apparitions and undead. Furthermore, monstrous incursions into the settled lands began to

increase as raiding parties of humanoids assaulted villages, and evil and fantastic monsters appeared from nowhere to prey upon the harried peasants. At the height of this unrest, Keraptis's tax collectors came forth with word of a new levy: one-third of all newborn children were henceforth to be turned over to the wizard.

That edict turned out to be the tipping point. As one, the people rose up to overwhelm the wizard's lackeys and marched on his keep, where, led by a powerful and good cleric and his ranger acolytes, they destroyed Keraptis's final guardians. The great wizard barely managed to escape, accompanied only by his personal bodyguard company of deranged and fanatical evil gnomes.

Keraptis fled to the cities of the south and west, but wherever he went, his reputation preceded him, and he was unable to stay anywhere for long. Once again moving north, he came to the shores of the Lake of Unknown Depths, where he heard tales about haunted White Plume Mountain. After investigating further, he at last found the refuge he was looking for in the tangled maze of volcanic tunnels beneath the cone. He and his gnomes vanished into the shadow of the Plume, and humankind heard no more of the evil wizard.

That was almost thirteen hundred years before the present day. Now, seemingly, the hand of Keraptis is once again interfering in human affairs. If it is in truth the ancient wizard at work here, can he be thwarted before his power grows once more? What is his purpose in presenting this bizarre challenge to the world's heroes? There is only one way to find out.

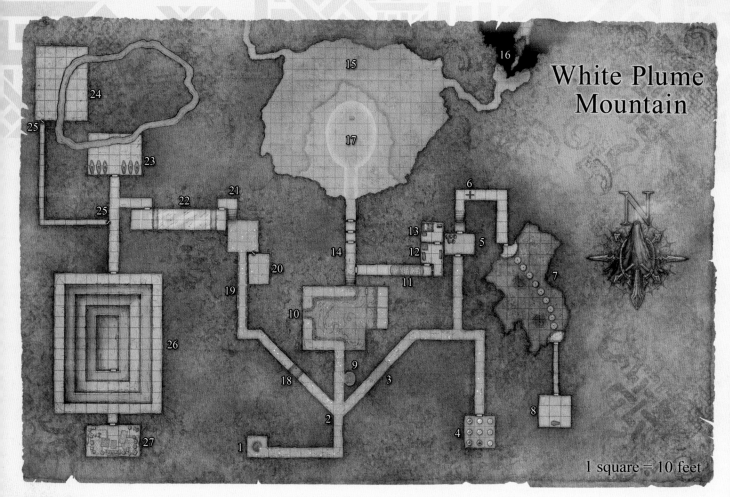

MAP 4.2: WHITE PLUME MOUNTAIN

Floating on the water are splotches of green and white subterranean algae. This algae or algae-like fungus also clings in patches to walls and ceilings. It is harmless, and can be found almost everywhere in the dungeon where there is water.

2. RIDDLING GUARDIAN

A rather mangy, bedraggled **gynosphinx** squats in the space where the three corridors converge. A wall of force along the south side separates the gynosphinx from those who approach from that direction. This wall of force is weaker than most, and can be brought down by *disintegrate*, *dispel magic*, or *passwall*.

The sphinx will let the characters pass (by removing the wall of force) if they can answer the following riddle:

Round she is, yet flat as a board
Altar of the Lupine Lords
Jewel on black velvet, pearl in the sea
Unchanged but e'erchanging, eternally

The answer is "the Moon." If the wall of force is destroyed or circumvented, the sphinx will attack.

3. HIDDEN SLIME

Midway along the corridor that runs northeast, the floor is covered by a large patch of green slime (see "Dungeon

Hazards" in chapter 5 of the *Dungeon Master's Guide*). Because the slime is covered by water, it is not easily detectable, and characters might walk through it and not even notice they have done so until it has eaten through their boots and started on their feet.

4. GLASS GLOBES

The door to this room appears normal on the way in: a large iron-bound oak door, swollen by dampness and difficult to open. When the characters have entered the room (or as many of them as are going in), the door will slam shut behind them. No tools, weapons, or magic available to the adventurers will open the door or prevent it from closing. Only the proper key inserted in the keyhole on the inside of the door will unlock it.

In the room, suspended from the ceiling by unbreakable wires, are nine silvered glass spheres, each about 2 feet in diameter. Unless otherwise noted, magically looking inside a sphere, such as with a *clairvoyance* spell or a *ring of x-ray vision*, will show that it contains some apparent treasure and a key. (Each sphere holds a key, but only one of the keys opens the door.) A good, hard crack with a weapon will shatter any of the spheres (each has AC 13 and 3 hit points), dropping its contents (if not caught) into the muck below.

Number the globes 1 through 9 for your own reference. The globes contain the following items:

Sphere 1. Three folded-up **shadows**, 300 worthless lead pieces, and a false key. (The shadows aren't visible to magical inspection.)

Sphere 2. A *spell scroll* of *fear* and a false key.

Sphere 3. Jewelry worth 12,000 gp, a false key, and an angry **air elemental**.

Sphere 4. A *potion of flying* and a false key.

Sphere 5. Eleven worthless glass gems and a false key.

Sphere 6. Phony glass jewelry, a false key, and a **gray ooze**. (The ooze fills the entire globe and isn't visible to magical inspection.)

Sphere 7. A *spell scroll* of *hold person* and a false key.

Sphere 8. The actual key and a silver ring. When the ring is released from the sphere, it speaks to the characters telepathically:

> "Stop before you put me on. I confer the following powers upon my wearer: *invisibility*, *haste*, immunity to charms, *fly* once per day, *detect magic*, and one *wish*. I also provide the benefits of protection and spell turning. The only drawback is that once a year I permanently eat a small part of your life. I must be worn before I can leave this room; merely carrying me away is not possible. If ever I am removed from my wearer's finger, however, all my powers are lost. So you must decide right now who will wear me forever."

This situation is a basic loyalty and intelligence test. Will the party members cut each others' throats over the ring? Will they be suspicious enough to simply leave it alone? If they take time to think about it, they'll likely realize that the ring must be a hoax.

Someone who puts it on can cause it to exhibit any of the powers mentioned above, except for the *wish* spell, as long as it remains in the room. While it is located here, the ring enables the wearer to produce the indicated spell effects at will (except for *fly*), and it also acts as a *ring of spell turning* and a *ring of protection*.

Once the ring leaves the area, however, it has no abilities and can't talk.

Sphere 9. Gems worth 600 gp and a false key.

5. NUMBERED GOLEMS

> Five flesh golems are clustered against the north wall. Each has a number on its chest: 5, 7, 9, 11, and 13. Number 5 says, "One of us does not belong with the others. If you can pick it out, it will serve you, and the others will allow you passage. If you pick the wrong one, we will kill you. You have sixty seconds."

The correct choice is 9, because it is not a prime number. Give the players an actual 60 seconds to figure it out.

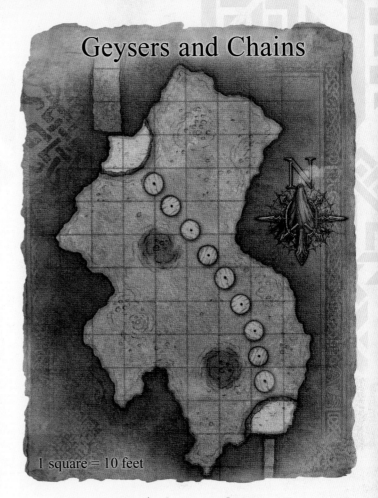

Geysers and Chains

1 square = 10 feet

MAP 4.3: GEYSERS AND CHAINS

If the characters give the wrong answer, roll initiative. The golems lumber forward to confront the intruders, trying to prevent anyone from moving through the door to the north. The monsters will pursue enemies that flee to the south, but they won't climb the stairs that led to area 6.

If the characters answer the riddle correctly, events unfold as promised: the golem numbered 9 becomes an ally of the party, accompanying the characters if they so desire, and the other four golems become inert again.

6. TURNSTILE

> A short flight of stairs leads up to a dry corridor. Just around the corner is a turnstile.

The characters will discover that the turnstile rotates in only one direction (counterclockwise). They can pass through it easily when moving to the east, but it will probably have to be destroyed on the way back. A golem or a strong character could rip it out with a successful DC 24 Strength (Athletics) check.

7. Geysers and Chains

> The door opens onto a stone platform in a large natural cave. Opposite the entrance in the distance is another stone platform. Between them, a series of wooden disks is suspended from the ceiling by massive steel chains. The cave floor seems to be covered by a pool of boiling mud.

The ceiling is 50 feet above the level of the platforms. The cave floor is 50 feet below. Two spots in the mud are the locations of geysers. The northern one erupts once every 5 minutes, the southern one every 3 minutes. The stone platform opposite the entrance is approximately 90 feet away.

The disks are about 4 feet in diameter and 3 feet apart. Each disk is attached to its chain by a giant staple fixed in its center. The disks swing freely and will tilt when weight is placed upon them.

The disks and the chains, as well as the walls of the cavern, are covered with a wet, slippery algal scum. This coating gives off a feeble phosphorescent glow. Climbing the chains or the walls requires a successful DC 15 Strength (Athletics) check.

When the geysers erupt, they reach nearly to the roof of the cavern, and creatures holding onto the disks or the chains might be washed off to fall into the boiling mud. The damage a creature takes from a geyser depends on how close a creature is to the geyser when it erupts (see the table below). Creatures that succeed on a DC 15 Dexterity saving throw take half damage.

In addition, a creature that is on a disk or holding onto a chain when a geyser erupts must succeed on a Strength saving throw (see the table for DCs) or be knocked off and fall into the boiling mud.

Location	Damage	DC
Adjacent to geyser	27 (5d10) fire damage	14
One disk away	22 (4d10) fire damage	13
Two disks away	16 (3d10) fire damage	12
Three disks away	11 (2d10) fire damage	11
Four disks away	5 (1d10) fire damage	10
Anywhere else in the area	3 (1d6) fire damage	—

Any creature that falls into the boiling mud takes 44 (8d10) fire damage at the start of each of its turns for as long as it remains in the mud.

8. Coffin

The door opens into an area of utter blackness.

The room beyond the door is the lair of a **vampire** named Ctenmiir. He is compelled by a curse to remain here in a trance except when roused to defend his treasure, which lies in a niche in the floor under his coffin. The vampire automatically awakes at the approach of intruders.

The room is affected by a *darkness* spell, which the vampire is not hindered by because he has truesight. If the vampire needs to leave this area to pursue intruders, the door to the room is littered with tiny holes through which he can pass in mist form. If the magical darkness is dispelled, it renews again automatically at dawn.

Treasure. The space beneath the coffin contains *Whelm*, a sentient warhammer (see "Sample Sentient Items" in chapter 7 of the *Dungeon Master's Guide*), 10,000 sp and 9,000 gp in six leather sacks, a *potion of mind reading*, and three *spell scrolls* (*conjure minor elementals*, *dispel magic*, and *magic mouth*).

9. Pool and Drain

As the characters move along the water-covered corridor, they can see that the water is deeper in a small circular area to the east. This space is a 10-foot-deep pit. At the bottom is a wheel connected to a valve. Turning the wheel requires a successful DC 20 Strength check.

When the wheel is turned, a channel will open, and all the water in the wet corridors will drain out in 1 hour. Also at the bottom of the pit is a secret door that is concealed by illusion magic. The door cannot be detected by sight, but can be discovered through the use of magic or by someone who examines the area by touch and succeeds on a DC 15 Intelligence (Investigation) check. The doorway leads to Keraptis's Indoctrination Center (see "Escaping the Dungeon" at the end of the adventure).

10. Deceptively Deep Room

Ahead is what appears to be a water-covered room, with steps rising out of the muck on the far side.

Most of the area is actually a 15-foot-deep pool. The only shallow spaces are those that run mostly around the perimeter of the room, where the water is only 1 foot deep.

The deep area that makes up most of the room is inhabited by two **kelpies** (see appendix B). As the characters move into the room, the kelpies will rise to the surface, and each will attempt to charm a character.

In the eastern wing of the pool are two partly enclosed areas with entrances that are accessible only from beneath the surface of the water. These areas are partially covered by a roof along the east edge, where the water is only 1 foot deep. The southern chamber is the kelpies' lair, which contains their treasure. The northern chamber is empty.

Treasure. Scattered about the kelpies' lair are 600 gp, a piece of jewelry worth 2,000 gp, and a suit of *+1 chain mail* armor.

11. Spinning Cylinder

The stone corridor changes abruptly to a spinning cylinder, apparently made of some light-colored metal. The inner surface rotates rapidly. It is painted in a dizzying black-and-white spiral pattern, and it glistens as if coated with some substance.

The 30-foot-long cylinder is 10 feet in diameter and spins counterclockwise at about 10 feet per second. The inner surface is covered with slippery oil. It is possible to slide through the cylinder by propelling oneself along the floor, but walking through this area without being knocked prone requires a successful DC 20 Dexterity (Acrobatics) check.

12. Burket's Guardpost

Watching through the arrow slit at the end of the passage is an alert guard named Burket (LE male human **veteran**). If he sees intruders approaching, he will wait until they are halfway through the spinning cylinder and then ignite the slippery oil with a flaming arrow.

Boiling Lake

1 square = 10 feet

MAP 4.4: BOILING LAKE

The oil burns for 2d4 rounds if the fire is not extinguished. On the first round, the burning oil deals 9 (2d8) fire damage to any creature that enters the spinning cylinder or starts its turn inside the cylinder. On later rounds, it deals 2 (1d4) fire damage to such creatures.

Development. After Burket shoots, he then warns his lover, the wizard Snarla, to close and lock the shutter over the arrow slit and move to defend the door that adjoins the corridor. They stand ready to engage anyone that enters.

Snarla is a **werewolf**, her Intelligence is 16 (+3), and she has the following additional feature, which increases her challenge rating to 5 (1,800 XP):

Spellcasting. Snarla is a 6th-level spellcaster. Her spellcasting ability is Intelligence (spell save DC 14, +6 to hit with spell attacks). She has the following wizard spells prepared:

Cantrips (at will): *fire bolt, light, mage hand, shocking grasp*
1st level (4 slots): *magic missile, shield, thunderwave*
2nd level (3 slots): *mirror image, web*
3rd level (3 slots): *dispel magic, fear, haste, stinking cloud*

If Burket is killed or if Snarla finds herself in a bad situation, she changes into werewolf form and attacks with desperate savagery, giving her advantage on all her attack rolls.

If she is captured alive and made to talk, she will tell the party only that she is charged with keeping the kelpies and other denizens of the dungeon fed. There are

strange gaps in her memory concerning her employer or any section of the dungeon other than her own. She has never been past the doors at area 14. Burket knows even less than she does.

Treasure. The room has a couple of benches and a table, upon which are a large candlestick (worth 10 gp) and Snarla's spellbook. The book contains the spells that she has prepared and no others. It is protected by an *explosive runes* glyph of warding that deals 5d6 fire damage.

13. SNARLA'S SANCTUM

> Unlike the room you just left, this place is beautifully decorated. The floor is covered by fine rugs, the walls by erotic tapestries and shimmering curtains, the ceiling by an intricate mosaic depicting a summer sky dotted with fleecy clouds. In the northeast corner is a large and lavishly covered bed, strewn with cushions. Next to it on a low table is a buffet of sweetmeats, cakes, and other delicious-looking comestibles. In the northwest corner of the room is a brass-bound oak chest.

Anyone who tries out the bed will find that it feels quite uncomfortable, and anybody who samples the food will be disappointed in the extreme, finding it tough and not very tasty.

In fact, the room is covered in illusions; a *true seeing* spell or similar illusion-piercing magic reveals that the opulent bed is only an old straw mattress, and the delicious treats are just ordinary rations. The walls, floor, and ceiling of the room are quite bare. A *dispel magic* spell will automatically remove the illusion.

Treasure. Only the brass-bound chest appears as it actually is. The chest must be opened while uttering a command word known only to Snarla, or it will emit a *stinking cloud* spell that lasts for 1 minute. Inside are 400 ep, 300 gp, and seven gems worth a total of 1,300 gp.

14. FLOOD DOORS

The three doors along the corridor are made of thick metal, their edges flanged so that they overlap the door jamb on the north side and thus can be opened only by pivoting them to the north. The north side of each door has a handle so that it can be pulled open from that direction.

These barriers are emergency doors, whose purpose is to prevent the dungeon from being flooded by the boiling lake at area 15, in case of an "accident."

15. BOILING LAKE

This boiling lake is several hundred feet deep, extending down to the red-hot rock below, and reaching nearly to the ceiling of the cavern it occupies, 50 feet above the level of the sunken ledge described in area 17. It is fed by an underground stream that enters from the northwest at a depth 100 feet below that of the ledge. Its run-

damage). Thereafter, any creature that enters the space with this stream of scalding water or that starts its turn there takes that damage. The skin will not "heal" once it is compromised. Major damage to the skin, as from a slash with a sword or an axe, will collapse the field like a deflating balloon in 1d6 rounds.

After 30 feet the corridor gives way to an oval-shaped, domed area enclosed by the protective skin. Here lives the guardian of the treasure, a Huge **giant crab** that has the following changes, which increase its challenge rating to 8 (3,900 XP):

- It has 161 (14d12 + 70) hit points.
- Its Strength and Constitution are 20 (+5).
- On one of its claws it wears a rune-covered copper band that makes it immune to being charmed, frightened, and paralyzed. (The copper band is worthless as a treasure, for the magic is keyed to this crab.)
- It has an improved claw attack:

Claw. *Melee Weapon Attack:* +9 to hit, reach 10 ft., one target. *Hit:* 27 (4d10 + 5) bludgeoning damage, and the target is grappled (escape DC 14). The crab has two claws, each of which can grapple only one target.

The crab will intelligently attack intruders, being careful not to bump the protective skin walls. The crab is experienced in fighting in this manner, as is evidenced by the bones scattered about, but the characters are not. You will have to watch for characters whose actions might rip the water skin, especially any foolish enough to use two-handed weapons or a violent spell such as *fireball* or *lightning bolt*. Such people are likely to get the whole party boiled.

Treasure. At the north end of the domed area is a heavy chest firmly attached to the floor. In it is *Wave*, a sentient trident (see "Sample Sentient Items" in chapter 7 of the *Dungeon Master's Guide*), 1,000 gp in small sacks, twenty gems (two big ones worth 1,000 gp each, one big one worth 5,000 gp, and seventeen others worth a total of 3,935 gp), *goggles of night*, and a *stone of good luck*.

Development. A character who grabs *Wave* while the protective skin is collapsing can save the lives of those nearby by using the trident as a *cube of force*. *Wave* will instantly make its bearer aware of this property and allow the bearer to instantly become attuned to it if that person worships a god of the sea or is willing to convert on the spot.

Characters protected by the cube will probably end up being blown out the geyser at the top of the mountain. The air-filled cube will float, drain down the cascade, and be ejected from the Plume—a rocky ride.

Characters could also survive the boiling lake with a combination of immunity to fire damage and the ability to breathe water.

18. Hall Pit

Halfway down the corridor that leads to the northwest is a 10-foot-long, 10-foot-deep open pit, filled with and hidden by water. If the characters aren't testing the floor ahead of them, those in the first rank must succeed on a DC 15 Dexterity saving throw to avoid falling into the pit.

off flows through a channel to the east, above the ledge, near the ceiling of the cavern.

Any creature that enters the boiling lake takes 44 (8d10) fire damage immediately and again at the start of each of its turns for as long as it remains in the lake.

16. Blow Hole

The run-off from the boiling lake cascades down through a series of near-vertical lava-tubes to the base of the blow hole, 800 feet below the level of the dungeon. There the water strikes molten rock and is instantly converted to steam. It is ejected up the blow hole and out the top of the volcanic cone, forming the continuous geyser of White Plume Mountain. The boiling water here is just as dangerous as the water in area 15.

17. The Boiling Bubble

A sunken stone ledge projects out into the boiling lake. The corridor from the dungeon continues out into the lake under a magical force field that keeps out the water by forming a sort of elastic skin. The shape of the corridor is not square in cross-section, but rather semicircular, as if a series of hoops were supporting the ceiling.

The protective skin is soft, resilient, and uncomfortably warm to the touch. Under any pressure it immediately becomes taut, and any character unwise enough to puncture it with a piercing weapon will cause a stream of scalding water to rush into the corridor, hopefully burning the idiot who made the hole for 2 (1d4) fire

19. METAL-HEATING CORRIDOR

> A series of copper-colored metal plates lines the walls of the path before you.

The plates are 6 feet high and 6 feet wide, and cannot be damaged or removed. They produce an invisible electrical field that extends from floor to ceiling throughout the 70-foot-long corridor. The field isn't directly harmful, but metal objects that pass between the plates become heated. Metal will become uncomfortably warm after moving 20 feet into the field, painfully hot after 30 feet, and hot enough to deal fire damage at 40 feet and beyond. The field affects armor, weapons, equipment, and even treasure made of metal.

A character in metal armor who tries to move through this corridor would take damage as follows: 4 (1d8) fire damage at 40 feet, another 9 (2d8) fire damage at 50 feet, an additional 16 (3d10) fire damage at 60 feet, and another 22 (4d10) fire damage at 70 feet.

Characters not wearing metal armor but carrying metal weapons or equipment will feel only slight discomfort when passing between the plates. Metal carried in wrappings of cloth will burn through by the 50-foot mark, and it will similarly burn through leather by the 60-foot mark. Armored characters might have no recourse other than to remove their armor, then drag, push, or use magic to get their metal armor and weapons through the corridor, and then suit up again. Armor pulled through the corridor by ropes will heat up enough to burn through the ropes at 60 feet, leaving a pile of hot metal lying in the water.

The only sovereign remedies for this dilemma are area effects that deal cold damage, such as *ice storm* or *cone of cold*, which will nullify the effect long enough for the party to dash through.

20. GHOUL AMBUSHERS

Behind the secret door, eight **ghouls** wait in ambush for intruders to come through the heat-induction corridor. These ghouls wear amulets that make them immune to the Turn Undead ability.

21. STAIRS UP

These stairs lead up out of the water to the dry corridor beyond.

22. FRICTIONLESS TRAP

When the characters pass through the door from area 21, describe the features of the room beyond depending on how much of the chamber they can see.

> The path to the west is broken by a sizable gap, and you can see the glint of metal at the bottom of the opening. The floor beyond this area has a silvery sheen.
>
> In the distance you can see another hole, beyond which is a patch of floor that adjoins the western wall.

The openings in the floor are pits, each 5 feet wide and 10 feet deep. Their bottoms are lined with rusty, razor-like blades. Anyone who falls in takes 6 (1d12) damage and must succeed on a DC 15 Constitution saving throw or contract a disease called super-tetanus (see below).

The walls, ceiling, and floor of the area between the pits are covered with a substance that is totally frictionless. This silvery stuff is inert and utterly unaffected by any force, magical or otherwise. Anything that alights on the surface will move in the direction of its last horizontal impetus, bouncing off the walls (if it strikes them) like a billiard ball, until it slides into a razor-pit. It is impossible for a creature even to stand still on the surface, for the slightest movement in any direction would unbalance it enough to send it moving in that direction.

Magic that augments movement (such as *fly*, *jump*, and *levitate*) and teleportation effects do not work in this room.

The line near the west edge of the room is the illusion of a wall—the actual wall is 10 feet farther away. Objects that make contact with the illusory wall will pass through it and seemingly disappear. This fact tends to frustrate (at least initially) any scheme for attaching a rope to the west wall from afar.

In fact, however, one way to get safely across is to get a rope strung through the room and fastened securely at both ends. Once this is done, characters can pull themselves across the floor and are able to control their speed. A clever party might be able to come up with other methods. Ingenuity is required.

Super-Tetanus. A creature that contracts the disease of super-tetanus is wracked with pain as its heart races and its muscles spasm hard enough to break its bones. The creature takes 11 (2d10) damage at the start of each of its turns. If a victim is not cured by other means, it can repeat the saving throw at the end of every minute after becoming exposed, ending the effect on itself with a successful save.

23. FLOATING STREAM

> Water not only flows through this room, it floats.
>
> Entering a hole in the western wall, two feet off the floor, is a stream seemingly suspended in mid-air. It flows out of another hole near the northeast corner. The water is about three feet deep. You can see a few blind cave fish being carried along in the brisk current.

On either side of the door are a total of six kayaks, each able to carry two riders, but there are no paddles to be found.

The stream is hemispherical in cross-section where it flows through the room. The entrance and exit holes are 6 feet in diameter; they are the ends of a tunnel that connects this room with area 24.

The water is lukewarm. Objects can be thrust through the sides of the stream, but no water other than a few drops will escape. It would even be possible to walk right through the stream, but only a very strong creature could do so without being swept off its feet (requiring a DC 15 Strength saving throw). The stream flows quite quickly from west to east.

If characters choose to go boating into the unknown tunnel, they will have to figure out how to get in the kayaks once the kayaks are placed in the stream, the surface of which is 5 feet off the floor. These vessels tip over easily. If they successfully board the kayaks, the characters will bump along through a twisting tunnel 6 feet across. They can regulate their speed by pushing against the walls. Eventually they will emerge into area 24.

24. Sir Bluto's Guardpost

A fallen knight named Sir Bluto Sans Pite (a NE **champion**; see appendix B) and his eight minions (NE human **knights**) wait here to ambush any who come through the tunnel. They will be alerted by disturbances in the flow of water as the party tampers with it upstream. The stream that flows through this room is suspended in the same manner as in area 23. It continues from north to south out of area 24 and back to area 23, completing the circuit.

Sir Bluto's knights work in two teams of four, with two team members on each side of the stream. When a kayak comes out, a team will throw a large net over it and attempt to drag it and its occupants out of the stream and down onto the floor. When it falls, they move in to finish off the occupants with swords. To escape from a net, a creature can use its action to make a DC 10 Strength check, freeing itself or another creature within its reach on a successful check. Dealing 5 slashing damage to the net (AC 10) also frees a creature without harming it; any other creature in the same net can then use its action to free itself through that opening.

Sir Bluto was a respected Knight of the Realm before his indictment in the River of Blood mass-murder case. His mysterious disappearance from prison left even the Royal Magician-Detectives baffled, and a reward of 10,000 gp was posted for his capture. Someone in the party is sure to recognize his one-of-a-kind face.

Treasure. In addition to his weapons and armor, Sir Bluto wears *boots of striding and springing*. In addition, he carries the key that opens the secret doors at area 25.

Aquarium and Prison

1 square = 10 feet

Map 4.5: Aquarium and Prison

25. Magical Secret Doors

The secret doors at either end of the narrow corridor will reveal themselves and open only to the bearer of Sir Bluto's magic key.

26. Terraced Aquarium

You are looking out and down into an enormous chamber defined by terraced steps that ring the entire area and descend toward a central enclosure.

A few feet south of the door, water laps at the edge of the stone floor. Looking to the side, you can see that the ring of the terrace that lies beyond is a ten-foot-deep ring of water held in by a nearly transparent wall. Another of these watery steps in the terrace is somewhat lower than the first; at the level in between these aquariums, the terrace steps are dry, but the area is still enclosed by a glassy wall like the others.

Each tier in the room is 10 feet in depth and width. The three middle levels are enclosed by 10-foot-tall glass walls that keep the inhabitants of those tiers confined. The two on either side are filled with water. All the creatures in this room have been charmed and ordered to stay in their areas as long as their glass walls are intact.

A 10-foot-square area of glass wall has AC 15, and 20 hit points. The glass can also be broken with a successful DC 15 Strength check.

The only exit from the room is the door that leads south out of the bottom tier. It opens into a corridor that passes under the higher tiers of the room.

Breaking Glass. If any of the glass walls are broken, a weak wall of force will activate immediately in front of the door on the bottom tier (preventing water from forcing the door open and escaping into the corridor beyond). If the glass is broken on both of the aquariums, the volume of water is sufficient to fill the two lower tiers and cover the floor of the middle tier to a depth of about 2 feet. The water will slowly drain out of four small drains in the corners of the bottom tier, but it will take a good three hours to do so. Of course, characters who

choose to wait will be subject to the possibility of random encounters. Once the water is finally gone, the wall of force will disappear.

If the characters destroy the wall of force, the pressure of the water will push open the door and the water will rush into the corridor beyond, pulling along any swimming characters and miscellaneous debris nearby. The water will collide with another wall of force that covers the door to area 27, and then begin draining out through a grating in the floor in the last 10 feet of the passage. The water will take only 20 minutes to drain out through this grating. (The water drains straight down through an old lava tube to a large cave with no other exits.) When the water is gone, the wall of force barring entry to area 27 dissipates.

Creatures. The occupants of each level will be randomly distributed when the party enters, but as the intruders come near, the monsters will move to follow, expecting to be fed. They are accustomed to live food, and will ignore dead meat or other nonliving sustenance. They consider any living creature that enters their domain as food, and will attempt to eat it.

No creatures inhabit the top tier of the terrace. The aquarium tier inside that area is occupied by six **giant crayfish** (see appendix B). The next lower tier is a dry level where the glass walls enclose six **giant scorpions**. Beneath and inside that is an aquarium that holds four **sea lions** (see appendix B).

On the bottom tier are three wing-clipped **manticores** that are unable to fly. The manticores will not hesitate to fire their spikes at any they recognize as intruders.

Treasure. A safe is set in the north wall opposite the door on the bottom tier. If it is opened incorrectly (that is, the trap not removed), a vibration device in the wall is triggered that will shatter the glass walls in this area in 1d6 rounds. The safe contains 6,000 sp and one piece of jewelry worth 3,000 gp.

27. LUXURIOUS PRISON

> Lavish furnishings and decorations are everywhere in this large room. The floor is strewn with rugs and cushions, and tapestries cover the walls. A hookah as tall as an adult human stands in one corner. The largest piece of furniture is a sumptuous divan.

The room is the residence of Qesnef, an **oni** who lost a bet with Keraptis and as a result must confine himself in these luxurious surroundings, guarding his treasure, for 1,001 years. A *magic mouth* spell warns him of the approach of trespassers, so he will disguise himself by using his Change Shape ability to take the form of a doughty halfling warrior, claiming to be someone who has been trapped by the evil wizard.

Treasure. Qesnef's valuables have been casually shoved beneath the divan. The hoard includes *Blackrazor*, a sentient greatsword (see "Sample Sentient Items" in chapter 7 of the *Dungeon Master's Guide*), 1,000 ep, 200 pp, four pieces of jewelry worth a total of 11,000 gp, a *potion of greater healing*, a *scroll of protection* (fiends), and *armor of vulnerability* (slashing).

In addition, Qesnef wears a *ring of protection* on his left hand and a *ring of spell storing* (with two *mirror image* spells in it) on his right.

ESCAPING THE DUNGEON

If the characters obtain two or even all three of the magic weapons and are finally leaving for good, they might be stopped at area 2 by the return of the wall of force. A voice will speak to them out of the air:

> "Not thinking of leaving, are you? You've been so very entertaining. I just couldn't think of letting you go, especially with those little items of mine. And since you've eliminated all of their guardians, why, you'll simply have to stay ... to take their places. I'll have to ask you to

> leave all of your ridiculous weapons behind and let Nix and Nox escort you to the Indoctrination Center. I'll be most disappointed if you cause me any trouble and Nix and Nox have to eliminate you. Don't worry—you'll like it here."

Creatures. The wall of force disappears, but coming up the south passage are Nix and Nox, two **efreet**. If the party can get past them, they're home free.

Of course, this whole episode can be omitted if the party has already taken too much damage. Conversely, if the characters have had too easy a time of it, this final challenge can be made tougher by the addition of one or two more efreet (called Box and Cox).

If, for some foolish reason, the party decides to comply with Keraptis's request and go with Nix and Nox to the Indoctrination Center, you will have to play it by ear. It's not too difficult—use your imagination and make it up as you go. Just make sure that the characters are extremely sorry they ever decided to submit to Keraptis's demands. They probably will end up as the brainwashed new guards in Keraptis's renewed version of White Plume Mountain's dungeon. 🅟

DEAD IN THAY

EAR THE VILLAGE OF DAGGERFORD ON
the Sword Coast, the Red Wizards of
Thay plotted to extend the evil reach of
their land and its master, the lich lord
Szass Tam. At a site called Bloodgate
Keep they built a powerful portal,
fueled by elemental nodes, that could
allow Thayans to instantly transport
whole armies into the very heart of the Sword Coast.
With this power, the Red Wizards would surely overthrow and take control of the North.

However, groups of heroes recently assaulted Bloodgate Keep and its master, the lich Tarul Var. With the
help of a renegade Red Wizard named Mennek Ariz, this
assault was successful. Bloodgate Keep fell, and Szass
Tam's plans of invasion were crushed.

What no one expected, though, was that despite the
fall of the keep itself, parts of the Bloodgate Nexus (an
interconnected series of teleportation circles) survived,
and a Thayan Resurrection cell leader named Syranna
devised a way to use it against Szass Tam. Syranna
had been part of the team that originally assembled the
Bloodgate Nexus, and knew that remaining nodes allowed direct access to a secret Thayan training ground
known as the Doomvault.

This adventure takes place in the Doomvault. It is designed for 9th-level characters. By the end of the story,
they are likely to advance to 11th level or perhaps higher
... if they don't end up dead in Thay.

SYNOPSIS

Kazit Gul, a Thayan archmage, built the Doomvault to
siphon the souls of those who perished within it for use
in his dark experiments. One of these was the creation
of an extradimensional vault in which he stored his
phylactery. Eventually, Szass Tam and his followers defeated and enslaved Gul. They changed the Doomvault
into a monstrous menagerie and arcane laboratory.
Although the space is still called the Phylactery Vault
of Kazit Gul, it now also holds the phylacteries of Szass
Tam and all his elite lich servants.

Syranna knows that if the characters can make their
way through the Doomvault and find the entrance to the
phylactery vault, they could strike a deathblow to Szass
Tam's hold on power. She can provide them access and
a little bit of guidance, but the bulk of the work is in their
hands. They must assault the Doomvault quickly—the
more word gets out about their activities, the more the
site's guards will be on alert.

Eventually, the characters will discover that Szass
Tam is siphoning the power of members of the Chosen,
mortals who have been invested with the power of the
gods so as to help shape the Realms to match the will of
their divine benefactors. The lich is using that power to

keep the vault hidden, warp the magic fueling the Doomvault, and power his pursuit of godhood.

CHARACTERS' GOALS

Over the course of the adventure, the characters try to
accomplish the following tasks:

- Explore the Doomvault and deal as much damage to
the Thayans as possible.
- Learn how to access the Phylactery Vault, and destroy
the phylacteries within it.

The villains' goals are straightforward: defend the
Doomvault and kill the intruders. Not all of the characters' potential foes share these goals, so the opportunity
exists to turn enemies into allies, or at least useful tools.

THE DOOMVAULT

After the fall of Bloodgate Keep, a Red Wizard named
Syranna, a leader in the Thayan Resurrection resistance movement, saw an unusual opportunity. Her
knowledge of the secret portal network of which the
Bloodgate was a part gave her the ability to open portals
directly into the Doomvault.

PLACING THE ADVENTURE

This adventure takes place in the Forgotten Realms, but it
can easily be transplanted—the site and the story alike—
into another setting.

Dragonlance. On Krynn, the Doomvault is likely to be the
work of renegade wizards, perhaps of more than one color,
with magic as their only alliance and moral compass. The
dungeon might exist underneath a ruined Tower of High
Sorcery, or it could be a haunt of Fistandantilus before his
failed attempt at godhood. If it is part of ruins, it could
even be the Tower of Istar, which Nuitari took at the end of
the Chaos War. Or it might be the same tower, after Mina
raised it and the black-robed wizards took it for their own.

Eberron. The Doomvault, lying beneath the Mournland,
might be the secret project of King Kaius of Karrnath.
Kaius I hid in the dungeon from the time the lich Vol made
him a vampire until he returned to take the throne from
his grandson. He's trying to become powerful enough
to thwart Vol's influence on him and become the preem-
inent monarch of Khorvaire. Kaius is draining powerful
dragonmarked scions instead of Chosen. Alternatively, the
Doomvault could be the Blood of Vol's headquarters in
Khorvaire. Vol uses the dungeon to harvest the power of
dragonmarks so she can become an undead god.

Greyhawk. Perhaps Rary the Traitor found the Doomvault—yet another vestige of ancient Sulm—under the
Bright Desert. Rary takes any chance to increase his power,
even as he claims the desire to destroy the accursed Scorpion Crown and return Sulm to its fertile state. Since his
betrayal of the Circle of Eight and the subjugation of the
people of the Bright Desert, Rary has made countless enemies who want him to fail even at noble aims. If he succeeds at destroying the crown, his tyranny will still remain.

The following sections contain details on the logistics of running an adventure set there. When you're familiar with these, continue with the characters' introduction to Syranna and their mission in Into The Doomvault.

DUNGEON CHARACTERISTICS

Locations in the Doomvault are identified on map 5.1. The following characteristics are common to all the areas, unless otherwise noted in a specific description.

Because of Szass Tam's suspicious nature, and the existential threat that discovery of the Phylactery Vault would pose, movement within the Doomvault is regulated with what one might call excessive precautions.

SECTORS, ZONES, AND AREAS

The Doomvault is divided into nine sectors that each focus on a different theme. A sector is split into four zones, that each explore one facet of that theme with a number of areas detailing a particular example. Magic gates separate zones from one another.

Sectors are labeled on the map: Abyssal Prisons, Blood Pens, Masters' Domain, Far Realm Cysts, Forests of Slaughter, Ooze Grottos, Predator Pools, Golem Laboratories, and Temples of Extraction. Zones are also labeled on the map. Areas are identified by numbers.

DIMENSIONAL BARRIERS

Magic secures the dungeon. No spell or trait allows anyone to evade the dungeon's security. For instance, a wizard might use a *dimension door* spell to teleport from one part of a zone to another, but no spell permits teleportation out of the zone in which the spell was cast. Similarly, a wizard might cast a *passwall* spell to burrow from one area to another. If the tunnel would pass from one zone to another, circumventing security, then the tunnel ends halfway between the origin point and the possible exit point. In any case, the caster knows why the spell didn't work as intended. Further, an incorporeal or ethereal creature can't pass between zones.

A *detect magic* spell can't penetrate the structure of the Doomvault to sense the dimensional barriers.

MAGIC GATES

Two types of magic gates, white and black, secure the Doomvault. Magic keys allow the manipulation of them.

Gate Features. Each gate is a 10-foot-wide circle of runes, drawn on the floor. This circle creates a magical energy field in its space from floor to ceiling. Someone who touches the edge of a gate's field can assess its nature with a successful DC 10 Intelligence (Arcana) check. The field can be disabled by the use of a glyph key (see below).

A creature that enters an active gate's energy field while not holding a properly attuned glyph key is pushed back 10 feet. The first time a creature does so on a turn, the creature takes 5 (2d4) force damage.

White Gates. White gates are placed in the dungeon to block passage between zones. When the characters see a white gate for the first time, read:

> A ten-foot-diameter circle of runes and clear quartz fragments is set into the floor. Within the circle, a luminous white mist shimmers, obscuring what lies beyond.

Thereafter, you can shorten the description of the gates they encounter to avoid repetition.

A white gate's misty energy field, when active, gives off dim light and renders its area heavily obscured. This field is also an impenetrable magical force that blocks passage (material and ethereal), sound, and scent.

If a glyph key attuned to the zone on either side of the gate is applied to the gate's field, the mist dissipates and the energy field becomes inactive while the key remains within the gate. Therefore, a creature that has a properly attuned glyph key can hold a white gate open for others.

Black Gates. The black gates were part of the Doomvault's original construction. They connect different areas of the complex. When the characters see a black gate for the first time, read:

> A ten-foot-diameter circle of runes and black onyx fragments is set into the floor. It exudes wisps of shadowy energy that look like curling black smoke.

Thereafter, you can shorten the description of the gates they encounter to avoid repetition.

MAP 5.1: THE DOOMVAULT

When a black gate's magical field is active, it gives off shadowy energy that lightly obscures the field's area.

A creature can render a black gate's field inactive by holding any glyph key to the field, whereupon the smoky energy dissipates. If the key is attuned to a zone containing a different black gate, then the creature holding the key can also open a magical portal that leads to the other black gate's area. While the portal is open, the destination gate's field also becomes inactive. A black gate's field remains inactive until no glyph key is applied to it. A portal created within a black gate remains open until the creature that opened the portal leaves the area of either connected black gate.

As the adventure progresses, the characters learn that disrupting a number of black gates is essential to reaching the Phylactery Vault, where the party can upset Szass Tam's plans and loosen his grip on power in Thay. Szass Tam's channeling of Chosen life force has created instability in the black gates' magic. To reach the Phylactery Vault, six black gates must be disrupted. Once those gates are disrupted, any black gate can be forced to connect the Temples of Extraction to the Phylactery Vault, which is otherwise accessible only to Szass Tam.

Once the characters learn that they need to disrupt the gates, anyone who understands the nature of the gates knows how to perform the disruption. As an action, a character who has the glyph key attuned to a black gate's zone can disrupt the gate. To do so, the character must touch the edge of the gate's energy field and succeed on a DC 15 Intelligence (Arcana) check. A *dispel magic* spell cast on the gate up to 1 minute beforehand grants advantage on this check. On a failure, the character performing the check takes 7 (2d6) force damage.

Creatures patrolling the Doomvault don't notice the disruption, since a disrupted black gate continues to function normally. However, the gate's active field deals 10 (3d6) force damage (instead of 2d6).

Gatehouse. Thanks to Syranna, the Red Wizard rebels maintain control of an unmapped magic gatehouse, which is how the characters first arrive in Thay and enter the Doomvault. The gatehouse contains several permanent teleportation circles. Syranna can key these circles to any entry point (listed below). Further, any creature that possesses a glyph key can use a black gate to teleport from the Doomvault to a permanent teleportation circle in the gatehouse.

The gatehouse also has a huge physical gate, facing east into Thay just west of Lake Thaylambar. This gate is built into a cliff about 30 miles northwest of Eltabbar and about 30 miles south of Keluthar. Syranna usually keeps this gate sealed, opening it only for emergencies. She raises this gate to allow characters out of the gatehouse and into Thay only if you decide she does so.

Entry Points. Choose a starting location for the party from among the seven entry points in the Doomvault. Black gates in the following areas have entry points labeled on the map: area 1 (Abyssal Prisons), area 23 (Blood Pens), area 33 (Masters' Domain), area 38 (Far Realm Cysts), area 49 (Forests of Slaughter), area 61 (Ooze Grottos), and area 77 (Predator Pools).

Glyph Keys. A magic crystal pendant on a bronze chain, a glyph key allows creatures to manipulate a handful of specific magic gates within the Doomvault. A glyph key is attuned to a zone or zones, allowing manipulation of gates within the attuned areas. For example, a glyph key attuned to the Temple of Chaos (areas 4 through 7) allows its user to use a functional black gate to open a portal to the black gate in area 7, as well as to pass through the white gates between area 4 and area 2, between area 6 and area 8 or area 16, and between area 7 and area 12.

Touching a glyph key provides a telepathic sense of the name of its attuned zone or zones. Thus, when the characters find glyph keys, they know which zones the keys are for.

A glyph key can hold multiple attunements, and attunements can be passed from one key to another. Only one attunement can be passed at a time. To pass an attunement, one creature must hold the originating key and another creature must hold the target key. The keys must touch. Then, as an action, the creature holding the originating key must make a DC 15 Intelligence (Arcana) check. If the check succeeds, each key shares the chosen attunement. If the check fails, the attunement remains in the originating key and each key's holder takes 2 (1d4) force damage. Also, if the check fails by 5 or more, the originating key is destroyed.

Temples of Extraction Glyph Keys. The Temples of Extraction are the site of Szass Tam's dark experiments with the Chosen of the gods, and security there is tighter than anywhere else in the Doomvault. Only four glyph keys to this sector, one for each zone, are outside the Temples of Extraction sector. They are in area 10, area 25, area 31, and area 63. The characters need to find these glyph keys to gain access to the temples.

COMMON FEATURES

This section details further generalities about the Doomvault. Descriptions in specific areas take precedence over this overview.

Atmosphere. Abjuration magic keeps the dungeon dry and at a comfortable temperature. A *detect magic* spell reveals this magic as a faint aura on all the Doomvault's surfaces.

Construction. Regular rooms and their features are of worked and finished stone, mostly marble. Caverns are rough-hewn stone.

Ceilings rise from 20 feet to vaults of 30 feet. Caverns have natural ceilings roughly 30 feet high. Corridor ceilings are 20 feet high.

Contact Stones. Each zone contains a circle of magical glyphs displayed on a wall or an object. These locations serve as contact stones, allowing someone who has a glyph key to contact the gatehouse. The characters can use any contact stone to contact Syranna and have her attune glyph keys to the zone where the contact stone is located.

When the characters see a contact stone on a wall for the first time, use the following description.

> Glowing glyphs form a circle on the wall about three feet off the floor.

Thereafter, you can shorten the description of the contact stones they encounter to avoid repetition.

Normal Doors. The Doomvault's doors are wood reinforced with steel, and they open easily. Most doors lack latches, bars, or locks. Those that are locked require a successful DC 15 Dexterity check to pick or a successful DC 20 Strength check to force open.

Secret Doors. A successful DC 20 Wisdom (Perception) check is required to find a typical secret door.

False Doors. A character must succeed on a DC 20 Intelligence (Investigation) check to determine that a door is real or false without opening it.

Light. Insubstantial magic orbs provide bright light in areas that indicate no other illumination conditions. Boxed text meant to be communicated to the players assumes that someone can see the described area.

Pit Traps. A typical pit trap is under a 5-foot-square section of floor, which forms a lid hinged on the inner side and lined with lead. A character within 5 feet of the lid might notice it with a successful DC 20 passive Perception check. A character who searches the area notices the lid with a successful DC 15 Wisdom (Perception) check. A lid can be jammed so that it remains closed by a character who makes a successful DC 15 Dexterity check. Otherwise, the lid falls open when a Small or larger creature places weight on it.

A creature that triggers the lid must succeed on a DC 15 Dexterity saving throw or fall 20 feet onto a bed of stone spikes, taking 7 (2d6) bludgeoning damage and 13 (2d12) piercing damage. The pit walls are smooth stone. The lid closes magically 5 minutes after being triggered. The lead on the lid prevents the magic of a closed trap from being detected.

DUNGEON DENIZENS

The Red Wizards, aided and abetted by their Thayan servants, hold sway over the Doomvault. In addition to battling the monstrous residents of the dungeon, the characters will need to contend with these humanoids.

Thayans as Foes. Thayan humanoids in the dungeon, especially Red Wizards, prefer to survive encounters with the characters. (All Thayans in the dungeon are non-good in alignment, and most of them are lawful.) When hard pressed, a few might be convinced to surrender, by the use of Charisma (Intimidation or Persuasion) checks. Under interrogation, however, most of these villains lie or otherwise mislead the characters, aiming to kill them with misinformation. Thayans who escape the characters' assault and have no other purpose either leave the Doomvault through the gatehouse or join patrols that attempt to hunt down the characters.

Prisoners. Most humanoid prisoners are terrified and have only enough strength to avoid battle. Prisoners do hard labor or end up as food for the dungeon's monsters. They have no glyph keys and can't leave their zone without help. If able, freed prisoners beg for aid in escaping. If given glyph keys, they head to the gatehouse. Use the **commoner** for prisoners if needed.

REDUCED-THREAT MONSTERS

A reduced-threat monster uses a normal monster's statistics, but it has half the normal hit point maximum and takes a −2 penalty on attack rolls, ability checks, saving throws, and saving throw DCs.

A reduced threat creature that is based on a creature bigger than Large is instead Large. Some specific reduced-threat creatures also make changes to the abilities they can use. A reduced-threat creature is worth half the normal XP earned for defeating it.

DUNGEON STATE

This adventure describes each area as it exists when the characters first arrive in the Doomvault. As they explore, they change the dungeon's state. Record the state each area is in when the characters leave. You need to track which rooms have been explored, which monsters have been defeated, which secrets remain undiscovered, what treasure has been taken, and so on. If the characters return to an area, your notes can remind you what is different from the original text.

RESTING

The incursion into the Doomvault is intended to be a fast-paced assault in which the characters have little time for typical rests. A few areas of the dungeon offer access to special magic that allows characters to gain the benefit of a rest.

The adventure assumes the characters stay in or close to the dungeon for the duration of their exploration. If you want the characters to be able to leave and return to the Doomvault, Syranna can use the circles in the gatehouse to send the party just about anywhere (except the Temples of Extraction or the Phylactery Vault). She can also allow the characters to return by giving them *spell scrolls* of *teleportation circle* keyed to the circles in the gatehouse. If you allow the characters to leave the Doomvault through the gatehouse, the characters can take normal rests outside the dungeon. Doing so has an effect on the alert level.

Resting within the Doomvault is risky, because of random encounters and the rising alert level (see below).

ALERT LEVEL

The Doomvault is an active complex. As effects of the characters' assault grow more widespread or easily detected, the alert level of the dungeon's inhabitants rises. This level starts at 0 and can go no lower than 0. It increases by 1 every 4 hours the characters spend inside the dungeon, including resting. The alert level affects the frequency and difficulty of random encounters.

For each 24 hours the characters spend outside the dungeon, the alert level decreases by 1. During this time, the Doomvault returns to a state more stable than when the characters left. Monsters might be recaptured or replaced, and new challenges could be set up to foil incursions. Alter the dungeon's contents as you see fit to account for the returning party's previous actions and the reactions of their foes.

A few other events specified in the adventure can raise or lower the alert level.

DREAD WARRIORS

Szass Tam devised the ritual that enables the creation of **dread warriors** (described in appendix B). The lich has since altered the process to make it possible for a Red Wizard to take control of a dread warrior. The effect creates a psychic link between the dread warrior and a Red Wizard, who can, for a time, experience the world through the dread warrior's senses, speak with its mouth, and cast spells through it. A powerful wizard can control more than one dread warrior at a time.

When a party in the Doomvault encounters a dread warrior that isn't in the company of a Red Wizard or Tarul Var, a special interaction may occur. If the dread warrior survives until end of the third round (or for more than 20 seconds), Tarul Var (see area 10) becomes aware of the group's presence. Var's attention raises the overall alert level by 1. In addition, Tarul Var takes control of the dread warrior by the start of its next turn. Instead of allowing the warrior to attack, Var uses the warrior's actions to cast his spells through it.

When Var becomes aware of the group through a dread warrior, the warrior's eyes glow with pale light. If someone casts counterspell or dispel magic on the dread warrior during this time, and successfully dispels a 5th-level spell, Var's connection is suppressed for 1 minute. Preemptively casting dispel magic on a dread warrior can have the same effect.

RANDOM ENCOUNTERS

Random encounters help determine if characters meet other creatures moving through the Doomvault. Consider rolling for an encounter in these circumstances:

- The party enters a zone within which they've previously defeated most of the monsters.
- The party moves between zones while the Doomvault has an alert level of 6 or higher.
- The alert level rises.

These encounters are more for atmosphere than challenge. Any random encounter should be foreshadowed with noise or other cues. If a result you roll makes no sense for a given area, select a different result that does.

At least one creature in a random encounter has a glyph key attuned to the zone it is in or an adjacent zone. In cases where foes have no way to enter an area, they instead follow the party into that area.

ENCOUNTER TYPE

If a random encounter is indicated, roll on the Encounter Type table, adding the current alert level to the roll. Then roll on the indicated table to determine the encounter specifics. Statistics for entries marked with (B) on the tables are found in appendix B of this book.

ENCOUNTER TYPE

2d4	Type
2–3	None
4–5	Minor encounter
6–7	Dread Legion patrol
8	Thayan patrol
9–10	Sector encounter
11+	Special encounter

MINOR ENCOUNTER

d4	Encounter
1	1 Thayan apprentice (B), 4 Thayan warriors (B), and 2d4 prisoners (commoners)
2–3	1 wight
4	1 wight and 2d4 skeletons or zombies

DREAD LEGION PATROL

d4	Encounter
1	2d4 gnolls
2	1 dread warrior (B) and 2d6 zombies
3	2d4 orcs
4	1 troll

THAYAN PATROL

2d4	Encounter
2	1 deathlock wight (B), 2d4 Thayan warriors (B), and 2d4 prisoners (commoners)
3–4	1 deathlock wight (B), 1d3 Thayan apprentices (B), and 2d4 Thayan warriors (B)
5–6	1 Red Wizard evoker (B), 1 Thayan apprentice (B), and 1d4 dread warriors (B)
7–8	1 wight and 1d4 dread warriors (B)

SECTOR ENCOUNTERS

If a sector encounter is indicated, roll on the table below that corresponds to the characters' current location. There are no random encounters in the Temples of Extraction.

Unless the dungeon is on high alert (level 6 or higher), a **Thayan apprentice** and 2d4 **Thayan warriors** (see appendix B for both stat blocks) accompany a monster in any sector or individual encounter entry marked with an asterisk.

ABYSSAL PRISONS*

d4	Encounter
1	1 reduced-threat hezrou
2	2d8 manes
3	1d4 quasits
4	1 reduced-threat vrock

BLOOD PENS

d4	Encounter
1	2d6 giant centipedes
2	1d4 giant spiders
3	Thayan patrol (roll on Thayan Patrol table)
4	1 shambling mound*

MASTERS' DOMAIN

d4	Encounter
1	1d4 shadows
2–4	Dread Legion patrol (roll on Dread Legion Patrol table)

Far Realm Cysts*

d4	Encounter
1	1 gibbering mouther
2	1 grell
3	1d4 gricks
4	1 otyugh

Forests of Slaughter*

d4	Encounter
1	1d2 hook horrors
2	1d4 cockatrices
3	1 displacer beast
4	1 troll

Ooze Grottos

d4	Encounter
1	1 black pudding*
2	1 gelatinous cube*
3–4	1d4 gray oozes

Predator Pools

d4	Encounter
1	2d4 giant crabs*
2	2d4 kuo-toa
3	1d2 merrow* (in water globes)
4	1 troll*

Golem Laboratories*

d4	Encounter
1	1 reduced-threat flesh golem
2	1 flesh golem
3	1 reduced-threat clay golem
4	1 clay golem

Special Encounters

If creatures leave their normal areas to roam the dungeon, add them to your notes as possible special encounters. If necessary, Syranna covertly helps such creatures move about the dungeon to add to the confusion and to aid the overall mission. When you roll a special encounter, you can choose from among the creatures in your notes or roll randomly. If a creature is eliminated, delete it from your list of possible special encounters. If you roll this result while no special encounters exist, then the group has an encounter of your choice.

Treasure

The adventure has some treasure built in, but the characters might be able to find more.

Changing Treasure. Feel free to change the treasure in the Doomvault or add more. It's especially appropriate to change treasure to something characters in the party can use, and it's satisfying to let them claim it from a defeated monster or Thayan. For instance, if you'd like to give a character a magic weapon, you can change a weapon-using monster to account for the treasure.

Thayans' Potions. Each group of Thayans has among them 1d4 − 2 potions (minimum 0), each one determined by rolling on the following table.

2d4	Potion
2	Flying
3–4	Climbing
5–7	Healing (1–3), greater healing (4–5), superior healing (6)
8	Invisibility

Red Wizards. Each Red Wizard encountered in the adventure carries 4d10 gp. A Red Wizard also carries 1d4–2 (minimum 0) spell scrolls, each containing a random arcane spell of 1st or 2nd level, most often darkvision, daylight, detect magic, identify, invisibility, or thunderwave. Twenty-five percent of Red Wizards (determine randomly using a d4) instead have one 3rd-level spell scroll, either of dispel magic or remove curse.

Dread Warriors. A dread warrior carries no gold, but some of them have weapons or armor, determined by rolling on the following table.

2d4	Item
2–6	None
7	+1 weapon (usually a battleaxe or a javelin)
8	+1 chain mail

Character Death

When a character dies, the player has a few options.

Soul Binding

The rebel Red Wizards can use the mighty magic of the Doomvault, which traps souls, to raise fallen adventurers as soul-bound dead. If a player chooses this option, the dead character returns to play with no changes.

Syranna warns such characters that a soul-bound creature created in this way will die permanently upon leaving the Doomvault. Furthermore, over the course of many weeks, a character who remains in this state loses any identity and becomes a wight under the control of the Red Wizards. To have any hope of exiting the dungeon, the character must end the soul-bound condition.

Syranna conveys that the undying laboratory (area 31) allows soul-bound characters to transform back to normal, but she lacks the knowledge of how this feat is accomplished.

New Character

The player selects or creates a new character who joins the group. Syranna coordinates uniting newcomers with a group in the dungeon. Such characters might be Thayan Resurrection members anxious to join the fight against Szass Tam. The new character could have been a prisoner in the Doomvault, released to help the rebels. Regardless of origin, the character arrives with the necessary resources and information to join the party.

Doomvault Lore

Some creatures that the characters encounter can divulge important information about the Doomvault. When you give out lore, reveal information appropriate to the creature being questioned based on its location and circumstance. You can make information more specific and useful, but the basics of the lore should be conveyed.

SECTORS

Some pieces of lore are threats and rumors known to those without firsthand experience of a sector. Creatures inside a sector are likely to know more specific details, especially about their neighboring zones; the DM is encouraged to provide appropriate details wherever creatures are noted to have lore to offer.

- In the Abyssal Prisons, the maze of undoing (area 15) has no easy exit, but fiends that can climb are said to have somehow escaped the magic there.
- In the Far Realm Cysts, the creatures of chaos keep intruders away from a powerful shrine.
- In the Forests of Slaughter, the most cunning hunters seek to steal glyph keys.
- In the Forests of Slaughter, magic pools can heal creatures that drink from them.
- In the Golem Laboratories, no Red Wizard will enter the glowing green archways.
- In the Masters' Domain, the Temples of Despair are used for the torture and execution of those who oppose Szass Tam.
- In the Masters' Domain, necromancy can be reshaped to restore life.
- In the Ooze Grottos, the power of the white pillar can heal or harm.
- In the Predator Pools, the hag seeks allies in her plot against the naga.
- In the Predator Pools, vats hold power over life.

TEMPLES OF EXTRACTION

Pieces of lore about the Temples of Extraction are presented in the order in which they should be revealed:

- The Temples of Extraction aren't temples at all but research facilities where Szass Tam's followers conduct profane magical experiments. Few know the specifics of what happens there.
- Only black gates allow access to the Temples of Extraction. Only Szass Tam's most trusted servants have the glyph keys attuned to that sector.
- Szass Tam's latest plan to become a god is his most ambitious. He intends to feed the souls of the Chosen into his phylactery through the Temples of Extraction.
- Szass Tam is making sure that his plan will work by channeling the souls of the Chosen into the phylacteries of his underlings, which are stored in the Phylactery Vault beneath the Doomvault.
- Disrupting the flow of soul energy into the phylacteries should destroy them, dealing an incalculable blow to Szass Tam's power.

PHYLACTERY VAULT

Pieces of lore about the Phylactery Vault are presented in the order in which they should be revealed:

- Beneath the Doomvault, the demilich Kazit Gul slumbers in his Phylactery Vault.
- Szass Tam repurposed the Phylactery Vault for his own magical experiments.

- The phylacteries of the highest-ranking liches in Szass Tam's service rest in the Phylactery Vault, protected by powerful magic. Szass Tam holds the phylacteries there to keep his lackeys in check.
- If enough black gates across the Doomvault are disrupted, the black gates in the Temples of Extraction can be forced to connect to the Phylactery Vault.

INTO THE DOOMVAULT

The characters arrive in the Doomvault through the Bloodgate Nexus or a similar magic portal. How and why they come is up to you. Perhaps the Thayan rebels call for help, alerting forces on the Sword Coast that some of those who assaulted the Bloodgate are alive but captive in the Doomvault. Maybe Syranna snatches heroes from somewhere in the world near another magic gateway. In any case, the characters arrive in the dungeon's gatehouse by teleportation.

To start the adventure, read:

> You arrive in a shadowy hall with glowing teleportation circles etched into the floor. Before you have time to consider your situation, the image of a female Red Wizard suddenly appears and speaks.
>
> "I am Syranna," she says. "It was I who brought you here. Welcome to Thay."

Syranna is present only as an image through which she can sense and communicate. She goes on as follows.

> "Many Red Wizards chafe under the rule of Szass Tam. Once, Thay was a land of learning and power. Now, death scours Thay while the lich lord ignores all concerns other than his quest to become a god. If his mad plans are left to run their course, none will be left alive here to worship him.
>
> "This is a magic gatehouse, from which I can send you to the Doomvault—the heart of the lich lord's domain deep beneath the Thaymount. The Doomvault is a secret laboratory and containment structure, beneath which lies a hidden storehouse where the phylacteries of Szass Tam's elite liches are held. There, the lich lord's power can be broken ... with your aid.
>
> "I offer you an opportunity to take the fight to the lich lord. I offer you the chance to help me see to it that Szass Tam's power is broken. The Phylactery Vault is where you can make that happen.
>
> "What say you?"

Syranna is a rebellion leader who knows that her life could end at any time. She means to make every moment count. She doesn't rest while the characters assault the Doomvault.

Syranna is lawful neutral. She has a sense of righteousness colored by fatalism. Her belief is that death

The Doomvault

Abyssal Prisons

Fiendish Arena

Halls of Conditioning

Pools of Devotion

Entry Point

Warrior Pools

Spawn Pools

Entry Point

Predator Pools

Blood Pools

Ooze Grottos

Augmentation Chambers

Inworld Caverns

Forest of Illusion

Forest of Recovery

Entry Point

Temple of Chaos

Entry Point

Abyssal Gates

Vermin Halls

Swine Run

Blood Pens

Hatchery

Entry Point

Dark Gardens

Temples of Anguish

Temples of Oppression

Temples of Despair

Temples of Turmoil

Temples of Extraction

Flesh Golem Mortuaries

Clay Golem Kilns

Temples of Nature

Masters' Domain

Hall of Necromancy

Golem Laboratories

Iron Golem Foundries

Hall of Obedience

Dread Legion Outpost

Entry Point

Stone Golem Churries

Culling Pens

Forest of Death

Lake of Madness

Warren of Eyes

Spawning Pools

Entry Point

Forests of Slaughter

Forest of Weakness

Prison of Filth

Far Realm Cysts

Caverns of Chaos

Map 5.2: Player Map

is better than being raised as another of Szass Tam's undead servants. With the characters, she is honest and forthright, as well as cynical.

Unfortunately for the characters, Syranna isn't familiar with the inside of the Doomvault. Her position as overseer of the gatehouse has given her only general knowledge of the dungeon. She explains that her ignorance is an intentional part of the dungeon's security structure. If given time, however, she can confirm Doomvault lore that the characters learn.

Syranna can relate the following information to the characters:

- For centuries, the Doomvault was a legend. Kazit Gul, a Red Wizard who spent his life studying the deadliest dungeons on many worlds, planned it. As a living human and a lich, Gul fashioned the vast complex based on his research. The purpose of the dungeon was to lure explorers to their deaths and harvest their souls to fuel Gul's phylactery.
- As Thay became more hostile to outsiders, fewer people sought the Doomvault. Eventually, unable to fuel his phylactery, Gul became a demilich. Szass Tam discovered the Doomvault and saw the opportunity to rebuild and repurpose it.
- The Doomvault is a vast, active complex of laboratories and menageries dedicated to creating the monstrous armies with which the Red Wizards plan to conquer first the North, then all of Faerûn. The dungeon is divided into sectors dedicated to the creation and control of specific types of monsters.
- Each sector is subdivided into protected zones for security, defending against attack from outside and betrayal from within, as well as the escape of confined creatures. Magical white gates block corridors, preventing physical access between zones. Magical black gates are teleportation circles that connect different parts of the dungeon. Syranna describes each gate type's appearance so the characters know the gates by sight.
- Magic crystals called glyph keys, when attuned to a zone, allow access to that zone's gates. Syranna describes the use of glyph keys, including how to transfer attunements. She also describes contact stones and how the characters can use them to contact her directly. Through contact stones, the characters can also gain glyph key attunements for the zone in which the contact stone is situated. Syranna initially provides the party with one glyph key.
- The characters have three goals: (1) Destroy the Red Wizards' monstrous creations and experiments to end the threat to Faerûn. (2) Gain access to the Phylactery Vault deep beneath the dungeon. (3) Destroy the phylacteries within the vault.
- Tarul Var's quarters lie in the Doomvault. Although the lich was defeated, he might have already rematerialized thanks to the power of his phylactery. Protected by his dread warriors, he is a deadly threat.
- Syranna provides information on dread warriors and how Tarul Var uses them.
- Szass Tam controls entry to the Phylactery Vault. Syranna knows the vault connects to the greater Doomvault, but hasn't discovered how to access it.

MAP 5.3: ABYSSAL PRISONS

- The rebels will use their power to stop magical communications to the outside and contain any enemies who escape from the Doomvault. They'll make sure that no one outside the dungeon knows of or reacts to what's happening until the characters succeed.
- Thayans have taken two adventurers, Shalendra Floshin and Kelson Darktreader, prisoner. They are likely dead or within the Doomvault.

Once the characters are finished talking, Syranna teleports in a map of the dungeon for the party (give the players map 5.2) and a glyph key attuned to the zone you chose as an entry point. She wishes the party well.

ABYSSAL PRISONS

Originally an area containing summoning traps, this sector has been changed into a place for confining demons. Thayans break the will of imprisoned fiends and bind them into service.

Locations in the Abyssal Prisons are identified on map 5.3.

Light. Dim light radiates from the walls, floors, and ceilings in this sector, a manifestation of strengthened dimensional barriers that prevent fiends from teleporting or summoning other demons within the sector.

FIENDISH ARENA

In this zone, a vampire named Issem culls the weakest demons using arena combat. When the demons fight, the battle can be heard in every chamber in this zone (see "Pit Battle" in area 2 to aid in narrating the noise).

1. Chandelier Chamber

> Scorched and shattered plaster shows faint signs of frescoes that once covered the walls here. A half-dozen ruined chandeliers hang from the cracked ceiling. In the northeast corner is a black gate.

Creatures. A **vampire spawn** keeps watch here, along with a **wight** and four **zombies**. A **quasit** perches invisibly on a chandelier.

Negotiation. Prisoners regularly move through the black gate here. The characters can bluff their way through by talking to Eldrath, a female human vampire spawn that challenges them. If the characters fail to talk their way through or make it obvious in any way that they don't belong here, the monsters attack.

2. Arena

> This area might once have been a columned temple. Its rotting tapestries show foul creatures tormenting humanoids in scenes of slaughter and sacrifice. At the center of this vast space, the stone floor has been hewn to create a pit. This pit is covered with the gory remains of past bloodshed.

Creatures. Issem, a pale human **vampire** in lavish clothes, is normally in this area, watching battles.

Negotiation. An old curse binds Issem to the Doomvault and to the service of the Thayans, but he hates the Red Wizards, so he is willing to talk. He can offer two pieces of lore (see "Doomvault Lore," page 115), and he allows prisoners and the characters to leave the area. He is willing to lie to any Thayans who seek the characters and help them cover their tracks.

Issem warns anyone who tries to enter area 3 against doing so. If someone does anyway, the vampire attacks.

Fighting Pit. This rough-hewn arena is 15 feet lower than the floor around it and imbued with magic. Any non-undead creature that approaches within 10 feet of the edge must succeed on a DC 13 Wisdom saving throw or be compelled to leap into the pit (a creature ignores this effect if immune to being charmed). Such a creature can't leave the pit until all the demons within it are destroyed. The pit is otherwise easy to climb.

Pit Battle. In the pit, a reduced-threat **vrock** (see "Reduced-Threat Monsters," page 113) is fighting ten prisoners, nine of whom are human **commoners**. The tenth is a gold elf **knight** named Shalendra Floshin. Half the humans each deal 1 slashing damage to the vrock each round, and Shalendra deals 10 damage to the vrock every round. The demon focuses on one target each round (roll randomly). If the characters join the battle, the vrock attacks them.

Glyph Key. Issem has a glyph key attuned to this zone. He is willing to share the key's attunement in return for a taste of fresh blood. Any character who agrees to this bargain suffers the effects of Issem's bite attack.

SHALENDRA FLOSHIN

Development. If the characters succeed in getting Issem to cover for them, the Doomvault's alert level decreases by 1.

Shalendra. Thayans captured Shalendra during the assault on the Bloodgate. She has managed to survive and help other prisoners stay alive. While doing so, she has learned one piece of lore. Shalendra asks for a glyph key; if given one, she goes to the gatehouse to recuperate. If not, she goes looking for a key on her own. Either way, before she leaves, she can help the party for a time if they (and you) wish.

White Gates. The corridor to the east contains a white gate that connects with the Temple of Chaos. Another white gate stands in the corridor that leads south to the Pools of Devotion.

3. Issem's Vault

Deadly traps, which Issem avoids while in mist form, protect the vampire's sarcophagus.

> This chamber has walls draped in black silk. Gleaming prisms float in midair, spinning slowly. At the center of the area, a great sarcophagus with its lid pushed ajar stands atop a stone dais. Along the upper edge of the sarcophagus, a series of arcane glyphs pulses with pale white light.

PENCHESKA, SUCCUBUS

Cursed Prisms. Unless Issem is in the room, each character who is in the room and can see the prisms must make a DC 13 Wisdom saving throw at the start each of his or her turns. The first time each character fails the save, a **wraith** that looks like a shadowy duplicate of that character erupts from a prism and attacks.

Pit Traps. As shown on the map, the floor has many pit traps.

Contact Stone. The glyphs on the sarcophagus cause it to serve as a contact stone.

Treasure. Inside the sarcophagus are six *spell scrolls* (three of *detect magic*, two of *comprehend languages*, and one of *greater restoration*). Also inside is a bottle of ink and an ink pen with fifteen sheets of parchment.

Glyph Key. In addition to its treasure, the sarcophagus holds a glyph key attuned to this zone.

TEMPLE OF CHAOS

Tarul Var reconfigured this zone for his use.

4. MYSTIC CIRCLES

> The wood-paneled walls of this long hall are scorched. Cracks in the panels reveal bare stone. Three mystic circles have been scribed in the floor, each edged with rough runes.

Locked Doors. These steel double doors are locked. Tarul Var (area 10) has a key in his possession.

Steel Orb. A magic steel orb is hidden in a recess in the ceiling 20 feet up. Spotting it requires a successful DC 20 Wisdom (Perception) check. The steel orb is part of the mystic circle trap.

Mystic Circle Trap. The circles are magical but misleadingly so. A successful DC 15 Intelligence (Arcana) check reveals that hidden among gibberish runes are warding glyphs that discharge lightning. If the check fails, the character discerns the false runes but doesn't notice the glyphs.

The trap activates 3 rounds after a creature enters the room. (Tarul Var's steel key disables the trap for 1 minute when it is used to open the door to area 5.) At the start of the fourth round, and every 2 rounds thereafter, one circle (chosen randomly) glows white. At the end of the same round, lightning discharges through the room from the steel orb in the ceiling. When the lightning discharges, any creature in the room must make a DC 10 Dexterity saving throw. On a failed save, a creature takes 7 (2d6) lightning damage.

A character who touches the steel orb and succeeds on a DC 15 Intelligence (Arcana) check can suppress the orb's magic, disabling the trap for 1d4 rounds. A *dispel magic* spell cast on the orb suppresses the magic for 1 hour. In both cases, the character doesn't know how long the suppression might last. The circles continue to glow at random.

White Gate. The corridor that separates this area from the Fiendish Arena contains a white gate.

5. SUCCUBUS VAULT

> The sweet scent of incense hangs in the hot air of this opulent chamber. The walls are covered with silk tapestries in green and yellow, and the floors are spread with cushions. To the south, two sets of sliding double wooden doors are set in the walls.

Creatures. Pencheska, a **succubus**, resides here with four **Thayan warriors** (see appendix B), who are in her thrall. Pencheska is an unwilling servant of Tarul Var.

If she is alerted to the characters' approach, the succubus takes on a humanoid form. She attempts to convince the characters that she is being held prisoner.

Pencheska isn't pleased with her situation and won't directly oppose the characters unless they attack her. She is willing to provide a piece of lore about the Phylactery Vault in the hope that the characters might destroy Tarul Var for good, freeing her to escape the Doomvault.

Closets. The sliding wooden doors open to reveal closets that contain fine female clothing in numerous styles and sizes. The easternmost closet contains a hemispherical stone in the middle of its back wall. The stone serves as a contact stone in this zone.

Heat. This chamber is uncomfortably hot due to the fire elemental in area 6. The heat grows more intense to the east and in the eastern secret passage.

Treasure. Pencheska's adornments include a gold gorget set with yellow topazes (500 gp), matching earrings (250 gp), a ruby ring (300 gp), an intricate jade necklace (400 gp) and two matching jade rings (200 gp each).

In the westernmost closet, hooks hold several items of jewelry, including a simple gold necklace and bracelet (250 gp each), a silver necklace with a garnet pendant (250 gp), and an ivory necklace (100 gp).

Glyph Key. Pencheska has a glyph key attuned to this zone, which hangs in the closet among her jewelry.

6. ELEMENTAL FURNACE

A character who listens at either doorway feels heat and hears a crackling roar.

> A blast of heat escapes as the door opens. A howling creature of flame roils at the center of a soot-streaked stone chamber whose walls are lined with glowing runes.

Creature. The **fire elemental** here flares out toward any creature it can see, but the runes on the wall glow more brightly when it does, and it stops short of making contact with any intruder. The elemental can't attack or leave the room. Instead, it babbles in Ignan (a dialect of Primordial), often using the word "home." Even though the elemental doesn't attack, any creature that ends its turn in the room takes 3 (1d6) fire damage as long as the elemental is present.

The runes on the wall are a set of arcane bonds that keep the elemental confined here. A character who makes a successful DC 15 Intelligence (Arcana) check discerns the connection. If a character who can cast spells then succeeds on three consecutive DC 15 Intelligence (Arcana) checks while continually touching the wall, the bonds are suppressed long enough for the elemental to leave the room. A *dispel magic* spell cast on the runes suppresses the bonds for 1 minute.

The elemental follows its rescuer, fighting alongside that person. If the elemental sees the rift in area 7, it uses the rift to leave the Doomvault and return to the Elemental Plane of Fire.

White Gate. A white gate is located east of this area at the junction of the corridors that lead to the Abyssal Gate and to the Vermin Halls.

7. CHAOS RIFT

Characters approaching this area can hear the roar of the elemental rift, which also generates bright light in the entire chamber.

> This enormous hall is set with rows of pillars carved in the shapes of elemental and demonic creatures. A great rift has been torn in the center of the stone floor. Through it, a stream of chaotic energy blasts upward, flowing into a similar rift in the vaulted ceiling forty feet above. Tendrils split off from the pulsing column of energy, lashing out to strike the nearest pillars.
>
> In the southwest corner is a black gate.

A character who succeeds on a DC 10 Intelligence (Arcana) check can tell that the rift is channeling elemental forces. If the check succeeds by 5 or more, the character knows that the rift is dangerous and is channeling extraplanar elemental forces.

If a non-elemental creature ends its turn inside the room, it takes 5 (2d4) damage of a random type (roll a d10: 1–2, acid; 3–4, cold; 5–6, fire; 7–8, lightning; 9–10, thunder).

Any creature that enters the rift can choose to remain here or go to an elemental plane. Characters who go to an elemental plane must use the rift to return on their next turn or they become trapped.

ABYSSAL GATE

Tarul Var oversees this zone, in which the Thayans have tapped Abyssal power.

8. SUMMONING CHAMBER

A character listening at the doors can hear the shrieks of any demons bound here.

> This area might once have been a great banquet hall, but its furnishings now lie in rotting piles along the walls. Between rows of pillars, six great magic circles glow brightly, illuminating the whole chamber.

Creatures. One **dread warrior** (see appendix B), two **wights**, and six **zombies** patrol the area.

Summoning Circles. Two summoning circles are empty. The other four contain creatures:

Circle A. One reduced-threat **hezrou** (see "Reduced-Threat Monsters," page 113)
Circle B. Four **quasits**
Circle C. One reduced-threat **vrock** (see "Reduced-Threat Monsters," page 113)
Circle D. Ten **manes**

A bound demon can't escape from its circle without assistance, and aside from attempts to communicate, nothing it does can affect anything outside the circle. All demons except for the manes ask to be released, promising to attack the Thayan forces if they are freed.

TARUL VAR, LICH

With a successful DC 10 Intelligence (Arcana) check, a character knows that, as an action, they can scuff the boundary of a circle to disrupt the circle's magic for 1 minute. During that time, a demon within the circle can break free with a successful DC 15 Wisdom check.

A freed demon attacks the nearest creature that isn't a demon.

Development. If any demon other than the manes remains free in this area, all the demons are eventually freed from their circles by the others. They spill out into the zone and attack any creature they find. That fact should be noted as part of the dungeon state.

White Gates. A white gate is located north of this area at the junction of the corridors that lead to the Temple of Chaos and to the Vermin Halls. Another gate lies in the passage to the east that connects with the Swine Run.

9. Dead End

A set of double doors is inlaid with brass filigree, marking out the shapes of angelic figures.

Advance Notice. A character who searches the floor in the eastern corridor and succeeds on a DC 15 In-

telligence (Investigation) or Wisdom (Survival) check ascertains that no other creatures have entered this side passage in a long time.

If examined with a *detect magic* spell, the area displays an aura of necromancy.

Stunning Shadow Trap. If the doors are opened, roll initiative. Darkness immediately fills the corridor out to 20 feet from the doors. Any non-undead creature that starts its turn in the area must succeed on a DC 15 Charisma saving throw or take 7 (2d6) necrotic damage and become paralyzed until the start of its next turn. The darkness remains as long as the doors are open.

10. Tarul Var's Quarters

Tapestries line the walls of these well-appointed living quarters. Standing screens divide the space into smaller sections containing couches, tables, and desks.

Creatures. Here resides the lich **Tarul Var** with his guards, four **dread warriors** (see appendix B for both stat blocks). Having lost the Bloodgate, Var is confined to this area because of his fear of Szass Tam, while he awaits his master's final judgment.

The lich attacks immediately. His guards emerge from various positions to screen him from direct attack. Tarul Var can cast any of his spells from one of the dread warriors.

The dread warriors attempt to drag any helpless characters to the pit in the intersection near this room or to area 9, where they throw open the doors.

Devious and arrogant, Tarul Var thinks all other creatures are beneath him. He berates the characters at every opportunity, and he drives his underlings to cruelty.

If reduced to 30 hit points or fewer, Var offers the party access to his glyph key's attunements and his steel key (see "Treasure" below), as well as two pieces of lore, in exchange for his freedom and his silence. If the characters let Var go, he flees the Doomvault, reasoning that the characters' disruptions will draw Szass Tam's attention away from him. If the lich is destroyed here, he might later be destroyed permanently if the party succeeds in collapsing the Phylactery Vault.

Contact Stone. A circle of glowing glyphs above Var's desk in the western section of the room serves as a contact stone.

Treasure. A search of the desk reveals several drafts of a letter to Szass Tam in which Var begs for another chance to bring the Sword Coast under Thayan domination. Inside the desk's several drawers are a *potion of mind reading* and a duplicate of the steel key that Var carries.

The largest drawer of the desk is held closed with an *arcane lock* spell (requiring a successful DC 25 Strength check to break). Inside is a flat box of black wood (see the next subsection) and a gold coffer wrought to look like a sleeping dragon with violet garnet eyes (worth 1,000 gp). The coffer holds 200 pp and a dark, smooth river rock (a *loadstone*; see appendix A).

True Name Box. If *detect magic* is used on the black box, the contents give off an aura of evocation magic. The box contains several pieces of parchment. A portion of the top page stored in the box has runes on it that, when read by anyone other than Tarul Var, cause the page to explode.

The runes can be neutralized by using *dispel magic* on the box or the page. Alternatively, a character who makes a successful DC 10 Intelligence check can remove the page from the box without inadvertently reading the runes. If the check fails, the character reads the runes accidentally, triggering the explosion.

If the page explodes, everyone within 10 feet of the box must make a DC 15 Dexterity saving throw, which the reader makes with disadvantage. A creature takes 21 (6d6) force damage on a failed saving throw and half as much damage on a successful one. The box and its contents are destroyed if the runes go off.

The box contains records of true names of minor devils and describes plans to use them in the attack on the Sword Coast. It also contains historical documents that indicate that Var was searching for the true name of a pit fiend called Baazka.

Keys. Tarul Var carries a glyph key attuned to this zone and to the Temples of Anguish (in the Temples of Extraction sector). He also has an ornate steel key (worth 5 gp) that opens the locked doors on the east wall of area 4.

11. Torture Chamber

A character who listens at the doors can hear the howls of the glabrezu if it's bound here.

> The walls of this torture chamber are hung with chains and spears encrusted with black ichor. In a few places, heavy black chains are fastened to the floor. In the northeast corner is a black gate.

Creatures. A **wight** and seven **skeletons** are tormenting a prone, reduced-threat **glabrezu** (see "Reduced-Threat Monsters," page 113) that is shackled and chained to the floor in four places. The undead attack interlopers, using pikes as weapons (1d10 piercing damage). The undead have magic weapons (see "Treasure" below).

Shackled Glabrezu. The bound glabrezu can't free itself. It can't cast spells or summon demons. It can attack only if a creature comes within 5 feet of it, which is why the undead are using pikes. When a battle starts, the demon demands to be freed, promising to "lay waste to these undead and their masters." If the characters refuse to aid it, the demon attacks them if it can.

To free the demon, a character must pick the locks of all four iron shackles (requiring a successful DC 15 Dexterity check for each). If it is freed, the glabrezu rampages, randomly attacking anyone in reach. Once free, it can cast spells, but it still can't summon demons.

Shackles. The ten sets of shackles and their chains are made of rune-scribed iron. A demon held in them can't escape them while the shackles are closed. The magic on the chains renders them unbreakable, so they can't be removed from this room.

Dungeon State. If the glabrezu is left free in this area, it eventually frees the demons in area 8 from their circles. That fact should be noted as part of the dungeon state.

Treasure. The skeletons' pikes are enchanted with *magic weapon* (+1) for 1 more hour. The wight wields a *+1 pike*.

Halls of Conditioning

After their initial subjugation, captured demons are held in the Halls of Conditioning, where they are properly broken to service.

12. False Pit Gauntlet

Communicate the boxed text before any character crosses the threshold into this room.

> The walls here consist of worked stone, but the thirty-foot-high ceiling of this broad chamber features rough rock hung with jagged stalactites. Seams in the floor tiles divide the space into squares five feet on a side. An open pit extends halfway across each of the four entryways, just inside the room.

Aura. A *detect magic* spell cast on this area reveals that magic permeates the entire room, focused most strongly at the open mouth of each pit.

False Pits. The pits appear normal, but an invisible force field extends across the apparently open space atop each pit. The horizontal field can hold the weight of any number of characters.

Gravity Trap. Any creature that enters the room and walks across the invisible field covering one of the open pits deactivates the gravity trap for 1 minute. Once deactivated, characters can move freely across the room for 1 minute before the trap reactivates. If the trap is active, any creature that enters the room without stepping onto the invisible field over one of the false pits is hurled toward the ceiling, taking 10 (3d6) piercing damage from the stalactites and remaining restrained on the ceiling for 1 minute. Then the creature is released and drops to the floor, taking 10 (3d6) falling damage and landing prone in a random square near the center of the chamber. Moving onto or over the floor triggers the gravity trap again, but the creature can remain safe if it stays in the space where it fell until another character deactivates the trap.

13. Sorlan's Haunt

The lock plainly visible on each of the double doors is false. The real locks and keyholes are hidden in the base of each door and detectable with a successful DC 15 Wisdom (Perception) check. If any attempt is made to pick a false lock or force the doors, any creature within 10 feet of the doors must succeed on a DC 14 Constitution saving throw (with disadvantage, if trying to pick a lock or force the doors) or take 5 (2d4) force damage and be knocked prone.

> This ruined chamber has tapestries and paintings that
> have been slashed and are shot through with black mold.
> The fine furnishings and cushions are rotted through and
> crumbling, and the air is heavy with the scent of decay.

Creature. Sorlan, a former adventurer who was imprisoned by the Red Wizards and subjected to horrible experiments, lives on as a **ghost** that is bound to this room. He hates the Red Wizards, and he immediately tries to attack all who enter his chamber, screaming that allies of the Red Wizards must die. If the characters convince Sorlan that they are opposed to the Red Wizards by making a successful DC 15 Charisma (Persuasion) check, the ghost stops attacking and can provide two pieces of lore, which he has overheard from passing Red Wizards.

Sorlan also tells the characters to avoid the maze of undoing (area 15), which is where he was captured while trying to escape the dungeon. He doesn't know the trick to overcoming the teleportation trap. If he is slain, Sorlan reappears in this area 24 hours later.

White Gate. The secret door on the west wall opens into a narrow corridor that leads to a white gate. Beyond the gate (and another secret door) is a corridor that connects with the Pools of Devotion.

14. DEMON CELLS

> Several cages line this chamber from floor to ceiling.
> Three of them hold various demons, which are raging
> futilely and silently against their confinement. The wall in
> the southwest corner contains a contact stone.

Creatures. One Red Wizard **conjurer** oversees one **deathlock wight** and one **Thayan apprentice** (see appendix B for all three stat blocks). The conjurer knows the pass phrase for the maze of undoing (area 15) and might provide it to the characters in exchange for mercy, knowing that freed demons will attack their "rescuers."

Cells. Cells that confine demons hold the following creatures:

Cell A. One **hezrou**
Cell B. Eight **quasits**
Cell C. Two **vrocks**

Each cell has iron, rune-scribed bars (warded against demons). Transmutation magic on the bars renders them unbreakable, so a demon can't escape the cell and, indeed, can't pass any part of its body between the bars. Further, no sound can pass out of a cell into the larger room. To free a demon, a character must pick the lock on the cage door (requiring a successful DC 20 Dexterity check). A freed demon attacks everyone in the room.

Keys. The Red Wizard has a glyph key attuned to this zone, as well as a ring of keys to the cells.

Dungeon State. If any demon remains free in this area, all the demons are eventually freed from their cells. That fact should be noted as part of the dungeon state.

15. MAZE OF UNDOING

> A short hall of gray granite runs perpendicular to this area's entrance, with six openings across from the entrance that lead deeper into the darkness. The cold stone ceiling looms thirty feet overhead.

Teleportation Maze. Conjuration magic infuses the area, emanating most strongly at the trigger points numbered 1 through 20, and at the two entry/exit trigger points labeled E on the map. In addition to the teleportation trigger points, the magic aligns gravity to the nearest surface. Therefore, creatures standing on the floor consider "down" to be beneath their feet, while creatures on the ceiling consider that surface to be "down" and are situated accordingly. The entire area was created to capture and hold demons.

Any creature that enters a trigger point on the floor teleports immediately to the ceiling above another trigger point (determined by a d20 roll). The creature must then succeed on a DC 15 Wisdom saving throw or take 5 (2d4) psychic damage and fall to the floor, taking 10 (3d6) falling damage and triggering another teleportation point. On a successful save, the creature takes no damage and can utilize the weird gravity until the end of its next turn, walking along the ceiling and walls as though they were the floor, and bypassing the teleportation triggers. If the creature is still above the floor at the end of its next turn, it falls the appropriate distance to the floor and triggers another teleportation point.

In addition to conjuration magic, the entry/exit points also radiate abjuration magic. Until someone utters the proper pass phrase (see area 14), a demon caught in the maze can't pass through either of the entry/exit points. For non-demons, leaving the maze can be accomplished by moving along the walls or ceiling and out of the area through either entry/exit point.

Creature. When the characters arrive, a **glabrezu** is trapped in the maze. The demon has learned how to navigate the maze, even though it can't escape the area. Place the demon on the ceiling above a random teleportation trigger point in the maze (roll a d20). Once the demon notices the characters, it moves toward characters it can see and in its rage and madness attacks any creatures it manages to reach.

Black Gate. A black gate is set into the southern alcove, not immediately visible from the entrance.

BLOOD PENS

The Red Wizards are breeding and raising monsters in their own foul nurseries.

Locations in the Blood Pens are identified on map 5.4.

VERMIN HALLS

The vermin-summoning magic of these halls now serves the Thayans.

16. GALLERY OF SWARMS
The Red Wizards no longer use this chamber.

Sounds. A character who listens at the door and succeeds on a DC 10 Wisdom (Perception) check hears distant chittering.

Light. None.

The sunken floor of this huge hall is covered in dead insects, their dried shells shifting and whispering in a faint breeze. Dozens of demonic faces are carved in the white marble walls of the chamber, slight gusts whistling from each of their open mouths. Down the center of the chamber, toward the doors at the far end, a series of black stone platforms are set like oversized stepping stones.

Demonic Faces. The mouths of these relief carvings are the source of the magical breeze.

Insect Floor. The floor is 2 feet below the level of the doors and filled completely with dead insects along with occasional bones, making it difficult terrain.

Pit Traps. Scattered through the room, hidden beneath the blanket of insect bodies, are several pit traps. It is impossible to notice a pit passively; finding one requires a successful DC 20 Wisdom (Perception) check. Each pit is filled with dead insects, so falling into one deals only half damage. Someone buried in a pit full of these husks can't breathe or see.

Trapped Platforms. Whenever a creature steps onto a platform, it must succeed on a DC 10 Constitution saving throw or be engulfed by a swarm of biting, stinging insects that emerge from the demonic faces. The creature takes 5 (2d4) piercing damage and 5 (2d4) poison damage, and must succeed on a DC 15 Dexterity saving throw or fall off the platform in a random direction. The insects die and fall to the ground immediately after their attack.

White Gates. A white gate is located west of this area at the junction of the corridors that lead to the Temple of Chaos and to the Abyssal Gate.

17. CRAWLING HALL

Two enormous pillars on the far side of this chamber emit brilliant white light that holds the attention of dozens of giant vermin crawling on and around them. The vermin occasionally fight among themselves, but most of these creatures move sluggishly, as if the light has subdued them.

Glowing Pillars. The pillars emit magical light, which pacifies the vermin and keeps their handlers safe.

Creatures. Two **Thayan apprentices** (see appendix B) are feeding the vermin scraps and pig excrement from buckets. Six **Thayan warriors** (see appendix B) guard the apprentices. All the Thayans attack as soon as they notice intruders. Each round of combat, the Thayans direct one **giant spider** and one **giant centipede** to join the fight.

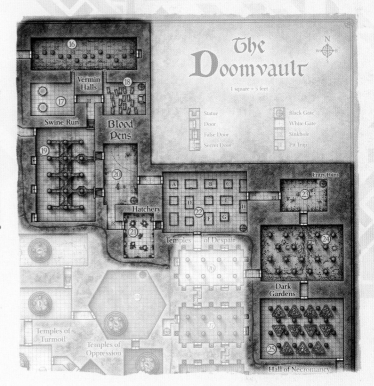

MAP 5.4: BLOOD PENS

Development. Vermin left in this chamber grow hungry, feeding on any dead creatures. Within a few hours, they begin killing and feeding on each other.

Glyph Key. One Thayan has a glyph key attuned to this zone.

White Gate. A white gate is located in the south branch of the corridor that leads east from this area toward the Swine Run.

18. BARRACKS

Rough cots scattered across the floor contrast with the decor in the east end of the room, which contains a great seat of white marble. Some of the magic lights are shrouded, so that side of the room is dimly lit.

In the northeast corner is a black gate. West of it is a contact stone.

Creatures. Six **Thayan apprentices** and eight **Thayan warriors** (see appendix B for both stat blocks) are resting here, watched over by a **wight**. Half the warriors and apprentices are asleep in the eastern side of the chamber. When the other creatures notice the characters, they attack. The sleeping Thayans awaken and join the fight over the course of 2 or 3 rounds.

Throne Swarm Trap. The 20-foot-tall white throne is a magic trap that the Thayans might use if desperate. When any non-undead creature climbs onto it, a swarm of stinging insects pours out of the back of the throne and quickly fills the chamber. Each creature in the room takes 9 (2d8) piercing damage and 9 (2d8) poison damage. For 1 minute thereafter, each creature that ends its turn in the room takes 4 (1d8) piercing damage and 4 (1d8) poison damage. The insects disappear after 1 minute, and the trap resets.

Glyph Keys. One Thayan has a glyph key attuned to this zone and the Swine Run. Another has a glyph key attuned to this zone and the Hatchery.

White Gate. A white gate is located in the south branch of the corridor that leads west from this area toward the Swine Run.

SWINE RUN

These adjoining halls have been converted into a pig farm to feed carnivorous monsters.

19. WALKWAY PEN

Sounds. The unmistakable squealing and grunting of pigs can be heard from outside any of the entrances.

Blocked Stairs. Slabs of stone, each 5 feet high, block the stairs that descend into this hall along the north and east sides. Climbing over a slab costs 10 feet of movement. Once over a slab, a character can step onto a plank bridge (see below).

Knocking a slab down requires a successful DC 20 Strength check. If a slab is knocked down, the bridge collapses and packs of pigs rush into the open area (see "Pigpens" below).

> What once must have been a great hall is now a great swine pen. Three rows of thick pillars support the ceiling. Each pillar is marked with a large X in red paint. Pigs, perhaps hundreds of them, are packed in here, shoulder to shoulder, on the floor. Ten feet above them, skeletal undead stand on a crude bridge of wooden planks, dumping food into the pigpen.

Creatures. Three **deathlock wights** (see appendix B) oversee six **skeletons**. They attack intruders.

Aura. A *detect magic* spell reveals a transmutation aura on the whole area, which is a simple magical effect to control the pigs' odor.

Bridges. A series of unsteady plank bridges runs 10 feet above the floor, lashed to the pillars and to the slabs of rock that block the eastern stairs. Any creature that falls unconscious while on a bridge has a 50 percent chance to fall into the pigpen.

Enchanted Pillars. A *detect magic* spell reveals that each pillar radiates an aura of enchantment magic. Any humanoid that touches a pillar must succeed on a DC 13 Wisdom saving throw or fall unconscious for 1 minute. (The Thayans marked the pillars as a reminder for themselves.) A *dispel magic* spell suppresses the magic of the pillars for 1 minute.

Floating Disk. An opaque, slightly concave, circular plane of magical force, 5 feet in diameter, floats on the northern side of the northern bridge to area 20. The

disk can hold up to 1,000 pounds. It is stationary and level with the bridge, but it can be mentally directed by anyone who can see it (DC 10 Intelligence) to float to the blocked stairway that leads up to the Vermin Halls (areas 16–18).

Pigpens. The pigs are maltreated, hungry, and irritated. They swarm any creature that enters the pen. Such a creature must succeed on a DC 13 Dexterity saving throw at the start of each of its turns or take 3 (1d6) bludgeoning damage and 3 (1d6) piercing damage. Characters who take 12 damage also are knocked prone. Single-target attacks against the pigs have little effect, but an area spell clears its area of pigs until the end of the caster's next turn.

The enclosed area beneath the bridge is filled with sows and piglets. The DC for the Dexterity saving throw here is only 8.

Drevin. One pig is much smaller than the others, and looks especially malnourished. A *detect magic* spell reveals that the creature radiates transmutation magic. The pig is in fact a lightfoot halfling named Drevin. He was a minstrel (use the **spy** statistics) who ran afoul of a Red Wizard transmuter. If freed of the *true polymorph* spell he is under, Drevin accompanies the characters until he is permitted to escape the Doomvault, at which point he departs amid promises to write great ballads about the characters' exploits.

Glyph Keys. Each wight has a glyph key attuned to this zone.

20. ABATTOIR

> Empty wall niches might once have held works of art, but this broad gallery has now been converted to an abattoir, its floor slick with filth and gore.
>
> In the southeast corner is a black gate. North of the gate is a contact stone.

If the pigs from area 19 rush into this room, they move unwittingly toward the skeletons, knocking half of them prone before retreating back into the pigpen.

Aura. A *detect magic* spell reveals a faint aura of transmutation magic on the whole area, which is a simple magical effect to control the odor of the butchery.

Creatures. Twelve **skeletons** are here, with a **wight** and a **deathlock wight** (see appendix B) overseeing them. Eight work to the east, stacking butchered pigs along the wall. To the west, four more work at a sluice that carries offal to the black gate, where it disappears (transported to area 41). Occasionally they toss some of the foul slop toward an **otyugh** chained to the floor.

The otyugh can move 40 feet from the northeast corner, anywhere within the area described by the dashed line on the map. It attacks any creature it can reach. If it can't attack, the otyugh uses its turn to attempt a DC 20 Strength check to break its chain while its captors are distracted.

With its childlike intellect and telepathy, the otyugh broadcasts its desire for more food. The characters are able to communicate with the creature, and if they offer to feed it, the otyugh ceases attacking for 1 round. Then the characters must periodically placate it with successful DC 10 Charisma (Persuasion) checks. A character who frees the otyugh learns that more of its kind are in the dungeon and receives a general impression of area 42, where more otyughs live. All these otyughs hate the Thayans.

Niches. The shallow niches are 3 feet off the floor and 5 feet high. Climbing into a niche costs 10 feet of movement.

Dungeon State. If the otyugh is given a glyph key to the Prison of Filth and told how to use a black gate, it teleports to area 41 and reaches area 42. Its presence there will change the characters' encounter with the other otyughs (see area 42).

Glyph Key. The wight has a glyph key attuned to this zone and the Prison of Filth.

White Gates. The corridor that leads east to area 22 in the Hatchery contains a white gate. Another white gate is situated in the southern passage that connects with area 21 in the Hatchery.

HATCHERY

Thayans tend and hatch the eggs of exotic monsters in these areas, rearing the young to serve Thay.

21. EGG CHAMBER

The two approaches to this area are warm and humid.

> Heat wafts from this chamber, and steam obscures parts of the room. Stone braziers built into the walls burn with orange flame, as do braziers in various places across the room. The floor is covered with sand, on which rest dozens of large eggs of various colors and textures.

Creatures. A Red Wizard **enchanter** (see appendix B), one **dread warrior** (see appendix B), and six **skeletons** oversee the eggs. If combat breaks out, the wizard sends the undead forward as a screen and uses targeted spells that won't harm the eggs.

Braziers. The magic stone braziers are built into the room and can't be moved. A creature that touches a brazier for the first time on a turn takes 3 (1d6) fire damage.

Eggs. Clusters of eggs make this area difficult terrain. None of the eggs is close to hatching. One person with a weapon could destroy all the eggs in about 5 minutes. Leaving the eggs untended also renders them lifeless. The eggs are those of an assortment of creatures, including hook horrors, remorhazes, wyverns, and basilisks, with 1d6 + 1 of each kind. Identifying a particular kind of egg requires a successful DC 20 Intelligence (Nature) check.

Steam. Steam renders this chamber lightly obscured.

Glyph Key. The Red Wizard has a glyph key attuned to this zone.

White Gate. In the corridor beyond the western exit is a white gate that separates area 21 from the Swine Run.

22. HATCHLING PENS

Anyone near the doors hears the shrieking and howling of the caged creatures.

> Relief carvings of angelic figures along the walls of this huge hall contrast with the crowded iron cages here. Half of these cells are packed with miniature, shrieking versions of deadly monsters.
>
> In the southeast corner is a black gate. North of the gate is a contact stone.

Aura. A *detect magic* spell reveals a transmutation aura on the whole area, which is a simple magical effect to control the odor of the hatchlings and their food.

Creatures. A Red Wizard **transmuter** oversees two **Thayan apprentices** in caring for the imprisoned hatchlings, while four **Thayan warriors** stand guard (see appendix B for all three stat blocks). They attack intruders. In a desperate battle, the Red Wizard might take the time to release hatchlings to add to the characters' opposition.

If the battle goes badly for the Thayans, the Red Wizard surrenders. Her name is Myrja, and her allegiance to Szass Tam is less than resolute. If the characters spare her, she offers the pass phrase to get by the trap and creatures in area 23 ("That which is dead, stay so") and one piece of lore.

Cages. Half the cages here are empty. The others hold the following young monsters, which are reduced-threat creatures (see "Reduced-Threat Monsters," page 113):

Cage A. One **remorhaz**
Cage B. Two **basilisks**
Cage C. Five **darkmantles**
Cage D. Five **ettercaps**
Cage E. Two **carrion crawlers**
Cage F. One **behir** (no Constrict or Swallow traits)
Cage G. Two **hook horrors**
Cage H. One **wyvern**

Each cage has rune-scribed bars of steel. Transmutation magic on the bars renders them unbreakable, so a creature inside can't physically or magically attack through the bars. To free the occupants of a cage, a character can pick the lock on the cage door, which requires a successful DC 15 Dexterity check.

If freed from their cages, the young attack the nearest creatures. If a Thayan and a character are equally close to a young creature, it targets the character.

Keys. Myrja has a glyph key attuned to this zone. She also carries a key to each of the cages in a ring on her belt.

White Gates. Area 22 is bordered by three white gates. One connects to the Swine Run, another to the Dark Gardens, and a third to the Temples of Despair.

Dark Gardens

Once an area of deadly gardens, these chambers have been altered to support the Blood Pens.

23. Dead Garden

Dead and blackened thorny vines cover the walls and floor, which are peppered with small, circular holes the size of a human fist.

In the northeast corner is a black gate.

Creatures. Seven **zombies** and two **wights** are focused on the doors to areas 22 and 24. Those who appear by way of the black gate can gain surprise if they attack immediately.

Unless the creatures are attacked, they grant free passage to anyone who appears to be a Thayan and knows the room's pass phrase (see area 22). The wights challenge those who know the phrase but look like intruders. It takes a successful DC 15 Charisma (Deception, Intimidation, or Persuasion) check to convince the wights to stand down.

Aura. A *detect magic* spell cast on this area reveals an aura of transmutation magic around each hole, hinting at the presence of a magical effect.

Blood Vines Trap. If a non-undead creature moves 10 feet or farther into the room without uttering the pass phrase, animated vines shoot out of the holes and into every part of the room. Each creature must say the phrase; it's not good enough for one character to say it for the whole group.

The vines ignore the undead. Any non-undead creature in the room when the vines emerge must succeed on a DC 13 Dexterity saving throw or become restrained by a vine. A creature takes 11 (2d10) piercing damage each time it starts its turn restrained in this way. As an action, a restrained creature can free itself or another creature with a successful DC 13 Strength (Athletics) check, or free only itself with a successful DC 13 Dexterity (Acrobatics) check. A vine that's restraining a creature can also be cut and killed; each vine has AC 15 and 8 hit points.

While the vines are present, the area is lightly obscured and difficult terrain. A creature takes 2 (1d4) piercing damage for every 5 feet it moves through the room. A creature that moves more than 15 feet on its turn must immediately make a DC 13 Dexterity saving throw. On a failed save, the creature becomes restrained as described above.

If no creature is restrained at the end of a round after the trap has been triggered, all the vines immediately die. The trap then goes dormant for 1 hour.

Glyph Keys. Each of the wights has a glyph key attuned to this zone.

White Gate. A white gate is located in the corridor to the west between this area and the Hatchery.

24. Pale Garden

The Red Wizards use this magical garden for food.

Light. The room is filled with dim light.

The scent of decaying plants hangs over an underground garden. White vines, trembling as if touched by an unfelt breeze, twine around cracked pillars that glow with pale light. Between the pillars, ashen flowers, sickly gray shrubs, and giant mushrooms stand in dense groves around a couple of gravel paths.

Many baskets full of plant matter are stacked on shelves carved into the walls near the doors.

Creatures. Twelve unarmed humanoid **skeletons** wander the area, harvesting plant material in large baskets. As they tear off growths, a crackling sound accompanies an increase in the glow of a nearby pillar, and the harvested plant starts to rapidly regrow.

The skeletons ignore intruders unless they are attacked or damaged, in which case they all attack trespassers in the room.

Two **shambling mounds** hide in the groves, ignoring the skeletons. These creatures are trained to disregard anyone who remains within 15 feet of any doorway, where the baskets are stored on the shelves. They wait to ambush any non-undead creature that ventures any farther into the room.

Dense Garden. Any area within 5 feet of a pillar and not shown on the map as part of the path is difficult terrain.

Pillars. The chamber's pillars respond when plant matter in the chamber is damaged. At the end of each round during which a shambling mound took damage, a discharge of energy ripples over the pillars, and each creature within 5 feet of a pillar takes 5 (1d10) lightning damage.

White Gate. The passage that leads west contains a white gate that connects with the Temples of Despair.

25. Dreaming Garden

A garden courtyard fit for a palace features walls of dark marble veined with gray. The ceiling of brass is supported on black marble pillars. Between the pillars, raised stone garden beds are filled with flowers and creeping vines in every color of the rainbow, their sweet scent hanging in the air.

Creatures. Thuria, a Red Wizard **enchanter** (see appendix B), lives here and oversees the Blood Pens. Two **dread warriors** (see appendix B) and eight robed **zombies** guard him, and a **black dragon wyrmling** is his personal pet. When the characters first arrive, the dragon has just killed a commoner.

Thuria spends much of his time in seclusion, and relishes the opportunity to fight intruders. If reduced to 20 hit points or fewer, he surrenders and offers two pieces of lore in exchange for his life. He is also willing to give up his treasure and share the attunements of his glyph key, turning over the actual key only under severe threat.

Dungeon State. If Thuria survives an initial encounter with the player characters, he and any surviving allies go on patrol, attacking any intruders in the Doomvault.

Garden Beds. Enchantment magic imbues the garden beds. Any living humanoid that spends more than 1 minute here must succeed on a DC 12 Wisdom saving throw or fall unconscious. The creature can repeat the saving throw at the end of each of its turns, ending the effect on itself on a successful save. On any successful save, the creature is immune to the effect for 24 hours. The creatures here are already immune to this effect.

Thuria's Repose. The middle garden bed among the three southernmost beds is full of plants shaped like pieces of furniture. A circular shrub is a resting couch, an angular one is solid enough to use as a desk, and others nearby serve as small chairs.

Contact Stone. On the southern wall near Thuria's place of repose is a circle of glowing glyphs that serves as a contact stone.

Treasure. Thuria wears a gold circlet set with rubies (worth 1,000 gp) and a gold cuff (100 gp). He carries a *spell scroll* of *fly* and a *potion of greater healing*.

One dread warrior has a *+1 longsword*, and each has a gold cuff that matches Thuria's.

In Thuria's "desk" are mundane records of important functions in the Blood Pens. Also within are *oil of etherealness* and a *potion of poison* disguised as a *potion of healing*. A bundle of entwined branches opens like a coffer to reveal 100 pp and a diamond (worth 1,000 gp).

Glyph Key. Thuria has a glyph key attuned to this zone, the Vermin Halls, the Swine Run, the Hatchery, and the Temples of Turmoil (in the Temples of Extraction sector).

White Gate. Beyond the exit to the south, a white gate lies in the corridor that leads to the Hall of Necromancy.

MASTERS' DOMAIN

This sector is the central sanctum of the Red Wizards in charge of the Doomvault.

Locations in the Masters' Domain are identified on map 5.5.

TEMPLES OF DESPAIR

Although the chambers in this zone are referred to as "temples," they are essentially security rooms designed to destroy the unwary.

Doors. All the doors in this zone are locked.

Aura. Divine Sense and *detect evil and good* reveal that this zone is thoroughly desecrated.

26. TEMPLE OF LIGHT

> Glowing pillars brightly light this chamber of white marble. Each pillar is carved in the likeness of a smiling figure with its hands held out, as if ready to accept an offering.
>
> In contrast to the beatific pillars, alcoves around the room contain statues of four-armed gargoyles.

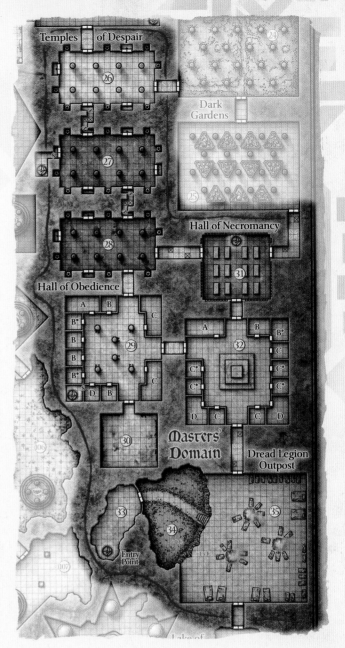

MAP 5.5: MASTERS' DOMAIN

Advance Notice. Characters who enter this area feel tranquility despite the gargoyles. If a player expresses doubt about the impression, that player's character can make a DC 15 Wisdom (Insight) check. On a successful check, the character realizes that the emotion is artificial and illusory.

Creatures. When the characters first enter this area, the eight four-armed gargoyles are true statues. After a door other than a secret door is opened in this area, four four-armed gargoyles (as normal **gargoyles** with 63 hit points and one extra claw attack, for a total of three attacks, with Multiattack) animate and attack. Another four-armed gargoyle animates whenever another such door is opened. This process continues for as long as any gargoyles remain in the alcoves. The gargoyles don't leave the room.

Pillars of Light. Seeming to offer a measure of protective power, the pillars have magic designed to prolong the torment of those trapped here. When a creature touches a pillar, the room pulses with light, and that creature gains 5 temporary hit points. Any slain gargoyle disappears when the light pulses, and a new statue appears in an empty alcove. This light pulses spontaneously once an hour, replenishing the gargoyles even if no one is present.

Body. Sprawled in front of one alcove, in a location where the characters see it only after entering the room, is the red-robed form of a male human. Vorja, a Red Wizard sent here to face execution, fell to the gargoyles but became stabilized after being left for dead. It takes healing magic or a successful DC 15 Wisdom (Medicine) check to bring him back to consciousness. He has only 1 hit point unless healing magic was used. Vorja is in no condition to fight, and his loyalty to Thay is tenuous.

If assisted, Vorja can reveal one piece of lore along with descriptions of the Hall of Obedience and the Hall of Necromancy. He knows nothing about this zone. If he is given a glyph key and taken to the black gate, he escapes the Doomvault and joins Syranna's forces.

Dungeon State. The nature of this area means the gargoyles can't be permanently slain.

White Gates. A white gate lies in the corridor to the north that connects with the Hatchery. Another white gate is in the eastern passage between this area and the Dark Gardens.

27. TEMPLE OF SHADOW

A creature near the doors into this area hears a faint moaning that rises in intensity as the creature moves closer to the doors.

> A wailing howl erupts from the shadows of this dim chamber, echoing from black marble walls. Dark pillars rise to the ceiling, each exuding shadow that twists in the air like smoke. Alcoves around the room hold statues of four-armed gargoyles shrouded in darkness.

Light. Dim light radiates from the pillars and fills the area. Any light source brought into or created in the room radiates only dim light unless it is a spell of 3rd level or higher.

Wailing. Pervading the chamber is a horrid wailing that has unnerving effects on non-undead creatures that hear it. Such creatures have disadvantage on melee attack rolls, Strength checks, and Dexterity checks. A character can take an action to make a DC 14 Wisdom check or Charisma check. On a successful check, the character can ignore the effect for 10 minutes.

Creatures. Shadows swirling around a pillar coalesce into a **wraith** after a door other than a secret door is opened in this area. Another wraith emerges from another pillar each round thereafter, until eight undead have appeared. The undead don't leave the room.

Pillars of Shadow. The pillars here are imbued with necromancy magic. An undead creature that touches (or passes through) the pillar gains 5 temporary hit points. A non-undead creature that touches a pillar takes 5

(1d10) necrotic damage and 5 (1d10) cold damage. A creature can take this damage only once per turn.

Black Gate. The space beyond the western false door contains a black gate.

Contact Stone. A contact stone is on the wall near the black gate.

28. TEMPLE OF BLOOD

> The coppery scent of blood hangs heavy in the air in this chamber of dark red marble. Pools of blood are spread across the floor around several dimly glowing red pillars that give off wispy vapors. Statues of four-armed gargoyles, each with mouths and claws dripping blood, stand in alcoves around the chamber.

Light. Dim, blood-red light radiates from the pillars and fills the area.

Blood. Due to the slick blood on the floor, a creature that moves across the ground at greater than half its normal speed must succeed on a DC 10 Dexterity saving throw or fall prone.

Creatures. The vapor swirling around two of the pillars coalesces into a pair of **vampiric mists** (see appendix B) after a door other than a secret door is opened in this area. Another vampiric mist appears whenever another such door is opened. This process continues until eight of the creatures have manifested.

Pillars of Blood. If a living humanoid creature touches a pillar, the part of its body that touched the pillar becomes stuck, and the creature is restrained. At the start of each of its turns, the restrained creature is drained of blood and must succeed on a DC 15 Constitution saving throw or take 5 (1d10) necrotic damage and have its hit point maximum reduced by the amount of the damage until the creature finishes a long rest. With a successful DC 15 Strength check, a creature can use an action to escape the pillar's hold, or another creature can use an action to pull a victim free.

White Gates. Two white gates adjoin area 28. One is in the south passage that leads to the Hall of Obedience, and the other is in the eastern corridor that connects with the Hall of Necromancy.

HALL OF OBEDIENCE

The Red Wizards use the magic of the Hall of Obedience to create zealous followers.

29. CONDITIONING COURT

> Doors surround a central courtyard here, creating the sense of a monastic sanctuary. Each of the glowing silver pillars that support the ceiling has a set of chains and manacles fastened to it. Thayans hang from four of the pillars, their seemingly dead eyes open wide as if in a state of intense focus.

Silver Pillars. Exuding enchantment magic that dulls will and perception, the silver pillars cause any creature in the courtyard to have disadvantage on Wisdom checks and saving throws. Being chained to the pillars causes hypnotic dreams that, after a period of weeks or months, improve combat skill and imbue most creatures with strong devotion to the Red Wizards.

Four Thayan warriors chained to the pillars are in an advanced state of entrancement. They can be treated as unconscious. If they are slain, a gong sounds in the chamber, alerting the inhabitants of the cells.

Cells. Several of the cells are quarters for Thayans who train and work here. Unless otherwise noted, each cell contains rough cots and footlockers that hold worthless personal possessions.

Any commotion in the area, or the sounding of the gong, alerts those in the cells. The Red Wizard emerges 1 round later, and the Thayan apprentice comes out during the following round. The residents of the other cells take 1d4 + 1 rounds to respond (roll separately for each).

The occupants of the cells are as follows:

Cell A. A Red Wizard **illusionist** dwells in this fine chamber with one **Thayan apprentice** (see appendix B for both stat blocks). The wizard is half asleep. Both have glyph keys attuned to the zone, as well as keys to the C cells. In combat, the apprentice uses an action to open the occupied C cell if able to do so without significant risk.

Cell B. Two **Thayan warriors** (see appendix B) sleep in each of four small rooms. The B cells marked with an asterisk are empty.

Cell C. The doors to these two cells are locked. Four **Thayan warriors** (see appendix B) are held in one of them when it's not their turn to be shackled to the silver pillars. The other C cell is empty.

Cell D. This cell contains bunks but is empty.

Black Gate. The space beyond the secret door in the southeast corner contains a black gate.

White Gates. The corridors that exit this area to the north and the east have white gates that connect with the Temples of Despair and the Hall of Necromancy.

30. Training Floor

> An arsenal of weapons and armor hangs from the walls in this broad chamber, the floor of which is stained with blood and black ichor. On the wall between two weapon racks to the east is a contact stone.

Creatures. Lahnis, a Red Wizard **evoker** (see appendix B), directs the brutal combat training here. Six **Thayan warriors** engage a **dread warrior** (see appendix B for both stat blocks) and seven **skeletons**. Lahnis orders the whole lot to attack intruders. Because they have been engaged in combat, each creature aside from Lahnis starts with current hit points equal to half its hit point maximum.

Lahnis initially stays back in combat, using lower-level spells and trying to assess the characters' motivations.

LAHNIS, RED WIZARD

His allegiance to Szass Tam has been flagging. He leans toward supporting the Thayan rebels, but he has not formally joined their ranks. He worries that some of his peers who are loyal to Szass Tam might suspect him.

Aware of Szass Tam's cunning, Lahnis first assumes the characters are testing his allegiance. Around the second round of combat, or if reduced to half his hit points or fewer, Lahnis directly asks the characters their purpose and admits a willingness to join the rebels. The characters can sway him with convincing talk and proof that they have overcome other parts of the dungeon. If the characters earn his trust, Lahnis turns against Szass Tam, having become convinced that the regent's plots will be the undoing of Thay.

He then turns on the Thayans here, whom he knows won't stand down, and helps the characters fight. Afterward, Lahnis provides two pieces of lore and the attunements on his glyph key, as well as his physical keys. He goes to the gatehouse through the black gate in area 29.

Treasure. Among the weapons here are a *+1 battleaxe*, a *+1 greatsword*, and a *+1 shortbow*. A heavily scarred suit of plate armor here is *armor of vulnerability* (your choice of type). In addition, Lahnis wears a *ring of protection*.

Keys. Lahnis carries a glyph key attuned to this zone, the Hall of Necromancy, and the Temples of Despair. He also carries a key that safely opens all the doors in the Temples of Despair, as well as a key to open the C cells in area 29.

Development. If Lahnis joins the rebels, he provides information that decreases the Doomvault's alert level by 1.

PHAIA, RED WIZARD NECROMANCER

HALL OF NECROMANCY

Red Wizards practice and refine their darkest magic in the Hall of Necromancy.

31. UNDYING LABORATORY

If Phaia and Kelson are here (see "Creatures" below), anyone who listens at the doors can hear screaming coming from the other side.

> The walls of this black marble mausoleum are lined with hundreds of niches, each holding an ivory urn set with gold, silver, and precious gems. A dozen gray marble tables arrayed across the floor are encrusted with blood and ichor.
>
> In the north side of the room is a black gate.

Creatures. Phaia, a Red Wizard **necromancer** (see appendix B), is drawing the soul from Kelson Dark-treader, a male half-elf lying on a stone table farthest from the door the characters use to enter. Kelson is unconscious and stable at 0 hit points. Phaia's magic is drawing forth from his body a wispy shape that resembles him, and this shape screams in an echoing voice. Strands of energy flow from the shape into the table and from there into other forms in the room.

A **deathlock wight** (see appendix B) on a nearby table is a Red Wizard in the process of being raised as undead. Also nearby, two reduced-threat **wights** (see

"Reduced-Threat Monsters," page 113) are being raised as warrior undead. These wights are only partially animated, so they respond only to Phaia when she orders an attack. One of them tries to throw an urn at a character each round (+4 to hit, range 10 feet/20 feet; one creature). A hit deals 3 (1d6) bludgeoning damage, and the target must make saving throws as noted in the "Urns" section. Phaia stays for a round or two to assess the party's capabilities and then moves to area 32 or uses the black gate in the room.

As a faithful servant of Szass Tam, Phaia follows the lich lord's philosophy that no magic is too dangerous and no experiment too dark if it promises power. Lawful evil, Phaia is as opportunistic as she is wicked.

She does anything she can to save herself from death, including using Szass Tam's secrets. She can reveal two pieces of lore and is willing to share her glyph key's attunements. Further, she can teach the characters the ritual that uses this area's magic to return soul-bound undead characters to life.

If she is allowed to do so, Phaia flees the Doomvault.

Aura. A *detect magic* spell reveals an aura of necromancy on the whole area, signifying the magic that helps in the creation of undead. Divine Sense and *detect evil and good* reveal that this area is desecrated.

Stone Tables. These 3-foot-high carved slabs channel the energy of life and undeath. They aid in rituals and spells to create undead.

With the proper knowledge, a creature can use the stone tables to transform a soul-bound character back into a normal creature. Doing so requires the aid of a Red Wizard or explicit written instruction, such as the scroll in Lahnis's room in area 32. The ritual takes 20 minutes and requires a spellcaster to make a DC 15 Intelligence (Arcana) check. The spellcaster must also expend a 3rd-level spell slot. On a successful check, the soul-bound creature returns to normal with all of its Hit Dice expended. On a failed check, the spell slot is expended but the creature remains soul bound.

Urns. The urns are magic and worthless but clever fakes that appear valuable, requiring a successful DC 20 Intelligence (Investigation) check to discern the truth. Any non-undead creature that touches an urn must succeed on a DC 17 Constitution or Wisdom saving throw (creature's choice) or take 10 (3d6) necrotic damage and become paralyzed for 1 minute. The creature can repeat the saving throw at the end of each of its turns, ending the effect on itself on a successful save. If this damage reduces a creature to 0 hit points, the creature dies and turns to dust.

Kelson. Despite his ordeal, Kelson Darktreader can be restored to health through normal means, although he is in no condition to help. He thanks the characters for saving him and offers two pieces of lore. He asks for a glyph key and goes to the gatehouse to recuperate.

Treasure. Phaia carries a *+1 dagger*, a *spell scroll* of *darkvision*, and a *potion of water breathing*.

Glyph Key. Phaia has a glyph key attuned to this zone and the Temples of Oppression (in the Temples of Extraction sector).

White Gates. The corridor that leads west has a white gate that connects with the Temples of Despair. In the northern leg of the corridor to the east is another white gate that leads to the Dark Gardens.

32. WIZARDS' COURT

> A stepped monument of gray marble shot through with red dominates an open courtyard surrounded by closed doors. Blue light shines from the top of the monument. The air around it hums with power, its vibration overwhelming other sensations. Red Wizards and other Thayans kneel on the lower two tiers, eyes fixed on the monument.

Stepped Monument. The monument amplifies magic in the courtyard, but those in the area have trouble with physical sensations and tasks, and they have disadvantage on Strength and Dexterity checks and saving throws. Meditating on the monument causes hypnotic dreams that, after a period of weeks or months, improve spellcasting capabilities and imbue most creatures with strong devotion to the Red Wizards.

Each tier of the monument is 5 feet high, and clambering onto it requires 5 extra feet of movement.

Creatures. Three **Thayan apprentices** (see appendix B) kneel on the lower tier of the monument. The Thayans attack intruders.

Cells. The cells around the perimeter of the court (rooms labeled A through D on the map) are quarters for Thayans who train and work here. Unless otherwise noted, each cell contains rough cots and footlockers holding worthless personal possessions. Cells marked with an asterisk on the map are empty.

Combat in the courtyard alerts the inhabitants of the cells. They take 1d4 + 1 rounds to respond (roll for each one):

Cell A. Lahnis (see area 30) uses these quarters, which contain a fine bed, a footlocker, and a desk. Searching the area uncovers one written piece of lore, as well as a *tome of the stilled tongue* and six *spell scrolls* (two each of *detect magic*, *identify*, and *remove curse*). Lahnis also has a scroll describing the ritual used to turn soul-bound undead back into non-undead creatures in area 31.

Cell B. One Red Wizard **evoker** (see appendix B) sleeps here.

Cell C. One **Thayan apprentice** (see appendix B) sleeps here.

Cell D. Each of these two rooms is a library. An hour spent examining a library's contents turns up two pieces of lore.

Contact Stone. Atop the monument is a circle of glowing glyphs that serves as a contact stone.

Glyph Key. The Red Wizard in cell B has a glyph key attuned to this zone.

White Gates. Two white gates separate area 32 from other zones. The gate in the corridor to the west leads to the Hall of Obedience. Beyond the doors to the south is a gate that connects with the Dread Legion Outpost.

KELSON DARKTREADER

DREAD LEGION OUTPOST

The Dread Legion, Thay's army, maintains a full company in the Doomvault.

33. CAVERN GUARD POST

> Glowing crystals set into the walls and floors light a rough stone cavern. To the south is a black gate.

Blue Crystals. The blue crystals brightly light the area.

Creatures. One **Thayan warrior** (see appendix B), five **gnolls**, and five **orcs** attack intruders on sight.

Glyph Key. The Thayan warrior has a glyph key attuned to this zone.

34. SHARD CAVERN
This cavern has no light.

> The walls and ceiling of this rough cavern are a mass of rock spines, the floor covered with rock dust and shards. A path has been worn through the rubble, winding between double doors to the west and a rough flight of stairs rising to the larger and lit open space to the east.

Path. Except on the path, the ground in the room is difficult terrain.

Shard Storm Trap. Transmutation magic infuses the room. Any creature that spends more than 1 round in this area triggers the trap. When the trap triggers, each creature in the room who isn't wearing a Thayan uniform must make a DC 15 Dexterity saving throw, taking 14 (4d6) piercing damage from flying shards on a failed save, or only half as much damage on a successful one. This effect repeats every round until the room is empty, when the trap resets.

The path becomes difficult terrain, and if the creatures in areas 33 and 35 can hear the trap go off, the guards have warning that intruders are in the area.

Stone Wall. A rough stone wall separates the lower cavern of area 34 from the higher finished chamber of area 35. The wall is 15 feet high.

35. DREAD LEGION BARRACKS

The light in this room can be seen from area 34. Unless the creatures here have a reason to be quiet, they are talking loudly.

> Three bonfires light this vast chamber, their smoke rising to vent through cracks in the ceiling. Scattered bedding and the stench of unwashed humanoids suggest that many creatures might dwell here.
>
> In the east, on the wall between two oversized bedrolls, is a contact stone.

Bonfires. Large fires brightly light this area. A creature that enters a bonfire for the first time on a turn, or starts its turn in a fire, takes 3 (1d6) fire damage.

Creatures. Resting in this chamber are a **Thayan warrior** (see appendix B) and a Dread Legion squad made up of five **orcs** and five **gnolls**. A **troll** is on post here to keep the other legionnaires in line.

Stone Wall. See area 34.

Dungeon State. The Dread Legion patrols throughout the Doomvault. If a squad resting in the barracks is slain, an identical squad arrives here within 1 hour.

Glyph Keys. The Thayan warrior has a glyph key attuned to every zone in this sector. The troll has a glyph key attuned to this zone.

White Gates. A white gate is located in the corridor to the south, leading to the Warren of Eyes. Another white gate is in the passage to the north that connects with the Hall of Necromancy.

FAR REALM CYSTS

The influence of the Far Realm has warped a portion of the Doomvault, where several star-shaped chambers have been turned into a weird mix of worked stone and glistening walls. Unless otherwise noted, these caverns are dark.

Locations in the Far Realm Cysts are identified on map 5.6.

LAKE OF MADNESS

An aboleth dwells in a watery crevasse, seething at its imprisonment and hungry to enslave the living.

36. DARK WATER

Water can be heard rippling in this dark area before the characters arrive.

> The walls of this cavern are the same dark shade of blue as the pool of water that fills the center of the area. Ripples spread across the surface as if the water has been recently disturbed. Around the cavern, narrow alcoves hold enormous globes of blue liquid suspended in the air.
>
> In the west side of the room is a black gate, and on the wall near it is a contact stone.

Creatures. One reduced-threat **aboleth** (see "Reduced-Threat Monsters," page 113) dwells deep in the pool. Within this room, the aboleth can use the water globes (see "Water Globes" below) to move around.

The aboleth's ordeal in the Doomvault has weakened it, making it a reduced threat. In addition, its hatred of the Red Wizards makes the aboleth a potential ally. With a successful DC 20 Charisma (Persuasion) check, or another successful and appropriate check, a character can convince the aboleth to stand down and negotiate. In exchange for sparing the characters, the aboleth demands to be freed and given a glyph key.

Pool. Over 350 feet deep, this pool has sheer sides that drop to its bottom. The water within 10 feet of the surface is a lightly obscured area, and deeper water is heavily obscured.

Water Globes. Floating 5 feet above the floor, these magic water globes are 15 feet in diameter. Red Wizards use them to hold aquatic creatures for transport through the black gates.

As an action, a creature that is within 5 feet of a globe and has an Intelligence score of 10 or higher can take control of the globe by succeeding on a DC 10 Intelligence check. As part of its movement and with a successful DC 10 Intelligence check, the controller can direct the globe to move with it, remaining within 5 feet of the controller. A globe's controller can enter and leave the globe at will. The controller can maintain control of the globe while within 100 feet of it. Another creature that qualifies as a controller can gain control of a globe by winning a contest of Intelligence checks against the current controller.

A creature that touches a globe but isn't its controller must succeed on a DC 15 Strength saving throw or be drawn into the globe and unable to pass back through its boundary. As an action, a trapped creature can free itself with a successful DC 15 Intelligence check. Also as an action, a globe's controller can release a trapped creature with a successful DC 10 Intelligence check. A creature inside a globe has half cover against effects that originate outside the globe. While inside a globe, a trapped creature can't contest for control of the globe.

Dungeon State. If the characters free the aboleth, it wanders the dungeon and attacks anyone it runs across.

White Gate. A white gate lies in the east–west corridor between this area and the Warren of Eyes.

37. COMPELLING LIGHT

Light. The dim light that fills the chamber can be seen before the room can.

> Dim light dances in the air, shimmering through the colors of the rainbow, gently lighting the walls of this cavern. A few piles of bones and scraps of gear litter the floor.

Creatures. The shimmering light here has affected two **wights**, two **dread warriors** (see appendix B), and six **zombies**. They attack if the trap's effect on them ends.

Compelling Light Trap. Any creature that sees the magical light while within this area must succeed on a DC 13 Wisdom saving throw or enter the cavern and stand there while ignoring all other stimuli. When an affected creature takes damage, the creature can repeat the saving throw, ending the effect on itself on a successful save. Any non-undead creature that ends its turn in the lighted room takes 10 (3d6) necrotic damage.

A *dispel magic* spell suppresses the light's effect for 10 minutes. Any spell that overwhelms or blocks the light also suppresses it in the spell's area for the duration of the spell.

Glyph Key. One of the dread warriors has a glyph key attuned to the Forest of Death.

White Gate. A white gate lies at the foot of the stairs leading west toward the Forest of Death.

WARREN OF EYES

Thaxalia, a beholder, has been summoned and imprisoned here.

Light. This zone is bathed in a weird green glow that provides dim illumination.

38. SINKHOLE CAVERN

> This rough cavern has an uneven floor with open holes in it. In the east, on a spar of rock, is a contact stone.

If the characters come from the north, add the following.

> Southwest of the doors is an alcove that contains a black gate.

Creatures. Eight **zombies** and two **ogre zombies** attack any intruders. Any combat warns Thaxalia (area 39) of the approach of intruders.

Sinkholes. These open sinkholes are 5 feet across and 10 feet deep. A creature that falls into a sinkhole is restrained in the narrow bottom. It takes a successful DC 13 Strength check or Dexterity check to work free,

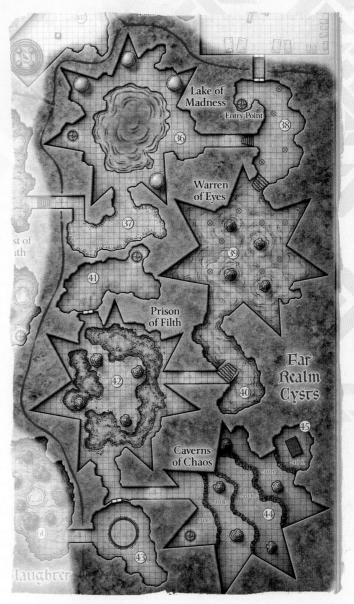

MAP 5.6: FAR REALM CYSTS

and a Small creature has advantage on this check. It's then an easy matter to climb out of the sinkhole.

White Gate. The passage that leads west has a white gate that connects with the Lake of Madness.

39. BEHOLDER'S DOMAIN

> Hundreds of unblinking eyes stare into this room from long walls of glistening green stone. The floor of this chamber is covered with viscous slime that drips from four stalagmites.

Beholder. Thaxalia, a reduced-threat **beholder** (see "Reduced-Threat Monsters," page 113) crippled by Thayan magic, floats near the ceiling, trying to remain unnoticed while intruders enter. Thaxalia's central eye and two of its eyestalks have been maimed by the Red

Wizards, rendering those eye rays (death ray and disintegration) powerless. If it has warning or is reduced to 50 hit points or fewer, it withdraws to area 40, leaving its spawn to deal with the threat.

After only 2 rounds, Thaxalia's hatred for the Red Wizards inspires the beholder to question the characters' purpose in the dungeon. If they reveal their goals, the beholder suggests an alliance, extolling its plans for revenge.

Fearing Thaxalia's ability to wreak havoc if it escapes this zone, the Red Wizards cursed the beholder with the inability to use glyph keys. Thaxalia doesn't know the solution, but a *remove curse* spell can eliminate the prohibition. The beholder then takes a glyph key from the wight in area 40 and asks the characters to provide it with more attunements. If refused, it becomes hostile and uses its powers to compel the characters to give it more attunements.

Beholder Spawn. Clinging to the cavern walls by the hundreds, between this world and the Far Realm, are the manifestations of beholder spawn. These spawn aren't independent creatures, but they can project weak eye rays that function as an area hazard. At the start of each of its turns, any creature other than Thaxalia in the cavern must succeed on a DC 12 Wisdom saving throw or suffer one of the following effects, rolled randomly.

2d4	Eye Ray
2–3	*Charm.* For its turn, the target moves toward its nearest ally and attacks with a weapon or a cantrip. The target can't check for danger as it moves.
4–5	*Telekinesis.* The target is pushed 5 feet in a random direction and falls prone.
6–7	*Slow.* Until the start of its next turn, the target's speed is reduced by 15 feet, and others make attack rolls against the target with advantage.
8	*Sleep.* The target falls unconscious until the start of its next turn.

Slime. Covering the rough floor is 1 foot of thick slime, which is difficult terrain and covers several hidden sinkholes. Any creature that starts its turn prone in or submerged in the slime takes 4 (1d8) poison damage.

Sinkholes. These open sinkholes are 5 feet across and 10 feet deep, and they are filled with slime. While moving near a sinkhole, a character who succeeds on a DC 20 Perception check notices the hazard due to the flow of slime in and around it. A creature that falls into a sinkhole is restrained in the narrow bottom and submerged in slime, unable to breathe. It takes a successful DC 15 Strength check or Dexterity check to work free, and a Small creature has advantage on this check. It then takes a successful DC 10 Strength check to climb out of the sinkhole.

Stalagmites. These 10-foot-diameter spires of rock rise 20 feet above the floor and exude the otherworldly slime. Their sides are slick and smooth, difficult to climb.

Dungeon State. If freed and given a glyph key, Thaxalia allows the characters free passage through this area. While Thaxalia is free in the Doomvault, it prefers to attack Thayans. If encountered again, the beholder might help the characters, given incentives.

The beholder spawn in this area are no longer a threat to those who freed Thaxalia. If Thaxalia is destroyed, the beholder spawn here disappear.

40. SLIME SLAVES

> Viscous slime covers this chamber. Rough stone steps lead up and out.

If Thaxalia left area 39, the beholder is in this location. It has been picking off Thayan patrols here. Amid the slime are five bodies: two of wights and three of Thayan warriors.

Slime. Covering the rough floor is 1 foot of thick slime. Any creature that starts its turn prone in the slime takes 4 (1d8) poison damage.

Glyph Key. One wight corpse has a glyph key attuned to this zone.

White Gate. A white gate lies in the corridor to the west, leading into the Prison of Filth.

PRISON OF FILTH

A pack of otyughs has been imprisoned here to reproduce in the filth.

Light. None.

Necrotic Essence. Viewed with *detect magic*, the area has an aura of necromancy. When non-undead creatures regain hit points in this zone, they regain only half as many.

41. GARBAGE TRANSFER

> This rough-walled cavern contains nothing that should make it stink of filth and rot as it does.
>
> Shadows curl like smoke from the walls. To the northeast, similar shadows whirl around a black gate. East of it is a contact stone.

Creatures. Twenty unarmed **skeletons** stand here, waiting to cart refuse that arrives from other areas through the black gate. They attack only if attacked.

If a character drops any moderate-sized object in front of the skeletons, as many of them as needed quickly seize the object and carry it into area 42. The otyughs are distracted while the skeletons move through area 42.

Doors. Abjuration magic on these locked doors causes them to open if an animate skeleton touches them.

Dungeon State. Unless destroyed with radiant damage, the skeletons here reassemble within 1 minute of being destroyed. Restored skeletons have no memory of their previous fate, so they attack only if attacked or if they witness other skeletons under attack.

42. Otyugh Lair

> Pools and piles of rotting garbage, offal, and filth cover the rough stone floor of this cavern. The air is heavy with an unbearable stench. Four stalagmites thrust up from the floor.

Creatures. Two **otyughs** and two reduced-threat **otyugh** young (see "Reduced-Threat Monsters," page 113) hide in the trash here. The reduced-threat monsters can't restrain with tentacles or use Tentacle Slam. The otyughs attack right away unless the otyugh from area 20 is here, in which case it may convince them to delay or even negotiate with the characters (depending on how the previous encounter went).

The otyughs use their telepathy to demand food like peevish children. If the characters offer to feed them, the otyughs stop fighting to see if the party is telling the truth (unless the party has slain one of the young). If the characters have killed one of the young, it takes a successful DC 20 Charisma (Intimidation or Persuasion) check to get the otyughs to stand down.

Stench. At the start of each of its turns in this area, any non-undead creature that isn't an otyugh must succeed on a DC 10 Constitution saving throw or be overpowered by the stench. On a failed save, a creature is poisoned until the start of its next turn. On a successful save, the creature is immune to this stench for 1 hour.

Trash. The waste in the area is difficult terrain.

Stalagmites. These 10-foot-diameter spires of rock rise 20 feet above the floor.

Dungeon State. If the otyughs are freed and given a glyph key, they go rampaging through the dungeon, devouring anything in their path, including Red Wizards.

White Gates. The open passages that lead away from area 42 both contain white gates. The northern route leads to the Warren of Eyes, and the southern path goes to the Caverns of Chaos.

43. Summoning Chamber

> A blood-red circle is scribed on the floor of this cavern, the twisted runes around its edge pulsing with sickly purple light.

A successful DC 15 Intelligence (Arcana) check allows a character to recognize the runes as symbols of dangerous magic that can be manipulated to call forth creatures of the Far Realm. The character further knows that using the summoning circle is impossible without the proper rituals, and that it can be disabled by defacing particular runes. The character is also aware that the process could unleash weird forces. Defacing the runes requires the use of a weapon or tools, such as thieves' tools, and a successful DC 20 Intelligence (Arcana) check.

Each time a character tries to disable the circle and fails, the circle unleashes a pulse of magical power that forces each creature in the area to succeed on a DC 15

Intelligence saving throw or suffer a severe break with reality. On a failed save, a creature has disadvantage on all Intelligence checks, Wisdom checks, and Charisma checks. In addition, the creature has disadvantage when rolling initiative and can't maintain concentration. *Remove curse, greater restoration*, or equivalent magic restores the creature to normal, as does finishing a long rest.

White Gate. A white gate stands in the passage that leads to the Forest of Weakness.

Caverns of Chaos

The creatures and forces of the Far Realm are held in these unlit caverns.

44. Chaos Lair

> Twisting ledges divide this chamber into multiple sections, creating a series of increasingly deep tiers. Stalagmites dot the floor.

Advance Notice. Those entering this area can hear the babble of the gibbering mouthers. A successful DC 10 Intelligence check confirms that the speech is gibberish in various languages.

Ceiling. Although the cavern floor steps down to the east as shown on the map, the ceiling stays level.

Creatures. Four **gricks** climb and wander on the top two steps, while two **gibbering mouthers** lurk on the third. One **grell** starts out flying above area 45. Six prisoners hide among the ledges, trying to avoid the aberrant monsters.

Aberrant Magic Field. Weird transmutation magic radiates from the entire cavern. Whenever a character gets a failure on an attack roll, a saving throw, or a check in this area, all the character's ongoing spells and magic items are suppressed until the end of the character's next turn. During this time, spells provide no effect and items don't impart their properties or powers.

Ledges. Each rough ledge is 10 feet high and easy to scale.

Stalagmites. These 10-foot-diameter spires of rock rise 20 feet above the floor.

Black Gate. A black gate is set into the western alcove, not immediately visible from the entrance.

White Gate. The exit from this area contains a white gate that connects with the Prison of Filth.

45. Eldritch Altar

> A slab of jet-black stone sits at the center of this cavern alcove. Its sides show relief carvings of familiar humanoid faces—your own.
>
> On the wall east of the altar is a contact stone.

Altar. This ancient altar to chaos is imbued with transmutation magic that reshapes its sides to show the faces of the most recent sentient humanoids to enter area 44.

The top of the altar slab shows the shadowy outlines of a dozen weapons, pendants, and other objects. An *identify* spell reveals that the altar imparts additional power into magic items placed on its surface. The caster must succeed on a DC 20 Intelligence (Arcana) check to further discern that when an item is empowered, the altar also draws in the life force of creatures near it.

When any magic item is placed on the altar for 1 minute, it takes on the following features:

- The item glows with dim purple light out to a radius of 5 feet.
- The item periodically and randomly alters its appearance in slight ways. The bearer has no control over these minor transformations, which don't affect the item's use or magical properties.
- The owner can communicate telepathically with the creature whose soul was consumed (see below).

When a magic item is transformed, randomly select one character within 50 feet of the altar. That person's soul is drawn into the item, and he or she drops into a deathlike coma, requiring a successful DC 15 Wisdom (Medicine) check to realize that the victim is still alive. An *identify* spell can be used to discern the whereabouts of the soul and how to cure the condition, temporarily or permanently.

Placing the transformed magic item in the victim's hand temporarily ends the coma. Thereafter, the character must continue to hold the object in hand or fall into a coma again. If the character breaks contact with the object for 1 hour, or if the object is destroyed, the character dies. *Remove curse*, *greater restoration*, or equivalent magic breaks the bond, returning the soul to its rightful place.

FORESTS OF SLAUGHTER

These caverns house a Thayan menagerie.

Locations in the Forests of Slaughter are identified on map 5.7.

Light. The cavern ceilings glow with magical light that varies in 12-hour cycles to simulate day and night. When the characters arrive, it is the start of the night cycle, and all areas of this sector are in dim light.

Magic Trees. Isolated stands of gnarled and vine-choked trees rise 15 to 20 feet high in the caverns. The trees are magic, having different powers in each zone, and targeting any intruders—creatures that aren't normally housed in the area. An area of trees is difficult terrain.

Magic Turf. The rocky cavern floors in this sector are covered in a layer of magic turf that uses transmutation magic to slowly absorb the waste of the creatures that dwell here.

Pools. Each of the rocky pools in these caverns is 1 foot deep and magically filled with cool, clean water. A pool is difficult terrain.

FOREST OF ILLUSION

Powerful illusion magic suffuses the trees in this zone. When an intruder ends its turn in an area of trees, the creature must make a DC 15 Wisdom saving throw. On a failed save, the creature becomes unable for 1 minute to see creatures hostile to itself. The creature repeats the saving throw at the end of each of its turns, ending the effect on itself on a successful save.

46. HOOK HORROR NEST

> The turf here is full of deep, enormous gouges.

Advance Warning. A character who succeeds on a DC 15 Wisdom (Survival) check can identify the gouges and tracks in the area as belonging to Large bipedal predators that use oversized clawed forelimbs to move like a gorilla might. A character who succeeds on a DC 15 Intelligence (Nature) check recognizes the traits of hook horrors.

Creatures. Four **hook horrors** hang from the walls here. They have grown lazy and distracted by their imprisonment, so characters have advantage on Dexterity (Stealth) checks made against the horrors until any character is spotted. The horrors hesitate to attack those dressed like Thayans but do so if no food is quickly offered.

The horrors fight mostly to defend a mound in the northwest section of the cavern, which contains their eggs. A character who can speak Undercommon and deal with the hook horrors' unsophisticated intellect can get them to stand down by guaranteeing the eggs' safety and making a successful DC 20 Charisma (Deception, Intimidation, or Persuasion) check. If the check fails, the horrors try to kill and eat the interlopers, but the negotiations can be renewed if two or more horrors are slain.

Black Gate. A black gate is set into the northeastern edge of the area, not immediately visible from the entrance.

Contact Stone. A contact stone is on the wall just north of the black gate.

Dungeon State. The hook horrors recognize a truce for only about 10 minutes. At that point, intruders have to renegotiate.

White Gate. The passage to the northeast contains a white gate that offers access to the Immortal Caverns.

47. COCKATRICE ROOST

> This treeless section of the cavern is set with natural ledges and indentations ten feet from the floor.

Creatures. Eight **cockatrices** roost on the ledges. They make no attempt to hide, and they attack as soon as they realize the characters have no food for them.

Ledges. Rough handholds make it easy to climb the walls in this area. A search of the ledges reveals sixteen cockatrice eggs.

MAP 5.7: FORESTS OF SLAUGHTER

48. GORGON LAIR

> At the pool's edge is a lifelike statue of a hook horror.

Creatures. Two adult **gorgons** attack intruders on sight, pursuing those who flee into area 46. Any hook horrors there attack only if the intruders slay or drive off the gorgons.

White Gate. A white gate is situated in the opening in the rock wall that leads to the Forest of Recovery.

FOREST OF RECOVERY

Powerful conjuration magic suffuses the trees in this zone. When an intruder ends its turn in an area of trees, the creature must make a DC 15 Wisdom saving throw. On a failed save, any damage the creature deals for 1 minute instead causes the target to gain 5 (1d10) temporary hit points per successful attack. The creature repeats the saving throw at the end of each of its turns, ending the effect on itself on a successful save.

49. GATE CAVERN

> Trees crowd the walls of this turfed cavern. To the southwest the turf gives way to a stone floor, where shadows curl up like smoke from a black gate. West of the gate is a contact stone.

Creatures. A **helmed horror** and a **wight** guard this area. The wight has orders to confront anyone who comes through the gate without pig carcasses or other items to feed to the zone's monsters. If such interlopers can't provide credible reasons for their presence, the wight orders the helmed horror to attack.

Glyph Key. The wight has a glyph key attuned to this zone.

50. BARGHEST RANGE

> The grassy turf grows high in this large cavern.

Creatures. Two **barghests** (see appendix B) lurk in the tall grass. A character who succeeds on a DC 20 Wisdom (Perception) check spots one or more of them. These creatures hesitate to attack only if the characters seem to be Thayans.

The barghests want to take revenge on the Red Wizards and then escape the Doomvault. If the characters offer to free them and succeed on a DC 20 Charisma check (any appropriate Charisma skill can apply), the fiends stand down. They want any glyph keys the characters have. If they are defied, the barghests are likely to renew their attacks.

Development. If the barghests are freed and given a glyph key, they stalk the dungeon for any prey they can find.

White Gate. A white gate is located in the opening in the rock wall that leads to the Forest of Illusion.

51. POOL OF RECOVERY

> A pool in this cavern glows with pale blue light.

The pool's magic grants non-undead creatures that drink from it the benefits of finishing a short rest. A creature can drink from the pool safely only once per tenday. The second time the creature drinks in a tenday, its hit point maximum is halved for one tenday (*remove curse* negates this effect). The third time the creature drinks in a tenday, it suffers the effects of a *harm* spell (save DC 15).

It isn't safe for an undead to drink from the pool. If the undead does, it gains no benefits and takes 22 (4d10) radiant damage.

White Gate. A white gate stands in the opening in the wall between this area and the Forest of Weakness.

52. DISPLACER BEAST DENS

> Bones are piled against the western walls of this cavern, forming low mounds.

Creatures. Two adult **displacer beasts** dwell here with three reduced-threat **displacer beasts** (see "Reduced-Threat Monsters," page 113). Each creature sits atop a different bone mound, and they all attack when it becomes clear that the characters have not brought food.

Bone Piles. These 1-foot-high piles of bones are difficult terrain.

White Gates. The northern exit from this area has a white gate that connects with the Culling Pens. The opening to the east has a white gate that leads to the Forest of Death.

FOREST OF DEATH

Powerful necromancy magic suffuses the trees in this zone. When an intruder ends its turn in an area of trees, the creature must make a DC 15 Constitution saving throw. On a failed save, the creature can't regain hit points for 10 minutes.

53. PERYTON ROOST

> Broad ledges run along the walls of this long cavern, twenty feet above the floor.

Creatures. The four adult **perytons** and four reduced-threat **perytons** (see "Reduced-Threat Monsters," page 113) that roost here have grown tired of their pork diet. If the characters don't appear to be Thayans, or if they fail to offer food within a few moments, the perytons attack.

Ledges. Rough handholds make it easy to climb the walls in this area. A search of the ledges reveals five peryton eggs.

White Gates. The southern passage has a white gate that leads to the Forest of Recovery. To the northwest, a white gate connects with the Culling Pens.

54. TROLL CAVERN

> Broken and gnawed bones are strewn across the turf in this forested cavern. Against the eastern ledge is a black gate. On the wall southwest of the gate is a contact stone.

Creatures. Three **trolls** live in this area, two males that fight constantly and one immense, dominant female that lazes near the black gate. They wait to be fed or given prisoners to play with, which allows the characters a few moments to decide on a course of action. If the party lingers, it's likely to dawn on the trolls that the characters are fair game.

Glyph Key. The female troll has a glyph key attuned to this zone, with which she and her allies can pursue fleeing characters.

White Gate. A white gate is situated in the opening in the wall that leads to the Forest of Weakness.

55. POOL OF CONSUMPTION

> A pool in this cavern glows with pale gray light.

The pool's necromancy magic grants undead creatures that drink from it the benefits of finishing a short rest. An undead creature can drink from the pool safely only once per tenday. The second time the creature drinks in a tenday, its hit point maximum is halved for one tenday (*remove curse* negates this effect). The third time the creature drinks in a tenday, it suffers the effects of a *harm* spell (save DC 15).

It isn't safe for a non-undead creature to drink from the pool. If the creature does, it gains no benefits and takes 22 (4d10) necrotic damage.

56. BEHIR LAIR

> The trees in this forested cavern are scorched and gouged. The turf is burned and overturned, revealing the stone floor in places.

A **behir** spends its days sleeping and eating in this chamber. The creature is asleep or otherwise preoccupied when the characters come here. It doesn't attack unless provoked.

White Gate. A white gate is located in the passage to the north that connects with the Iron Golem Foundries.

FOREST OF WEAKNESS

Powerful transmutation magic suffuses the trees in this zone. When an intruder ends its turn in an area of trees, the creature must make a DC 15 Strength saving throw. On a failed save, the creature becomes paralyzed for 1 minute. The creature repeats the saving throw at the end of each of its turns, ending the effect on itself on a successful save.

57. LEUCROTTA LAIR

> This area resembles a tranquil meadow dotted with a few trees.

Tracks. The ground seems to be covered with the tracks of large deer or elk, but a successful DC 25 Intelligence (Nature) check reveals that these tracks are those of leucrottas.

Creatures. Four **leucrottas** (see appendix B) lurk here among the trees. They make noises that sound like the calls of pained humans, which their handlers normally ignore. The creatures gleefully attack anyone they succeed in tricking.

White Gates. A white gate sits in the opening to the north that leads to the Forest of Death. Another gate lies to the south, giving access to the Forest of Recovery.

58. POOL OF RENEWAL

> A pool in this cavern glows with pale yellow light. Northeast of the pool, the turf gives way to a stone floor with a black gate set into it. East of the gate is a contact stone.

Pool. The pool's magic grants creatures that drink from it the benefits of a *greater restoration* or a *lesser restoration* spell (creature's choice). A creature can drink from the pool safely only once per tenday. The second time the creature drinks in a tenday, its hit point maximum is halved for one tenday (*remove curse* negates this effect). The third time the creature drinks in a tenday, it suffers the effects of a *harm* spell (save DC 15).

59. CHOKER GROTTO

> This big side chamber has a few small copses of trees and a few piles of bones.

Bones. The gnawed bones of six humans are here. Each has crushed neck vertebrae, which someone can discern with a successful DC 15 Wisdom (Medicine) check.

Creatures. Six **chokers** (see appendix B) live here, two lurking in each of the two treed areas near the pool and two on the walls near the pool. They wait and watch, attacking when the characters move within reach, which their handlers rarely do. The chokers in the trees try to pull victims into the treed areas.

60. OWLBEAR GROVE

> The trees grow closer together in this cavern, giving it the look of a silent forest. A monstrous owlbear crouches low at a pool of still water, its razor-sharp beak and bright eyes on display as its gaze tracks you.

Two adult **owlbears** and three reduced-threat **owlbear young** (see "Reduced-Threat Monsters," page 113) lurk among the trees here. They wait long enough to see if food is being handed out, and they attack if none seems forthcoming. The young are hidden, and they join the fight from the flanks after their parents attack.

White Gate. The passage that leads east has a white gate that connects with the Prison of Filth.

OOZE GROTTOS

The Red Wizards use the magic of this sector to breed and control oozes.

Locations in the Ooze Grottos are identified on map 5.8.

Ooze Prod. An *ooze prod* is a quarterstaff that deals 1d4 force damage instead of the normal damage of that weapon. The prod suffers no damage from contact with oozes. In addition, an ooze hit by a prod has its speed reduced to 0 until the end of its next turn, and it can't benefit from bonuses to speed during that time. If an *ooze prod* is used as a weapon, it breaks the first time a natural 1 is rolled on an attack roll with it.

Interactions. Most living Thayans assigned to this sector hate being here. Thayans who surrender here hate the sector so much that they are more inclined to give truthful information about it.

Sentient Oozes. One of the many experiments in the Doomvault is an effort to infuse oozes with intelligence. The Red Wizards have met with some success, though the process requires the sacrifice of many subjects. The sentient oozes that result from this process are the same as normal versions of such monsters, except that they have Intelligence 5, can understand basic communication in Common, and are no longer immune to being charmed.

AUGMENTATION CHAMBERS

The magic of these chambers allows Thayans to bestow glimmers of intelligence into living oozes, making them obedient and more capable combatants.

61. BONE ROOM

> Cracked and decaying bones are piled throughout this chamber. In the northwest corner is a black gate.

Creatures. Three sentient **ochre jellies** and a **wight** guard this area. The wight confronts anyone who enters but stands down if the characters look like Thayans and give a credible reason for being here. Otherwise, the creatures attack.

MAP 5.8: OOZE GROTTOS

63. SPAWN VATS

The sound of flowing and bubbling liquid is audible from the northern hallway leading to this chamber.

> This enormous chamber of gray stone is filled with square vats made of the same material. At the center of the chamber, a great fountain spews black liquid that lands in a wide stone pool. Trenches cut into the floor run from the fountain bowl to the vats. The eastern wall of the chamber is partly covered by a long black curtain.

Creatures. Two **deathlock wights** (see appendix B) and four **skeletons** move among the vats, using *ooze prods* to poke the mixtures. They challenge any intruders. If the undead become distracted, oozes might attack (see "Vat System" below).

Sarkalla, a Red Wizard **transmuter** (see appendix B), is working behind the black curtain, but she peeks out in response to the wights' challenge. She whispers to order the lead wight to attack. A character who succeeds on a DC 20 Wisdom (Perception) check notices Sarkalla while she does so.

Quite mad, Sarkalla cares only for her experiments and her "precious children"—the oozes that she is working to imbue with intelligence in order to create "the perfect assassins." If she and her wights have the upper hand in combat, or if all the wights are destroyed, she calls for a break in hostilities. She proudly talks of the sentient oozes that will wreak havoc for Thay. She promises the characters positions as assistants and bodyguards to the Ooze Master (see area 65). If the characters accept, they are allowed to leave and go to area 64. Sarkalla otherwise attacks again and fights until killed.

Vat System. A 10-foot-high, circular magic fountain forms the center of a vat system. Around it are 3-foot-high square vats. Trenches, each 2 feet wide and 1 foot deep, connect the fountain to the vats. The whole system contains necrotic essence that prepares oozes for binding to undead.

A creature that enters the necrotic essence for the first time on a turn, or starts its turn there, takes 5 (2d4) necrotic damage and must succeed on a DC 11 Constitution saving throw or become paralyzed until the start of its next turn.

Six of the eight square vats each contain one ooze, all of them reduced-threat versions of the creatures (see "Reduced-Threat Monsters," page 113). Two vats hold black puddings (marked B on the map), one has a gray ooze (G), and three contain ochre jellies (O). Usually, wights use *ooze prods* to keep the oozes in the vats. If the wights are engaged in combat, roll a d6 at the end of every round. If the indicated ooze is still in a vat, it escapes and tries to attack the nearest creatures.

d6	Ooze
1–2	Black pudding
3	Gray ooze
4–6	Ochre jelly

Bone Piles. Here lie fragments of bone left from bodies destroyed in attempts to infuse oozes with humanoid intelligence. The piles are 3 feet high. It costs 15 feet of movement to move 5 feet across a pile. A creature that enters or starts its turn in a pile takes 4 (1d8) acid damage. A creature can take this damage only once per turn.

White Gate. A white gate stands at the junction in the corridor to the northeast, leading to the Spawn Pools and to the Blood Pools.

62. OOZE TEMPLE

> This chamber has stone benches, columns, and a raised altar, all suggesting it might have once been a temple or forum. Skeletons are arrayed across the benches.

Creatures. Two **deathlock wights** (see appendix B) with buckets and stone boots move among dozens of skeletons. They pour steaming ooze over the bones. Two sentient **ochre jellies** and two sentient **gray oozes** are pooled near the benches.

Spilled Ooze. The spilled ooze essence makes the area around the benches difficult terrain. Any creature that ends its turn in the area of the spilled ooze takes 4 (1d8) acid damage. The wights aren't affected, thanks to their boots.

Raised Altar. This raised altar is 10 feet above the floor. It has sides of smooth stone.

White Gate. The corridor to the east contains a white gate that leads to the Spawning Pools.

Black Curtain. Beyond a heavy black curtain, Sarkalla has her quarters, which contain a bed, a table strewn with writing implements and books, and shelves piled with bound volumes and scrolls.

Contact Stone. A circle of glowing glyphs above Sarkalla's southern table is a contact stone.

Treasure. Sarkalla's table and shelves contain two pieces of lore, four *spell scrolls* (two each of *dispel magic* and *greater restoration*), a *potion of greater healing*, a *potion of heroism*, and six valuable tomes on underground exploration and natural history (worth 120 gp each).

Glyph Key. Sarkalla has a glyph key attuned to this zone, the Immortal Caverns, the Spawning Pools, and the Temples of Nature (in the Temples of Extraction sector).

White Gate. The passage to the south has a white gate that connects with the Immortal Caverns.

IMMORTAL CAVERNS

Horrifying by-products of the Red Wizards' dark ooze experiments are found here.

64. WHITE MAW
This area is unlit.

> The cavern walls here are dry white stone, as is the clean floor. Toward the center, a massive, cracked black pillar rises to the dark ceiling.

Creature. The cavern is occupied by **White Maw** (see appendix B), a gray ooze so enormous that it covers the entire floor and much of the walls. Unlike the other sentient oozes, this one is quite intelligent (Intelligence 12) and has the ability to communicate telepathically to creatures within 50 feet of it.

As soon as the last character enters, solid white "stone" closes over each exit as White Maw seals the characters within itself. The ooze is insane and displays multiple personalities of the creatures that were sacrificed to imbue it with sentience. Although it might communicate briefly with the characters, eventually madness takes hold and it attacks, slamming the characters with pseudopods that manifest from the floor or walls. The characters attack it by targeting the floor or walls of the cavern.

When White Maw drops to 0 hit points, cracks shoot through the smooth white stone, which collapses to white dust, exposing the exits and dropping the characters 1 foot to the actual floor of dark stone.

Black Pillar. The black pillar is infused with psionic energy. Any creature that touches it for the first time on a turn takes 9 (2d8) psychic damage and is knocked prone.

White Gates. The opening to the north contains a white gate that connects with the Augmentation Chambers. To the northeast is another white gate that leads to the Spawning Pools.

65. RED MASTER

> An enormous pillar of thick red liquid stretches from floor to ceiling in this cavern. Embedded within the pillar is a whispering, crimson-robed humanoid form.
>
> To the northeast is a black gate. East of the gate is a contact stone.

Creature. A Red Wizard known only as the **Ooze Master** (see appendix B) has melded with the pillar of red ooze. He uses his powers to make sure the red pillar consumes those who come here.

The Ooze Master is the result of a failed experiment to blend a Red Wizard with ooze. When the characters arrive, the Ooze Master assumes they are Thayan apprentices come to join him "in immortality." He greets them and honors their "great sacrifice." The Ooze Master knows if White Maw has been killed (though not who did it), and vows to use the characters' power, once it is consumed, to seek out and punish those responsible. He also speaks of "the great transformation," when all Red Wizards will be joined with oozes.

Red Pillar. The red pillar flows like viscous fluid. When a creature moves within 10 feet of the pillar, the creature feels its body soften. Whenever a creature starts its turn within 10 feet of the pillar, the creature must succeed on a DC 15 Constitution saving throw or take 7 (2d6) acid damage. A creature that drops to 0 hit points due to this effect dies and collapses into a puddle of gooey red liquid. The fluid then flows into the pillar.

Dungeon State. The Ooze Master is a sort of lich. If destroyed, he remains in the red pillar but doesn't regain consciousness. His unconscious form whispers as if dreaming. The Ooze Master dies only if the Phylactery Vault is disabled at the end of the adventure.

White Gate. In the passage to the southeast is a white gate that leads to the Forest of Illusion.

66. BLACK ELDER

> In the brilliant light shed by the white pillar at the center of this cavern, a pool of mottled black liquid gleams.

Light. The white pillar fills this area with bright light.

Pool. Silvery calm water forms this highly reflective, 1-foot-deep pool. Until a character looks into the pool and notices its mirrorlike nature, it takes a successful DC 20 Wisdom (Perception) check to notice that quality.

Creature. An elder **black pudding** (Huge size; 130 hit points) lurks on the ceiling here, reflected in the pool. Unless a character looks up and sees the ooze, it quickly slides down the pillar and attacks with surprise.

White Pillar. A creature that starts its turn within 20 feet of the pillar regains 1d6 hit points. If this effect restores a wounded creature to its hit point maximum, the creature must succeed on a DC 15 Constitution saving throw or become blinded until it finishes a short rest.

SPAWNING POOLS

In these connected chambers, Red Wizards breed oozes for their experiments.

Noise. Anyone near area 68 can hear the loud sound of steel grinding flesh and bone, rising and falling at intervals. The noise means that Thayans here fail to perceive sounds of combat from nearby areas.

Glyph Keys. Every one of the Red Wizards in this zone has a glyph key attuned to this zone.

67. LABORATORY BARRACKS

Dozens of fine gilt mirrors stand between silk hangings along the walls of this once-splendid salon. A dozen rough cots are spread across the center of the room. Shrouded magic lights are set into floor stands between them, dimly lighting the area.

Near a niche along the eastern wall is a black gate.

Advance Notice. Any character who studies the room for a moment and succeeds on a DC 10 Wisdom (Perception) check notices that all the cots and lights are 10 feet or more away from the walls.

Creatures. One Red Wizard **transmuter** and three **Thayan apprentices** sleep here (see appendix B for both stat blocks). When roused, they tip the cots over and cast their spells from behind cover. They try to force or draw the characters close to the walls and the magic mirrors, hoping to summon the deadly defenders of this area.

Cursed Mirrors. Cursed mirrors are on all the walls except those within 5 feet of the exit points, including the black gate and the secret door. Conjuration magic in the mirrors works such that any living humanoid that moves within 5 feet of one must succeed on a DC 15 Wisdom saving throw, or a howling **specter** emerges from the mirror to attack. Once they have collectively called forth five undead, the mirrors all become dormant for 1 hour.

White Gates. The corridor leading west has a white gate that connects with the Augmentation Chambers. Beyond the secret door to the east is a gate that offers access to the Blood Pools.

68. ARCH OF BLADES

A large archway of worked stone stands at the center of this curving cavern. A stack of pig carcasses is piled haphazardly along the eastern wall. Buckets are arrayed on the northern side of the arch, as well as along the southern wall.

On the wall to the west of the arch is a contact stone.

Creatures. One Red Wizard **transmuter** oversees two **Thayan apprentices** (see appendix B for both stat blocks) and six **skeletons** here. Four skeletons drag pig carcasses toward the arch and heave them through, while blades scythe across the opening and reduce each body to a heap of blood, flesh, and bone that collects on the far side. Two skeletons then pick up shovels and collect the gore in buckets, making the flesh easier to transport.

If the characters watch long enough, the apprentices eventually carry full buckets toward the southern entrance and retrieve empty buckets stacked there.

Arch of Blades. The 3-foot-thick, 15-foot-diameter arch is a former trap imbued with enchantment magic. The Red Wizards suppressed the magic, but they couldn't do away with it completely. Any non-undead creature that starts its turn within 5 feet of the arch must succeed on a DC 15 Wisdom saving throw or be compelled to run through the opening (a creature ignores this effect if immune to being charmed).

The magic blades in the arch come to life when any creature comes within 5 feet of the opening. A creature that moves through the arch must make a DC 15 Dexterity saving throw, taking 33 (6d10) slashing damage on a failed save, or half as much damage on a successful one. A creature compelled to run through the arch must make another DC 15 Wisdom saving throw after doing so. On a failed save, the creature stops moving while still within 5 feet of the arch. The creature can willingly move farther away only after the start of its next turn.

A creature that succeeds on two Wisdom saving throws against the arch's effect becomes immune to the effect for 24 hours.

White Gate. The passage to the northeast contains a white gate, which connects with the Culling Pens.

69. SPAWN CAVERN

Broad, circular pools are spread across this cavern, each filled with dark goo. The area smells of blood.

Creatures. One Red Wizard **transmuter** (see appendix B) oversees two **Thayan apprentices** (see appendix B) in this cavern. They walk a circuit around the pools, carefully jabbing down into them with the *ooze prods* they carry.

Spawn Pools. These 5-foot-deep pools are filled with ravenous ooze spawn that are nourished into full-grown oozes by feeding them pig meat. Each pool contains gray oozes, ochre jellies, or black puddings. The pools are magically warded to keep the spawn from climbing up the interior walls, but that doesn't keep them from striking out at nearby creatures with their pseudopods. Any creature that starts its turn adjacent to a spawn pool must succeed on a DC 13 Dexterity saving throw or take 7 (2d6) acid damage. If a creature strikes a pool with an *ooze prod*, the pool's pseudopod attacks are suppressed until the end of that creature's next turn.

A creature that enters a pool for the first time on a turn, or starts its turn in one, takes 9 (2d8) acid damage.

White Gate. The route to the southwest contains a white gate that connects with the Immortal Caverns.

Culling Pens

Young oozes feed on each other in the great pools that fill these caverns.

70. Battle Pool

If creatures occupy this area, those that approach it can hear the sounds of thrashing in liquid.

> A jet-black pool that roils like a storm-tossed sea takes up half this cavern.

Creatures. One Red Wizard **transmuter** (see appendix B) and two **Thayan apprentices** (see appendix B) are focused on the black pool with their *ooze prods*. When the Thayans turn away to deal with the characters, a Medium reduced-threat **black pudding** (see "Reduced-Threat Monsters," page 113) emerges from the ooze pool at the start of the second round. Another such pudding emerges at the start of the fourth round, and another at the start of the sixth round. The Thayans try to keep the characters between themselves and the pool, since the oozes see all other creatures as prey.

Ooze Pool. Filled with reduced-threat black puddings, the pool is 2 feet deep and difficult terrain. Transmutation magic on the pool keeps most of the puddings in a torpid state so that they react only to stimulation from a nearby source. A creature that enters the pool for the first time on a turn, or starts its turn there, takes 13 (3d8) acid damage. In addition, every time a creature moves 5 feet in the pool, the creature is subject to an opportunity attack from a black pudding.

Black Gate. A black gate is set into the western alcove, not immediately visible from the entrance.

White Gate. To the southwest, a white gate separates this area from the Spawning Pools.

71. Dead Pool

> A reeking, acrid pool of slime and sludge fills most of this cavern, leaving only a rocky ledge to both sides.
>
> East of the pool is a contact stone.

Noise. Unless areas 72 and 73 have been cleared, combat noise in those areas can be heard here.

Acidic Vapor. The air contains acidic vapors. A creature that starts its turn here must succeed on a DC 10 Constitution saving throw or take 2 (1d4) acid damage. A creature that holds its breath or doesn't need to breathe has advantage on the saving throw.

Ooze Pool. Filled with the remains of dead oozes, the pool is 2 feet deep and difficult terrain. A creature that enters the pool for the first time on a turn, or starts its turn there, takes 9 (2d8) acid damage and 9 (2d8) poison damage.

Development. Any noise in this area alerts creatures in areas 72 and 73.

White Gate. The exit to the south has a white gate that connects with the Forest of Recovery.

72. Ooze Duel

> This cavern bears minor signs of multiple combats.

Creatures. One Red Wizard **transmuter** (see appendix B) and two **dread warriors** (see appendix B) watch from near the eastern wall as four **Thayan warriors** (see appendix B) battle a **gelatinous cube**. Two of the four warriors have been engulfed, and all are at half hit points (as is the ooze). If the wizard notices the characters aren't Thayan, he orders the others to attack them instead. The cube views everyone in the area as a foe.

73. Jelly Pit

> A rough pit takes up half of this cavern.

Creatures. One Red Wizard **transmuter** (see appendix B) and two **Thayan apprentices** (see appendix B) use *ooze prods* to keep three Medium reduced-threat **ochre jellies** (see "Reduced-Threat Monsters," page 113) in the pit and fighting. When the Thayans start combat with the characters, each of the three oozes emerges from the pit 1d4 rounds later (roll for each). The oozes see all other creatures as prey.

Jelly Pit. Filled with young, reduced-threat ochre jellies, living and dead, the pit is 3 feet deep and difficult terrain. Transmutation magic on the pit keeps most of the jellies in a torpid state so they react only to stimulation from a nearby source. A creature that enters the pool for the first time on a turn, or starts its turn there, takes 9 (2d8) acid damage. In addition, every time a creature moves 5 feet in the pit, the creature is subject to an opportunity attack from an ochre jelly.

White Gate. The corridor that leads southeast holds a white gate that provides access to the Forest of Death.

Predator Pools

The Red Wizards' plans involve the disruption and control of the Sword Coast's trade. To that end, the Thayans are spawning an aquatic army.

Locations in the Predator Pools are identified on map 5.9.

Pools. The saltwater pools in this sector are 50 feet deep, and the surface of each pool is 1 foot below the surrounding floor. It takes 5 extra feet of movement to move from a pool onto the floor. Unless otherwise noted, transmutation magic in each pool keeps the water clean.

The pools also exude enchantment magic. Living in the water causes hypnotic dreams that, after weeks or months of exposure, improve combat skill and imbue most creatures with strong devotion to the Red Wizards.

Reactions. Creatures in this sector usually hesitate to attack those who seem to be Thayan but quickly overcome this reticence if the characters linger and fail to act according to type. Most aquatic monsters prefer to drag foes into the water.

Water Globes. Floating 5 feet above the floor, these magic water globes are 15 feet in diameter. Red Wizards

A creature that touches a globe but isn't its controller must succeed on a DC 15 Strength saving throw or be drawn into the globe and unable to pass back through its boundary. As an action, a trapped creature can free itself with a successful DC 15 Intelligence check. Also as an action, a globe's controller can release a trapped creature with a successful DC 10 Intelligence check. A creature inside a globe has half cover against effects that originate outside the globe. While inside a globe, a trapped creature can't contest for control of the globe.

POOLS OF DEVOTION

A spirit naga oversees this zone and its creatures.

74. KRAKEN POOL

> Beyond a broad round pool in the center of this circular chamber is a black gate.

A **malformed kraken** (see appendix B) is held in this saltwater pool. Although it responds to specific orders from Red Wizards, it attacks anyone in the room who looks over the edge of the pool.

White Gates. The corridor that connects this area with the Fiendish Arena has a white gate. Another one is to the east, behind a set of doors and a secret door, in the passage that leads to the Halls of Conditioning.

75. DRAGON TURTLE PRISON

If the dragon turtle occupies this area, characters approaching can hear the rattle and clank of immense chains.

> Gigantic steel bolts have been driven into the stone floor of this immense area, attached to heavy chains. These trail down into the water of a vast pool situated between curving northern and southern staircases that lead up to double doors. Two enormous globes of blue liquid are suspended in the air to the east.

Creatures. One reduced-threat **dragon turtle** (see "Reduced-Threat Monsters," page 113)—it has no tail attack—recently taken from Lake Thaylambar, has been chained here while the insidious mind control magic of the pools takes effect. Not yet under the sway of Thay, it grows agitated when any creature enters this chamber, and it's likely to attack.

The dragon turtle wants freedom, and it is small enough to use a black gate. Any offer of freedom, including the use of a glyph key, causes a break in hostilities while the creature listens. If it is freed, unless the characters know of the circle in area 82, the dragon turtle goes to area 76 and escapes through the gatehouse.

The turtle knows that Ihanvas, the naga overseer of this zone, dwells in area 76. It can be persuaded with a successful DC 17 Charisma (Persuasion) check to fight the naga if it is lured into this chamber.

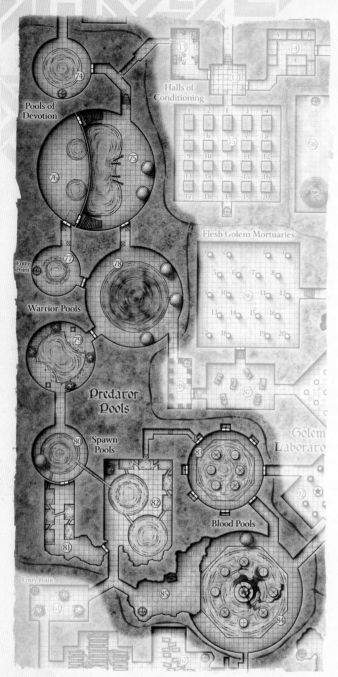

MAP 5.9: PREDATOR POOLS

use them to hold aquatic creatures for transport through the black gates.

As an action, a creature that is within 5 feet of a globe and has an Intelligence score of 10 or higher can take control of the globe by succeeding on a DC 10 Intelligence check. As part of its movement and with a successful DC 10 Intelligence check, the controller can direct the globe to move with it, remaining within 5 feet of the controller. A globe's controller can enter and leave the globe at will. The controller can maintain control of the globe while within 100 feet of it. Another creature that qualifies as a controller can gain control of a globe by winning a contest of Intelligence checks against the current controller.

Chains. Magic infuses the chains, which are long enough to allow the dragon turtle free run of the chamber. When the dragon turtle moves, any creature within 10 feet of its path must succeed on a DC 12 Dexterity saving throw or be knocked prone.

The dragon turtle can't harm or break the binding chains. The characters can open each of the two pin locks with a separate successful DC 20 Dexterity check.

White Gate. Behind the doors to the south is a white gate that connects with the Warrior Pools.

76. Naga's Den

If the spirit naga occupies this area, anyone who listens at the entry doors hears a scream of pain.

> The magical light shimmers off two circular pools in this chamber. A glowing glyph covers a broad area of the floor in the south. On the eastern wall is a contact stone.

Creatures. Ihanvas, the **spirit naga** overseer of this zone, is eating a prisoner. The naga attacks any intruders. Ten **commoners** also linger in the pools here. Ihanvas's Charisma, combined with the magic water, has turned them into the naga's willing devotees. They defend their master in any battle.

Southern Interior Door. The southern door to area 77 is locked.

Curse Glyph. Ihanvas wants to block direct access to her lair from area 77, so a magic glyph has been placed in the area marked on the map. Any creature that enters the marked area must succeed on a DC 15 Wisdom saving throw or have disadvantage on attack rolls against the naga, while the naga has advantage on saving throws against the creature's capabilities. The effect is a curse that lasts until Ihanvas dies.

Pools. A lip around the interior edge of each pool forms a 5-foot shelf where the water is only 3 feet deep. Further, a tunnel connects each pool to the other at the bottom, so the two pools are really one U-shaped structure, which Ihanvas can use to move through the room.

Treasure. The naga wears a platinum circlet set with sapphires (worth 1,000 gp) and matching earrings (500 gp for the pair).

Hidden at the bottom of the pools' connecting tunnel, Ihanvas's treasure includes 200 pp, five tourmaline jewels (100 gp each), *+1 plate* and a sealed ivory case that holds seven *spell scrolls* (two each of *detect magic*, *identify*, and *lesser restoration*, and one of *remove curse*).

Glyph Key. Ihanvas carries a glyph key attuned to this zone, the Warrior Pools, the Spawn Pools, and the Blood Pools.

White Gate. Behind the doors to the south is a white gate that connects with the Warrior Pools.

Warrior Pools

This gruesome zone is packed with the foulest of the aquatic soldiers.

Light. Unless otherwise noted, this zone has no light sources.

77. Scrag Pool

> A circular pool in this chamber has foul slime filled with bits of bone along its edge. To the west is a black gate.

Creatures. Two **trolls**, a male and a larger female, lurk in the pool. These trolls are of an aquatic variety known as scrags. In addition to the statistics of a normal troll, each has a swim speed of 30 feet and can breathe underwater.

Pool. The floor within 5 feet of the pool is crusted with the remains of the scrags' meals. If a creature makes a Dexterity saving throw while on the floor in this area and the saving throw fails, the creature falls prone. If the save fails by 5 or more, the creature then slides into the pool.

White Gate. The corridor leading north has a white gate that separates this area from the Pools of Devotion.

78. Undead Pool

> The stench of death is overwhelming here. The pool at the center of this chamber is a blackened sea of floating corpses. Three enormous globes of blue liquid are suspended in the air to the east.
>
> West of the pool, just south of a set of double doors, is a contact stone.

Creatures. Eight **ghouls** here float like corpses in the water until they catch the scent of non-undead creatures. These ghouls are of an aquatic variety known as lacedons. In addition to the statistics of a normal ghoul, each has a swim speed of 30 feet.

Pool. The necromancy magic in this pool is intended not to keep it clean but to kill intruders. Any creature that makes an attack dealing radiant damage in this area must succeed on a DC 15 Wisdom saving throw or move to the pool and jump in as soon as it can. A creature that enters the pool for the first time on a turn, or starts its turn there, takes 9 (2d8) necrotic damage.

Development. Any combat that lasts more than 3 rounds attracts the scrags in area 77. They enter the fray here at the start of the fifth round.

White Gates. The corridor leading north has a white gate that separates this area from the Pools of Devotion. To the south, a white gate stands in the corridor that leads to the Flesh Golem Mortuaries.

79. Bone Pool

> The floor of this sweltering chamber and its pool are spread with a fine layer of shattered bone. The faint illumination from a pair of low-burning braziers reveals piles of animal skulls set around the edge of the water.

Creatures. Four **merrow** entertain themselves by decorating their lair and chewing bones.

Pool. The magic of the pool has failed, and the water is filthy. Any non-undead creature that starts its turn in the pool must succeed on a DC 10 Constitution saving throw or be poisoned until the start of its next turn.

Bones. Pig bones and humanoid bones are scattered across the floor, but a few 1-foot-high piles are difficult terrain.

Braziers. The magic stone braziers are built into the room and can't be moved. A creature that touches a brazier takes 3 (1d6) fire damage. A creature can take this damage only once per turn.

White Gate. A white gate stands in the corridor that leads south to the Spawn Pools.

SPAWN POOLS

The Red Wizards refocused the magic of these once-deadly pools to spawn aquatic creatures under the supervision of a sea hag.

Spawning Essence. Blue glowing water in this zone is spawning essence, the transmutation magic of which causes spawn to grow quickly and strengthens their predatory nature. A creature that drinks spawning essence gains the benefit of finishing a short rest. A humanoid can safely gain this benefit only once per tenday. If a creature drinks again within that time, it gains no benefit and must succeed on a DC 15 Wisdom saving throw or suffer the effects of a *confusion* spell for 1 minute. The creature can repeat the saving throw at the end of each of its turns, ending the effect on itself on a successful save.

Spawn Pools. The round pools in this zone are cut 10 feet deep into the surrounding stone floor. Spawn pools are filled with spawning essence.

Spawn Pits. Rectangular 5-foot-deep spawn pits are filled with spawning essence. Each pit holds juvenile predatory fish. A creature that enters a pit for the first time on a turn, or starts its turn there, takes 2 (1d4) piercing damage from the attacks of these fish.

80. BLACK GATE POOL

Beneath walls set with relief carvings of humanoid couples romantically entwined, the bottom of a slimy, dimly luminous pool is shrouded in shadow. Trenches from the pool flow into one-foot-diameter tubes in the wall. An enormous globe of blue liquid is suspended in the air to the west.

Creatures. Five **kuo-toa** are on guard. Another four are sleeping on the bottom of the pool. All of them are loyal to Thay and expect to be asked to escort those who pass through this area. They attack anyone who makes no such request.

Black Gate. This zone's black gate is underwater at the bottom of the pool.

Development. If combat lasts longer than 3 rounds, the activity draws the attention of the creatures in area 81. They open the southern doors during the fourth round of combat and retreat to draw characters into the spawn pits in area 81.

White Gate. A white gate stands in the corridor that leads north to the Warrior Pools.

81. SPAWN HALL

Relief carvings along this arch-roofed hall show scenes of demons and humanoids engaged in debauchery. Five pits cut into the floor are filled with glowing water. South of these pools on a rough wall is a contact stone.

Creatures. A **dread warrior** (see appendix B), two **wights,** and four **zombies** guard this area. They attack anyone who isn't escorted by kuo-toa or the sea hag, pursuing such interlopers to any area of the zone.

Glyph Key. The dread warrior has a glyph key attuned to this zone.

82. SEA HAG LAIR

Two large pools fill a chamber whose walls are carved with reliefs of humanoids frolicking with cherubic angels. Water from the pools flows into pits that spread along the walls from one corner. A foul pile of debris and bones stands in the opposite corner of the chamber.

Creatures. Two male **merrow** dwell in the south pool. A **sea hag** named Tanjus luxuriates under the surface of the north pool with her pets, six **giant crabs.** She oversees the spawning pools in this zone and yearns to overthrow Ihanvas (area 76) for control of the Predator Pools and their monsters.

During combat, Tanjus offers the characters a temporary truce. She asks them to find and kill Ihanvas, because Tanjus wants to be the dominant force in this portion of the dungeon. The hag offers two pieces of lore and promises that none of her creatures will leave this sector. She also says that the characters can move freely through this zone once the naga is disposed of.

Development. If combat lasts longer than 3 rounds, the activity draws the attention of the creatures in area 81. They open the southern doors during the fourth round of combat and attack unless Tanjus orders them not to.

North Pool. A magic circle is scribed on the bottom of the north pool. It's a combination summoning circle and teleportation circle, but it's currently dormant. A spellcaster who succeeds on three DC 20 Intelligence (Arcana) checks can reactivate the circle's conjuration magic. The character then becomes aware that the circle allows teleportation to the sea floor off Bezantur, deep down in the Sea of Fallen Stars.

Debris Pile. Any creature that starts its turn in this disgusting pile, which is difficult terrain, must succeed on a DC 10 Constitution saving throw or be poisoned until the start of its next turn. Creatures that live in this zone are immune to this effect.

Secret Door. The secret door in the north wall is built just above the surface of the contents of the spawn pit.

Treasure. Tanjus has a black pearl (500 gp), a golden gorget set with aquamarines (1,000 gp), and a *staff of charming*.

A character who succeeds on a DC 15 Wisdom (Perception) check while searching the debris discovers five *potions of water breathing* and two *spell scrolls of water walk*.

Glyph Key. Tanjus has a glyph key attuned to this zone and the Pools of Devotion.

Dungeon State. If the characters leave Tanjus alive and Ihanvas is killed, the hag and her merrow allies relocate to area 76. No matter what else happens, Tanjus and her monsters attack any characters who return to this zone.

White Gates. A white gate stands at the junction in the corridor to the south, which leads to the Augmentation Chambers and to the Blood Pools. Another white gate is located in the corridor to the north behind the secret door that leads toward the Blood Pools.

BLOOD POOLS

The Red Wizards have the allegiance of sahuagin that are exiled from Aleaxtis in the Sea of Fallen Stars.

Light. Unless otherwise notes, this zone has no light sources.

83. BARON'S COURT

> The pool that takes up most of this circular chamber is filled with clear water. Stone pillars rise from the bottom to break the surface. Sets of double doors are spaced evenly around the room's perimeter.

Creatures. Six **sahuagin** swim along the surface around the edge of the pool, while a **sahuagin baron** and two **hunter sharks** swim deeper down.

Enmity between the baron and the priestess (area 84) means that these sahuagin make no attempt to call for aid.

The sahuagin know the hazards of the pillars. They aren't aware of the secret door.

Paralysis Pillars. The tops of the pillars are even with the floor around the edge of the pool, so they protrude 1 foot above the surface of the water. The remnants of an old magical trap exist in the three pillars marked with an X on the map. A creature that ends its turn touching the top of one of those pillars must succeed on a DC 15 Constitution saving throw or become paralyzed for 1 minute. A paralyzed creature slips into the water and sinks to the bottom of the pool. The creature can repeat the saving throw at the end of each of its turns, ending the effect on itself on a successful save.

Treasure. The baron wears *+1 leather armor* (shark skin and chitin) and a crown-like helm of ivory, coral, leather, and gold (worth 500 gp).

At the bottom of the pool is a stone coffer that contains a stash of 100 pp and eight large pearls (100 gp). It also has a crystal phial that contains a *potion of diminution*.

Glyph Key. The sahuagin baron has a glyph key attuned to this zone.

White Gates. In the corridor behind the secret door is a white gate that connects with the Spawn Pools. In the passage that leads east, a white gate stands between this area and the Stone Golem Quarries.

84. ALTAR POOL

If the sahuagin occupy this area, those approaching can hear chanting.

> An octagonal pool fills this chamber. A slick of blood darkens the water around a stepped stone altar that sits on a broad pillar rising from the pool. Smaller pillars are spread around the central one. An enormous globe of blue liquid is suspended in the air to the north.

Creatures. Four **sahuagin** stand and chant along with a **sahuagin priestess** on the altar pillar. Another five sahuagin and two **hunter sharks** dwell in the pool. A **commoner** is bound on the altar.

The chanting that precedes the sacrifice takes 3 rounds to complete. If the characters deal at least 20 damage to the priestess in that time, she breaks off the ritual to lead a counterattack. Otherwise, the prisoner is slain and thrown to the sharks. Any sahuagin on the altar then gains the effects of the *aid* and *bless* spells.

Enmity between the priestess and the baron (area 83) means that these sahuagin make no attempt to call for aid.

Altar Pillar. The outside area of the pillar is 1 foot above the surface of the water. The central altar rises 3 feet above the outside pillar. It takes 5 extra feet of movement to move from the outside pillar to the top of the altar.

Paralysis Pillars. See area 83.

Prisoner. If the prisoner is saved, he is in the same mental state as the prisoners in area 85. He can't aid the characters or answer questions.

Ledge. A 10-foot-high rough ledge separates this area from area 85.

Treasure. The priestess carries a *dagger of venom* and wears a headdress of ivory, coral, leather, and gold (worth 500 gp).

Glyph Key. The sahuagin priestess has a glyph key attuned to this zone.

White Gates. The narrow exit to the south opens onto a white gate that offers access to the Spawning Pools. The northeast corridor contains a white gate that connects with the Stone Golem Quarries.

85. PRISONER CAVERN

> On the north wall of this cavern is a black stone shrine set with relief carvings of roses. On the wall about a foot above the arcane shrine is a contact stone. To the south is a black gate.

Creatures. A **dread warrior** (see appendix B) keeps watch with seven **skeletons**. They do little but confront creatures moving toward or appearing from either magic gate. The characters can enter and leave this area from the east without fighting, even with the prisoners in tow.

Part of the deal the Red Wizards struck with the sahuagin involves providing prisoners for dark rites and horrid meals. The magic of the black shrine keeps ten **commoners** standing around it in a catatonic state.

Black Shrine. Any non-undead creature that moves to within 20 feet of the black shrine or ends its turn in such a location must make a DC 15 Intelligence saving throw. On a failed save, the necromancy magic of the shrine lowers the creature's Intelligence, Wisdom, and Charisma scores by 1d6 each (roll once for all three). A creature can be affected only once per round. If any affected score is reduced to 2 or lower, the character becomes paralyzed. A character who leaves the area recovers in 1 minute.

Ledge. A 10-foot-high rough ledge separates this area from area 84.

Glyph Key. The dread warrior has a glyph key attuned to this zone.

GOLEM LABORATORIES

In these formerly cursed temples and workshops, the Red Wizards create golems.

Locations in the Golem Laboratories are identified on map 5.10.

Golems. If a golem is inactive, it is unconscious. If a golem is listed as being a reduced-threat monster, it is because the construct is incomplete.

Dungeon State. When these areas are cleared, any golems that remained inactive become inert and can't be activated thereafter.

Treasure. The treasure in this sector consists of materials and tools used in the creation of the golems. As such, the value of the treasure is less than what might be expected.

White Gate. A white gate stands at the junction in the corridor to the west, leading to the Augmentation Chambers and to the Spawn Pools.

FLESH GOLEM MORTUARIES

Red Wizards bind and reanimate dead flesh and bone in these halls.

86. HALL OF TELEPORTATION

The walls of this massive hall are carved with reliefs of humanoid monarchs adorned with jeweled crowns and other finery, while servants bow at their feet. Huge white pillars rise to the ceiling.

Creatures. Two reduced-threat **helmed horrors** and a reduced-threat **flesh golem** (see "Reduced-Threat Monsters," page 113) stand inactive here in front of pillars. The golem hopes to draw on the pillars' lightning effect to become fully empowered. They come to life if attacked or when the teleportation magic of the pillars is triggered.

Teleporting Pillars. The first time a creature moves within 5 feet of a pillar on its turn, the creature must succeed on a DC 17 Wisdom saving throw or be teleported to a random space next to another pillar (roll a d20). The creature also takes 5 (2d4) lightning damage. If the destination pillar is the same as the origin pillar, the creature takes double damage.

White Gate. The corridor that leads east has a white gate that connects with the Clay Golem Kilns.

87. GOLEM VAULT

Relief-carved walls showing nobles at a great feast make a stark counterpoint to the stench of preservatives with a hint of rot. Flesh golems in their first gruesome stages of assembly are on a few of the tables. Other tables contain only prepared body parts and bones.

A contact stone is set in the midpoint of the southern wall.

Creatures. A Red Wizard **necromancer** (see appendix B) and two **Thayan apprentices** (see appendix B) are in this area, moving among the tables working or selecting parts. Four **skeletons** keep watch from the corners, while a **ghoul** mops gore from the floors. Golems in this area can't be activated and are no threat.

Treasure. One table contains special unguents and bindings used in the creation of the golems. A character who succeeds on a DC 15 Intelligence (Arcana) check realizes that these materials, which weigh 10 pounds, are worth 1,500 gp.

Glyph Key. The Red Wizard has a glyph key attuned to this zone.

White Gate. The eastern corridor holds a white gate that leads to the Clay Golem Kilns.

88. BLACK PRISON

A large stone block on the floor between the room's double doors prevents them from fully closing. Within, rusted black iron cages hang by heavy chains from the ceiling of this dark-walled chamber. In the northeast corner is a black gate.

Creatures. A **wight** commands eight **zombies** who guard this chamber while some members of their squad recover in the cages. One **deathlock wight** (see appendix B) and two wights rest in the cages.

Cages. The bottoms of these unlocked cages hang 3 feet above the floor. Necromancy magic on the cages restores 20 hit points per hour to an undead creature in a cage. A non-undead creature in a cage takes the same amount of necrotic damage at the end of each minute it remains in the cage.

Doors. If the 800-pound stone block holding these doors open is removed, they magically slam shut. It takes a successful DC 25 Strength (Athletics) check to force the doors open. A *knock* spell disrupts the magic briefly, lowering the check DC to 15 for 1 minute.

Glyph Keys. The wight and the deathlock wight each have a glyph key attuned to this zone. The deathlock wight's key is also attuned to all the zones in the Ooze Grottos.

White Gate. The exit to the north has a white gate that connects with the Warrior Pools.

Clay Golem Kilns

Red Wizards have twisted this zone's magic toward the creation of clay golems.

89. Transmutation Pits

> Two sides of this chamber have collapsed to form shallow, rough-walled pits filled with clay. Near the northern and southern corners are circles of sigils that glow with red light.
>
> In the eastern corner is a small array of urns and boxes. Above them on the wall is a contact stone.

Creatures. A Red Wizard **transmuter** (see appendix B) works here with a dwarf cleric of Grumbar, a deity associated with caverns and earth. The dwarf assists in the creation of clay golems, which require divine spellcasting. The dwarf **priest**, whose name is Gorvan Ironheart, was recruited by the Red Wizards and offered a substantial sum of money for assistance in crafting the golems. If he is questioned, he lies, claiming to be a prisoner of the Red Wizards. If the characters spare him, he accompanies the party until he sees an opportunity to escape.

Also present is a reduced-threat **clay golem** (see "Reduced-Threat Monsters," page 113). The wizard or the cleric can activate the golem by using an action and succeeding on a DC 15 Intelligence check.

Clay Pits. These 3-foot-deep pits channel powerful transmutation magic that converts rock walls and floor to clay for use in golem construction. The soft clay is difficult terrain.

A creature that starts its turn in a clay pit must succeed on a DC 13 Strength or Dexterity saving throw (creature's choice) or take 5 (2d4) bludgeoning damage and become restrained in the clay until the start of its next turn. A creature can escape the clay by succeeding on the saving throw or by taking an action to make a successful DC 15 Strength check or Dexterity check. Another creature can try to pull a restrained creature free by taking an action to do so and succeeding on a DC 15 Strength check. A creature that dies while trapped in the clay is transformed into a rough clay statue.

Teleportation Circles. Set into the floor, these magic teleportation circles have been partially disabled. A creature that enters a circle's area is pushed back 10 feet and knocked prone. The first time a creature does so on a turn, the creature takes 5 (2d4) force damage.

Treasure. In the eastern corner are a few jars of rare oils and boxes of rare powders used in the creation of

MAP 5.10: Golem Laboratories

the golems, along with some empty containers. A character who succeeds on a DC 15 Intelligence (Arcana) check realizes that these materials, which weigh 15 pounds, are worth 3,000 gp.

Glyph Key. The Red Wizard has a glyph key attuned to this zone.

White Gate. The corridor leading west contains a white gate, which leads to the Flesh Golem Mortuaries.

90. Golem Pen

> Pillars of white marble glow with an intense white light that brightly illuminates the area. The light is so bright that it almost obscures the arcane glyphs carved in the archways that lead into the room.

Pillars of Light. The intense bright light, created by evocation magic in the pillars, causes disadvantage on ranged attack rolls and ability checks made to search or see in this area. In addition, whenever a creature starts its turn in the chamber proper (not in an entryway next to the glyphs), it must succeed on a DC 13 Constitution saving throw or become blinded until the start of its next turn.

Arcane Glyphs. In the entryways, arcane glyphs on the wall can be used to control the pillars. When someone touches the glyphs, the pillars flicker. It takes a successful DC 10 Intelligence (Arcana) check to understand exactly how the glyphs function. A *detect magic* spell shows that the abjuration aura of the glyphs is connected to the evocation magic of the pillars, thereby revealing the function of the glyphs without a check.

A character who understands how the glyphs work can take an action to touch the glyphs and subdue the pillars with a successful DC 10 Intelligence (Arcana) check or deactivate them with a successful DC 15 Intelligence (Arcana) check. Subdued pillars shine less intensely for 1 minute, and the DC for the saving throw against them becomes 8. While the pillars are subdued, golems in this area regain 5 (2d4) hit points at the start of each of their turns. Deactivated pillars go dark for 1 minute, then are subdued for another minute, and then return to normal function.

Creatures. A clay golem in this area activates the first time a character fails a saving throw against the pillars, deactivates them, or subdues them.

White Gates. The corridor to the west has a white gate that provides access to the Flesh Golem Mortuaries. The passage heading southeast has a white gate that connects with the Stone Golem Quarries.

91. HALL OF SKULLS

Three of the skulls here connect to corridors, which the Thayans simply avoid. Characters who approach this room see the following.

> Ahead is a broad archway of dimly glowing green stone. Inside it is a field of dead gray mist.

Any creature that moves within 5 feet of the mist must succeed on a DC 20 Strength saving throw or be pulled into it and shunted violently into area 91, falling prone and taking 3 (1d6) bludgeoning damage.

Inside the room is the following scene.

> Six enormous fiendish skulls are set into the walls of this vast rectangular hall, two on each long side and one on each short side. Each skull is twenty feet high and carved of dimly glowing green stone, and it has a wide-open fanged mouth filled with dead gray mist.
>
> In the center of the chamber is a black gate.

Fiendish Skulls. The fiendish skulls are imbued with powerful magic. When any character steps into a skull's mouth, macabre laughter erupts from the northwest corner. The character is teleported to the mouth of a different skull (roll a d6) and comes tumbling back into the room, falling prone and taking 3 (1d6) bludgeoning damage.

The character must then succeed on a DC 15 saving throw (the ability is tied to the skull's number; see the table) or suffer the skull's curse. The curses are cumulative, imposing a −1d4 penalty to checks and saving throws of the indicated ability. If a character has a penalty of −5 or greater to a single ability, the character also suffers the curse's secondary effect.

Skull	Ability	Secondary Effect
1	Strength	Fall prone whenever hit by an attack
2	Constitution	Reduce hit point maximum to three-quarters of normal
3	Dexterity	Move at half speed or fall prone at the end of the movement
4	Intelligence	Unable to speak or understand languages
5	Wisdom	Unable to perceive anything more than 30 feet away
6	Charisma	Gain the Stench trait of a **troglodyte**

Secret Door. In the northwest corner, 20 feet above the floor, a secret door is hidden. The door is nearly impossible to find from the floor, requiring a successful DC 30 Wisdom (Perception) check. The smooth wall is hard to climb without aid, but the vaulted ceiling provides places where a grappling hook might catch.

Beyond the secret door, a teleportation circle set into the floor of a small chamber glows with a deep red light. A creature that steps into the circle is teleported into one of the two circles in area 89 (determine randomly).

Black Gate. Because it must be activated before it can be used, the black gate here doesn't exude shadowy energy. Any character who successfully assesses the gate knows that it must be activated and how to do so. A character who succeeds on a DC 20 Intelligence (Arcana) check while holding a glyph key, which need not be attuned to this zone, can reactivate the gate. The DC decreases by 2 each time a character in the room enters the mouth of a fiendish skull. Once the gate reactivates, it also attunes the activator's glyph key to this zone.

White Gates. Each of the corridors on the southeast wall has a white gate. One connects with the Stone Golem Quarries, the other with the Iron Golem Foundries.

STONE GOLEM QUARRIES

The Red Wizards have manipulated this zone's magic to enable the creation of stone golems.

92. TIMELESS PRISON

> A statue of an angelic female stands on a raised dais in the center of this chamber, the walls of which glow dimly with golden light. Six cracked pillars support the crumbling ceiling, each carved in its lower portions to resemble a four-armed gargoyle shrieking in rage.
>
> To the northeast is a black gate.

Light. When the characters first enter this area, the walls give off dim light.

Creatures. When any non-undead creature enters this area (which the Thayans avoid), a four-armed gargoyle (as a normal **gargoyle** with 63 hit points and one extra claw attack, for a total of three attacks, with Multiattack) emerges from a random pillar and attacks. At the start of each round thereafter, another random pillar transforms until all six gargoyles have emerged.

Because the Red Wizards are drawing off the magic in this area to create stone golems, the ceiling is close to giving way. Whenever a gargoyle emerges from a pillar, crumbling stone falls from the ceiling above that pillar, making the area around the pillar difficult terrain. Any creature next to the pillar must succeed on a DC 12 Dexterity saving throw or take 10 (3d6) bludgeoning damage.

Deva Statue. Anyone who succeeds on a DC 15 Intelligence (Religion) check recognizes the statue as that of a **deva**.

The last gargoyle to appear uses its initial action to touch the statue, which ends the curse that holds the creature in stasis. This deva's name is Lumalia. After she is freed, the walls shed bright light instead of dim. The deva shrieks, unable to act until her turn, at which point she attacks the nearest creatures. (The gargoyles avoid her.)

A character who succeeds on a DC 13 Wisdom (Insight) check understands that the deva is crazed from captivity. The characters can try to influence her to direct her attacks against the gargoyles, but doing so takes a successful DC 15 Charisma (Persuasion) check to calm her and refocus her attention. Once she is lucid and able to talk to the characters, she vows to aid them by sowing chaos through the Doomvault on her own.

Lumalia decides that her first task will be to inflict justice upon the Thayans. She is immortal, but her anger and regret over the time she has lost during her imprisonment seems very humanlike. In the thick of combat, she can become lost in her thirst for vengeance on the current owners of the Doomvault. Lumalia was lawful good when she was imprisoned, but she is now chaotic good.

Dungeon State. The magic of the Doomvault resonates within Lumalia. She needs no glyph key to move through the magic gates in the dungeon, although she can't take others with her. If she is freed, her resonance creates feedback in the gate system, making it harder to find intruders in the dungeon, and the Doomvault's alert level decreases by 1.

White Gates. The corridor leading west has a white gate that connects with area 83 in the Blood Pools. In the corridor to the south and west, a white gate leads to area 84 in the Blood Pools.

93. STONE QUARRY

If the giants occupy this area, the sounds of their labor are audible from either doorway even with the doors closed.

> A deep pit surrounded by loose rock and rubble scars the smooth marble floor of this chamber. A heavy rope descending into the pit is connected to a system of winches and pulleys.

LUMALIA, DEVA

Creatures. One **stone giant** operates the pulley system to haul stone out of the pit while a second giant cuts stone away from the pit walls. Both are occupied with their noisy work.

The giants joined the Dread Legion willingly, but they hate their duties. Initially, they relish the chance to take their wrath out on the party, but they listen to offers of freedom. They need a glyph key to leave the dungeon.

Pit. Filled with rubble, which is difficult terrain, the pit is 30 feet deep with rough, gently sloped sides. The ropes and pulleys above the pit are attached to a gigantic bucket used to transport the rock. It takes a successful DC 15 Strength check to raise the bucket when it is filled with stone.

Rubble. The area within 10 feet of the pit is full of rock debris, so it is difficult terrain.

94. GOLEM ASSEMBLY

If the Thayans are here, the sounds of their labor are audible from any open hallway leading into the room.

> White stones frame the four open archways that lead into this chamber. The four stones at the corners of each arch pulse with white light. The walls in this vast space are

set with panels of copper that reflect the lights, revealing several piles of stone blocks on the floor.

A contact stone is located in the eastern corner of the room.

Glowing Archways. Any creature that steps through one of the four archways that open into this chamber is hurled 10 feet into the room. The first time a creature does so on a turn, the creature must also succeed on a DC 15 Constitution saving throw or take 5 (2d4) force damage and fall prone.

Touching any one of an archway's four glowing stones causes that stone to change color for 1 round. Number the stones from 1 to 4 and make the players specify which stones are touched. Select colors as you see fit, pretending to consult your notes each time. (The color changes have no effect on the encounter.)

Creatures. A Red Wizard **transmuter** (see appendix B) and two **Thayan apprentices** (see appendix B) are distracted by their work here shaping a reduced-threat **stone golem** (see "Reduced-Threat Monsters," page 113), but they do notice if anyone is hurled into the room. These apprentices are armed with light hammers instead of daggers. The wizard can activate the golem by succeeding on a DC 15 Intelligence (Arcana) check made as an action.

Stone Piles. The 3-foot-high piles of rough stone blocks are difficult terrain.

Copper Panels. If a creature touches a copper panel, the creature takes 2 (1d4) lightning damage, and the archway stones flash. Until the end of the creature's next turn, it can pass through any archway in this room without being pushed or taking damage. The Thayans know that touching a panel with a wooden item or some other nonconductor provides the benefit of the panel without causing damage.

Treasure. Each Thayan has a fine chisel (worth 50 gp). At the feet of the golem are a few jars of rare oils and boxes of rare powders. A character who succeeds on a DC 15 Intelligence (Arcana) check realizes that these materials, which weigh 10 pounds, are worth 2,500 gp.

Glyph Key. The Red Wizard has a glyph key attuned to this zone.

White Gates. The exits to the northwest and northeast both hold white gates that connect with areas 90 and 91 in the Clay Golem Kilns. The passage to the southeast has a white gate that leads to the Iron Golem Foundries.

Iron Golem Foundries

Deadly elemental fire fuels the creation of iron golems to serve the Red Wizards. The roar of flames is audible throughout this zone, and firelight provides illumination in many places.

95. Efreet Prison

Characters approaching this area can hear the roar of flames.

A low, round pool of molten material sits at the center of this chamber. Tendrils of smoke curl up from it, moving in unnatural ways. In three of the corners stand several red urns, most of them cracked and empty but a few still closed and glowing with eldritch glyphs.

Gout of Flame. A gout of flame blocks the passage that leads to area 97. A creature can jump over the flame easily but takes 2 (1d4) fire damage when doing so. A creature that enters the flame during its turn, or starts its turn there, takes 21 (6d6) fire damage.

Creatures. An **efreeti** is bound to the smoke at the center of the room. It can't leave this area or use its powers against anyone outside the room.

Binding Smoke. The smoke tendrils form chains that have no solidity, but their abjuration magic holds the efreeti in this area. While it is bound in this smoke, the creature is susceptible to the *charm person* spell and has disadvantage on the saving throw. If it isn't charmed, the efreeti orders anyone present to grant it freedom and attacks if its demand isn't met.

The efreeti has no means to break the binding smoke. It knows, however, that the feat can be accomplished with spells, such as *dispel magic* (save DC 17), *gust of wind*, *knock*, or any spell that can push the efreeti out of the area of the pool. The smoke dissipates if the efreeti is slain.

Molten Pool. The pool has a 3-foot-high wall. A creature that enters the pool for the first time on a turn, or starts its turn there, takes 35 (10d6) fire damage.

Urns. Two unbroken funeral urns stand in each corner. Glyphs in the Primordial language on the urns suggest that they are binding vessels for efreet, and *detect magic* reveals that they have an aura of abjuration. The wax-seal stopper of an urn is broken easily, and an urn can be broken like any clay vessel of the sort. When an urn is opened or broken, the act releases a gas that causes any creature within 10 feet of the urn to gain resistance to fire damage for 1 hour. Each urn is 1 foot tall and weighs 5 pounds.

Dungeon State. The magic of the Doomvault resonates within the efreeti, which has been here since before the Thayans came to power in the dungeon. It needs no glyph keys to move through the gates in the dungeon but can't enable others to accompany it. If it is freed, the efreeti rampages through the dungeon, preferring Thayan targets.

White Gate. The opening on the northwest wall contains a white gate that connects with the Clay Golem Kilns.

96. Fire Vortex

This rough cavern splits off from the smooth walls of the adjacent chamber. Its floor is covered in a layer of ash.

Ash. Elemental ash covers the floor to a depth of 6 inches, concealing how uneven the floor is. This entire area is difficult terrain.

Cavern Walls. The extremely rough walls make it possible to traverse the cavern horizontally without touching the floor.

Elemental Vortex. When any creature moves onto the floor at the center of the cavern, the walls suddenly erupt in a maelstrom of elemental fire that lasts for 5 rounds. Any creature that starts its turn in the cavern during this time must make a DC 15 Dexterity saving throw, taking 21 (6d6) fire damage on a failed save, or half as much damage on a successful one.

97. Golem Forge

> At the center of this fiery hall is a huge crucible that emits vapors. Dozens of molds and piles of armor plate are spread out before six hulking armored figures that stand along the walls.
>
> To the southwest is a black gate. North of the gate is a contact stone.

Creatures. A Red Wizard **conjurer** (see appendix B) and two **Thayan apprentices** (see appendix B) work on an inactive iron golem in this area.

A charmed **efreeti** (see area 95) is at work boiling metal in the crucible. The efreeti fights for its Thayan friends. If freed of the charmed condition, it snatches up a falchion intended for the golem and attacks the Thayans. If the efreeti is alive when the other foes in the area are slain, it rampages like its kin in area 95.

Crucible. The 5-foot-high crucible contains molten metal. As an action, a creature can attempt to spill the contents by tipping the crucible over, taking 21 (6d6) fire damage in the process. On a successful DC 15 Strength check, the crucible tips, and on a successful DC 20 Strength check, a creature can also push the crucible 5 feet before it tips. Molten metal quickly spreads from the mouth of the crucible over an area 30 feet by 30 feet in size, including the crucible and the space within 5 feet of it.

Anyone caught in the molten metal takes 21 (6d6) fire damage and must succeed on a DC 15 Constitution saving throw or fall prone. The floor of the area is covered in molten metal. For the next 5 rounds, a creature that enters the area for the first time on a turn, or starts its turn there, takes 10 (3d6) fire damage. For 5 rounds after that, the damage is 3 (1d6), and then it drops to none.

Fire Vent. See area 95.

Treasure. A search of the molds throughout the room reveals vials of rare tinctures and admixtures used in the construction of iron golems. A character who succeeds on a DC 15 Intelligence (Arcana) check realizes that these materials, which weigh 30 pounds, are worth 5,000 gp.

Glyph Key. The Red Wizard has a glyph key attuned to this zone.

White Gates. At the top of the stairs to the south is a white gate that connects with the Forest of Death. The corridor that leads northwest has a white gate that leads to the Stone Golem Quarries.

Temples of Extraction

The so-called "Temples of Extraction" are profane laboratories that fuel Szass Tam's schemes for ascending to godhood. Szass Tam and his closest associates have reshaped this sector's magic to collect the divine essence of the Chosen of various deities. The Thayan regent believes that this essence may be the key to becoming a god.

Locations in the Temples of Extraction are identified on map 5.11.

Creatures. The Thayans here are the most loyal and fanatical servants of Szass Tam. They all know that no one is authorized to be in this sector, so the characters have a hard time fooling them. Except for the cowardly Red Wizard Shalok (area 103), the Thayans in this sector are unlikely to surrender and are unwilling to help intruders even at the cost of their lives.

The Red Wizards in this sector might feign surrender to put the characters off their guard. For example, they might fall to their knees and hold up their hands. Then, when the characters close in, the wizards cast area spells that include themselves and the party.

If a shrine of binding (see below) exudes a magical effect to which creatures in the room can become inured, the creatures that guard the shrine are already immune to the effect.

Doors. All the doors in this sector are locked.

Random Encounters. No random encounters occur in the Temples of Extraction.

Black Gates. Only four external glyph keys (one for each zone, in areas 10, 25, 31, and 63) allow access to the gates in this sector. Some Red Wizards here carry glyph keys to their zones and guard them zealously.

Contact Stones. There are no contact stones in this sector.

Shrines of Binding

Each chamber of this zone features an identical 3-foot-high shrine whose arcane power extracts energy from a Chosen creature that is strapped to the shrine. This energy is what powers the Doomvault but, even more, is also what both creates and keeps hidden the Phylactery Vault. The characters will have to examine the shrines to determine how these abilities function.

When the characters see a shrine of binding for the first time, use the following description.

> A three-step stone dais is set with four pillars, all carved of black jet. Glowing arcane runes surround the top edge of this shrine. Between the pillars, an unconscious humanoid is suspended in a roiling field of golden light.

Thereafter, you can shorten the description of the shrine, but be sure to specifically describe the Chosen that is bound inside it.

Entering a Shrine. While there is someone trapped on the shrine, the whole structure is surrounded by a tangible magical energy. Stepping onto the shrine re-

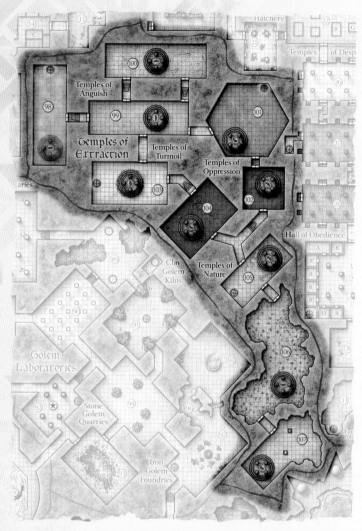

MAP 5.11: TEMPLES OF EXTRACTION

quires a successful DC 10 Charisma check, and unless this check succeeds by 5 or more, the shrine counts as difficult terrain. On a failed check, the creature is knocked prone next to the shrine and takes 5 (2d4) force damage.

Effects of a Shrine. Channeling the energy of the trapped Chosen, each shrine creates magical effects and light within its area (see each area descriptions for details) and throughout the complex—in particular they help to obfuscate the location of the Phylactery Vault. A successful DC 10 Wisdom check allows a character to intuit the effects of a working shrine, including how it channels the life essence of the trapped Chosen to another place and how to disable it. When a shrine is disabled, its magical effect in the area ends, and the Chosen bound inside it is freed.

Disabling a Shrine. The process for disabling a shrine is the same in each area. Characters who are standing on the shrine may disable its magic by making three successful DC 15 ability checks: Strength to smash the pillars, Dexterity to remove elements and disable key arcane runes, or Intelligence to disrupt the flow of magical energy. A character can make multiple

checks of the same type or any combination. On any failed check, the character who attempted the check is pushed off the shrine and knocked prone next to it, taking 5 (2d4) force damage.

Reaching the Phylactery Vault. Once a Shrine of Binding has been disabled, a character who closely examines the shrine and succeeds on a DC 15 Intelligence (Arcana) check discerns how these shrines and the black gates in this sector work together to shield the Phylactery Vault. The character understands that if the black gates in the Temples of Extraction can be overloaded, those gates will attune themselves to the location where the power of the Chosen is being directed—the vault itself.

In order to create that overload, six black gates in other sectors must be disrupted simultaneously (as described at the beginning of this adventure). Once that is accomplished, any glyph key can be used on any of the black gates in the Temples of Extraction, and the user will be taken to the Phylactery Vault.

THE CHOSEN

In each area of the Temples of Extraction, one of the Chosen of the gods is being drained to grant power to Szass Tam. Some of these Chosen would be deadly adversaries, but the binding ordeal leaves most of them physically and mentally weakened to the point that they pose no real danger. The Chosen have no memory of how they came to be in the Doomvault, so they can offer no information about the dungeon.

Many of the helpless Chosen are thoroughly evil, and good-aligned characters might balk at seeing them freed. Take advantage of this situation to create opportunities for interesting interactions.

If combat statistics become necessary, a helpless Chosen has AC 10, has 5 hit points, and makes checks and saving throws with a +0 modifier. If you plan to use this adventure in a continuing campaign, killing a helpless Chosen can later bring the characters into conflict with other agents of that Chosen's deity.

The magic of the Doomvault resonates within all of the Chosen. A Chosen needs no glyph key to move through the gates in the dungeon, although that individual can't enable others to accompany it.

TEMPLES OF ANGUISH

The Chosen of deities who are associated with torment have been imprisoned in these chambers.

98. TEMPLE OF POISON

> The air in this white marble chamber hangs heavy with a dark mist that burns the eyes. To the north is a black gate.

Creatures. A Red Wizard **necromancer** (see appendix B) works here, guarded by a **helmed horror**. They are immune to the Dark Mist, and the Red Wizard has the Venomous Touch trait (see below).

Dark Mist. The shrine exudes poisonous mist that makes the area lightly obscured. Any creature that starts its turn in the room must succeed on a DC 15 Constitution saving throw or become stunned until the start of its next turn. If the save succeeds, the creature is immune to this effect for a day and gains the following trait. Constructs and undead can't gain this trait.

Venomous Touch. When the creature hits with a weapon attack, that attack also deals 5 (2d4) poison damage.

Chosen of Zehir. The Chosen of Zehir is a male **yuan-ti malison** (type 3) named Oussa. Zehir is the serpentine god of poison, darkness, and murder. He is worshiped primarily by yuan-ti. If Oussa is rescued and then realizes that the characters aren't Zehir's faithful sent to help him, he uses his unholy power to instantly assume snake form and attacks the party.

Glyph Key. The Red Wizard has a glyph key attuned to this zone.

99. TEMPLE OF SUFFERING

> Stripes of red mist appear in the air in this white marble chamber, as if someone is whipping the air and it is bleeding.

Creatures. A Red Wizard **enchanter** and a **Thayan apprentice** work here, guarded by two **dread warriors** (see appendix B for all three stat blocks).

The Red Wizard here is Mennek Ariz, the rebel wizard who helped assault the Bloodgate. He was captured during the assault and brainwashed. A character who succeeds on a DC 15 Wisdom (Insight) check can discern that he isn't acting of his own volition. Only magic, such as *dispel magic* or *charm person*, can break the effect. If he is freed of the brainwashing, Mennek can reveal two pieces of lore.

Suffering Aura. Whenever a creature in this room deals damage to one or more creatures, it must make a DC 15 Wisdom saving throw. If the saving throw fails, the attacker takes radiant damage equal to one-quarter of the greatest amount of damage it dealt to a single target. If the save succeeds, the attacker instead regains a number of hit points equal to one-quarter of the greatest amount of damage it dealt to a single target.

Chosen of Ilmater. The Chosen of Ilmater is a lawful good male human named Kieren. Ilmater, also known as the Crying God, is the god of suffering, martyrdom, and perseverance. He offers succor and calming words to those who are in pain, oppressed, or in great need.

Treasure. Mennek carries a *wand of binding*.

Keys. Mennek has a glyph key attuned to this zone, as well as a skeleton key that unlocks all the doors in this zone.

White Gates. Behind the doors to the south is a white gate that leads to the Temples of Turmoil. The eastern doors open onto a white gate that connects with the Temples of Oppression.

MENNEK, RED WIZARD ENCHANTER

100. TEMPLE OF PAIN

> A tangible feeling of unease and discomfort fills the air of this scarred marble chamber.

Creatures. A **deathlock wight** (see appendix B) keeps watch here. One **wraith** and four **shadows** circle around the shrine, streaks of crimson trailing from their spectral forms.

Web of Pain. Whenever a non-undead creature in this area takes damage, it must make a DC 15 Constitution saving throw. On a failed save, the creature makes attack rolls, Strength and Dexterity saving throws, and ability checks with disadvantage until the end of its next turn. In addition, others make attack rolls against the creature with advantage until the end of its next turn.

Chosen of Loviatar. The Chosen of Loviatar is a lawful evil female half-elf named Irisoth. Loviatar, the Maiden of Pain, is the god of hurt and agony, and the patron of torturers. Loviatar teaches that the world is filled with pain and torment, and the best that one can do is to suffer those blows that can't be avoided, and then deal as much pain back to those who offend.

Temples of Oppression

The dark of living night and deadly abominations fuels the shrines in the Temples of Oppression.

101. Temple of Ooze

> The walls in this hexagonal hall of gleaming gray marble shudder occasionally. To the northeast is a black gate.

Creatures. A Red Wizard **transmuter** (see appendix B) works here, with a **wight** leading two sentient **gray oozes** and two sentient **ochre jellies** to guard her. Sentient oozes are the same as normal versions of such monsters, except that they have Intelligence 5, can understand basic communication in Common, and are no longer immune to being charmed. Myrra, the Red Wizard, is especially cruel and likely to toy with the characters even when she is losing.

Ooze Walls. The first time a creature moves within 15 feet of any wall on a turn, that act provokes an opportunity attack as if made by a gray ooze with a reach of 15 feet. The attack roll is made with advantage.

Chosen of Ghaunadaur. The Chosen of Ghaunadaur is a sickly and chaotic evil male drow named Therzt. Ghaunadaur is a strange god worshiped primarily by male drow that seek power outside the confines of a society dominated by females. Ghaunadaur is a malignant and unknowable deity that desires living sacrifice and destruction due to monstrous causes, particularly oozes.

If he is freed, Therzt babbles about the weakness he demonstrated in being captured and declares that he must die. As an action, Therzt casts *Melf's acid arrow* on himself while screaming his devotion to Ghaunadaur. The acid consumes him utterly as unholy energy pulses out to touch the walls, producing two **gray oozes** at the center point of each wall. The oozes treat all creatures remaining here as prey.

Keys. The Red Wizard has a glyph key attuned to this zone, as well as a skeleton key that unlocks all the doors in this zone.

White Gate. Beyond the doors to the west is a white gate that leads to the Temples of Anguish.

102. Temple of Shadows

Light. This area has no light sources. Bright light from a source other than a spell of 3rd level or higher becomes dim light if it is produced in or carried into this chamber.

> The shrine of binding takes up a large portion of this black marble chamber.

Creatures. Six **shadows** lurk here.

Poisoned Shadows. Whenever a non-undead creature in this area takes damage, it must make a DC 15 Wisdom saving throw. On a failed save, the creature takes 5 (2d4) poison damage, and it is blinded for 1 minute. A creature can repeat the saving throw at the end of each of its turns, ending the effect on itself on a success.

Chosen of Ibrandul. The Chosen of Ibrandul is a chaotic evil female drow named Ashdra. Ibrandul is a god of darkness and underground places once primarily worshiped by humans in southern lands such as Calimshan. He was worshiped as a comforter and protector of those who travel and work in darkness.

White Gate. The doors to the south open onto a corridor that runs southwest and joins with two other passages. At the junction is a white gate that connects with the Temples of Turmoil and with the Temples of Nature.

Temples of Turmoil

The magic of Szass Tam turns different facets of chaos to absolute evil in these great halls.

103. Temple of Fortune

> A pattern of shadow swirls around a shrine of binding and plays out across the white-and-gold marble floor of this hall. To the west is a black gate.

Creatures. A Red Wizard **necromancer** (see appendix B) works here, guarded by a **flesh golem**. Shalok, the Red Wizard, is a coward. If the fight goes badly for him, he surrenders. He offers his skeleton key and one piece of lore if he's allowed to flee to the gatehouse.

Curse of Fortune. High and low d20 results matter more in this area:

- A creature that rolls a natural 1 on an attack roll takes the damage from its attack.
- A creature that scores a critical hit can roll the extra damage die twice instead of just once.
- A creature that rolls a 1 on a saving throw suffers the worst possible effect, such as maximum damage from a spell.
- If a creature rolls a 20 on a saving throw, the creator of the effect that caused the saving throw suffers the effect instead.
- If a creature rolls a 1 on an ability check, it suffers the worst possible outcome of the attempted action.
- If a creature rolls a 20 on an ability check, it accomplishes a particularly spectacular and favorable outcome.

Chosen of Tymora. The Chosen of Tymora is a chaotic good male halfling named Curran Corvalin. Tymora is the goddess of good fortune, skill, and victory. She is the patron of all who take risks. Although considered to be a good deity who favors those who take bold action, she is also seen as somewhat capricious.

Curran was captured by the Red Wizards a few weeks ago. He never considered himself to be a Chosen of Tymora, since he never had any special powers. He always just assumed he had unnaturally good luck.

Curran is eager to return home, but he is too weak to help the party. If taken to the gatehouse, he awaits the party's triumph there.

Keys. Shalok has a glyph key attuned to this zone, as well as a skeleton key that unlocks all the doors in this zone.

104. Temple of Savagery

This chamber of red marble rings with the dying screams of humanoids. The sounds arouse feelings of violence.

Creatures. A Red Wizard **evoker** (see appendix B) has command over two **dread warriors** (see appendix B) here. A **shadow** lurks at each pillar on the shrine of binding, for a total of four.

Curse of Bloodlust. If combat occurs in this area, a creature takes 5 (2d4) psychic damage at the end of each of its turns when it doesn't deal damage to another creature.

Curse of Betrayal. Any creature that ends its turn in this area must make a DC 15 Charisma saving throw. If the saving throw fails, the creature treats all other creatures as enemies for the purpose of opportunity attacks and makes any opportunity attack available to it, with advantage on the attack roll, until the end of the creature's next turn. It can use no other reactions during this time.

Chosen of Bhaal. This shrine contains a Chosen of Bhaal named Torlin Silvershield, who was formerly a duke of Baldur's Gate. He has become a **wight**. The creature hisses an oath to Bhaal and attacks characters who free it.

Bhaal is the Lord of Murder and a patron of assassins.

White Gate. The doors on the eastern wall open onto a corridor that joins with two other passages. At the junction is a white gate that connects with the Temples of Oppression and with the Temples of Nature.

Temples of Nature

The power of nature is stripped down to its most destructive core in this zone.

105. Temple of Plague

A glowing green mist drifts around a shrine of binding in this white marble chamber. To the southwest is a black gate.

Creatures. A Red Wizard **necromancer** (see appendix B) and a **deathlock wight** (see appendix B) work here, guarded by a **dread warrior** (see appendix B) and four **zombies**. Thutai, the Red Wizard, is the overseer of this sector. He cares little for his underlings, including them in area effects if it means harming more characters. If the fight goes badly, he uses the black gate to flee.

Curse of Death. Characters have disadvantage on death saving throws while in this area.

Plague Mist. The shrine exudes poisonous mist that makes the area lightly obscured. Each creature that starts its turn in the room must make a DC 13 Constitution saving throw. On a failed save, the creature takes 5 (2d4) poison damage and spends its turn incapacitated and retching. If a creature accumulates three failed saves against this mist, its hit point maximum is lowered by the amount of poison damage it has taken from the mist. A creature that makes three successful saving throws against the mist becomes immune to its effects for 4 hours.

Chosen of Yurtrus. The Chosen of Yurtrus is a neutral evil male orc named Bandagh. Yurtrus is the orc deity of disease, decay, rot, and death. Orcs fear Yurtrus, and his priests have protected status in the tribe even though they are often weak or infirm in some way. Bandagh is pockmarked from years of disease, and is in no condition to pick a fight if he is freed.

Treasure. Thutai wears *bracers of defense* and has *spell scrolls* of *remove curse* and *speak with dead*.

Keys. Thutai has a glyph key attuned to every zone in this sector, as well as a skeleton key that unlocks all the doors in this zone.

White Gate. The doors on the western wall open onto a corridor that joins with two other passages. At the junction is a white gate that connects with the Temples of Oppression and with the Temples of Turmoil.

106. Temple of the Forest

Gnarled vines thrust from the rough floor of this green cavern, and roots dangle from the ceiling. The vines move as if in a breeze, though you feel no such thing.

Creatures. A **wraith** and three **will-o'-wisps** guard this chamber. The wisps start out invisible.

Clutching Vines. While on the ground, a creature that moves more than half its speed or misses with a melee attack causes the branches within 5 feet to elongate and grasp. Each creature on the ground in the area must succeed on a DC 13 Strength saving throw or become restrained in the vines. The area becomes difficult terrain. A restrained creature can take an action to make a DC 13 Strength check, freeing itself on a success.

Chosen of Rillifane Rallathil. A neutral good female wood elf **druid** named Eira is the Chosen of Rillifane Rallathil, the elven god of the woodlands and of the harmony of nature. He is seen as a calm and steady deity, quite unlike his more mercurial fellow elven deities.

As part of the experiments in this sector, Eira has been infused with the essence of a Chosen of Talona who was sacrificed. The binding process has left Eira at half her hit points but otherwise in good shape. She begs to accompany the characters in the fight against the Red Wizards.

If Eira joins the party, when she enters combat, the Talona side surfaces and contests for control. She argues out loud with herself, and half the time she acts evilly and without concern for her saviors. While talking to herself, she reveals what happened to her as well as one piece of lore. If Eira drops to 0 hit points, she disintegrates, her body turning to ash.

107. Temple of Winter

A blast of freezing air comes through the open doors to this chamber, where the walls are covered with ice.

Creatures. A Red Wizard **evoker** (see appendix B) and a **Thayan apprentice** (see appendix B) work here, with three trained **yetis** as bodyguards. Aduna, the Red Wizard, and her apprentice prefer to stand near the braziers.

Braziers. The magic stone braziers are built into the room and can't be moved. A creature that touches a brazier for the first time on a turn takes 3 (1d6) fire damage.

Chill Metal Aura. A creature within 10 feet of a brazier ignores this effect. Any other creature wielding a metal weapon or wearing metal armor must succeed on a DC 13 Constitution saving throw at the start of each of its turns or take 5 (2d4) cold damage. If the saving throw fails by 5 or more, the creature has disadvantage on Strength- and Dexterity-based attack rolls, ability checks, and saving throws until the start of its next turn.

Chosen of Auril. The Chosen of Auril is a chaotic evil female human named Hedrun Arnsfirth. Auril is a callous and cold-hearted bringer of winter. Most humans propitiate Auril with offerings or prayers when the first frosts come and curse her name during blizzards.

Hedrun is now a **deathlock wight** (see appendix B). If freed, she screams an oath to Auril and attacks the characters.

Treasure. Aduna wears a *robe of summer* (see appendix A).

Keys. Aduna has a glyph key attuned to this zone, as well as a skeleton key that unlocks all the doors in this zone.

THE PHYLACTERY VAULT

Once the characters disrupt six black gates throughout the dungeon, they can use the gates in the Temples of Extraction to travel to the Phylactery Vault. Before they make that journey, Syranna uses *sending* to call the characters back to the gatehouse and brief them on their final task. Syranna interacts with the party as follows:

> Syranna's image appears before you and speaks.
>
> "Hello again," she says. "I confess that I'm surprised at how well you have persevered. Your actions have significantly disrupted activity in the Doomvault. But the task is not yet complete.
>
> "You have a chance to deal a heavy blow to Szass Tam and the liches of Thay. The black gates have been disrupted, allowing entry into a chamber deep beneath the Doomvault. Accessible only by magic, this room is called the Phylactery Vault because it houses the phylacteries of many of Szass Tam's high-ranking lich servants.
>
> "You must enter the vault, defeat its guardians, and disrupt the magic there. You can enter through any black gate in the Temples of Extraction when you are ready."

The characters can ask questions, but at best Syranna knows only a little more than they do. (You can use this opportunity to give out information you want the players to know before proceeding.)

ENTERING THE VAULT

The Phylactery Vault is a tetrahedral space—like standing inside a hollow pyramid—and the characters are inside that space when they arrive. Each face of the vault has its own gravity. In effect, every surface is a floor. See the "Gravity" section for more details.

Maps 5.12 and 5.13 depict the inside of the Phylactery Vault and indicate how those floors connect with the other surfaces. The characters arrive on floor 1.

Begin by describing the area:

> The vast, four-sided pyramidal space has a floor of rough-hewn white marble set with low circular pedestals of the same material. At the three corners of the floor stand sepulchers of white marble, each a three-sided pyramid that mirrors the shape of the vault. Engraved into each sepulcher's double doors is a four-armed gargoyle, poised to attack. A pool of dark liquid churns in the center of the floor.
>
> Each other surface of the vault is nearly identical. Rubble of black rock scattered near the wall and the pool on each side stay in place. It seems apparent that each side has its own gravity.

Make sure the players understand the relative gravity of each floor.

Adjacent Floors. The directions that lead to other floors in the vault are indicated on the map for floors 1 and 2.

If the characters are on floor 3, they can reach floor 1 by traveling north, floor 4 by going southwest, and floor 1 by traveling southeast.

If the characters are on floor 4, they can reach floor 3 by traveling south, floor 1 by going northwest, and floor 2 by traveling northeast.

GENERAL FEATURES

Each floor inside the Phylactery Vault has the following features.

Dark Pools. A dark pool is 1 foot deep and difficult terrain. Any creature that starts its turn in a dark pool takes 9 (2d8) necrotic damage. A creature in a dark pool can't regain hit points.

Pedestals. The 3-foot-high pedestals store radiant energy, which is released in the presence of undead intruders. If an undead creature other than Kazit Gul ends its turn within 5 feet of a pedestal, the creature must succeed on a DC 13 Charisma saving throw or take 11 (2d10) radiant damage.

Rubble Piles. Along the edge of each floor, a pile of loose chunks of black marble rises to a height of 3 feet as it crosses to the adjacent floor. This rubble is difficult terrain.

Sepulchers. The double doors to these tetrahedral pyramids are locked (requiring a successful DC 17 Dexterity check to pick the lock or a successful DC 20 Strength check to burst it). If either of the two doors on a sepulcher is opened, each door on that sepulcher

Phylactery Vault

1 square = 5 feet

To Floor 2

To Floor 3

To Floor 4

Floor 1

To Floor 3

To Floor 4

Floor 2

To Floor 1

Map 5.12: The Phylactery Vault

Phylactery Vault

1 square = 5 feet

To Floor 2

Floor 3

To Floor 4

To Floor 1

To Floor 1

Floor 4

To Floor 2

To Floor 3

Map 5.13: The Phylactery Vault

transforms into a four-armed **gargoyle** (as a normal gargoyle with 63 hit points and one extra claw attack, for a total of three attacks, with Multiattack) and attacks.

Within each sepulcher is a set of phylacteries. See the "Phylacteries" section.

GRAVITY

Each floor in the vault's tetrahedral space has its own gravity. This phenomenon also has the following effects.

Flying. A creature flying from one floor to land on another must succeed on a DC 10 Dexterity (Acrobatics) check or fall prone upon landing.

Ranged Attacks. Due to the weird gravity, creatures have disadvantage on ranged attack rolls made against targets on a different floor.

Moving between Floors. The edges of the tetrahedron are lined with piles of rubble. Crossing to the rubble pile onto an adjacent floor requires a successful DC 13 Strength (Athletics) or Dexterity (Acrobatics) check. On a failed check, the creature falls prone in that rubble pile.

PHYLACTERIES

Within each sepulcher is a scene like the following:

> The sepulcher walls hum with arcane power. On stone shelves are leather cases, amulets, daggers, scroll tubes, unholy symbols, and other ornate objects. These are the phylacteries of Szass Tam's lich servants.

The phylacteries can't be harmed while they are protected by the magic of the sepulcher. However, a successful DC 10 Intelligence (Arcana) check made while examining a sepulcher reveals that disrupting the flow of eldritch energy within a sepulcher will disable the structure.

Disrupting the energy flow requires intense concentration. It takes three successful DC 15 Intelligence (Arcana or Religion) checks performed by a character who is proficient in that skill and is touching the target sepulcher. On each failed check, the character takes force damage equal to the amount by which the check failed. After making one check, a character realizes that every glyph key he or she holds will grant a +1 bonus to the check.

When the group disables its first sepulcher, read:

> Fountains of shadowy energy burst from the dark pools to form an inky vortex in the open air at the vault's center.
>
> A gleaming black humanoid skull flies out of the vortex. It has a ruby in each of its eye sockets and eight oversized glowing diamonds in place of teeth.

KAZIT GUL

Kazit Gul, a **demilich**, has entered the vault and immediately attacks the characters. If the demilich is destroyed, read:

> The skull turns to black ash that floats away, and the eight gems embedded in it fall to the ground.

The gems that contain souls gleam with inner light. If such a gem is crushed, the soul is released. The soul departs for the afterlife unless its body is intact and within 10 feet of the crushed gem.

ENDGAME

In order to destroy the Phylactery Vault, first Kazit Gul must be destroyed, and then three sepulchers must be disabled. When those conditions are met, the magic coursing through the Phylactery Vault unravels:

> The white pedestals crumble to rubble and the dark pools dissipate, leaving behind black ash. The vortex overhead collapses, spilling black ash and diamonds onto the floor. Your glyph keys pulse with blue light and subtle vibrations. The black gates begin to pulse in time with the keys.

A character can make a DC 13 Intelligence (Arcana) check to assess the failing magic and confirm that the Phylactery Vault is collapsing.

If all eight of the demilich's gems have been destroyed when the Phylactery Vault begins to collapse, then Kazit Gul is permanently slain. The characters can hear a distant wail and sense Gul's passing.

At this juncture, the characters' glyph keys allow them to use any black gates to escape this quickly collapsing extradimensional space, but the only place they can go is the gatehouse.

AFTERMATH

With the Phylactery Vault destroyed, Syranna is true to her word and uses *teleport* to send the characters (as well as any NPCs they saved from the Doomvault) to a location of their choice. She invites any characters who proved useful, particularly those with arcane talents, to remain in Thay under her leadership. She promises them power and influence if they throw in support for her.

Any fallen characters who were raised as soul-bound undead can't leave the Doomvault without dying permanently. Syranna assures such characters who choose to stay that she will see that they are restored to life, once she gains sufficient power to do so. 🜚

Against the Giants

IANTS HAVE BEEN RAIDING CIVILIZED lands in bands, with giants of different sorts in these marauding groups. Death and destruction have been laid heavily upon every place these monsters have visited. This has caused great anger in high places, for life and property loss means failure of the vows of noble rulers to protect the life and goods of each and every subject—and possible lean times for the rulers as well as the ruled. Therefore, a party of the bravest and most powerful adventurers has been assembled and given the charge to punish the miscreant giants. Characters whose homes lay in the devastated land probably need little more motivation to face their oppressors.

The first stage of the characters' mission is an infiltration and assault of the Steading of the Hill Giant Chief. From there, if they succeed, the adventurers can advance to test their mettle against the even more formidable giants of frost and fire, but that is of no concern right now—the steading awaits, and its perils are plentiful.

Running the Adventures

This is a series of three linked adventures. It is designed for a group of four or five player characters of 11th level. If the characters persevere, they are likely to advance in level at the end of each section of the story. Only strong and experienced characters should adventure into these giants' areas if the party consists of no more than four characters. The characters should have magic items to help them overcome the challenges they face. For a small party, the most important qualities are experience and caution. A group of four well-played characters can expect a reasonable chance of survival if they use their knowledge and cunning to best advantage.

These adventures were designed for strategic play, so some areas of the giant settlements are very dangerous even for characters of the recommended level. Further, adventurers who call too much attention to themselves are likely to be doomed. It takes only one or two extra giants in an encounter to turn a manageable situation into a very deadly one.

Therefore, be free with information the players need to make informed decisions. For example, any seasoned adventurer can see that the giants in the great hall of the steading represent an overwhelming challenge. So, the question becomes how to accomplish punishing the giants and discovering what is influencing them without having to face so many at once. The adventure contains some possible answers.

Keep track of the fate of important giants and their allies or captives. Escaping adversaries will generally flee to the next higher-ranking stronghold (from the steading to the rift and from the rift to Snurre's hall);

freed captives may join forces with their rescuers (this is a good way to introduce replacement player characters). This assumes survival of the individuals, of course, as well as opportunity for them to act. Some provision for the movement of surviving giants is given in the latter scenarios, but you will have to modify these according to the outcome of previous adventuring by your group.

Customizing the Giants

If you want to add some variability to the encounters in these adventures, a good way to do this is by modifying the armor and weapons the giants use. In particular, the servants and the young that are found among the giants might not be outfitted with the gear described in the statistics used for them. Servants could use improvised weapons, such as giant-sized tools and utensils they have available. If you decide to change any giant's melee weapon to some other giant-sized weapon, adjust its damage accordingly: Huge giants deal three times normal weapon damage, and Large giants, such as ogres, deal twice normal weapon damage.

When a giant uses the statistics of an ogre, that creature might use throwing rocks for ranged attacks (assuming any are on hand) rather than the ogre's standard weaponry. If projectiles are available, throwing rocks is always a giant's best (and preferred) ranged attack.

Giants' Bags

Many opportunities arise throughout these adventures for the characters to search miscellaneous bags and

---

Placing the Adventures

The preferred habitats of hill giants, frost giants, and fire giants exist in virtually every D&D setting, so it's not too difficult to find locations for the strongholds and the events in *Against the Giants*.

Dragonlance. On Krynn, the alliance of giants could center on the Kharolis Mountains, bringing Abanasinia, Qualinesti, Thorbardin, Kharolis, and Tarsis into the conflict. The ultimate villains in the Dragonlance setting would have to be dark exiles of an even more unexpected sort than those described in this adventure.

Eberron. The giant conspiracy could have its roots in faraway Xen'drik, with an outpost in Breland serving as the hill giant steading. Or the giants could be from Droaam, perhaps acting against the wishes of the Daughters of Sora Kell due to another sinister influence.

Forgotten Realms. In Faerûn, the giants could be raiding the Sword Coast after emerging from the Sword Mountains or the Sunset Mountains or the Spine of the World. They might be preparing to move on Damara from out of the Galena Mountains, or to descend upon the Dalelands and Cormyr from the Stormhorns or the Thunder Peaks.

Greyhawk. The giants might threaten Geoff, Sterich, or other nearby realms from out of the Crystalmists, the Jotens, or even the infamous Barrier Peaks.

chests that belong to giants. The contents of these containers can be determined randomly by using the following table. Roll 3d4 to determine the number of different items among the contents, then roll d100 for each item and refer to the table to determine its nature. Either apply the result of the roll or use it as inspiration for something along the same lines.

Giant's Bag Contents

d100	Item in Bag
01–03	Old axe blade for use as hand chopper
04–17	1d4 small boulders
18–19	Battered tin or pewter bowl and spoon
20–21	Various and sundry bent brass items
22–23	1d6 large iron caltrops
24–25	Hard cheese, slightly moldy and stinky
26–30	Shabby wool or hide cloak
31–32	Bone comb and hairpins
33–40	Iron cooking pot
41–43	Drinking horn
44–47	Skinning knife
48–53	Various soiled and patched linens
54–60	Haunch of meat
61–64	Coins, copper (100 to 400 pieces)
65–67	Coins, silver (20 to 80 pieces)
68–69	Coins, gold (10 to 40 pieces)
70–76	Fur pelt, worthless and mangy
77–83	Coil of very strong rope (10 feet to 120 feet)
84–85	Salt (small bag or box)
86–90	Old sandals
91–98	Wineskin or water skin (full)
99–00	1d8 animal teeth or tusks (no ivory value)

Steading of the Hill Giant Chief

To send them off with every possible advantage, patrons outfit the characters with all standard items needed for both wilderness and dungeon exploration; and each member of the party has likewise been given the finest horse available. Guides are available to help, and the party has a splendid map showing the exact location of the great timber fortress of the chief of the hill giants.

This chief, one Nosnra, is a grossly fat and thoroughly despicable creature, sly and vicious, loving ambush and back-stabbing. Furthermore, the party has been cautioned to expect a secret force, some motivational power behind this unusual banding of different races of giants. Finally, the party has been instructed to keep any and all loot they chance upon, this being their reward for the perils they are to face. They are to follow any clues that point toward the sinister hand suspected of guiding the uprising, but are to return at once if they determine exactly the reason or force behind the unholy alliance. Some relic of great evil might be at hand.

Running the Adventure

There is considerable information contained herein with respect to what the players see as they explore the steading, and what the inhabitants do if they become aware of the intruders. This does not mean that you, as Dungeon Master, must surrender your creativity and become a mere script reader. You will have to make up certain details for areas and items that characters thoroughly examine and explore. There will inevitably be player actions which the script has not anticipated, and you will have to judge their results. Finally, you can amend and alter monsters and treasures as you see fit, with an eye towards your home campaign and your particular players. If time permits, the giants organize traps, ambushes, and last-ditch defenses against continuing forays into their stronghold.

Adventure Start

It is assumed that the party has safely arrived at a spot near the giants' stronghold—a small cave, well hidden, where they can hide mounts and equipment. They come to the place of the giants just at dusk. No windows are visible, nor can giants or any other creatures be seen about the place, although occasional bursts of shouting and laughter can be heard faintly from within. The characters have been warned to expect guards at the great doors to the steading, but none are visible. (If the party returns to the stronghold after an initial foray, there will

About the Original

Against the Giants, by Gary Gygax, was originally produced in 1981 as a compilation of three adventures written in the earliest days of the game. Those adventures were created and originally released in 1978, during the time when Gary

Gygax was still writing the *Player's Handbook* for the original AD&D game. Despite being (in a sense) older than the game itself, these adventures continue to hold a special place in the hearts and memories of D&D players of all ages.

be guards present on the second and subsequent visits.) The time has come to see what is afoot!

If the party decides to retire between forays against the steading, they can retreat to the relative safety of the hidden cave base camp to rest and regain spells—provided they take moderate precautions not to leave a plain trail or be followed to this sanctuary. Failure to take such basic precautions may lead to disaster! The characters are assumed to have brought sufficient supplies for several weeks' stay with them.

UPPER WORKS: GENERAL FEATURES

Map 6.1 shows the layout of the huge timber stronghold of the local clan of hill giants. All outer walls are of logs at least 3 feet in diameter. Inner walls dividing rooms are about 2 feet thick. All inside floors are of stone.

The steading is in a nasty, damp area, where hard rain is a daily occurrence and wet fog a nightly event. As a result, all wood in the place is very damp and difficult to set aflame.

Ceilings. Ceiling height varies from about 16 feet at the edges to 32 feet at the center, the roof being held up by great, smoke-blackened rafters. The open yard (area 22) has no roof.

Doors. Doors are great iron-bound log affairs 1 foot in thickness, each about 7 feet wide and 16 to 18 feet high.

A Medium or smaller creature must succeed on a DC 10 Strength (Athletics) check to open any of the doors on the upper level due to their great size and weight. Doors stay open if left that way.

Illumination. Fireplaces are indicated on the map, but the locations of other light sources such as cressets and braziers are not.

Secret Doors. Secret doors in the upper level of the stronghold are relatively easy to find due to the crude construction of the place. It requires a successful DC 12 Wisdom (Perception) check to find such a door.

RANDOM ENCOUNTERS

On the upper level of the stronghold, the chance of a random encounter occurs on an hourly basis. At the end of each hour, roll a d6. On a roll of 1, which indicates a random encounter, consult the section below that corresponds to the characters' current location.

Entryway and Long Corridor. If the characters are in area 1 or in the corridor that leads to area 11, choose from the following possibilities:

- Two hot-headed **hill giants** heading for the weapons room (area 13) from the great hall (area 11), intending to fight an impromptu duel
- The **cloud giant** from the great hall (area 11) heading for the front gate (area 1)
- The **stone giant** from the great hall (area 11) heading for the front gate (area 1)

Eastern Section. If the characters are in areas 2 through 10, choose from the following possibilities:

- Grutha, the chief's wife, coming from the great hall (area 11) to get her pet cave bear from her room (see area 7)
- A **hill giant** with four **dire wolves** from the open yard (area 22) going to the barracks (area 4)

- Chief Nosnra (see area 11) and two **ogres** going to get some trophies from the chief's hall (area 6) to show off in the great hall
- 1d4 + 1 young hill giants (use the **orc** statistics) from the dormitory (area 3) heading through the open yard (area 22) to raid the pantry (area 18A)

Western Section. If the characters are in areas 12 through 21, choose from the following possibilities:

- 2d6 orc slaves (**commoners**) rushing to get shields (from area 12 or 13) to use as platters
- Two **hill giants** from the great hall (area 11) going to sleep off a drunk (in area 15 or 16)
- Three **ogres** from the great hall (area 11) going to get one of the guards from the entryway (area 1)
- A **hill giant** from the great hall (area 11) taking a stroll to clear his head

Yard and Barracks Rooms. If the characters are in areas 22 through 25, they might encounter a **hill giant** from the great hall (area 11) heading for bed.

LOCATIONS ON THE UPPER LEVEL

The following locations are identified on map 6.1.

1. FRONT GATE AND FOYER

Most of the floor in the entryway is bare, but various items of giant outerwear (capes, cloaks, and the like) and bags hang from the many pegs along the walls. Use the Giant's Bag Contents table to randomly determine what's inside any bag or sack the characters happen to open. Any noise the characters make could awaken the sleeping guards in the area.

Guards at the Gate. Two snoring **hill giants**, supposedly guarding the entrance, lie curled up blissfully asleep just inside the front gate, a nearly empty keg of ale between them. If these guards are attacked and not killed in a single round, they alert the third guard (posted in the watch tower at area 1B).

1B. TOWER GUARD

Steps in the western end of the foyer lead up to the watch tower, where a **hill giant** guard is dozing, an empty flagon smelling of mead still in his hand. An iron hoop and a straight bar hang on ropes from a rafter above; striking them together will alert everyone in the upper level.

Treasure. The guard wears a belt with a gem-set gold buckle (worth 400 gp).

2. SUBCHIEF'S ROOM

This place contains a scattering of furnishings: hides on the floors, a bear skin on the wall, a chair, a stool, a huge chest, and a vast bed mounted with furs.

Under the furs on the bed is a sleeping **hill giant**. It requires successful DC 8 Dexterity (Stealth) checks for characters to enter this room without waking her, as well as when the characters do anything else that might make enough noise to rouse her. Any loud noise wakes her immediately.

Treasure. On a shelf 9 feet above the floor are a beaten silver comb set with four gems (worth 100 gp), a copper mirror (20 gp), and a large gold hairpin set with

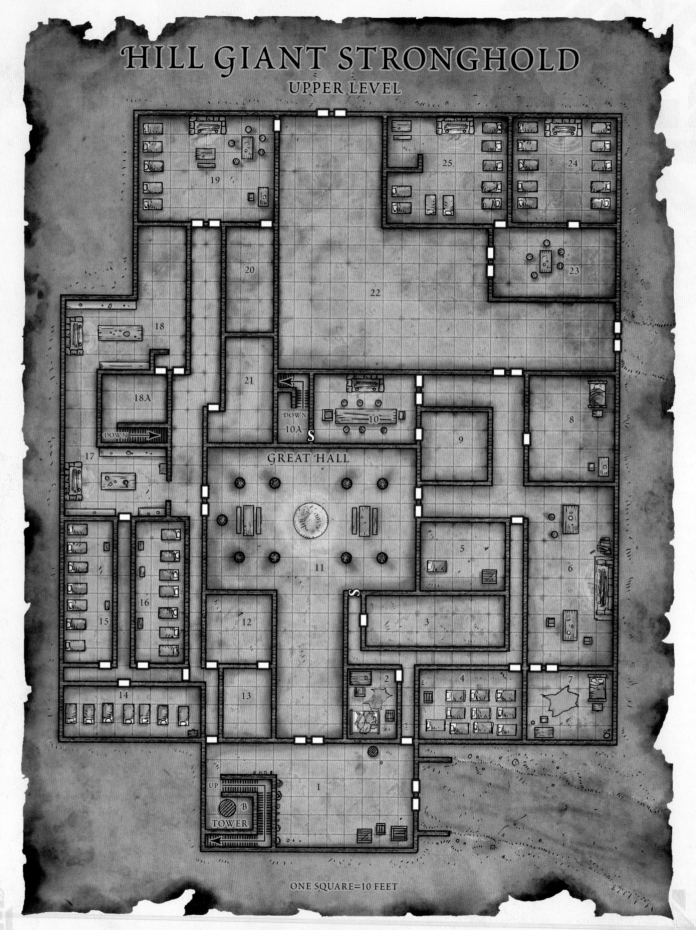

HILL GIANT STRONGHOLD
UPPER LEVEL

19

25 24

20

23

22

18

18A

21

17

10A

DOWN

10

S

8

9

GREAT HALL

5

6

11

16

15

12

3

14

13

2

4

7

1

UP

B

TOWER

ONE SQUARE = 10 FEET

MAP 6.1: HILL GIANT STRONGHOLD, UPPER LEVEL

a pearl (total value 200 gp). The chest contains 980 cp, 320 sp, and 400 gp.

3. Dormitory

Here twelve young hill giants (use the **orc** statistics) are rollicking; beefy smacks, and shouts, laughter can easily be heard through the corridor outside. All these youngsters have weapons and will readily attack any intruders they spot. Noise coming from here, even shrieks and swords clashing, will be regarded by others as the kids simply having fun.

4. Barracks

Two soundly sleeping, loudly snoring **hill giants** occupy two of the ten beds in the barracks. Typical giant clothing hangs from the walls, and a couple of torches smolder in wall-mounted cressets. A wooden chest stands near the western wall.

Treasure. A small pouch in the chest contains 40 pp.

5. Maids' Chamber

Three hill giant servants (use the **ogre** statistics) are in this room, along with the usual furnishings. Only the nasty old matron, a normal **hill giant**, is inclined to fight, but she dominates the others and orders them to attack if necessary. If the matron is slain, the three others cease hostilities and cooperate with the characters by describing Chief Nosnra's sanctum (areas 8, 9, and 10) and telling how to get there safely—if they are allowed to have the matron's hoard.

Treasure. The matron's valuables are stashed in a locked iron chest under the matron's bed. The matron carries the key to the chest; it can also be unlocked by a character who succeeds on a DC 15 Dexterity check using thieves' tools. The chest holds 800 gp, three platinum bracelets (worth 1,000 gp each), and four potions: *healing*, *superior healing*, *poison*, and *mind control* (hill giant) (see appendix A). The maids can be persuaded to part with the potions.

6. Hall of the Chief

Numerous interesting things fill this place, which is dominated by an enormous fireplace. The mantel of the fireplace holds a few items, including a shiny brass jar and a humanoid skull. The room has two tables, several chairs, and two stools, as well as rugs, hides, and skins on the floors and walls.

The tables have pottery flagons and platters on them; pots and kegs are all about the place. The walls display various trophies: heads of humanoids and other creatures, skulls, skins, and some arms and armor. Directly across from the fireplace, eight shields are mounted on the wall.

Treasure. One of the shields on the wall is a *+1 shield*. The brass jar on the mantel of the fireplace might catch the characters' eye, but it has no value. The skull on the mantel is also valueless, but inside it is a large gem worth 500 gp—one of the kids was playing with this bauble and stuck it inside the skull, where it has lain forgotten ever since.

7. Chamber of the Chief's Wife

Grutha, the chief's wife, is at feast in the great hall (area 11), while her pet cave bear (use the cave bear variant with the **polar bear** statistics) stays in her room. The creature acts as a guard and immediately attacks any intruder, for it can smell the person at the door. The bear makes no noise until it attacks.

The room has a bed, a small table, a chair, a stool, two chests, and a coffer, plus rugs, hides, and the like. The chests contain only clothing, since she is wearing her jewelry at the banquet.

Treasure. Hidden in the bed's straw mattress is a leather pouch with twenty-nine gems in it: one worth 1,000 gp, three 500 gp each, four 250 gp each, eight 50 gp each, and thirteen of 10 gp value.

8. Chief's Chamber

The room where the chief sleeps is hung with rugs and skins, and there are hides on the floor. It holds a bed, two chairs, a small table with a tun of cheap wine on it, a chest for clothing, and other clothing hanging on pegs. A thick chain (for the chief's cave bear) is set into one wall. An old shield and some of the chief's well-used weapons lie on the floor near one of the corners.

9. Arms Room

The chief's best personal armor, shields, and weapons are stored in a chamber that can be accessed only by going through the dining room (area 10). There are also four huge fur capes among the dozen or so items in the place.

Treasure. A *javelin of lightning* is wrapped in an old rag, which is stuffed under a cloak thrown into a far corner and shielded from sight by three spears and a club leaned against the wall in front of it. One of the capes, made of a giant otter pelt, is worth 400 gp.

10. Small Dining Room

The room beyond the double doors is used for meals and also the council meetings of the chief. It contains a long table, a great chair, a lesser chair, and six stools. A rough map of the area drawn on a large animal skin, showing past and planned raids, hangs on the wall opposite the fireplace. Several shelves, a smaller table and chair, and some miscellaneous items (a mug, some paper scraps, an old knife, a rock paperweight) round out the furnishings. There are hides on the walls and the floor.

Hidden Door. Near the southwest corner is a door concealed behind a manticore hide hung on the wall. Someone looking around the room can notice the shape of the door behind the hide with a successful DC 20 Wisdom (Perception) check. Someone who handles or looks behind the manticore skin finds the door without needing to make a check.

10A. Secret Stairs

Several scroll tubes are concealed in this room under a stack of logs in the alcove to the northwest. Someone who glances at the logs notices the bone tubes with a successful DC 15 Wisdom (Perception) check, and any search of the pile reveals them.

One tube, sealed and marked with a triangle surrounding a Y, holds instructions on the next raid, written in Giant and signed *Eclavdra*. Also inside is a map of the floor plan of this level of the steading. All the other tubes are empty.

The steps lead to the secret area of the steading's dungeon level (areas 29 through 33).

11. Great Hall

The long corridor that leads north from area 1 is dim, shadowy, and generally deserted and ignored, for all of the feasting and fun lies beyond, in the great hall itself. A few torches burn smokily high up along either wall.

The vast room at the end of the corridor contains trestle tables, benches, stools, and the like. Here and there stand barrels and kegs of ale, beer, and mead. All of the tables are crowded with various sorts of meat, cheese, bread, and drinking containers. Singing, talking, laughing, shouting, arguing, wrestling, joking, and the like are going on, so the place is a veritable din of noise. To the north of the central firepit (where a whole ox, two sheep, and four pigs roast on huge spits) is a higher table reserved for the chief, his wife, and their guests.

Creatures. The following creatures are in the hall:

- Chief Nosnra fights as a **frost giant** with no immunities. He has AC 17 from splint armor. The chief is seated at the head table.

- Nosnra's wife, Grutha, is a **hill giant**. She sits beside the chief.
- The chief's cave bear (use the cave bear variant with the **polar bear** statistics) is licking up spills under the head table at Nosnra's feet.
- The subchief, also seated at the head table, is a hill giant that fights as a **stone giant**, without Stone Camouflage. His AC is from splint armor.
- A **cloud giant** ambassador stands near the firepit.
- A **stone giant** visitor is seated at the head table.
- Seven **hill giants**, including the sergeant from area 25 (who has AC 16 from chain mail and 115 hit points), six hill giant servants (use the **ogre** statistics), and eight **ogres** are scattered around the room.

There are no throwing rocks here, aside from the few that some of the giants, especially the stone giant, might carry. On the wall directly behind the chief is a small ballista, which he uses as a heavy crossbow (2d10 piercing damage). It fires spears instead of bolts, and six of those projectiles are ready to hand.

Treasure. Each giant wears one to four pieces of jewelry worth 250 gp each. Ogres each wear one or two pieces worth 100 gp each. The subchief, decked out for the occasion, has four pieces. Nosnra and Grutha also wear four pieces of jewelry each, worth 1,000 gp per item. The bear has a jewel-studded collar with six rubies, worth a total of 250 gp.

The largest ogre has a key to the chest in area 21.

12. Arsenal Room

Thirty helmets, twenty-six shields, twenty-two spears, nine clubs, and three great axes are stored in the arsenal, scattered around the place. All are giant-sized.

13. Weapons Room

Spears, shields, clubs, and axes are abundant here—no fewer than a dozen of each, all sized for giants. There are four great swords (two-handed with respect to human-sized creatures), two huge iron maces (Strength 17 required to lift), and a sheaf of 6-foot-long spears that the giants use for javelins. All the shields are leaning against the walls.

Treasure. Behind the seventh shield that the characters check is a *+1 warhammer*. Another hammer is out of sight in a corner and only seen on close inspection of the room. Under the scrutiny of a *detect magic* spell, it radiates an aura of illusion magic due to a *magic mouth* spell placed on it. If picked up by a dwarf it barks out, "Here's a kiss for you, runt!"

14. Main Guest Chamber

The cloud giant ambassador and the stone giant visitor (currently in the great hall, area 11) are lodged here. In all, the room holds seven beds and various small furnishings including chairs, nightstands, and chests. One torch burns at the west end of the room in a sconce; on the opposite wall is a sconce holding a large, unlit torch. Various skins and hides cover the floors. Several others hang on the walls alongside giant garments on pegs. All are worthless, as are the contents of all the chests and the bags tucked under four of the beds. Still, a valuable reward waits for those who can find it.

Treasure. The unlit torch is an illusion, and making physical contact with it reveals it as such. Someone who examines the image without touching it can determine that it is an illusion by making a successful DC 15 Intelligence (Investigation) check. The sconce is actually the sheath for a weapon that belongs to the cloud giant: a sentient greatsword named *Waythe* (see appendix A).

15. Common Room

The place contains several cots, boxes, and stools, a table, two benches, and various odds and ends.

16. Common Room

This place is almost identical to the matching room across the hall (area 15), with the addition of a few cloaks plus some hides on the floors and walls.

Treasure. A small chest on a stool in the northeast corner contains some dwarf and elf ears, and one of them has an earring still attached with a gem in it (worth 50 gp).

17. Kitchen

This is a typical giant kitchen with counters along the walls, several tables, benches, a stool or two, and various items for cooking and baking (pots, kettles, bowls, knives, forks, spoons, ladles, spits, and so forth).

Twenty-nine orc slaves (**commoners**) work about the place, but they run away from conflict. Five hill giant servants (use the **ogre** statistics) and six young ogre ser-

vants (use the **orc** statistics) also run, but they call loudly for help as they flee.

18. Kitchen Workroom

The storage area north of the kitchen doubles as an eating place for servants. It includes three tables, a long counter, stools, benches, and an assortment of kitchen gear. Numerous sacks, boxes, and barrels contain flour, dried meat, dried fruit, honey, and other foodstuffs. Various cheeses, smoked meats, and sausages hang from the rafters. Several casks and tuns hold a wide variety of potables—ale, beer, mead, and wine—all of giant strength. Loaves of bread, still warm from the ovens, are stacked on one table.

18A. Pantry

The room to the south contains more provisions of the same types found in the kitchen workroom (area 18), as well as stairs that lead to the dungeon level.

19. Servants' Quarters

A large common room in the extreme north end of the stronghold has various cots, tables, chairs, stools, and the like. It is cluttered with old clothing and junk. Six hill giant servants (use the **ogre** statistics) are here, and a few are flirting with a handsome male **hill giant**. The giant enters combat to show off for his admirers. He will not call for help unless his current hit points drop to less than half of his hit point maximum. On the round when this happens, he begins to shout. Some of the servants aid him if he starts to cry out, but others prefer to avoid direct conflict, perhaps taking the opportunity to hurt or disadvantage a character from the blind side.

The giant warrior is the keeper of the wolves in area 22. His whip is hanging beside the door in the southeast corner of this room; this whip need only be shown to the wolves to make them whimper, cower, and fall back.

20. Orc Slave Quarters

This hall is a messy and smelly place filled with pallets and junk. The two orc slaves (**commoners**) currently in this place are too injured to work (since giants' kicks break bones). All the other slaves are elsewhere, helping with the feast.

The two slaves will happily aid the characters if allowed to do so. These orcs know about the rebellion in the dungeons, and they tell the party that any orcs they see down there should be hailed as friends. Aside from that, they are familiar with only the servants' quarters (area 19), the kitchen (area 17), and the great hall (area 11).

21. Ogre Quarters

The hill giants employ ogres as scouts, messengers, servants, and the like, for the ogres are trusty flunkies as well as hard workers and fighters. In addition to those in the great hall (area 11) and the youngsters at work in the kitchen (area 17), five more **ogres** are in their quarters playing at knucklebones and drinking beer. Ogres are a rowdy lot; hence, noise from this place attracts no attention. Scattered on the floor of the room are nearly a dozen heaps of skins on which the ogres sleep, and a locked iron chest is tucked into one corner.

Treasure. Hidden inside one of the heaps of skins is a leather sack containing a *potion of storm giant strength* and a *potion of invisibility*. There are ten such heaps, and the sack is hidden in the seventh one that the characters search.

One ogre wears a gem (worth 250 gp) on a thong around his neck. The creatures have 381 cp between them as the stakes for their game.

The lock on the chest can be opened by a character who succeeds on a DC 15 Dexterity check using thieves' tools, or by someone who uses the key that is carried by one of the ogres in the great hall (area 11). The chest holds 955 sp, 202 gp, and 19 pp.

22. OPEN YARD

Fourteen **dire wolves** run free here, and they immediately attack any humanoid that enters their area. If they see the whip from area 19, however, they cower and whimper, allowing the intruders to pass unchallenged.

23. GUARD ROOM

A huge horn rests upon the small table in the center of the room; blowing it calls the dire wolves. Eight stools and two benches line the walls, and a sheaf of eighteen spears is leaning against the wall by the door. A line of seven giant-sized shields and four clubs stands along the south wall. The guards that would normally be stationed here have gone to the celebration in the great hall.

24. BARRACKS ROOM

No one currently occupies the hill giants' barracks room. The place contains ten beds, equal numbers of chests and stools, two tables, a bench, and miscellaneous junk. A few hides decorate the floors and walls, and several broken weapons and dented helmets are strewn about.

25. BARRACKS ROOM

This room's contents are similar to those in area 24 (see above), except for the partially enclosed area to the northwest. This alcove belongs to the sergeant of the guards, who is now away feasting. There are three chests in the space, all filled with clothing and equipment for the troops and herself. Giant-sized boots are gathered in a sack that hangs from the wall.

Treasure. One of the boots near the bottom of the sack has 300 gp and two gems (worth 100 gp each) stuffed inside it. Another sack under the sergeant's cot has nothing but old (human-sized) helmets in it, mementos from foes she has slain.

DUNGEON LEVEL: GENERAL FEATURES

Map 6.2 shows the layout of the steading's lower level. The stonework is ancient but holding up well, patched in places with new mortar or shored up with newly hewn stone. All natural cave areas have stalagmites, but for ease of passage the giants have removed stalactites from the central caverns (areas 19–21).

Ceilings. Passageways have ceilings that are arched, and buttressed every 10 feet, with the peak of the arch about 18 feet overhead. The ceiling height in most small-ish rooms in the dungeon is 20 feet or so, again arched and buttressed. In the large rooms and chambers, the ceilings are 30 feet high. The roof in the natural caverns to the southeast (areas 19–21) is of varying height, the passages about 15 feet high and the large areas some 20 feet or more. The roof of the carrion crawlers' lair (area 23) is about 40 feet high.

Doors. Unless otherwise noted, doors on the dungeon level are the same as those on the upper level, made of iron-bound logs and each about 7 feet wide and 16 to 18 feet high.

Illumination. Torches and braziers provide light in several locations, and a few areas are illuminated by other means, as indicated in the area descriptions. The caverns of unworked stone (areas 19, 20, 21, and 23) are unlit.

Secret Doors. Secret doors on the dungeon level are hidden well. It requires a successful DC 20 Wisdom (Perception) check to find such a door.

RANDOM ENCOUNTERS

On the dungeon level, the chance of a random encounter occurs on an hourly basis. At the end of each hour, consult the section below that corresponds to the characters' current location.

Excavated Rooms and Passages. If the characters are in areas 1 through 18, area 22, or areas 24 through 33, roll a d12. On a roll of 1, which indicates a random encounter, choose from the following possibilities:

- Four **ogres** seeking some orcs
- The Keeper (see area 2), out inspecting, accompanied by an **ape** (one of his pets)
- Twelve rebel **orcs** out raiding for food, two armed with heavy crossbows and poisoned bolts

Caverns. If the characters are in areas 19 through 21 or area 23, roll a d20. On a roll of 1, which indicates a random encounter, choose from the following possibilities:

- 1d4 young **giant lizards** from area 21
- 1d3 **carrion crawlers** coming from area 22 by way of the sinkholes

LOCATIONS ON THE DUNGEON LEVEL

The following locations are identified on map 6.2.

1. MARSHALING AREA

At the bottom of the stairs that lead from area 18A on the upper level is a room where slaves are rounded up and sent about their tasks under guard. It is also used for the revels of the off-duty dungeon crew. A few smoky torches burn along the walls. Several benches and tables are pushed out of the way against the walls, revealing a floor of black stone, much worn by the tread of countless feet.

2. CHAMBER OF THE KEEPER

A cluttered room near the marshaling area has skins on the floor, a bed, a table and chair, two wooden boxes, several crates and barrels, a chest, and odds and ends of armor, weapons, furniture, tableware, and so forth.

Residing here is the Keeper, a ghastly hill giant (use the **stone giant** statistics, without Stone Camouflage) that is hunchbacked and twisted, and has only one good eye. He is thoroughly wicked, strong, and remorseless. In his lair, he is never without his two pet **apes** (which have 30 hit points each). One is on guard to the north of the door, the other resting on a platform built above the door.

The Keeper wears a thick chain mail shirt (accounting for his AC), and he fights with a giant-sized *+1 battleaxe* that gives him a +10 bonus to hit. He has a reach of 15 feet with the weapon, which deals 20 (3d8 + 7) slashing damage on a hit.

Treasure. Beneath a loose stone in the floor is a hole that contains 1,250 gp, three 250 gp gems, two 100 gp gems, and a large earthenware jug that holds four *potions of water breathing*.

3. CELL BLOCK

In the outer guard room are two **bugbears**, initially located in the eastern end of the area. If not engaged immediately, they will raise an alarm by striking a large brass gong that hangs near the door. If they are prevented from doing so and are faced by an obviously superior enemy, the bugbears feign surrender and direct the characters' attention to the fourth cell (see below), where—so they say—treasure is to be had. Then, when the characters are occupied fighting the monsters that await within that cell, the bugbears will strike the alarm and flee. In addition to the alarm gong, the guard room contains a table, two stools, torches, and a ring of keys that open four of the five cell doors.

The cells, from left to right, have the following occupants:

First Cell. A human merchant (**noble**), taken prisoner some time ago and now quite insane from mistreatment, is in the cell nearest the door.

Second Cell. A second human prisoner, an engineer (**commoner**), is kept alive to help with the excavation of new areas of the dungeon. He cannot aid his rescuers, but he will repay them with service.

Third Cell. An elf **knight** is chained to the wall. He is wounded from torture (currently down to 14 hit points). He gladly takes up arms to aid his rescuers and is willing to serve his rescuers for one year without pay in gratitude for his freedom.

Fourth Cell. The bugbear guards will say that they have been instructed to keep three "magical skeletons" in one of the cells safe from would-be thieves. To back up their tale, they point out—quite truthfully—that they have no key to this cell. Indeed, there are three skeletal creatures lying on the floor, each one wearing a shiny ring set with a large gemstone.

The lock on the door can be opened by a character who succeeds on a DC 10 Dexterity check while using thieves' tools, or the door can be forced by someone who makes a successful DC 15 Strength [Athletics] check.

The three creatures are **wights** that spring to attack anyone who enters the cell. The rings they wear are nothing but brass, and the gems gemstone (glass).

Fifth Cell. Five captured **orc** rebels are crammed into the easternmost cell. Three others of their number have

already been tortured to death and eaten, so they will be very willing to help any creature promising them escape from the toils of the giants. These orcs can lead the characters south and east to the rebels' hideout (area 19) and will see them safely past the guards behind the barricade to the south (at the location marked B) if the characters can handle the bugbear at the watch post (W) to the west of that place.

BUGBEAR COMPLEX (AREAS 4–8)

Each of the five areas of the bugbear community has a few torches and braziers burning. Hides and skins decorate walls and floors, while mounds of straw and similar litter serve for bedding. Rounding out the furnishings are a few stools and small crates, boxes, and the like, a scattering of (worthless) personal belongings, and tables with scraps of food and odds and ends of eating utensils upon them.

4. Outpost. This room holds eight **bugbears**, alert and ready for trouble. They carry 2d4 gp each.

5. Barracks. This small barracks holds nine sleeping **bugbears**.

6. Barracks. This small barracks is similar to area 5, with eight sleeping **bugbears**.

7. Chamber of the Bugbear Captain. Currently, five bugbears—the captain (a **bugbear chief**) and four lieutenants (**bugbears**)—are sitting around a crude table drinking ale and discussing a plan to wipe out the rebel orcs in area 19. All these bugbears have longswords that deal 11 (2d8 + 2) slashing damage on a hit. All five are carrying 50 gp each. The captain also has thirty-one 10 gp gems hidden in a pouch under his armor.

HILL GIANT STRONGHOLD
DUNGEON LEVEL

ONE SQUARE = 10 FEET

MAP 6.2: HILL GIANT STRONGHOLD, DUNGEON LEVEL

8. Outpost. Six **bugbears** watch this point. These alert fellows are readying for an attack on the rebel orcs. One of them is always stationed in the corridor outside the south exit (at the place marked W on the map), watching the barricade (B) to the east for any signs of activity.

OBEDIENT SLAVE QUARTERS (AREAS 9–11)

The three chambers south of the bugbear complex are occupied by orc slaves that are considered docile by their captors. As such, these rooms are not heavily guarded. Each door is barred on the outside with a heavy iron rod.

Each room has a few smoky torches on the walls and moldy straw strewn on the floor. Some crude benches are built into the walls.

The occupants of these rooms are subdued to the point of being nearly helpless. They will defend themselves if harmed, but they offer no resistance otherwise.

9. Barracks. This room holds twenty-four unarmed orc slaves (six **orcs**, eighteen orc **commoners**).

10. Barracks. This room holds thirty unarmed orc slaves (seven **orcs**, twenty-three orc **commoners**).

11. Barracks. This room holds twenty-five unarmed orc slaves (five **orcs**, twenty orc **commoners**).

Barricade. East of these three rooms (near the place marked B on the map), the corridor is blocked by an accumulation of boulders and debris.

UNRULY SLAVE QUARTERS (AREAS 12–14)

Three enclosures to the west of the bugbear complex are used to house orc slaves that have proved themselves to be troublesome; as such, this area is under heavy scrutiny. A **bugbear** guard, watching for trouble, is stationed at each position marked W on the map.

Each of the barracks is secured by a barred gate through which the bugbears can keep an eye on the slaves. Each set of bars is secured by a lock and a bolt. The lock can be opened by a character who uses thieves' tools and succeeds on a DC 15 Dexterity check, or the gate can be forced open by someone who makes a successful DC 25 Strength (Athletics) check.

The rooms are unlit, have only scanty straw, and are quite noisome with the scent of unwashed orc.

The slaves housed in these rooms are not as meek as those in the chambers to the south. If their guards are dispatched and they are freed, some of them might be willing to take up arms against the giants.

12. Barracks. This chamber holds forty-eight unarmed orc slaves (thirteen **orcs**, thirty-five orc **commoners**).

13. Barracks. This chamber holds twenty-four unarmed orc slaves (five **orcs**, nineteen orc **commoners**).

14. Barracks. This chamber holds sixteen unarmed orc slaves (ten **orcs**, six orc **commoners**). If released, they are particularly eager to attack their captors. They know of a haven for orc refugees somewhere to the south but not the exact location of the rebel headquarters.

15. TORTURE CHAMBER

This large area contains various implements for torturing prisoners large and small—an iron maiden, two racks, thumbscrews, iron boots, chains, whips, branding irons, strappados, and so forth. A firepit in the center of the room lends it all a hellish light.

Huddled next to the northwest and southwest walls, two **hill giants** are dozing.

Treasure. One giant wears a gold chain set with a fire opal in the manner of a watch fob (worth 500 gp).

16. ARMORY AND SMITHY

Stacks of giant arms and armor, either newly made or in need of repair, clutter this place. The alcove north of the entrance holds several pike-sized spears, battleaxes, two-handed swords, and other weapons and armor usable only by giants. Some helmets are balanced on shields, each propped up by a warhammer or a mace.

The armorer and the smith, two **fire giants**, are occupied in the eastern section of the room when the characters enter. If any of the armor and weapons in the northern section are touched, they collapse with a clatter that warns the armorer and the smith of trouble. The giants immediately shout and come out fighting.

Also in the room, near the forge and bellows in the southwest corner, are five dwarves chained to the floor and forced to labor making weapons. Four of them are dwarf **commoners** intent only on escaping if they are released, but the fifth is a **veteran** who volunteers to stay with the characters as long as he receives a share of treasure equal to that of a character and a chance to fight giants.

Treasure. The armorer and the smith each have a sack filled with 1,000 gp.

17. BLOCKED PASSAGE

The rebel orcs have piled finished and rough stones against the north side of this door to keep it closed. The wooden door is bound with moldering bands of bronze, and a heavy bronze bolt secures it. Beyond the door, the corridor that leads to the southwest is disused, dusty, and reeks disgustingly.

17A. WEIRD ABANDONED TEMPLE

This room is lined with faintly glowing purplish-green stone, engraved with disturbing shapes and signs that seem to stare out from the walls and columns and to shift positions when the viewer's back is turned. Touching the walls sends a chill up a character's spine, and touching a pillar brings on nausea—a creature that does so must make a DC 15 Constitution saving throw. On a failed save, the creature becomes poisoned for 1 hour.

At the far west end of the temple is an altar of pale, yellow-gray translucent stone. It feels greasy to the touch but has no obvious effect upon those who touch it. Behind this altar is a flight of low, uneven stairs that lead to a semicircular alcove with a back wall made of a purplish-black, glassy-appearing substance. Anyone who stands before this wall and gazes upon it for 1 round sees a writhing, amorphous form of sickly mauve and violet stretching its formless members to embrace the viewer. This sight forces a character to succeed on a DC 15 Intelligence saving throw or be cursed with insanity (as the *symbol* spell's insanity effect, but permanent until ended with *remove curse, greater restoration, heal,* or similar magic).

Treasure. The first character who views the wall and does not go mad discovers that a *ring of mind shielding* has appeared on the altar. Any other character who undergoes the ordeal and succeeds on the saving throw is rewarded with a 1,000 gp gem that appears on the altar.

18. Buried Vestry
The visible walls of the corridor leading south bear faint traces of disgusting murals and bas-relief depictions of nasty things. After about 40 feet, the way is completely blocked by tons of stone blocks and rubble.

19. Natural Cavern
In their excavations, the ancient builders of the stronghold stumbled upon an enormous expanse of natural caves and caverns. The southern part of this network is now inhabited by seventy-eight escaped orc slaves, including two **orogs**, twenty-six **orcs**, and fifty orc **commoners**, for whom the place is a sanctuary.

The orcs, making ready for a rebellion against the giants, are armed with clubs, axes, daggers, and various cast-off weapons, as well as seven highly prized crossbows. They obtain food from raids, supplemented by fungus they find in a subterranean cave accessed through the sinkhole along the southwest edge of the cavern.

The rebel orcs have an uneasy truce with the nearby troglodytes (see area 20) and trade food to these creatures in exchange for water. If the orcs are approached in a non-hostile manner, they become agreeable immediately if the characters mention the possibility of fighting against bugbears or giants.

Guard Posts. The orcs have guards at several locations (marked G on the map) whose main function is to act as lookouts in case of incursion from any of the adjoining areas. These orcs will flee into area 19 to warn the others if they spot trouble.

Treasure. The orcs' scavenged loot amounts to 119 cp, 23 sp, and 45 gp.

20. Troglodyte Cavern
A tribe of troglodytes dwells in the central portion of the cavern complex. The group includes twenty-three adult **troglodytes** and fourteen young (use the **kobold** statistics). Trapped as they are between the orcs in area 19 and the lizards at area 21, they are trying to make do until they can escape.

Treasure. The tribe's leader has four gems worth 100 gp each. Nine of the other troglodytes have single gems, seven worth 50 gp each and two 10 gp ones. These gems are regarded as holy things by the troglodytes, and any other creature that touches one of them will be savagely attacked.

21. Lizards' Lair
A mated pair of exceptionally old and large subterranean lizards have chosen this spot to raise their young. The adults use the statistics for **giant crocodiles**, except that they have a climbing speed of 30 feet, no swimming speed, and darkvision out to a range of 60 feet. Their four young use the statistics for **giant lizards**.

These reptiles occasionally dart forth on forays to hunt and devour troglodytes or orcs, but their main

hunting ground is the series of caves beneath their own, the entrance to which is through the sinkhole on the eastern edge of their lair. Those unmapped lower caverns wander off into the darkness, and are barren of treasure or anything of interest aside from many different types of fungus. The lizards feed on the fungus when more substantial fare is unavailable.

22. Partially Cleared Passage to Cistern
The well-like chamber at the end of the broad corridor is filled with a deep pool of water. This dark liquid is cool and wholesome to drink, and only a few albino tadpoles dwell in it. It is an emergency water supply fed from several spouting springs that come through holes in the wall to the west.

The pool is 14 feet deep, and at the bottom is an outlet large enough for a Medium humanoid to pass through, The opening is finished stone, obviously constructed. This outlet slants upward, providing access to the stream that flows through area 23. Anyone who travels downstream, along a route that is underwater the whole time, comes out about three miles below the stronghold in a small pond.

23. Cavern of the Carrion Crawlers
In the northern end of the cavern complex, two sinkholes lead down to an even larger area where a number

of carrion crawlers lurk. They come up to this area from time to time to breed or to devour prey that the creatures have dragged here to consume at leisure. All sorts of bones, human and otherwise, are heaped and piled here and there. Seldom does any other sort of creature venture into the place, for any that do usually end up by adding their bones to the litter.

Two **carrion crawlers** are in the northeast finger of the cavern when the characters first enter. Every 10 minutes, there is a 30 percent chance that 1d3 more of these monsters appear from either the northern or southern sinkhole.

Treasure. Significant treasure has accumulated in the creatures' lair over the centuries, but it can be hard to find among all the bones and other debris. It takes three persons 30 minutes to thoroughly search the entire area. If such a search is conducted, refer to the Treasure Hoard: Challenge 5–10 table in Chapter 7 of the *Dungeon Master's Guide*. Roll once for each type of coin, then roll d100 to determine whether any gems, art objects, or magic items are also found.

24. STORAGE ROOM

The chamber at the end of the corridor leading northwest contains various tools for digging and stone masonry—shovels, pickaxes, hammers, drills, chisels, baskets, and so forth, many sized for giants but some for smaller creatures.

The door to the north is locked with a huge padlock. Unlocking it requires thieves' tools and a successful DC 15 Dexterity check. The door can be forced open by someone who succeeds on a DC 25 Strength (Athletics) check.

25. WINE CELLAR

A padlocked door identical to the one at area 24 blocks entry to the wine cellar. Inside, in addition to several large barrels, and various kegs, thirteen casks of exceptional wine, holding 5 gallons each, are stored here. Each of the casks has a bung seal with a blob of black wax impressed with a death's head.

The wine is black, has a slightly earthy smell, tastes like no other drink, and is of such excellence that it is difficult to stop drinking it. A character who tastes the wine must succeed on a DC 15 Constitution or Wisdom saving throw (drinker's choice) to keep from becoming intoxicated. (One quart is enough to make a giant reel, while a pint will make a human drunk.) On a failed save, the drinker becomes drunk (poisoned) for 1 hour, and must then repeat the saving throw.

On a successful save after 1 hour, a character stops drinking and is no longer drunk. On a failed save after 1 hour, the character continues to drink until falling unconscious for several hours, then awakens and remains drunk for 1 hour thereafter.

Once a character's drunken state ends, whether after 1 hour or several hours, the drinker suffers one level of exhaustion.

Treasure. This wine is a gift to Chief Nosnra, in return for his good services, from the creatures that are masterminding the attacks by the giants, although at best the characters can only guess at this fact. Due to its potency and quality, it has a market value of 500 gp per cask if characters can transport it safely out of the dungeon and back to civilization.

26. GALLERY UNDER CLEARANCE

The north face of this area is being cleared, and a few tools are scattered about. The place is otherwise unremarkable and empty.

27. CHAMBER UNDER CLEARANCE

Another unlit and unremarkable place with a few tools left lying around.

28. QUARTERS FOR STONE GIANT MINERS

The chamber at the end of the corridor holds piles of skins, five cots, several stools, two tables, and several chests and sacks containing personal gear (including several huge, thin books on mining techniques written in Giant, with many illustrations).

Two **stone giants**, subordinates of the one currently in the great hall, make this room their abode. These giants are the master miners and engineers for all work in the dungeon. They are not interested in fighting for the hill giants and politely decline combat with intruders unless they are attacked or extorted.

Treasure. If characters search through the personal gear, the third chest opened contains the giants' accumulated pay, amounting to 4,800 gp.

29. FALSE TREASURE

If the characters descend the stairs in area 10A and follow the obvious route, they come to a large chamber in which a faint glint of light shines from the far western wall. A collection of coffers can be found in that area, one tipped so that some of the gems it held are strewn before it. (The gems are worthless rocks, and the unopened coffers hold more of the same.)

To the south, thick iron bars separate this room from another chamber that is shrouded in darkness.

If a character touches one of the coffers or the spilled contents, thick iron bars drop from above the entrance. This portcullis can be lifted by someone who makes a successful DC 25 Strength (Athletics) check. At the same time, the bars that block entry into the adjacent room (area 30) lift into the ceiling, allowing the creatures therein to emerge and attack.

30. IMPRISONED GUARDS

Four **manticores** are confined here by Nosnra to serve as guards for his treasure. Fed kitchen garbage dumped down a chute from above, these monsters are wild with rage at their captivity and attack any creature if the opportunity presents itself. The manticores can fire their tail spikes through the gaps in the bars but cannot attack through the bars with bites or claws.

If the bars across the entrance are down, they can be lifted by someone who makes a successful DC 25 Strength (Athletics) check. A separate check is required for each 10-foot section.

31. MINOR TREASURE ROOM

The place that the manticores are supposed to guard is the storage area for the chief's excess coinage.

Treasure. The room contains seven chests and some empty boxes. The chests have the following contents:

- The first chest holds bags of coins (amounting to a total of 13,000 cp).
- Opening the second chest triggers a scything blade trap that targets the opener (+7 to hit), dealing 10 (3d6) slashing damage on a hit. With a successful DC 20 Wisdom (Perception) check, a character spots alterations to the hinges that are part of the trap mechanism. Thieves' tools can be used to disable the trap, along with a successful DC 20 Dexterity check. The chest holds bags of coins (totaling 9,100 sp).
- The third chest holds loose coins (a total of 2,400 ep) and an unlabeled potion (actually a *potion of poison*).
- Inside the fourth chest are twenty-seven copper ingots worth 400 cp each.
- The fifth chest is empty.
- The sixth chest holds eleven ivory tusks worth 250 gp each.
- The seventh chest is locked, and the lock is trapped with a poison needle (see "Sample Traps" in chapter 5 of the *Dungeon Master's Guide*). The needle deals 1 piercing damage and delivers a dose of drow poison (see "Sample Poisons" in chapter 8 of the *Dungeon Master's Guide*). Inside the chest are loose gems, three hundred twenty-five in all, worth 1 gp each.

32. SECRET ROOM

This hideaway is equipped with spy-holes for the chief so he can look out upon areas 1 or 29. (There are also smaller spy-holes at about 5 feet off the ground that the hill giant has never noticed.)

Two levers are set in the west wall. These control the thick portcullises that can block off entry to area 29 or release the manticores in area 30.

33. CHIEF'S SECRET TREASURE ROOM

Beyond the secret door to this room waits a hidden pit, 30 feet deep, with a trapdoor cover that snaps shut once someone has fallen through it. A character who succeeds on a DC 15 Wisdom (Perception) check can discern the edge of the trapdoor. In addition, someone who prods a pit lid forces the pit open with a successful DC 10 Strength check. The lid can be wedged shut with a piton or similar shim. A character doing so must succeed on a DC 15 Strength check to place the shim, or else the shim fails if someone treads on the pit. A creature that falls in takes falling damage plus 11 (2d10) piercing damage from the spikes. The spikes are also poisoned, so someone injured by them must make a DC 15 Constitution saving throw, taking 22 (4d10) poison damage on a failed save, or half as much damage on a successful one.

Treasure. The room holds a number of valuable items, including:

- 8,000 gp in loose coins inside a large chest
- 1,000 pp in a locked iron box (requiring thieves' tools and a successful DC 15 Dexterity check to open)
- Eleven 100 gp gems, four 500 gp gems, and two 1,000 gp gems in a small coffer
- Seven pieces of jewelry (worth 500 gp each) in another small coffer

In addition, a large growth of yellow mold seems to cover the southwest corner of the room. Making physical contact with this image reveals its illusory nature. Someone who examines the image without touching it can determine that it is an illusion by making a successful DC 15 Intelligence (Investigation) check. On a successful check, the illusion fades for that character, becoming transparent enough to see through.

The illusion conceals the following items, which are hung upon the wall: a quiver of eleven *+1 arrows,* a *+2 spear,* and a *flame tongue shortsword.* A character attuned to this sword can use an action to mentally command it to detect gems and jewels. Someone who does so learns the kind and number of such objects within 60 feet of the sword.

Finally, what appears to be a broken barrel rests in the southeast corner. This is another illusion, concealing a well-made, watertight cask that holds a map showing the location of the frost giants' glacial rift and an obsidian box.

Inside this latter container is a long, thin chain made of weird black metal and instructions written in Giant (using Dwarvish script) on a sheet of human skin. The instructions indicate that the chain is a magical device meant to be placed on a flat surface and looped into a figure-8 shape. (It radiates an aura of conjuration to the use of *detect magic.*) Thus configured, it can transport up to one giant or six human-sized persons standing in each loop of the figure-8 to the glacial rift, if one of their number is holding the map. (Nosnra uses this method of escaping if he finds himself in desperate straits.)

THE GLACIAL RIFT OF THE FROST GIANT JARL

Dozens of leagues to the north and west of the Steading of the Hill Giant Chief, amid the tallest mountain peaks, is the stronghold of Grugnur, Lord of Frost Giants. As frost giants have been among those who have been in the reaving bands, the party is to deal with them as they did the hill giants: death and destruction are to be meted out to the frost giants in the same measure they gave these things to the peoples below. Those members of the party who have participated in the raid on the steading should know by now that their most important mission is to garner intelligence as to what or who is behind the unholy alliance of hill, stone, frost, and possibly other types of giants as well. Any such information gained is to be delivered by the fastest means to the nobles sponsoring the expedition, while the party is to follow up clues in order to prosecute offenders. Any treasure taken is to be kept by the party; this is their reward for the perils they must face—and they are bound to face many in the weird ice caves and rocky caverns of the jarl. The evil root is deeply grown here, far worse than among the hill giants.

RUNNING THE ADVENTURE

As with the first part of the adventure, you should feel free to make substitutions as you see fit. Note that if the giants here have learned of the fate that befell the hill giants, or if survivors from the steading reached them,

they will be on the alert. Furthermore, the frost giants will organize traps, ambushes, and last-ditch defenses against continuing forays into their stronghold, taking full advantage of the treacherous terrain (ice slides, rigging tunnels to collapse on the party, and so forth). They will also make active efforts to locate the characters' base of operations (winter wolves make good trackers) and, if successful, attack it at the most inopportune time. Finally, make sure to keep track of the fate of important giants and their allies or captives; those who survive might play roles later in the adventure.

START

It is assumed that the party has either followed the map obtained at the steading or used the magical chain found there to arrive in the neighborhood of the glacial rift. If they spend a few hours searching the area, they discover a hidden cave in which they can safely hide themselves, their mounts, equipment, and even treasure if they take minimum precautions with respect to keeping their hiding place secret (do not lead pursuers to the spot, allow a light to show, make undue noise there, etc.). In any event, the same search will also reveal the rift.

The party can travel on the surface of the glacier-mountain (over the caves shown) to circumvent the whole rift if they so desire. Ropes can be lowered to gain the ledges below—a distance of some 50 to 150 feet depending on position. Every hour the party moves along the icy terrain, randomly choose one character to make a DC 10 Dexterity (Acrobatics) check. If the check fails, the character slips and falls. If the check fails by 5 or more, the character goes over the edge of the rift.

The whole place is windy and very cold. Visibility atop the rift is about 150 feet. The wind at the bottom of the rift is worse still, and visibility there is only 30 feet. The floor of the rift is a maze of snow and ice hillocks and mounds, with peaks of ice and rock thrusting up here and there like fangs. All movement in the rift is hampered by this difficult terrain. Due to wind force and eddying currents, attempts at levitation or flying cause movement in a random direction equal to half the distance traveled (use a d8 to determine direction: 1 north, 2 northeast, 3 east, and so on).

If the party is on the floor of the rift and fleeing from pursuing monsters, the blizzard-like conditions in this area makes the characters hard to catch. The characters have advantage on Dexterity (Stealth) checks to evade pursuit. At the same time, winter wolves are considered to have passive Perception scores 4 higher than normal when they are pursuing the characters.

The map the characters have shows only the location of the rift and the entrance to the place, and they have no other idea as to which path they should follow. Other than a few traces of giant footprints, the ice and wind-driven snow hide all traces of who or what uses the ledges to gain access to the caves. The characters must learn for themselves what lies in store.

If the adventurers decide to fall back between forays into the rift, they can use their hidden cave as a base if they have seen to its provisioning.

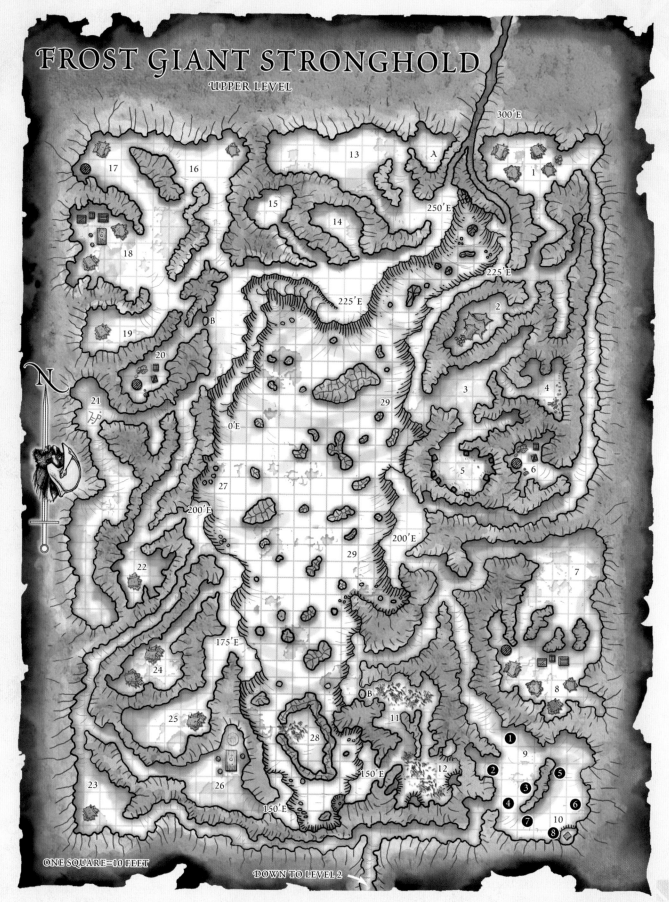

FROST GIANT STRONGHOLD
UPPER LEVEL

300'E

13   A

17   16

250'E

15

14   225'E

18   225'E   2

B

19   3   4

20

21   5   6

0'E   29

27

200'E   7

22   200'E

29

175'E

24

B

25   11

28   ①

9

② 150'E   12   ②
③
④   ⑤
④   ⑥
⑦   ⑥
23   26   ⑦   ⑩
150'E   ⑧

ONE SQUARE=10 FEET

DOWN TO LEVEL 2

MAP 6.3: FROST GIANT STRONGHOLD, UPPER LEVEL

Upper Level: General Features

Map 6.3 shows the layout of the upper level of the glacial rift. The passage from the northeast at the top of the map indicates the beaten path that the giants follow to enter the glacial rift. The path forks inside the entrance, each side leading to one of the icy ledges along either face of the rift. The caves and caverns herein are basically formed from ice, with a few areas of rock outcropping here and there.

Both ledges slope gradually downward, as indicated by the elevation markers on the map, from a height of 250 feet above the bottom of the rift at their northern beginnings to about 150 feet above the rift at the ledges' far ends to the south. The central area is the rift itself, and the openings along it are the entrances to the caves and tunnels in its face.

Boulders. Several cave mouths on this level are blocked by huge boulders (at the places marked B on the map). For Medium or smaller creatures, moving these obstructions out of the way requires a successful DC 20 Strength (Athletics) check.

Ceilings. Caves and caverns have ceilings from 30 to 45 feet high, while tunnels and passages are from 25 to 30 feet high.

Illumination. Throughout this level a faint greenish light penetrates from above, making torches or similar lights unnecessary.

Secret Doors. Secret doors in the rift are coated in ice and snow, and thus difficult to find. It requires a successful DC 20 Wisdom (Perception) check to find such a door.

Slippery Ice. *Fireball* spells or other fire effects used in these icy areas will make the footing within the area of effect very slippery. A creature hit by an attack or that moves more than half its speed over slippery ice must succeed on a DC 10 Dexterity (Acrobatics) check or fall prone. For 5 minutes after such magical fire is used, the area will also be filled with fog that renders the area heavily obscured.

Tokens of Free Passage

In a few locations within the rift, the characters can find and obtain special items that enable them to move through the stronghold without raising an alarm. If one member of a group displays a token of free passage, its privilege extends to the entire group. Those individuals are safe from attacks by the giants or the giants' allies as long as they take no aggressive action.

Random Encounters

On the upper level of the frost giant stronghold, the chance of a random encounter occurs on an hourly basis. At the end of each hour, roll a d12. On a roll of 1, which indicates a random encounter, choose from the following possibilities:

- 1d4 + 1 **yetis**
- One **frost giant**
- 1d4 + 1 **ogres**
- 1d6 + 1 **winter wolves**

Locations on the Upper Level

The following locations are identified on map 6.3.

1. Guardroom Ice Cavern

One **frost giant** keeps watch here at all times to prevent any unauthorized use of the long passage that leads south. If combat goes against the giant, he flees through this passage to give a warning of intruders to the guards at areas 9 and 10.

The room contains piles of hides, a giant sack, and a pile of rocks and ice chunks for hurling. The guard certainly hurls missiles if not immediately forced into melee. His treasure is at area 6. Note that the giant in area 2 will hear sounds of combat here and rush to aid his comrade (and vice versa).

2. Guardroom Ice Cave

One **frost giant** waits here on standby guard. On the floor of the cave are a pile of sleeping skins and two bags. The guard has an ample supply of rocks and ice blocks at hand for hurling at opponents.

If the giant hears noise from area 1, he rushes there to help; conversely, if attacked, he will raise a cry to bring the guard from area 1 to aid him.

Treasure. Under the pile of skins is a silver belt worth 250 gp. The giant wears a jeweled chain on his wrist (a 500 gp necklace), and one of the sacks holds 950 gp.

3. Empty Ice Cave

If loud noise is made in the unoccupied chamber south of the guardroom, the ceiling of ice and icicles in this area partially collapses. A creature beneath the ceiling must make a DC 15 Dexterity saving throw, taking 16 (3d10) bludgeoning damage on a failed save, or half as much damage on a successful one. Softer noises or visual clues could give warning of the unstable ice.

4. Small Ice Cave

This bone-strewn cave is the den of two adult **winter wolves** and their three half-grown pups (use the **dire wolf** statistics). If the young are harmed, the parents fight recklessly, risking opportunity attacks and ganging up to kill quickly.

5. Ice Caverns

In a chamber southeast of the wolves' lair, the giants have preserved eight corpses of mutilated victims, standing them upright and enclosing them in blocks of transparent ice. These exhibits are meant to frighten off any trespassers. The bodies are obviously hacked and very dead, not merely frozen whole.

Treasure. Each of these corpses has some valuable item with it in the ice. Beginning with the northernmost one and proceeding clockwise, the ice blocks contain:

- A dwarf and a *+1 battleaxe*
- An elf with a long case at its feet (containing a *staff of frost*)
- A human wearing a jeweled belt (worth 1,000 gp)
- A human with a tube in its hand that contains a *scroll of protection* (elementals)
- A dwarf that has a spilled pouch of gems at its feet (thirty-seven in all, worth 10 gp each)

- A human wearing a *ring of resistance* (fire)
- A half-elf grasping a sack with a burst seam showing silvery coins (471 sp)
- A human wearing gleaming armor that is actually *armor of vulnerability* (DM's choice)

Strong vibrations here, such as from loud noise, can cause a cave-in like that described in area 3.

6. PROVISIONS

Various pieces of frozen meat, some bales of cloth, piles of hides, and a few odd boxes and barrels of foodstuffs are stashed in an out-of-the-way cave.

Treasure. If the characters move any of the boxes and barrels around, the third container moved will reveal a hole filled with 600 gp, four 250 gp gems, and a silver tube (worth 50 gp) that holds a *spell scroll* bearing a 3rd-level *cure wounds* spell.

7. CAVERN

This natural rock cavern is covered with ice formations, so unless the characters pay particular attention, only the lack of light will tip them off that they are no longer surrounded by solid ice. On the floor near the southeastern end of the place are four big heaps of furry hides (or more, if ogres from the steading survived and relocated here).

The hides cover four sleeping **ogres**, who are awaiting an audience with the jarl. Any noise will awaken them, and they will give the alarm to their fellows in area 8 as well as attempting to give the party the slip and warn the giants too.

Treasure. Each ogre has 200 gp and a gem worth 100 gp.

8. SOUTH CAVERN

Ogre mercenaries that serve Jarl Grugnur dwell here. There are currently six **ogres** here. All fight fiercely when ordered to do so, or when they come upon intruders. Also in the place are five chests, twelve sacks, and three barrels, as well as many piles of the usual skins and hides used for beds.

Treasure. Some of the containers in this cavern have items of value or possible interest.

The second chest opened contains an ear collection, and the fourth holds 1,300 cp, 1,000 sp, 150 ep, and 1,000 gp.

The ninth sack examined contains six pieces of silver jewelry (worth 50 gp each) and eight pieces of gold jewelry (worth 100 gp each).

The first barrel opened contains a collection of skulls.

Hidden under the tenth pile of skins are two *potions of healing* and an armband made of gold fabric with a clasp fashioned from ivory and amber sculpted in the form of a bear. The armband is worth 500 gp, and it serves as a token of free passage.

CAVERN GUARD POST (AREAS 9 AND 10)

Giants encountered here are always alert (not sleeping). To determine the position of each guard when the characters first enter, roll a d4 twice. Use one of the results as the location of the guard in area 9. Add 4 to the other roll and use it as the location of the guard in area 10. These guards will cooperate and attempt to set up ambushes.

9. Northwest Chamber. One **frost giant** keeps a sharp lookout here. The giant has its greataxe plus a boulder ready at hand, with plenty of additional boulders piled near the entrances (guard positions 1 and 4).

10. Southeast Chamber. One **frost giant** is stationed here. If alerted, the guard moves into area 9 and joins the fray.

Treasure. The guard wears an armband that is a token of free passage like the one described at area 8. Eight bags are piled along the south wall (near guard position 8), each holding 200 gp.

A rock ledge on the southeast wall, 9 feet off the ground, has a stone box atop it. The stone box cannot be seen by a human-sized creature standing on the floor. Inside this box are two more armbands and a pouch of five gems (worth 100 gp each).

Exit to Lower Level. The passage leading west from this area intersects with a down-sloping tunnel that descends 100 feet before opening onto area 1 of the lower level (see map 6.4).

11. CAVE OF BONES

This place is the disposal area for unwanted bodies and similar refuse tossed into the place by the various giants in the upper area. If the characters decide to look through the refuse, it takes 10 minutes to search a 10-foot-square area, and the toads from area 12 come into the place to look for food if they hear any noise. Even if the characters are quiet, there is a cumulative 15 percent chance for every 10 minutes that passes that the toads will come looking for food.

Treasure. Although it certainly appears that some valuables might be scattered among all the bones, in truth there are only a few coins to be had—1d6 each of copper, silver, and gold—and some broken weapons, pottery shards, and the like.

12. Lower Bone Cave

This place has many bones and skulls littering it and serves as the lair of five **giant ice toads** (see appendix B). These creatures feed on the leavings in area 11. The toads rest on small ledges from 8 to 12 feet above the cave floor, and they will hop down and savagely attack anything that touches it.

Treasure. The creatures have one item of value, a naturally shaped piece of reddish-purple amethyst (worth 1,000 gp) that resembles a toad. It sits on a protuberance in the middle of their cave, and they worship it as a god.

13. Ice Cavern

This place is the home of six **yetis** that act as scouts for the frost giants. The yeti leader at the location marked A has a *frost brand greatsword*. It fights with this weapon instead of its claws, dealing 11 (2d6 + 4) slashing damage plus 3 (1d6) cold damage on a hit, and carving great chunks out of those held fast by his Chilling Gaze.

Treasure. The yeti leader has a hoard of eleven ivory tusks, each weighing 2 pounds and worth 200 gp, buried under a mound of snow.

14. Misty Ice Cave

Escaping hot air from somewhere beneath filters into this place through numerous cracks in the floor, making it full of damp, cold fog. The cracks are about 1 foot wide, not enough to hamper movement. The fog renders the area heavily obscured, and the floor is very slippery.

A creature hit by an attack when on the slippery ice or that moves more than half its speed over the ice must succeed on a DC 10 Dexterity saving throw or fall prone. If a character's save fails by 5 or more, the character drops an object in hand, which falls into one of the cracks. The object tumbles somewhere into the bowels of the earth, forever lost.

15. Ice Cave

This is the den of two large snow leopards (use the **tiger** statistics), which serve as pets of the yetis in area 13. These creatures lair on a ledge above the floor of the cave, and they try to take intruders by surprise.

Barracks Complex (Areas 16–19)

This section of the stronghold houses a group of frost giants readying for a raid. Each of the separate areas has piles of hides for sleeping, a table and stools, and a few extra giant-sized weapons around. Each giant here has 2d4 rocks to hurl.

16. Outer Sleeping Area. One **frost giant** resides in the northeast cavern.

17. Upper Sleeping Area. The northwest cave holds one **frost giant**.

18. Middle Sleeping Area. Two **frost giants** occupy the largest of these caverns. At the back of this cave is a clear spring of water about 2 feet deep, at the bottom of which are two hundred seventy-eight clear rock crystals worth 10 gp each.

19. Lower Sleeping Area. One **frost giant** is in the southernmost chamber.

20. Ice Storage Cave

This place is full of large and small pieces of frozen meat. Some of the chunks resemble parts of human and other humanoid bodies.

21. Ice Cavern

A warning carved into the icy floor in Giant with Dwarvish runes clearly shows that this place is to be shunned. Ten feet beyond where the passage turns to the southwest, the walls appear to be crusted with rough old ivory—in fact, this is an infestation of brown mold (see "Dungeon Hazards" in chapter 5 of the *Dungeon Master's Guide*). The floor is dotted with mounds of what look like old snow with the ends of bones sticking out of them. These are the bony remains of various creatures, covered by the growth.

22. Guard Ice Cave

Two **frost giants** are stationed here; one watches at the cave mouth, while the other naps on a pile of hides. Eight throwing rocks are within reach in the cave.

Treasure. Each giant has a sack. No other valuables are present.

23. Guard Cave

Two **frost giants** rest here. One giant watches down each passage while the other sleeps on a heap of skins. Each has a weapon and four rocks to hurl.

Treasure. There are four sacks in the cave, but nothing else of value.

Exit to Lower Level. The passage leading east from this area eventually intersects with a down-sloping tunnel that descends 100 feet before opening onto area 1 of the lower level (see map 6.4).

24. Visitors' Cave

Two **hill giants** and their three hill giant servants (use the **ogre** statistics) are camped here awaiting a summons from the jarl. The cave has five heaps of hides and five giant-sized bags.

Treasure. The fourth bag searched contains a gold-inlaid skull with a report from Chief Nosnra to Jarl Grugnur on a piece of parchment rolled up inside it. This document serves as a token of free passage to the hall of the fire giants. The biggest hill giant knows that they are bound south to King Snurre's realm after seeing the jarl, intending to take a message to the fire giant king.

In addition, each hill giant wears a fur cloak worth 1,000 gp.

25. Visitors' Cave

Two **stone giants** have come to the rift to pay their respects to the jarl and to see how well the frost giants are doing in their war on humankind. They will report their observations to other stone giants if they get the opportunity. They fight only if attacked. Each has a stone greatclub and three rocks handy.

FROST GIANT STRONGHOLD
LOWER LEVEL

UP TO LEVEL 2

ONE SQUARE = 10 FEET

Treasure. Hidden among the piles of skins in the cave is a jeweled platinum crown (worth 3,000 gp) that the stone giants intend to give to the jarl as a gift if he appears to be doing well.

26. Special Visitors' Cave

This location is warmed somewhat by volcanic activity and lit by dim reddish light. In it are a **fire giant** messenger and his fire giant servant (as a **hill giant** with fire immunity) who have delivered their message and are about to depart for their own land. There are two piles of furs and skins in the place, a rude table, a bench, three stools, a large brazier, and two sacks.

Treasure. One giant's sack contains 1,500 gp and the other 500 gp, in addition to the usual contents. In a padded bag at his belt, the messenger carries a symbol of the jarl's fealty to King Snurre: a solid silver statue of a bear, rampant, with topaz eyes (worth 1,500 gp).

27. Winter Wolf Pack

Along the western side of the rift floor is the lair of a pack of five **winter wolves**. The wolves are encouraged to roam the place by the frost giants.

28. Snow-Covered Dome of Ice

This hollowed-out ice formation has been created by the creature that lairs inside—a **remorhaz** that has recently moved into the rift. A number of charred skeletons are strewn around its icy den.

29. White Puddings

The two spots marked with numbers along the east edge of the rift floor are the locations of a pair of Huge white puddings. A white pudding uses the statistics for a **black pudding**, and its coloration gives it perfect camouflage in these icy conditions. While a white pudding remains motionless, it is indistinguishable from a mound of snow.

Lower Level: General Features

Map 6.4 shows the layout of the lower level of the glacial rift. This area has basically natural formations, with some rough-hewn connecting passages and enlargements made here and there.

Boulders. Some passageways on this level are blocked by huge boulders (at the places adjacent to boulders that are marked B on the map). For Medium or smaller creatures, moving these obstructions out of the way requires a successful DC 20 Strength (Athletics) check.

Ceilings. Passages have ceilings that are about 25 feet high. Ceilings of small caverns are 30 to 40 feet high, and those of the large caves 45 to 60 feet.

Illumination. Light in this area comes from torches and from cressets that are actually cages for giant fire beetles (the latter mostly in the part inhabited by the jarl).

Random Encounters

On the lower level of the frost giant stronghold, the chance of a random encounter occurs on an hourly basis. At the end of each hour, roll a d10. On a roll of 1,

which indicates a random encounter, choose from the following possibilities:

- One **frost giant**, a guard making the rounds
- 1d4 + 1 **ogres** on an errand for the jarl
- One **frost giant** and two **ogre** servants out for a walk
- If the giants know intruders are about, one **frost giant** and three **winter wolves** search for those intruders.

Locations on the Lower Level

The following locations are identified on map 6.4.

1. Grand Entry Cavern

The entrance to the lower level is obviously meant to be impressive, as its walls bear carvings of battle and hunting scenes in bas-relief. These carved scenes show giants slaying enemies, hunting dragons and other fearsome monsters, and engaged in similar activities. Torches burn at intervals along the length of the cavern.

Survivors of attacks on the level above will most likely make a stand in the grand entry cavern if they are still in relatively good shape.

Secret Exits. The boulders that close off the passages to the east and west are well concealed and look much like the normal cavern walls, so each must be discovered by characters as though it were a secret door.

2. Vaulted Cavern

The noise of moving the boulder that closes the place off from the rest of the complex awakens a mated pair of **young white dragons** that are kept here, along with a great pile of treasure. If they have enough warning, both the dragons hide and wait to see who enters.

The only intruders that the dragons do not object to are frost giants coming to feed them or bearing treasure to add to the dragons' hoard. Unless the male dragon is hiding, he sits proudly atop a heap of valuable items in the north end of the cavern. The female rests nearby on a ledge that projects from the western wall of the chamber (see area 2A).

Treasure. The dragons' hoard includes the following items:

- 15,000 sp and 12,400 gp in loose coinage
- Eight silver boxes filled with ivory (weighing 20 pounds apiece, each box worth 300 gp plus 100 gp for the ivory inside it)
- An alabaster statue depicting a winged woman (a deva), worth 800 gp
- Seven white marble statues of no great worth
- A scattering of three hundred fifty gems, worth 1 gp each
- Eleven pewter serving pieces of small worth
- Twenty-four various weapons (a *+2 dagger* among them)
- Nine shields
- Eight suits of armor (including a silvered set of *+2 chain mail*)
- Twenty-seven urns of small value
- Sixty-one bottles and flasks, valueless except for one that holds a *potion of poison*, another that is a *potion of resistance* (fire), and two more that hold *potions of diminution* and *growth* respectively

2A. DRAGON'S LEDGE

A ledge about 30 feet above the floor of the cavern has a cave-like nook at the back. On the elevated area, the female dragon hides and watches. If roused to action, she joins the battle as stealthily as she can.

Treasure. The female has hidden twelve gems worth 250 gp each (eight opals and four diamonds) behind her on the ledge.

3. ABANDONED STORAGE CAVE

The place contains some remnants of carcasses, a few broken boxes with spoiled provisions, some split sacks containing moldering grain, casks of wine turned to vinegar, and ale barrels that have been stove in.

If any of the denizens from above fled to this level and are injured or were being hotly pursued, they attempt to avoid notice by hiding in this storeroom.

4. DESERTED CAVERN

Broken items of giant-sized furniture litter this place—the remnants of tables, benches, stools, and chairs. Soot-covered wall cressets hold burned-out torches. Three skeletons of frost giants are plainly visible near the center of the cavern.

Treasure. Loose coins amounting to 500 gp, spilled from a rotted sack, are scattered around the frost giant skeletons. Note that the monsters at area 4B will attack any creatures that poke around in these bones.

4A. STONE RUBBLE

A frost giant skeleton rests in the far south end of the chamber, half-buried under stone rubble. It appears that the giant was trying to flee from the cave-in of a passage to the south (behind the rubble) but failed to make it and was killed by falling rocks.

Treasure. One of the giant's skeletal hands clutches an iron tube containing a map that shows areas 1, 2, 3, and 4 of the lower level. Area 1 is labeled (in Common) as "Grand Entry," area 2 as "Storage Place," area 3 as "Provisions," and area 4 as "Great Hall of the Jarl." The map also shows a passage leading south from this chamber (along the way now blocked by rubble), which after some 60 feet reaches a complex of caves and caverns, including various barracks room, the jarl's private chambers, and a treasure room.

This map is actually a fake, a ruse perpetrated by the jarl to mislead would-be robbers. If the characters attempt to dig out the rubble to find the supposed treasure room, they succeed only in making a lot of noise—no passage beyond can be unearthed.

4B. HUNGRY AND HOPPING

Six **giant ice toads** (see appendix B) lair in the northern extreme of this chamber. They are very hungry and seek to kill and devour any creatures that enter the cavern, forcing themselves to wait only long enough for intruders to be distracted by the glint of gold and lure of bone in the center of the main cavern.

5. ENTRANCE CAVERN

Hidden by a camouflaged boulder from prying eyes, this chamber is the actual entrance to the jarl's complex. It is always guarded by a **frost giant** equipped with a weapons and throwing stones, plus a giant's bag. If a conflict erupts, the giant tries to sound a great iron horn suspended from the ceiling on iron chains in the center of the cavern. The giant has to use an action to blow the horn.

6. EMISSARIES' CAVERN

An **oni** and its four **ogre** servants are staying here. They have had an audience with the jarl, and after a special wassail to be held on the morrow they will depart for home with a treaty scroll. This scroll is signed (with a special mark) by the jarl and offers the Lord of the Oni 25,000 gp worth of gems, plus whatever loot the lord's minions garner, if they will join the war on humankind.

Treasure. The oni wears a *necklace of fireballs* with five beads remaining that it will not hesitate to use. The oni also bears a pouch containing six 500 gp gems (gifts from the jarl).

A small iron casket among the oni's belongings holds a gift to the Lord of Oni—a trick box made out of eighteen plates of platinum, eighteen plates of electrum, and eighteen plates of silver. The box is opened by sliding certain plates on the left side, then the top, then the right side in a particular sequence. The correct order is platinum–electrum–silver on each end, and silver–electrum–platinum on the top.

The box has properties similar to those of a *bag of holding*—although the container is but 10 inches long by 6 inches wide and 4 inches deep, it holds 3 cubic feet of material or 60 pounds, whichever is the lesser. At present the box contains 500 gp, a *potion of mind control* (frost giant) (see appendix A), and a *potion of cloud giant strength*.

7. Guest Cavern

A torch-lit place adorned with tapestries, this comfortable chamber has skins and hides covering the floor and a bed heaped with soft pelts. Furnishings include a chest, a bag, a table, two chairs, and a small cabinet. The **cloud giant** who is the current guest has just agreed to join the jarl as his chief henchman.

Treasure. The chest holds 2,200 gp, and the giant wears a silver belt set with ivory and gems (worth 600 gp).

8. Prison Cavern

Torches light the place dimly. A female **storm giant** is chained on the north wall with huge manacles at her wrists and ankles. A fur rug in the middle of the place bears a table and two chairs. Upon the table are heaps of food on six golden platters and in three silver bowls. Two huge flagons of ivory set with gems have been filled with fine wine; the scents from the food and the wine fill the chamber.

These refreshments have been set out to tantalize the giant into submitting to the jarl's will and becoming his leman, but she has not been won over—quite the opposite is true. Being subjected to this durance vile makes her a friend to any who rescue her, although she despises evil. Thus, the presence of evil characters in the party will cause her to fulfill her obligation as quickly as possible and depart. By contrast, she might strike up a long-term friendship with a party of good-aligned characters.

Treasure. The platters are worth 500 gp each, the bowls 50 gp apiece, and the flagons have a value of 100 gp each.

9. Servants' Quarters Cavern

Eight **ogres** dwell here. Each has its own pile of hides and rags for sleeping, a wooden box for goods, a peg to hang outer garments, and a bag. The ogres serve the jarl willingly and fight fiercely.

Treasure. Each ogre has 1d100 sp, 1d100 ep, and 1d100 gp in its box or its bag.

10. Antecavern

A **frost giant** guard is alert inside this oblong cavern at all times. He has a greataxe and one throwing rock. He shouts to alert the guards to the south if intruders enter the area.

11. Great Cavern of the Jarl

This is where all the special functions and feasts hosted by the jarl take place. Various tables and benches line the east and west walls, pushed out of the way for now until they are needed. Caged fire beetles dimly illuminate the place, which appears to be deserted.

Guard Posts. The ledges marked A and B are more than 30 feet above the floor and hidden in dark shadow. Each of the ledges holds a watchful **frost giant** with a supply of six rocks to throw.

12. Audience Alcove and Throne Dais

A stone outcrop partially encloses an area in the south of the jarl's cavern. A enormous ivory and bone throne, decorated with skulls, silver, and gems, rests near the south wall of this alcove. Hung behind it, spread out against the rough wall, is a white dragon hide. Before the throne on the floor is the skin of a huge polar bear. Three ivory stools are off to one side of the throne; these are the seats of the jarl's lieutenants.

Treasure. The gems that decorate the throne consist of sixty worth 50 gp each, fifteen worth 100 gp each, three of 500 gp value, and one 1,000 gp gem.

13. Guard Area

One **frost giant** guard stationed in the far southern end of this chamber looks east and west at varying times. He has two rocks. If an intruder is seen, he will sound a large gong on the north wall (possibly with a thrown rock).

14. Kitchen

Two fire giant servants (use the **hill giant** statistics, plus immunity to fire damage) and four **ogres** labor in the kitchen, roasting a horse over the natural firepit and otherwise readying the jarl's food. Various foodstuffs, furniture, and utensils are scattered about in all the nooks that lead away from the firepit. Amid heaps of foodstuffs to the north are four human captives (**commoners**) in a cage, being saved for a feast. They can warn the characters about what lies in areas 15, 16, and 17.

15. Weapons Cave

Herein are stored sixty-two throwing rocks, eight shields, fifteen spears, five clubs, and five helmets, all of frost giant size. The cave also holds six battleaxes (which the giants can hurl) and a well-made chain shirt of giant size.

16. Common Quarters Caverns

Currently one **frost giant**, two frost giant servants (use the **hill giant** statistics, plus immunity to cold damage), and three young frost giants (use the **ogre** statistics, plus immunity to cold damage) call this place home. If the frost giant is killed, the others weepily surrender, not fighting thereafter unless they are attacked.

In addition to the giants, the room holds piles of skins and hides, a few stools, eleven large boxes, five chests, and many pegs (currently with fourteen capes and nine bags hanging from them).

Treasure. Under the ninth box moved by the characters is a hole in the floor that contains 3,500 gp.

17. Kennel Cave

The jarl's hunting pack—four huge **polar bears** with 65 hit points each—lairs here.

Treasure. Each bear wears a gem-studded collar worth 200 gp.

Caverns of the Carls (Areas 18 and 19)

Two large caverns provide quarters for the frost giant gentry. Each inhabitant has a cot, a chest, a chair or a stool, and several hides and skins for bedding. The whole area is lit by torches and a few fire beetles, with many pegs holding cloaks, capes, and bags along the walls. Three huge lockers, three hampers, and six wardrobes make up the rest of the furnishings. The giants, some of them warriors and some of them servants, are

willing to negotiate to protect the young, which they fight to the death to protect or avenge.

Treasure. Each giant warrior in the place has 1,000 gp plus an armband that is a token of free passage (identical to the one described at area 8 of the upper level). Each other adult giant has 500 gp. The young have no treasure.

18. West Chamber. This large cave is occupied by two **frost giants** and three frost giant servants (use the **hill giant** statistics, plus immunity to cold damage) along with three young frost giants (use the **ogre** statistics, plus immunity to cold damage).

19. East Chamber. This slightly smaller area holds one **frost giant**, one frost giant servant, and two young frost giants.

20. JARL'S ANTECAVERN AND TROPHY HALL

Jarl Grugnur receives visitors in a chamber on the southern edge of the lower level. The eastern half of the cavern is a private audience hall, with pelts and skins on the walls and floor, a table, and four chairs. Some worthless scrolls are on the table, and on the walls of this area hang two normal shields, a heavy crossbow, two normal two-handed swords, and a pair of huge ivory tusks of no value. A few worthless furs and tapestries hang on the short sections of wall to the north. Both halves of the hall are illuminated by caged fire beetles. To the east a

set of well-worn steps, each about 3 feet high, lead up to an exit screened by thick, leathery hides.

The western spur of the chamber is the jarl's trophy hall. Here, the jarl often sits in a comfortable chair and ruminates over past glories and future plans; the floor in this area has actual rugs. The walls of the alcove are adorned with a host of trophies, including a cave bear pelt of enormous size, a wyvern skin, the rack from a giant stag, the mandibles and claws of an umber hulk, giant scorpion claws, the horn of a woolly rhinoceros, a pair of mammoth tusks, a pair of mastodon tusks, a giant boar head, a griffon skin, the wings of a giant eagle, a giant lynx pelt, and the jaws from a subterranean lizard,

Treasure. In addition to all the trophies of kills mentioned above, the place holds several items that are valuable or potentially useful. Many of them are weapons or armor of normal (nonmagical) sort, including:

- A bow and a quiver with sixteen arrows
- Three shields
- A light crossbow and fourteen bolts
- A greataxe, two spears, and a flail
- A huge iron mace
- A suit of splint armor sized for a dwarf
- A suit of plate armor sized for a human

Other items of interest, because of their magical nature or unusual appearance, are as follows:

- A *+1 shield* that is trapped (see below)
- The skull of a dwarf wearing an iron crown (no value)
- Eleven *+1 bolts*
- Two walrus tusks that are trapped (see below), one of which is an ivory-covered bronze *horn of Valhalla*
- A white dragon skull that has an aura of abjuration magic about it
- A suit of *+1 plate armor* sized for an elf
- Three elaborate tapestries (one worth 400 gp, anoher valued at 100 gp, and one that is worthless)

Trapped Shield. If the magic shield is taken down from the wall, that act releases a spear trap that fires straight ahead to a range of 60 feet. The spear has a +10 bonus to hit and deals 10 (3d6) piercing damage on a hit. The trap mechanism can be seen by someone who examines the shield and succeeds on a DC 15 Wisdom (Perception) check. Given 1 minute or so, a character who uses thieves' tools and succeeds on a DC 15 Dexterity check can jam the mechanism so the spear can't launch. If the check fails by 5 or more, the spear launches even if the shield is still on the wall.

Trapped Tusks. If either of the walrus tusks is touched, the dragon skull screams "Alarm! Robbers!" in Giant until the skull is smashed to pieces, which continue to quietly whimper for some time thereafter.

21. Jarl Grugnur's Private Cavern
The chief of the frost giants and his lady reside in a secluded chamber on the southeast edge of the stronghold's lower level.

Living Area. The western part of this chamber contains a huge table, four chairs, three wardrobes, five chests, five trunks, and seven coffers. The walls are hung with heavy tapestries and various pelts and skins, all of no particular worth.

Jarl Grugnur (use the **cloud giant** statistics, plus immunity to cold damage but without Keen Smell and Innate Spellcasting) sits at the table in his chain mail jack with his *arrow-catching shield* nearby (AC 18, or AC 20 against ranged attacks, with his shield; AC 16 without it). At his hip is his *+2 longsword*. The jarl has a +14 bonus to hit with the weapon and deals 23 (3d8 + 10) slashing damage on a hit. In his hand is a platinum drinking horn set with eight gems.

Across the table is Estia, his lady (use the **cloud giant** statistics, altered as for Grugnur), a fierce beauty with a cloak of saber-tooth tiger hide about her and an iron *+2 morningstar* at her hip. On the table in front of her is a gold flagon set with eight gems (1,200 gp).

Two **winter wolves** are crouched under the table.

Treasure. The jarl's drinking horn has a value of 2,000 gp, and his lady's flagon is worth 1,200 gp.

All the various containers in the room contain clothing and other unremarkable items, except as follows:

- The second chest searched holds 700 pp.
- The fifth chest has 3,200 gp.
- The fourth trunk has a thick layer of old socks, underneath which are eight potions (*speed, superior healing, storm giant strength, poison, oil of slipperiness, healing,* and a *philter of love*).

- The second coffer has nine pieces of jewelry (worth 1,000 gp each).
- The sixth coffer holds one hundred ninety-eight gems (one hundred four worth 10 gp each, fifty-one of 50 gp, thirty-six of 100 gp, six of 250 gp, and one of 1,000 gp value).

Sleeping Area. The eastern portion of the cavern is partially screened off by hangings. This cozy nook holds a rumpled bed, a small table, a chair, two stools, a chest, a trunk, and various odds and ends of clothing, armor, and weapons here and there. The walls are hung with pelts and rugs of no particular value.

Treasure. The lid of the trunk has a secret drawer in it that contains six scroll tubes. The jarl will take these items if he is forced to flee and has time to get them. The contents of the tubes are as follows:

- Number 1 is empty.
- Number 2 holds a key to the invisible chest in the hidden escape tunnel (see below).
- Number 3 contains a map marking the location of the Hall of the Fire Giant King.
- Number 4 holds a *scroll of protection* (fiends).
- Number 5 contains a scroll of gibberish with an *explosive runes* glyph of warding on it (spell save DC 15).
- Number 6 has two *spell scrolls*, one of *delayed blast fireball* and one of *finger of death*.

Hidden Escape Tunnel
Behind the wall hangings in the northeast end of the chamber is a natural passage about a mile long that turns south and exits at the base of the glacier, out of sight of anyone near the rift. Someone who looks around the room can notice the opening in the wall through gaps in the hangings with a successful DC 15 Wisdom (Perception) check. Someone who handles the hangings in this area or looks behind them finds the opening without needing a check.

The alcove to the northwest just inside the tunnel has a thick iron bar protruding from the wall about 10 feet off the ground. To a casting of *detect magic*, the bar has a strong aura of conjuration. Noticing the bar without specifically looking up for it requires a successful DC 15 Wisdom (Perception check). If the bar is pushed downward, that act transports whatever or whoever is standing on the floor of the alcove to a spot some 50 feet distant from the entrance to Snurre's hall (the Hall of the Fire Giant King).

An apparently empty ledge high in the southwest wall is the resting place of an iron box that is invisible, has no magical aura, and is locked (requiring a successful DC 20 Dexterity check to open). Those who investigate the ledge can find the box only if they blunder into it or they are able to see invisible objects. The chest becomes visible when opened. It has a *glyph of warding* (save DC 17) inside the lid. The glyph triggers if the chest is opened without its key. If triggered, the glyph casts *cloudkill* (spell save DC 17) centered on itself. The box's contents are meant to be taken to the fire giants' stronghold and given as gifts to the powers behind the uprising.

Treasure. In the iron box are a *pearl of power*, a set of *Nolzur's marvelous pigments*, and a *wand of paralysis*.

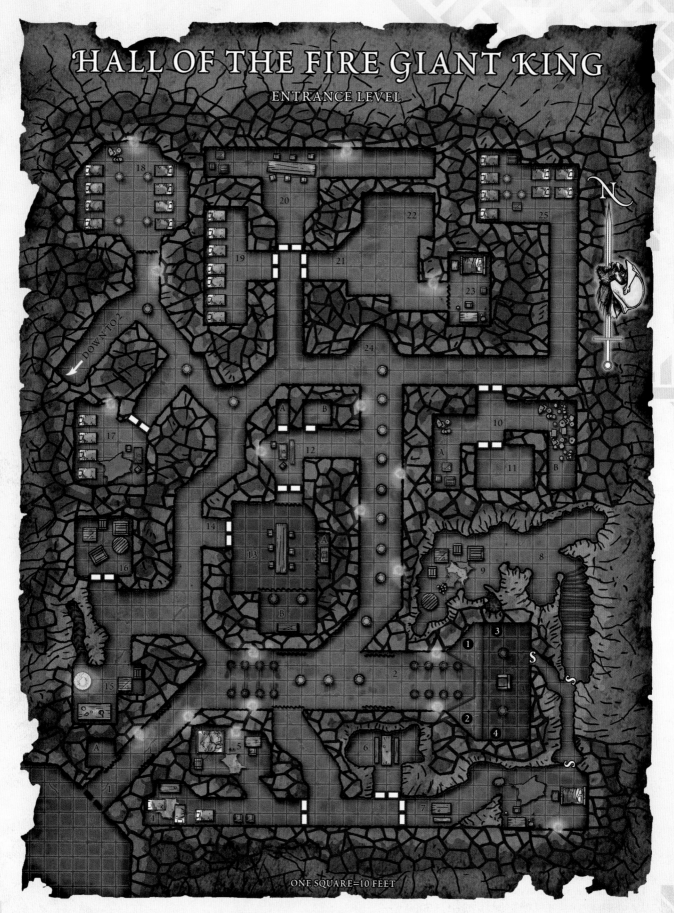

HALL OF THE FIRE GIANT KING

ENTRANCE LEVEL

DOWN TO 2

ONE SQUARE=10 FEET

MAP 6.5: HALL OF THE FIRE GIANT KING, ENTRANCE LEVEL

HALL OF THE FIRE GIANT KING

Just as the trail led from the Steading of the Hill Giant Chief to the frozen wastes wherein was found the Glacial Rift of the Frost Giant Jarl, so the adventure in the latter place has led (or transported) the intrepid party to what they hope will be their last challenge. They are about to venture into the hot and smoking barrens which are in effect Muspelheim, the home of the fire giants. In the vast rocky halls of the fire giants' doughty liege lord, the dread King Snurre Iron Belly, they hope to find not only great treasure but the answer to the question of what or who is behind the strange alliance of many different types of giants. Surely here in the stronghold of the fire giants will be encountered the evil genius or geniuses controlling the uprising and planning the well-executed attacks, for Snurre is said to be far stronger than smart.

It is a sad fact that the characters can expect all encounters here to be worse than those the party has faced elsewhere, for fire giants are ferocious opponents, and their associates and helpers will undoubtedly be proportionately stronger and more fearsome than those of the lesser hill and frost giants—a sobering thought indeed! Surely the rewards for success cannot fail to be greater, for the fire giants—and their masters, perhaps?—have more loot for the taking.

If the party (or one or more members thereof) has been to the other two places, the characters will know that there is a charge upon them to report definite information to the rulers who have sent them forth to inflict punishment on the rapacious giant raiders. Their mission: to slay fire giants and all who associate with them. Failure means death, not from the nobles, but from the monsters the party must face. Success means the right to keep all the loot they find, plus the possibility of reward from the rulers of the lands being ravaged by the giant bands.

And now the adventurers stand before the black and smoking slag hill that holds the Hall of the Fire Giant King. They have penetrated near the heart of the matter—into a fell realm where even the strongest need beware!

RUNNING THE ADVENTURE

As with the previous adventures in this series, it is up to you to add to the considerable detail given herein, filling in any needed information to color the whole and bring it to life. You, as Dungeon Master, must continue to improvise and create, for your players will certainly desire more specifics, seek to do things not provided for herein, and generally defy expectation. The script is here, but you will direct the whole, rewrite parts, and sit in final judgment on characters' actions.

If you have already taken your players through the first two adventures, be particularly mindful of how their behavior there will have altered what is described here. Use the parameters given to design your own epic. Be disinterested, and be just. This is a very difficult scenario, and the players might rue thoughtless actions,

but do not allow this reaction to temper what you have before you. Likewise, do not set about to entrap the characters in a hopeless situation—allow their actions to dictate their fate.

Remember also that these giants are not only the toughest so far encountered but also have the best advice immediately available to them. As soon as the party strikes and then retires, the attack will be assessed and countermeasures taken. Even when the party first enters the hall, you will have to gauge the reaction of the giants if and when they learn that intruders are within. How will they react? From whence will they call in guards? Where will Snurre go? Most assuredly, he will not remain seated upon his throne when an attack is in progress! You have not ceased being a Dungeon Master by using this prepared scenario; you have simply had some details handled for you so that you can better script the more important material.

When the party retires from the hall to rest, the fire giants will lay whatever traps and ambushes they are able to prepare under the circumstances. Lights will be smothered, sentries posted, and so forth. In the original playtest, the giants who survived the first foray by the (exceptionally strong and well-played) party set several ambushes, each surprise being timed to allow them to retreat quickly behind a turn in a passage or through a set of doors, gradually falling back to the corridor to the lower level. While the characters offered no quarter and slew every giant or other creature encountered with absolute ruthlessness, their opponents fought with reckless abandon and self-sacrifice.

How you manage this conflict in your game must be based on knowledge that only you can have. The upshot of this whole series of adventures is a fight to the finish. Only the leaders and those they take with them will normally seek to move to a place of safety; the rest will stand fast and battle to the end.

ADVENTURE START

The party might have arrived before the huge obsidian valves that bar entrance to the hall by means of the transporter found in the lair of the frost giant jarl. In this case, they will have to search to find a place of safety to rest and recover their strength between forays into the hall.

If the group journeyed hence by some other method, they will have noted such a place of refuge about two miles distant from Snurre's sooty palace. This hidden site should initially prove to be safe from detection as long as the characters leave no plain trail to it and as long as they are not followed to it. There is a limit, though, to how far they can push their luck. Each time they venture forth from their refuge to raid the fire giant hall, there is a 10 percent cumulative chance that the hidey-hole will be found by the giants (a 10 percent chance after the first raid, 20 percent following the second, and so forth).

A nearby ravine leads directly from the safe cave to the spiny, broken heap of slag indicated on the characters' map as the site of the hall. A wide, well-trod path winds its way across the barren land up to two great slabs of black stone—the obsidian portals that give access to Snurre's hall. Each valve is 29 feet tall, 10 feet wide, and no less than 3 feet thick. Normal human strength cannot even budge them; for Medium or smaller creatures to open them requires at least two characters working together to make a successful DC 25 Strength (Athletics) check. On the second and any successive raids upon the place, there is a 50 percent likelihood that the gates will be ajar, and some guard will be watching for attackers in order to alert the hall.

The plain around the stronghold is most evil and drab in appearance. The sky is gray and filled with sooty clouds. A distant volcano can be seen, and far to the south a glowing river of molten lava moves sluggishly down a slope and out of sight. The air is hot and smells of heated rock and metal. The ground is covered with cinders and sharp rocks that make walking cross-country difficult (and noisy). The area is lit by night with dim red light, both from flaming gases that shoot forth out of the bowels of the earth and from the glow of molten rock.

The pile of lava, slag, and jutting black rock that houses the Hall of Snurre is a steeply rising hill about 300 feet high at its summit. It is difficult to scale. Smoking vents are everywhere, and some of these holes spurt out jets of flame from time to time. The characters will never locate any entrance into the place other than by the main gate, and there is a 33 percent chance that any member investigating a vent hole will be struck by flaming gases for 7 (2d6) fire damage.

ENTRANCE LEVEL: GENERAL FEATURES

Map 6.5 shows the layout of the uppermost level of the fire giant stronghold. The floors, walls, and ceilings throughout the place are of black, reddish-black, dark gray, and dull brown rock. In some places the stone has been hewn, but in others it appears to have been fused by heat.

Ceilings. Passageways in the hall have vaulted ceilings 30 feet high. Caves, chambers, and rooms are 40 to 60 feet high.

Doors. All doors are made of iron plates. A Medium or smaller creature must succeed on a DC 15 Strength (Athletics) check to open any of the doors in this place due to their great size and weight. Doors stay open if left that way.

Illumination. The upper level of Snurre's hall is lit by torches, braziers, and natural gas jets.

Locks. The hall contains numerous well-made locks. Someone using thieves' tools can pick a lock with a successful DC 20 Dexterity check.

Secret Doors. Secret doors in the hall are precisely crafted. Unless otherwise noted, it requires a successful DC 20 Wisdom (Perception) check to find such a door.

RANDOM ENCOUNTERS

On the entrance level of the fire giant stronghold, the chance of a random encounter occurs on an hourly basis. At the end of each hour, roll a d12. On a roll of 1, which indicates a random encounter, choose from the following possibilities:

- One **fire giant** guard
- One **fire giant** with 12 **gnoll** workers
- Four young fire giants (use the **ogre** statistics, plus immunity to fire damage) with two **hell hounds**
- One **cloud giant**, one **frost giant**, or one **stone giant**, a visitor looking around

LOCATIONS ON THE ENTRANCE LEVEL

The following locations are identified on map 6.5.

1. ENTRY PASSAGE

The floor here is polished obsidian, and great wall hangings can be seen by the characters as soon as they enter. The tapestries displayed between the torches are rendered in bloody colors and show victorious fire giants. The door guard is hidden in the alcove (area 1A).

1A. ALCOVE

The tapestry that covers the opening to this guard post is of loose weave, allowing the **fire giant** guard in the dark recess to clearly see whoever enters the corridor. If intruders are spotted, he sounds his great bronze horn to warn the hall (see area 2). The giant has four rocks for throwing.

If the characters are returning after severely defeating the giants, a ballista (from the arsenal at 10A) will be set up at the far end of the hallway in anticipation of a second raid. This weapon is triggered by a nearly invisible tripwire set 30 feet inside the entrance, and someone must succeed on a DC 20 Wisdom (Perception) check to find the wire. Once the wire is found, it can be avoided, but cutting it sets off the ballista. The ballista fires an array of bolts down the length of the hall, so each creature in it is subjected to one attack at a +6 bonus to hit, dealing 11 (2d10) piercing damage on a hit.

2. GRAND HALL

Two **ettins** are always in the hall that runs east–west off the entry passage, using their four heads to watch in all directions. If the guard at the gate sounds the alarm, these creatures move to hold the mouth of the entryway until help arrives from area 3, area 18, or areas 21–25.

The floor of the grand hall is of reddish-black, highly polished stone. The pillars are carved into the shapes of dwarves, each straining to hold up the figure atop it. Light flickers weirdly from burning gases that spurt from the walls. One of the tapestries on the south wall screens the entrance to the royal apartment (areas 4–7).

3. THRONE ROOM AND AUDIENCE CHAMBER

Two steps of white-veined black marble lead up to an area where the floor is of deep red polished stone, Between two pillars of polished obsidian sits a massive throne made of jet and black-and-white-banded onyx, the whole inlaid with various large gems. The walls are inlaid with colored stone laid out to show various scenes of victory by King Snurre over his foes. On the wall directly behind the throne is depicted the flaming skull which is Snurre's own device, flanked by fire giants with clubs over their shoulders. The northern one of these inlaid giant-images conceals a secret door hidden in the wall; a cresset to the left of it, when pulled down, causes the portal to swing inward.

King Snurre is seated on the black seat of the throne. Over 19 feet tall, he is hugely muscled and extraordinarily ugly—very broad, with bandy legs. His teeth are tusk-like and protruding, his side whiskers and beard bright orange and full. Snurre is clad in black iron plate armor, and he wields a huge greatsword that displays flames running along its blade when it is swung. The king wears a necklace of coral skulls and has a broad girdle set with small gems. Around his shoulders is a cape made of white dragon hide.

When he sits on the throne, he wears his jewel-studded crown of iron. Otherwise the crown is in his bag and his bald pate covered by an iron helmet.

King Snurre is a **fire giant** with the following changes, which increase his challenge rating to 11 (7,200 XP):

- He has 187 (15d12 + 90) hit points.
- He has resistance to cold damage.
- He can speak Common and Giant.
- His greatsword deals an extra 7 (2d6) fire damage on a hit.

Two **fire giants** guard the king at all times; their positions are indicated by the circled numbers 1 and 2. Each giant has a carved stone to throw. Crouching at positions 3 and 4 are a pair of **hell hounds**, the king's constant companions.

Treasure. Snurre's crown is set with six rubies (worth 500 gp each), six diamonds (500 gp each), and a huge jacinth (1,000 gp). His necklace has a value of 1,000 gp, and his girdle is decorated with sixty-six garnets (worth 10 gp each). His magic cape grants resistance to cold damage.

The gems embedded in Snurre's throne include twelve pieces of sard (worth 100 gp each), twelve fire opals (worth 250 gp each), and twelve rubies (500 gp each).

4. Chamber of the Queen's Servants
The walls of the grand hall are covered with hide rugs and wall hangings, one of which screens the entrance to the queen's private chamber.

Inside this entryway are torches on the walls, and six chairs and three small tables along the hallway. At the end of the route westward is a chamber that holds four beds, four chests, two wardrobes, and four stools.

Three fire giant servants (use the **hill giant** statistics, plus immunity to fire damage) are present here, one waiting outside the queen's chamber and two more in the end chamber. Each fights fiercely to protect the queen, with those at the end chamber rushing to aid the other. The servants wield longswords that deal 18 (3d8 + 5) slashing damage on a hit.

Treasure. Each of the servants wears three pieces of jewelry worth 250 gp apiece. Amid the eighty-one hides, pelts, skins, and furs in the end chamber are five of value—the seventeenth, twenty-fourth, fortieth, fifty-ninth, and seventy-seventh items that the characters examine are worth 200 gp each.

5. Queen's Chamber
The floors and walls in the chamber north of the servants' quarters are covered with rich rugs and tapestries

of no great value. The place is well lit by torches and a large brazier, and this makes it very hot indeed (just right for fire giants!).

Queen Frupy, who resides here, is a veritable harridan, a sly and cunning **fire giant**. She is, if anything, uglier than Snurre. Topped by a huge mass of yellow-orange hair that looks like a fright wig, Queen Frupy's face is a mass of jowls and wrinkles set in the middle of a very large head that seems to grow directly out of her shoulders without the benefit of any neck. Her body is lumpy and gross, her skin covered with bristles the color of her hair. Her little pig eyes, however, are bright, suggesting intelligence unusual in a giant.

Her chamber contains a giant-sized bed covered with furs, a table and two chairs, a stool, and a dressing table with a huge *mirror of seeing* (weighing 100 pounds) that functions similarly to a *gem of seeing*, so that even unseen creatures and objects are reflected in it. (Frupy uses it if she suspects invisible creatures are about.) Also here are an ebony and mother-of-pearl wardrobe (filled with her clothing), an iron strongbox, a chest of twelve drawers, four small coffers of copper on the table, and two bronze caskets. Each bronze casket has a **poisonous snake** inside, which must be dealt with before the contents can be accessed (see "Treasure").

The queen wears garments of black dragon hide set with iron studs (giving her an AC equivalent to that of plate armor). She wields an iron scepter as a weapon (treat as a maul with the same statistics as a fire giant's greatsword, except that it deals bludgeoning damage). Out of sight under the bed are Frupy's two pets, a pair of **giant weasels** that obey her every command.

If intruders enter the place, Queen Frupy will command them to kneel in her august presence and state their business, so that she may fairly address their humble requests. Any who are so foolish as to do so will be sorry, as Frupy will call forth her pets and herself strike at the intruder who appears to be the most powerful. (A kneeling character is considered to be prone in this situation.) She will then bellow for her servants to come to her aid.

Treasure. One of the bronze caskets holds 400 cp, and the other one has 300 pp concealed beneath a layer of 100 cp.

If the lid of the strongbox is opened by anyone but Frupy, a *glyph of warding* inside is triggered, producing a *fireball* spell centered on the chest (save DC 15). The strongbox itself holds nothing of value, but it has a trick panel in the side, which requires a successful DC 20 Wisdom (Perception) check to find.

The panel, if opened, allows access to a jade box (worth 500 gp). This box has a false bottom, found with another successful DC 20 Wisdom (Perception) check, that contains *spell scrolls* of two random 7th-level spells of a particular class (DM's choice).

All but one of the copper coffers contain unguents and the like; the third coffer examined contains four pieces of gem-set gold jewelry worth 750 gp each.

The drawers in the chest hold worthless personal articles, except for the fifth drawer from the bottom, where under some underthings Queen Frupy has concealed three potions: *resistance* (fire), *mind control* (mammal),

and *mind control* (fire giant), the latter of which she plans to use on the king (see appendix A for the latter two potions).

Finally, Frupy wears six pieces of gem-set jewelry worth 500 gp each.

6. CHAMBER OF THE KING'S GUARDS
Beyond the doors that lead north, along the east and west walls of the short hallway, are a total of twelve throwing rocks lined up ready for use. Two **fire giants**, off-duty guards, relax in the adjoining chamber. Each has a carved throwing rock and a greatsword nearby.

A table and two benches sit in the center of the room. The table has several platters and flagons on it, along with a small cask of wine and a wheel of cheese covered with mold. Two wooden lockers are tucked under the table.

Treasure. Hidden inside the cheese in a hollowed-out space are five 100 gp gems. (This is the repository for the wealth of the on-duty guards.)

Each of the lockers contains ordinary clothing and 150 gp. Each guard carries three gems worth 100 gp each in a belt pouch,

7. KING SNURRE'S PRIVATE QUARTERS
The great iron doors to this place bear the blazon of the flaming skull also found in the throne room. The doors open into an outer hall where six **hell hounds** roam.

The walls in the outer hall are set with torches in cressets and draped with crude tapestries. Six chairs and two benches lie along the walls, along with three tables—each with a keg of ale, beer, or mead and drinking vessels of horn or leather at hand. A small step up on either side of a natural stone column of reddish stone marks the end of the outer hall and the entry to the king's private chamber.

The bedchamber of the king is lit in an eerie manner by flaming jets of gas and a huge iron brazier full of glowing coals. The room contains a huge, fur-covered bed, a table, a small throne of ebony and three lesser chairs, a tall cabinet, four trunks, an iron chest at the foot of the bed, and a bench near the entry. The floor is covered with pelts, and the walls are hung with tapestries and trophies: two shields, an axe, four swords, a flail, and a hammer. All these items are sized for giants. A ledge on the south wall 9 feet above the floor holds thirty-nine skulls (human, dwarf, elf, giant, and other various and sundry creatures), eight helmets and helms, and five sets of armor (chain mail, splint, or plate as you desire).

The containers in the room hold the personal gear of King Snurre, consisting of clothing, footwear, and bits of armor. Arrayed on the table are several small items including pieces of carved ivory, animal teeth, bits of wood, and stones. Together these items, the king believes, can be made to serve as a divination device.

Treasure. Aside from all the mundane armor and weapons, the only item of value to be had here is one of the stones on the table, which is an uncarved piece of carnelian worth 100 gp.

Secret Exit. A stone projects out of the wall to the left of the secret door, 12 feet above the floor. Pushing the stone in causes the portal to pivot, revealing an opening 10 feet wide and 10 feet high.

8. Hydra Cave

A **hydra** lurks in either the north or the south alcove of this area if it hears any creature coming up the steps toward its lair. The creature is very vicious, as the king beats it and torments it for fun, and it hopes to take revenge on virtually any other living thing.

9. King Snurre's Treasure Cave

The chamber to the west of the hydra's lair is filled with stuff, much of which is valueless or nearly so—a pile of 2,800 cp, three mounds of 4d4 worthless tapestries and furs, several dozen bales of valueless cloth, scores of various vessels and containers, and urns and vases of pewter and brass and bronze, plus ten urns of silver (worth 50 gp each) and two of gold (worth 500 gp each).

A chimney in the southeastern part of the cave leads up through the roof.

Treasure. The real wealth in the room is held inside nearly twenty different containers—eight iron trunks, six smaller chests, and five even smaller coffers. As the characters investigate and attempt to open them, they discover features and contents as follows. Opening a locked one requires a successful DC 20 Dexterity check using thieves' tools.

Trunk 1 is locked. It contains 7,200 sp.

Trunk 2 is locked. It contains nothing.

Trunk 3 is unlocked and has no defenses. At the bottom is s sack holding ten pieces of jewelry (worth 500 gp each). It is buried under a heap of 6,000 cp.

Trunk 4 is locked and trapped. It contains 3 cubic feet of silk, worth 300 gp per cubic foot. If the trunk is opened without the key, a blade springs from the lid and chops down at one target, with a +11 bonus to hit and dealing 13 (3d8) slashing damage on a hit. With a successful DC 20 Wisdom (Perception) check, a character can spot alterations to the lock and hinges that are part of the trap mechanism. A successful DC 20 Dexterity check by someone using thieves' tools can be used to disable the hinge mechanism. If the trap goes off but the blade misses, it chops through 2 cubic feet of the silk, ruining it.

Trunk 5 is locked. It contains eight pieces of rare wood, each the size of a mace and inlaid with mother-of-pearl (worth 100 gp apiece).

Trunk 6 is unlocked and has no defenses. It contains 1,300 ep.

Trunk 7 is locked. It contains ten fine ivory tusks each weighing 5 pounds and worth 150 gp.

Trunk 8 is unlocked. When it is opened, it initially appears empty because all of its contents are invisible. The chest holds six pieces of jewelry worth 250 gp each as well as nine **poisonous snakes**.

Chest 1 is unlocked and trapped. If its lid is lifted, poisonous gas billows forth and spreads out to fill a 10-foot-radius area around it. Those within the cloud when it erupts must succeed on a DC 15 Constitution saving throw or become poisoned until they finish a short or long rest. The chest is empty.

Chest 2 is locked. It contains worthless rocks.

Chest 3 is unlocked and trapped. If its lid is lifted before the trap is disabled, acid sprays out from small holes in the sides, splattering anyone within 10 feet of the chest. Those in the affected area must make a DC 15 Dexterity saving throw, taking 7 (3d4) acid damage on a failed save, or half as much damage on a successful one. With a successful DC 20 Wisdom (Perception) check, a character discovers that the hinges are connected to a valve, disguised as a decoration, that pressurizes the acid in the chest walls. The trap can be disabled by someone who uses thieves' tools and succeeds on a DC 20 Dexterity check.

To determine the contents of the chest, consult chapter 7 of the *Dungeon Master's Guide*. Roll four times on Magic Item Table A, two times on Table B, two times on Table C, once on Table D, and once on Table E. Any result that is not a potion or a scroll should be disregarded but not rerolled.

Chest 4 is unlocked and trapped. It contains 1,600 gp. If its lid is lifted before the trap is disabled, numerous spikes shoot forward, backward, and to each side. Each spike has a range of 15 feet and a +11 bonus to hit, dealing 7 (2d6) piercing damage on a hit. Anyone within 15 feet of the chest might be hit. With a successful DC 20 Wisdom (Perception) check, a character notices that the hinges are connected to four valves, disguised as decorations, that pressurize the spikes in the chest walls. Thieves' tools and a successful DC 20 Dexterity check can be used to disable the valves.

Chest 5 is locked. It contains nothing.

Chest 6 is locked and trapped. It contains a *cloak of elvenkind* and a pair of *boots of elvenkind*. The lock and the chest's handles are coated with oil of taggit (see "Sample Poisons" in chapter 8 of the *Dungeon Master's Guide*). With a successful DC 20 Wisdom (Perception) check, a character spots the oil. A character who succeeds on a DC 15 Intelligence check, or any character who has proficiency with a poisoner's kit, knows that the oil can be wiped off with alcohol, although doing so without wearing protective clothing is risky, requiring a successful DC 15 Dexterity check. On a failed check, the character is exposed to the poison.

Coffer 1 is unlocked and trapped. It contains thirty gold rings, one of which is a *ring of protection*. The others are ordinary rings worth 50 gp each. If the treasure is touched before the trap is disabled, a poison needle shoots from the inner side of the coffer, hitting the extremity that was extended. The needle deals 1 piercing damage and delivers a dose of purple worm poison (see "Sample Poisons" in chapter 8 of the *Dungeon Master's Guide*). With a successful DC 20 Wisdom (Perception) check, a character discovers the recess in the coffer wall that holds the needle. A character can remove the needle, thereby disabling the trap, by using thieves' tools and making a successful DC 15 Dexterity check.

Coffer 2 is locked. It contains 200 pp concealed beneath a layer of 500 cp.

Coffer 3 is locked. It holds packets of leaves and seeds and husks—various hot spices worth a total of 100 gp.

Coffer 4 is unlocked. It contains six small, highly crafted, carved statues of unknown mineral and workmanship. All register as desecrated objects to the scrutiny of Divine Sense or a *detect evil and good* spell. Each idol is associated with a different ability score. While one is carried, its bearer has disadvantage on all d20 rolls involving that particular ability score.

Coffer 5 is locked. It holds sixteen gems (worth 250 gp each) concealed beneath a layer of two hundred gems worth 10 gp each, further topped by five hundred gems of good size and fine appearance but worth only 1 gp each.

10. ARSENAL COMPLEX

A **fire giant** is always at the ready inside the entrance to this storage area. If summoned or attacked, the guard fetches the chimera from area 11. The guard has three throwing rocks at hand. Torches provide light, and a bench offers a place to sit down.

10A. West Arsenal. The western wing contains fifteen huge swords, a ballista, twenty spears, three maces, five greataxes, and a quantity of giant-sized throwing rocks.

Treasure. Hidden in the far southwestern corner under the spears are a *+1 longbow* and a quiver of twenty *+1 arrows.*

10B. East Arsenal. The eastern wing has another supply of throwing rocks, five massive clubs, nine fire giant helmets, two chain shirts, eight shields, and eight studded leather jacks—all giant-sized. Eight big barrels of oil are stored along the east side of the area.

Treasure. One of the giant-sized shields is actually a *shield of missile attraction.*

11. CHIMERA PEN

The fire giants keep a **chimera** here. This creature attacks intruders on sight, since it hates everyone except fire giants.

12. ADVISOR'S QUARTERS

A corridor heads westward from the pillared hallway. The corridor and the chamber beyond contain furnishings of various sizes. The smallest of them are a table, a plush chair with a footstool, and a couch. Other items are more or less human-sized, including a long table, two benches, two chairs, and twelve chests. Finally, there are four huge chairs, a table, and a footstool sized for giants. Rugs on the floor, tapestries on the walls, and bronze cressets with flaming torches complete the decor.

Eight **gnoll** servants/bodyguards are lounging in this area, awaiting orders. They obey only the commands of King Snurre, Queen Frupy, or the Advisor—who is is a grossly fat but very strong and quite fast renegade mountain dwarf named Obmi (see area 12A).

Treasure. The chests contain the treasure of each gnoll (amounting to 50 gp each) plus the gnolls' personal gear. The third, eighth, tenth, and twelfth chests that the characters examine are locked; they contain bottles of wine and spirits.

12A. OBMI'S STUDY

The door to this study appears to be locked from the outside, suggesting that the place is vacant (Obmi is very clever). He can see through the door by means of a peephole, and if he sees intruders who are battling the gnolls and winning he will yell for them to help him, claiming to be a victim and a prisoner of the giants.

In fact, at first sight, this chamber appears to be a cell rather than a truly comfortable study. Obmi is at work in the room, poring over several scrolls atop his plain wooden desk, searching for solutions for the problems besetting his King. The dwarf has been Snurre's advisor for twenty-five years, having spent five years as a slave before that. A case against the north wall contains various maps, scrolls, and papers, all written in Giant or Dwarvish.

If he finds himself at a disadvantage, Obmi (use the **assassin** statistics, with 16 Strength and Charisma and the ability to make three melee attacks using Multiattack) tells the characters that the giants have held

him—a prince of his people—captive for ten years, trying to trick information out of him or to subvert his loyalty to dwarfdom when torture failed. He further claims that several humans in black robes aid the giants in their questioning. Finally, he asks to be allowed his armor and weapons in order to gain sweet revenge upon Snurre, and he claims to know exactly where the king will be.

While in his study, Obmi has only a studded leather jacket and a long knife (the equivalent of a shortsword, coated with one dose of the poison noted in the assassin statistics). If worst comes to worst, he bolts for room 12B and bars the door once he is inside.

Treasure. Obmi uses a plain wooden box as a footstool. It seemingly holds only old clothes of his—but beneath a false bottom, which requires a successful DC 15 Wisdom (Perception) check to find, some gems are hidden: two worth 500 gp each, eight worth 100 gp each, twenty-three worth 50 gp each, forty-one worth 10 gp each, and eighteen worth 5 gp each.

12B. OBMI'S BEDCHAMBER
In a larger chamber adjacent to his study, the renegade dwarf has a soft bed, a small stand, a table and chair, a cabinet, two iron chests, and an arming rack. His *dwarven plate* and *+1 shield* (AC 20, or AC 23 with his shield) are laid on the rack near the door, and his *+1 battleaxe* and *+1 warhammer* (each deals 1d8 + 4 damage in Obmi's hands) hang on the wall above. Underneath the armor are his *gauntlets of ogre power* (giving him an additional +1 to attack and damage rolls with melee weapons). His *ring of invisibility* is on a small stand near his bed.

Upon entering the room Obmi will palm the ring, don the armor, put on the gauntlets, thong the axe to his belt, heft the hammer, and grab the shield. At the first good opportunity he will attack the party and raise a cry for help, but he will do so only when he knows help will be able to come. He knows a bit about the drow, and he will bargain with that information, or anything else, to save his life. If offered no quarter, he will fight to the very end.

Treasure. In addition to Obmi's magical gear, both of the iron chests contain valuables. One chest holds 900 gp. The other holds 100 pp and a bejeweled silver ewer and silver bowl (each item worth 500 gp).

13. COUNCIL ROOM
The king and his council meet in this large chamber, but the place is now empty. A long table near the center of the room has five great chairs around it. Hides cover parts of the polished black floor. Rude tapestries adorn the walls and are also hung across the openings around the perimeter of the room. There are several torches in the place, but none are lit.

13A. WEST ALCOVE
Within the alcove to the west is a table with a flat chest on it, locked and full of stones (weighing 200 pounds). If the chest is lifted or moved, a pressure plate underneath it shifts, causing six poisoned arrows to shoot out from the north wall. Each arrow has a range of 100 feet and a +11 bonus to hit; it deals 5 (1d10) piercing damage on a hit, and the target struck must make a DC 11 Consti-

tution saving throw, taking 10 (3d6) poison damage on a failed save, or half as much damage on a successful one). The arrows strike the south wall and shatter if they miss interposing creatures.

The holes for the arrows are sealed with a thin crust of mortar. A character who examines the wall spots them with a successful DC 20 Wisdom (Perception) check. Someone who looks carefully at the base of the chest can spot the pressure plate with a successful DC 20 Wisdom (Perception) check. The holes can be blocked by hammering iron pitons or similar objects into them. The pressure plate can be wedged in place with the use of at least two such objects. In either case, a character attempting to disarm the trap must succeed on a DC 10 Strength check. On a failed check, the trap operates anyway when the attempt to block it fails.

Treasure. A map of the area around the stronghold hangs on the western wall. Two locked chests rest against the north and south walls—the northern one filled with 850 sp, the southern one holding 500 gp and six bone batons with Dwarvish runes upon them.

Each of the batons is a token of free passage whose runes read, in Giant, "Official Business on Behalf of King Snurre the Fearsome." Any individuals or groups that display one of these items are safe from attacks by the giants or the giants' allies as long as they take no aggressive action.

13B. SOUTH ALCOVE
Four extra chairs for the council table are stored in the alcove to the south, and a huge cabinet holds eighty-three scrolls and three hundred sixty-seven pieces of paper or parchment.

Most of the cabinet's contents are worthless and of no import, but the sixty-eighth scroll tube contains instructions for King Snurre, telling him to gather forces of hill, stone, frost, and fire giants, along with whatever strength he can raise in ogres, oni, cloud giants, and any other creatures for an all-out attack on humankind. The message further promises powerful help from the dark elves. It is signed "Eclavdra."

The papers are copies of messages to and replies from various types of giants and giant-kin. One, in Dwarvish, reads, "The fire giant of stone left and left elbow."

14. DOOR GUARD
A **fire giant** stands guard at all times outside the doors to the council chambers.

15. KITCHEN
Benches, counters, a table, several stools, three cupboards, various bins and barrels, and miscellaneous kitchen gear are scattered around the kitchen. The area to the west is a natural firepit, where flaming gases are used to roast whole creatures.

The place is typically occupied by busy workers: a **fire giant** matron, two fire giant servants (use the **hill giant** statistics, plus immunity to fire damage), and seven **gnoll** thralls. The servants and the gnolls fight only under the direction of the matron, fleeing or surrendering if she falls.

Slippery Exit. The chute to the northwest goes down to the lava pool on the second level (area 6 on map 6.6).

Six feet in diameter, it is slippery and greasy from garbage and empties out 2 feet above the lava.

16. Storage Chamber

The room near the kitchen is jammed full of barrels of ale and mead, boxes, sacks, hampers, and wheels of cheese. Overhead hang smoked sides of meat, smoked fish, strings of sausages, and the like. There are smaller boxes of salt, and a screw-top copper container filled with spices (wonderfully hot peppers). Tuns of wine and casks of beer are kept handy near the door. The most common item, heaps of hard bread, is everywhere.

17. Guest Chamber

The doors to this room are closed on the outside by a great bar, because King Snurre does not fully trust his guest, a **rakshasa**, that resides herein. Naturally, most adventurers will assume a creature thus imprisoned might become a trusted associate—an attitude the rakshasa will encourage by taking some benign form (such as that of a fellow adventurer, a kindred soul, who has been deprived of equipment) to gain the characters' confidence before it attacks.

Inside are four beds, a table and two chairs, two stools, and other furnishings including three chests and a footstool (in reality a treasure chest). Rugs and tapestries adorn the floor and walls, and flaming torches in sconces provide light.

Treasure. The rakshasa carries 50 gp and two gems (worth 100 gp each). The disguised chest holds a jeweled scepter worth 1,000 gp, three potions (*superior healing*, *mind reading*, and *invulnerability*), and five *spell scrolls* (*zone of truth*, *true seeing*, *darkness*, *cure wounds* cast at 4th level, and *symbol*).

18. Barracks

Currently two **fire giants** and two fire giant servants (use the **hill giant** statistics, plus immunity to fire damage) are housed here. They typically lounge around sharpening weapons and telling lies about their amatory prowess.

The room has eight cots, four stools, and four hampers. Each cot is heaped with skins. The hampers contain the giants' personal gear. Pegs on the walls hold their bags and cloaks. There are five clubs, three axes, six spears, and eight shields scattered about, mostly along the north wall. The place is lit by flaming gas jets.

Treasure. One of the clubs, noticeably lighter than the others, has been hollowed out to serve as a treasure cache. It holds 15 pp, 30 gp, 15 ep, 25 sp, 184 cp, and three 100 gp gems.

19. Servants' Quarters

This room currently holds four fire giant servants (use the **hill giant** statistics, plus immunity to fire damage). The others that live here are presently at work in the kitchen (area 15). This torch-lit chamber has seven cots, various pieces of smaller furniture, and pegs on the walls that hold garments and the like.

Treasure. Each servant has a piece of silver jewelry worth 100 gp.

20. Communal Quarters

Three fire giant servants (use the **hill giant** statistics, plus immunity to fire damage) care for six young fire giants (use the **ogre** statistics, plus immunity to fire damage) in this vast chamber. All have weapons (kids' toys for the youngsters) and will fight with enthusiasm.

There are three beds and six cots along the walls. In each wing is a bench, three chairs, six stools, a long table, and various boxes, hampers, and cupboards.

Treasure. Each servant has a piece of silver jewelry worth 100 gp.

21. Entry Hall of the Kennels

Four **hell hounds** scuffle and play just inside the doors. They are part of the pack at area 22 and will flee thereto by the safest route if threatened.

22. Kennel Chamber

Four **hell hounds** are here. If those in area 21 are attacked and yelp for assistance, these beasts split into pairs and station themselves in the north and south ends of the open area, from where they spring to the aid of the others. The hell hounds love their handler at area 23 and come to his rescue if he whistles.

The kennel contains no treasure, other than the hounds' prized bones (of interest only to other hell hounds).

23. Kennel Keeper's Quarters

Herein dwell the Keeper and his mate, two **fire giants** who will rush to the aid of their charges if they hear a commotion outside. Their chamber contains a large bed, a table, two chairs, a bench, a chest, a cabinet, three barrels (beer, mead, and ale), two buckets (his and hers), and a crate (holding dried meat for the hounds). Burning torches light the place. Pegs on the walls hold wearing apparel and the giants' bags. A shield, a battleaxe, and a javelin lean against the wall to the north. Hides and pelts decorate the floor and walls, and a number of skins and furs are heaped on the bed and the bench.

Treasure. The second bucket has a false bottom, which requires a successful DC 15 Wisdom (Perception) check to find. Beneath it are stored 20 pp and eight gems (worth 100 gp each).

The javelin leaning against the wall is actually a *javelin of lightning*.

One of the six cloaks on the bench is a *hell hound cloak* (see appendix A). Wrapped inside this cursed cloak is a *sword of vengeance*. There are three other hell hound hides in the chamber (those of beloved departed pets), all quite normal.

24. Guardpost

A **fire giant** is on duty here at all times with four throwing rocks nearby. An iron cylinder hanging near the north wall is a gong to be sounded if intruders are seen.

25. Barracks

Two **fire giant** warriors and two fire giant servants (use the **hill giant** statistics, plus immunity to fire damage) are lounging among the cots, chests, and other furniture that fill this place. Several pegs here and there hold cloaks, capes, shields, and four giants' bags. There are only worthless giant-sized items in the chests and other containers.

One warrior has a greatsword, and the other one fights with a human-sized *+2 greataxe*. The weapon gives the giant a +13 bonus to hit and deals 22 (3d8 + 9) slashing damage. The room also has twenty-one throwing rocks, which all the giants will use if the opportunity presents itself.

Treasure. The easternmost of the three pillars has a secret hatch (equivalent to a secret door) concealing a hollowed-out space that contains 800 gp and three pieces of gem-studded jewelry (worth 500 gp each).

SECOND LEVEL: GENERAL FEATURES

Map 6.6 shows the layout of the second level of the fire giant stronghold. The floors, walls, and ceilings throughout the area are of black, reddish-black, dark gray, and dull brown rock. In some places the stone has been hewn, but in others it appears to have been fused by heat.

Ceilings. Passageways have vaulted ceilings 30 feet high. Caves, chambers, and rooms are 40 to 60 feet high.

Doors. All doors are made of iron plates. A Medium or smaller creature must succeed on a DC 15 Strength (Athletics) check to open any of the doors in this place due to their great size and weight. Doors stay open if left that way.

Illumination. Light is provided by torches, braziers, natural gas jets, and molten lava.

Locks. The hall contains numerous well-made locks. Someone using thieves' tools can pick a lock with a successful DC 20 Dexterity check.

Secret Doors. Secret doors on this level are precisely crafted. Unless otherwise noted, it requires a successful DC 20 Wisdom (Perception) check to find such a door.

RANDOM ENCOUNTERS

On the second level of the fire giant stronghold, the chance of a random encounter occurs on an hourly basis. At the end of each hour, roll a d12. On a roll of 1, which indicates a random encounter, choose from the following possibilities:

- One **fire giant** and one fire giant servant (use the **hill giant** statistics, plus immunity to fire damage)
- One **troll** escorting one **hill giant**, one **stone giant**, or one **frost giant**
- One **troll** with ten **gnolls**
- One **drow mage** with five **wererats**

LOCATIONS ON THE SECOND LEVEL

The following locations are identified on map 6.6.

1. HALL OF THE DEAD

This dark hall contains twenty huge sarcophagi standing upright against the walls, and four even larger ones lying on the floor in the center of the chamber. Those four are made of stone, and the northern two have likeness of fire giants carved into their lids, while the southern two are blank.

Of the sarcophagi that line the walls, half are made of stone, six are crafted from bronze, two are brass, and two are iron. All of them bear likenesses of fire giant kings and queens.

Examination will reveal that each of these burial vaults contains only the remains of a king or a queen, moldering garments, a few corroded weapons, and similar worthless items (wererat grave robbers stole anything of value long ago).

Secret Exit. The tunnel behind the secret door in the southeast corner is about 5 feet in diameter. It twists and turns so that any person using it will lose all sense of direction before exiting at area 2 on map 6.7.

2. ETTIN GUARDS' CHAMBER

Four **ettins** reside here when they are not on duty near the main entrance to the grand hall (map 6.5, area 2). Two are asleep, their weapons within easy reach, while the other two quite alert. The chamber has a rude table, a bench, two stools, and four cots. Torches light the place. Nine pegs on the walls hold clothing and six giants' bags.

Treasure. In the northwest corner is a hamper with six sacks, each holding 600 cp (which is the ettins' accumulated pay).

3. VISITORS' CHAMBER

The doors to the north open into a room that houses two **stone giants** who have been working for King Snurre as engineers. The room, lit by torches, contains four cots, a large table, other furnishings, and pegs that hold clothing and two giants' bags. Eleven throwing rocks are scattered on the floor. A haunch of meat rests on the table along with mugs and platters of tin.

Treasure. Each giant has 250 gp and a gem (worth 100 gp).

4. STORAGE ROOM

This room, illuminated by four torches set in wall cressets, has been cleaned out to serve as quarters for four **hill giants**. If they survived or escaped the assault on the steading, Chief Nosnra and his wife are among the occupants.

If only ordinary hill giants are here, the room contains nothing more than four heaps of skins for bedding, a table, and two chests.

If Nosnra and Grutha are present, the place has two cots, two heaps of skins, a trunk, a chain, a table, and two chests.

Treasure. Ordinary hill giants carry 100 gp each but have no other treasure. The chief, if present, will have brought along whatever of his valuables he could salvage and carry here.

5. COMMUNITY QUARTERS

In this large area are housed a **fire giant** warrior, three fire giant servants (use the **hill giant** statistics, plus immunity to fire damage), and four young fire giants (use the **ogre** statistics, plus immunity to fire damage). All are armed with various weapons, even the young, and there are twenty throwing rocks in the chamber.

The place holds several beds, two large cabinets, two tables, miscellaneous smaller furniture, a crate, and

HALL OF THE FIRE GIANT KING

SECOND LEVEL

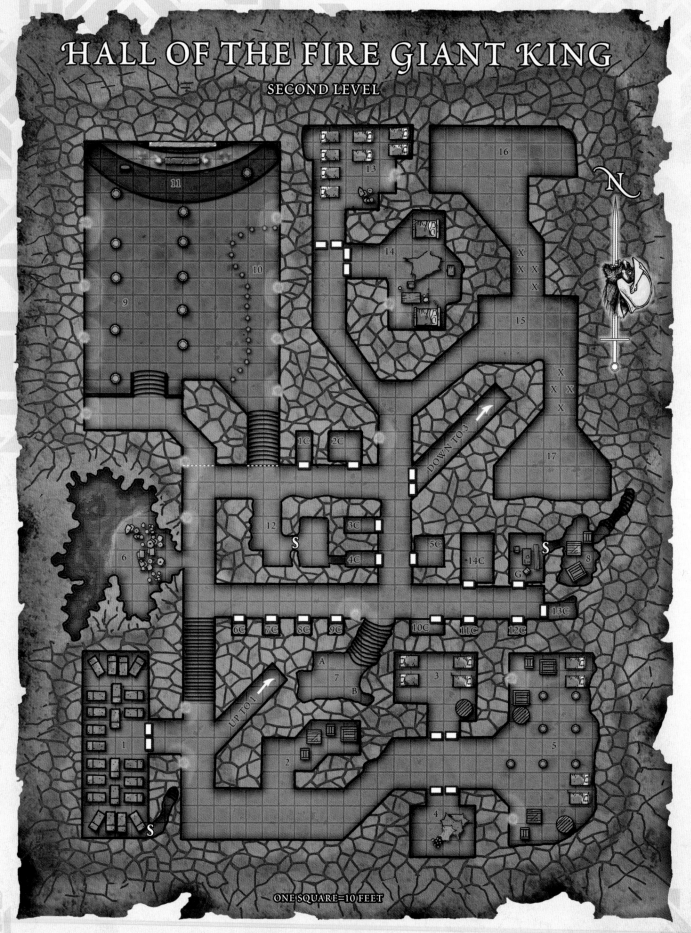

ONE SQUARE = 10 FEET

Map 6.6: Hall of the Fire Giant King, Second Level

three small boxes. Lit torches are set along on the walls, as well as pegs that hold clothing and four giants' bags. Bits of gear, eating utensils, and odds and ends are scattered about the place too.

Treasure. The fire giant warrior has 200 gp in his bag, and the other three adults have 100 gp each hidden in their personal effects.

6. SMITHY

As the characters approach the natural cavern on the west side of the stronghold, they hear an intermittent hammering sound, made by a metallic object, coming from the other side of the opening. The hall outside this place is tinged a bloody red by the light emitted from the lava pool and the flaming gas jets that are found inside.

A knotty-limbed, burly **fire giant**, King Snurre's weaponsmith, is working here. He uses the molten lava to heat the items he works. With him are two **trolls** that serve as his assistants. Currently in his forge, in various stages of completion, are three giant-sized swords, some pieces of armor, and several axe and spear heads.

Treasure. The weaponsmith has in his possession a special *+2 mace*, made of strange black metal, that he is doing some repair work on. If he is attacked and the fight goes against him, there is a 33 percent chance per round that he uses his action to toss the mace into the lava and destroy it, rather than let it fall into the hands of his enemies.

7. TORTURE CHAMBER

At the midpoint of the east–west corridor, steps lead down to the south, ending at a cluttered room with a 50-foot-high ceiling (which enables even very tall victims to be suspended on chains well above the floor). The stairway and the chamber are lit by torches, but the area is lightly obscured due to steam and murk.

The gloomy chamber contains a large (giant-sized) rack, a smaller (human-sized) one, an iron maiden (at the location marked A), and a stone-rimmed well (at the location marked B). Various chains, bats, irons, whips, ropes, wires, and the like are strewn about the place. A table, two chairs, a stool, and a large barrel of ale complete the picture.

Two **fire giants**, the King's Torturer and the Royal Headsman, are crouched in the center of the room, playing knucklebones on the floor with stakes of jewelry gems scattered in front of them. The headsman has his gigantic *+2 greataxe* at hand—a weapon that can be employed only by a creature at least as strong and massive as he is. He has a +13 bonus to hit with the weapon, and it deals 28 (3d12 + 9) slashing damage on a hit. His friend the torturer has a greatsword nearby.

If the torturer is engaged in melee, he grapples his opponent and attempts to carry or throw the character into the iron maiden and slam it shut, dealing 55 (10d10) piercing damage to the unlucky victim. A victim can't open the iron maiden from within.

If the headsman is closely pressed, he grapples his opponent and tosses the character headfirst down the well. Anyone flung into the well falls 90 feet into an underground pool of water.

After the torturer uses the iron maiden, he begins tossing as many characters as possible down the well until the room is cleared of opponents. The headsman, by contrast, uses his axe after tossing one victim down the well.

Treasure. The stakes of the game include six pieces of jewelry (worth 250 gp each) and ten gems (worth 50 gp each).

CELL COMPLEX

A number of small chambers are clustered around the center of this level of the stronghold. These rooms, labeled 1C through 14C, are cells meant to hold prisoners. In addition, the guardroom for the cell complex is marked with a G. Each cell has a thick wooden door with a high, barred window (about 15 feet up, too high for the average human to peek through without some climbing). Inside these rooms are rings set in the walls, chains attached to the rings, buckets, heaps of straw, and precious little else.

The occupants and other contents of the cells and the guardroom are as follows.

Cell 1C. The female elf in this cell is destined for sacrifice in the Temple. She is a **noble**, and she promises that if she is rescued, she will send her rescuers a reward of 1,000 gp, twenty *+1 arrows*, an *arrow of giant slaying*, a *cloak of elvenkind*, and a pair of *boots of elvenkind*. The reward will come to the characters a month or two after she is able to leave the stronghold and return home.

Cell 2C. Eight male elf **commoners** are awaiting sacrifice in the Temple. They have no treasure, but they promise to sing their rescuers' praises.

Cell 3C. A merchant is being held for ransom. He is a human **commoner** whose goods have all been seized by the giants, and thus he can pay his rescuers only with eternal gratitude.

Cell 4C. The cell is empty. On the west wall is a secret door that opens only with a key held by the drow high priestess at area 12.

Cell 5C. Two noble **centaurs** imprisoned here are bound for torture and execution. They offer help to any who free them.

Cell 6C. The cell is empty.

Cell 7C. Three **gnolls** being punished for insubordination were thrown in here. One is already dead from the aftereffects of torture; the other two will serve any rescuer who can tolerate their habits.

Cell 8C. The cell is empty.

Cell 9C. In this cell sits a **troll** that is used for torture practice from time to time. It is mindless and enraged, so it will attack instantly if given a chance. Otherwise, it remains motionless.

Cell 10C. Seven **gnolls** caught stealing gold await their fate in this cell. They run away as fast as possible.

Cell 11C. Two human skeletons lie on the floor, twined in each other's arms.

Cell 12C. A female human **assassin** is chained to the wall. She cheerfully admits to being a thief who was caught trying to find the king's treasure room ("Know where it is?") and volunteers to aid the party faithfully in exchange for a chance to escape. Thereafter, if the opportunity presents itself, she will heist as much in gems and magic as she can and then slip away—but until then she will help the characters to the best of her ability (both to better her own chances of staying alive in this awful place and to win their trust). During this time she will be casing the characters to learn what they carry.

Cell 13C. The king's chief lieutenant, a **fire giant** named Boldo, hangs in chains as punishment for failing to be properly deferential to Snurre. He will do anything to get back into Snurre's favor. Thus, he will happily lie to the party and tell them he is here because he tried to prevent Snurre from taking his current hostile course. If freed, he tells the characters, he can get several other fire giants to aid them in overthrowing the king and restoring the peace. In fact, Boldo will betray the party at his earliest opportunity. He is quite bright, and he will not be rash.

Cell 14C. Chained in the cell next to the guardroom is an **empyrean** (of chaotic good alignment). It has been drugged and is effectively unconscious. A character who succeeds on a DC 15 Wisdom (Medicine) check can identify the effects of exposure to a virulent form of oil of taggit (see "Sample Poisons" in chapter 8 of the *Dungeon Master's Guide*). Magic, such as *protection from poison* or *lesser restoration*, can remove the poison from the empyrean's system. Otherwise, he recovers naturally in 12 hours. If awakened, he helps any party destroy the inhabitants of this place, although he would not mind seeing evil characters in the party die also.

Guardroom (G). One **fire giant** guard and three **wererats** in human form (appearing as female humans in tattered clothing) are conversing here by torchlight. The giant has two rocks nearby. In the room are a table, a chair, a stool, a bench, three kegs on the floor, and a small, covered jar on the table. The first keg holds small beer, the second one water, and the third one mead. The jar contains oil of taggit; anyone who opens the jar is exposed to the poison and has disadvantage on the saving throw. On the walls are pegs holding a giant's bag, a cape, a shield, keys to the cells, and a shirt.

If the guard is subdued and interrogated, he knows nothing of the secret tunnel to area 8 (and thus does not volunteer that information). If the disguised wererats are conversed with, they claim to be captives forced to labor for the giants as scullions. If they are attacked, the wererats assume the form of giant rats and escape through a drain hole in the northwest corner of the room, traveling from there to alert the drow of intruders.

The secret door to the east opens into a passage about 2 feet wide and 1½ feet high. It is rough, and a human in armor could not hope to pass along its length; even a halfling would have to struggle to get through it.

Treasure. A loose stone in the floor to the east of the door hides a cache of 30 ep, 60 gp, and 21 pp. The guard wears a gemmed brooch (worth 100 gp) on his cloak.

8. SECRET ROOM

This place, pitch dark, is the lair of seven **wererats**. If the encounter is going badly for them, survivors flee down the northeast passageway to area 15 on the third level (map 6.7) and warn the drow.

Aside from stolen cloaks piled here and there like nests, the chief features in this secret room are three heavy iron chests. All are locked, and each key is on a different wererat. The chests are also trapped with poison needles (see "Sample Traps" in chapter 5 of the *Dungeon Master's Guide*). The poison on these needles is oil of taggit (see "Sample Poisons" in chapter 8 of the *Dungeon Master's Guide*).

The third chest the characters investigate is additionally trapped so that two poisoned darts fire upward from the inside when the lid is opened. Each dart has a range of 30 feet and a +8 bonus to hit. It deals 2 (1d4) piercing damage on a hit and subjects its victim to exposure to drow poison (see "Sample Poisons" in chapter 8 of the *Dungeon Master's Guide*). The mechanism for this trap is inside the chest, thus it cannot be detected from the outside. A character who succeeds on a DC 20 Wisdom (Perception) check while beginning to open the lid notices that it opens stiffly, with resistance from the inside. Those near the chest have a brief moment of warning before the lid springs fully open and the darts shoot forth; anyone who ducks down or lunges away from the chest can avoid being hit.

Treasure. The first chest holds six pieces of jewelry worth 250 gp each, eight pieces worth 500 gp each, and three large pouches stuffed with 100 gp each.

The second chest contains a *potion of poison*, 800 gp (loose), and a cursed *scroll of protection* (lycanthropes). Someone who reads the scroll must succeed on a DC 15 Wisdom saving throw or become afflicted with wererat lycanthropy.

The third chest is empty, but a permanent *invisibility* spell covers writing on the inside of the lid. If the invisibility is dispelled, the information tells where a stone in the wall along the stairs down can be removed to reveal a *ring of shooting stars*, a *spell scroll* of seven cleric spells (DM's choice), and a metal case holding six potions (*healing*, *diminution*, plus four more of the DM's choice).

A secret compartment in the lid of the box that contains the potions holds *pipes of the sewers*. A character who succeeds on a DC 20 Wisdom (Perception) check while examining the box finds the compartment.

TEMPLE OF THE EYE (AREAS 9–11)

Illusionary walls (represented by dashed lines on the map) screen the temple area from discovery. Making physical contact with these images reveals their illusory nature. Someone who examines either image without touching it can determine that it is an illusion by making a successful DC 15 Intelligence (Investigation) check. On a successful check, the illusions fade for that character, becoming transparent enough to see through.

Beyond the illusions, the whole place is illuminated by a strange, swirling light that seems to be part of the very air. Eddies of luminosity drift here and there, causing the whole scene to be difficult to perceive. Distances and dimensions are tricky to determine in the shifting light of rusty purple motes and lavender rays. Globs of mauve and violet seem to seep and slide around. The ceiling of the temple is out of visual range, 50 feet high at its lowest point and well over 65 feet where it vaults upward in the center.

9. Giants' Worship Area. Each pillar radiates a sense of unease and insecurity in a 5-foot radius (simulate this by making players uneasy in whatever way you find best). The wall to the west is a mural showing giants bowing before a black cairn, offering sacrifices and giving gifts. The floor in the western half of the area is of porphyry, and the pillars are made of serpentine. Their well-polished surfaces reflect the strange light that permeates the place. The scenes on the west wall grow more gruesome as the viewer proceeds north, culminating in scenes showing human and giant sacrifice near the end closest to the altar (area 11).

10. Servants' and Thralls' Worship Area. The polished floor of red and black hornblende seems to flow between the thin pillars of obsidian that border this area. Each of these pillars radiates an aura of mild fear in a 2-foot radius, and if one is touched the creature who comes into contact with it must succeed on a DC 15 Wisdom saving throw or be affected as if by a *fear* spell with the pillar as the object of its fear. Passing between two pillars causes a creature to take 5 (2d4) lightning damage, or double that if it is wearing metal armor.

The wall to the east shows a scene of various creatures submitting to a trio of huge, vaguely squid-like creatures, each with ten hairy tentacles and mottled in various shades and tints of purple and violet. In the forefront of this mass self-sacrifice are elves and humans, but there are also dwarves, gnolls, orcs, trolls, halflings, ogres, goblins, and other creatures among the crowd. Those near the front of the line are being torn apart and the bloody gobbets eaten as dainty morsels.

11. Priests' Area. The northern end of the temple is tiered, with three low steps that lead up toward the center of the north wall. This wall, made of cloudy purple stone, displays an inlay of a huge inverted triangle with a Y shape enclosed in it and touching the triangle's sides. Hanging beneath this symbol, suspended on chains from the ceiling, is a black metal triangle and cylinder.

The floor of the first tier is black stone shot through with veins of violet. A great drum of blackened skin and chitinous material rests on the western side of the first tier. On the eastern side is a rack from which hang nine silver cylinders, apparently a set of chimes. (these chime tubes are hollow and are worth 100 gp each).

The large pillar to the east on the first tier is made of malachite and is covered with graven signs and sigils. A casting of *detect magic* reveals that the glyphs radiate an aura of conjuration magic. If the correct pair of gylphs are touched, the creature touching them will be transported to area 18 on the third level (see map 6.7). You should devise the twenty-four glyphs upon this pillar and select which two are the trigger mechanism.

The second tier is dark gray stone, with specks of lilac and orange and purple. It holds a huge stone altar block of dull, porous-looking, somewhat rust-colored black mineral. To either side of the altar are large bronze braziers whose corroded green coloration is particularly nauseating in this setting. Flanking the braziers, in the form of triangles pointing downward, are two sets of candelabra, each candelabrum having three branches.

These are made of bronze that is green with age, and each branch holds a fat black candle that burns with a flame of leaping lavender and deep glowing purple but never grows shorter.

The third tier is dull black stone with whorls of plum and lavender and splotches of red. The metal triangle stands upon the third tier. If the altar stone is touched by living flesh or hit by a weapon (or any object), it begins to fade in color, and in 3 rounds becomes a translucent amethyst color with a black, amorphous center. A creature that touches or strikes the altar when it is in this form must succeed on a DC 15 Wisdom saving throw or become paralyzed for 1 hour.

If the drum on the first tier is beaten, the chimes are rung, and the triangle is struck while the altar is in this translucent state, a glowing golden eye swims into view in the stone's writing center. For each creature that sees the eye, roll a d12 and consult the following table. The creature is affected as if by a *symbol* spell of the indicated type (save DC 15):

d12	Result
1	Death
2	Discord
3	Fear
4	Hopelessness
5	Insanity
6–12	No effect (looked away in time)

Except for the death effect, these effects are curses and can be removed only as such.

If the three *tentacle rods* from area 12 are in the characters' possession when the eye appears, and the braziers remain lit, then the altar becomes a means of summoning an Elder Elemental God—it turns a transparent heliotrope in color, the black mass at the center grows larger and shows swollen veins of purple, and the eye is a fiery red-orange. Then a tentacle comes out of the altar and grabs the nearest living creature. The tentacle has a reach of 20 feet and a +11 bonus to hit. A creature hit by the tentacle is drawn into the stone—totally gone, destroyed.

If a creature is drawn into the altar, the altar returns to its dormant state, and atop it will be the thing most wished for by the party—or something that will enable the characters to attain the end or state they most desire.

If a second summoning of this Elder Elemental God is attempted within the same day, roll a d12 and apply the indicated result from the table below.

d12	Result
1	Tentacles try to seize and devour 1d4 more creatures within the minute, but entity does not grant any additional desires.
2	Entity strikes everyone present permanently blind and does not grant any additional desires.
3	Entity raises one ability score of each character present by 1 point and takes no sacrifice.
4–12	Entity ignores the whole thing.

Treasure. The only items of value in the temple that can be salvaged are the silver chimes. Each hollow silver cylinder is worth 100 gp.

HALL OF THE FIRE GIANT KING

THIRD LEVEL

N

A

20

18

17

2

16

19

5

15

4

G

G

3

7

6

8

14

1

9

10

UP TO 2

S

2

11

13

12

ONE SQUARE=10 FEET

MAP 6.7: HALL OF THE FIRE GIANT KING, THIRD LEVEL

12. Drow Clerics' Area

The entrance to this chamber is protected by a wall of tentacles (not depicted on the map). It appears as rough brown-purple stone. This magic wall is like two **ropers** combined into one creature, giving it two bite attacks and eight tendrils that it can employ every round (though the tendrils have a range of only 20 feet). The wall has resistance to bludgeoning, piercing, and slashing damage from nonmagical weapons. A casting of *dispel magic* deals the wall 50 damage, and *disintegrate* deals it 100 damage.

Drow can freely pass through the wall. If any other creature touches it, the wall attacks and emits a hissing and champing noise to alert the occupants of the chamber beyond it. If its current hit points drop to half its hit point maximum or lower, the wall casts *darkness* on itself (affecting only the outside of the wall, not its inner surface).

The chamber south of the wall is lit by the same ever-burning black candles that are found in the temple (area 11), so the illumination is eerie and dim. The walls are hung with purple cloth, and the floor is thickly carpeted in black. The inner room to the east is screened off from the outer room by a brocaded hanging of black with orange, gold, lilac, and mauve.

Outer Chamber. The antechamber is the quarters of a **drow elite warrior** and a **drow mage** who assist their priestess, Eclavdra. Each has a *tentacle rod* in addition to its usual gear and weaponry.

A smoldering copper brazier near the door gives off an incense-like smoke that is sweet, cloying, decayed-smelling, disgusting, alluring, and euphoric all at once. In the candlelit room are two low black couches, each inlaid with silver. To one side sit a round table and two armchairs. At the foot of each couch is a low table with a basin and ewer made of jasper. Small stools and enameled coffers provide a bit of decoration.

Treasure. The jasper basins and ewers are worth 300 gp per set. The first coffer examined holds a *spell scroll* of *word of recall* and three bars of adamantine, each weighing 5 pounds and worth 500 gp each. The second coffer contains 100 cp, 100 sp, 10 ep, 20 gp, and 10 pp, each type of coin in its own black leather pouch, as well as a pouch of ten gems (worth 50 gp each).

Inner Chamber. The inner room, lavishly furnished and decorated, is the sanctuary of Eclavdra, the **drow priestess of Lolth** who has fomented all the trouble with the giants. Like her assistants, she also carries a *tentacle rod* in addition to her other equipment.

Here the light from candles is supplemented by two small braziers of black and silver. Tapestries of a suggestive nature adorn the walls. The furnishings include a large bed, two small tables, three coffers, a buffet, a cabinet, a large wardrobe, two divans with a low chest between them, a dressing table and chair, a large mirror, two hampers, and two chests. All furnishings are of ebony or black stone, and most have silver inlay. The wardrobe holds feminine clothing and the priestess's vestments of mauve, black, and plum, stitched with gold.

A small screen of ebony inlaid with amber (weighing 10 pounds and worth 150 gp) sets off a dressing area in

the southeast corner near the wardrobe, where a low-backed chair stands with a gown thrown over it. This screen effectively hides the location of the secret door, which enables the priestess to slip in and out unseen.

Treasure. Many of the items in Eclavdra's chamber are of significant value.

The priestess's ceremonial garment is set with ten violet garnets (worth 50 gp each), ten topazes (50 gp each), ten black opals (100 gp each), and ten amethysts (100 gp each); it is covered with a plain black wrapper to protect it from dust and damage.

A coffer on the low chest between the divans has a *glyph of warding* on the inside of the lid, so if anyone other than Eclavdra opens it, the glyph casts *insect plague* (spell save DC 14). The container holds three *spell scrolls* (*gate*, *divine word*, and *greater restoration*).

A coffer near her bed contains six potions: *poison*, *mind control* (fire giant) (see appendix A), *growth*, *heroism*, and two *philters of love*.

On the dressing table are two combs, a brush, four pins, and ten jars that hold unguents and cosmetics. These items are of onyx and silver, set with tiny gems. Each is worth 50 gp.

Beside her bed on a small table are a basin, a ewer, and a goblet made from lapis lazuli (each is worth 500 gp). The ebony-and-amber screen around the dressing area weighs 10 pounds and is worth 150 gp. The large mirror of silver is worth 50 gp.

13. Guest Chamber

If Jarl Grugnur and his lady, Estia, survived the assault on the glacial rift, they will be sequestered in this chamber, accompanied by a **frost giant** that serves as a door guard. If the jarl and his lady are not present, the room contains two **frost giants**, recently arrived messengers.

The place is dimly lit by a few torches. It holds eight cots, a long table, two benches, two chairs, three stools, two buckets, six chests, a large box, and a cabinet. Hides on the floors and pelts on the cots help to make this place more comfortable and familiar for frost giant guests. Pegs hold clothing and three giants' bags.

Treasure. Each giant carries 100 gp. In addition, the jarl and his lady will have whatever loot they managed to salvage from their stronghold.

14. Guest Chamber

Two **cloud giants**, a noble and his traveling companion, have come to hear from King Snurre why his warfare will profit them and make them more powerful. The giants have two **lions** serving as watch-animals at the door. The noble has a chain mail coat (AC 16), and both have their great morningstars and throwing rocks nearby.

The chamber contains two very large beds, two wardrobes, two small tables, a large table, two chairs, two stools, two buckets, a cabinet, a bench, and four chests. The place is illuminated by torchlight, and there are tapestries on the walls, rugs and hides on the floor, and furs on the beds.

Treasure. On the small table near the bed to the south is a platinum box set with moonstones and sunstones (worth 1,000 gp) that holds ten gems (worth 100 gp each), which are a present to the visitors from the king.

15. Trolls' Chamber

Six **troll** guards nest in this room. Two of them keep watch in the northern passage (within the area marked by Xs) and two others do the same in the southern passage. The other two monsters are in the central chamber. Dozens of various polearms, morningstars, and swords lie heaped in the middle of the room. (These are used to arm the gnolls currently penned in areas 16 and 17.)

Treasure. Each troll has a nest of sticks, bones, hide and skin scraps, and other nauseating material in which is hidden 50 gp.

16. Thrall Pen

Sixteen unarmed **gnolls** dwell here. Each has nothing but a heap of straw and a hide coverlet. Although these creatures are slaves of the giants, they identify with their masters' cause and will never help humans for any reason—in fact, they will gladly take up arms to fight intruders if given the chance.

17. Thrall Pen

Ten unarmed **gnolls** dwell here. They will behave in all respects like their kin in area 16.

THIRD LEVEL: GENERAL FEATURES

Map 6.7 shows the layout of the lowest level of the fire giant stronghold. This place is entirely natural, the tunnels and caverns showing no marks of being hollowed out, except for the entranceway to the level from above and around the exit beyond the River of Lava.

As is usual with natural areas, do not worry overmuch about describing direction of passages and walls of caves and caverns, let alone size and shape. Primitive mapping techniques under stress conditions would develop just about the same sort of chart as your players will when their characters explore this level . . . wretched, but sufficient to get from place to place. If they have made it this far, they do not need any help from the DM!

Ceilings. All passages are at least 20 feet high, small caves being 25 feet or so from floor to ceiling vault and large caverns anywhere from 25 to 75 feet high (areas 7, 19, and 20 are among the highest).

Illumination. Most areas here are dark and still; only a few are lit, such as the lava cavern (areas 19 and 20) and the giants' final refuge in a crisis (area 5). If you like, add a few patches of phosphorescent growth as dungeon dressing—the light making it possible to see movement across it but not sufficient to illuminate an area.

Sounds. If the characters were to remain still, they might hear water dripping, and perhaps once and once only a far distant echoing of stone striking stone.

RANDOM ENCOUNTERS

On the third level of the fire giant stronghold, the chance of a random encounter occurs on an hourly basis. At the end of each hour, roll a d12. On a roll of 1, which indicates a random encounter, choose from the following possibilities:

- Two wandering **trolls**
- A **fire giant** patrolling with two **hell hounds**
- One **drow elite warrior** and three **drow** that use stealth to remain undetected and avoid confrontation

LOCATIONS ON THE THIRD LEVEL

The following locations are identified on map 6.7.

1. CAVERN

This cavern is fairly colorful, having many reddish, pale yellow, and shining blue-gray rock formations that glisten in the light of torches or lanterns. Three **ropers** dwell here and conceal themselves among the natural stalagmite formations. They wait until prey approaches the center of the area before attacking.

Treasure. Each roper has one gem (worth 100 gp) in its internal digestive organ.

2. GLOWING CAVE

This small offshoot of the larger cavern that runs north and south is filled with luminous plant growth and contains twelve hungry **giant fire beetles**. Some will be on the ceiling and drop upon any creatures entering their lair. These creatures served as a source of gifts for the frost giants in the past. They have no treasure.

3. CAVERN END

The long cavern hooks eastward and terminates. Near the dead-end wall is an abandoned subterranean lizard's nest that contains several dozen shiny rocks (but none of value).

4. CAVE

Four **hell hounds** are on guard here, immediately giving voice if they detect any intruders.

5. CAVERN

Two **fire giants** are stationed here as a reserve on Snurre's order (acting on instructions from the drow, of course). One rests in the northeast end while the other keeps watch, patrolling between the spots marked G. Each has several rocks nearby for throwing. They have a typical giant's bag apiece, and the room also has piles of hides for bedding, a hamper or two, and some personal gear.

In a crisis situation, this is where King Snurre, Queen Frupy, Obmi, and other important fire giants and guests will retreat to, along with whatever valuables they can salvage.

6. GREAT VAULTED CAVERN

In the middle of this place is a permanent illusion of a huge red dragon dozing atop a mound of treasure (appearing like area 7, below). What is actually in that spot is a **gorgon** that obeys drow and has been instructed to ignore the presence of such creatures as hell hounds and fire giants and trolls. If any other kind of creature speaks to it from a distance in Common or Draconic, it has been instructed to stand quietly but then to breathe upon intruders as soon as they are within range. The illusion disappears once the gorgon attacks.

7. TREASURE TROVE CAVE

This room is actually an extradimensional space, ten times larger than shown on the map. Anyone entering will notice first the enormous pile of treasure that fills the central part of the area and second the **adult red dragon** sleeping upon it.

Brazzemal is the dragon's name. If the boulder across the entrance is moved, requiring the strength of a fire giant, he will certainly awaken. He will not immediately reveal that he is aware of intruders, preferring to wait until they are at the edge of his breath weapon's range before addressing them.

Brazzemal is persuasive and deceitful, and his real desire will be to slay and devour the party and take their treasures to add to his already considerable hoard. Few adventurers ever face a dragon of his size in battle and live to tell about it; make sure that players and characters are well aware that they face a truly terrifying foe. Characters who are suitably flattering and ransom themselves by handing over the bulk of their wealth and magic items may be allowed to withdraw.

If the dragon is cornered and in desperate straits, he will swear to anything in order to save his life, but his information is not to be trusted (although he will word things in such a way as to avoid uttering any magically detectable lie).

Treasure. Brazzemal's hoard is an enormous heap, most of its volume consisting of loose coins. All the best treasures are buried, and a thorough search through the pile will take a very long time. It contains:

- 69,830 cp
- 34,600 sp
- 1,870 ep
- 9,240 gp
- 200 pp in a malachite box that is itself worth 100 gp
- Twenty-three loose gems worth 10 gp each
- Five gems worth 100 gp each in a gold-chased silver egg (the two halves unscrew) that is itself worth 100 gp
- Twelve pieces of assorted jewelry worth 100 gp each
- Five jeweled weapons, human-sized, worth 200 gp each
- Two silver mirrors worth 50 gp each)
- A ten-piece gold service worth 150 gp per piece
- Ten ivory statues with inlays of gems and precious metals worth 200 gp each
- Four jade carvings and figurines worth 500 gp each inside a small chest
- An idol carved of bloodstone worth 200 gp
- Seven *spell scrolls* of wizard spells (DM's choice) in a crystal casket worth 500 gp
- A *dragon slayer* (DM's choice of sword type) in a jeweled scabbard worth 500 gp
- A *brazier of commanding fire elementals*
- Four *potions of resistance* (fire) in a coffer
- Eight jars of rare unguents and perfumes worth 100 gp each
- A suit of *+2 armor*, sized for a human (DM's choice of armor type)

In addition, Brazzemal has six hundred sixty-six gems (worth 1 gp each) pressed into his stomach to protect it. Destructive magical attacks against the dragon will certainly destroy from 60 percent to 90 percent of these gems as well as wreaking havoc with the hoard as a whole.

8. CAVE

This is a drow guardroom, currently housing three **drow elite warriors** and six **drow**. All are clothed in black capes, shod with soft boots of black hide, and wear hoods over their helmets. Two sentries are on duty at all times near the entrance. The room holds only bedrolls and some miscellaneous gear.

Treasure. Each elite warrior carries 40 pp, and each other drow carries 5 pp.

9. WIDE PASSAGE

Twelve **piercers** make their home in a cul de sac, where they patiently await unwary prey. The floor of the place is strewn with shattered skulls and bones.

Treasure. Amid the gleaming white remains lies a gold necklace set with five gems (worth 250 gp in total).

10. SINGING CHAMBER

This small place has excellent acoustics, and the drops of water falling into the pool along the southern portion of the wall make a faint, pleasant musical sound that can be heard for 120 feet in silence (or from 60 feet away in normal conditions). The pool's edge is lined by a huge patch of **gray ooze**, and another lies along a ledge 11 feet high in the southeast of the place.

STINKING CAVERNS (AREAS 11–13)

The large spaces along the southern side of this level are inhabited by troll servants of King Snurre. The stink that comes from these creatures, their nests, and the offal and remnants of rotted meat they leave about is noticeable from as far away as the head of the corridor that leads southwest from near area 9.

These caverns are very dangerous. If the trolls hear suspicious noises, or if any of them are assaulted, they split up to use the multiple passages in these areas to surprise and surround their attackers, leaping out of the darkness to tear them to shreds. An assault from nine trolls is nothing to sneeze at, even for a high-level party.

Treasure. Each troll's nest holds about 1,000 gp worth of mixed coins. The nest of the large troll in area 13 also contains fifteen gems worth 100 gp each and a jeweled mace worth 500 gp.

11. Troll Annex. Three **trolls** lounge herein, each with the typical messy mound of sticks and bones and other noisome things.

12. Troll Central. Two **trolls**. This room, and its inhabitants, are much the same as those in area 11.

13. Troll Heaven. Four **trolls**, including a dominant one that is particularly large (120 hit points), reside here. Conditions are similar to those in areas 11 and 12, except even more noisome.

14. NARROW CAVERN

The corridor leading north from the troll dens is striated with layers of blue and green and greenish-blue deposits and streaks. Patches of green slime (see "Dungeon Hazards" in chapter 5 of the *Dungeon Master's Guide*) grow on the roof of the passage and in the pool of water at its end. The slime on the ceiling covers an area about 40 feet wide just south of the pool. The pool holds thirty-six agates (worth 10 gp each), which sparkle in the presence of any light-source. Any creature that reaches in to get these stones is 50 percent likely to blunder into the slime in the pool, which blends in with the greenish rock.

15. GRAY CAVERN

This dark-walled place is the drow strong point, and a **drow** watches each of the six routes that meet at this cavern. Four more drow are stationed in the chamber itself, for a total of ten.

In addition, the eastern alcove serves as a field headquarters for two **drow elite warriors** (the female is in command) and a **drow mage**. Near this alcove, a narrow passage leads east and then south, ending at a set of rough-hewn stairs that ascend to the second level, emerging near area 8 on map 6.6.

Treasure. The warriors and the mage carry 40 pp apiece, and each drow has 5 pp.

16. SMALL CAVERN

The arrows to the north of the entry passage on the map mark the location of a trap. A character must succeed on a DC 20 Wisdom (Perception) check to spot a tripwire made of fine spidersilk that is stretched across the entrance of the cavern. If an intruder steps on the wire, the act triggers a torrent of small iron spheres, each ¼ inch in diameter, that pour out of hidden containers on the eastern wall. These little spheres coat the floor in the final 40 feet of the passageway and the first 20 feet of the cavern itself.

If they fall, the iron balls make a loud noise, and any creature moving across the affected area must succeed on a DC 10 Dexterity saving throw or fall prone. A creature that moves through the area at half speed doesn't need to make the saving throw.

There are nine female drow in the place. Five are normal **drow**, and three others are **drow elite warriors**. These eight guards protect Nedylene, a **drow priestess of Lolth** who is opposed to anything Eclavdra attempts. She is here to check up on her rival, and she will be suspicious of any creature entering her current abode. On the other hand, she will not be averse to seeing her rival's plans go wrong, so negotiation is a possibility.

Nedylene wields a *+2 whip* and carries a *staff of swarming insects* in addition to her other gear.

17. Jeweled Cavern

If light strikes the walls of this cavern, mineral deposits make the place glitter and sparkle as if it were sown with jewels. This breathtakingly beautiful place is the current lair of two **mind flayers** who have decided to see what is going on with their friendly enemies, the drow. They plan to observe events, and the dark elves ignore them.

Treasure. Each mind flayer carries 250 gp (bribe money), and they have a *tome of clear thought* in a black metal box that can be opened only by a creature that has Intelligence 18 or higher.

18. Small Cavern

The cave at the end of the passage to the northeast is another drow guardroom, with occupants and contents identical to area 8: three **drow elite warriors** and six **drow**, two of which are on duty at all times near the entrance.

Treasure. Each elite warrior carries 40 pp, and each other drow carries 5 pp.

19. Salamander Central

The huge cavern in the northwest corner of this level is lit up in reddish light from the bubbling, steaming river of molten lava that flows through the place. The cavern stinks of sulfur and heated rock, and the temperature here is very hot, although a strong draft cools it somewhat. The roof is no less than 60 feet high.

A rope bridge is suspended about 15 feet above the lava river, offering safe access to the northern chamber (area 20). The ropes have been specially treated to keep them from bursting into flame. A creature that comes within 10 feet of the lava for the first time on a turn, or starts its turn within 10 feet of the lava, takes 11 (2d10) fire damage. A creature that enters or touches the lava for the first time on a turn, or starts its turn in the lava, takes 33 (6d10) fire damage.

Amid this vaporous inferno in the area to the southeast are two **salamanders** enjoying a change of clime.

The flames and smoke render the area lightly obscured. The salamanders are totally indifferent with respect to whom they attack, although they know and respect the drow.

20. Council Chamber and Drow HQ

The secluded section of the cavern to the north serves as the meeting place and council chamber for Eclavdra and her minions. If things have gone badly for the drow and Eclavdra has escaped, she will be here with any surviving followers.

A constant watch is kept on the east entry to the cavern—if intruders come, the dark elves will know of it. If threatened by powerful characters, the drow will cut the rope bridge, then flee to safety back along the passage to the north-northwest (at the location marked A), descending deep into the Underdark.

Currently in this place (at the least) are six **drow** and four **drow elite warriors**, one of which is a female commander who has 110 hit points. The commander has a *+2 shortsword*, a *+1 hand crossbow*, and three magic bolts, as follows:

- A *bolt of holding*, which casts *hold person* on a target hit with the bolt, as well as up to two other targets within 30 feet of that target
- A *bolt of blinding*, which casts *blindness/deafness* to blind on a target hit with the bolt, as well as up to two other targets within 30 feet of that target
- A *bolt of vapors*, which casts *stinking cloud* centered on the point it hits

Each of these effects has a spell save DC of 15 and a duration of 1 minute.

Treasure. In addition to bedding and a small amount of personal gear, a chest holding 200 pp and ten gems worth 100 gp each is hidden behind a rock formation in the far northeastern corner of the place. (Anyone who looks there will find the chest.)

The commander has a small coffer that contains two *potions of speed* and two *potions of superior healing*. These will be used by the drow if necessary (and if she is able to dispense them).

Pursuing the Drow

A pair of hoists—derrick-like machines with straps strong enough to hold cargo of any sort (even giants!)—are tucked into nooks on either side of the river of lava. If any of the dark elves escape and the characters want to follow them, they can use these hoists to transport their possessions over the lava. It will take several hours to set the devices into working position, but thereafter characters will be able to move supplies and pack animals across the river and begin their pursuit of the drow.

If the characters choose not to chase the dark elves, assume that the drow collapse the tunnel behind them, sealing off the Underdark and ending the threat of coordinated giant attacks thereafter. In any case, surviving characters are to be congratulated on the success of their mission.

TOMB OF HORRORS

N THE FAR REACHES OF THE WORLD, UNDER A lost and lonely hill, lies the sinister Tomb of Horrors. This labyrinthine crypt is filled with terrible traps, strange and ferocious monsters, rich and magical treasures, and somewhere within rests the demilich.

The legend of the tomb is an old story with many parts, some of which may be lost or obscured. Characters attempting to glean special information by consulting sages or through *legend lore* spells may still have difficulty obtaining as much background as they desire, for the scraps of information thus gained are often minimal and mystical.

The essentials of the legend can be furnished to the players from the following section.

LEGEND OF THE TOMB

Somewhere under a lost and lonely hill of grim and foreboding aspect lies a labyrinthine crypt. It is filled with terrible traps and not a few strange and ferocious monsters to slay the unwary. It is filled with rich treasures both precious and magical, but in addition to the aforementioned guardians, there is said to be a demilich who still wards his final haunt. Be warned that tales have it that this being, called Acererak, possesses powers that make him nearly undefeatable!

All accounts conclude that it is quite unlikely any explorers will ever find the chamber where the demilich lingers, for the passages and rooms of the tomb are fraught with traps, poison gases, and magical protections. Furthermore, the demilich has so well hidden his lair that even those who avoid the pitfalls will not be likely to locate their true goal. Only large and well-prepared parties of the bravest and strongest should even consider the attempt, and if such a group does locate the tomb, they must be prepared to fail. Any expedition must have magical protections and weapons, and must be equipped with every sort of device possible to ensure survival.

THE TRUTH BEHIND THE LEGEND

Ages ago, a human wizard/cleric of surpassing evil took the steps necessary to preserve his life force beyond the centuries he had already lived, and this creature became the lich known as Acererak. Over the scores of years which followed, the lich dwelled with hordes of ghastly servants in the gloomy stone halls of the very hill where the tomb is.

Eventually even the undead life force of Acererak began to wane, so for the next eight decades, the lich's servants labored to create the Tomb of Horrors. Then Acererak destroyed all his slaves and servitors, magically hid the entrance to his halls, and went to reside in his final haunt, while his soul roamed strange planes unknown

to even the wisest of sages. If the characters gain access to the innermost part of the tomb where the lich's crypt lies, their actions along the way will have caused his soul to be called back to the Material Plane and alerted Acererak, now a demilich, that interlopers have invaded his resting place.

RUNNING THE ADVENTURE

As clever players will gather from the information in the "Legend of the Tomb," this dungeon has more tricks and traps than it has monsters to fight. This is a thinking person's adventure, and if your group is a hack-and-slay gathering, they will be unhappy! Only high-level characters stand a chance of surviving, but every player who braves the tomb will have the experience of a lifetime.

Negotiation of the tomb will require quite a long time, so be prepared to spend several sessions with this material. When the game ends for the day, assume the expedition is spending the intervening time resting and recovering until play again commences. Since there are no monsters to be randomly encountered within the tomb, the party might be able to encamp close to the entrance without fear of being disturbed, but if you do so opt, do not inform the players of this.

As characters enter the various areas, read aloud appropriate sections of text, but never give any additional

---

PLACING THE ADVENTURE

In the original *Tomb of Horrors*, Gary Gygax suggested six possible, far-flung locations for the adventure in the Greyhawk setting—proof in itself that the tomb is liable to turn up just about anywhere. Those possibilities are as follows:

- Inside the highest hill on the Plains of Iuz
- On an island (unmapped) in the Nyr Dyv
- In the Bright Desert
- At the western border of the Duchy of Geoff
- Somewhere in the Vast Swamp south of Sunndi
- On an island beyond the realm of the Sea Barons

Other settings offer choices that are just as varied.

Dragonlance. The tomb on Krynn might be in the foothills near the Eastwall Mountains, in the Cursed Lands of Newsea, or in the Shadowglades of Krynn, where a renegade wizard who served Takhisis was said to dwell.

Eberron. Appropriate sites for the tomb in Eberron include the Ashen Spires of Karrnath, among the tors in the Vile Marsh between Droaam and the Shadow Marches, or among Shargon's Teeth. Eberron's Boneyard could hide the tomb and thus speak to Acererak's enmity for Eberron's dragons.

Forgotten Realms. The tomb could be in the Serpent Hills or the Trielta Hills on Faerûn. It could be in the High Moor or amid the isles that make up the Korinn Archipelago in the Moonshaes. It might be somewhere in the Anauroch desert, perhaps tying Acererak to ancient Netheril.

information that player characters would have no way of knowing, and avoid facial expressions or voice tones that might either give helpful hints or mislead players. The real enjoyment of this adventure is in managing to cope, and those players who do so with even moderate success will appreciate your refereeing properly and allowing them to "live or die" on their own.

The starting information given here simply assumes that the expedition has arrived at the site of the Tomb of Horrors. After relating the salient features of the "Legend of the Tomb," you may fill in whatever other background is needed to get the characters to the site.

ADVENTURE START

The characters have arrived at the site of the demilich's last haunt. Before them is a low, flat topped hill, about 200 yards wide, 300 yards long, and 60 feet high. Only ugly weeds, thorns, and briars grow upon the steep sides and bald top of the mound. There are black rocks upon the top of the hill, and if these are viewed from a height of about 200 feet or so above the mound, it will be seen that the whole is shaped like a human skull, with piles of rock appearing as eyeholes, a nose hole, and the jagged teeth of a grinning death's head.

A thorough inspection and search of the entire area reveals only that the north side of the hill has a crumbling cliff of sand and gravel about 20 feet high in the middle of the whole. (This cliff face is represented by the northern edge of map 7.1.) A low stone ledge overhangs this eroded area, and shrubs and bushes obscure it from observation at a distance.

It takes 10 minutes for characters to search each 10-foot-wide space along the cliff face. This examination must be done from a distance, using a long spear or a 10-foot pole to poke into the sand and gravel, looking for an opening. Any prodding into the cliff face must be suf-

DEMONIC ATTENTION
Characters who become astral or ethereal in the tomb might attract a demon. Roll a d20 whenever this occurs. On a roll of 1 to 16, no demon appears. Otherwise the following demons could appear: 17, a **vrock**; 18, a **hezrou**; 19, a **glabrezu**; or 20, a **nalfeshnee**.

ficiently high off the ground in order to collapse enough material to expose a portion of a tunnel entrance. Once an entrance is exposed, it takes about 1 hour for characters to thoroughly clear the passage that lies beyond, but a crawl space can be opened in 10 minutes.

Probing of the gravel and sand face can begin wherever the characters choose—east side, west side, middle, several locations at once or merely a single one at a time. Leave this strictly to the players to decide. The best manner to handle it is to ask where they will search, once they have determined that they will investigate the area and they have stated how it will be done and with what. Remember that probing low to the ground, or probing with short implements (daggers, swords, and the like) will not reveal anything.

As soon as any entrance is cleared and entered, go to the appropriate location on map 7.1: either area 1, area 2, or area 3.

LOCATIONS IN THE TOMB

The following locations are identified on map 7.1.

1. FALSE ENTRANCE TUNNEL
If the characters clear the passage on the west side of the cliff face, read:

> The corridor before you is made of plain stone, roughly worked, and it is dark and full of cobwebs. The ceiling overhead is obscured by hanging strands of webbing.

Casual observation will not reveal that the ceiling, 20 feet overhead, is composed of badly fitting stones. The cobwebs must be burned away for someone to be able to inspect the tunnel ceiling. Anyone who does so and succeeds on a DC 10 Intelligence (Investigation) check realizes that the ceiling is unstable and in danger of collapse.

Daylight is sufficient to reveal a pair of oaken doors at the end of the passageway. The doors open outward by means of great iron ring pulls. When either door is opened, it is revealed to be a false door, and the trap is triggered.

ABOUT THE ORIGINAL
Tomb of Horrors was born in Gary Gygax's home campaign and introduced to the world at the first Origins game convention in 1975. Since its original publication in 1978, *Tomb of Horrors* has risen to legendary status among D&D players and is generally regarded as one of the greatest adventures of all time.

In the words of its creator, "This is a thinking person's adventure." It was designed not for player characters of a certain level—though high-level adventurers are certainly necessary—but for players who enjoy a mental challenge and DMs who want to put their own spin on this truly unique dungeon.

Tomb of Horrors

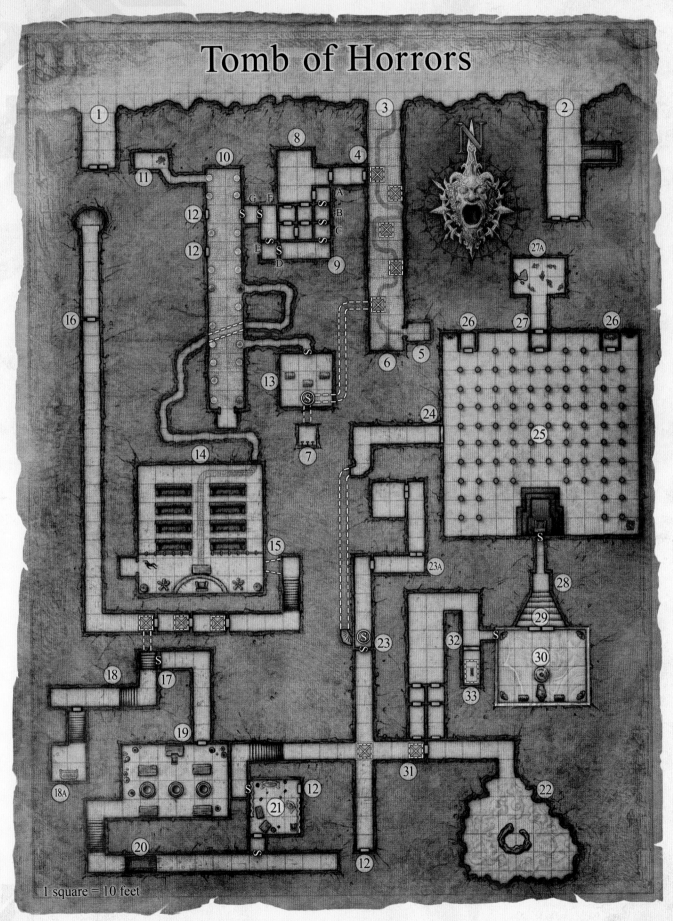

1 square = 10 feet

Map 7.1: Tomb of Horrors

Ceiling Trap. If the ceiling is prodded with any force, or if the doors are opened, the ceiling of the tunnel collapses. Creatures under the collapse must make a DC 15 Dexterity saving throw, taking 27 (5d10) bludgeoning damage on a failed save, or half as much damage on a successful one. The trap mechanism is beyond the doors and inside the ceiling, so it can't be disabled from outside.

2. FALSE ENTRANCE TUNNEL
If the characters clear the passage on the east side of the cliff face, read:

> The corridor before you is made of plain stone, roughly worked and mortared, with a 10-foot-high ceiling.

Daylight will enable adventurers to dimly see what appear to be two separate doors at the end of the corridor.

The paving stones on the floor 50 feet south of the entrance are unmortared and shift slightly when characters tread upon the surface. A character who inspects the floor in this section and succeeds on a DC 15 Wisdom (Perception) check notices the change in the floor. A character can use thieves' tools to keep the stones from shifting by taking 1 minute and succeeding on a DC 20 Dexterity check. On a failed check, the shims are put in place but they fail when someone moves across the stone, and the trap is triggered.

Sliding Block Trap. If the paving stones shift when someone moves across them, a 10-foot-thick block of stone emerges from the midpoint of the eastern wall and begins to slide into the corridor. Have the players roll initiative. On each initiative count, the block slides 6 inches to the west, until at initiative count 1, it completely blocks the corridor. The block's movement can be stopped by using an iron bar or a similarly sturdy normal object, but only if the object is placed on the floor where it can be wedged into the space between the block and the floor. If the block moves far enough to prevent the characters from escaping, they have to devise a means to bypass it. It can't be moved or forced backward.

The doors at the end of the passage are false ones.

3. ENTRANCE TO THE TOMB OF HORRORS
Even a bit of light entering through a crawl space or provided by a torch will reveal that an unusual tunnel lies ahead. If the characters clear the passage near the center of the cliff face, read:

> Bright, brilliant colors are to be seen everywhere, the stones and pigments undimmed by the passage of decades. The floor of the corridor is a colorful mosaic of stone, with a distinct, winding path of red tiles about two feet wide snaking its way south down the corridor. No stonework can be seen on the walls or the ceiling twenty

feet above, for some sort of cement or plaster has been smoothed over all of these surfaces and then illustrated.

The scenes show fields with kine grazing, a copse with several wolves in the background, workers of various races and strange human-animal mixtures—pig-human, ape-human, and dog-human—going about various tasks. Certain of the frescoes show rooms of some building—a library filled with many books and scrolls, the door of a torture chamber, and a wizard's work room. There are chairs, windows, boxes, bales, doors, chests, birds, bats, spiders, and all manner of things shown on the walls.

This corridor contains five covered pits (see the sidebar). On the west wall adjacent to the northernmost pit is where the torture chamber is painted. The wall hiding the passage to the west shows a depiction of an iron door that evidently confines some sort of horrid creature (its taloned and scaled hands grasp the bars of its small window). If the plaster and lath beneath this image is broken away, a normal, inward-opening door will be revealed. If the plaster remains intact, the door can be discovered only by magical means.

Message from Acererak. If the path of red tiles on the floor is carefully observed and studied all the way from the entrance to where the path forks toward areas 5 and 6, the individual with such perseverance will be rewarded by suddenly understanding that a message is contained in barely noticeable runes in the mosaic floor.

The message reads:

Acererak congratulates you on your powers of observation, so make of this whatever you wish, for you will be mine in the end no matter what!

Go back to the tormentor or through the arch, and the second great hall you'll discover.

Shun green if you can, but night's good color is for those of great valor.

If shades of red stand for blood, the wise will not need sacrifice aught but a loop of magical metal—you're well along your march.

Two pits along the way will be found to lead to a fortuitous fall, so check the wall.

These keys and those are most important of all, and beware of trembling hands and what will maul.

If you find the false you find the true, and into the columned hall you'll come, and there the throne that's key and keyed.

The iron men of visage grim do more than meets the viewer's eye.

You've left and left and found my tomb, and now your souls will die.

4. Fresco of the Wizardly Work Room

> The most outstanding feature in this location is actually outstanding! Two jackal-headed human figures are painted so as to appear to be holding a real bronze chest that protrudes from the wall.

Covered Pits

Pit traps throughout the tomb, except where otherwise noted, are constructed as covered pits. Each one is 10 feet deep and concealed by a counterweighted trapdoor that looks like the floor and opens as soon as any person steps on it.

A character who succeeds on a DC 15 Wisdom (Perception) check discerns the edges of a pit's lid. In addition, someone who prods a pit lid can force the lid to open with a successful DC 10 Strength check. The lid can be wedged shut with a piton or a similar object. A character must succeed on a DC 15 Strength check to place the shim properly. On a failed check, the shim fails if someone treads on the lid.

Each pit is spiked at the bottom, so someone who falls in takes falling damage plus 11 (2d10) piercing damage from the spikes. The spikes are also poisoned, so someone injured by them must make a DC 15 Constitution saving throw, taking 22 (4d10) poison damage on a failed save, or half as much damage on a successful one.

Poison Needle Trap. If the chest is examined closely, the viewer will note that it is hinged on the bottom so as to allow the lid to swing down if a catch on the top is pressed. The catch has an easily seen poison needle trap—the needle sticks 3 inches out of the wall—and the needle can be avoided easily by pressing the catch with the pommel of a dagger. Disabling the trap by taking the needle out of the mechanism requires the use of thieves' tools and a successful DC 10 Dexterity check.

The needle deals 1 piercing damage and 11 (2d10) poison damage if it hits someone. Someone who takes this poison damage must succeed on a DC 15 Constitution saving throw or become poisoned for 1 hour.

Deep Covered Pit. If the chest is opened, it appears to be empty, but a character who actually feels inside the chest will find a rod that protrudes vertically from the bottom. This lever moves easily, and if it is pulled with any force it will open a trapdoor in this square that covers a 30-foot-deep covered pit (see the sidebar). Someone who falls in takes damage from a 30-foot fall as well as from the spikes and the poison.

The trapdoor over this pit is 3 feet thick and can't be detected by sounding, and it is technically not a trap, so a *find traps* spell doesn't reveal it. A *true seeing* spell reveals a tiny rectangular gap where the door meets the floor. Once the trapdoor falls away, the pit remains open thereafter.

5. The Arch of Mist

One section of the path shown on the floor leads directly into a stone archway. If any character stands within 2 feet of the entranceway upon the path, read:

> The stone archway before you is filled with a veil of thick vapors. The stones on either side of the base and the keystone protrude slightly from the stones around them. As you move to within touching distance, the left-hand base stone begins to glow yellow, the right-hand base stone orange, and the keystone seven feet above blue.

Nothing will cause the vapors to clear, nor will any sort of magic allow sight into the area, until the glowing stones are pressed in the proper sequence: yellow, blue, orange. If this is done, the vapors disappear, and the path appears to go eastward.

If the archway is entered when it is clouded, those characters doing so will be instantly teleported to area 7. If it is passed through after pressing the glowing stones in proper sequence, those who step through while following the path will be teleported to area 11, and those who pass through off the path will be sent back to area 3.

6. THE FACE OF THE GREAT GREEN DEVIL

The path of red tiles leads south from the fork. If any character comes within 2 feet of the southern wall, read:

> On the wall before you is a relief sculpture of a devil face formed of mosaic tiles. The face has a huge O of a mouth, inside of which the space is dead black.

Aura. The devil face radiates an aura of transmutation magic if *detect magic* is used on it, and a casting of *detect evil and good* or a paladin's use of Divine Sense reveals it as a desecrated place.

Mouth Trap. The mouth opening is similar to a *sphere of annihilation*, but it is about 3 feet in diameter—plenty of room for those who wish to leap in and be completely and forever destroyed. A character who examines the mouth and succeeds on a DC 20 Intelligence (Arcana) check identifies the trap for what it is.

7. THE FORSAKEN PRISON

> This miserable cubicle appears to have absolutely no means of egress. Three iron levers, each about one foot long, protrude from the south wall of the chamber.

Even a magical means of detection will not indicate any way out of this place.

Levers. The iron levers can be moved horizontally or vertically, singly or in combination. Only the act of moving all three together upward or downward has any results. Moving them up opens a small trapdoor in the center of the ceiling 10 feet above. Pushing them simultaneously down opens the entire floor to a 100-foot-deep pit with no exit. The floor returns to a closed position in 10 minutes, sealing any victim inside the pit until another creature triggers the floor trap again.

Crawl Space. The ceiling route is a crawl space some 3 feet square. At the place it turns east there is a plug in the ceiling, which can be detected only with magic or if a character has sense enough to check for secret doors. A character who succeeds on a DC 20 Wisdom (Perception) check can find the door. Also, anyone who raps or sounds on the ceiling in the door's area hears it is hollow, indicating a space beyond. Eventually the small tunnel leads to a magical one-way door, which opens in the pit side as shown, and players are back to square one.

8. GARGOYLE LAIR

When any door leading to the lair is opened, it frees the room's occupant from temporal stasis.

> What appeared to be a statue an instant ago comes to life before your eyes. The creature flaps its wings and stares at you.

Creature. A mutated, four-armed **gargoyle** attacks anyone who enters its lair. This creature uses Multiattack to make three attacks: one with its bite and two with its claws.

Treasure. Around the creature's neck is a collar studded with ten gleaming gems (blue quartz stones of 100 gp value each).

Hidden in a secret compartment of the collar is a slip of parchment with the following written on it in magical code (requiring *comprehend languages* to understand): "Look low and high for gold, to hear a tale untold. Take the archway at the end, and on your way you'll wend." Beneath the runes, the initial "A" is inscribed.

9. COMPLEX OF SECRET DOORS

If someone opens the door on the east wall of area 8, read:

> The small room beyond the door is empty and appears to have no other exits.

The south wall contains the first in a series of secret doors. Each of these portals requires a successful DC 20 Wisdom (Perception) check to find and must be opened by hand using a particular method, as follows:

A. Pull down and inward (hinged on bottom)
B. Pivot on central hinge
C. Pull inward and up at bottom (hinged on top)
D. Slide up
E. Pull double panels inward (hinged on sides)
F. Slide left
G. Door has seven studs in a row—press all at once and door opens, but press 1 and 7 and the door falls inward. A character pressing the studs or near enough to do so must succeed on a DC 15 Dexterity saving throw or take 10 (3d6) bludgeoning damage from the falling door.

Bolts from Above. Each round that characters are in any of the rooms inside the complex of secret doors, a number of bolts will be fired into the area from hidden devices in the walls and ceilings, and there is a 50 percent chance that one character, randomly determined, in each such area must succeed on a DC 20 Dexterity saving throw or take 5 (1d10) piercing damage. There is no way to prevent the bolts from being triggered.

10. GREAT HALL OF SPHERES

This area is similar to area 3, for the floor is of inlaid tiles and the walls and ceiling are painted with figures of animals, strange signs and glyphs (which mean absolutely nothing), and humans and human-like creatures posing with spheres of different colors. These globes are two-dimensional, of course, and their significance and pattern are described below. From north to south, with the west wall being the left-hand column, and the east the right-hand, the spheres are colored and positioned as follows:

West Wall	East Wall
Gold, held high overhead[1]	Pale blue, held at shoulder
Orange, held waist high	Silver, at feet
(False door)	(Secret one-way door[2])
Purple, at feet	Green, held high overhead
(False door)	Yellow, held at shoulder
Bronze, held waist high	Pink held high overhead
Gray, held at shoulder	Black, at feet[3]
(None)	Pale violet, held at shoulder
Bright blue, at feet	(None)
White, held high overhead	Red, held waist high[4]
Turquoise, held at shoulder	Buff, at feet
Scarlet, held waist high	(None)
Pale green, at feet	Indigo, held high overhead

[1]An illusion covering a crawlway to area 11

[2]This door can be opened by a *knock* spell or destroyed with *disintegrate*

[3]An illusion covering a crawlway to area 14

[4]An illusion covering a crawlway to area 13

The false doors and secret doors can be found with successful DC 20 Wisdom (Perception) checks. If anyone makes physical contact with an illusion in this area, its nature becomes apparent. Also, a character who examines an illusory image without touching it can make a DC 20 Intelligence (Investigation) check. On a successful check, the illusion becomes faint to the character, who can then easily see the crawlway beyond the illusion.

Magic Archway. On the south wall is a stone archway similar in appearance to area 5, also filled with cloudy vapors that block vision or detection of what lies beyond. When a character moves to within 3 feet of the arch, read:

> As you come close, three stones in the archway in front of you begin to glow. The left-hand base stone shines with an olive hue; the one on the right glows citron, and the keystone seven feet overhead gives off russet light.

No matter how the stones are manipulated, the archway remains clouded and veiled with a haze which nothing can enable the onlookers to see through. All living matter which goes through the arch will be teleported to area 3, while nonliving matter is teleported simultaneously to area 33—meaning that characters stepping through will appear at the start totally nude, while everything else with them will go to the crypt of the demilich. (Cruel, but most entertaining for the DM.)

11. The Three-Armed Statue

> This small room holds what appears to be a statue of a gargoyle, eight feet tall, with four arms. One of the arms is broken off and lies on the floor in front of the statue.

No amount of fooling around with the broken arm will enable it to be replaced, and the statue will do nothing at all meanwhile.

Ten Gems for One. A close look at the open and outstretched hands of the statue will determine that a large gem (a 100 gp blue quartz fits perfectly) will fit in a carved depression in each of the three remaining hands, while the broken one has no such concavity. If three large gems of any sort are placed within the hands, the stony digits will close and crush them to powder, dump the remains on the floor, and return to their normal positions.

If this process is repeated until ten gems (or more) are crushed, a *magic mouth* spell is triggered and speaks the following words: "Your sacrifice was not in vain. Look to the fourth to find your gain."

As these words are uttered, an invisible *gem of seeing* will come into being in the palm of the broken-off arm. The gem must be found, and the character so doing will need to wipe it free of a magical substance before it can be seen or used. Note that if the arm is carelessly moved, the gem will fall out and roll away. *See invisibility* or any other sort of searching except by careful feeling will be useless. Describe the gem, once it is wiped clean and visible, as an oval diamond, with two flat and polished sides, very clear, and about 1 inch in diameter by a quarter-inch thick. It will operate only twelve times, then shatter.

12. TRAPPED FALSE DOORS

In four locations in the tomb, there are false doors which screen a spear trap. When one of these doors is opened, a spear will shoot out, and the door opener or someone standing nearby is subject to be struck. Determine at random, if need be, which character is the target. The trap has a range of 60 feet, has a +11 bonus to hit, and deals 9 (2d8) piercing damage. If the door is closed and reopened, another spear will fire. The mechanism can be jammed by a character who uses thieves' tools and succeeds on a DC 20 Dexterity check.

13. CHAMBER OF THREE CHESTS

When the party enters the illusory crawlway hidden by the red sphere, they will come to an apparent dead end, but a successful DC 10 Wisdom (Perception) check reveals the presence of a secret door.

The character who opens the door will fall to the floor 10 feet below due to a tilting stone at the mouth of the crawlway, taking falling damage (a mere annoyance, but it erodes the strength of the party).

Three large chests are affixed firmly to the floor; the western one is gold (plate covering iron), the center one is silver (plate over iron), and the eastern one is of oak bound with thick bronze bands. Each is about 4 feet long, 2 feet wide, and 3 feet high.

Gold. Opening the gold chest releases a **swarm of poisonous snakes** that slither out and attack next round. They continue biting until all are killed.

Silver. Inside the silver chest is a clear crystal box (worth 1,000 gp) that holds a *ring of protection*. Someone who succeeds on a DC 15 Wisdom (Perception) check while examining the box and the chest notices the box is set into the chest bottom. When this box is lifted from the supposed bottom of the chest, eight darts will fire upward, and the one or two characters leaning over the chest so as to be in the line of fire will take 1d4 attacks each if they are exposed to the path of these missiles. The darts have a range of 60 feet, a +11 bonus to hit, and deal 3 (1d6) damage on a hit. The trap mechanism is under the crystal box and can't be disabled without first removing the box.

Oak. When the lid of the oak chest is opened, an animated **giant skeleton** (see appendix B) will be instantly teleported into the room, and it strikes with surprise.

14. CHAPEL OF EVIL

After passing through the illusory black sphere the party will have crawled along the small tunnel until reaching the end, only to find it is solid stone. It requires a successful DC 20 Wisdom (Perception) check to find the secret door at the end of the passage—no form of magic will detect it, save for a *gem of seeing*. If the characters open the door and enter the room, read:

> You see what is obviously some form of temple area. There are scenes of normal life painted on the walls, but the people have rotting flesh, skeletal hands, worms eating them, and so forth. Yet there are also depicted various religious symbols of good alignment. There is a mosaic path leading between four rows of wooden pews that face the worship area. In front of the pews, a wooden railing divides the room. South of it is an altar in front of a tiered dais, on which sits a wooden chair.

If the characters move farther into the room so they can see the features in the south end, continue:

> The chair is nicely carved and padded but seems unremarkable. On either side of the dais are large, free-standing large brass candelabras each holding five white candles. In each corner on the southern wall is a large white pottery urn stoppered with a brass and wood plug. Sprawled on the floor near the west wall is human skeleton in black chain mail that is badly rusted and damaged. The skeleton's outstretched arm points to a stone archway set in the wall. The opening is filled with opaque, bright orange vapors.

Aura. A casting of *detect evil and good* or a paladin's use of Divine Sense identifies the chapel as a consecrated place. (What a puzzle! Could the demilich actually have been of good alignment?)

Pews. Simple examination indicates that all of the benches have hinged seats. If a character examines either of the pews in the front row before opening the lid, a successful DC 15 Wisdom (Perception) check reveals that the hinges on this pew are larger than the ones on the pews in the other rows.

Gas Trap. The hinges on the front pews are larger and stronger because they include rods that are connected to valves inside the pew. If the seat on either of the front pews is lifted up, a cloud of poison gas fills the whole room in 2 rounds. A character caught in the gas must succeed on a DC 15 Constitution saving throw or become poisoned for 48 hours.

If the hinges are noticed and then disassembled, requiring 1 minute and a successful DC 15 Dexterity check using thieves' tools for each hinge, the trap can't trigger. A failed check results in no progress at the task, but if the check fails by 5 or more, the trap goes off explosively, blowing the lid open.

Treasure. The back pair of pews have 4,000 sp each hidden therein, the next pair have 3,000 ep each, and the pair closest to the trapped pews have 2,000 gp each.

Altar. The centerpiece of the chapel is a block of strange material that glows with an inner light of opalescent blue. (If the altar is specifically targeted by a *detect evil and good* spell, it registers very faintly as a desecrated object.) If the altar is touched by living matter, a *lightning bolt* spell (save DC 15) will streak down the center aisle. After this bolt comes forth, the altar turns a fiery blue-red, and if it thereafter is touched by any object it will explode as a *fireball* spell (save DC 15).

Archway. Just as in other locations around the tomb, the mists that obscure the archway can't be penetrated with any sort of vision or magic. (If a character moves close to the archway and asks about it, explain that none of the stones of the arch glow.) The skeleton, of course, misleads the party, for any character passing through the portal will enter a 10-foot-by-10-foot room where their sex and alignment are reversed by a powerful magic. Exiting the room and reentering the archway will restore original alignment, but also deals 3 (1d6) psychic damage. Going back a third time will reverse sex again, but the individual will be teleported in the manner of the archway in area 10. Only a *wish* spell will restore both alignment and sex. If alignment is restored by entering the orange portal, a *remove curse* or *greater restoration* spell will then restore original sex.

Wall Slot. A character who inspects the eastern wall directly opposite the archway and succeeds on a DC 10 Wisdom (Perception) check finds a small slot with the letter O faintly traced above it. This is the location of a moving stone block described below. The block can't be magically detected, nor will it open by physical or magical means other than the method given in area 15.

15. STONE GATE

As shown on the map, the stone that forms part of the eastern wall of the chapel is 2 feet wide, 4 feet high, and 10 feet thick in a wedge shape. It is impregnated with strong antimagic that prevents its detection or removal or its change to another form or substance. The wall slot (see above) is of sufficient size to accept a coin or a disc-shaped gem. It is also just right for the insertion of a magic ring of any sort. Only such an item will trigger the mechanism, which causes the block to sink slowly into the floor so as to allow entry into the passage beyond. The object deposited into the slot is forever lost, as the sinking stone crushes all to pieces. The gate opens easily from the other (east) side, and no special item is required to trigger its opening from that side.

Doors and Pits. Beyond the gate stone, the corridor widens to 10 feet and turns southward where steps lead down steeply to a corridor that goes west. Each of the three doors in the corridor opens easily if any pushing force is applied to it, and a creature that does so stumbles into the pit on the other side unless it succeeds on a DC 15 Dexterity saving throw. If a door isn't violently pushed against, it can be opened safely by pulling it inward, and the party will have standard chances of falling in when the characters leading the way step on the pit cover.

By the time the westernmost door and pit have been reached, the characters will certainly expect the pit, and will be likely to bypass and ignore it. This carelessness would prevent them from examining the pit from within. On the south wall of the pit is a wooden door painted to look like stone, which is easily discovered by anyone who looks at this wall while inside the pit or who makes a tactile investigation of the wall from outside the pit.

Crawl Space. Beyond the painted door is a narrow passage that emerges at the top of a short flight of stairs leading down.

16. LOCKED OAKEN DOOR

> The thick wooden door ahead of you is heavily bound with iron bands, and there are several locks keeping it shut.

Aura. The door is found to radiate an aura of abjuration magic if a *detect magic* spell is cast upon it.

Sounds from Beyond. A character who listens with an ear to the door will hear far-off music and happy singing, obviously coming from the other side of the door.

No amount of forcing or spells will open the door. The only way to continue northward is to use a *disintegrate* spell on the door or physically destroy it (it has 100 hit points).

If the characters destroy the door, read:

> As the door falls away, you can hear sounds of confusion and distress coming from the north. A faint glow, like that of a small flame, shines in the distance. The walls of the passage ahead of you are of smooth white alabaster, and the floor is highly polished, smoke-gray marble.

The destruction of the door triggered a *minor illusion* spell that produced the noises of distress, which are designed to lure the characters onward.

The tunnel floor is a counterweighted beam. Its overbalancing point is the third square north of the door. When one or more characters move there, the floor beyond the door will begin to tilt downward, with the north end slowly sinking. If this occurs, quickly state how the floor is beginning to slant, and have the characters roll initiative. On initiative count 10, all characters north of the door fall prone and slide 10 feet to the north.

A character can attempt to scramble back up the ramp to the south by making a successful DC 10 Strength (Athletics) check, or two successful checks if using the Dash action. Those who succeed still slide 10 feet north on initiative count 10 in each round, but they can also climb upward according to the normal rules for doing so. A character whose check fails by 5 or more slides an extra 5 feet to the north. Those who slide to the fourth square north of the door take 3 (1d6) fire damage, then 11 (2d10) fire damage in the fifth square. Characters who slide farther than that are plunged into a pit of molten lava which will absolutely snuff them out.

17. MAGICAL SECRET DOOR

This entrance to the remainder of the tomb is on the wall adjoining the stairway that leads down. It can be found by mundane means, requiring a successful DC 20 Wisdom (Perception) check, but nothing will enable it to be opened until either the area is viewed through a *gem of seeing*, a *true seeing* spell is cast, or a *detect magic* spell is used to determine the door's magic aura (abjuration).

After the magic of the door is identified, a *dispel magic* or *remove curse* spell is needed to remove the guard that prevents the door from being opened. Once this is accomplished, the secret door can be opened easily from either side.

18. CORRIDOR PROTECTED BY FEAR GAS

If the characters travel south from the secret door, they reach a landing at the top of a stairway.

> Stairs descend to the west. The corridor that extends past the bottom of the steps is slightly cloudy.

The corridor is filled with fear gas. Unless characters announce they are holding their breath before entering its 40-foot length, they will breathe in the gas. A creature exposed to the gas must succeed on a DC 15 Constitution saving throw or become frightened for 1 minute.

A creature frightened in this way must take the Dash action on each of its turns to retrace its steps, moving away from this area of the tomb by the safest route possible. The creature can repeat the saving throw at the end of each of its turns, ending the effect on itself on a successful save. Once the effect ends, the creature is immune to the gas for 1 hour.

Beyond the first 10 feet, the gas becomes thicker, and it irritates the eyes. The area is lightly obscured, so it requires a successful DC 10 Wisdom (Perception) check to notice the south door that leads into area 18A. Once that door is opened, the gas dissipates.

18A. FALSE CRYPT

> Beyond the door, a stairway leads down. The way is blocked by thick webbing that fills the area from steps to ceiling.

The steps down to the chamber at the end are filled with *webs* (as the spell) which can only be removed by magical fire (a *burning hands* spell, a *flame tongue* sword, or the like). Any character trying to break through them will become hopelessly entangled and can't get loose unless the webs are burned away or the character is freed by a *wish* spell.

If the characters clear away the webs and descend to the foot of the stairway, read:

> Lying on the floor at the bottom of the stairs is an iron mace inlaid with silver. South of this location is a modest-sized room. What you can see of it is filled with rotting and decayed furnishings.

The mace will begin to glow with a bright golden light when it is picked up by any character. (Whenever this weapon is swung at the occupant of this chamber, it will hit.)

Characters who enter the room will see a solid gold couch along the back wall. A skeletal figure that resembles a lich, wearing a crown on its head, slowly rises from the couch (and throws up its hands in apparent fear if the mace is being carried). A booming voice seeming to emanate from the whole of the chamber will demand: "Who dares to disturb the rest of Acererak? It is your death which you have found!"

Creature. The false crypt is the home of a false lich that is actually a magically prepared **greater zombie** (see appendix B). Between strikes the creature will gesture with its hands as if readying a spell. If it is struck by the golden mace it will make a roaring bellow (produced by a *magic mouth* spell), and the weapon will obviously stagger it (roll dice and shake your head ruefully) every time the mace is used. The third time it is struck by the glowing mace, the false lich will instantly wither and disappear in a puff of dust, and the mace will shatter.

If the characters investigate the room's contents, they can see a jade coffer, the dead monster's fallen crown, and a fine leather bag (its condition is a give-away—it isn't rotten) all within easy reach. The furnishings and decorations are of no value.

Collapse. At the moment when the false lich disappears, the room will start to shake and stones will begin to come down from the ceiling. Obviously the place is beginning to collapse, but take your time detailing the increasing rumblings, tremors, grinding noises, falling hunks of ceiling, and so forth to the players.

Now begin counting slowly to 10, and it is odds on that there will be a stampede up the stairs to get away! A *programmed illusion* spell affecting the entire false crypt will produce the full effects of a cave-in, complete with tactile components. Actual dust will billow up the stairs, while bits of stone begin to fall in the east–west tunnel and then in the north–south tunnel and the stairs reached from the pit. If the party runs out, ask them if they thought it was too hard a dungeon.

Treasure. The jade coffer is worth 5,000 gp and contains six *potions of healing*. The crown is set with gems and worth 25,000 gp. (The gold that makes up the couch is worth 50,000 gp, but it can't be moved or damaged.) The small sack holds 278 pp, twenty-nine gems worth 10 gp each, seven *spell scrolls* (all of 1st- and 2nd-level wizard spells), and a map showing a location several hundred miles away that supposedly has a rich treasure (it is a fake, naturally).

False Ending. If this outcome doesn't make the players suspicious enough to take another run through to check things out, put the adventure away for use when you have a different group (or the same ones) inquiring about one of the references in the "Legend of the Tomb." Note that something so simple as a *commune* spell will reveal that the demilich has not been destroyed.

19. LABORATORY AND MUMMY PREPARATION ROOM

Although there is only one item of eventual use within this totally plain and cluttered place, the volume of items within it is calculated to waste time for the players. Describe the features of the room as the characters investigate.

All of the walls are lined with shelves, and upon these are old jars filled with dust and impotent ingredients of all sorts. There is a large desk and stool, two workbenches, and two mummy preparation tables. Clay pots and urns on these tables and the floor obviously once contained unguents, ointments, oils, perfumes, and the like. Linen wrappings are in rolls or strewn about. Dried herbs of unidentifiable nature, bones, skulls and the like litter the workbenches.

Vats. In the south part of the room are three vats of about 7 feet in diameter and 4 feet in depth that contain murky liquids. The vats are affixed to the floor and too heavy to move. The western one holds only dirty water.

The middle vat contains a slow-acting acid which will deal 3 (1d6) acid damage on the round after a creature's flesh comes into substantial contact with it (by immersing an arm, being splashed on, and so forth)—minor contact (dipping a finger) will cause only a mild itch. At the bottom of this vat is one-half of a golden key.

The eastern vat contains a grayish substance that is actually an **ochre jelly** that sits atop the other half of the golden key.

Treasure. The key parts are magical and will not be harmed by anything. If the parts are joined together they form one solid key, hereafter called the *First Key*. Because the acid will harm even magic weapons, the players will have to figure some way to neutralize or drain off the contents of the second vat to acquire the key, as a

reach-in-and-grope-for-it technique has only a 1 percent cumulative chance per round of being successful.

20. HUGE PIT FILLED WITH SPIKES

If the characters proceed through the laboratory, they come upon a descending staircase that ends at a corridor heading east. Assuming they can see what lies ahead of them, read:

> A ten-foot-deep, empty pit completely fills the passageway and extends so far as to make jumping across it impossible for most creatures.

Spike Trap. The characters might deduce that the pit can be crossed by climbing down and walking across the bottom, then climbing up the other side. Simple! Wrong—any footstep upon the last 5 feet (east portion) of the pit presses a pressure plate, causing a volley of spikes to discharge upward. If the plate is triggered, each person in the pit or leaning over its edge is likely to be struck by the spikes, which have a +11 bonus to hit and deal 11 (2d10) piercing damage. New spikes will come up out of the floor every time if the plate is pressed more than once.

A character who succeeds on a DC 20 Wisdom (Perception) check discovers the pressure plate. It can then be wedged shut by a character who is adjacent to the plate and succeeds on a DC 20 Dexterity check while using thieves' tools. On a failed check, it's apparent that the block didn't work—unless the check fails by 5 or more, in which case the job seems solid but fails when someone walks on the plate.

21. The Agitated Chamber

The secret door to this place can be found with a successful DC 15 Wisdom (Perception) check.

> The room appears to be filled with funerary offerings and furniture. There are four rotting sofas, a couple of throne-like chairs, and a jumble of stands, small tables, and vases and urns that are dented, chipped, and broken. Only the rather plain tapestries hanging on the east and west walls appear to have been spared a rough looting. Amid the general havoc are scattered several trunks and a larger number of coffers.

Heaving Floor. The weight of the characters upon the balanced floor of this room sets a mechanism into motion. Each round they remain in the place, on initiative count 0, roll a die. An odd-numbered result means that the floor of the room will jump and buck up and down violently. When the floor does so, each creature in the room must succeed on a DC 10 Dexterity saving throw or fall prone and take 1 bludgeoning damage from abrasions and contusions.

Tapestries. The wall hangings, which depict weed-grown rocks and green and golden tan scenes of undersea life, are special, antimagic-treated creations made of green slime and brown mold (see "Dungeon Hazards" in chapter 5 of the *Dungeon Master's Guide*).

If either tapestry is torn down, it instantly turns into green slime and covers a 20-foot-long, 10-foot-wide area of floor when it falls. Note that the tapestries can be handled normally without risk, just not yanked so as to tear them (and they are well affixed at the top); if any character is holding one when the room becomes agitated, however, it is 75 percent probable that the jerking motion will tear the thing.

If these hangings are subjected to burning, they instantly turn to brown mold that covers the same area.

The secret door behind the tapestry on the west wall requires the tapestry to be removed, but thereafter can be found as easily as the entry door.

Treasure. The trunks are empty, but the smaller coffers hold various items. Roll a d6 each time one is opened. On a roll of 1–3, the coffer contains 1d3 **poisonous snakes**. On a roll of 4–5, 8d10 pp are found. On a roll of 6, the coffer holds 2d4 gems (worth 10 gp each).

22. The Cavern of Gold and Silver Mists

> A thick silver mist, shot through with delicate streamers of gold, partially blocks your view of the area that lies ahead.

The mists make the entire area heavily obscured. A *detect evil and good* spell cast in the area, or a paladin's use of Divine Sense, indicates that this is a consecrated place.

Any creature that steps into the mist must make a DC 15 Intelligence saving throw. On a failed save, the crea-ture's Intelligence and Charisma scores become 1. The creature can't cast spells, activate magic items, understand language, or communicate in any intelligible way. The creature can, however, identify its friends, follow them, and even protect them. This effect lasts until the character can breathe the clean air above ground under the warm sun.

Creature. At the center of the cavern is a small grotto in which dwells the fey being **Siren** (see appendix B). As a private joke, Acererak placed her in this cavern under an enchantment. She must be asked to come out of the chamber in order to break the spell, and she can give no clues as to the nature of her durance. If the characters come close enough, they can see that two sacks, a large one and a small one, are lying on the floor next to her.

Siren will converse in a friendly fashion, asking how characters are and if they find the going hard in the tomb. Because of the enchantment, she will answer any direct questions with an evasive reply: "I cannot say," "That is unknown to me," "Possibly," and so forth unless she is freed. She knows nothing of the tomb in any event.

If the characters ask her to come with them and are kind, she will do so and stay with them through the rest of the adventure.

Treasure. Both of Siren's sacks contain treasure, but it isn't possible to acquire more than one of hem—and in fact both of the sacks will disappear if she is asked to accompany the party. If a character touches one of the sacks before she is asked to come along, she and the other sack immediately disappear.

The large sack contains 50 pieces each of copper, silver, electrum, gold and platinum. It appears to be a normal sack, but it has a magical aura if it is checked, for it is a *bag of holding*.

To determine the contents of the small sack, roll a d10:

d10	Contents
1–2	Filled with wool
3–4	Five pieces of jewelry
5–6	1d6 *potions of greater healing*
7	1d6 *spell scrolls*, each of a wizard spell of 5th level or lower (DM's choice)
8	4d12 gems (worth 100 gp each)
9	*Bracers of defense*
10	*Ring of feather falling*

It isn't possible to gain both the large and the small sacks by any means. If a character or characters state they will grab them simultaneously, roll dice to see which sack is touched a fraction of a second sooner. The other disappears—along with Siren—forever.

23. False/True Door

When the party opens the door that promises to offer access to the north, it is probable that they will believe it to be nothing more than a false door, but the seemingly blank wall of solid stone behind the false door hides a secret door, which can be found with a successful DC 15 Wisdom (Perception) check.

Secret Trapdoor. On the other side of the secret door is a secret trapdoor in the floor of the corridor, requiring a successful DC 20 Wisdom (Perception) check to find.

The trapdoor opens onto a steep flight of narrow stairs that spiral down to a 5-foot-wide tunnel which emerges at area 24.

23A. KNOCKOUT CORRIDOR

If the characters don't find the tunnel or choose not to follow it, they move through a door that leads east and then come upon a set of double doors in the north wall. When the doors to the north are opened, sleep gas billows forth from the other side. Each creature in the east-west passage must succeed on a DC 15 Constitution saving throw or fall unconscious for 2d4 × 10 minutes.

Rolling Stone. Every 10 minutes after the gas is released, roll a d4. On a roll of 4, a stone juggernaut (rather like a steam roller) comes out of the 20-foot-square room to the north and rolls 1d6 × 10 feet south, then west. Everything it rolls over is squashed to a pulp. There is no appeal.

24. ADAMANTINE DOOR

The tunnel from the south emerges into a corridor that then heads east. The door at the end is a great block of adamantine. It has permanent antimagic effects on it, and there is no magical or physical way of forcing entry.

There are three slots in the door at about waist height. If sword blades are shoved simultaneously into all the slots, the 1-foot-thick door will swing open. Five rounds later, the door slams shut. There is no way of opening it from the east side.

25. PILLARED THRONE ROOM

> You look upon an enormous chamber colored in pastels. A forest of massive, many-hued columns support the ceiling.

Aura. Each of the 3-foot-diameter pillars radiates an aura of transmutation magic when such is detected for.

Upwardly Mobile. Any character who touches a pillar with or without intent will uncontrollably float upward (as if affected by a *levitate* spell), then bounce gently around on the ceiling, 30 feet above, just as a helium balloon. To stop this effect, a *dispel magic* or *remove curse* spell must be placed upon each such individual.

There seems to be a gentle breeze in the room, for any character floating among the many-hued columns will begin drifting toward the northwest or northeast corner of the room. From the entry an observant character with a suitable light source will be able to observe part of the dais on the south wall and the door at area 27.

Northwest Devil Face. About 24 feet above the floor in the northwest corner, on the north wall, is a mosaic relief sculpture of a green devil's face which appears to be exactly the same as that first encountered in the entrance hall to the tomb (area 3). Any creature that comes within 3 feet of its gaping mouth will be sucked in and instantly teleported, to be "spat out" nude at area 6, while all non-living matter in the character's possession goes to area 33.

Northeast Devil Face. The sculpture in the northeast corner is identical in size and placement to the one in

the other corner, but it is tinged with a bluish color over the green. Any character that enters the mouth opening of this devil face is teleported to area 27A.

Charred Remains. Strewn near the southeast corner is a heap of charred bones and skulls, plus the crisped and blackened remains of clothing and gear, arms and armor—a thoroughly awful and frightening sight. A character who comes close enough to examine the remains will find a huge, glowing orange gem at the center of the destruction.

Cursed Gem. The gem can be easily claimed. Casting a *detect evil and good* spell reveals it to be a desecrated object. On a casting of *detect magic*, the gem gives off a strong aura of conjuration—so strong that the detecting character will get the vague feeling that the *wish* spell is involved in the gem's magic.

The gem is actually a cursed magic item. If any character touches it and attempts to cast a *wish* spell using it, a reversed or distorted version of the wish's fulfillment will bring harm to that character and all named in the wish.

Then, immediately after the evil *wish* spell has transpired, the gem begins to pulse with reddish lights, growing progressively stronger, brighter and hotter. Roll initiative. On initiative count 1, the stone explodes, absolutely killing any character within a 15-foot radius in a wave of searing radiation and flames. The gem remains as a noisome mass of stinking purplish mold which bubbles and chuckles. In one week the mass will again re-form as a glowing orange gem.

Ebony Dais and Silver Throne. When the characters come close enough to see the details on the dais, read:

> Contrasting with the pastel colors of the floor and pillars of the hall is the stark blackness of the huge dais on the south wall, atop which sits an obsidian throne inlaid with silver and ivory skulls. Upon the throne rest a crown made of gold and a scepter made of electrum, with a gold knob on one end and a silver cap on the other.

Aura. The crown and both ends of the scepter prove to be magical if such is detected for. In addition, the crown and the gold knob of the scepter radiate an aura of abjuration magic, and the silver end of the scepter has an aura of necromancy magic.

Crown and Scepter. The crown negates the pillars' levitation effect for anyone who dons it and enables the wearer to see within the hall as if in normal daylight—but outside this place the wearer is blind. As soon as a creature puts on the crown, the wearer knows that the crown can be removed only by touching the scepter to it, but doesn't find out the exact procedure.

If the golden knob is touched to the crown, the wearer can remove the headgear. If the silver end of the scepter is touched to the crown, the wearer is instantly snuffed out, turning to a fetid powder that can't be brought back to life no matter what (*wish* spells notwithstanding).

Treasure. Each of these items is obviously valuable (25,000 gp for the crown, 12,500 gp for the scepter), but both are cursed. If they are removed from the tomb, the possessor of either item will be visited by a **vrock** sent to reclaim the item and return it to the throne room—or by two such demons if a single character has both items.

Throne Passage. A character who examines the throne and succeeds on a DC 15 Wisdom (Perception) check discovers a small replica of the crown inlaid in silver on the lower front panel of the seat. If the silver end of the scepter is applied to this inlay, the throne sinks down and reveals a 5-foot-wide passageway that leads south.

26. Small Room with a Door of Electric Blue

The two doors near the northern corners of the throne room look the same. When a character comes within 10 feet of either one, it can be seen that the door actually shimmers with a faint blue light. When the door is touched, this glimmering grows bright. A brass pull beckons to be used, and the door will open easily. Inside the western room there is nothing but dust. The eastern room is another matter.

If the eastern door is opened, the characters will see a low stone table upon which rests a wooden sarcophagus. Various broken and looted urns and coffers are scattered about. Inside the sarcophagus are the parts of a mummy (not an undead, exactly, for at this time it is the mummified remains of a human) with wrappings partially undone and tattered.

Treasure. A huge amethyst, worth 5,000 gp, is barely visible between the wrappings that cover the mummy's head. A character who examines the mummy and succeeds on a DC 20 Wisdom (Perception) check can discover it in one of the eye sockets.

Creature. The gem has an evil magic placed upon it, and if it is removed from the mummy, the remains become a true **mummy lord** that has no spells and no legendary actions (defeating it awards half XP). Magic upon the mummy lord's wrappings makes them nonflammable, and the creature wears a *ring of resistance* (fire).

27. The Portal of Scintillating Violet

The door in the center of the north wall of the throne room appears to lead to another small room. Like the two near the corners, this one gives off a faint glow when viewed from 10 feet away, though this light is of a lilac color.

When this door is touched, the light changes to a bright and coruscating purple with tinges of sickly green. If a character opens the door, read:

> You see a bare chamber, with a small door on the north wall, and pairs of swords crossed behind shields hung upon the walls. There are three such sets on each of the walls to either hand, and two sets on the north wall, one flanking each side of the door.

Creatures. If the threshold of the chamber is crossed by any creature, one set of swords will fly off the wall and attack the individual so doing. The two **flying swords** will both attack, and the shield (statistics as the swords, but no attacks) will interpose itself to take hits meant for the swords. This trio will attack until they are destroyed or the one who violated their area is dead. Surviving weapons and shields return to their former positions after the offender is hacked to pieces.

Worse still, if the threshold is crossed a second time, another pair of blades and a shield will attack, and each set gains a cumulative +1 bonus to attack and damage rolls, as well as 1 hit point more than the previous set.

Only the following spells will affect these items: *telekinesis* sends all three items of a set back to their original position; *heat metal* will cause one item to fall to pieces; *disintegrate* will destroy all items of a set; *magic weapon* will cause a sword to become a plain iron weapon.

27A. Chamber of Hopelessness

Any creature unfortunate enough to be teleported here from area 25 is doomed, for its fate is clearly stated in glowing letters magically written on the north wall of the place. If someone arrives here, read:

> "You who dared to violate my tomb now pay the price. Stay here and die slowly of starvation, or open and enter the door to the south, where certain but quick death awaits.
>
> "Whichever you choose, know that I, Acererak the Eternal, watch and scoff at your puny efforts and enjoy your death throes."

Fountain. A small stream of water spills from a wall outlet into a basin and drains away through side holes, so there is always plenty to drink. (It is impossible to flood the place, for there are hundreds of small drain holes in the walls and floor.)

Treasure. There are numerous skeletons here, rotting equipment, and 30d10 each of sp, ep, gp, and pp hurled about. Searching through the remains will yield 2d10 gems (worth 10 gp each), a *potion of diminution,* and a *+1 flail.*

Swords and Shields. If the door to the south is opened from this side, all the swords and shields in area 27 swoop from the walls to attack, but they cease as soon as the door opener retreats into the chamber to the north.

28. THE WONDROUS FOYER

The narrow passage behind the throne leads to a 10-foot-wide landing and a series of steps which become wider to the south as they ascend. When a character reaches the landing and is able to see the steps, read:

> The walls of the area ahead are untarnished and gleaming copper panels set between rare woods inlaid with ivory. The ceiling is silver, formed so as to reflect and amplify light brought into the place. The chamber widens to the south, where a set of gently sloping steps leads upward. The six steps, from nearest to farthest, are made of onyx, pink marble, lapis, black marble, yellow serpentine, and malachite.

Upon the black marble step is a large, cylindrical key of bronze, hereafter called the *Second Key,* for all to behold. It has an *antipathy/sympathy* spell cast upon it (save DC 17) that repels humanoids (the antipathy effect). At the head of the steps are a pair of huge doors.

29. THE VALVES OF MITHRAL

The doors at the top of the stairs are 14 feet wide and 28 feet tall. They are made of solid mithral, 3 feet thick, and impregnated with great magics in order to make them absolutely spell- and magic-proof.

Keyhole. Where these valves meet, at about waist height, is a cup-like depression, a hemispherical concavity with a central hole. The hole appears to fit the *Second Key,* but if it is inserted, the character so doing will take 5 (1d10) lightning damage. Anyone so foolish as to insert the *First Key* (from area 19) will take double that amount of damage.

True Key. The real key to these great gates is the scepter from area 25. If the gold knob is inserted into the depression, the mithral doors will swing silently open. If the silver end of the scepter is touched to the hemispherical cup the holder of the instrument will be teleported instantly to be spat out of the devil's mouth at area 6, nude, while all non-living materials with the individual go to area 33, and the crown and the scepter reappear on the throne.

Blood Trap. If the door is attacked by force it will not budge, but if it is scratched or nicked it will turn red in that spot, and if it is cut by a sharp weapon it will begin to gush forth blood—the blood of all those who have died within the tomb! The red flow will cascade down the steps and fill the area to the top of the southernmost step in 6 rounds, and each round thereafter it will rise higher and encompass one more step. If unchecked, the flow of blood will fill the foyer to the ceiling in 20 rounds.

Fire of any sort, magical or otherwise, turns the blood to a poison gas, which is fatal, and all characters in the foyer area are dead, with no saving throw, while any in the 5-foot-wide passage to the throne room are slain unless they succeed on a DC 17 Constitution saving throw.

Casting one or more *cure wounds* spells on the door in any combination that expends four spell slots (such as four 1st-level castings, two 2nd-level, or one 4th-level) will stanch the flow of blood, as will a *heal* spell. If other magic is used against the blood, only the following spells will have any effect:

Cone of cold freezes the blood and halts the flow for 3 rounds.

Create or destroy water turns the blood to water.

Disintegrate destroys all the blood.

Levitate coagulates the blood and causes it to rise up as a Huge red **ochre jelly**.

Polymorph changes the blood into seven **wights**, which attack immediately.

Purify food and drink turns all the blood to poison gas. A character caught in the gas must succeed on a DC 15 Constitution saving throw or become poisoned for 48 hours.

Raise dead or *resurrection* destroys all the blood and causes a shade to appear on the top stair. The shade blesses the characters so that they benefit as if they had just finished a long rest.

30. FALSE TREASURE ROOM

> This imposing chamber has a silvered ceiling, just as the foyer has, so it is brightly illuminated by reflected light. The walls are of ivory with gold inlaid. The floor is polished agate. In each corner stands a statue of black iron, easily nine feet tall. That to the northeast stands with a saw-toothed two-handed sword raised to strike; that to the northwest a huge, spike-ended mace; to the southeast the sculpture holds a wickedly spiked morning star, and the one in the southwest has a voulge.
>
> Near the center of the room is a large bronze urn filigreed in gold. A thin stream of smoke issues from a tiny vent in its brass stopper. On the southern wall stands a granite sarcophagus that appears to be damaged. Flanking the sarcophagus are two large iron chests.

The room is lined with lead and has antimagic properties, so no spells will work within the room, and no magical properties of items of any sort will properly function except those that detect an aura of magic or a place of desecration.

Statues. Each statue has a magical aura, but they are merely hunks of metal; they do nothing. Each registers to the casting of *detect evil and good* as a desecrated object, and the visage of each of these iron statues is most fearsome and terrifying.

Moving a statue can be done, but it requires a combined Strength of 48. Moving the statue in the northwest corner reveals a ring pull in the western wall which will raise a small plug of stone and enable the party to enter a small chute which takes them into the corridor that goes west.

Bronze Urn. A character who examines the urn can use an action to pry loose the stopper. If the stopper is removed, an **efreeti** will come forth. If the urn has been battered, knocked about, shaken, overturned, or otherwise roughly handled, the creature will be in a fury and will attack. If not, it will grant three wishes for the party and then depart.

Sarcophagus. Examining the lid of the sarcophagus reveals that glyphs spelling "ACERERAK" are inset on it in platinum. (The metal, worth 100 pp in total, can be pried out.) The end of the thing nearest the wall is stove in and shattered. Inside can be seen bits of a wooden inner shell, a few bones, destroyed jewelry (the stones pried out), torn bits of robes and windings, dust, and a broken *staff of the magi* (evident from the runes upon it). A shattered skull will roll out if the contents are moved around. (Why, the demilich has long been destroyed, but his magical traps somehow survived!)

Iron Chests. Each of these massive boxes is embedded into the stone. Neither can possibly be moved, and both show marks of prying, battering, and similar treatment. Each chest is triple-locked, and each lock contains a poison needle trap (see "Sample Traps" in chapter 5 of the *Dungeon Master's Guide*). If the trap is triggered by a failed check, it deals 1 piercing damage and delivers a dose of purple worm poison (see "Sample Poisons" in chapter 8 of the *Dungeon Master's Guide*).

Treasure. Both chests have treasure, the true nature of which doesn't become apparent until the spoils are moved at least 13 miles away from the tomb.

The eastern chest holds 10,000 gems, which will initially appear to be of not less than 50 gp value each. Each is actually a 1 gp piece of quartz. The other chest contains 10,000 copper pieces magicked to appear as platinum when they are first discovered.

31. One-Way Doors

Characters who traverse the east–west corridor have no chance of discovering the north–south route that adjoins it. The two doors to the north are magical, such that they don't exist except for characters who approach and open them from the north.

Phasing Pit. The covered pit depicted on the map doesn't exist until someone opens either of the one-way doors or opens the door in the corridor while traveling east to west. When one of those events occurs, the covered pit comes into phase where shown. This pit is otherwise exactly the same as others in the place.

32. Secret Door

The portal to the south can't be detected by any magical means, but a successful DC 15 Wisdom (Perception) check enables a character to notice that the wall at this location has a small opening that is metal-lined—obviously a keyhole!

Following this discovery, any attempt to force the door open by physical or magical means will be useless. But if the *First Key* (from area 19) is inserted in the hole and then removed, the door will sink into the floor, revealing itself to be a stone-sheathed adamantine slab of tremendous thickness. There can be no real doubt that the end of the adventure—one way or another—is near.

33. The Crypt of Acererak the Demilich

> Beyond the door is a smallish, rectangular chamber with a ceiling that extends twenty-five feet overhead. There is a small depression a few inches deep and about two feet square in the center of the floor.

A successful DC 15 Wisdom (Perception) check enables a character to discover a small hole in the middle of this depression—another keyhole!

If the *First Key* is inserted herein, the key explodes, and the individual doing so takes 17 (5d6) bludgeoning damage.

The *Second Key* (from area 28) will fit within the hole, and nothing untoward will occur. In fact, nothing whatsoever will happen until it is turned three times to the right in succession. If this is done, read:

> As you finish turning the key, the floor begins to tremble, and then abruptly it starts to rise toward the ceiling.

Roll initiative. On initiative count 10, anyone still on the southern 15 feet of the crypt floor is crushed against the roof and slain. If any characters survive, read:

> The rising of the floor in the southern part of the room reveals a mithral vault. There is a door in the center of the device, with a ring set into it.

A hard pull will open the door.

> A low, dust-covered bench is near the back wall of the vault. On and around it are an abundance of items. Resting on one end of it is a human skull.

Creature. The skull belongs to Acererak, the demilich who lies in wait for the characters. When they joined the halves of the *First Key*, that act called his soul back to the Material Plane, and their use of the *Second Key* to enter the vault alerted him that he must be prepared to do battle in order to survive yet more centuries.

All that now remains of Acererak the lich are the dust of his bones. This bit is enough! If any of the treasure in the crypt is touched, the dust swirls into the air and forms a man-like shape. If this shape is ignored, it will dissipate in 3 rounds, for it can only advance and threaten, not harm. Any physical attack will give it 1 point of energy, however, and a damaging spell cast on it gives it a number of points of energy equal to the level of the spell slot expended (1 point for a cantrip). Each point of energy is equivalent to a hit point, and if 50 hit points are thus gained, the dust will form into a **ghost** controlled by Acererak, and this thing will attack immediately. (The dust will seem to waver and fall back if it is struck by blow or spell, as if suffering actual damage, so formation of the ghost isn't too improbable.)

If any character is so foolish as to touch the skull of the demilich, a terrible thing occurs. Acererak rises into the air upon the touch, and it slowly scans the party prior to attacking. The **demilich** has the Trap the Soul action and access to its lair actions, but not lair traits. It can tell which members of the party are the most powerful, and it uses Trap the Soul on them first.

There are two jewels set into the skull's eye sockets (50,000 gp rubies) and six pointed (marquis cut) diamonds set as teeth in the jaw (each diamond is worth 5,000 gp). If all these gems are filled with souls and the skull is still intact and still being opposed, it will pronounce a curse upon the remaining characters which will teleport them randomly in a 300-mile radius, each

subjected to a *bestow curse* spell (save DC 17) that lasts until dispelled. If the curse is removed, the character must make a DC 17 Wisdom saving throw. On a failed save, the character must permanently decrease one ability score by 2, or two ability scores by 1 each. This secondary effect is instantaneous and can't be dispelled.

Treasure. Characters who survive the demilich's wrath can claim any loot they can carry. Inside the vault are these items:

- All items possessed by characters who were teleported nude
- Ninety-seven small gems worth 10 gp each
- Three huge gems—a 10,000 gp peridot, a 50,000 gp emerald, and a 100,000 gp black opal
- Four magic weapons—a *defender*, a *sword of vengeance*, a *berserker axe*, and a *spear of backbiting* (see appendix A)

In addition, the hoard contains several magic items of your choosing (except that none can be of legendary rarity), including:

- Twelve potions
- Six *spell scrolls*, each of a wizard spell of 5th level or lower
- One magic ring, one magic rod, one magic staff, and three wondrous items

This ends the expedition to the Tomb of Horrors. We hope you and your players have found it exciting, challenging, and rewarding.

APPENDIX A: MAGIC ITEMS

The magic items that are introduced in this book are detailed here in alphabetical order. The adventure in which an item appears is given at the end of its description.

AMULET OF PROTECTION FROM TURNING
Wondrous item, rare (requires attunement)

While you wear this amulet of silver and turquoise, you have advantage on saving throws against effects that turn undead.

If you fail a saving throw against such an effect, you can choose to succeed instead. You can do so three times, and expended uses recharge daily at dawn.

Each time an effect that turns undead is used against you, the amulet glows with silvery blue light for a few seconds. (*The Hidden Shrine of Tamoachan*)

BALANCE OF HARMONY
Wondrous item, uncommon

This scale bears celestial symbols on one pan and fiendish symbols on the other. You can use the scale to cast *detect evil and good* as a ritual. Doing so requires you to place the scale on a solid surface, then sprinkle the pans with holy water or place a transparent gem worth 100 gp in each pan. The scale remains motionless if it detects nothing, tips to one side or the other for good (consecrated) or evil (desecrated), and fluctuates slightly if it detects a creature appropriate to the spell but neither good nor evil. By touching the scales after casting the ritual, you instantly learn any information the spell can normally convey, and then the effect ends. (*The Hidden Shrine of Tamoachan*)

BRACELET OF ROCK MAGIC
Wondrous item, very rare (requires attunement)

While you wear this gold bracelet, it grants you immunity to being petrified, and it allows you to cast *flesh to stone* (save DC 15) as an action. Once the spell has been cast three times, the bracelet can no longer cast it. Thereafter, you can cast *stone shape* as an action. After you have done this thirteen times, the bracelet loses its magic and turns from gold to lead.

Curse. The bracelet's affinity with earth manifests as an unusual curse. Creatures of flesh that are strongly related to earth and stone, such as stone giants and dwarves, have advantage on the saving throw against *flesh to stone* cast from the bracelet. If such a creature's save is successful, the bracelet breaks your attunement to it and casts the spell on you. You make your saving throw with disadvantage, and on a failed save you are petrified instantly. (*The Hidden Shrine of Tamoachan*)

EAGLE WHISTLE
Wondrous item, rare

While you blow an *eagle whistle* continuously, you can fly twice as fast as your walking speed. You can blow the whistle continuously for a number of rounds equal to 5 + five times your Constitution modifier (minimum of 1 round) or until you talk, hold your breath, or start suffocating. A use of the whistle also ends if you land. If you are aloft when you stop blowing the whistle, you fall. The whistle has three uses. It regains expended uses daily at dawn. (*The Hidden Shrine of Tamoachan*)

HELL HOUND CLOAK
Wondrous item, rare (requires attunement)

This dark cloak is made of cured hell hound hide. As an action, you can command the cloak to transform you into a hell hound for up to 1 hour. The transformation otherwise functions as the *polymorph* spell, but you can use a bonus action to revert to your normal form.

Curse. This cloak is cursed with the essence of a hell hound, and becoming attuned to it extends the curse to you. Until the curse is broken with *remove curse* or similar magic, you are unwilling to part with the cloak, keeping it within reach at all times.

The sixth time you use the cloak, and each time thereafter, you must make a DC 15 Charisma saving throw. On a failed save, the transformation lasts until dispelled or until you drop to 0 hit points, and you can't willingly return to normal form. If you ever remain in hell hound form for 6 hours, the transformation becomes permanent and you lose your sense of self. All your statistics are then replaced by those of a hell hound. Thereafter, only *remove curse* or similar magic allows you to regain your identity and return to normal. If you remain in this permanent form for 6 days, only a *wish* spell can reverse the transformation. (*Against the Giants*)

LOADSTONE
Wondrous item, rare

This stone is a large gem worth 150 gp.

Curse. The stone is cursed, but its magical nature is hidden; *detect magic* doesn't detect it. An *identify* spell reveals the stone's true nature. If you use the Dash or Disengage action while the stone is on your person, its curse activates. Until the curse is broken with *remove curse* or similar magic, your speed is reduced by 5 feet, and your maximum load and maximum lift capacities are halved. You also become unwilling to part with the stone. (*Dead in Thay*)

MIRROR OF THE PAST
Wondrous item, rare

The holder of this platinum hand mirror can learn something about the history of a specific object or creature by taking an action to gaze into the mirror and think of the target. Instead of the holder's reflection, the mirror presents scenes from the target's past. Information conveyed is accurate, but it is random and cryptic, and presented in no particular order. Once it is activated, the mirror gives its information for 1 minute or less, then returns to normal. It can't be used again until the next dawn. (*The Hidden Shrine of Tamoachan*)

NIGHT CALLER
Wondrous item, uncommon

This whistle is carved from transparent crystal, and it resembles a tiny dragon curled up like a snail. The name

Night Caller is etched on the whistle in Dwarvish runes. If a character succeeds on a DC 20 Intelligence (Arcana or History) check, the character recalls lore that says the duergar made several such whistles for various groups in an age past.

If you blow the whistle in darkness or under the night sky, it allows you to cast the *animate dead* spell. The target can be affected through up to 10 feet of soft earth or similar material, and if it is, it takes 1 minute to claw its way to the surface to serve you. Once the whistle has animated an undead creature, it can't do so again until 7 days have passed.

Once every 24 hours, you can blow the whistle to reassert control over one or two creatures you animated with it. (*The Sunless Citadel*)

POTION OF MIND CONTROL
Potion, rarity varies

When you drink a *potion of mind control*, you can cast a *dominate* spell (save DC 15) on a specific creature if you do so before the end of your next turn. If you don't, the potion is wasted.

A *potion of mind control* produces the effect of a *dominate beast*, a *dominate person* (humanoid), or a *dominate monster* spell (see the table below). If the target's initial saving throw fails, the effect lasts for 1 hour, with no concentration required on your part. The charmed creature has disadvantage on new saving throws to break the effect during this time. (*Against the Giants*)

Potion of ...	Rarity
Mind control (beast)	Rare
Mind control (humanoid)	Rare
Mind control (monster)	Very rare

ROBE OF SUMMER
Wondrous item, rare (requires attunement)

This elegant garment is made from fine cloth in hues of red, orange, and gold. While you wear the robe, you have resistance to cold damage. In addition, you are comfortable as if the temperature were that of a balmy day, so you suffer no ill effects from the weather's temperature extremes. (*Dead in Thay*)

SHATTERSPIKE
Weapon (longsword), uncommon (requires attunement)

You have a +1 bonus to attack and damage rolls you make with this magic weapon. If it hits an object, the hit is automatically a critical hit, and it can deal bludgeoning or slashing damage to the object (your choice). Further, damage from nonmagical sources can't harm the weapon. (*The Sunless Citadel*)

SPEAR OF BACKBITING
Weapon (spear or javelin), very rare (requires attunement)

You gain a +2 bonus to attack and damage rolls made with this magic weapon. When you throw it, its normal and long ranges both increase by 30 feet, and it deals one extra die of damage on a hit. After you throw it and it hits or misses, it flies back to your hand immediately.

Curse. This weapon is cursed, and becoming attuned to it extends the curse to you. Until the curse is broken with *remove curse* or similar magic, you are unwilling to part with the weapon, keeping it within reach at all times. In addition, you have disadvantage on attack rolls made with weapons other than this one.

Whenever you roll a 1 on an attack roll using this weapon, the weapon bends or flies to hit you in the back. Make a new attack roll with advantage against your own AC. If the result is a hit, you take damage as if you had attacked yourself with the spear. (*Tomb of Horrors*)

STONE OF ILL LUCK
Wondrous item, uncommon (requires attunement)

This polished agate appears to be a *stone of good luck* to anyone who tries to identify it, and it confers that item's property while on your person.

Curse. This item is cursed. While it is on your person, you take a −2 penalty to ability checks and saving throws. Until the curse is discovered, the DM secretly applies this penalty, assuming you are adding the item's bonus. You are unwilling to part with the stone until the curse is broken with *remove curse* or similar magic. (*The Hidden Shrine of Tamoachan*)

WAND OF ENTANGLE
Wand, uncommon (requires attunement by a spellcaster)

This wand has 7 charges. While holding it, you can use an action to expend 1 of its charges to cast the *entangle* spell (save DC 13) from it.

The wand regains 1d6 + 1 expended charges daily at dawn. If you expend the wand's last charge, roll a d20. On a 1, the wand crumbles into ashes and is destroyed. (*The Sunless Citadel*)

WAYTHE
Weapon (greatsword), legendary (requires attunement)

Waythe is a unique greatsword most recently in the possession of a high-ranking cloud giant ambassador.

You gain a +1 bonus to attack and damage rolls made with this magic weapon. When you hit a creature of the giant type with it, the giant takes an extra 2d6 slashing damage, and it must succeed on a DC 15 Strength saving throw or fall prone.

The sword also functions as a *wand of enemy detection*. It regains all of its expended charges at dawn and isn't at risk of crumbling if its last charge is used.

Sentience. *Waythe* is a sentient weapon of neutral good alignment, with an Intelligence of 12, a Wisdom of 2, and a Charisma of 14. It has hearing and darkvision out to a range of 120 feet.

The weapon can speak and understand Giant and Common, and it can communicate telepathically with its wielder.

Personality. This sword believes in freedom and allowing others to live as they see fit. It is protective of its friends, and wants to be friends with a like-minded wielder. (It takes only 1 minute for a good-aligned character to gain attunement with the sword.) *Waythe* is courageous to the point of foolhardiness, however, and vocally urges bold action. It is likely to come into conflict with an evil or a timid wielder. (*Against the Giants*)

APPENDIX B: CREATURES

This appendix details creatures and nonplayer characters that are mentioned in this book and that don't appear in the *Monster Manual*. That book's introduction explains how to interpret a stat block.

Some of these creatures are available in *Volo's Guide to Monsters* but are reproduced here for your convenience.

The creatures are presented in alphabetical order.

ANIMATED TABLE

Some of the defenders of the fortress in *The Forge of Fury* are animated objects that were crafted long ago by the dwarf mage Arundil. They include the animated table.

Constructed Nature. An animated table doesn't require air, food, drink, or sleep.

BARGHEST

Vicious and intelligent canines from the Lower Planes, barghests can be encountered inside the Doomvault. Unlike other creatures of their ilk, the barghests in *Dead in Thay* can be bargained with because they resent their imprisonment, and thus they might become allies (after a fashion) of the player characters.

ANIMATED TABLE

Large construct, unaligned

Armor Class 15 (natural armor)
Hit Points 39 (6d10 + 6)
Speed 40 ft.

STR	DEX	CON	INT	WIS	CHA
18 (+4)	8 (–1)	13 (+1)	1 (–5)	3 (–4)	1 (–5)

Damage Immunities poison, psychic
Condition Immunities blinded, charmed, deafened, exhaustion, frightened, paralyzed, petrified, poisoned
Senses blindsight 60 ft. (blind beyond this radius), passive Perception 6
Languages —
Challenge 2 (450 XP)

Antimagic Susceptibility. The table is incapacitated while in the area of an *antimagic field*. If targeted by *dispel magic*, the table must succeed on a Constitution saving throw against the caster's spell save DC or fall unconscious for 1 minute.

False Appearance. While the table remains motionless, it is indistinguishable from a normal table.

Charge. If the table moves at least 20 feet straight toward a target and then hits it with a ram attack on the same turn, the target takes an extra 9 (2d8) bludgeoning damage. If the target is a creature, it must succeed on a DC 15 Strength saving throw or be knocked prone.

ACTIONS

Ram. Melee Weapon Attack: +6 to hit, reach 5 ft., one target. *Hit:* 13 (2d8 + 4) bludgeoning damage.

BARGHEST

Large fiend (shapechanger), neutral evil

Armor Class 17 (natural armor)
Hit Points 90 (12d10 + 24)
Speed 60 ft. (30 ft. in goblin form)

STR	DEX	CON	INT	WIS	CHA
19 (+4)	15 (+2)	14 (+2)	13 (+1)	12 (+1)	14 (+2)

Skills Deception +4, Intimidation +4, Perception +5, Stealth +4
Damage Resistances cold, fire, lightning; bludgeoning, piercing, and slashing from nonmagical attacks
Damage Immunities acid, poison
Condition Immunities poisoned
Senses blindsight 60 ft., darkvision 60 ft., passive Perception 15
Languages Abyssal, Common, Goblin, Infernal, telepathy 60 ft.
Challenge 4 (1,100 XP)

Shapechanger. The barghest can use its action to polymorph into a Small goblin or back into its true form. Other than its size and speed, its statistics are the same in each form. Any equipment it is wearing or carrying isn't transformed. The barghest reverts to its true form if it dies.

Fire Banishment. When the barghest starts its turn engulfed in flames that are at least 10 feet high or wide, it must succeed on a DC 15 Charisma saving throw or be instantly banished to Gehenna. Instantaneous bursts of flame (such as a red dragon's breath or a *fireball* spell) don't have this effect on the barghest.

Keen Smell. The barghest has advantage on Wisdom (Perception) checks that rely on smell.

Innate Spellcasting. The barghest's innate spellcasting ability is Charisma (spell save DC 12). The barghest can innately cast the following spells, requiring no material components:

At will: *levitate, minor illusion, pass without trace*
1/day each: *charm person, dimension door, suggestion*

ACTIONS

Bite. Melee Weapon Attack (true form only): +6 to hit, reach 5 ft., one target. *Hit:* 13 (2d8 + 4) piercing damage.

Claws. Melee Weapon Attack. +6 to hit, reach 5 ft., one target. *Hit:* 8 (1d8 + 4) slashing damage.

CENTAUR MUMMY

In *The Hidden Shrine of Tamoachan*, characters must contend with a mummified centaur that wants to prevent them from moving any farther into the dungeon. Combining the most lethal features of two creature types, the centaur mummy can attack nearby targets with its melee weapons while trying to use its Dreadful Glare against enemies that hold back.

Undead Nature. A mummy doesn't require air, food, drink, or sleep.

CENTAUR MUMMY
Large undead, lawful evil

Armor Class 13 (natural armor)
Hit Points 85 (10d10 + 30)
Speed 30 ft.

STR	DEX	CON	INT	WIS	CHA
20 (+5)	12 (+1)	16 (+3)	5 (−3)	14 (+2)	12 (+1)

Saving Throws Wis +5
Damage Vulnerabilities fire
Damage Resistances bludgeoning, piercing, and slashing from nonmagical attacks
Damage Immunities necrotic, poison
Condition Immunities charmed, exhaustion, frightened, paralyzed, poisoned
Senses darkvision 60 ft.; passive Perception 12
Languages Common, Sylvan
Challenge 6 (2,300 XP)

Charge. If the centaur mummy moves at least 20 feet straight toward a target and then hits it with a pike attack on the same turn, the target takes an extra 10 (3d6) piercing damage.

ACTIONS

Multiattack. The centaur mummy makes two melee attacks, one with its pike and one with its hooves, or it attacks with its pike and uses Dreadful Glare.

Pike. *Melee Weapon Attack:* +8 to hit, reach 10 ft., one target. *Hit:* 10 (1d10 + 5) piercing damage.

Hooves. *Melee Weapon Attack:* +8 to hit, reach 5 ft., one target. *Hit:* 12 (2d6 + 5) bludgeoning damage plus 10 (3d6) necrotic damage. If the target is a creature, it must succeed on a DC 14 Constitution saving throw or be cursed with mummy rot. The cursed target can't regain hit points, and its hit point maximum decreases by 10 (3d6) for every 24 hours that elapse. If the curse reduces the target's hit point maximum to 0, the target dies, and its body turns to dust. The curse lasts until removed by the *remove curse* spell or similar magic.

Dreadful Glare. The centaur mummy targets one creature it can see within 60 feet of it. If the target can see the mummy, the target must succeed on a DC 12 Wisdom saving throw against this magic or become frightened until the end of the mummy's next turn. If the target fails the saving throw by 5 or more, it is also paralyzed for the same duration. A target that succeeds on the saving throw is immune to the Dreadful Glare of all mummies (but not mummy lords) for the next 24 hours.

CHAMPION

One of the most remote locations inside White Plume Mountain is the hideout of a band of criminals led by the fallen champion Sir Bluto, an alleged mass murderer and a fugitive. Sir Bluto and his companions will do everything in their power to ensure that anyone who happens upon their sanctum doesn't live to tell of it.

CHAMPION
Medium humanoid (any race), any alignment

Armor Class 18 (plate)
Hit Points 143 (22d8 + 44)
Speed 30 ft.

STR	DEX	CON	INT	WIS	CHA
20 (+5)	15 (+2)	14 (+2)	10 (+0)	14 (+2)	12 (+1)

Saving Throws Str +9, Con +6
Skills Athletics +9, Intimidation +5, Perception +6
Senses passive Perception 16
Languages any one language (usually Common)
Challenge 9 (5,000 XP)

Indomitable (2/Day). The champion rerolls a failed saving throw.

Second Wind (Recharges after a Short or Long Rest). As a bonus action, the champion can regain 20 hit points.

ACTIONS

Multiattack. The champion makes three attacks with its greatsword or its shortbow.

Greatsword. *Melee Weapon Attack:* +9 to hit, reach 5 ft., one target. *Hit:* 12 (2d6 + 5) slashing damage, plus 7 (2d6) slashing damage if the champion has more than half of its total hit points remaining.

Shortbow. *Ranged Weapon Attack:* +6 to hit, range 80/320 ft., one target. *Hit:* 5 (1d6 + 2) piercing damage, plus 7 (2d6) piercing damage if the champion has more than half of its total hit points remaining.

Choker

The choker (from *Dead in Thay*) is a malevolent, otherworldly creature that relies on stealth and strangulation to put down its enemies. Two long arms extend from its scrawny body, functioning like tentacles that enable the choker to strike from a distance. The creature's primary tactic is to grab a target around the throat and hold on until its prey is dead.

Conjurer

Conjurers are specialist wizards who summon creatures from other planes and create materials out of thin air. Some conjurers use their magic to bolster armies or destroy enemies on battlefields, while others use summoned creatures to guard their lairs.

Conjurer

Medium humanoid (any race), any alignment

Armor Class 12 (15 with *mage armor*)
Hit Points 40 (9d8)
Speed 30 ft.

STR	DEX	CON	INT	WIS	CHA
9 (−1)	14 (+2)	11 (+0)	17 (+3)	12 (+1)	11 (+0)

Saving Throws Int +6, Wis +4
Skills Arcana +6, History +6
Senses passive Perception 11
Languages any four languages
Challenge 6 (2,300 XP)

Spellcasting. The conjurer is a 9th-level spellcaster. Its spellcasting ability is Intelligence (spell save DC 14, +6 to hit with spell attacks). The conjurer has the following wizard spells prepared:

Cantrips (at will): *acid splash, mage hand, poison spray, prestidigitation*
1st level (4 slots): *mage armor, magic missile, unseen servant**
2nd level (3 slots): *cloud of daggers,* misty step,* web**
3rd level (3 slots): *fireball, stinking cloud**
4th level (3 slots): *Evard's black tentacles,* stoneskin*
5th level (2 slots): *cloudkill,* conjure elemental**
*Conjuration spell of 1st level or higher

Benign Transportation (Recharges after the Conjurer Casts a Conjuration Spell of 1st Level or Higher). As a bonus action, the conjurer teleports up to 30 feet to an unoccupied space that it can see. If it instead chooses a space within range that is occupied by a willing Small or Medium creature, they both teleport, swapping places.

Actions

Dagger. *Melee or Ranged Weapon Attack:* +5 to hit, reach 5 ft. or range 20/60 ft., one target. *Hit:* 4 (1d4 + 2) piercing damage.

Choker

Small aberration, chaotic evil

Armor Class 16 (natural armor)
Hit Points 13 (3d6 + 3)
Speed 30 ft.

STR	DEX	CON	INT	WIS	CHA
16 (+3)	14 (+2)	13 (+1)	4 (−3)	12 (+1)	7 (−2)

Skills Stealth +6
Senses darkvision 60 ft., passive Perception 11
Languages Deep Speech
Challenge 1 (100 XP)

Aberrant Quickness (Recharge after a Short or Long Rest). The choker can take an extra action on its turn.

Spider Climb. The choker can climb difficult surfaces, including upside down on ceilings, without needing to make an ability check.

Actions

Multiattack. The choker makes two tentacle attacks.

Tentacle. *Melee Weapon Attack:* +5 to hit, reach 10 ft., one target. *Hit:* 5 (1d4 + 3) bludgeoning damage plus 3 (1d6) piercing damage. If the target is a Large or smaller creature, it is grappled (escape DC 15). Until this grapple ends, the target is restrained, and the choker can't use this tentacle on another target (the choker has two tentacles). If this attack is a critical hit, the target also can't breathe or speak until the grapple ends.

DEATHLOCK WIGHT

In *Dead in Thay*, two kinds of wights serve the Red Wizards as guards and workers. The deathlock wight resembles a normal wight, except that its undead form courses with dark magic.

Undead Nature. A wight doesn't require air, food, drink, or sleep.

DEATHLOCK WIGHT
Medium undead, neutral evil

Armor Class 12 (15 with *mage armor*)
Hit Points 37 (5d8 + 15)
Speed 30 ft.

STR	DEX	CON	INT	WIS	CHA
11 (+0)	14 (+2)	16 (+3)	12 (+1)	14 (+2)	16 (+3)

Saving Throws Wis +4
Skills Arcana +3, Perception +4
Damage Resistances necrotic; bludgeoning, piercing, and slashing from nonmagical attacks
Damage Immunities poison
Condition Immunities exhaustion, poisoned
Senses darkvision 60 ft., passive Perception 14
Languages the languages it knew in life
Challenge 3 (700 XP)

Innate Spellcasting. The wight's innate spellcasting ability is Charisma (spell save DC 13). It can innately cast the following spells, requiring no verbal or material components:

At will: *detect magic, disguise self, mage armor*
1/day each: *fear, hold person, misty step*

Sunlight Sensitivity. While in sunlight, the wight has disadvantage on attack rolls, as well as on Wisdom (Perception) checks that rely on sight.

ACTIONS

Multiattack. The wight attacks twice with Grave Bolt.

Grave Bolt. *Ranged Spell Attack:* +5 to hit, range 120 ft., one target. *Hit:* 7 (1d8 + 3) necrotic damage.

Life Drain. *Melee Weapon Attack:* +4 to hit, reach 5 ft., one creature. *Hit:* 9 (2d6 + 2) necrotic damage. The target must succeed on a DC 13 Constitution saving throw or its hit point maximum is reduced by an amount equal to the damage taken. This reduction lasts until the target finishes a long rest. The target dies if this effect reduces its hit point maximum to 0.

A humanoid slain by this attack rises 24 hours later as a zombie under the wight's control, unless the humanoid is restored to life or its body is destroyed. The wight can have no more than twelve zombies under its control at one time.

DREAD WARRIOR

The Red Wizards (*Dead in Thay*) make use of several kinds of undead minions, including the special servants known as dread warriors. After being created by a secret ritual, a dread warrior is further enchanted so that a Red Wizard can employ the creature in the fashion of a spellcaster's familiar. By creating a psychic link with a dread warrior, a Red Wizard can experience the world through the creature's senses and direct the warrior.

Undead Nature. A dread warrior doesn't require air, food, drink, or sleep.

DREAD WARRIOR
Medium undead, neutral evil

Armor Class 18 (chain mail, shield)
Hit Points 37 (5d8 + 15)
Speed 30 ft.

STR	DEX	CON	INT	WIS	CHA
15 (+2)	11 (+0)	16 (+3)	10 (+0)	12 (+1)	10 (+0)

Saving Throws Wis +3
Skills Athletics +4, Perception +3
Damage Immunities poison
Condition Immunities exhaustion, poisoned
Senses darkvision 60 ft., passive Perception 13
Languages Common
Challenge 1 (200 XP)

Undead Fortitude. If damage reduces the dread warrior to 0 hit points, it must make a Constitution saving throw with a DC of 5 + the damage taken, unless the damage is radiant or from a critical hit. On a success, the dread warrior drops to 1 hit point instead.

ACTIONS

Multiattack. The dread warrior makes two melee attacks.

Battleaxe. *Melee Weapon Attack:* +4 to hit, reach 5 ft., one target. *Hit:* 6 (1d8 + 2) slashing damage, or 7 (1d10 + 2) slashing damage if wielded with two hands.

Javelin. *Melee or Ranged Weapon Attack:* +4 to hit, reach 5 ft. or range 30/120 ft., one target. *Hit:* 5 (1d6 + 2) piercing damage.

DUERGAR SPY

Medium humanoid (dwarf), lawful evil

Armor Class 15 (studded leather)
Hit Points 33 (6d8 + 6)
Speed 25 ft.

STR	DEX	CON	INT	WIS	CHA
10 (+0)	16 (+3)	12 (+1)	12 (+1)	10 (+0)	13 (+1)

Damage Resistances poison
Skills Deception +5, Insight +2, Investigation +5, Perception +4, Persuasion +3, Sleight of Hand +5, Stealth +7
Senses darkvision 120 ft., passive Perception 14
Languages Dwarvish, Undercommon
Challenge 2 (450 XP)

Cunning Action. On each of its turns, the spy can use a bonus action to take the Dash, Disengage, or Hide action.

Duergar Resilience. The spy has advantage on saving throws against poison, spells, and illusions, as well as to resist being charmed or paralyzed.

Sneak Attack. Once per turn, the spy can deal an extra 7 (2d6) damage when it hits a target with a weapon attack and has advantage on the attack roll, or when the target is within 5 feet of an ally of the spy that isn't incapacitated and the spy doesn't have disadvantage on the attack roll.

Sunlight Sensitivity. While in sunlight, the spy has disadvantage on attack rolls, as well as on Wisdom (Perception) checks that rely on sight.

ACTIONS

Multiattack. The spy makes two shortsword attacks.

Enlarge (Recharges after a Short or Long Rest). For 1 minute, the spy magically increases in size, along with anything it is wearing or carrying. While enlarged, the spy is Large, doubles her damage dice on Strength-based weapon attacks (included in the attacks), and makes Strength checks and Strength saving throws with advantage. If the spy lacks the room to become Large, it attains the maximum size possible in the space available.

Shortsword. *Melee Weapon Attack:* +5 to hit, reach 5 ft., one target. *Hit:* 6 (1d6 + 3) piercing damage, or 10 (2d6 + 3) piercing damage while enlarged.

Hand Crossbow. *Ranged Weapon Attack:* +5 to hit, range 30/120 ft., one target. *Hit:* 6 (1d6 + 3) piercing damage.

Invisibility (Recharges after a Short or Long Rest). The spy magically turns invisible until it attacks, deals damage, casts a spell, or uses its Enlarge, or until its concentration is broken, up to 1 hour (as if concentrating on a spell). Any equipment the spy wears or carries is invisible with it.

DUERGAR SPY

Combining the natural abilities of the duergar race with the specialized training of a spy, the duergar named Ghared is a force to be reckoned with inside Khundrukar (*The Forge of Fury*).

ENCHANTER

Enchanters are specialist wizards who understand how to alter and control minds using magic. They might be personable and interesting, using magic to manipulate people only when banter and conventional persuasion fails, or they might be rude and demanding, using and relying on charmed, obedient minions.

ENCHANTER

Medium humanoid (any race), any alignment

Armor Class 12 (15 with *mage armor*)
Hit Points 40 (9d8)
Speed 30 ft.

STR	DEX	CON	INT	WIS	CHA
9 (−1)	14 (+2)	11 (+0)	17 (+3)	12 (+1)	11 (+0)

Saving Throws Int +6, Wis +4
Skills Arcana +6, History +6
Senses passive Perception 11
Languages any four languages
Challenge 5 (1,800 XP)

Spellcasting. The enchanter is a 9th-level spellcaster. Its spellcasting ability is Intelligence (spell save DC 14, +6 to hit with spell attacks). The enchanter has the following wizard spells prepared:

Cantrips (at will): *friends, mage hand, mending, message*
1st level (4 slots): *charm person,* mage armor, magic missile*
2nd level (3 slots): *hold person,* invisibility, suggestion**
3rd level (3 slots): *fireball, haste, tongues*
4th level (3 slots): *dominate beast,* stoneskin*
5th level (2 slots): *hold monster**
*Enchantment spell of 1st level or higher

ACTIONS

Quarterstaff. *Melee Weapon Attack:* +2 to hit, reach 5 ft., one target. *Hit:* 2 (1d6 − 1) bludgeoning damage, or 3 (1d8 − 1) bludgeoning damage if used with two hands.

REACTIONS

Instinctive Charm (Recharges after the Enchanter Casts an Enchantment Spell of 1st Level or Higher). The enchanter tries to magically divert an attack made against it, provided that the attacker is within 30 feet of it and visible to it. The enchanter must decide to do so before the attack hits or misses.

The attacker must make a DC 14 Wisdom saving throw. On a failed save, the attacker targets the creature closest to it, other than the enchanter or itself. If multiple creatures are closest, the attacker chooses which one to target.

EVOKER

Evokers are specialist wizards who harness magical energy and elemental forces to destroy. Many tend to be hotheaded and aggressive. Others are cold and reserved, unleashing their power at just the right moment to exploit an opponent's weakness.

GIANT CRAYFISH

The giant crayfish appears in *The Hidden Shrine of Tamoachan* and in *White Plume Mountain*.

GIANT ICE TOAD

In a cavern within the glacial rift (*Against the Giants*), a group of ice toads vigorously guard their territory. Waves of cold radiate from the creature, afflicting those that try to approach it, and anyone unfortunate enough to be swallowed suffers injury from cold as well as from the toad's digestive juices.

EVOKER

Medium humanoid (any race), any alignment

Armor Class 12 (15 with *mage armor*)
Hit Points 66 (12d8 + 12)
Speed 30 ft.

STR	DEX	CON	INT	WIS	CHA
9 (−1)	14 (+2)	12 (+1)	17 (+3)	12 (+1)	11 (+0)

Saving Throws Int +7, Wis +5
Skills Arcana +7, History +7
Senses passive Perception 11
Languages any four languages
Challenge 9 (5,000 XP)

Spellcasting. The evoker is a 12th-level spellcaster. Its spellcasting ability is Intelligence (spell save DC 15, +7 to hit with spell attacks). The evoker has the following wizard spells prepared:

Cantrips (at will): *fire bolt,** *light,** *prestidigitation, ray of frost**
1st level (4 slots): *burning hands,** *mage armor, magic missile**
2nd level (3 slots): *mirror image, misty step, shatter**
3rd level (3 slots): *counterspell, fireball,** *lightning bolt**
4th level (3 slots): *ice storm,** *stoneskin*
5th level (2 slots): *Bigby's hand,** *cone of cold**
6th level (1 slot): *chain lightning,** *wall of ice**
*Evocation spell

Sculpt Spells. When the evoker casts an evocation spell that forces other creatures it can see to make a saving throw, it can choose a number of them equal to 1 + the spell's level. These creatures automatically succeed on their saving throws against the spell. If a successful save means a chosen creature would take half damage from the spell, it instead takes no damage from it.

ACTIONS

Quarterstaff. *Melee Weapon Attack:* +3 to hit, reach 5 ft., one target. *Hit:* 2 (1d6 − 1) bludgeoning damage, or 3 (1d8 − 1) bludgeoning damage if used with two hands.

GIANT CRAYFISH

Large beast, unaligned

Armor Class 15 (natural armor)
Hit Points 45 (7d10 + 7)
Speed 30 ft., swim 30 ft.

STR	DEX	CON	INT	WIS	CHA
15 (+2)	13 (+1)	13 (+1)	1 (−5)	9 (−1)	3 (−4)

Skills Stealth +3
Senses blindsight 30 ft., passive Perception 9
Languages —
Challenge 2 (450 XP)

Amphibious. The giant crayfish can breathe air and water.

ACTIONS

Multiattack. The giant crayfish makes two claw attacks.

Claw. *Melee Weapon Attack:* +4 to hit, reach 5 ft., one target. *Hit:* 7 (1d10 + 2) bludgeoning damage, and the target is grappled (escape DC 12). The crayfish has two claws, each of which can grapple only one target.

GIANT ICE TOAD

Large monstrosity, neutral

Armor Class 14 (natural armor)
Hit Points 52 (7d10 + 14)
Speed 30 ft.

STR	DEX	CON	INT	WIS	CHA
16 (+3)	13 (+1)	14 (+2)	8 (−1)	10 (+0)	6 (−2)

Damage Immunities cold
Senses darkvision 60 ft., passive Perception 10
Languages Ice Toad
Challenge 3 (700 XP)

Amphibious. The toad can breathe air and water.

Cold Aura. Any creature that starts its turn within 10 feet of the toad takes 5 (1d10) cold damage.

Standing Leap. The toad's long jump is up to 20 feet and its high jump is up to 10 feet, with or without a running start.

ACTIONS

Bite. *Melee Weapon Attack:* +5 to hit, reach 5 ft., one target. *Hit:* 10 (2d6 + 3) piercing damage, and the target is grappled (escape DC 13). Until this grapple ends, the target is restrained, and the toad can't bite another target.

Swallow. *Melee Weapon Attack:* +5 to hit, reach 5 ft., one Medium or smaller creature the toad is grappling. *Hit:* 10 (2d6 + 3) piercing damage, the target is swallowed, and the grapple ends. The swallowed target is blinded and restrained, it has total cover against attacks and other effects outside the toad, and it takes 10 (3d6) acid damage and 11 (2d10) cold damage at the start of each of the toad's turns. The toad can have only one target swallowed at a time.

If the toad dies, a swallowed creature is no longer restrained by it and can escape from the corpse using 5 feet of movement, exiting prone.

GIANT LIGHTNING EEL

Large beast, unaligned

Armor Class 13
Hit Points 42 (5d10 + 15)
Speed 5 ft., swim 30 ft.

STR	DEX	CON	INT	WIS	CHA
11 (+0)	17 (+3)	16 (+3)	2 (−4)	12 (+1)	3 (−4)

Damage Resistances lightning
Senses blindsight 60 ft., passive Perception 11
Languages —
Challenge 3 (700 XP)

Water Breathing. The eel can breathe only underwater.

ACTIONS

Multiattack. The eel makes two bite attacks.

Bite. *Melee Weapon Attack:* +5 to hit, reach 5 ft., one target. *Hit:* 10 (2d6 + 3) piercing damage plus 4 (1d8) lightning damage.

Lightning Jolt (Recharge 5–6). One creature the eel touches within 5 feet of it outside water, or each creature within 15 feet of it in a body of water, must make a DC 12 Constitution saving throw. On failed save, a target takes 13 (3d8) lightning damage. If the target takes any of this damage, the target is stunned until the end of the eel's next turn. On a successful save, a target takes half as much damage and isn't stunned.

GIANT SKELETON

Huge undead, neutral evil

Armor Class 17 (natural armor)
Hit Points 115 (10d12 + 50)
Speed 30 ft.

STR	DEX	CON	INT	WIS	CHA
21 (+5)	10 (+0)	20 (+5)	4 (−3)	6 (−2)	6 (−2)

Damage Vulnerabilities bludgeoning
Damage Immunities poison
Condition Immunities exhaustion, poisoned
Senses darkvision 60 ft., passive Perception 8
Languages understands Giant but can't speak
Challenge 7 (2,900 XP)

Evasion. If the skeleton is subjected to an effect that allows it to make a saving throw to take only half damage, it instead takes no damage if it succeeds on the saving throw, and only half damage if it fails.

Magic Resistance. The skeleton has advantage on saving throws against spells and other magical effects.

Turn Immunity. The skeleton is immune to effects that turn undead.

ACTIONS

Multiattack. The skeleton makes three scimitar attacks.

Scimitar. *Melee Weapon Attack:* +8 to hit, reach 10 ft., one target. *Hit:* 15 (3d6 + 5) slashing damage.

GIANT LIGHTNING EEL

The giant lightning eel (*Tamoachan*) can electrify the water around it.

GIANT SKELETON

In the Tomb of Horrors, treasure sometimes presents itself for the taking. In one such location, the "reward" for an attempt to grab some valuables turns out to be the animated skeleton of a giant—deadly not only because of its size and strength, but because it has defenses normally possessed only by undead of much greater power.

Undead Nature. A skeleton doesn't require air, food, drink, or sleep.

GIANT SUBTERRANEAN LIZARD

The giant subterranean lizard (*Forge of Fury*) is an enormous reptile with a powerful tail attack.

GIANT SUBTERRANEAN LIZARD

Huge beast, unaligned

Armor Class 14 (natural armor)
Hit Points 66 (7d12 + 21)
Speed 30 ft., swim 50 ft.

STR	DEX	CON	INT	WIS	CHA
21 (+5)	9 (−1)	17 (+3)	2 (−4)	10 (+0)	7 (−2)

Skills Stealth +3
Senses passive Perception 10
Languages —
Challenge 4 (1,100 XP)

ACTIONS

Multiattack. The lizard makes two attacks: one with its bite and one with its tail. One attack can be replaced by Swallow.

Bite. *Melee Weapon Attack:* +7 to hit, reach 5 ft., one target. *Hit:* 16 (2d10 + 5) piercing damage, and the target is grappled (escape DC 15). Until this grapple ends, the target is restrained, and the lizard can't bite another target.

Tail. *Melee Weapon Attack:* +7 to hit, reach 10 ft., one target not grappled by the lizard. *Hit:* 12 (2d6 + 5) bludgeoning damage. If the target is a creature, it must succeed on a DC 15 Strength saving throw or be knocked prone.

Swallow. *Melee Weapon Attack:* +7 to hit, reach 5 ft., one Medium or smaller creature the lizard is grappling. *Hit:* 16 (2d10 + 5) piercing damage, the target is swallowed, and the grapple ends. The swallowed target is blinded and restrained, it has total cover against attacks and other effects outside the lizard, and it takes 10 (3d6) acid damage at the start of each of the lizard's turns. The lizard can have only one target swallowed at a time.

If the lizard dies, a swallowed creature is no longer restrained by it and can escape from the corpse using 10 feet of movement, exiting prone.

GREATER ZOMBIE

Many of those who brave the Tomb of Horrors believe they have reached their ultimate destination when they disturb a skeletal figure inside a secluded crypt. It is, in fact, a greater zombie, a creature magically created from a humanoid corpse to be far more resilient than a typical zombie.

Undead Nature. A zombie doesn't require air, food, drink, or sleep.

ILLUSIONIST

Illusionists are specialist wizards who twist light, sound, shadow, and even minds to create false and quasi-real effects. They can be flamboyant and use their powers in spectacular and obvious ways, or quiet and subtle, using their magic to conceal the truth.

GREATER ZOMBIE
Medium undead, neutral evil

Armor Class 15 (natural armor)
Hit Points 97 (13d8 + 39)
Speed 30 ft.

STR	DEX	CON	INT	WIS	CHA
18 (+4)	10 (+0)	17 (+3)	4 (−3)	6 (−2)	6 (−2)

Saving Throws Wis +1
Damage Resistances cold, necrotic
Damage Immunities poison
Condition Immunities charmed, exhaustion, frightened, paralyzed, poisoned
Senses darkvision 60 ft., passive Perception 8
Languages understands the languages it knew in life but can't speak
Challenge 5 (1,800 XP)

Turn Resistance. The zombie has advantage on saving throws against any effect that turns undead.

Undead Fortitude. If damage reduces the zombie to 0 hit points, it must make a Constitution saving throw with a DC of 5 + the damage taken, unless the damage is radiant or from a critical hit. On a success, the lich drops to 1 hit point instead.

ACTIONS

Multiattack. The zombie makes two melee attacks.

Empowered Slam. *Melee Weapon Attack:* +7 to hit, reach 5 ft., one target. *Hit:* 7 (1d6 + 4) bludgeoning damage and 7 (2d6) necrotic damage.

ILLUSIONIST
Medium humanoid (any race), any alignment

Armor Class 12 (15 with *mage armor*)
Hit Points 38 (7d8 + 7)
Speed 30 ft.

STR	DEX	CON	INT	WIS	CHA
9 (−1)	14 (+2)	13 (+1)	16 (+3)	11 (+0)	12 (+1)

Saving Throws Int +5, Wis +2
Skills Arcana +5, History +5
Senses passive Perception 10
Languages any four languages
Challenge 3 (700 XP)

Spellcasting. The illusionist is a 7th-level spellcaster. Its spellcasting ability is Intelligence (spell save DC 13, +5 to hit with spell attacks). The illusionist has the following wizard spells prepared:

Cantrips (at will): *dancing lights, mage hand, minor illusion, poison spray*
1st level (4 slots): *color spray,* disguise self,* mage armor, magic missile*
2nd level (3 slots): *invisibility,* mirror image,* phantasmal force**
3rd level (3 slots): *major image,* phantom steed**
4th level (1 slot): *phantasmal killer**
*Illusion spell of 1st level or higher

Displacement (Recharges after the Illusionist Casts an Illusion Spell of 1st Level or Higher). As a bonus action, the illusionist projects an illusion that makes the illusionist appear to be standing in a place a few inches from its actual location, causing any creature to have disadvantage on attack rolls against the illusionist. The effect ends if the illusionist takes damage, it is incapacitated, or its speed becomes 0.

ACTIONS

Quarterstaff. *Melee Weapon Attack:* +1 to hit, reach 5 ft., one target. *Hit:* 2 (1d6 − 1) bludgeoning damage, or 3 (1d8 − 1) bludgeoning damage if used with two hands.

KALKA-KYLLA

Adventurers who get inside the halls of the Hidden Shrine of Tamoachan are likely to find a unique opportunity—the chance to communicate with a crustacean that can speak. If Kalka-Kylla is coaxed out of its hiding place and not attacked, it might provide visitors with a bit or two of possibly useful information.

KELPIE

A kelpie (*White Plume Mountain*) is a form of intelligent, aquatic plant life that resembles a pile of wet seaweed. It is able to shape its body into various forms, often assuming the aspect of a beautiful humanoid in order to lure people into deep water.

KALKA-KYLLA
Large monstrosity, neutral

Armor Class 15 (natural armor)
Hit Points 85 (10d10 + 30)
Speed 30 ft., swim 30 ft.

STR	DEX	CON	INT	WIS	CHA
17 (+3)	12 (+1)	16 (+3)	15 (+2)	16 (+3)	12 (+1)

Skills Deception +3, Insight +5, Stealth +3
Senses blindsight 30 ft., passive Perception 13
Languages Olman
Challenge 3 (700 XP)

Amphibious. Kalka-Kylla can breathe air and water.

False Appearance. While Kalka-Kylla remains motionless and hidden in its shell, it is indistinguishable from a polished boulder.

Shell. Kalka-Kylla can use a bonus action to retract into or emerge from its shell. While retracted, Kalka-Kylla gains a +4 bonus to AC, and it has a speed of 0 and can't benefit from bonuses to speed.

ACTIONS

Multiattack. Kalka-Kylla makes two claw attacks.

Claw. *Melee Weapon Attack:* +5 to hit, reach 5 ft., one target. *Hit:* 10 (2d6 + 3) bludgeoning damage, and if the target is a Medium or smaller creature, it is grappled (escape DC 13). Until this grapple ends, the target is restrained. Kalka-Kylla has two claws, each of which can grapple only one target.

KELPIE
Medium plant, neutral evil

Armor Class 14 (natural armor)
Hit Points 67 (9d8 + 27)
Speed 10 ft., swim 30 ft.

STR	DEX	CON	INT	WIS	CHA
14 (+2)	14 (+2)	16 (+3)	7 (–2)	12 (+1)	10 (+0)

Skills Perception +3, Stealth +4
Damage Resistances bludgeoning, fire, piercing
Condition Immunities blinded, deafened, exhaustion
Senses blindsight 60 ft., passive Perception 13
Languages Common, Sylvan
Challenge 4 (1,100 XP)

Amphibious. The kelpie can breathe air and water.

Seaweed Shape. The kelpie can use its action to reshape its body into the form of a humanoid or beast that is Small, Medium, or Large. Its statistics are otherwise unchanged. The disguise is convincing, unless the kelpie is in bright light or the viewer is within 30 feet of it, in which case the seams between the seaweed strands are visible. The kelpie returns to its true form if takes a bonus action to do so or if it dies.

False Appearance. While the kelpie remains motionless in its true form, it is indistinguishable from normal seaweed.

ACTIONS

Multiattack. The kelpie makes two slam attacks.

Slam. *Melee Weapon Attack:* +4 to hit, reach 10 ft., one target. *Hit:* 11 (2d8 + 2) piercing damage. If the target is a Medium or smaller creature, it is grappled (escape DC 12).

Drowning Hypnosis. The kelpie chooses one humanoid it can see within 150 feet of it. If the target can see the kelpie, the target must succeed on a DC 11 Wisdom saving throw or be magically charmed while the kelpie maintains concentration, up to 10 minutes (as if concentrating on a spell).

The charmed target is incapacitated, and instead of holding its breath underwater, it tries to breathe normally and immediately runs out of breath, unless it can breathe water.

If the charmed target is more than 5 feet away from the kelpie, the target must move on its turn toward the kelpie by the most direct route, trying to get within 5 feet. It doesn't avoid opportunity attacks.

Before moving into damaging terrain, such as lava or a pit, and whenever it takes damage from a source other than the kelpie or drowning, the target can repeat the saving throw. A charmed target can also repeat the saving throw at the end of each of its turns. If the saving throw is successful, the effect ends on it.

A target that successfully saves is immune to this kelpie's hypnosis for the next 24 hours.

LEUCROTTA

The leucrotta is every bit as horrible as its grotesque appearance would suggest: the body of a hyena perched atop the spindly legs of a deer and topped with the head of a giant badger. A group of these creatures lurks inside a location in the Doomvault (*Dead in Thay*), where they use their talent for mimicry to call for help—enticing would-be prey to come to their rescue before discovering the truth of the matter.

LEUCROTTA
Large monstrosity, chaotic evil

Armor Class 14 (natural armor)
Hit Points 67 (9d10 + 18)
Speed 50 ft.

STR	DEX	CON	INT	WIS	CHA
18 (+4)	14 (+2)	15 (+2)	9 (−1)	12 (+1)	6 (−2)

Skills Deception +2, Perception +3
Senses darkvision 60 ft., passive Perception 13
Languages Abyssal, Gnoll
Challenge 3 (700 XP)

Keen Smell. The leucrotta has advantage on Wisdom (Perception) checks that rely on smell.

Kicking Retreat. If the leucrotta attacks with its hooves, it can take the Disengage action as a bonus action.

Mimicry. The leucrotta can mimic animal sounds and humanoid voices. A creature that hears the sounds can tell they are imitations with a successful DC 14 Wisdom (Insight) check.

Rampage. When the leucrotta reduces a creature to 0 hit points with a melee attack on its turn, it can take a bonus action to move up to half its speed and make an attack with its hooves.

ACTIONS

Multiattack. The leucrotta makes two attacks: one with its bite and one with its hooves.

Bite. *Melee Weapon Attack:* +6 to hit, reach 5 ft., one target. *Hit:* 8 (1d8 + 4) piercing damage. If the leucrotta scores a critical hit, it rolls the damage dice three times, instead of twice.

Hooves. *Melee Weapon Attack:* +6 to hit, reach 5 ft., one target. *Hit:* 11 (2d6 + 4) bludgeoning damage.

MALFORMED KRAKEN

The Doomvault (*Dead in Thay*) contains a number of denizens that don't have all the traits or abilities of normal creatures of their kind. By far the most powerful of these "inferior" creatures is a malformed kraken that is kept in a saltwater pool and is not as large or as durable as a true kraken.

MALFORMED KRAKEN
Huge monstrosity, chaotic evil

Armor Class 17 (natural armor)
Hit Points 172 (15d12 + 75)
Speed 20 ft., swim 40 ft.

STR	DEX	CON	INT	WIS	CHA
25 (+7)	11 (+0)	20 (+5)	11 (+0)	15 (+2)	15 (+2)

Saving Throws Str +11, Con +9, Int +4, Wis +6, Cha +6
Damage Resistances bludgeoning, piercing, and slashing from nonmagical attacks
Damage Immunities lightning
Condition Immunities frightened, paralyzed
Senses truesight 60 ft., passive Perception 12
Languages understands Common but can't speak; telepathy 60 ft.
Challenge 10 (5,900 XP)

Amphibious. The kraken can breathe air and water.

Siege Monster. The kraken deals double damage to objects and structures.

ACTIONS

Multiattack. The kraken makes three tentacle attacks. One of them can be replaced with a bite attack, and any of them can be replaced with Fling.

Bite. *Melee Weapon Attack:* +11 to hit, reach 5 ft., one target. *Hit:* 16 (2d8 + 7) piercing damage.

Tentacle. *Melee Weapon Attack:* +11 to hit, reach 20 ft., one target. *Hit:* 14 (2d6 + 7) bludgeoning damage, and the target is grappled (escape DC 16). Until this grapple ends, the target is restrained. The kraken has ten tentacles, each of which can grapple one target.

Fling. One Medium or smaller object held or creature grappled by the kraken's tentacles is thrown up to 60 feet in a random direction and knocked prone. If a thrown target strikes a solid surface, the target takes 3 (1d6) bludgeoning damage for every 10 feet it was thrown. If the target is thrown at another creature, that creature must succeed on a DC 16 Dexterity saving throw or take the same damage and be knocked prone.

Lightning Storm. The kraken creates three bolts of lightning, each of which can strike a target the kraken can see within 150 feet of it. A target must make a DC 16 Dexterity saving throw, taking 16 (3d10) lightning damage on a failed save, or half as much damage on a successful one.

Martial Arts Adept

Within a lavish chamber inside the Hidden Shrine of Tamoachan, two dust-covered bodies are found reclining. If their rest is disturbed, the bodies awaken from a state of suspended animation and reveal themselves to be monks of considerable capability.

Nereid

One of the most inviting locations in the Hidden Shrine of Tamoachan is a gently illuminated pool of water, beside which sits a lovely being singing a pleasant tune. The figure is a nereid—a fey water creature that can shape its environment to suit its needs. Whether male or female, a nereid bears an otherworldly beauty.

Martial Arts Adept
Medium humanoid (any race), any alignment

Armor Class 16
Hit Points 60 (11d8 + 11)
Speed 40 ft.

STR	DEX	CON	INT	WIS	CHA
11 (+0)	17 (+3)	13 (+1)	11 (+0)	16 (+3)	10 (+0)

Skills Acrobatics +5, Insight +5, Stealth +5
Senses passive Perception 13
Languages any one language (usually Common)
Challenge 3 (700 XP)

Unarmored Defense. While the adept is wearing no armor and wielding no shield, its AC includes its Wisdom modifier.

Actions

Multiattack. The adept makes three unarmed strikes or three dart attacks.

Unarmed Strike. *Melee Weapon Attack:* +5 to hit, reach 5 ft., one target. *Hit:* 7 (1d8 + 3) bludgeoning damage. If the target is a creature, the adept can choose one of the following additional effects:

- The target must succeed on a DC 13 Strength saving throw or drop one item it is holding (adept's choice).
- The target must succeed on a DC 13 Dexterity saving throw or be knocked prone.
- The target must succeed on a DC 13 Constitution saving throw or be stunned until the end of the adept's next turn.

Dart. *Ranged Weapon Attack:* +5 to hit, range 20/60 ft., one target. *Hit:* 5 (1d4 + 3) piercing damage.

Reactions

Deflect Missile. In response to being hit by a ranged weapon attack, the adept deflects the missile. The damage it takes from the attack is reduced by 1d10 + 3. If the damage is reduced to 0, the adept catches the missile if it's small enough to hold in one hand and the adept has a hand free.

Nereid
Medium fey, any chaotic alignment

Armor Class 13
Hit Points 44 (8d8 + 8)
Speed 30 ft., swim 60 ft.

STR	DEX	CON	INT	WIS	CHA
10 (+0)	17 (+3)	12 (+1)	13 (+1)	14 (+2)	16 (+3)

Skills Acrobatics +5, Nature +3, Stealth +5, Survival +4
Senses darkvision 60 ft., passive Perception 12
Languages Aquan, Common, Elvish, Sylvan
Challenge 2 (450 XP)

Amphibious. The nereid can breathe air and water.

Aquatic Invisibility. If immersed in water, the nereid can make itself invisible as a bonus action. It remains invisible until it leaves the water, ends the invisibility as a bonus action, or dies.

Mantle Dependent. The nereid wears a mantle of silky cloth the color of sea foam, which holds the creature's spirit. The mantle has an AC and hit points equal to that of the nereid, but the garment can't be directly harmed while the nereid wears it. If the mantle is destroyed, the nereid becomes poisoned and dies within 1 hour. A nereid is willing to do anything in its power to recover the mantle if it is stolen, including serving the thief.

Shape Water. The nereid can cast *control water* at will, requiring no components. Its spellcasting ability for it is Charisma. This use of the spell has a range of 30 feet and can affect a cube of water no larger than 30 feet on a side.

Speak with Animals. The nereid can comprehend and verbally communicate with beasts.

Actions

Blinding Acid. *Melee or Ranged Spell Attack:* +5 to hit, reach 5 ft. or range 30 ft., one target. *Hit:* 16 (2d12 + 3) acid damage, and the target is blinded until the start of the nereid's next turn.

Drowning Kiss (Recharge 5–6). The nereid touches one creature it can see within 5 feet of it. The target must succeed on a DC 13 Constitution saving throw or take 22 (3d12 + 3) acid damage. On a failure, it also runs out of breath and can't speak for 1 minute. At the end of each of its turns, it can repeat the save, ending the effect on itself on a success.

Water Lash. The nereid causes a 5-foot cube of water within 60 feet of it to take a shape of its choice and strike one target it can see within 5 feet of that water. The target must make a DC 13 Strength saving throw. On a failed save, it takes 17 (4d6 + 3) bludgeoning damage, and if it is a Large or smaller creature, it is pushed up to 15 feet in a straight line or is knocked prone (nereid's choice). On a successful save, the target takes half as much damage and isn't pushed or knocked prone.

Necromancer

Necromancers are specialist wizards who study the interaction of life, death, and undeath. Some like to dig up corpses to create undead slaves. A few use their powers for good, becoming hunters of the undead and risking their lives to save others.

Ooze Master

The Immortal Caverns inside the Doomvault (*Dead in Thay*) are home to a number of bizarre creatures, of which the Ooze Master is perhaps the strangest. It initially appears in the form of a pillar composed of thick, red, ooze-like stuff. The creature is actually inside the pillar, and when it is roused, it emerges with evil intent.

Undead Nature. The Ooze Master doesn't require air, food, drink, or sleep.

NECROMANCER

Medium humanoid (any race), any alignment

Armor Class 12 (15 with *mage armor*)
Hit Points 66 (12d8 + 12)
Speed 30 ft.

STR	DEX	CON	INT	WIS	CHA
9 (−1)	14 (+2)	12 (+1)	17 (+3)	12 (+1)	11 (+0)

Saving Throws Int +7, Wis +5
Skills Arcana +7, History +7
Damage Resistances necrotic
Senses passive Perception 11
Languages any four languages
Challenge 9 (5,000 XP)

Spellcasting. The necromancer is a 12th-level spellcaster. Its spellcasting ability is Intelligence (spell save DC 15, +7 to hit with spell attacks). The necromancer has the following wizard spells prepared:

Cantrips (at will): *chill touch, dancing lights, mage hand, mending*
1st level (4 slots): *false life,* mage armor, ray of sickness**
2nd level (3 slots): *blindness/deafness,* ray of enfeeblement,* web*
3rd level (3 slots): *animate dead,* bestow curse,* vampiric touch**
4th level (3 slots): *blight,* dimension door, stoneskin*
5th level (2 slots): *Bigby's hand, cloudkill*
6th level (1 slot): *circle of death**
*Necromancy spell of 1st level or higher

Grim Harvest (1/Turn). When necromancer kills a creature that is neither a construct nor undead with a spell of 1st level or higher, the necromancer regains hit points equal to twice the spell's level, or three times if it is a necromancy spell.

ACTIONS

Withering Touch. *Melee Spell Attack:* +7 to hit, reach 5 ft., one creature. *Hit:* 5 (2d4) necrotic damage.

OOZE MASTER

Huge undead, lawful evil

Armor Class 9 (natural armor)
Hit Points 138 (12d12 + 60)
Speed 30 ft., climb 30 ft.

STR	DEX	CON	INT	WIS	CHA
16 (+3)	1 (−5)	20 (+5)	17 (+3)	10 (+0)	16 (+3)

Saving Throws Int +7, Wis +4
Skills Arcana +7, Insight +4
Damage Resistances lightning, necrotic; bludgeoning, piercing, and slashing from nonmagical attacks
Damage Immunities acid, cold, poison
Condition Immunities blinded, charmed, deafened, exhaustion, frightened, paralyzed, poisoned, prone
Senses blindsight 120 ft., passive Perception 10
Languages Common, Primordial, Thayan
Challenge 10 (5,900 XP)

Corrosive Form. A creature that touches the Ooze Master or hits it with a melee attack while within 5 feet of it takes 9 (2d8) acid damage. Any nonmagical weapon that hits the Ooze Master corrodes. After dealing damage, the weapon takes a permanent and cumulative −1 penalty to damage rolls. If its penalty drops to −5, the weapon is destroyed. Nonmagical ammunition that hits the Ooze Master is destroyed after dealing damage.

The Ooze Master can eat through 2-inch-thick, nonmagical wood or metal in 1 round.

Instinctive Attack. When the Ooze Master casts a spell with a casting time of 1 action, it can make one pseudopod attack as a bonus action.

Spellcasting. The Ooze Master is a 9th-level spellcaster. Its spellcasting ability is Intelligence (spell save DC 15, +7 to hit with spell attacks). It has the following wizard spells prepared:

Cantrips (at will): *acid splash, friends, mage hand, poison spray*
1st level (4 slots): *charm person, detect magic, magic missile, ray of sickness*
2nd level (3 slots): *detect thoughts, Melf's acid arrow, suggestion*
3rd level (3 slots): *fear, slow, stinking cloud*
4th level (3 slots): *confusion, Evard's black tentacles*
5th level (1 slot): *cloudkill*

Spider Climb. The Ooze Master can climb difficult surfaces, including upside down on ceilings, without needing to make an ability check.

ACTIONS

Pseudopod. *Melee Weapon Attack:* +7 to hit, reach 10 ft., one target. *Hit:* 13 (3d6 + 3) bludgeoning damage plus 10 (3d6) acid damage.

REACTIONS

Instinctive Charm. If a creature the Ooze Master can see makes an attack roll against it while within 30 feet of it, the Ooze Master can use a reaction to divert the attack if another creature is within the attack's range. The attacker must make a DC 15 Wisdom saving throw. On a failed save, the attacker targets the creature that is closest to it, not including itself or the Ooze Master. If multiple creatures are closest, the attacker chooses which one to target. On a successful save, the attacker is immune to this Instinctive Charm for 24 hours. Creatures that can't be charmed are immune to this effect.

Sea Lion

A sea lion is a fearsome monster with the head and forepaws of a lion and the lower body and tail of a fish. Adventurers who delve beneath White Plume Mountain might discover a group of these creatures confined in a watery cage.

Sharwyn Hucrele

A young adventurer whose group ran afoul of a band of goblins, Sharwyn Hucrele now finds herself enslaved deep inside the Sunless Citadel, an unwitting supplicant of the Gulthias Tree. The corrupting influence has turned her skin thick and rough, as though she were affected by a *barkskin* spell, and has turned the normally good-aligned Sharwyn into an evil adversary.

Sea Lion

Large monstrosity, unaligned

Armor Class 15 (natural armor)
Hit Points 90 (12d10 + 24)
Speed 10 ft., swim 40 ft.

STR	DEX	CON	INT	WIS	CHA
17 (+3)	15 (+2)	15 (+2)	3 (−4)	12 (+1)	8 (−1)

Skills Perception +4, Stealth +5
Senses passive Perception 14
Languages —
Challenge 5 (1,800 XP)

Amphibious. The sea lion can breathe air and water.

Keen Smell. The sea lion has advantage on Wisdom (Perception) checks that rely on smell.

Pack Tactics. The sea lion has advantage on an attack roll against a creature if at least one of the sea lion's allies is within 5 feet of the creature and the ally isn't incapacitated.

Swimming Leap. With a 10-foot swimming start, the sea lion can long jump out of or across the water up to 25 feet.

Actions

Multiattack. The sea lion makes three attacks: one bite attack and two claw attacks.

Bite. *Melee Weapon Attack:* +6 to hit, reach 5 ft., one target. *Hit:* 12 (2d8 + 3) piercing damage.

Claw. *Melee Weapon Attack:* +6 to hit, reach 5 ft., one target. *Hit:* 12 (2d8 + 3) piercing damage.

Sharwyn Hucrele

Medium humanoid (human), neutral evil

Armor Class 16 (Barkskin trait)
Hit Points 13 (2d8 + 4)
Speed 30 ft.

STR	DEX	CON	INT	WIS	CHA
11 (+0)	13 (+1)	14 (+2)	16 (+3)	14 (+2)	9 (−1)

Skills Arcana +5, Insight +4, Persuasion +1
Senses passive Perception 12
Languages Common, Draconic, Goblin
Challenge 1/2 (100 XP)

Barkskin. Sharwyn's AC can't be lower than 16.

Special Equipment. Sharwyn has a spellbook that contains the spells listed in her Spellcasting trait, plus *detect magic* and *silent image*.

Spellcasting. Sharwyn is a 1st-level spellcaster. Her spellcasting ability is Intelligence (spell save DC 13, +5 to hit with spell attacks). She has the following wizard spells prepared:

Cantrips (at will): *light, prestidigitation, ray of frost*
1st level (2 slots): *color spray, magic missile, shield, sleep*

Tree Thrall. If the Gulthias Tree dies, Sharwyn dies 24 hours later.

Actions

Dagger. *Melee Weapon Attack:* +4 to hit, reach 5 ft., one target. *Hit:* 4 (1d4 + 2) piercing damage.

SIR BRAFORD

While traveling in the vicinity of the Sunless Citadel, Sir Braford and his companions were captured by goblins. The young paladin of Pelor has been corrupted by the sinister Gulthias Tree and now swings his magic sword, *Shatterspike*, on behalf of a different sort of "deity."

SIREN

Imprisoned inside a mist-filled chamber in the Tomb of Horrors, Siren serves as evidence of Acererak's heartless sense of humor. This mysterious fey creature yearns to be released, but an enchantment laid on her by the demilich prevents her from telling visitors how to accomplish that task. If anyone succeeds in freeing her, she vows to be a lifelong friend.

SIR BRAFORD
Medium humanoid (human), neutral evil

Armor Class 18 (chain mail, shield)
Hit Points 19 (3d8 + 6)
Speed 30 ft.

STR	DEX	CON	INT	WIS	CHA
16 (+3)	9 (−1)	14 (+2)	10 (+0)	13 (+1)	14 (+2)

Skills Athletics +5, Perception +3
Senses passive Perception 13
Languages Common
Challenge 1/2 (100 XP)

Barkskin. Sir Braford's AC can't be lower than 16.

Special Equipment. Sir Braford wields *Shatterspike*, a magic longsword that grants a +1 bonus to attack and damage rolls made with it (included in his attack). See appendix B for the item's other properties.

Tree Thrall. If the Gulthias Tree dies, Sir Braford dies 24 hours later.

ACTIONS

Longsword. *Melee Weapon Attack:* +6 to hit, reach 5 ft., one target. *Hit:* 8 (1d8 + 4) slashing damage, or 9 (1d10 + 4) slashing damage if used with two hands.

REACTIONS

Protection. When a creature Sir Braford can see attacks a target other than him that is within 5 feet of him, he can use a reaction to use his shield to impose disadvantage on the attack roll.

SIREN
Medium fey, chaotic good

Armor Class 14
Hit Points 38 (7d8 + 7)
Speed 30 ft., swim 30 ft.

STR	DEX	CON	INT	WIS	CHA
10 (+0)	18 (+4)	12 (+1)	13 (+1)	14 (+2)	16 (+3)

Skills Medicine +4, Nature +3, Stealth +6, Survival +4
Senses darkvision 60 ft., passive Perception 12
Languages Common, Elvish, Sylvan
Challenge 3 (700 XP)

Amphibious. Siren can breathe air and water.

Innate Spellcasting. Siren's innate spellcasting ability is Charisma (spell save DC 13). She can innately cast the following spells, requiring no material components:

1/day each: *charm person, fog cloud, greater invisibility, polymorph* (self only)

Magic Resistance. Siren has advantage on saving throws against spells and other magical effects.

ACTIONS

Shortsword. *Melee Weapon Attack:* +6 to hit, reach 5 ft., one target. *Hit:* 7 (1d6 + 4) piercing damage.

Stupefying Touch. Siren touches one creature she can see within 5 feet of her. The creature must succeed on a DC 13 Intelligence saving throw or take 13 (3d6 + 3) psychic damage and be stunned until the start of Siren's next turn.

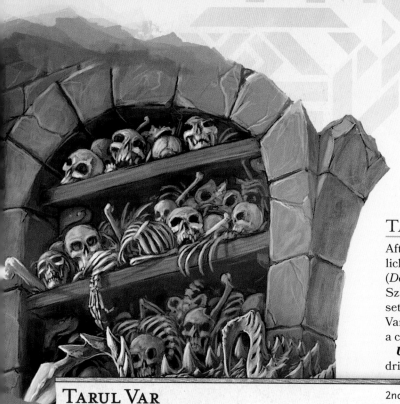

TARUL VAR

After failing in an earlier task for the Red Wizards, the lich Tarul Var is sequestered within the Doomvault (*Dead in Thay*), where he tries to avoid the attention of Szass Tam. Interlopers who discover his quarters are set upon by the lich and his dread warrior guards, but if Var is brought to the brink of death, he might bargain for a chance to escape the dungeon.

Undead Nature. A lich doesn't require air, food, drink, or sleep.

TARUL VAR

Medium undead, neutral evil

Armor Class 16 (natural armor)
Hit Points 105 (14d8 + 42)
Speed 30 ft.

STR	DEX	CON	INT	WIS	CHA
11 (+0)	16 (+3)	16 (+3)	19 (+4)	14 (+2)	16 (+3)

Saving Throws Con +8, Int +9, Wis +7
Skills Arcana +9, History +9, Insight +7, Perception +7
Damage Resistances cold, lightning, necrotic; bludgeoning, piercing, and slashing from nonmagical attacks
Damage Immunities poison
Condition Immunities charmed, exhaustion frightened, paralyzed, poisoned
Senses darkvision 60 ft., passive Perception 17
Languages Abyssal, Common, Infernal, Primordial, Thayan
Challenge 13 (10,000 XP)

Focused Conjuration. While Var is concentrating on a conjuration spell, his concentration can't be broken as a result of taking damage.

Legendary Resistance (3/Day). If Var fails a saving throw, he can choose to succeed instead.

Rejuvenation. If Var is destroyed but his phylactery remains intact, Var gains a new body in 1d10 days, regaining all his hit points and becoming active again. The new body appears within 5 feet of the phylactery.

Spellcasting. Var is a 12th-level spellcaster. His spellcasting ability is Intelligence (spell save DC 17, +9 to hit with spell attacks). He has the following wizard spells prepared:

Cantrips (at will): *fire bolt, mage hand, minor illusion, prestidigitation, ray of frost*
1st level (4 slots): *detect magic, magic missile, shield, unseen servant**

2nd level (3 slots): *detect thoughts, flaming sphere,* mirror image, scorching ray*
3rd level (3 slots): *counterspell, dispel magic, fireball*
4th level (3 slots): *dimension door,* Evard's black tentacles**
5th level (3 slots): *cloudkill,* scrying*
6th level (1 slot): *circle of death*
*Conjuration spell of 1st level or higher

Turn Resistance. Var has advantage on saving throws against any effect that turns undead.

ACTIONS

Paralyzing Touch. *Melee Spell Attack:* +9 to hit, reach 5 ft., one creature. *Hit:* 10 (3d6) cold damage. The target must succeed on a DC 17 Constitution saving throw or be paralyzed for 1 minute. The target can repeat the saving throw at the end of each of its turns, ending the effect on itself on a success.

Benign Transposition. Var teleports up to 30 feet to an unoccupied space he can see. Alternatively, he can choose a space within range that is occupied by a Small or Medium creature. If that creature is willing, both creatures teleport, swapping places. Var can use this feature again only after he finishes a long rest or casts a conjuration spell of 1st level or higher.

LEGENDARY ACTIONS

Var can take 3 legendary actions, choosing from the options below. Only one legendary action option can be used at a time and only at the end of another creature's turn. Var regains spent legendary actions at the start of his turn.

Cantrip. Var casts a cantrip.
Paralyzing Touch (Costs 2 Actions). Var uses Paralyzing Touch.
Frightening Gaze (Costs 2 Actions). Var fixes his gaze on one creature he can see within 10 feet of him. The target must succeed on a DC 17 Wisdom saving throw against this magic or become frightened for 1 minute. The frightened target can repeat the saving throw at the end of each of its turns, ending the effect on itself on a success. If a target's saving throw is successful or the effect ends for it, the target is immune to Var's gaze for the next 24 hours.

Tecuziztecatl

Clinging to the wall of a water-filled chamber inside
the Hidden Shrine of Tamoachan is Tecuziztecatl, also
known as the Lord of Snails. This giant slug is not only
intelligent, it's capable of speech. If faced with enemies
that are too much of a threat for it, the slug might offer to
provide assistance, or it might submerge itself to avoid
further harm.

Thayan Apprentice

The Red Wizards have a number of helpers that super-
vise tasks in the Doomvault (*Dead in Thay*). Thayan
apprentices have a measure of spellcasting ability, and
many strive to become full-fledged wizards one day.

Tecuziztecatl

Large monstrosity, neutral

Armor Class 13 (natural armor)
Hit Points 102 (12d10 + 36)
Speed 30 ft., climb 30 ft., swim 30 ft.

STR	DEX	CON	INT	WIS	CHA
17 (+3)	10 (+0)	16 (+3)	15 (+2)	16 (+3)	13 (+1)

Skills Deception +3, Stealth +2
Damage Resistances bludgeoning from nonmagical attacks
Damage Immunities acid
Senses blindsight 30 ft., passive Perception 13
Languages Olman, Primal
Challenge 4 (1,100 XP)

Amphibious. Tecuziztecatl can breathe air and water.

Glowing. Tecuziztecatl sheds dim light within 20 feet of itself.

Flexible. Tecuziztecatl can enter a space large enough for a Medium creature without squeezing.

Spider Climb. Tecuziztecatl can climb difficult surfaces, including upside down on ceilings, without needing to make an
ability check.

Actions

Multiattack. Tecuziztecatl makes two pseudopod attacks.

Pseudopod. *Melee Weapon Attack:* +5 to hit, reach 10 ft., one
target. *Hit:* 12 (2d8 + 3) bludgeoning damage.

Spit Acid (Recharge 4–6). Tecuziztecatl exhales acid in a 30-foot
line that is 5 feet wide. Each creature in that line must make a
DC 13 Dexterity saving throw, taking 18 (4d8) acid damage on a
failed save, or half as much damage on a successful one.

Thayan Apprentice

Medium humanoid (human), any non-good alignment

Armor Class 12 (15 with *mage armor*)
Hit Points 27 (5d8 + 5)
Speed 30 ft.

STR	DEX	CON	INT	WIS	CHA
10 (+0)	14 (+2)	12 (+1)	15 (+2)	13 (+1)	11 (+0)

Skills Arcana +4
Senses passive Perception 11
Languages Common, Thayan
Challenge 2 (450 XP)

Doomvault Devotion. Within the Doomvault, the apprentice
has advantage on saving throws against being charmed or
frightened.

Spellcasting. The apprentice is a 4th-level spellcaster. Its spellcasting ability is Intelligence (spell save DC 12, +4 to hit with
spell attacks). It has the following wizard spells prepared:

Cantrips (at will): *fire bolt, mage hand, prestidigitation,
    shocking grasp*
1st level (4 slots): *burning hands, detect magic, mage ar-
    mor, shield*
2nd level (3 slots): *blur, scorching ray*

Actions

Dagger. *Melee or Ranged Weapon Attack:* +4 to hit, reach 5 ft. or
range 20/60 ft., one target. *Hit:* 4 (1d4 + 2) piercing damage.

THAYAN WARRIOR

The Red Wizards have a number of helpers that perform tasks in the Doomvault (*Dead in Thay*). Thayan warriors provide muscle when it's needed and often serve beside Thayan apprentices.

THAYAN WARRIOR

Medium humanoid (human), any non-good alignment

Armor Class 16 (chain shirt, shield)
Hit Points 52 (8d8 + 16)
Speed 30 ft.

STR	DEX	CON	INT	WIS	CHA
16 (+3)	13 (+1)	14 (+2)	10 (+0)	11 (+0)	11 (+0)

Skills Perception +2
Senses passive Perception 12
Languages Common, Thayan
Challenge 2 (450 XP)

Doomvault Devotion. Within the Doomvault, the warrior has advantage on saving throws against being charmed or frightened.

Pack Tactics. The warrior has advantage on an attack roll against a creature if at least one of the warrior's allies is within 5 feet of the creature and the ally isn't incapacitated.

ACTIONS

Multiattack. The warrior makes two melee attacks.

Longsword. *Melee Weapon Attack:* +5 to hit, reach 5 ft., one target. *Hit:* 7 (1d8 + 3) slashing damage, or 8 (1d10 + 3) slashing damage if used with two hands.

Javelin. *Melee or Ranged Weapon Attack:* +5 to hit, reach 5 ft. or range 30/120 ft., one target. *Hit:* 6 (1d6 + 3) piercing damage.

THORN SLINGER

A corridor inside the Hidden Shrine of Tamoachan is the site of a long, narrow pit with a number of large bushes along its floor. Though they might appear harmless at first, these thorn slingers are doubly dangerous, as anyone who falls into the pit or tries to traverse it soon discovers.

THORN SLINGER

Large plant, unaligned

Armor Class 11
Hit Points 32 (5d10 + 5)
Speed 10 ft.

STR	DEX	CON	INT	WIS	CHA
13 (+1)	12 (+1)	12 (+1)	1 (−5)	10 (+0)	1 (−5)

Condition Immunities blinded, deafened, frightened
Senses blindsight 60 ft. (blind beyond this radius); passive Perception 10
Languages —
Challenge 1/2 (100 XP)

Adhesive Blossoms. The thorn slinger adheres to anything that touches it. A Medium or smaller creature adhered to the thorn slinger is also grappled by it (escape DC 11). Ability checks made to escape this grapple have disadvantage.

At the end of each of the thorn slinger's turns, anything grappled by it takes 3 (1d6) acid damage.

False Appearance. While the thorn slinger remains motionless, it is indistinguishable from an inanimate bush.

ACTIONS

Thorns. *Melee or Ranged Weapon Attack:* +3 to hit, reach 5 ft. or range 30 ft., one target. *Hit:* 8 (2d6 + 1) piercing damage.

TRANSMUTER

Transmuters are specialist wizards who embrace change, rail against the status quo, and view magical transmutation as a path to riches, enlightenment, or apotheosis.

TRANSMUTER

Medium humanoid (any race), any alignment

Armor Class 12 (15 with *mage armor*)
Hit Points 40 (9d8)
Speed 30 ft.

STR	DEX	CON	INT	WIS	CHA
9 (−1)	14 (+2)	11 (+0)	17 (+3)	12 (+1)	11 (+0)

Saving Throws Int +6, Wis +4
Skills Arcana +6, History +6
Senses passive Perception 11
Languages any four languages
Challenge 5 (1,800 XP)

Spellcasting. The transmuter is a 9th-level spellcaster. Its spellcasting ability is Intelligence (spell save DC 14, +6 to hit with spell attacks). The transmuter has the following wizard spells prepared:

Cantrips (at will): *light, mending, prestidigitation, ray of frost*
1st level (4 slots): *chromatic orb, expeditious retreat,** *mage armor*
2nd level (3 slots): *alter self,* *hold person, knock**
3rd level (3 slots): *blink,* *fireball, slow**
4th level (3 slots): *polymorph,* *stoneskin*
5th level (1 slot): *telekinesis**
*Transmutation spell of 1st level or higher

Transmuter's Stone. The transmuter carries a magic stone it crafted that grants its bearer one of the following effects:

- Darkvision out to a range of 60 feet
- An extra 10 feet of speed while the bearer is unencumbered
- Proficiency with Constitution saving throws
- Resistance to acid, cold, fire, lightning, or thunder damage (transmuter's choice whenever the transmuter chooses this benefit)

If the transmuter has the stone and casts a transmutation spell of 1st level or higher, it can change the effect of the stone.

ACTIONS

Quarterstaff. *Melee Weapon Attack:* +2 to hit, reach 5 ft., one target. *Hit:* 2 (1d6 − 1) bludgeoning damage, or 3 (1d8 − 1) bludgeoning damage if used with two hands.

VAMPIRIC MIST

In a loose manner of speaking, the vampiric mist is the embodiment of the vampire's hunger for blood. It exists only to seek out creatures and drain the life from them, and its insubstantial nature enables it to pursue prey through the tiniest of openings.

When first encountered, a vampiric mist appears as a billowing mass of light clouds. As the creature feeds, its coloration darkens to a deep crimson. In the Temple of Blood inside the Doomvault (*Dead in Thay*), several clouds of vampiric mist appear and attempt to engulf any who don't escape the place quickly.

Undead Nature. A vampiric mist doesn't require air or sleep.

VAMPIRIC MIST

Medium undead, chaotic evil

Armor Class 13
Hit Points 45 (6d8 + 18)
Speed 0 ft., fly 30 ft. (hover)

STR	DEX	CON	INT	WIS	CHA
6 (−2)	16 (+3)	16 (+3)	6 (−2)	12 (+1)	7 (−2)

Saving Throws Wis +3
Damage Resistances acid, cold, lightning, necrotic, thunder; bludgeoning, piercing, and slashing from nonmagical attacks
Damage Immunities poison
Condition Immunities charmed, exhaustion, grappled, paralyzed, petrified, poisoned, prone, restrained
Senses darkvision 60 ft., passive Perception 11
Languages —
Challenge 3 (700 XP)

Blood Sense. The vampiric mist can sense living creatures that have blood or similar vital fluids in a radius of 60 feet.

Forbiddance. The vampiric mist can't enter a residence without an invitation from one of the occupants.

Misty Form. The vampiric mist can occupy another creature's space and vice versa. In addition, if air can pass through a space, the mist can pass through it without squeezing. Each foot of movement in water costs it 2 extra feet, rather than 1 extra foot. The mist can't manipulate objects in any way that requires hands; it can apply simple force only.

Sunlight Hypersensitivity. The vampiric mist takes 20 radiant damage when it starts its turn in sunlight. While in sunlight, the mist has disadvantage on attack rolls and ability checks.

ACTIONS

Blood Drain. One creature in the vampiric mist's space must make a DC 13 Constitution saving throw (undead and constructs automatically succeed). On a failed save, the target takes 10 (2d6 + 3) necrotic damage, its hit point maximum is reduced by an amount equal to the necrotic damage taken, and the mist regains hit points equal to that amount.

This reduction to the target's hit point maximum lasts until the target finishes a long rest. It dies if this effect reduces its hit point maximum to 0.

White Maw

In their laboratories inside the Doomvault (*Dead in Thay*), the Red Wizards experiment with a process to create sentient oozes. The creature they call White Maw is one of their early achievements—a gray ooze of enormous size that has intelligence and can communicate. These talents are considerably diminished by the fact that the creature is utterly insane.

Ooze Nature. White Maw doesn't require sleep.

Yusdrayl

The kobolds that occupy a portion of the Sunless Citadel are not a combative lot, as long as they are not attacked. That attitude is shared by their leader, Yusdrayl. She is not automatically hostile to strangers who enter her throne room, and in fact is looking for some help from a group of outsiders that can help her contend with the goblins that live nearby. But if she or any other kobolds are threatened or set upon, Yusdrayl defends herself and her tribe as fiercely as she can.

White Maw

Gargantuan ooze, chaotic neutral

Armor Class 5
Hit Points 217 (14d20 + 70)
Speed 10 ft.

STR	DEX	CON	INT	WIS	CHA
18 (+4)	1 (–5)	20 (+5)	12 (+1)	10 (+0)	3 (–4)

Damage Resistances acid, cold, fire
Damage Immunities poison
Condition Immunities blinded, charmed, deafened, exhaustion, frightened, poisoned, prone
Senses blindsight 60 ft. (blind beyond this radius), passive Perception 10
Languages telepathy 50 ft.
Challenge 10 (5,900 XP)

Amorphous Form. White Maw can occupy another creature's space and vice versa.

Corrode Metal. Any nonmagical weapon made of metal that hits White Maw corrodes. After dealing damage, the weapon takes a permanent and cumulative –1 penalty to damage rolls. If its penalty drops to –5, the weapon is destroyed. Nonmagical ammunition made of metal that hits White Maw is destroyed after dealing damage.

White Maw can eat through 2-inch-thick, nonmagical metal in 1 round.

False Appearance. While White Maw remains motionless, it is indistinguishable from white stone.

Killer Response. Any creature that starts its turn in White Maw's space is targeted by a pseudopod attack if White Maw isn't incapacitated.

Actions

Pseudopod. *Melee Weapon Attack:* +8 to hit, reach 10 ft., one target. *Hit:* 22 (4d8 + 4) bludgeoning damage plus 9 (2d8) acid damage. If the target is wearing nonmagical metal armor, its armor is partly corroded and takes a permanent and cumulative –1 penalty to the AC it offers. The armor is destroyed if the penalty reduces its AC to 10.

Yusdrayl

Small humanoid (kobold), lawful evil

Armor Class 12 (15 with *mage armor*)
Hit Points 16 (3d6 + 6)
Speed 30 ft.

STR	DEX	CON	INT	WIS	CHA
8 (–1)	15 (+2)	14 (+2)	10 (+0)	10 (+0)	16 (+3)

Skills Arcana +2, Insight +2, Stealth +4
Senses darkvision 60 ft., passive Perception 10
Languages Common, Draconic
Challenge 1 (200 XP)

Spellcasting. Yusdrayl is a 2nd-level spellcaster. Her spellcasting ability is Charisma (spell save DC 13, +5 to hit with spell attacks). She knows the following sorcerer spells:

Cantrips (at will): *mage hand, prestidigitation, ray of frost, shocking grasp*
1st level (4 slots): *burning hands, chromatic orb, mage armor*

Sunlight Sensitivity. While in sunlight, Yusdrayl has disadvantage on attack rolls, as well as on Wisdom (Perception) checks that rely on sight.

Pack Tactics. Yusdrayl has advantage on an attack roll against a creature if at least one of her allies is within 5 feet of the creature and the ally isn't incapacitated.

Actions

Dagger. *Melee Weapon Attack:* +4 to hit, reach 5 ft., one target. *Hit:* 4 (1d4 + 2) piercing damage.